REPRESENTATIVE VERSE OF
CHARLES WESLEY

CHARLES WESLEY, 1786
*Engraved by Jonathan Spilsbury from
his own portrait*

[*Frontispiece*

Hymns, Poetry

REPRESENTATIVE VERSE OF

Charles Wesley

SELECTED AND EDITED
WITH AN INTRODUCTION BY

FRANK BAKER

B.A., B.D., Ph.D.

ABINGDON PRESS
New York   Nashville

FIRST PUBLISHED IN 1962

© THE EPWORTH PRESS 1962

Book Steward
FRANK H. CUMBERS

FOR
NELLIE

PRINTED IN ENGLAND BY
HAZELL WATSON AND VINEY LTD
AYLESBURY AND SLOUGH

PREFACE AND ACKNOWLEDGEMENTS

THE basic aim of this volume is to provide in compact form the means for an adequate appreciation of Charles Wesley as a poet. This is attempted by the provision in three separate sections of

(*a*) a carefully documented corpus of his hymns,

(*b*) characteristic specimens of his devotional verse, and

(*c*) a selection of miscellaneous poems, whimsical, satirical, political, ecclesiastical, controversial, topical, and personal, which at the same time present a summary of Charles Wesley's life and of his reactions to men and movements of the day.

In the interests of making this selection as representative as possible, I have carefully read through, not only the 4,600 poems which he himself published, and the 3,000 which were published posthumously, but over 1,300 so far unpublished, a total of over 180,000 lines of verse. In every case the text is that of the first published edition, where one exists, together with careful collations with all other major editions, and with all known manuscripts—quite frequently there are two or three manuscripts of his poems, and occasionally four.

Because Charles Wesley's most valuable contribution to English literature is undoubtedly his hymns, a critical history of all those hymns selected (which include the most well known) is given by collating them with the six 'general' hymn-books prepared by the Wesleys, with their successors in the main Wesleyan stream down to the *Methodist Hymn-book* of 1933, and with the main stream of Anglican hymnology as represented by Whitefield's *Hymns* (1753), Madan's *Collection* (1760 and 1763), and the eight different editions of *Hymns Ancient and Modern* from 1861 to 1958.

Interwoven with the three main approaches to Charles Wesley's verse is an attempt to illustrate his important place in the history of English prosody, by incorporating examples of all the hundred stanzaic patterns which he employed—many of them apparently original—in a century comparatively sterile of the lyric. (For 'stanzaic pattern' I normally use the term 'metre'.)

I must emphasize that this selection includes not only some of Charles Wesley's best verse, but some of his worst. Most students will probably agree with me that his greatest literary achievements are to be found among the hymns and sacred poems of his middle years, and it would easily have been possible to fill a volume twice this size with noteworthy poetry of this type. Nevertheless it seemed desirable to include a number of inferior items in order to illustrate metrical experiments which were relatively unsuccessful, or points of topical importance. Let me repeat, therefore: this selection does not pretend to offer 'the best of Charles Wesley' but 'representative verse'.

It will be realized that this has involved an immense amount of labour not only for the editor but for many others. My warmest acknowledgements are especially due to Dr Frank Cumbers and Dr J. Alan Kay of the Epworth Press and to the members of their staff for more kindnesses than it is possible to list, including ready access to the priceless wealth of

Charles Wesley MSS under the care of Dr Cumbers. Particular mention should be made of the meticulous care of Mr H. A. W. Robinson in seeing the work through the Press. Nor have I received anything but ready and sometimes abounding co-operation from all whom I have approached for the use of manuscripts and rare editions—Dr Harold Roberts and the Rev. Norman Goldhawk of Richmond College, Surrey; Professor Victor Murray, President of Cheshunt College, Cambridge; the Rev. Frederic Greeves, Principal of Didsbury College, Bristol; Dr Maurice Frost, of Deddington; the Rev. John T. Wilkinson, former Principal of Hartley-Victoria College, Manchester; Dr Elmer T. Clark, of Lake Junaluska, North Carolina; and the staffs of the British Museum, of Duke University Library, North Carolina, of Emory University Library, Georgia, and of the Rylands Library, Manchester. I am also grateful for generous assistance in the unravelling of historical knots, even though on occasion the tangles proved intractable, from the following:

The Keeper of Printed Books, Bodleian Library, Oxford; Professor Benjamin Boyce, of Duke University; W. S. Haugh, B.A., F.L.A., City Librarian, Bristol; H. Sargeant, F.L.A., City Librarian, Portsmouth; Mr Donald Baker, B.A., of Weymouth; the Rev. Dr Oliver A. Beckerlegge, of Camborne; the Rev. L. H. Bunn, B.A., of Crook, the editor of the forthcoming revised edition of Julian's *Dictionary of Hymnology;* Mr Clifford B. Freeman, M.A., of Hull; the Rev. Griffith Roberts, M.A., B.D., for inquiries undertaken at the National Library of Wales; the Rev. Wesley F. Swift, of Lytham St Annes; and (for photographic help) Mr Alan Marshall, of Hull.

My cordial thanks to all!

Duke University
Durham, North Carolina   FRANK BAKER

N.B. *Critical Apparatus*

Titles supplied by the editor are given within square brackets.

The *sources* listed before each item have all been collated with the basic source, denoted by an asterisk in the margin.

Any *footnotes* by Charles (or John) Wesley are given first. Elucidations of these, and any other explanatory notes by the editor, follow in square brackets.

The *variant readings* include only the more important variants, not differences of spelling or capitalization unless there is some special significance about these points. The *abbreviations* used in the variant readings should prove self-explanatory, since they relate only to the authorities listed at the head of each item. One point calls for special mention, however: to avoid undue repetition, '1780, &c.' is used where *all* 'Wesleyan' volumes from 1780 onward employ the same variant reading—and so with '1831, &c.' and later dates. Similarly, 'A & M 1861, &c.' implies that *all* editions of *Hymns Ancient and Modern* from 1861 onward use that line (if they use it at all) in the same form.

CONTENTS

ILLUSTRATIONS

INTRODUCTION

THE DISCOVERY OF CHARLES WESLEY

THERE IS little difficulty in securing enthusiastic tributes to the outstanding merits of Charles Wesley as a hymn-writer, even though these tributes are frequently tempered by the over-bold assertion that hymns cannot be poetry and the completely false assumption that Charles Wesley confined himself to hymns. Methodist admirers have waxed rhapsodical in his praise. Since these may well be accused of partiality, I refrain from quotation. Let the informed 'outsider' speak. It was a cautious Unitarian, Dr Alexander Gordon, who thus described Charles Wesley's hymns: 'Rich in melody, they invite to singing, and in the best of them there is a lyrical swing and an undertone of mystical fervour which both vitalize and mellow the substratum of doctrine.'[1] It was a shrewd and scholarly Congregational layman, Bernard Lord Manning, who claimed that the 1780 *Collection of Hymns for the use of the People called Methodists* —almost pure Charles Wesley—'ranks in Christian literature with the Psalms, the Book of Common Prayer, the Canon of the Mass. In its own way it is perfect, unapproachable, elemental in its perfection. You cannot alter it except to mar it; it is a work of supreme devotional art by a religious genius.'[2] And it was an Anglican, Dr John Julian, outlining the hymnological contribution of the Wesley family for his monumental *Dictionary of Hymnology*, who placed the bardic wreath on his head: 'But, after all, it was Charles Wesley who was the *great* hymn-writer of the Wesley family—perhaps, taking quantity and quality into consideration, the great hymn-writer of all ages.'

Since the time of Stopford Brooke's *Theology in the English Poets* (1874) there has been a growing awareness of the important place of Charles Wesley in the history of English verse in general, an awareness accompanied by a recognition of the fact that hymns even of a quality far lower than the average compositions of Charles Wesley play an essential part both in the development of literary taste and in the shaping of literary achievement. Certainly Charles Wesley's competence as a verse-writer has been increasingly recognized, and Professors of English literature have come to agree with John Wesley that in the compositions of his brother there are to be found not only 'the purity, the strength, and the elegance of the English Language', but in some of them 'the true Spirit of Poetry'.[3] Edmund Gosse acknowledged that 'the sacred songs of Charles Wesley . . . reach at their noblest the highest level of Protestant religious poetry in this country since George Herbert'.[4] W. J. Courthope described him as 'the most admirable *devotional* lyric poet in the English language'.[5] George Saintsbury treated Wesley as the leader of the small group of truly inspired writers of religious verse, who in the eighteenth

[1] *Dictionary of National Biography*, article on Charles Wesley.
[2] *The Hymns of Wesley and Watts* (1942), p. 14.
[3] Preface to the 1780 *Collection*.
[4] *History of Eighteenth Century Literature* (1891), p. 230.
[5] *History of English Poetry*, Vol. V (1905), p. 343.

century became 'more positively poetical than most of the profane'.[6] Oliver Elton placed Charles Wesley 'at the head of all English hymnologists', illustrating the statement that he 'often attains to poetry, and is much oftener on the brink of it' by references to his 'verbal music and easily rememberable sound', his 'ringing vowels', and his ear for rhythm, which 'often keeps the hymn going when the language flags'.[7]

From the quotations already presented it is obvious that Charles Wesley already has an important niche in the history of English poetry. The magnitude of his achievement, however, has only been opening up to students of English literature in general during the last two or three decades, and even now there is a vast hinterland waiting to be explored. Although a revered Methodist professor, Dr Henry Bett, had for over a generation been proclaiming the literary riches to be found in Wesley's hymns, their real discovery by the world of letters may be traced to the writings of Bernard L. Manning, quoted above, and to those of Mr George Sampson, particularly his Warton Lecture on English Poetry, delivered before the British Academy in 1943. Under the title 'A Century of Divine Songs' Mr Sampson outlined the contribution made to English literature during the eighteenth century by the hymn—'the poor man's poetry' and 'the ordinary man's theology'. Taking as his (unannounced) text George Saintsbury's dictum quoted above, Mr Sampson claimed that eighteenth-century hymns (particularly those of the Wesleys, to whom over half the lecture is devoted) constituted a far more important literary achievement than any contemporary secular verse, and that they 'helped to form the very texture of the English mind'. And yet, he complained, 'this extraordinary outburst of religious poetry is ignored in most histories of English literature as if it had never existed'.

Since the pronouncements of Mr Manning and Mr Sampson students of our literature have paid more attention to the work of hymn-writers, and particularly to the verse of Charles Wesley, the greatest of them all. Among other studies that of Dr Donald Davie—*Purity of Diction in English Verse* (1952)—may be noted as an important contribution to the theory of poetry. Dr Davie takes Charles Wesley as the first major example of a restrained classicism in verse which achieves its effects not through luxuriant metaphor but through 'purity of diction'. This is no sign of literary poverty, but of artistic economy in words and metaphors. Dr Davie illustrates the wide range of Wesley's language, his powerful use of simple words, the sophistication of his verse structure, his use of the *dénouement* in the closing line, his wealth of allusion, and his ability to resuscitate a dead metaphor. It can safely be prophesied that the exploration of Charles Wesley's vast contribution to English literature will continue to increase, and will continually be unearthing new treasures.

CHARLES WESLEY'S LITERARY OUTPUT

One of the major problems of any student of Charles Wesley's verse, however, is that of his enormous literary output. The hundreds of his hymns in the older Wesleyan hymn-books are still only small selections; the 13 volumes of his *Poetical Works* omit over 1,300 poems available

---

[6] *History of English Prosody*, Vol. II (1923), p. 501. Cf. pp. 507, 530–1.
[7] *Survey of English Literature, 1730–1780*, Vol. II (1928), pp. 224–6.

only in manuscript. Even a widely representative collection like the present volume is quite inadequate for the research student who seeks to do more than acquire the basic 'feel' of Wesley's writing. It is well at the outset to understand something of the magnitude of the task of even *reading* all Wesley's verse, let alone studying it.

Many have smiled over George Saintsbury's characteristic dictum: 'They say Charles Wesley wrote between 6,000 and 7,000 hymns—a sin of excess for which he perhaps deserved a very short sojourn in the mildest shades of Purgatory, before his translation upwards for the best of them.'[8] Actually this fabulous figure is both understatement and overstatement. It is an exaggeration to speak of 6,000 'hymns' if that term is to be used in a narrowly specific sense, as defined below; it is a serious understatement if by 'hymn' we mean (as most people who make such statements about Charles Wesley's writings usually do mean) his verse compositions as a whole, or even those with more or less religious content.

I dare not claim that my own statistics contain no element of error—the task of compilation is beset with multifarious problems—but the figure of 8,989 of his poems which I have read is near enough to 9,000 to proclaim that 'round' number as the total of his extant poems *as he left them*. The last cautionary phrase is necessary because of the many alterations to which they have been subjected, division into separate parts here, combination of smaller units into a larger unit there, and extracts everywhere. In particular it is fairly common knowledge that many of his compositions were (to use his own description) 'Short Hymns' of only one or two stanzas. In order to gain an adequate understanding of the scope of his literary output, therefore, it is necessary to count the lines, not the poems. To summarize the results of such a wearying though (I believe) necessary undertaking, we may take it that Charles Wesley wrote (again in round figures) 9,000 poems, containing 27,000 stanzas and 180,000 lines. This is something like three times the output of one of our most prolific poets, William Wordsworth, and even more than that of the redoubtable Robert Browning. Moreover, unlike both these poets, Charles Wesley's verse consists almost solely of lyrics in stanzaic form—a mere 7,500 lines are extant in various couplet forms. Taking the average— and it must be stressed that this is an *average*, not a description of normal practice—Charles Wesley wrote ten lines of verse every day for 50 years, completing an extant poem every other day.

Much has been written about the dangers of facility in verse, and most of it applies to Charles Wesley. He left scores of poems incomplete—many of them published in that form without any suggestion that the author had originally intended an addition or continuation. There are hundreds that he could have improved, should have improved, and almost certainly would have improved had he deliberately prepared them for publication. Oliver Elton's comment contains much truth, though it is far from being the whole truth—'Charles Wesley has the note of the *improvisatore*, with whom it is hit or miss. . . . He goes wrong, not through over-elaboration, but through neglect of finish.' For the defence we can produce thousands of poems which Charles Wesley carefully revised time and time again,

[8] *History of English Prosody*, Vol. II (1923), p. 531.

particularly the 3,500 manuscript poems on the Gospels and the Acts, whose five volumes were worked through and touched up eight times between their completion in 1764 and his death in 1788. His extant manuscripts abound in erasures, alterations, and alternative words—as may be seen from some of the texts and collations in the anthology which follows. Even these frequently revised poems, however, often betray signs that they were originally composed in the saddle rather than in the study, and are more memorable for their flow and pace than for their depth or their polish.[9] Many a poem came to him white-hot, and its original casting has only been tampered with to its detriment. It cannot even be said that all Charles Wesley's own revisions were obvious improvements, though this is more nearly true of the editorial emendations of his brother John. Henry Moore preserves an interesting picture of Charles Wesley at work on his verse from youth to age:

When at the University, in early youth, his brother (as he informed me) was alarmed whenever he entered his study. *Aut insanit homo, aut versus facit.* [Moore's footnote translates: 'The man is mad, or making verses.'] Full of the muse, and being short-sighted, he would sometimes walk right against his brother's table, and, perhaps, overthrow it. If the 'fine phrenzy' was not quite so high, he would discompose the books and papers in the study, ask some questions without always waiting for a reply, repeat some poetry that just then struck him, and at length leave his brother to his regularity. . . . When he was nearly fourscore, he retained something of this eccentricity. He rode every day (clothed for winter even in summer) a little horse, grey with age. When he mounted, if a subject struck him, he proceeded to expand, and put it in order. He would write a hymn thus given him, on a card (kept for the purpose) with his pencil, in shorthand. Not unfrequently he has come to our house in the City-road,[10] and, having left the poney in the *garden* in front, he would enter, crying out, 'Pen and ink! Pen and ink!' These being supplied, he wrote the hymn he had been composing. When this was done, he would look round on those present, and salute them with much kindness, ask after their health, give out a short hymn, and thus put all in mind of eternity.[11]

CLASSICAL TRAINING

Between those two pictures of the poet at work, as an Oxford tutor in his early twenties and as a veteran Anglican clergyman and Methodist preacher on the verge of eighty, there is much more than a gulf of fifty years' writing experience—there is a complete transformation, both in content, in form, and in inspiration. Yet it must be claimed that the academic exercises and experiments of the Student of Christ Church, Oxford, his myopic absorption in the classics of Greece and Rome, and especially in the Latin poets, tilled the soil for what became his life's blossoming. It has usually been assumed that Charles Wesley suddenly became a poet at his conversion in 1738, that 'Where shall my wond'ring Soul begin?' was, in fact, practically his first venture in verse. Nothing could be farther from the truth, although this assertion is not susceptible of absolute proof. He was already, I am convinced, a matured poet. Already he had written hundreds of competent poems, mainly versifica-

[9] Examples will be found in Nos. **185** and **187**; for a much more carefully constructed poem see No. **195**; cf. Nos. **240** and **254**, the former left permanently unfinished, the latter an 'imperfect hymn just as it came to [his] mind', later revised for publication.

[10] I.e. Wesley's House adjoining Wesley's Chapel, City Road, London.

[11] *Life of the Rev. John Wesley*, Vol. II (1825), pp. 368–9.

tions of the classics in the manner of Dryden or Pope. This seems to have been a major preoccupation of his nine years at Oxford, the foundation having been laid by thirteen years at Westminster School under his elder brother Samuel, himself a noteworthy classicist and poet, as was their father before them. At Westminster Charles Wesley had become saturated with the classics of Greece and Rome as he was later to become saturated with the classics of Samaria and Jerusalem. In both cases his enthusiasm found expression in a series of occasional poems inspired by his meditations on purple passages. His *Short Hymns on Select Passages of the Holy Scriptures* and his five subsequent volumes on the Gospels and the Acts have survived. His youthful volumes on the classics have disappeared, and only fragments remain.[12] Those fragments, however, form a reminder of the deep classical scholarship, and of the real poetical talent, displayed while he was still an Oxford tutor. Doubtless he dreamed of an academic future when he would gather the heady literary fruits of his solid classical studies at Westminster and Oxford. He did reap his harvest; but it was not the kind that he had expected.

Any full understanding of the verse of Charles Wesley must begin with this classical background, and with an educational system that insisted on aspects of literary study which are now regarded as unimportant sidelines if not the veriest eccentricities. In Wesley's youth the swing in higher education toward mathematics and modern languages was only in its infancy. The classics still held the field, together with the arts of thinking, of writing, and of speaking, which went with them. Rhetoric, in particular, which we hardly consider a basic academic subject, was then a most important part of education both at grammar school and university level, and those strange 'exercises' before graduation at Oxford and Cambridge were largely modelled on the practice of the Schools of Rhetoric organized in Athens by Marcus Aurelius. The study of rhetoric was essential to the matter, as well as to the manner, of the 'acts' and 'opponencies' at Oxford, and colleges offered prizes for 'declamations'. This was the academic atmosphere in which both Wesleys breathed freely. In their days there were no examinations in 'practical' or 'applied' subjects, and their mother tongue was almost a foreign language. All was 'pure' and as far away from the realities of daily living as dead languages could make it. Even though there were symptoms of academic decay at Oxford, and although the medieval system was on its way out, one of the basic elements of the Methodist reformation at the university was a revival of learning as well as of religion, and of learning moulded on traditional classical lines. The classics continued to provide genuine inspiration to both Wesleys, and when John Wesley founded his own grammar school at Kingswood it was on classical lines. Vossius's *Rhetoric* was prescribed as a text-book for the senior class, whose pupils had to 'learn to make themes and declaim'.

The picture may seem slightly overdrawn, but this will serve to underline the fact that Charles Wesley's art of versification was quite consciously an *art*, and a carefully practised art, long before he was fired with religious inspiration. When we refer to rhetorical devices in the verse of Charles Wesley, devices with fearsome titles such as anadiplosis and aposiopesis, chiasmus, epizeuxis, oxymoron, and parison, it is no perversity of the

[12] See Nos. 232–3 in this anthology.

enthusiastic researcher who is imagining minutiae which do not really exist, and thus making the process of Charles Wesley's verse-making sound much more complicated than it really was. Nor is it that Wesley had accidentally stumbled upon a way of saying things which had a peculiar structure and therefore a peculiar effect. It was all there in his classical training, a training so thorough that the vocabulary, the style, and the structure of his verse were markedly affected by it. This is not to suggest, of course, that every rhetorical device, every Latinism or metrical effect, was deliberately thought out by Wesley, any more than they are by other poets. But a particular mode of writing, the classical mode, had become so ingrained that even when he wrote unpremeditated verse, as often as not there were features that recalled the classical tutor's study almost as much as the prayer-room or the pulpit.

As experiences accumulated for Charles Wesley with the passing of the busy years—ordination, travel, 'heart-warming', evangelical preaching, marriage, family joys and anxieties, deep concern over the pattern of contemporary Church life, political shocks—the young Oxford tutor developed out of all recognition. His verse gained new notes, experimented with new techniques, acquired a new depth—and height. Gradually the Bible came to mean to him even more than the Classics had meant, saturating his language in speech and in verse. Yet the Scriptures never completely ousted the Classics, either in thought or in composition— witness the quotations from Horace and Virgil and Ovid prefixed to the political verse of his seventies.[13] They remained parallel streams watering the broad and fertile acres of his post-conversion years.

THE SPIRITUAL IMPETUS

Although the beginnings of his capacity for the making of memorable verses must be sought in his classical training, the name of Charles Wesley could hardly have been known and loved in millions of homes across two centuries and five continents without the quickening of his talent through a spiritual impetus. For any great poetry to be written there must be both consummate craftsmanship and a powerful urge. Without the spiritual urge that was born at Whitsuntide 1738 and which continued through varying phases to his life's end, Charles Wesley would have been both more and less successful as a poet than he actually became. He would (I believe) almost certainly have achieved widespread recognition as a minor poet, possibly as one of the major poets; he would have written some really great love poems (always assuming that he had fallen in love!); and he would have made a name chiefly by his scintillating satire— a more polished Butler or Swift, a more virile companion for Gray, Goldsmith, and Collins. He would have been admired, feted and feared in the literary circles of his own day, and applauded by the literary historians of every day. This did not happen, however, and it is of course impossible to prove that it would have happened. In the event his talents as a poet were both enriched and engulfed by his discovery of a rapturous personal religion. Henceforth all other pursuits, no matter how deeply felt, how vividly expressed in verse at the time, assumed but secondary importance compared with his spiritual obsession. This spiritual obsession brought

[13] See Nos. 292, 302, 310-11.

a new note into English secular verse and swelled immeasurably the rising tide of hymnody—hymnody which overflowed into sacred poetry and became a formative influence in the literary education of the average Englishman.

Both Charles Wesley's chief strength and the main reason for the comparative neglect of his poetry by literary students are to be found in the basic content of his published work. In his day it was considered 'enthusiastic' to undergo deep religious emotion, and most indecorous to *write* about such things. Yet the Wesleys and their followers did undoubtedly experience deep religious emotions, just as they thought deeply upon theological problems (which was socially permissible), and they became convinced that the conventional inhibitions and reticences about personal religion were at least partly to blame for the cold frustrations of the century. Therefore they must broadcast the good news of personal salvation from sin through faith in the Lord Jesus Christ, the normality of a personal assurance of that saving faith, and the possibility of the crowning spiritual experience of what was variously called 'holiness', 'Christian perfection', or 'perfect love'.

It was the profound conviction of the Wesleys that a personal experience of God's saving and sustaining love was possible not only for an elect few, but for all men. In their theological thought they went to the very brink of Calvinism, endorsing its emphasis upon the sovereignty of God, but then drew back. Salvation must be 'free', but it must also be 'for all', otherwise it was hardly a gospel. Both became key-notes of Methodist preaching and Methodist singing. As a result the theological atmosphere of English religion was changed from the rigid Calvinism of the seventeenth century to the Arminianism and modified Calvinism of the nineteenth century. In this theological revolution no two men played a greater part than the brothers Wesley, and it seems likely that the hymns of Charles were even more influential than the sermons of John.

This gospel, illustrated from Scripture, from theological reasonings, and from personal experience, formed the one theme of Charles Wesley's hymns. When Dr J. E. Rattenbury writes of *The Evangelical Doctrines of Charles Wesley's Hymns* it is with no implication that there were any other doctrines of essential importance to him. Everything else was bent to this: the ventures into the Arminian-Calvinist controversy, the more academic hymns on the doctrine of the Holy Trinity, the mysticism and sacramentarianism of the *Hymns on the Lord's Supper*, nearly every paraphrase and meditation based on the Old Testament as well as on the New—all was seen through the Gospel glow, every event was brought to its focus in the Cross, the Divine Act on behalf of Man. Even Wesley's love poems needed only a few light touches to transform them into hymns; even his poems of spiritual despair have a substratum of assurance; hardly a topical or a controversial or a political poem but eventually leads to the Cross and to the final Crown in Heaven. Charles Wesley did write poems, many more poems than has generally been realized, which were not strongly tinctured with the glowing colours of his own deep faith— but he did not publish them. His published work was a weapon of his evangelism, both in creating the atmosphere and in reinforcing the message of the Methodist preacher. Indeed in some respects the exhortation from the pulpit was a far less effective weapon than the song in the pew.

The subsequent lowering of the spiritual temperature, even within Methodism, made it somewhat difficult after a few generations to sing many of Charles Wesley's greatest hymns without either hypocrisy or at least a faintly uneasy self-consciousness—a 'defect' from which the hymns of Isaac Watts do not suffer, since they enshrine, not the heights and depths of the human soul, but 'average religious sentiment'.[14] One example of this debasing of Wesley's spiritual currency is to be seen in his preoccupation with Heaven. One of the most characteristic features of his hymns is the way in which, no matter with what earthly subject they commence, they end in Heaven. Not only a clear belief in an after-life, but frequent and fervent thoughts about it were common both to saint and sinner in Wesley's day. Death, as the entrance to this after-life, obtruded itself much more upon the attention of adults and children alike then than now—quite apart from the fact of a much higher average of mortality. Gradually agnosticism has laid its cold hand on the man in the street, and even the man in the pew neither wishes to be reminded too frequently about death nor has very clear views about heaven or about hell. As a result our hymn-books have required drastic revision. Many hymns (such as 'Ah! lovely appearance of death!' though not 'Rejoice for a brother deceased') have been completely banished. Others have been truncated by the omission of the closing references to heaven. Yet heaven for Charles Wesley was not simply a place of rest—or even of joy—after death. Heaven was a relationship between God and man, a relationship summed up in the word 'love', just as the Person of Christ is summed up as 'Love', and just as the perfect life of the Christian is summed up as 'love'. In other words, heaven was in some sense present in the Christian's earthly communion with God, and the real heavenliness of the after-life was the enlargement and enrichment of this communion. This is seen constantly in Charles Wesley's poems, including the excised portions, such as this final stanza (omitted from the hymn-books) of his 'O for a Thousand Tongues':

> With me, your Chief [i.e. chief of sinners], you then shall *know*,
>   Shall feel your Sins forgiven;
> Anticipate your Heaven below,
>   And own, that Love is Heaven.[15]

Not only did Wesley's conversion introduce him to depths and heights of personal emotion. Not only did it help him to view those emotions in the context of eternity. It also enlarged the boundaries of his experience horizontally upon earth as well as vertically into heaven, by making him more susceptible to the emotions of others. Nor is 'susceptible' a large enough word; he was more responsive to the emotions of others, deeply, desperately concerned about them, for they were the potential children of God, and lived on the threshold of eternity. So powerful was the sympa-

---

[14] J. E. Rattenbury, *Evangelical Doctrines of Charles Wesley's Hymns* (1941), pp. 59–60.
[15] No. 17. See G. H. Findlay, *Christ's Standard Bearer* (1956), pp. 67–74.

thetic link between Charles Wesley and others that it is sometimes exceedingly difficult to be sure whether in his verse he is describing his own experience or identifying himself with that of someone else. Occasionally clues of time or place or circumstance make it clear that he writes of himself. In other instances it is just as clear that he is thinking and feeling himself into the personality of another—as when he writes for wives and widows, coal-miners and criminals, lay preachers, Loyalist soldiers, or the scholars at Kingswood School. There remains a large body of verse, however, where—unless new evidence is forthcoming, such as is sometimes available in his manuscripts—it is impossible to be sure whether he portrays personal or vicarious experience. Dr Rattenbury has pointed out that his use of the first person singular is often 'a piece of dramatic personation', as when he writes:

> Pity my Simplicity,
> Suffer me to come to Thee.

On the other hand Dr Rattenbury has also stressed the fact that the penitential hymns written by Charles Wesley in the first person are usually far more powerful and convincing than those in the third person, and are therefore the more likely to have emerged from his own experience. Be that so, his faculty of convincing 'personation' remains. There is little doubt that Charles Wesley's personal discovery of religious faith brought such a heightening of sensitivity that his identification with the emotions of others led to the development in his verse of what can justly be described as a form of dramatic art. 'It is in this dramatic poetry, combining liturgy and evangelism,' says Mr T. S. Gregory, 'that we can discern the genius of Charles Wesley.'[16]

CHARLES WESLEY'S VOCABULARY

Having thus sketched in the academic and spiritual background to Charles Wesley's ventures into verse, it is desirable to analyse some of the literary characteristics of his work, and thus to demonstrate in some small way the manner in which his heritage was transmuted into genuine poetic achievement. Dr Donald Davie claims that Wesley takes a Latin word and 'refurbishes' it so that 'the blunted meaning or the buried metaphor comes sharp and live again, by a sort of Latinate pun'.[17] Dr Henry Bett gives many examples of such words—'expressed' (a shape struck out with a die), 'illustrate' (illuminate), 'secure' (free from care), 'tremendous' (terrifying), 'virtue' (manliness or power).[18] Most of these words have suffered from continuous debasement, so that it is difficult to recapture the shade

---

[16] J. E. Rattenbury, *Evangelical Doctrines of Charles Wesley's Hymns* (1941), pp. 28–31; T. S. Gregory, article on 'Charles Wesley's Hymns and Poems' in the *London Quarterly Review* (1957), pp. 253–62. This same identification with the deepest spiritual experiences of every man is one of the reasons why Charles Wesley's poetry can be so effectively used in private devotions. The cover of Dr J. Alan Kay's *Wesley's Prayers and Praises* (1958)—an anthology of lesser-known poems for devotional use—claims that Wesley 'speaks to our condition with a directness which is without parallel'.
[17] *Purity of Diction in English Verse* (1952), pp. 76–7.
[18] *The Hymns of Methodism* (1945), pp. 35–46.

of meaning which they had for Wesley, and in some cases well-nigh impossible without a footnote—a notable example is 'pompous', recalling the due dignity of a magnificent procession, without any overtones of ostentation.

Wesley displayed a Miltonic facility for incorporating polysyllabic Latinate words into the texture of his verse in such a manner that they illustrated his theme, introduced a modulation into the verbal music, and varied without disrupting the rhythm. Adjectives and adverbs ending in '-able, -ably' and '-ible, -ibly' were particular favourites, but nouns and verbs were employed with similar effect. A well-known and deservedly praised example is found in the opening stanza of one of his *Nativity Hymns* (No. **39**):

> Let Earth and Heaven combine,
> Angels and Men agree
> To praise in Songs divine
> Th'Incarnate Deity,
> Our GOD contracted to a Span,
> Incomprehensibly made Man.

This illustrates what Dr Davie describes as the threading of Latinisms on the staple Anglo-Saxon of his diction so that both 'criss-cross and light up each the other's meaning'—witness, 'songs/divine', 'contracted/span', and 'incomprehensibly/man'. Moreover every word is used precisely, not only (as we shall see later) carefully chosen and carefully placed, but so carefully chosen and placed that clear thought about its exact meaning is demanded of the reader, and always rewarded. Wesley's is the art of the etcher, sharp and definite rather than vague and suggestive.

Some people are basically afraid of precision and profundity in hymns, and are also apt to confuse a lengthy word with prolixity. An interesting example is to be found in 'O Thou who camest from above' (No. **96**). Wesley wrote:

> There let it for thy glory burn
> With inextinguishable blaze.

This was too much for the compilers of the ill-fated 1904 edition of *Hymns Ancient and Modern*, who substituted tautology—'with ever-bright, undying blaze'. This meddlesome botch (as John Wesley would undoubtedly have called it) did not find its way into the 'Standard Edition' of *Hymns Ancient and Modern*, and has happily been refused entry to the 1950 edition, which has restored a few other of Wesley's original readings. Unfortunately, however, as Mr Findlay points out,[19] it has been retained in the *BBC Hymn Book*.

It must be granted that Wesley's introduction of Latinisms in order to point and illustrate his thought does not always 'come off', mainly because he is writing above our heads. Most of us lag far behind him in our familiarity with the Classics; it needs, therefore, not only a mental effort, but the consultation of a lexicon, in order to appreciate fully some of his words and phrases. We are in much the position of the rank and file of Wesley's converts; we get the gist of his thought through the sturdy Anglo-Saxon, and

[19] *Christ's Standard Bearer*, p. 16.

are swept past the finer points of the Latin allusion. Unlike most sermon-tasters, we understand the argument, but not the illustration. A few familiar examples may be quoted, prefaced by the warning that because they are familiar we may miss their fuller significance:

> Blest with this Antepast of Heaven! (No. **1**)
> Bear'st them thro' Life's disparted Wave (No. **11**)
> Unmark'd by Human Eye,
>   The latent Godhead lay.[20]
> Concentred all thro' JESUS' Name. (No. **71**)

Greek words are nothing like so frequent in Wesley's verse as those from ancient Rome, and they almost always come from the Greek of the New Testament. A familiar example is his use of 'panoply' (the original is πᾶνοπλία) in 'Soldiers of Christ, arise' (No. **30**). Another occurs in a favourite stanza of both Dr Bett and Mr Manning, taken from one of Wesley's *Hymns Occasioned by the Earthquake* (1750), where he describes the unshaken house awaiting the Christian in the City of God:

> Those amaranthine bowers,
>   Inalienably ours,
> Bloom, our infinite reward,
>   Rise, our permanent abode,
> From the founded world prepared,
>   Purchased by the blood of God.

Both Bett and Manning point out the Latinism of 'founded' and the retention of the original Greek in the musical 'amaranthine'. I may add the point that this latter retention is quite deliberate, since the English translation 'never-fading' would have fitted Wesley's metre equally well.[21]

Very occasionally there are references to or reminiscences of the Hebrew text of the Old Testament. In some stanzas on Isaiah 9[6-7], 'The mighty God, the everlasting Father', Wesley prefixed the normal translation of the Authorized Version, but in the poem itself instead of 'everlasting Father' used the literal translation from the Hebrew, 'Father of Eternity'. Similarly, in the phrase from Psalm 85 about man being made 'a little lower than the angels' he preferred the original (which is followed by the Revised Version), and read 'a little lower than God', somewhat to the consternation of the non-Hebraists among the Methodists.[22]

When all has been said, however, it must be reasserted that the basic texture of Wesley's speech was provided by Anglo-Saxon, in which every now and then was woven a bright pattern of classical words. Wesley's Anglo-Saxon was derived (like that of many of our greatest writers) from

[20] No. **39**. The phrase about the 'latent Godhead' is apparently a reminiscence of St Thomas Aquinas, who in his hymn *Adoro te devote* used the words *'latens Deitas'*. See Bett, *The Hymns of Methodism*, pp. 112–14.

[21] For fuller details of Charles Wesley's use of the Greek NT see Bett, op. cit. pp. 81–92.

[22] See No. **119**, line 40 and footnote. For these and other references to Wesley's use of the Hebrew see Bett, op. cit. pp. 76–8. It should be noted that Wesley's approach to the Hebrew text was strongly influenced by Matthew Henry—see Rev A. Kingsley Lloyd's article in *London Quarterly Review*, 1946, p. 333.

the Bible, and—in spite of his careful study of the original tongues—from the King James Version of the Bible. This was partly because Bible words and phrases permeated the atmosphere which he breathed as a boy at Epworth, and partly because the solid purity of their diction appealed to his clean, direct mind. Even his pre-conversion translations from the classics are more Anglo-Saxon than Latin in their vocabulary. Certainly after his conversion he deliberately chose home-spun diction, both because it was the language of the English Bible and because it was the surest way to the mind of the ordinary man. Although Wesley is occasionally Miltonic in his use of the sonorous Latin word, in general he is much more akin to his distant relative Daniel Defoe in his use of robust though rarely colloquial common speech. Charles Wesley's Latinisms generally enforced and illustrated for the educated man the basic meaning conveyed in staple Anglo-Saxon to the illiterate worshipper. The deliberate Latinisms, therefore, are comparatively few, though always significant.

This predominant use of the mother tongue was the more noteworthy in an era of neo-classicism, when scholars were fond of larding their weighty tomes with Greek and Latin quotations. John and Charles Wesley sometimes used Latin and Greek in conversation and in correspondence for the sake of privacy or precision, and knew as many classical tags as the next Master of Arts, but both carefully refrained from any form of classical ostentation. Just as their volumes were reduced in size, so their sentences were freed from superfluity and ambiguity for the sake of the 'man in the street'. They wrote plain English for plain people. This economy in words was the result in part of training, in part of a purified taste, and in part of deliberate restraint for the purposes of evangelism. The result both in prose and verse was a lucid, direct, forceful style whose influence on the spread of Methodism, as even on English literature, was greater than has often been recognized.

Moreover, Anglo-Saxon is direct and monosyllabic compared with the elaborations and profundities of Latin and Greek. Words derived from Anglo-Saxon are therefore likely to be more vigorous than those from the classical languages, whose strength is found in the ability to express a finer precision of thought. The one is more suitable for action, the other for contemplation. For the most part Charles Wesley's verse was not mystical or quietly contemplative; certainly it does not embody an eager pursuit of knowledge for its own sake. The note of wonder and awe is never far away, but primarily Wesley's hymns are poems of action—of theological action, the action of God in Christ, matched by the responding action of man.[23]

This marriage of common speech to the timeless realities of personal religion, rather than the jargon of the *literati* harnessed to the latest academic or scientific fashion, almost preserves Wesley from the charge of being 'dated'. Almost, but not quite. His verse contains a few less happy Latinisms and some archaic grammatical constructions. He frequently introduces ideas which are distasteful to modern congregations, such as 'bowels', 'blood', and 'worms'—though the criticism here must be levelled

[23] Cf. Manning, *The Hymns of Wesley and Watts*, pp. 24–6. For a study of Charles Wesley's use of the verbs 'feel' and 'prove' see Findlay, *Christ's Standard Bearer*, pp. 39–46.

at the Bible rather than at the eighteenth century.[24] Nevertheless there is surely much truth in Dr Bett's claim that Wesley's vocabulary is 'distinctly the most modern diction to be found in eighteenth-century verse',[25] and in Mr George Sampson's comment in his Warton lecture that the language of the common man for which Wordsworth sought so painfully, since the belles-lettres of the eighteenth century merely echoed the *patois* of the drawing-room, was nevertheless enshrined in verse in the hymns of the Evangelical Revival. In some of these hymns (as in those of John Cennick) it was used at its most colloquial or with the exaggerated technicalities and sentimentalities of contemporary piety at its worst, but in those of Charles Wesley it was normally purified and strengthened, yet rarely stilted or erudite.

Nevertheless Charles Wesley was ready to experiment with uncommon words, particularly with lengthened and strengthened forms of common words, even though they involved the wedding of Anglo-Saxon and Latin. Some such words were already available for him, though they might be archaic. Such was 'implunge', used in his brief but exhilarating response to the invitation of Revelation 22[17], 'And let him that is athirst come', where nothing but the biggest words would do for the rapturous climax:

> Thy call I exult to obey,
>   And come in the Spirit of prayer,
> Thy joy in that happiest day
>   Thy kingdom of glory to share;
> To drink the pure river of bliss,
>   With life everlasting o'erflow'd,
> Implung'd in the chrystal abyss,
>   And lost in an ocean of God![26]

Occasionally he would coin a word. One very interesting example, not noted in the *Oxford English Dictionary*, occurs in a well-known poem, but has been almost lost either through carelessness or timidity. In 'Soldiers of Christ, arise' (No. **30**) Wesley originally wrote:

> Extend the Arms of mighty Prayer
> Ingrasping all Mankind.

Although in Wesley's day 'grasp' *might* be used for 'embrace', the normal meaning was 'to inclose in the Hand, to take hold on with the Hand, to seize on' (Bailey's *Dictionary*, 15th edn, 1753). Wesley could perfectly well have used the word 'embracing', but its sentimental connotations might well have cheapened his climax; he therefore set aside the conventional word for the bold experiment, and his coined 'ingrasping' is both a robust word, and creates a clear mental image of the mighty arms of prayer spreading wide enough to hold all men within their embrace. Yet in face of the orthodoxy of printers and the obstinacy of congregations he seems eventually to have acquiesced in the splitting of this powerful coining into its two components.

[24] Cf. Bett, *The Hymns of Methodism*, pp. 35–49; G. H. Vallins, *The Wesleys and the English Language* (1957), pp. 21–4, 70–4.
[25] Bett, op. cit. p. 34.   [26] *Scripture Hymns* (1762), II.430.

Whether derived from Anglo-Saxon, Latin, Greek, or Hebrew, from a combination of two of them, or out of his own eager mind, Charles Wesley was constantly searching for *le mot juste*. As a tribute to his precision, his flexibility, and his economy in the use of words, we can do no better than to quote John Wesley's Preface to the 1780 *Collection*, remembering that these words applied principally to his brother's verses, which formed the bulk of the volume:

Here is no doggerel, no botches, nothing put in to patch up the rhyme, no feeble expletives. Here is nothing turgid or bombast on the one hand, nor low and creeping on the other. Here are no *cant* expressions, no words without meaning. . . . Here are (allow me to say) both the purity, the strength, and the elegance of the English Language: and at the same time the utmost simplicity and plainness, suited to every capacity.

This tribute, of course, covers far more than the vocabulary, and summarizes also the style, or the use made of that vocabulary, to which we now turn.

LITERARY ALLUSIONS

One of the delights of reading is to be moving in two dimensions at once—in the dimension of the immediate reality of the story being told or the theme being expounded, and in the dimension of allusions, which light up different aspects of the subject from the view-point of other writings or experiences, and thus make it three-dimensional, solid, alive. As in his vocabulary, so in his literary illustrations, Charles Wesley draws from wide reading, but again primarily from the Bible. We have already seen that Wesley often used single words from Latin and Greek as metaphors in miniature. Sometimes this allusive quality of his verse extends to a phrase, a sentence, or even several sentences. Dr Bett shows how a famous passage in the *Aeneid* (vi. 724–9) has coloured one of Wesley's poems (No. **127**), and he has also drawn attention to the influence both of Horace and Young on another (No. **90**). He suggests that Horace's '*Caelum, non animum mutant, qui trans mare currunt*', recalled either consciously or unconsciously, was the probable origin of some striking lines in one of the *Earthquake Hymns*:

> In vain ye change your place,
>   If still unchanged your mind:
> Or fly to distant climes, unless
>   Ye leave your sins behind.

There is a possible allusion to the *Iliad* (viii. 19) in Wesley's 'golden chains' (No. **127**), and a more sustained reference in one of the *Nativity Hymns* (No. **40**) to the Greek legend of Hercules strangling in his cradle the snakes sent to destroy him—a legend typically transformed to Christian uses, though this particular stanza was marked by John Wesley for future omission:

> Gaze on that Helpless Object
> Of endless Adoration!
>   Those Infant-Hands
>   Shall burst our Bands,
> And work out our Salvation;

> Strangle the crooked Serpent,
> Destroy his Works for ever,
> And open set
> The Heavenly Gate
> To every True Believer.[27]

Dr Bett also garners echoes in Charles Wesley's verse of several English poets, particularly Shakespeare, Milton, Herbert, Dryden, Pope, Prior, and Young.[28] It is almost inevitable that the phraseology of a man's favourite authors should find their way, sometimes unnoticed, into his own writings, though the results in the case of Charles Wesley are occasionally quite surprising to the modern reader. Most of us are familiar with the fact that 'Love Divine, all Loves excelling' follows the metre as well as echoes the opening words of Dryden's 'Fairest Isle', but very few of us would realize unaided the debt of 'Jesu, Lover of my Soul' to Prior's *Solomon*, in its direct quotation of the phrase 'the nearer waters roll'. It was undoubtedly a direct quotation, for *Solomon* was a favourite poem with both Wesleys; it occupies 100 pages of John Wesley's *Collection of Moral and Sacred Poems*,[29] and Charles Wesley urged his daughter Sally to memorize it completely![30] Another familiar echo of Prior's *Solomon* is to be found in the closing lines of 'Christ, from whom all blessings flow' (No. **19**):

> Love, like Death, hath all destroy'd,
> Render'd all Distinctions void:
> Names, and Sects, and Parties fall;
> Thou, O CHRIST, art ALL in ALL!

A glance at Prior's own lines makes the debt unmistakable:

> Or grant thy passion has these names destroy'd:
> That Love, like Death, makes all distinction void.

Charles Wesley's elder brother Samuel also influenced him greatly, and that not only by teaching him to appreciate and practise the compressed, balanced, epigrammatic verse modelled on the Classics. Constant reminiscences of Samuel's poems appear in those of Charles. Dr Bett's *Hymns of Methodism* (pp. 151-5) points out some of them, including the striking debt in 'Christ the Lord is ris'n today' (No. **9**). He strangely omits to mention that one of Charles Wesley's most telling phrases—'Our God contracted to a span' (No. **39**)—quotes the last four words from Samuel Wesley's *Hymn to God the Son*, though he does point out its more remote possible ancestry, the phrase 'contract into a span' used in a quite different context in George Herbert's 'The Pulley'.

Once more, however, it is the Bible that provides Wesley with a never-failing source of allusions as of vocabulary. A detailed familiarity with the

[27] Bett, *The Hymns of Methodism*, pp. 124-9; cf. p. 163.
[28] Ibid., pp. 130-69; cf. Davie, *Purity of Diction in English Verse*, pp. 73-5.
[29] Vol. I, pp. 91-192.
[30] Letter of 1st October, 1778, where his request that she should begin with Book I must be read against the background of his commendation of Miss Morgan's example a week or so earlier.

Bible was the 'extra poetic dimension' (to use Dr Davie's phrase) in which Wesley could move at will and be fairly certain that others could follow him, both the more educated of his readers and—to some extent at least—the few among the Methodist worshippers who were content to remain illiterate.[31] Through the Scripture-saturated hymns of Charles Wesley the Bible-reading and the hymn-singing of the Methodists were mutually enriched.

Much has already been written about the wealth of Scripture allusion in Wesley's hymns, and undoubtedly much more will yet be written. There is no need to labour the point, but two illustrations may be given. In Wesley's day it was quite unnecessary to expound to a Methodist congregation the closing lines of 'Sing to the great Jehovah's praise' (No. **89**), which are usually omitted nowadays either because of their theology of the Second Advent or because of the misleading Latinate construction of the second line. As so often, the hymn ends in heaven, with the Second Coming of our Lord, but this is illustrated by a doubled metaphor from the Old Testament:

> 'Till JESUS in the clouds appear
> To Saints on earth forgiven,
> And bring the grand Sabbatic year,
> The Jubilee of Heaven.

More subtle is the way in which Charles Wesley equates his conversion with the Spirit of God brooding over the face of the waters when the earth was without form and void (Genesis 1[2]):

> Long o'er my Formless Soul
> The dreary Waves did roll;
> Void I lay and sunk in Night:
> Thou, the overshadowing Dove,
> Call'dst the Chaos into Light,
> Bad'st me Be, and live, and love.[32]

There are even echoes of Bible commentaries in Wesley's verse. Dr Bett notes his allusions to Luther on Galatians in 'O Filial Deity' (No. **3**), as also his use of Bengel. The Rev A. Kingsley Lloyd and Dr Erik Routley have demonstrated Wesley's indebtedness to the better-known commentary of Matthew Henry in 'Wrestling Jacob' (No. **25**), 'Captain of Israel's Host' (No. **94**), 'A Charge to Keep' (No. **97**), and other poems.[33] Allusions to the Primitive Fathers, the liturgies, and the mystics are also noted by Dr Bett.[34] When we have added all the allusions and quotations from all the commentators and Christian writers through the centuries to all those from the poets, philosophers, and historians both classical and modern,

[31] The Wesleys exerted a great though often indirect pressure toward wider literacy, for converts wanted to be able to read their Bibles and their hymn-books.

[32] No. *4*, stanza 2.

[33] Bett, *The Hymns of Methodism*, pp. 94–7; *London Quarterly Review* (October, 1946), pp. 330–7. Dr Routley's article was first published in Bulletin 69 of the Hymn Society for Autumn 1954, pp. 193–9, and reprinted in the *Congregational Quarterly* for October 1955, pp. 345–51.

[34] Op. cit. pp. 98–123.

however, we find that they are as a drop in a bucket beside Wesley's use of the Scriptures. This is the vast ocean from which he draws. His verse is an enormous sponge filled to saturation with Bible words, Bible similes, Bible metaphors, Bible stories, Bible ideas. In the thirty-two lines of 'With glorious clouds incompast round' (No. **111**) Dr W. F. Moulton found references to no fewer than fifty verses of Scripture.[35] Indeed, in the memorable words of Dr J. E. Rattenbury, 'A skilful man, if the Bible were lost, might extract much of it from Wesley's hymns. They contain the Bible in solution.'[36]

THE ART OF RHETORIC

Wesley's classical background was of some importance, as we have seen, in his choice of vocabulary and his employment of allusion. It was far more important however, indeed it was a dominant factor, in the more artificial (a better word might be 'artistic') elements of his style—the subtle or startling changes in the normal usage of words, the careful arrangement of both words and ideas so as to bring richer meaning by parallels or contrasts or sequences, or even by somewhat complicated interlockings, and particularly by the many changes rung on the art of repetition. Most of this artistic use of words is so skilful that it is only noticed when pointed out, yet it is the secret of Charles Wesley's most characteristic effect, the compact tautness of his verse, the epigrammatic intensity, as if a powerful steel spring had been compressed into his lines, so that they were always trying to burst their restraints. This is by no means true of all his poems, but it is true of a far greater number than might be generally recognized, as the following selection will show. In some few of them the spring (to continue the metaphor) has been allowed to shoot out and quiver at its full extent. Or, to change the metaphor, some poems give the effect of a spate of words tumbling over one another, or of a smoothly flowing stream, rather than of a huge weight of water dammed up so that a mere fraction gushes through under terrific pressure. Wesley's anapaestic verses are almost all of them examples of this looser, more rapid flow.

It must be insisted that this characteristic effect of restrained energy, both in its general intention and in its particular application, was deliberate—though there may well be scores and hundreds of undesigned examples. Wesley's style was consciously moulded on that of the ancient classics, and he copied many or most of their rhetorical devices. Not that he was constantly saying to himself, 'We must have an oxymoron here, and a chiasmus there', or 'Here at last is a good opportunity for an aposiopesis!' By the time Charles Wesley came to write his greatest poems he was thirty years old, and nearly twenty years of close application to classical studies had made this literary discipline an integral part of his mental processes, just as an experienced preacher almost unconsciously breaks up his thoughts into 'points'. The appreciation, the terminology, and the practice of rhetoric had become almost as essential an element of

[35] *Proceedings* of the Wesley Historical Society, I.26–7.

[36] Rattenbury, *Evangelical Doctrines of Charles Wesley's Hymns*, pp. 47–52, especially p. 48. Cf. Bett, *The Hymns of Methodism*, pp. 71–97. Manning, *The Hymns of Wesley and Watts*, pp. 37–42, Davie, *Purity of Diction in English Verse*, p. 73. See also John W. Waterhouse, *The Bible in Charles Wesley's Hymns* (1954).

his approach to literature as his A B C. Willy-nilly he worked that way—and working that way was one of the chief reasons for his success.

The Art of Rhetoric was a common title for text-books which helped the school-boys and undergraduates of the sixteenth, seventeenth, and eighteenth centuries to choose and marshal their words, both in speech and writing, with the fullest effect. There were over three hundred different terms by which they could describe the 'tropes' and 'figures' and 'fine turns' used by the ancients to make language clear, forceful, and beautiful. The peak period for the use of these devices in English was probably the late sixteenth century, about the time of Puttenham's *Arte of Poesie*, which describes over a hundred of them. Gradually the art of rhetoric was transmuted from the poet's dream to the schoolboy's nightmare, and eventually faded into the light of common day, becoming a memory and an aroma difficult for men of our scientific era to recapture. Even after the middle of the eighteenth century, however, the rhetoricians, though fewer, were far from extinct. In 1755 a grammar school master named John Holmes published an *Art of Rhetoric* in which he listed (with explanations and examples) over 250 rhetorical terms. Some of these have found their way into ordinary speech—such words as enigma, irony, sarcasm. More are among the technical terms still used by grammarians—like apostrophe, ellipsis, euphemism, periphrasis, and even hyperbole, synecdoche, and prolepsis. Others are almost completely forgotten.

In defence of *The Art of Rhetoric* it should be stated that technical terms have great importance in simplifying the complications of life. It is therefore a serious mistake to assign more than its value as satire to the words of one of Wesley's favourite poems, Butler's *Hudibras:*

> For all a Rhetorician's Rules
> Teach nothing but to name his Tools.

This displays excellent rhetoric—in the unfortunate derogatory sense of that word—but poor intelligence. For it *is* important, as any surgeon would insist, to know the names as well as the uses of one's tools. It is a great economy of time and effort if a single word can be used instead of a complicated description, perhaps supported by an illustrative example. Yet many of the Greek, Latin, or Latinized Greek terms which were the rhetorician's tools have not found their way even into the larger English dictionaries. Granted that some of them had synonyms, and others were too finicky to be of permanent value; yet not all those laid aside were useless or cumbersome. How, for instance, would we describe a long succession of subordinate clauses whose meaning is at last made clear by the completion of the sentence? A good example is 'If . . . if . . . if . . . if . . . —You'll be a man, my son!' It hardly seems satisfactory to define this as 'the rhetorical device which forms the basis of Kipling's "If".' But 'the Greeks had a word for it'—a word which was adopted by the Romans, and which came into English with the rest of the paraphernalia of rhetoric, but has now been thrown out as lumber. The word was *'hirmos'* or *'hirmus'*, which is not even to be found in the monumental *Oxford English Dictionary*. Many other terms, for figures of thought or speech which are much more complicated, have no place in our larger standard dictionaries. We therefore tend to overlook the fact that these were among the common-places of literary appreciation and practice in past centuries. It will not be possible here to do more than name a few of the more common rhetorical devices by which Wesley transmitted both energy and polish to his verses.

To follow Holmes's *Art of Rhetoric*, there were three main classes of such devices—tropes, figures, and 'fine turns'. He lists seven main tropes, or 'saying one thing and meaning another': metaphor, its extension the allegory, metonymy, synecdoche, irony, hyperbole, and catachresis. In describing each principal trope he mentions others which are associated with them, and goes on to refer to others sometimes classed as tropes. This abnormal usage of words in order to convey a vivid mental image is, of course, basic to the creative vision of poetry, and many interesting examples can be found in Wesley, whereby he gives poetic force to abstract statements. Sometimes this is in single phrases such as 'our inward Eden' (No. **110**). At other times it is in a more fully developed metaphor, as when he describes the Incarnation of our Lord in terms of dressing and undressing—a metaphor dignified, as well as somewhat disguised—by his use of slightly uncommon words:

> He laid his Glory by,
> He wrap'd Him in our Clay. (No. **39**)

The same poem contains one of his favourite sea-going metaphors of 'sounding the depths':

> See in that Infant's face
> The Depths of Deity,
> And labour while ye gaze
> To sound the Mystery.

This occurs in much simpler form in the lines:

> And sound, with all Thy Saints below,
> The Depths of Love Divine. (No. **13**)

Although on occasion Charles Wesley would mix his metaphors, or at least pass rapidly from one to another, we find many examples of carefully sustained metaphors which almost become allegorical. Such is that in 'Rejoice for a brother deceased':

> Our Brother the Haven hath gain'd,
>   Outflying the Tempest and Wind . . .
>   And left his Companions behind;
> Still toss'd on a Sea of Distress,
>   Hard toiling to make the Blest Shore . . .
> There all the Ship's Company meet,
>   Who sail'd with the Saviour beneath . . .
> The Voyage of Life's at an End . . . (No. **65**)

Metaphor is undoubtedly the most important of the 'tropes' employed by Wesley, though examples of others constantly recur. For instance there is the antonomasia of 'Come all ye *Magdalens* in lust' (No. **1**), where a proper noun is used as a general epithet; there is the synecdoche of 'The mournful, broken Hearts rejoice' (No. **17**), where a part is used instead of the whole; and there is the somewhat annoying metonymy of speaking about 'the stony' instead of 'the stony heart', as in No. **62**. Hyperbole is a favourite device, as in the soaring anapaestics describing the ecstasies of conversion, for which no ordinary language is sufficient:

> I rode on the Sky
> (Freely justified I!)
> Nor envied *Elijah* his Seat;
> My Soul mounted higher
> In a Chariot of Fire,
> And the Moon it was under my Feet. (No. **73**)

John Holmes lists twenty 'principal and most moving figures in speech' and many more either related to these, or unrelated but of minor importance, to which he adds the terms brought over into rhetoric from grammar and logic. Again a few examples must suffice. It is by now a commonplace to point out Wesley's use of exclamation marks—ecphonesis, to use the rhetorician's term. It was impossible to confine the rapture of the Christian experience of God to a mere statement of fact, and sometimes it could only be expressed (and quite imperfectly at that) in a series of exclamatory phrases which had ceased to be a part of a normal sentence. A good example is to be found in the closing four stanzas of 'The Invitation' (No. **62**), where the theme of 'His proffer'd Benefits' announced in stanza 6, and outlined in the following four stanzas, is almost forgotten in the spate of exclamations.[37] Wesley frequently uses the device of hypotyposis or 'lively description', bringing a scene immediately before our eyes:

> See! He lifts his Hands above!
> See! He shews the Prints of Love!
> Hark! His gracious Lips bestow
> Blessings on his Church below! (No. **10**)

Wesley's parentheses are often masterly:

> He left his Father's Throne above,
> (So free, so infinite his Grace!)
> Empty'd Himself of All but Love,
> And bled for *Adam*'s helpless Race: (No. **5**)

One of his favourite devices in this category is to paint a damning generalized picture of sin—or of God's forgiving grace—and then to bring himself into the picture in a dramatic final parenthesis:

> He died for Crimes like Yours—and Mine. (No. **1**)

Wesley can even make a periphrasis add energy to his lines instead of obscuring and weakening them, though he is very sparing in his circum-

[37] There is a similar construction in the closing two stanzas of No. **76**. See also Chapter 2 of G. H. Findlay's *Christ's Standard Bearer*.

locutions, preferring direct phrases. In the much-discussed 'Ah! lovely
Appearance of Death' (No. **64**) he pictures the powdered, rouged, and be-
dizened ladies of fashion, contrasting them very unfavourably with the
bare and seemingly brutal simplicity of death:

> Not all the gay Pageants that breathe
> Can with a dead Body compare.

Perhaps the sentiment does not command our admiration today, but we
can still feel (when we realize what he's about) the force of the contrast
between the deliberately elaborate periphrasis of 'the gay pageants that
breathe' and the directness of 'dead body'.

Figures of thought and speech involving a contrast held a particular
attraction for Charles Wesley—or perhaps we should say that only thus
could he approach an adequate expression of the basic paradoxes of the
Christian faith. Simple contrasts of ideas, or antitheses, are woven into
most of his verse. Sometimes they are obvious and normal, as that
between the verbs and the nouns in:

> Raise the Fallen, chear the Faint,
> Heal the Sick, and lead the Blind. (No. **15**)

Often they are much more subtle. 'How happy are the little Flock' (No.
91), one of the *Hymns for the Year 1756*, furnishes several examples. The
opening lines of stanza 3 contain a simple statement:

> The Plague, and Dearth, and Din of War
> Our SAVIOUR's swift approach declare,
> And bid our Hearts arise.

The following three lines continue the same theme, with the 1755 earthquakes as the subject this time, but with far more subtlety:

> Earth's Basis shook confirms our Hope,
> Its Cities fall but lifts us up,
> To meet Thee in the Skies.

The contrast between the physical fall of the city and the spiritual rise of
the Christian soul is on quite a different level from 'Raise the fallen, chear
the Faint', and the other antithesis can easily be missed, namely that
between 'shook' (which was then grammatically acceptable for 'shaken')
and 'confirms', which still retained something of the physical solidity of
its original Latin meaning, and was certainly so used here by Wesley. The
following stanza repeats the claim that these cataclysmic events foreshadow
the Second Advent of Christ. and encloses within the statement antithetical demonstrations from the four calamities already named:

> Thy Tokens we with Joy confess,
> The War proclaims the Prince of Peace,
> The Earthquake speaks thy Power,
> The Famine all thy Fulness brings,
> The Plague presents thy healing Wings,
> And Nature's final Hour.

Occasionally such antitheses are practically indistinguishable from paradox:

> Dead is all the Life they live,
> Dark their Light, while void of Thee. (No. **4**)

The pure paradox or self-contradiction is also to be found, as in No. **102**:

> Yet when the work is done,
> The work is but begun.

The antithesis also shades off into the oxymoron or combination for special purposes of words which seem to be contradictory. Many examples could be given, from 'the guiltless Shame, the sweet Distress' of No. **62**, and 'confident in self-despair' of No. **25**, to 'their humbled LORD' and 'th'Invisible appears' of No. **38**. Some would limit the term oxymoron to 'adjective + noun' or 'adverb + adjective', as in 'Victim divine' (No. **57**) and 'Death Divine' (No. **54**), or—one which describes the strange blend of opposites to be found in his own verse—'I want a calmly-fervent Zeal' (No. **78**). It may bear the wider connotation, however, and so can be applied to antitheses pushed to the *n*th degree, as in 'Impassive, He suffers; Immortal, He dies' (No. **61**). Whatever terminology is employed the terse vigour and imaginative power of such phrases cannot be gainsaid. And once again it is the supreme mysteries of the Incarnation and the Atonement which constantly demand expression in this way—for how can an Eternal Being either be born or die?

> Beings Source *begins to* Be,
> And GOD himself is BORN! (No. **38**)

In many ways the most interesting group of Wesley's rhetorical devices are those classed by Holmes as 'fine turns', in other words the various types of repetition. These not only add strength and vigour to individual phrases, but also serve to bind together both lines and stanzas. Holmes names fourteen 'chief repetitions', and adds eight minor types. One of the simplest forms is common to most poets, namely anaphora, or the repetition of the same word at the commencement of consecutive phrases or sentences, or (in the case of poetry) lines. One example from Wesley must suffice:

> Enough for all, enough for each,
> Enough for evermore. (No. **95**)

The immediate repetition of a word or phrase within the same sentence, or epizeuxis, is another common method of securing emphasis—'Who for Me, for Me hast dy'd' (No. **3**). Less common generally, but frequent in Wesley, is epanadiplosis, the beginning and ending of a clause or line with the same word:

> Come, Desire of Nations, come (No. **8**)
> Hide me, O my Saviour, hide (No. **15**)
> Go, by Angel-Guards attended,
> To the Sight of JESUS go! (No. **81**)

Repetition of a word or words at the end of lines or phrases is known as epistrophe. A good example occurs in the opening stanza of No. **5**:

> And can it be, that I should gain
> An Int'rest in the Saviour's Blood!
> Dy'd He for Me?—who caus'd his Pain!
> For Me?—who Him to Death pursu'd.
> Amazing Love! how can it be
> That thou, my GOD, shouldst die for Me?

It will be noticed that the phrase 'for me', although in each case it comes at the end of a phrase—indeed in the second instance it constitutes the complete phrase—is actually introduced in three different positions in the line, and only comes at the end when it is most needed for emphasis, in the very last line. One reason is that Wesley (like his father before him, *vide* his *Essay on Poetry*) knew the dangers of double rhymes, except in humorous verse. The other, and chief reason, is that Wesley used subtlety in his repetitions, so that they knocked at the back door of the sub-conscious mind, and gained admittance without the master of the house always being aware of how the divine visitation had occurred. Even more subtle is the effect of wonder created in the same stanza by the mesodiplosis or repetition of the phrase 'can it be' in the middle of successive sentences, once near the beginning of a line, and once at the end, first with the note of questioning predominant, and then with the note of wonder that it really has happened.

Another less common device which is very popular with Wesley is that of using the last word of one clause as the first of the following, thus ensuring both the emphasis of an important point and the continuity of the argument:

> Earnest Thou of Joys Divine,
> Joys Divine on me bestow'd. (No. **4**)

This taking up of an announced theme is very useful as a means of binding stanzas together, as may be seen in No. **18**:

> We our Dying LORD confess,
> We are JESU'S Witnesses.

> 4 Witnesses that CHRIST hath died,
> We with Him are crucified:

People have racked their brains to find a descriptive title for this feature of Wesley's verse. Mr Findlay (who has gathered seventy examples from the 1876 *Collection*) uses what he agrees is the 'rather obscure heading' of 'Last and first words'.[38] Wesley himself knew the name of this most useful rhetorical tool, and we need not be ashamed of using it after him. The technical term for this device is anadiplosis, or epanastrophe.

[38] *Christ's Standard Bearer*, pp. 38–9.

The rhetoricians had terms for several less obvious forms of repetition, but we will mention only three more. The repetition of a phrase in reverse order was known as antistrophe. It occurs in a number of Wesley's well-known hymns, as in 'Thine to Ours, and Ours to Thine' (No. **8**), and it constantly forced itself upon him in his Trinitarian verse—'One in Three, and Three in One' (No. **58**), and 'Three in One, and One in Three' (No. **108**). (The corresponding pattern in thoughts rather than words is chiasmus, mentioned below.) Ringing the changes on different forms of the same word was known by the Latin term *traductio*, an example of which is found in No. **17**:

> My Second, Real, Living Life
> I then began to live.

Familiar to all writers of verse, good and especially bad, is the other device of repetition which we shall mention, the refrain, or (as the rhetoricians termed it) epimone. Wesley's use of the refrain really demands an essay in itself. He employed it in strict moderation, knowing how easily a refrain can become forced or feeble, or the cloak for poverty of thought or craftsmanship. Wesley's are always strong phrases which readily stand up to repetition in a prominent position, though they are often movingly simple, like that to 'O Love Divine, what hast Thou done?', which is an adaptation from Ignatius' *Epistle to the Romans*—'My Lord, my Love is crucified'. He never allows a refrain to be repeated too frequently, as may well be seen from the variations of the last line in 'Wrestling Jacob' (No. **25**). And he is adept at transforming a strong refrain into an even stronger climax. A good example is 'Rejoice, the Lord is King' (No. **59**), whose opening word is taken up in the refrain:

> Lift up your Heart, lift up your Voice,
> Rejoice, again, I say, Rejoice.

We notice how this refrain is itself consolidated by the balanced phrases with their anaphora in the first line, and by the epanadiplosis in the second line. After five such refrains the poem is rounded off with a new couplet, which takes us from earth to heaven, but finishes on that same trumpet-word with which the poem began, an extended epanadiplosis:

> We soon shall hear th'archangel's Voice,
> The Trump of GOD shall sound, Rejoice.

So far we have looked at fairly straightforward examples of the basic types of 'fine turns' or repetition. With an ear as sensitive and a mind as subtle as Charles Wesley's, however, the real mastery is shown in the combination of such devices, and in their extension to other devices which have as yet been given no name. Here (from No. **17**) is an echo of Luther's comment on St Paul, which meant so much in the conversions both of John and Charles Wesley. It shows not only the ringing of the changes on *me* and *my* (traductio), and the powerful wrenching of the correct grammatical order of the words (anastrophe) in order to underline the marvel of God doing that for *him;* there is also a modified anaphora and a double epizeuxis:

> I felt my LORD's Atoning Blood
> Close to *my* Soul applied;
> *Me, me* he lov'd—the Son of GOD
> For *me,* for *me* He died!

Wesley's anaphora itself is frequently, we might almost say usually, accompanied by a subtle change, not only in the word-music, but in the meaning also. It is not *mere* repetition, but repetition with a difference, or —as the Greeks and the rhetoricians called it—antanaclasis. Here is an example combined with antistrophe. The last line of stanza 8 of 'CHRIST the Lord is ris'n today' (No. **9**) runs 'Hid our Life with CHRIST in GOD!' Most of these words are repeated in the first line of the following stanza, 'Hid; till CHRIST our Life appear'. Not only is the sequence of words changed, however; a completely new meaning is given to the phrase 'our life', which in the first instance has a human, in the second a divine, connotation. Many similar examples could be quoted where an echo is combined with slight change both in words and meaning, as in No. **15**:

> All my Trust on Thee is stay'd;
> All my Help from Thee I bring.

Here the change is from passive to active, from rest to movement. Again in No. **20**:

> We all *must* own that GOD is True;
> We all *may* feel, that GOD is Love.

Here the shift within the basic repetition is from universal compulsion to individual choice. This is a frequent sequence of thought with Wesley— 'For all the world—and me!'

One very interesting feature of Wesley's repetitions is a progression by which several words of one line are taken up and extended in the following line, a process which is repeated—a kind of enlarged and extended ana-diplosis which might perhaps be termed epiploce. Stanza 2 of 'God of un-exampled love' (No. **54**) ends 'Was never love like Thine!' This is taken up by the opening line of stanza 3 with the addition of the term 'sorrow' and the amplification of 'Thine':

> Never Love nor Sorrow was
> Like that my JESUS show'd.

Often the patterns of repetition are interlaced in such a way that it is almost impossible to notice them all at a first reading, though all have their unrealized impact. A good example is furnished by the following stanza from 'O Love Divine, how sweet Thou art' (No. **63**):

> Thy only Love do I require
> Nothing on Earth beneath desire,
> Nothing in Heaven above:
> Let Earth and Heaven, and all Things go,
> Give me thine only Love to know,
> Give me thine only Love.

The bold repetition of all but the last two words of the fifth line in the closing line strikes us immediately. We realize on examination that the whole stanza furnishes an example of epanadiplosis, the same phrase being used for the beginning and the end—with the slight variation of 'thy' to 'thine'. Then we see that Charles Wesley has also contrived to give us an intermediate stage by using that same key phrase 'thine only love' in the very middle of the penultimate line, just as it is at the beginning of the opening line and the closing of the last line. Then, perhaps, we notice the anaphora of 'Nothing . . . Nothing', linked in turn with the antithetical 'Earth beneath' and 'Heaven above', which are then gathered together in one phrase: 'Earth and Heaven.' This latter device of accumulating single ideas for summarizing as a compound unity is paralleled by the more frequently employed reverse procedure—announcing the compound idea first, and then taking each term singly for development. An example of this is provided in 'Come on, my Partners in Distress' (No. **80**), where the closing lines of the first stanza read:

> And look beyond the Vale of Tears
> To that celestial Hill.

The verb and the preposition are each taken up (in inverse order) and expanded in the opening lines of the following stanza:

> Beyond the Bounds of Time, and Space,
> Look forward to that happy Place,
> The Saints secure abode.

When (as often) Charles Wesley wants to emphasize the universality of Christ's Saviourhood, he keeps hammering the word 'all' and the phrase 'for all' into our minds, yet with all his insistence contrives to vary his theme so skilfully that the reader or singer does not fully realize how his subconscious mind is being bombarded. (Let us call this, as does Holmes, 'tautotes', and reserve 'tautology' for clumsiness in repetition, which Wesley's is certainly not.) In 'Let Earth and Heaven agree' (No. **22**) stanza 6 introduces the theme quietly:

> For Me, and All Mankind,
> The Lamb of GOD was slain . . .
> Loving to All, He none pass'd by . . .

(In passing we note that the 'all' is implicit in the closing negative clause.) Stanza 7 closes on the same note:

> What Thou for all Mankind hast done!

Stanza 8 repeats the word 'all' in the second syllable of each of the last three lines, but with a different word of introduction on each occasion:

> For this alone I breathe
> To spread the Gospel-sound,
> Glad Tidings of Thy Death
> To all the Nations round;
> Who All *may* feel Thy Blood applied,
> Since All are freely justified.

At last in stanza 9, before the quiet closing 'Amen!' of stanza 10, the full battery is brought into play, taking up the simple second syllable 'all' in the second line (with yet a different introductory word), and letting it expand into an emphatic 'for all' (introduced in stanza 7) at the end of the fourth line. The phrase is hammered home at the beginning of the following line, and for good measure there is a two-fold repetition to open the last line:

> O for a Trumpet-voice,
>   On all the World to call,
> To bid their Hearts rejoice
>   In Him, who died for All!
> For All, my Lord was crucified,
> For All, for All my Saviour died.

The devices of repetition crowd one upon another—tautotes, anadiplosis, anaphora, epizeuxis. Yet though the effect is there and is strongly felt, we are conscious of no straining for effect. Indeed it is hard to realize that just over half of the last fifteen words consist of 'for all'. This is indeed the art that conceals art!

Sometimes *two* words are thus woven into a pattern of repetition, a double tautotes, with many of the associated 'fine turns'. In the third stanza of 'Father, Son, and Holy Ghost' (No. **58**) Wesley has already played on the theme 'all', and this is continued and even intensified in the following stanza, with the addition of a twin theme, 'take', introduced by an epanadiplosis on the preparatory word 'claim'—the just demand that leads to the only adequate response. The marriage of the two key words as 'take all' is hinted at or assumed throughout, though we never see the pair thus side by side:

> If so poor a Worm as I
>   May to thy great Glory live,
> All my Actions sanctify,
>   All my Words and Thoughts receive:
> Claim me, for thy Service claim
> All I have, and all I am.
>
> Take my Soul and Body's Powers,
>   Take my Mem'ry, Mind, and Will,
> All my Goods, and all my Hours,
>   All I know, and all I feel,
> All I think, and speak, and do;
> Take my Heart—but make it new.

It will be seen that repetition was one of the chief means by which Charles Wesley ensured the powerful impact of the best of his verse. This also was one of the secrets of its continuity and cohesion. It is necessary to examine in a little more detail the architecture both of stanza and of poem, bearing in mind the fact that repetition provides the basic mortar binding together the whole structure and its several components.

STRUCTURE

Charles Wesley's education had involved another important mental discipline which is less common today, though by no means so rare as the study of rhetoric. He was trained, and to a small extent helped to train others, in the art of logic, though he never pretended to be the equal of his brother John in this field. The very *size* of his stanzas was conditioned by his logical approach. He wanted a stanza in which a theme could be announced, developed, and satisfactorily concluded—with a foreshadowing of the theme for the following stanza. He therefore showed a marked preference for the longer stanza, rather than for the somewhat cramping limits of the conventional four lines. On the other hand he carefully avoided as too heavy for lyrical verse the iambic pentameters so beloved of later hymn-writers, and only used lines of more than eight syllables in strongly reflective poems or in his anapaestics, where the length was counteracted by the speed. Such was his fondness for lengthy stanzas that he not only doubled the 8.8.8.8 8.8 metre, but even the already doubled short metre, making a stanza of sixteen lines. Yet he mercifully allowed a central pause. This stanzaic caesura is to be found also in most of his eight-lined stanzas—which is why later editors have so easily halved them, though not always without some slight disruption of their thought. Charles Wesley wrote several hundreds of poems in four-lined stanzas, but so appreciated intellectual elbow-room that of his total production of some 27,000 stanzas the over-all average is almost exactly six lines per stanza.

Within the stanzas themselves we find an orderly synchronization of thought and verse. In general every line contains a complete idea, is in fact a clause or a sentence. Similarly every stanza is a paragraph, and the whole poem a logically constructed essay in verse, or—to use the contemporary word of his grammar school and university days—a 'theme'. Charles Wesley seldom uses the run-on line or enjambment in order to link his lines together—indeed this is in the opinion of Dr Bett one of the differentiae between the verse of John and Charles Wesley. Instead he uses the devices of repetition and similar figures, either of words or of thought. Corresponding with the verbal device of anaphora is the figure of thought termed parison. This balancing of clauses is the reverse of antithesis, where the thought of one forms a contrast to the thought of the other. Wesley normally combines it with some kind of verbal repetition. One example has already been quoted in the refrain of No. **59**—'Lift up your Heart, lift up your Voice'. Others will readily occur to the mind: 'Fightings without, and Fears within' (No. **86**), and

> Publish at his wondrous Birth
> Praise in Heaven and Peace on Earth. (No. **46**)

Parison is a favourite device with Wesley for knitting more closely the looser texture of the longer anapaestic lines:

> Your Debt He hath paid, and your Work He hath done. (No. **61**)
> The sweat of our brows, and the work of our hands. (No. **112**)

Mr Manning has already drawn attention to Charles Wesley's skilful use of chiasmus. This device (from the Greek letter X or 'chi') is the crossing of clauses in the pattern $\frac{A}{B} \times \frac{B}{A}$. It is almost the equivalent in thought of the verbal figure of antistrophe. The pattern ABBA is often readily distinguishable, as in the For + persons—mercy—mercy—For + person of:

> For All thy tender Mercies are
> If Mercy is for me. (No. 74)

or in the four nouns of

> Let Earth and Heaven agree
> Angels and Men be join'd. (No. 22)

As Mr Manning points out, even in that supposedly non-literary poem, 'Jesu, Lover of my Soul' (No. 15), there is a very interesting example—nor is this the only one in the hymn:

> Just, and Holy is Thy Name   A
> I am all unrighteousness,   B
> False, and full of Sin I am, B
> Thou art full of Truth, and Grace. A

Not only is there the crossed pattern in the four lines as a whole—Saviour, Sinner, Sinner, Saviour. Mr Manning points out that there are further examples of chiasmus in these same four lines: one in each of the two pairs AA, BB—personal pronoun, epithet, epithet, personal pronoun.[39] Actually there are two further examples of a similar type (not noted by Mr Manning) in each of the *consecutive* pairs of lines, AB, BA, in this case epithet, personal pronoun, personal pronoun, epithet.

The question immediately arises, 'Did Wesley think all that out?' The answer must be, I believe, 'No'. But his mind was so accustomed to thinking in the intertwined formulae of logic as well as in the figures of rhetoric that his sentences often quite unconsciously assumed this form of patterns within patterns. Almost always the chiasmus in arrangement is combined with an antithesis in meaning, as in 'Sow in Tears, in Joy to reap' (No. 31), and

> Who built the Skies,
> On Earth he lies. (No. 40)

The chiasmus is one of the natural outworkings both of the essential paradoxes of the Christian faith, and of the antithetical processes of Charles Wesley's literary art.

With this sense of balance in thought as well as in word we are not surprised to note how carefully Charles Wesley articulates his stanzas. As an

---

[39] *Hymns of Wesley and Watts*, pp. 21–3; cf. Findlay, *Christ's Standard Bearer*, p. 32.

example we may quote No. **2**, whose opening stanza provides a chiasmus in lines 1–2, another in lines 3–4, and a parison in lines 5–6:

> Thee, O my GOD and King,
> My Father, Thee I sing!
> Hear well-pleas'd the joyous Sound,
> Praise from Earth and Heav'n receive;
> Lost, I now in CHRIST am found,
> Dead, by Faith in CHRIST I live.

This stanza is in two distinct sections, as are all the stanzas in this poem, and almost every stanza which he wrote in this metre. The opening couplet introduces the theme—in this case a statement of intention—and the succeeding lines develop that theme, in this instance first by expanding the idea of praise introduced in 'sing', and then by showing the reason for that praise, the restoration of a modern prodigal to his Heavenly Father through faith in Christ. The following stanza similarly announces the theme of 'father and son' carried over from this stanza, and then develops it by an extension of the idea of the wandering of the son and the welcome of the father. And so it goes on, the careful articulation of each stanza, and of the stanzas into the poem as a whole.

In this particular metre the turning-point in Wesley's thought is almost always the close of the first couplet, where the opening iambics are succeeded by the four trochaics, thought thus carefully matching metre—or *vice versa!* In other stanza-forms the articulation of Charles Wesley's thought is quite different, though it is always present—there is no woolliness in his thinking, no meandering. Particular stanza-forms were chosen (doubtless almost subconsciously) because they matched particular lines of thought. Thus Wesley's favourite 8.8.8.8.8 8 iambic metre announces and develops the thought during the first four lines, and then usually clinches the matter in the closing couplet. Looking for an example at random the first stanza on which my eye fell was No. **12**, in the trochaic counterpart of the metre for which I sought:

> CHRIST, whose Glory fills the Skies,
> CHRIST, the true, the only Light,
> Sun of Righteousness, arise,
> Triumph o'er the Shades of Night:
> Day-spring from on High, be near:
> Day-star, in my Heart appear.

Here the theme of Christ the 'light of the world' is introduced by the invocation in lines 1–2, developed into a general prayer in lines 3–4, and in the parison of the closing couplet the movement from the general to the personal is clinched by the direct appeal, 'in *my* heart appear'.

Wherever we look in Charles Wesley's verse we find this development of thought. He does not simply choose his subject and walk round it, describing it from different viewpoints as he comes to them; even less does he drift on by the undisciplined process of the association of ideas; he analyses his theme carefully, and moves in logical succession from one aspect to another. Movement, indeed, is one of the great characteristics of his verse. It is not merely evocative of emotion in a vague way, but takes us step by step along a planned pathway to a definite goal. This is what Mr Manning means when he speaks of the 'liturgical action' of 'Victim Divine', but which he describes perhaps even more felicitously as a 'dramatic and architectural' quality.[40] For it has the virtues of both these realms of art— there is the balanced solidity of a carefully designed building, and there is the purposeful movement of a good play. Constantly we are reminded of the technique of drama. We see the plot unfold before our eyes, stanza-scene after stanza-scene to the final denouement, always an important feature of his verse. Sometimes it is unexpected, more often a heightening of emotion at the inevitable climax, sometimes the evocation of a mood of calm resolution to follow the vision that has been given. Like all good dramatists, Wesley watched his curtain lines, though one could hardly expect them all to be of equal quality. Mr Manning points out how in 'See how great a flame aspires' every stanza closes with 'a knock-out blow'— 'all the preceding lines lead by steps to an emphatic concluding phrase'.[41] Even more powerful is the closing phrase of stanza 7 of 'Come on, my partners in distress' (No. **80**), where Wesley describes the rapture of heaven:

> The Father shining on his Throne,
> The glorious co-eternal Son,
> The Spirit one and seven,
> Conspire our Rapture to compleat,
> And lo! we fall before his Feet,
> And Silence heightens Heaven.

There is enough theological and scriptural allusion there to keep us busy for some time; in addition, if we've got our allusions right, and if we've ever been hushed in a soaring Gothic cathedral, we can hardly miss the awe and the rightness of the last line.

It is not surprising that Dr Davie quotes Wesley as an illustration of Ezra Pound's definition of 'scenario' in literary construction—'so arranging the circumstance that some perfectly simple speech, perception, dogmatic statement appears in abnormal vigour'. Dr Davie draws attention to 'the poignant simplicity which is one of [Wesley's] best effects, . . . brought about by sudden and calculated descent from a relatively elaborate level of language', akin to Lear's 'Pray you, undo this button'. As an example he quotes the following:

> Sinners, believe the gospel word,
> Jesus is come your souls to save!
> Jesus is come, your common Lord;
> Pardon ye all through Him may have,
> May now be saved, whoever will;
> This Man receiveth sinners still.

His comment is: 'The piercing directness of that last line is an achievement in literary form.'[42] That this is quite deliberate is confirmed by the fact

[40] *The Hymns of Wesley and Watts*, p. 69.   [41] Ibid. pp. 39–40.
[42] *Purity of Diction in English Verse*, pp. 72–3. The stanza quoted begins a cento in common use until the *Methodist Hymn-book* of 1904; it comes from 'See, sinners, in the gospel glass', No. 10 in *Hymns on God's Everlasting Love*, 1741.

that in this particular stanza Wesley deserts his normal articulation for this form, and instead of pairing his thoughts for a closing couplet he makes the last line stand starkly isolated.

Wesley's closing lines are frequently epigrammatic, particularly in his satirical verse, but also in his more devotional poems. In No. 2 he follows the closing words of his prototype (the parable of the Prodigal Son), but makes them evangelical, personal, and epigrammatic, by means of two balanced antitheses:

> Lost, I now in CHRIST am found,
> Dead, by Faith in CHRIST I live.

A poem on the death of his child (No. 255) closes on a typical note, though one we might hardly expect in such a context:

> Love our Eden here would prove,
> Love would make our heaven above.

Love is frequently his closing thought, occasionally in vivid phraseology, as in No. 161, 'In speechless eloquence of love'. No. 170 is a challenge to those who boast of their Christian Perfection, and one feels that the antitheses of the closing epigram are worthy of a better cause:

> Humility your whole delight,
> And your ambition's utmost height
> To weep at Jesus' feet.

Actually Charles Wesley was at his most epigrammatic in his satirical verse, especially upon subjects which moved him greatly, as did the controversy over predestination. 'The Horrible Decree' (No. 117) contains some outstanding examples of vigorous closing lines to the DSM stanzas:

> And mockest with a fruitless Call
> Whom Thou hast doom'd to die.

> Thou shew'st him Heaven, and say'st, go in—
> And thrust's him into Hell.

Indeed the whole of what Charles Wesley calls the 'other Gospel' of the fiend is a sustained epigram, one of the most powerful pieces of theological invective in the English language:

> Sinners, abhor the Fiend,
> His *other* Gospel hear,
> *The GOD of Truth did not intend*
> *The Thing his Words declare,*
> *He offers Grace to All,*
> *Which most cannot embrace*
> *Mock'd with an ineffectual Call*
> *And insufficient Grace.*

> *The righteous GOD consign'd*
> *Them over to their Doom,*
> *And sent the Saviour of Mankind*
> *To damn them from the Womb;*
> *To damn for falling short,*
> *Of what they could not do,*
> *For not believing the Report*
> *Of that which was not true.*

> *The GOD of Love pass'd by*
> *The most of those that fell,*
> *Ordain'd poor Reprobates to die,*
> *And forc'd them into Hell.*
> *He did not do the deed*
> *(Some have more mildly rav'd,)*
> *He did not damn them—but decreed*
> *They never should be saved.*

Dr Newton Flew has enabled us to see another frequent element in the structure of Charles Wesley's verse, not this time dramatic but homiletic. He was, of course, a preacher, both a logical and a challenging, forceful preacher, and it seems obvious (when someone has pointed it out!) that he should prepare many of his poems as he prepared his sermons. One of the best examples is 'What shall I do my God to love' (No. **74**), even though it is a hymn adopted (and slightly adapted) from the closing stanzas of a longer poem. In this closing section he is thinking of Ephesians 3^{18-19}; 'To apprehend . . . the breadth and length and height and depth, and to know the love of Christ which passeth knowledge.' He announces his text and even outlines his points in the opening stanza:

> What shall I do my God to love,
> My loving God to praise !
> The Length, and Breadth, and Height to prove,
> And Depth of Sovereign Grace !

The following stanza is his 'firstly'—the *length* of God's love, which 'to all extends'. Next comes his 'secondly', its *breadth*—'Throughout the world its breadth is known, Wide as infinity.' Then his 'thirdly', the *height*, both of his own sin, 'grown up to heaven', but even higher still—'far above the skies'—the soaring mercies of God in Christ. And 'fourthly', 'The *depth* of all-redeeming love', in two verses, the second of which (usually omitted from our hymn-books) underlines this idea of depth—'Deeper than hell . . . Deeper than inbred sin'. Having made his points, like any good preacher Charles Wesley applies them in a prayer of supplication, and for a final knock-down blow (again omitted from most hymn-books) he works his spatial relationships into a paradox parallel to (though quite different in content from) St Paul's paradox about knowing the love which passes knowledge:

> And *sink* me to Perfection's Height,
> The *Depth* of Humble Love.[43]

[43] R. Newton Flew: *The Hymns of Charles Wesley: a study of their structure* (1953), pp. 18–25, 56–9. Cf. Nos. **13**, **141**.

Sometimes the sermon remains in embryo, as in an instance noted by Mr Findlay, who points out that the repeated 'Thou' opening three of the lines is for all the world like a preacher announcing his 'heads':

> Saviour in temptation Thou:
> Thou hast saved me heretofore,
> Thou from sin dost save me now,
> Thou shalt save me evermore.[44]

(Nor should we overlook the concealed artistry of this stanza: the two basic words, 'Thou' and 'save' are both introduced in the opening line, in reverse order, so that there is not only both the anaphora and the anadiplosis on 'Thou', and the traductio and mesodiplosis on 'Saviour', 'saved', 'save'; there is also a chiasmus between 'Saviour' and 'Thou' in the opening line, and each of the following three lines.)

Wesley is not alone in this kind of structure, of course. There are even more notable examples in Christopher Smart's *A Song to David*. Indeed they are perhaps *too* notable—the machinery tends to creak. The opening lines of stanza 4 furnish us with a catalogue of David's virtues:

> Great, valiant, pious, good, and clean,
> Sublime, contemplative, serene,
> Strong, constant, pleasant, wise!

The following 12 stanzas each deal (in the same order) with one of these virtues, and to ensure that the reader does not miss the point, each epithet opens its respective stanza, followed by a dash. Charles Wesley is never as obvious as that, and is a far greater artist as a result.

We can be left in no doubt that Charles Wesley was an adept in marshalling thoughts, as he was of words, and (as we shall see) of sounds, yet at the same time extremely versatile in varying the methods of his structure to the material which he was using and the purpose for which it was intended. He was undoubtedly a master craftsman in verse. This mastery is made even more impressive when we consider those deft touches of musical mortar with which he bonded together his structure of thought, whether in stanza or in poem—the 'patterns of sound', to use Mr Findlay's phrase. Wesley's skilful use of repetition for the purpose of emphasis has been sufficiently dealt with, but its use for cohesion has only been hinted at. Many examples could be quoted both of stanzas and of whole poems whose theological theme is accompanied by a musical theme which renders the verse both continuous and compact. One of each must suffice. For a stanza we turn to the following, based on Ephesians 4[4–6]:

> Build us in One Body up,
> Call'd in one high Calling's Hope;
> One the Spirit whom we claim,
> One the pure Baptismal Flame,
> One the Faith, and Common LORD,
> One the Father lives, ador'd
> Over, thro', and in us all,
> GOD Incomprehensible.[45]

[44] *Christ's Standard Bearer*, p. 37. (From *Hymns and Sacred Poems* (1742), p. 238.)
[45] 'The Communion of Saints', Part I, *Hymns and Sacred Poems* (1740), p. 188.

The theme is announced in the opening line, and is taken up by the fivefold repetition of 'one' in the five following lines. Wesley is careful, however, not to overdo this repetition, allowing St Paul's 'one Lord' to enter in disguise—'One the Faith, and Common LORD'—even though 'One the Faith and one the Lord' would have fitted the metre perfectly, and would have been nearer to his original.

This disciplined use of repetition, constantly varied just before it is becoming too obvious, is one of Wesley's strong points, appreciated all the more when turning from Christopher Smart. Stanzas 51–71 in Smart's *A Song to David* overdo the word 'ADORATION' (always printed in capitals) and the following stanzas dwell at length on the adjectives 'sweet' (72–4), 'strong' (75–7), 'beauteous' (78–80), 'precious' (81–3), 'glorious' (84–6), and their comparatives. It is all a little too mechanical and obvious, as if he were saying: 'See how clever I am!' Wesley is much more subtle and self-effacing. Wesley's delicately modulated repetitions are one of the great secrets of the success of his 'Wrestling Jacob' (No. **25**), underlining its deep emotion, yet never allowing that emotion to become maudlin. The two themes are thus announced in the closing couplets of stanzas 1 and 2:

> With Thee all Night I mean to stay,
> And wrestle till the Break of Day.

And:

> But who, I ask Thee, who art Thou,
> Tell me Thy Name, and tell me now.

The succeeding three stanzas all end with a combination of these two themes:

> Wrestling I will not let Thee go,
> Till I Thy Name, Thy Nature know.

This refrain is omitted from stanza 6, and only partially taken up in the closing couplet of stanza 7:

> I stand, and will not let Thee go,
> Till I Thy Name, Thy Nature know.

Stanza 8 provides a hesitant answer to half of this recurrent question:

> And tell me, if Thy Name is LOVE.

The following stanza triumphantly transforms the question into a proclamation:

> Thy Nature, and Thy Name is LOVE.

The constant ringing triumph of this same line closes each of the remaining five stanzas, always with a varied introductory line lest the thing become a mechanical refrain. This is only one element in the poem's literary achievement, but it is a very important one, as it is in many another of Wesley's most successful poems.

METRE

Another major factor in the literary achievement of Charles Wesley is his metrical versatility and even—the word is not too strong—genius. Although he could make no great musical claims as vocalist, instrumentalist, or composer, his musical sons acknowledged that his ear was impeccable. And because there was music in his soul, lilting, rapturous, divine music, he could not be confined to the humdrum in verse. The lyric was his *métier*. Both his inventiveness and his mastery in lyrical form were without parallel in the verse of that century, and perhaps only paralleled by Shelley in the century that followed. A list of Charles Wesley's extant metres, with some introductory notes on technical details, is given at the end of this volume.[46] It is sufficient here to make some general observations about his important place in the story of English prosody, and to illustrate this by some statistics.

By far the greatest bulk of Charles Wesley's verse is in the traditional iambic measure,[47] dignified, safe, though capable of great beauty and power in the hands of an accomplished poet. This is where most versifiers both begin and end. Even the great Isaac Watts rarely ventured outside iambics. His thousand poems include only 22 in trochaic metres and five in anapaestics, while his iambics themselves are almost confined to common, long, and short metre. In his best-known collections—the *Psalms* and the *Hymns and Spiritual Songs*—only 30 out of some 700 compositions are not in these three basic metres, these 30 being spread over four other metres—8 8.8.8 8.8; 6 6.8.6 6.8; 6.6.6.6.4.4 4.4; and 10 10.10 10.10 10. Even when we turn to his famous *Horae Lyricae*, so deservedly praised by Dr Johnson, only eight other metres are found, with 13 examples, apart from the 38 pindarics, whose irregular forms place them in a different category. The *Divine Songs* are restricted to the conventional, but the *Moral Songs* add five examples of four anapaestic stanza-forms, and three examples of two trochaic stanza-forms. To summarize, Watts used 20 different stanza-forms, in addition to pindarics and three varieties of couplets. It is fairly clear that he was capable of much more in the way of lyrical experiment, but his position as a pioneer of hymn-writing, at a time when few tunes were available, restricted nine-tenths of his production to the three common forms. With Charles Wesley both the spiritual impulse and the lyrical versatility were greater, and the result was a burst of new measures, for some of which the tunes were specially composed, while the remainder were an enrichment of religious verse rather than of congregational worship.

Charles Wesley wrote in no fewer than 45 iambic metres, and in each of 15 of them wrote over a thousand lines of verse. The most prolific

---

[46] Pp. 396ff. The first 'Attempt at a Classification of Charles Wesley's Metres' was made in a valuable article by the Rev Dr O. A. Beckerlegge, in the *London Quarterly Review* for July 1944, pp. 219–27. To this I remain greatly indebted, even though fuller research has made it necessary to amplify, rearrange, and very occasionally correct, Dr Beckerlegge's pioneer study.

[47] The basic nature of English verse has not yet been settled with anything like unanimity, and it seems that in any final formula T. S. Omond's plea for scansion by time-spaces will need to be accommodated to the conventional scansion by syllabic accent. In this book, however, the conventional scansion is retained, though with the realization that it has its drawbacks, and is not absolutely foolproof.

of all was his favourite form of six 8's—8.8.8.8.8 8, rhyming ABABCC. In this metre he composed over 1,100 poems, a total of nearly 23,000 lines, most of them with a vigour, a flexibility, yet a disciplined compactness, that proved this to be the instrument fittest for his hand. It is the metre of what Watts considered Wesley's masterpiece, 'Wrestling Jacob', and is represented by one-tenth of the poems in this present anthology, just as it represents more than one-tenth of his total output. His next most prolific form was the old romance metre, 8 8.6.8 8.6, rhyming AABCCB, a metre which moves more rapidly than 8.8.8.8.8 8, but loses in sturdiness what it gains in speed. In this—the metre of Smart's *Song to David*—Charles Wesley wrote over 20,000 lines in 900 poems, including 'O Love Divine, how sweet thou art', and 'Be it my only wisdom here'. The iambic metres next most popular with him (in order of preference) were the cross-rhyming double long metre ('O Thou who camest from above' in its original double form), the double short metre ('Soldiers of CHRIST arise' and other magnificent 'marching' poems), and the double common metre ('All praise to our redeeming LORD' and 'Sing to the great Jehovah's praise' in their original double form). The production here ranges from just over to just under 13,000 lines each. The only rival to these forms was one of the mixed iambic-trochaic metres. Only after these firm favourites with their six or eight lines do we come to the four-lined stanzas—common metre (7,000 lines), and the cross-rhymed long metre (9,000 lines); the consecutive-rhyming long metre comes well below nine other metres with 2,500 lines, and the four-lined short metre is among the 'also-rans' with a mere 364 lines.

Putting aside the many experiments which Charles Wesley did not follow up to any great extent, it seems desirable to draw attention to three other iambic metres of which he made considerable use. Only once did he employ the rather flimsy form 6.6.6.6, and very rarely its doubled or consecutively rhyming variations. When strengthened and clinched with a closing octosyllabic couplet, however, it became one of his favourite stanza-forms, used to great effect in (for example) 'Let earth and heaven agree', 'Arise, my soul arise', and 'Rejoice, the Lord is King'. Altogether he wrote over 3,000 lines in this metre, and a mere 198 in the consecutively rhymed variant, 6 6.6 6.8 8. Wesley wrote almost 2,000 lines in the form 7.6.7.6.7.6.7.6, yet never seemed thoroughly happy in it, certainly not as happy as was Cowper in his 'Sometimes a light surprises'. Dr Beckerlegge suggests that Wesley may have been influenced to its use by German example, though he points out that it was also employed (in continuous form) as the medium for Vaughan's 'My soul, there is a country'. In one other even more unusual (and apparently original) stanza-form Wesley did achieve real success. This was the metre of 'Head of Thy Church triumphant', 7.7.4 4.7 D, in which each half verse is introduced by one of the unrhyming lines so uncommon in Charles Wesley's verse. In this metre he wrote 40 poems amounting to over 1,000 lines.

Although the bulk of Charles Wesley's verse was written in iambic metres, however, and although the form 8.8.8.8.8 8 was both his most prolific and his most generally successful one, his more original contributions to the development of English prosody were in other types of metre, where his productivity was not so great in quantity, and on the whole not on such a consistently high level of quality. He wrote over 1,000 poems, some 22,000 lines, in 16 trochaic metres, in seven of them writing over 1,000 lines each. Again his favourite was an eight-lined stanza, eight 7's, cross-rhymed, in which he wrote over 7,000 lines. The best-known example is 'Jesu, Lover of my soul'. One of his more interesting experiments in trochaics is the 8.3 3.6 metre, which he seems to have introduced into English from the German, though John Cennick was also a pioneer in its use—it is the metre of Cennick's 'Ere I sleep, for every favour'.

It is now fairly well known that Charles Wesley played an important part in introducing some anapaestic metres into religious verse, and into hymns in particular, though Professor Elton is hardly accurate in speaking of 'his favourite lolloping anapaestics'. We have seen that Watts wrote five anapaestic poems. Even Prior and Swift, to whom is generally assigned the chief merit for elevating anapaestics from their crudest and clumsiest form in the street-ballad to an instrument fit for drawing-room satire, fell very far short of Charles Wesley. Actually their entire combined output of anapaestics does not match in quantity the 90 poems published by Wesley in his most popular anapaestic form. Moreover, his technical mastery is far in advance of theirs, and it is only with Wesley that we really get away from the rather loose 11's and 12's, either in couplets or in stanza-form, to something more taut and shapely. Of the type of stanza formed from two short lines followed by a long one, the solitary examples in Prior and Swift (each of whom seems to have written one only) is in the form 5 5.9.5 5.9. Neither has anything to compare with Wesley's regular eight 8's, which he wisely and skilfully disciplined to a uniformly iambic opening, thus avoiding the looseness which sometimes characterizes Shenstone's 'Pastoral Ballad' of 1743—Wesley's possible model. Wesley's popularization of the anapaest in his hymns seems to have been at least as important in improving its status as the somewhat hesitant use made of it by secular poets, and he was a pioneer in making it the medium for the irrepressible lilt of emotions which burst the bonds of conventional verse, as they did of conventional religion. If not responsible for its introduction, it fell to his lot to bring it under firmer discipline, and to train it for unaccustomed tasks.

Wesley's experimentation with anapaests began in 1741 with what became easily his most productive form, 5.5.5.5.6.5.6.5, cross-rhymed, and occasionally set out as 10 10.11 11. It was, of course, an adaptation of the old anapaestic ballad form, with the introduction of what we may call regularized variety, making the stanza both more satisfying and more amenable to congregational use. In this form he wrote no fewer than 4,000 lines, his hymns including 'O Heavenly King' and 'Ye Servants of God'. The only other of his 11 anapaestic metres which top the thousand-line mark are the cross-rhyming eight 8's mentioned above (exemplified by 'Thou Shepherd of Israel' and the best known of his *funeral* hymns), and the doubled 5 5.5 11 metre of the well-known watch-night hymn, 'Come, let us anew'. Altogether Wesley wrote some 10,000 lines of ana-paestic, or rather iambic-anapaestic, verse.

Even more important for the student of prosody is Charles Wesley's fertile experimentation with mixed metres, particularly mixed iambic and trochaic. Once the ear has become accustomed to the syncopated rhythm of these alternations between a rising and a falling beat, there is no gainsaying the force and virility of their challenge. Charles Wesley's first introduction to this alternating beat almost certainly came through the singing of the Moravians, but he made it completely his own, both simplifying it by concentrating on a few basic patterns, and at the same time extending the application of those patterns. His first such experiment was in 1739, with the form 6 6.7.7.7.7, an iambic couplet quickened and strengthened by a cross-rhymed trochaic quatrain. This remained one of his favourite metres, in which he wrote 168 poems, a total of nearly 4,000 lines, including 'O Filial Deity'.[48] He next discovered the robust 7.6.7.6.7.7.7.6, cross-rhymed throughout, but with a group of three consecutive trochaic lines opening the second half and breaking the alternating trochaic-iambic sequence. In this he wrote 3,500 lines, including 'God of unexampled grace' and 'Meet and right it is to sing'. He much preferred, however, the variant on which he quickly embarked, in which the alternation both of rhyme and beat was constant throughout, the fourth trochaic 7 being replaced by an iambic 8. This metre was used also by John Cennick from the same year of 1741 in which Wesley published his first example. Altogether Wesley wrote over 10,000 lines in this metre, which thus ranks as his sixth most prolific. Among the 680 poems are 'Lamb of God, whose bleeding love' and 'God of glorious majesty'.[49] None of his other mixed metres are of very frequent occurrence, with the exception of one which seems at first like a variant of the romance metre, 8 8.6.8 8.6, the second line being altered from an iambic 8 to a trochaic 7. This alteration, however, was undoubtedly an attempt—and a successful attempt—to secure an effect quite distinct from the smoothly running iambics, and Wesley wrote 67 poems (nearly 1,500 lines) with this as the basic pattern. Of this, as of the other mixed metres, it is simple to point to a typical example (No. 237, 'Far from my Native Land remov'd') but *not* to a widely known example, because these unconventional mixtures have not been readily assimilated as hymns, no matter how effective they may be as poems. In mixed metres generally Wesley wrote some 20,000 lines— about the same as his output in trochaic verse.

MODULATIONS

There is one very important footnote which should be added to any study of Charles Wesley's command of metre. He was for the most part in such perfect command that he did not let it master him. In other words he was a poet, rather than a versifier terrified lest an accent might fall 'incorrectly'. Any musician knows that if he remains in the same key for too long monotony sets in. This he avoids by modulations, passages in a different, though related key, passages short or long, obvious or subtly

[48] I am fairly confident that he also wrote No. 2, 'Thee, O my God and King', although it has always been claimed for John Wesley, on the mistaken assumption that Charles never translated German hymns.

[49] Mr Findlay has pointed out (*Christ's Standard Bearer*, p. 22) that this metre can be regarded as trochaic throughout by looking upon the iambic lines as a continuation of the trochaic lines; they would then be designated 13 13.7.7.13 and 13 13.15 13. The same is true of some other of the mixed metres.

concealed beneath the melody, varying both with the occasion and with the technical command and musical sensitivity of the composer. The same kind of thing is true in verse. 'Modulations', as we may call them, are obviously more necessary in longer lines and longer poems, which otherwise would degenerate to a jog-trot. The need is not quite so self-evident in lyrical verse, but even here their complete absence has a sterilizing effect.

Hymns are in a peculiar category, since they are made for singing to relatively simple tunes, to which each stanza must conform. Hymn-writers in general, therefore, tend to ignore (or to remain in ignorance of) the values of modulation. The slavery to the tune is one very important reason for the widespread assumption that hymns cannot be poetry, an assumption based on the (sometimes unrealized) nature of poetry as a constantly varying compromise between the naturalness of common speech and the artificiality of strictly metrical speech; at the one extreme lies prose, at the other the hurdy-gurdy. It is broadly true that hymns with no modulation are as unsatisfactory for reading as those with excessive or violent modulations are for singing. 'Modulation in moderation' is the motto for the hymn-writer with a feeling for poetry.

Charles Wesley was not simply a hymn-writer with a feeling for poetry, however, but a true poet who wrote hymns. In his couplets modulation is therefore inevitable, and the same is true of his 'sacred poems', i.e. the 'hymns' which were in fact not really intended for regular congregational singing. Even in the true hymns, however, modulation is present. The syncopated beat of the mixed metres is itself a form of modulation. It is to be found also in many hymns where it is both unexpected and unrealized, being overlaid by the beat of the music, which is normally remembered even when the verse is being read. If we *do* conscientiously try to dismiss the tune from our head for the moment, however, we can hardly fail to realize the variations in stress and duration of corresponding syllables. One of the most frequent modulations in Wesley's iambic verse— as in iambic verse generally—is the use of an opening choriambus, or a foot consisting of a trochee followed by an iambus.[50] This is one of the methods by which he injects trochaic vigour into the otherwise docile iambics of the double short metre, witness:

> Soldiers of CHRIST, arise,
> And put your Armour on,
> Strong in the Strength which GOD supplies
> Thro' his Eternal Son;
> Strong in the LORD of Hosts,
> And in his mighty Power,
> Who in the Strength of JESUS trusts
> Is more than Conqueror. (No. **30**)

This is by no means 'regular' verse, as many unsuspecting folk assume. Out of the eight lines four commence with the deliberately misplaced beat of a choriambus, the 1st, 3rd, 5th, and 7th. This looks at first almost like a regular pattern of misplaced beats, but no! In the 2nd stanza it is the

[50] Called by Mr Findlay (*Christ's Standard Bearer*, pp. 25–6), a 'hammer-head'.

1st and 7th lines only, in the 3rd stanza the 1st, 3rd, and 7th, the 4th line opening with what is more like a spondee; in the 4th stanza only the first line commences with a choriambus, and in the 5th stanza there is no example at all, though there are two pyrrhic feet, consisting of relatively unstressed syllables. Usually these accentual variations are not sufficiently marked to cause a worshipper discomfort. In this particular instance the hymn has been set in the *Methodist Hymn-book* to a tune which follows the misplaced accentuation of this first stanza, and so misfires (though only slightly) in other stanzas. This particular 'hymn', of course, was originally written as a long poem, in the course of which Wesley felt it necessary, as well as permissible, to vary his scheme of accentuation.

The opening choriambus is by no means confined to this metre, as may be seen from the opening lines of two of the famous hymns upon his conversion—'Where shall my wond'ring Soul begin' (No. 1) and 'O for a Thousand Tongues to sing' (No. 17). The *Methodist Hymn-book* has unfortunately tried to squeeze the other famous conversion hymn into the same mould, as represented by the tune SAGINA (No. 5). 'And can it be that I should gain', however, is a perfectly regular iambic line, and only the closing stanzas have an introductory choriambus, though that same modulation is to be found in other parts of the hymn. Often it is combined with less noticeable variations, as in 'Pardon, and Holiness, and Heaven'. Here, in addition to the opening choriambus, there is a distinct lightening of the emphasis on '-ness', where the beat falls, though there is a compensatory lengthening of the syllable through the presence of a closing sibilant.

This brief discussion of only one form of modulation enables us to see that there is more of the mystery of music in many of Charles Wesley's hymns than is at first obvious, especially when the ear is deafened by a familiar tune. That Wesley's employment of modulation is something of importance to the general history of prosody can be seen by quoting some words from Mr Sampson's *Concise Cambridge History of English Literature:*

To us the substitution of a three-syllabled foot for a two-syllabled foot and the replacing of an 'iamb' with its 'rise' by a 'trochee' with its 'fall' are neither faults nor anomalies, but the touches that transmute metre into rhythm. In listening to Chatterton and Blake and Coleridge we must not take these things for granted; we must make an imaginative retreat in audition, and hear the liberties of the new poetry as they first fell upon ears attuned to the regularity and smoothness practised by the poets who came after Pope, and prescribed by the theorists who formulated the principles they expected the poets to practise. But the end of the century saw many signs of revolt against mechanical regularity (p. 774).

The signs had been there long before the poets named; indeed in the variety and freedom of his metre, as well as in the rapturous content of his verse, Charles Wesley may be regarded as one of the heralds of the Romantic Revival. It is somewhat strange that in spite of his recognition of Charles Wesley's literary stature Mr Sampson seems to have missed the fact that in this matter of 'substitution' (as he prefers to call it) Charles Wesley was well in the vanguard of the reformers.[51]

[51] There had been many others before him, of course, even among the hymn-writers—witness Bishop Ken's well-known Morning and Evening Hymns, and Watts's 'Our God, our help in ages past'.

As a pendant I should perhaps add that not all the modulations which today we find in Wesley's verse were intentional. Many are the result of a shift in accent since his day. One example may be given. In 'Come, Sinners, to the Gospel-Feast' Charles Wesley wrote the following balanced iambic couplet, each line opening with a choriambus:

> This is the time, no more delay,
> This is the Acceptable Day. (No. 72, lines 93–4)

This is perfectly all right so long as we stress the first syllable of *acceptable*, as did eighteenth-century Englishmen. With the modern shifting of the accent to the second syllable, however, the effect is to have one stressed followed by three unstressed syllables, and the remainder of the line thrown out of joint. In actual fact Methodists did sing this until 1933, when the line was amended to 'This is the Lord's accepted day'. Not every such example was amended, however. In No. 156 of the 1933 Hymn-book a similar line is left unchanged, so that it reads like an anapaestic rather than an iambic line:

> Make this the acceptable hour;
> Come, O my soul's physician Thou!

The chief sinners in this matter of shifted accent are listed by Dr Bett as *ac'ceptable*, *ce'mented*, *con'fessor*, *obdu'rate*, and *suc'cessor*.[52]

RHYMES

Most of us find it far easier to detect the music of the rhyme than the more subtle music of the rhythm, with its variations in stress and tempo. Charles Wesley, however, recognized rhythm as a far more important element in poetry than rhyme, even though he never experimented in blank verse, and never took the easy way followed by Watts and others of being content with two rhyming lines per quatrain. It is, I believe, his matured sense of the respective importance of these elements of rhythm and rhyme, rather than his subordination of poetry to piety (as suggested by G. H. Vallins) that leads to the frequent imperfection of his rhymes. If rhyme had been all-important he would have thrown overboard many otherwise good lines, or remodelled them, but he knew that rhyme was a useful auxiliary rather than of the essence of poetry, and so (as Vallins succinctly remarks) 'he used it as a servant, but did not submit to it as a master'.[53]

Some Charles Wesley enthusiasts have proclaimed him as a master of rhyme in a quite different sense; they can find no spot or blemish in this aspect of his verse. Alas! this is surely blind (or deaf) worship! I admit, of course, that several cautions must be entered before criticizing the rhymes of Wesley's day—or, for that matter, of any day but our own. Many rhymes perfectly acceptable to an eighteenth-century ear sound clumsy now because of the changing usages in ordinary speech. Sometimes

[52] *The Hymns of Methodism*, pp. 54–6.
[53] *The Wesleys and the English Language* (1957), p. 85.

1

these changes are mere nuances of pronunciation, but occasionally they are much more obtrusive, involving not only the transformation of vowel sounds, but also (as we have seen) the shift of accent from one syllable to another. Dr Henry Bett carefully analysed both aspects of this subject, and pointed out the following as perfectly good rhymes for the meticulous Pope and his contemporaries: 'join/mine' and 'oil/smile', 'shower/pour', 'wound/found', 'convert/heart', 'great/feet', 'God/rod' *and* 'God/road'.[54]

Another possible source of unjustified criticism is the failure to recognize the poets' agreement that an 'eye-rhyme' like 'come/home' might occasionally serve as understudy for an 'ear-rhyme'. Obviously this is a convention which must not be abused, for poetry is after all an appeal to the ear, even when it approaches the ear silently by way of the eye and the mind.

There is still another point of criticism to be considered in this matter of Wesley's rhymes. A number of them are perfect to the ear, but not to the mind, since they break accepted grammatical conventions. As an example we turn to the second stanza of 'Jesus, united by Thy grace', which would doubtless be much more popular but for one jarring word:

> Still let us own our common Lord,
> And bear Thine easy yoke,
> A band of love, a threefold cord,
> Which never can be broke.

This sounds either careless or criminal to the literary purist of today, yet caused no offence in Wesley's own time. His contemporaries knew that 'broke' had not merely hobbled in to patch up the rhyme—it was a valid alternative for 'broken'. Within, as well as at the end of his lines, Charles Wesley continually uses unfamiliar grammatical forms, or, more frequently, familiar forms in an unfamiliar setting. He chooses that particular form for a particular reason, whether rhythm, rhyme, or music, but we can be sure that in almost every case he was not in his own day considered guilty of any solecism. It is always wise when coming across what seems a peculiar grammatical usage in the writings of either of the Wesley brothers (or of other scholarly writers in that and previous ages) to assume that it is an example of changing customs rather than of error. The Wesleys lived in a period of grammatical flux, and in his verse Charles Wesley sometimes made the best of both worlds. The fluidity was most noticeable in the past participle, which was frequently assimilated to the past tense—Gray's famous 'Elegy' was originally described as 'wrote in a country churchyard'.[55]

When all the excuses have been made, however, Charles Wesley must be adjudged guilty of having written, writ, or wrote many imperfect rhymes. Without labouring the point, we may instance the opening stanza

[54] Bett, *The Hymns of Methodism*, pp. 50–6. The variations in accent have been noted already on the preceding page.

[55] See further Chapter 8, 'Eighteenth-Century Language', in J. H. Whiteley's *Wesley's England*, especially pp. 232–7; cf. Bett, *The Hymns of Methodism*, pp. 47–9; G. H. Vallins, *The Wesleys and the English Language*, pp. 21–4, 50–68; and the poem of Dr Byrom's quoted in part by both Whiteley and Bett, which will be found in the *Gentleman's Magazine* (1758), p. 487.

of a well-known hymn (No. **34**) where *every* rhyme is faulty, though one is an 'eye-rhyme':

> Behold the Servant of the LORD!
> I wait Thy guiding Hand to feel,
> To hear, and keep Thine every Word,
> To prove, and do Thy perfect Will.
> Joyful from all my Works to cease,
> Glad to fulfil All Righteousness.

Wesley, like other verse-writers, also found some difficulty in achieving sufficiently varied and pleasing feminine rhymes—the double rhyme consisting of an accented followed by an unaccented syllable. In any case he much preferred the masculine ending, apart from the fact that the accent on the closing syllable was simpler, necessitating a rhyme for that one syllable only. Indeed because of this strong preference it is usually possible to say from a glance at the syllabic structure of his stanzas whether they are iambic, trochaic, or mixed: 6 or 8 syllables normally mean three or four iambic feet, ending with an accented syllable; 7 usually means three trochaic feet, again ending with an accented monosyllable; and a combination of 6 and/or 8 with 7 normally means a combination of iambic and trochaic, again with a closing accent for each line. This is by no means invariable, of course, with a poet of his versatility, but it is true in well over ninety per cent of his verse.

Nevertheless Wesley was at least moderately succesful with the feminine rhyme, particularly in the lighter form of Hudibrastic verse, where such rhymes as 'walk in/talking' and 'wearing/appear in' do not seem so incongruous as they would do in hymns, even hymns in the light-hearted anapaestic measure. As a matter of fact both examples quoted *do* appear in a hymn, 'O what shall I do my Saviour to praise', from *Hymns and Sacred Poems* of 1742. They are there printed as *internal* rhymes, however, where mere assonance might suffice. If we turn to the trochaic forms which forced him to frequent feminine rhymes we see Wesley beset with the same kind of difficulty, and often apparently not really worried whether he overcomes it smoothly or not. His best known hymn in that metre is probably 'Love Divine, all Loves excelling' (No. **69**). In that poem he uses the following imperfect feminine rhymes: 'compassion/salvation', 'deliver/never', 'blessing/ceasing', 'glory/before Thee'. I do not add 'Spirit/inherit' because this *was* a good rhyme, the contemporary pronunciation of 'spirit' approximating to 'sperit'. Occasionally his feminine rhymes consist of diphthongs like 'fires/desires', which is tolerable, and 'cares/snares', which to a modern ear certainly sounds like a masculine rhyme.

It is noteworthy that the rare stanza-forms in which Wesley used an unrhyming line were so framed in order to avoid the necessity of an added feminine rhyme, namely the iambic 7.7.4 4.7 D (Metre No. 36) and the related iambic-anapaestic variant 7.7.5 5.8 (Metre No. 72): the un-rhyming line in the trochaic example, 8.7.8.7.4.7 (Metre No. 54), also has a feminine ending. Only in the first form noted did Wesley write any considerable number of poems—40, a total of over 1,000 lines. It led him to some strange expedients, as may be seen by looking at his most well-known hymn in that metre, 'Head of Thy Church triumphant' (No. **33**): 'adore Thee/Glory', 'fire/nigher', 'favour/ever', 'Stephen/heaven'. It also led to the ingenuity of the 'verb plus preposition' rhyme in one of his *Hymns for Times of Trouble:*

> Some put their trust in chariots,
> And horses some rely on,
>   But God alone
>   Our help we own,
> God is the strength of *Sion.*

We may sum up Wesley's attitude to feminine rhymes by saying that he did not really enjoy himself when he was writing under this type of discipline, and much preferred the strong masculine ending. Altogether he wrote a mere 300 poems in metres which called for them, out of a total of some 9,000.

A few sentences at least should be added about the more subtle forms of verbal music. To Wesley's sensitive ear individual words had a musical as well as a factual content, and occasionally their musical outweighed their mental value. We never find him deserting sense for sound, but he frequently rejected a word of simple sense and simple music for another which was harder to understand but contained more subtle or more rousing music. This is true of his classical vocabulary, examples being the beauty of 'amaranthine' and the sinewy strength of polysyllables like 'inextinguishable' and 'incomprehensible'. It is true also of his use of many biblical names such as Jeshurun and Zerubbabel. This also was an important factor in his manuscript revisions. Even his images were as likely to appeal to the ear as to the eye, for as a handmaid of religion music attracted him far more than did art.[56]

THE PROBLEM OF CLASSIFICATION

It can be proved conclusively that Charles Wesley wrote far more than 'between six and seven thousand hymns', even after subtracting John Wesley's known contribution and after defining a hymn as 'a lyrical poem with mainly religious content', thus disqualifying the few hundreds of his 9,000 poems which are not even faintly religious. On the other hand it can also be demonstrated that the use of a still narrower definition will reduce Charles Wesley's quota of hymns to the more modest proportions of some 3,000 or 4,000; the actual figure will depend in part on the assessment of many borderline cases, and must therefore be left somewhat vague. Nor is this simply a matter of statistics, so that what is lost on the roundabouts of one definition is gained on the swings of another. Not only Charles Wesley, but the literate public at large, has suffered from the conventional attitude that Charles Wesley was a hymn-writer who occasionally touched the realms of poetry through his hymns. Professor H. N. Fairchild, for instance, in the second volume of his *Religious Trends in English Poetry* (1942), confesses that 'the hymns of

[56] See J. E. Rattenbury, *Evangelical Doctrines of Charles Wesley's Hymns*, p. 53. Even the example of motes dancing in a sunbeam which Dr Rattenbury quotes as a visual word-picture was in fact taken direct from a German original—see No. **122.**

Charles Wesley . . . may so often be regarded as personal religious lyrics, and good ones, that here I have been tempted to abandon my policy of excluding hymnody from the scope of these studies'; he adds in a footnote that his scheme does not prevent him from glancing 'at the hymns of poets like Cowper, who also wrote non-liturgical religious poetry'. Yet in actual fact Charles Wesley wrote much more 'non-liturgical religious poetry' than Cowper, and Professor Fairchild might therefore with an easy conscience have followed his intuition. Far from being a writer of hymns only, albeit very good ones, we believe that Charles Wesley was primarily a devotional poet, though he deliberately diverted some of his output for congregational use, and other poems were so diverted for him. He wrote, however, because he *had* to, not mainly because he wanted to provide singable spiritual ditties for the people called Methodists. Both his hymns and his poetry are better understood and appreciated if this is borne in mind.

Some attempt at defining a hymn is obviously necessary if we are to assess Charles Wesley's position in the history of religious verse. How should a hymn be defined? (Perhaps we should ask instead, 'How *can* a hymn be defined?' since even Julian's *Dictionary of Hymnology* makes no attempt to tell us what hymns really are!) The *Shorter Oxford English Dictionary* offers the following definition: 'song of praise to God; spec[ifically] a metrical composition adapted to be sung in a religious service.' The first part of this definition (based on that of St Augustine) is both too general and too restricted, since it overlooks the frequent elements of confession or prayer in hymns. The specific definition brings us much nearer to what most of us understand by the term, though it seems nevertheless desirable to attempt a closer analysis of the elements of such a composition. The normal English hymn can be distinguished from related species of verse, I suggest, by reference to four criteria, two having regard to its content, and two to its form:

1. It is *religious*, an act of worship.
2. It is *communal* in its approach to religion, containing sentiments which may be shared by a group of people, even though they may all be expected to sing 'I' instead of 'we'.
3. It is *lyrical*, written to be sung, not chanted or intoned.
4. It is comparatively *regular* both in metre and in structure.

All these criteria may admit of slight variation, but they form the basic ingredients of what we usually recognize as a hymn, a species which includes the variety known as the 'metrical psalm'. If all four elements are not present to a marked degree, then it would be better to speak of the composition as anthem, chant, chorus, doxology—several terms both specific and generic are available—or else (to use Charles Wesley's own term) as a 'sacred poem'.

No such definition can be so absolutely satisfactory as to erect a watertight barrier between hymns and poems, and there will still be room for disagreement in its application to particular compositions. In practice, also, many of Charles Wesley's poems slip without warning from one category to another. In spite of overlapping and uncertainty, however, the religious verse of Charles Wesley undoubtedly falls into two main categories. It seems clear also that Charles Wesley himself fully recognized this fact. The first two volumes of religious verse edited and published by John Wesley (in 1737 and 1738) were both entitled *A Collection of Psalms and Hymns*. When Charles Wesley began to share the responsibility of publication in the following year his name appeared on an altered title-page—*Hymns and Sacred Poems*. Three volumes with this title, and over the names of the two brothers, appeared in rapid succession, in 1739, 1740, and 1742, and a further anonymous one (mainly a selection from the 1739 volume, for use in Ireland) in 1747. To make the responsibility for this title clearer, Charles Wesley used it for the two-volume work which was published in his name alone in 1749. John Wesley's own predilection seems to have been for 'Collection'—one might say that he was the born editor, as Charles was the born creator. John issued another *Collection of Psalms and Hymns* in 1741, and this title was retained even after the second edition of 1743 saw the addition of Charles Wesley's name to the title-page and the filling out of the work with his poems. Nor did John forsake the word in issuing his three-volume anthology in 1744; it was still a 'Collection' of 'Moral and Sacred Poems'. The same key word designated his most famous 1780 hymn-book—*A Collection of Hymns for the use of the People called Methodists*.

The religious lyrics in which Charles Wesley excelled, therefore, were described by him as 'Hymns and Sacred Poems', the two terms flowing into each other rather than forming mutually exclusive categories. Their varied character may be illustrated from the contents of the 1749 volumes. Perhaps half are hymns in the specific sense as defined above; a few are paraphrases of scripture; and a great many are poems written on particular occasions, such as 'After a deliverance from death by the fall of an house' or 'Written in going to Wakefield to answer a charge of treason'. While recognizing and proclaiming that his compositions were by no means all hymns, however, Charles Wesley does tend to use the term 'hymn' in a generic rather than in a specific sense. Of the 455 pieces in the two volumes, 392 are explicitly described by that term; in actual fact most critics would probably agree that many of these are really 'sacred poems', even though parts of them at least might have been used on rare occasions as 'hymns'. For Charles Wesley himself, as for others, there were many compositions at each end of the scale which must be described either as hymn or sacred poem; in the middle, however, were many which could be described as both, or either, and the choice of term would depend on the use made of the composition—a sacred poem could be sung as a hymn, and a hymn could be used in private like a devotional poem. Because of this extensive overlapping Charles Wesley eventually came to use the shorter and simpler term 'hymn' as a generic term embracing the 'sacred poem'. Both instalments of *Hymns on God's Everlasting Love* (1741) contain items which cannot possibly be described as hymns in any specific sense; it is likely that Wesley considered *Hymns and Sacred Poems on God's Everlasting Love* as a possible title, but if so he rejected it in the interests of brevity. Similarly, although the first *Funeral Hymns* (1746) did in fact consist exclusively of hymns (many of them with a strongly individual connotation), the second series (1759) contains many which are really elegies, though it seems just possible that they may have been used on a single occasion in public worship. In his *Short Hymns on Select Passages of the Holy Scriptures* (1762) Charles Wesley acquiesced in the general usage of the term 'hymn' to describe what he preferred to call a 'sacred poem'. The bulk of that particular collection consists of poems which are either irregular in form, complicated in metre, or far from communal in theme, and in fact very few were ever used as hymns. The term 'sacred poem', however, had been dropped, apparently for good, and the literary world henceforth thought of Charles Wesley as a 'mere' writer of hymns.

In this anthology two-thirds of the selected items come under the general heading of 'Hymns and Sacred Poems'. They have deliberately been separated into these categories in order to illustrate Wesley in his character of 'sacred poet' as well as of hymn-writer. Those included in Part 1 are almost all hymns which have come into fairly common use either throughout the English-speaking Churches or at least in Methodist worship. A few are examples of 'sacred poems' of which a part has come into common use as a hymn, such as No. **17**, 'For the Anniversary Day of One's Conversion', a personal poem from which was extracted the hymn 'O for a Thousand Tongues to sing', and No. **20**, 'Father, whose Everlasting Love', a theological manifesto which was abridged for congregational worship. There are also examples of hymns sung on particular occasions only (e.g. Nos. **90** and **105**), or by quite restricted groups (e.g. Nos. **78** and **110**), and also of verses undoubtedly written for group singing but never actually published by Wesley (Nos. **109** and **112**).

Under the heading of 'Sacred Poems', Part 2 contains items of a purely personal character, or those where the biblical or theological or devotional content seems to have been shaped for individual use rather than for congregational worship. In a number of cases these poems might have been placed in Part 1, just as some might thence have been transferred to Part 2. Examples are 'Thou God of Truth and Love' (No. **144**), composed as a personal love-poem, and touched up for congregational use, and 'How can a Sinner *know*' (No. **141**), written as a defence of Methodist teaching on the doctrine of assurance, and later simplified in its metre to fit it for congregational worship.

The third part of this anthology also uses one of Charles Wesley's own titles—'Miscellaneous Poems'. Into this part have been gathered examples of poems written on events in Wesley's personal life, and on controversial, ecclesiastical, political, and topical subjects. Many of these might well have been included in Part 2, particularly some of the personal and theological poems. The criterion has been whether the poem was intended for general *devotional* use, thus making it a 'Sacred Poem', or was more nearly personal or polemical, when it has been included among the 'Miscellaneous Poems'. I have also made a deliberate attempt in this part to present a brief summary of Charles Wesley's personal and family history, and of his reactions to some of the main events in the ecclesiastical, political, social, and cultural history of the eighteenth century. For that purpose I have retained for Part 3 some compositions which were undoubtedly written and used as 'hymns' for particular national events such as the 1745 Rebellion (Nos. **234–6**), the Seven Years War (Nos. **264–5**), and the War of American Independence (Nos. **304–5**). As might be expected, hardly any of these hymns have come into general use.

THE PROBLEM OF SELECTION

Inequality is inevitable in such a vast output of verse as that of Charles Wesley, but it is a mistake to assume that most of it must be of poor quality, so that a few outstanding poems will naturally rise to the surface, while the remainder can safely be forgotten. One of the surprising things is how different critics will make different choices even of the highlights of Charles Wesley's verse, and what some rate as passably good are placed by others among his very best. The position seems to be that the *majority* of Charles Wesley's verse is both technically competent and contains a spark of real poetic genius. Dr Rattenbury has not overstated the case:

'It would be possible today to publish hundreds of his forgotten hymns which, if their authorship were unrecognized, would be hailed as exceptionally fine, and if wedded to melodious tunes would certainly become popular.'[57]

But nobody, not even a Methodist, wants to sing hymns by one man all the time; and nobody, not even the most ardent Charles Wesley enthusiast, wants to read sacred poems by one man all the time. Some process of arbitrary choice is therefore forced upon the reader, and this usually takes the form of selection—and rejection—by non-poetical criteria, incidental features of a poem, particularly of its subject-matter, which either attract or repel. Even Professor Elton, after speaking of Wesley's 'favourite lolloping anapaestics' as being 'dangerous', proceeds to quote a stanza to which his main objection seems to be the use of the word 'worm' as applied to a human being in the manner typical of an eighteenth-century evangelist. Similar references to blood and bowels inevitably repel most modern readers, but we must recognize this as the prejudice resulting from cultural changes rather than some poetical defect inherent in the words themselves. From the point of view of poetry proper it would be more pertinent to draw attention to Charles Wesley's acceptance of much of the poetic licence normal in his day, of which the outstanding example is his frequent transformation by elision of 'spirit' into a mono-syllable.

While it is possible, therefore, to isolate a small group of Wesley's hymns on the grounds of their popularity, it is impossible to do so on grounds of poetic merit alone. A. E. Bailey's *The Gospel in Hymns* attempts the first task, on the basis of ten American and Canadian hymnals. Similarly Arthur Temple's *Hymns We Love* lists 100 hymns shown to be most popular throughout the English-speaking world by the evidence of radio hymn-singing programmes. But if ten informed lovers of Wesley's verse were asked to choose his 50 best hymns there is not the slightest doubt that every list would be different. Nor would the situation be very greatly eased if the choice were enlarged to 100, 200, or even more. That is one reason why the title of this present volume contains the word 'representative' rather than 'best'.

The selection of the examples presented, therefore, has not been carried out with any pretence that in a volume of this size it is possible to offer 'the best of Charles Wesley'. Indeed the volume contains a number of items which are among his poorest, yet nevertheless 'representative'.

[57] *Evangelical Doctrines of Charles Wesley's Hymns*, p. 60.

Several principles have been observed in the selection. The poems have been chosen from all periods of Charles Wesley's life, springing from many different moods, upon widely varying subjects, from almost every one of his 50 publications and many of his unpublished manuscripts, and representing each of his 100 metres. Subjects and metres which commanded a major portion of his writing are given a weightier share of this anthology. One of his hymn-tracts—*Hymns for the Nativity of our Lord*, to which John Wesley took exception—is presented in its entirety. Two of his longer works in decasyllabic couplets—the *Epistles* to John Wesley and to George Whitefield—are also given in full. An honest attempt has been made to offer *representative verse* rather than a collection of purple passages. Nor has there been any attempt to weed out the occasional poor verse from an otherwise good poem: every poem selected has been given in its entirety with the sole exception of the lengthy *Elegy* on Whitefield (which has been reduced by about half) and the inclusion of 'Part 1' only of a few of the longer poems written in several parts.

JOHN OR CHARLES WESLEY?

So far as it is possible to ascertain the authorship, nothing has here been included which came from the pen of John Wesley, though a number of the poems were edited by him. It is probably desirable that something should be said about the vexed problem of the joint authorship of the Wesley poetry. Between 1739 and 1745 the brothers published five volumes as joint authors, with no indication of the extent of their respective contributions. These five volumes, together with John Wesley's *Moral and Sacred Poems* of 1744, which again contained compositions of un-differentiated Wesley authorship, between them present some 700 poems which are either original or are adaptations from earlier poets. These 700 pieces include many of the best known Methodist hymns, as well as some of the most valued sacred poems. After this date it seems that John Wesley wrote practically no verse (an exception is his lament for the loss of Grace Murray in 1749) and confined himself to editing earlier poems for the successive general hymn-books of Methodism—in addition to praising or criticizing particular examples of his brother's lavish output. In agreeing not to distinguish their respective contributions to the joint publications, the brothers did nothing to ease the lot of inquisitive students anxious to bestow credit where it truly belongs. The great bulk of the Wesley verse can be assumed or almost proved to be by Charles Wesley; huge masses of it are extant in his manuscript, sometimes in two or three stages of composition, and there are sufficient clues for us to be almost sure that most of the anonymous productions are pure Charles Wesley and quite sure that some of them are, e.g. the *Nativity Hymns*. That early and important nucleus of one-twelfth of the total, however, remains a problem, a problem which is perhaps insoluble in every detail, though some of its features are gradually becoming clearer.

In his *Hymns of Methodism* Dr Henry Bett made the bold experiment of isolating the known compositions of John Wesley and seeking for some canons of judgement by which they might be distinguished from those of Charles. He commenced with the assumption that all the known 33 poems translated from the German were by John. I have given reason and example (in the introduction to items **121–2**) for disputing this assumption, and on the basis of what I believe to be the proof that Charles Wesley did both read and translate from the German I would claim for him (mainly on metrical grounds) 'Thou, Jesu, art our King' (No. **2**). Yet I find it impossible to dissent from Dr Bett's main contention, that in general the translations both from German and Spanish may be assumed to be the work of John Wesley. To these translations Dr Bett added 'Father of all! whose powerful voice' and the Grace Murray poem.[58] There are available also a few juvenile poems of John's, making a total of some 1,600 lines of verse, inadequate for any dogmatizing, yet useful for assessing tendencies.

The 'canons' formulated by Dr Bett after a detailed comparison of this 'Johannine corpus' with Charles Wesley's *Hymns and Sacred Poems* of 1749 are as follows. John Wesley's verse shows:

(1) *A strong preference for simpler measures.*
(2) *A preference for couplet rhyming.* (After some criticism by Dr Rattenbury, Dr Bett agreed that this criterion should not be stressed as much as the others.)
(3) *Division of an octosyllabic line into two equal feet, with a central pause,* Charles Wesley's lines being more fluent.
(4) *A tendency to elaborate and repeat a thought,* Charles being freer and more spontaneous.
(5) *A tendency to begin a succession of lines with parallel expressions.*
(6) *Frequent enjambment.*
(7) *A minor point: the last verse echoing the first.*
(8) *Another minor point: the use of favourite words* such as 'duteous', 'dauntless', 'boundless'.

To these original 'canons' further study led Dr Bett to add others, which may be summarized thus:

(9) *Avoidance of noun-verb compounds and 'all-' compounds.*
(10) *Avoidance of polysyllabic words,* of which Charles Wesley was fond.
(11) *Use of adjectives beginning with 'un-',* Charles preferring 'in-'.
(12) *Use of triads of nouns and less frequently of verbs.*
(13) *'A certain stiffness of movement.'*
(14) *Formal phrases of 'poetic diction',* such as 'ethereal blue' and 'solar fire'.
(15) *The use of 'I'd', 'I'll'.*

In addition to these specific clues to the authorship of one or other of the brothers Dr Bett makes the valid point that there was a tendency in these volumes for compositions by the same author to be arranged in blocks rather than singly.

Testing the 1780 *Collection* by these canons, Dr Bett came to the conclusion that nine-tenths of the hymns therein were by Charles. We should expect at least this, and really more, from the tenor of John Wesley's

---

[58] I think that we might almost certainly also add to the work of John Wesley the 43 adaptations from George Herbert's poems.

famous preface. He also named 16 hymns which he believed to be by John, including the following given in this anthology:

'And can it be, that I should gain' (No. **5**)
'Eternal Beam of Light Divine' (No. **6**)
'Father, whose Everlasting Love' (No. **20**)
'Jesu, if still the same Thou art' (No. **14**)

Much study is still necessary before anything like certainty can be achieved on many of these conjectures. We should be on much safer ground if we were able to formulate canons based on the ascertained work of Charles Wesley, particularly if this were done in such a way as to reveal the variations brought by maturity and age. Although I personally cannot pretend to have undertaken the necessary detailed study, after reading 180,000 lines of his verse, and collating many thousands of them many times over, and in addition compiling huge masses of statistics subdivided in several ways, I have found myself with certain convictions which may at least be mentioned as pointers. Two warnings must first be issued, however: I have included all but the undisputed work of John as if it were by Charles; and I have (with one exception) assumed for general purposes that all work in the handwriting of Charles Wesley was actually his composition, although in fact this is not a universally valid assumption.

From study spreading over some years, though nothing like so many as those which Dr Bett devoted to the subject in a more microscopic way, I believe that we should discount or at the very least treat with severe caution Dr Bett's 'canons' numbered 4, 5, 7, 9, and 12. As I have mentioned elsewhere, there is a strong tendency in Charles Wesley toward longer stanzas, and particularly toward a doubling of the normal CM, SM, and LM—though there is evidence to suggest that in his earlier years he wrote much in the ordinary long metre. There is, I believe, a strong tendency in Charles Wesley to prefer cross-rhyming (Dr Bett's term is 'alternate rhyme') to consecutive-rhyming. This is revealed in a very strong preference for the six-8's rhyme-pattern of 8.8.8.8.8 8, and a comparative shying away from the form 8 8.8.8 8.8, except in its doubled form. I think we may take it that almost without exception the verse in anapaestic and mixed metres is by Charles Wesley, and nearly all that in trochaic metres. This is really a confirmation of Dr Bett's point about John Wesley's preference for 'simpler measures', in which I would insert the word 'iambic'. It is also necessary, as Dr Rattenbury pointed out, to take note of the actual content of the poems, and to place them alongside the known predispositions and temperaments of the two brothers: thus I believe that we can in this way confirm Charles Wesley's authorship of the translation from the German of 'Melt, happy Soul, in Jesu's Blood'. Even when these points are added to those of Dr Bett, however, they remain for the most part 'tendencies', whose force in isolation is small, though fairly strong when many or all are combined. As Dr Rattenbury claimed, of the hymns published during the first ten years of the Methodist Revival not more than 50 can at present be shown to be by John, and it is likely that the total number did not reach 100.[59]

[59] Bett, *Hymns of Methodism*, pp. 21–33; Rattenbury, *Evangelical Doctrines of Charles Wesley's Hymns*, pp. 21–5, 58–84. Cf. Flew, *The Hymns of Charles Wesley*, pp. 26–31.

CONCLUSION

Poetry is sometimes described as the compromise between the demands of a regular adherence to a metrical form and the opposing urge of a mind fired by strong emotions. True poetry is the result of extreme tension. Without the discipline of metre the emotion might be expressed in lyrical prose; without the emotion it would remain an exercise in verse.

In the verse of Charles Wesley at his best we see the happiest results of this tension. On the one hand there is the classical restraint, the chaste, often sombre diction, strangely allied with the artificiality of the rhetorician's stock-in-trade. On the other there is the wide range of deep and high emotions, covering the realms of the family and public life, but at their most intense in the alternating longings, despairs, and raptures of the soul's contact with God. These emotions burst the fetters of conventional verse, demanding expression in a rich and daring variety of lyrical forms.

It is true of Wesley as of Wordsworth that his reputation has suffered because he allowed much of his weaker writing to survive. With him a live metaphor sometimes degenerates into a dead cliché; he is guilty of many flat lines, many clumsy, a few maudlin. John Wesley's pungent criticism of his brother's often-corrected manuscript hymns on the Gospels and the Acts applies to his work as a whole: 'Some are bad, some mean, some most excellently good'—though it should be noted that 'mean' signified 'average'. My final word, however, must be to echo John Wesley's considered tribute to the spirit of poetry breathing through his brother's verse, even though he rated this as second in importance to the spirit of piety: 'Lastly, I desire men of taste to judge (these are the only competent judges;) whether there is not in some of the following verses, the true Spirit of Poetry: such as cannot be acquired by art and labour; but must be the gift of nature.'[60]

---

[60] John Wesley's *Journal* (Standard Edn), VII.456–7; *Collection of Hymns for the Use of the People called Methodists* (1780), Preface.

PART ONE
HYMNS

This hymn, which opens Part II of the *Hymns and Sacred Poems* of 1739, is probably the hymn to which Charles Wesley refers in his *Journal* for Tuesday 23rd May 1738, where he speaks of his experience on Whitsunday, two days earlier, an experience which seems to have released his powers of evangelical verse:

'At nine I began an hymn upon my conversion, but was persuaded to break off, for fear of pride. Mr Bray coming, encouraged me to proceed in spite of Satan. I prayed Christ to stand by me, and finished the hymn. . . . In His name, therefore, and through His strength, I will perform my vows unto the Lord, of not hiding His righteousness within my heart.' (With this last phrase cf. lines 17–18 of the hymn.)

The following evening, 24th May, John Wesley's heart was 'strangely warmed', and Charles records in his *Journal*:

'Towards ten, my brother was brought in triumph by a troop of our friends, and declared, "I believe". We sang the hymn with great joy, and parted with prayer.'

* *Hymns and Sacred Poems* (1739), pp. 101–3.
  Poetical Works, I.91–3.
  Hymns and Spiritual Songs (1753): No. 32.
  Hymns for those to whom Christ is all in all (1761), No. 6, vv. 1–4.
  Collection (1780): No. 29, omitting v. 6.
  Collection (1831): No. 30, as 1780.
  Collection (1876): No. 30, as 1780.
  MHB (1904): No. 358, omitting vv. 4, 6, 8.
  MHB (1933): No. 361, as 1904.

Metre 10: 8.8.8.8.8 8
A B A B C C

1 Where shall my wond'ring Soul begin?
   How shall I All to Heaven aspire?
A Slave redeem'd from Death and Sin,
   A Brand pluck'd from Eternal Fire,
How shall I equal Triumphs raise,   *5*
And sing my great Deliverer's Praise!

2 O how shall I the Goodness tell,
   Father, which Thou to me hast show'd,
That I, a Child of Wrath, and Hell,
   I should be call'd a Child of GOD!   *10*
Should know, should feel my Sins forgiven,
Blest with this Antepast of Heaven!

3 And shall I slight my Father's Love,
   Or basely fear his Gifts to own?
Unmindful of his Favours prove?   *15*
   Shall I the hallow'd Cross to shun
Refuse his Righteousness t'impart
By hiding it within my Heart?

1. 1780: 'my wandering soul'; corrected to 'wondring' in the 2nd edn (1781).
6. 1780, &c.: 'Or sing'.
7. 1753 (from 3rd edn, 1754), 1780: 'thy goodness'.

4 No—tho' the Antient Dragon rage
    And call forth all his Hosts to War,   20
Tho' Earth's self-righteous Sons engage;
    Them, and their God alike I dare:
JESUS the Sinner's Friend proclaim,
JESUS, to Sinners still the same.

5 Outcasts of Men, to You I call,   25
    Harlots and Publicans, and Thieves!
He spreads his Arms t'embrace you all;
    Sinners alone his Grace receives:
No Need of Him the Righteous have,
He came the Lost to seek and save!   30

6 Come all ye *Magdalens* in Lust,
    Ye Ruffians fell in Murders old;[1]
Repent, and live: despair and trust!
    JESUS for you to Death was sold;
Tho' Hell protest, and Earth repine,   35
He died for Crimes like Yours—and Mine.

7 Come O my guilty Brethren come,
    Groaning beneath your Load of Sin!
His bleeding Heart shall make you room,
    His open Side shall take you in.   40
He calls you Now, invites you home—
Come, O my guilty Brethren, come!

8 For you the purple Current flow'd
    In Pardons from his wounded Side:
Languish'd for you th'Eternal GOD,   45
    For you the Prince of Glory dy'd.
Believe: and all your Guilt's forgiven,
Only Believe—and yours is Heaven.

[1 This line is borrowed from a poem on Bishop Francis Atterbury's birthday, written by Charles Wesley's eldest brother Samuel. (See his *Poems* (1862), p. 433; cf. *Arminian Magazine* (1778), p. 283.)]

20. 1753, 1761, 1780, &c.: 'all his host'.
42. In the first edition this line is incorrectly indented.
47. 1753, 1780, &c.: 'your sin's forgiven'.

2   HYMN OF THANKSGIVING TO THE FATHER

This is an example of the first 'mixed metre' attempted by Charles Wesley (or by the two Wesleys), and is one of a trilogy of hymns in the same metre to the three Persons of the Trinity. The calm iambic beat of the first two lines is succeeded by the martial tramp of the closing four trochaic lines. This type of metrical form, and this metre in particular, seems to have been copied from the German hymns sung by the Moravians in Georgia. One example was included in John Wesley's *Collection of Psalms and Hymns*, published in London in 1738. It has been assumed that this translation from the German of Johann Scheffler (1624–77) was by John Wesley himself. It is, however, the only poem in this metre claimed for John Wesley, and its position in the *Hymns and Sacred Poems* of 1739 (in a group of hymns in the same metre and of similar subject-matter) suggests that it might in fact have been by Charles Wesley. However that may be, this translation, 'Thou, Jesu, art our King', followed Scheffler's *'Dich, Jesu, loben wir'* (Herrnhut *Gesangbuch* (1737), No. 68), not only in thought and language, but even in metre—an unusual procedure for either of the Wesleys. Scheffler's poem was slightly different, 6 6.8.7.8.7, rhyming AAbcbc, but the likeness is unmistakable. Even in the *Gesangbuch* there is only one example of this metre. Whether Charles Wesley was responsible or not for the pioneer experiment of 'Thou, Jesu, art our King', he was soon making regular use of this metre, and was trying out with great success other adaptations or original ventures into mixed metres.

* *Hymns and Sacred Poems* (1739), pp. 107–8.
  Poetical Works, I.96–7.
  Hymns and Sacred Poems (Dublin, 1747), pp. 12–13.
  Hymns for those to whom Christ is all in all (1761): No. 7.
  Collection (1780): No. 184, omitting v. 5.
  Collection (1831): No. 191, as 1780.
  Collection (1876): No. 191, as 1780.

Metre 75: 6 6.7.7.7.7
A A b c b c

1   Thee, O my GOD and King,
      My Father, Thee I sing!
Hear well-pleas'd the joyous Sound,
    Praise from Earth and Heav'n receive;
Lost, I now in CHRIST am found,   *5*
    Dead, by Faith in CHRIST I live.

2   Father, behold thy Son,
      In CHRIST I am thy own.
Stranger long to Thee and Rest,
    See the Prodigal is come: *10*
Open wide thine Arms and Breast,
    Take the weary Wand'rer home.

3   Thine Eye observ'd from far,
      Thy Pity look'd me near:
Me thy Bowels yearn'd to see,   *15*
    Me thy Mercy ran to find,
Empty, poor, and void of Thee,
    Hungry, sick, and faint, and blind.

4   Thou on my Neck didst fall,
      Thy Kiss forgave me all: *20*
Still the gracious Words I hear,
    Words that made the Saviour mine,
Haste, for Him the Robe prepare,
    His be Righteousness Divine!

5   Thee then, my GOD and King,   *25*
      My Father, Thee I sing!
Hear well-pleas'd the joyous Sound,
    Praise from Earth and Heav'n receive;
Lost, I now in CHRIST am found,
    Dead, by Faith in CHRIST I live.   *30*

3   HYMN TO THE SON

* *Hymns and Sacred Poems* (1739), pp. 108–10.
    Poetical Works, I.97–9.
    Hymns for those to whom Christ is all in all (1761): No. 8.
    Collection (1780): No. 186, omitting v. 9.
    Collection (1831): No. 193, as 1780.
    Collection (1876): No. 193, as 1780.
    MHB (1904): No. 115, omitting vv. 2, 9.
    MHB (1933): No. 97, as 1904.

Metre 75: 6 6.7.7.7.7
A A b c b c

1   O Filial Deity,
        Accept my New-born Cry!
    See the Travail of thy Soul,
        Saviour, and be satisfy'd;
    Take me now, possess me whole,   5
        Who for Me, for Me hast dy'd!

2   Of Life Thou art the Tree,
        My Immortality!
    Feed this tender Branch of thine,
        Ceaseless Influence derive,   10
    Thou the true, the heav'nly Vine,
        Grafted into Thee I live.

3   Of Life the Fountain Thou,
        I know—I feel it Now!
    Faint and dead no more I droop: 15
        Thou art in me: Thy Supplies
    Ev'ry Moment springing up
        Into Life Eternal rise.

4   Thou the Good Shepherd art,
        From Thee I ne'er shall part: 20
    Thou my Keeper and my Guide,
        Make me still thy Tender Care,
    Gently lead me by thy Side,
        Sweetly in thy Bosom bear.

5   Thou art my Daily Bread;   25
        O CHRIST, Thou art my Head:
    Motion, Virtue, Strength to Me,
        Me thy Living Member flow;
    Nourish'd I, and fed by Thee,
        Up to Thee in all things grow.   30

6   Prophet, to me reveal
        Thy Father's perfect Will.
    Never Mortal spake like Thee,
        Human Prophet like Divine;
    Loud and strong their Voices be,   35
        Small and still and inward Thine!

3. 1831: 'of my soul'.

7   On Thee my Priest I call,
       Thy Blood aton'd for all.
  Still the Lamb as slain appears,
    Still Thou stand'st before the Throne,   *40*
  Ever off'ring up thy Pray'rs,
    These presenting with thy own.

8   JESU! Thou art my King,
       From Thee my Strength I bring!
  Shadow'd by thy mighty Hand,   *45*
    Saviour, who shall pluck me thence?
  Faith supports, by Faith I stand
    Strong as thy Omnipotence.

9   O Filial Deity,
       Accept my New-born Cry!   *50*
  See the Travail of thy Soul,
    Saviour, and be satisfy'd;
  Take me now, possess me whole,
    Who for Me, for Me hast dy'd!

41. 1780, &c.: 'my prayers', correcting what seems to have been a misprint.
    [The 1st and 2nd edns retain 'thy prayers', but the 3rd edn (1782), contains the correction.]
42. 1831, &c.: 'thine own'.
43. 1761, 1831: 'Jesus, Thou art'.

HYMN TO THE HOLY GHOST   **4**

* *Hymns and Sacred Poems* (1739), pp. 111–13.
  Poetical Works, I.99–101.
  Hymns for those to whom Christ is all in all (1761): No. 9.
  Pocket Hymn Book (1785): No. 66, vv. 1, 2, 7, 9–11.

                    Metre 75: 6 6.7.7.7.7
                            A A b c b c

1   Hear, Holy Spirit, hear,
       My Inward Comforter!
  Loos'd by Thee my stamm'ring Tongue
    First essays to praise Thee now,
  This the New, the Joyful Song,   *5*
    Hear it in thy Temple Thou!

2   Long o'er my Formless Soul
       The dreary Waves did roll;
  Void I lay and sunk in Night:
    Thou, the overshadowing Dove,   *10*
  Call'dst the Chaos into Light,
    Bad'st me Be, and live, and love.

11. 1761: 'Call'd'.

7

3   Thee I exult to Feel,
      Thou in my Heart dost dwell:
There Thou bear'st thy Witness true,   *15*
     Shed'st the Love of GOD abroad;
I in CHRIST a Creature New,
     I, ev'n I am Born of GOD!

4   Ere yet the Time was come
      To fix in Me thy Home,   *20*
With me oft Thou didst reside:
     Now, my GOD, Thou In me art!
Here Thou ever shalt abide;
     One we are, no more to part.

5   Fruit of the Saviour's Pray'r,   *25*
      My Promis'd Comforter!
Thee the World cannot receive,
     Thee they neither know nor see,
Dead is all the Life they live,
     Dark their Light, while void of Thee.   *30*

6   Yet I partake thy Grace
      Thro' CHRIST my Righteousness;
Mine the Gifts Thou dost impart,
     Mine the Unction from above,
Pardon written on my Heart,   *35*
     Light, and Life, and Joy, and Love.

7   Thy Gifts, Blest Paraclete,
      I glory to repeat:
Sweetly Sure of Grace I am,
     Pardon to my Soul apply'd,   *40*
Int'rest in the spotless Lamb;
     Dead for All, for me He dy'd.

8   Thou art Thyself the Seal;
      I more than Pardon feel,
Peace, Unutterable Peace,   *45*
     Joy that Ages ne'er can move,
Faith's Assurance, Hope's Increase,
     All the Confidence of Love!

9   Pledge of thy Promise giv'n,
      My Antepast of Heav'n;   *50*
Earnest Thou of Joys Divine,
     Joys Divine on Me bestow'd,
Heav'n and CHRIST, and All is mine,
     All the Plenitude of GOD.

22. 1761: 'in me Thou art'.
23. 1761: 'shall abide'.
49. 1761, 1785: 'the promise'.

10 Thou art My Inward Guide,   *55*
  I ask no Help beside:
Arm of GOD, to Thee I call,
 Weak as Helpless Infancy!
Weak I am—yet cannot fall
 Stay'd by Faith, and led by Thee!   *60*

11 Hear, Holy Spirit, hear,
  My Inward Comforter!
Loos'd by Thee my stamm'ring Tongue
 First essays to praise Thee now;
This the New, the Joyful Song,   *65*
 Hear it in thy Temple Thou!

57. 1761: 'on Thee'.
59. 1785: 'but cannot fall'.

FREE GRACE   **5**

Dr Henry Bett believed that this, rather than No. 1, was 'the hymn' associated with the conversion of Charles and then of John Wesley. The balance of the evidence, however, seems to favour the priority of 'Where shall my wond'ring Soul begin'.

* *Hymns and Sacred Poems* (1739), pp. 117–19.
 Poetical Works, I.105–6.
 Hymns and Sacred Poems (Dublin, 1747), pp. 59–60.
 Hymns for those to whom Christ is all in all (1761): No. 10.
 Collection (1780): No. 193, omitting v. 5.
 Collection (1831): No. 197, as 1780.
 Collection (1876): No. 201, as 1780.
 MHB (1904): No. 360, as 1780.
 MHB (1933): No. 371, as 1780.

Metre 10: 8.8.8.8.8 8
A B A B C C

1 And can it be, that I should gain
  An Int'rest in the Saviour's Blood!
Dy'd He for Me?—who caus'd his Pain!
  For Me?—who Him to Death pursu'd.
Amazing Love! how can it be   *5*
That Thou, my GOD, shouldst die for Me?

2 'Tis Myst'ry all! th'Immortal dies!
  Who can explore his strange Design?
In vain the first-born Seraph tries
  To sound the Depths of Love Divine.   *10*
'Tis Mercy all! Let Earth adore;
Let Angel Minds enquire no more.

3 He left his Father's Throne above,
  (So free, so infinite his Grace!)
Empty'd Himself of All but Love,   *15*
  And bled for *Adam*'s helpless Race:
'Tis Mercy all, immense and free!
For O my GOD! it found out Me!

9

4 Long my imprison'd Spirit lay,
    Fast bound in Sin and Nature's Night: *20*
Thine Eye diffus'd a quick'ning Ray;
    I woke; the Dungeon flam'd with Light;
My Chains fell off, my Heart was free,
I rose, went forth, and follow'd Thee.

5 Still the small inward Voice I hear,   *25*
    That whispers all my Sins forgiv'n;
Still the attoning Blood is near,
    That quench'd the Wrath of hostile Heav'n·
I feel the Life his Wounds impart;
I feel my Saviour in my Heart.   *30*

6 No Condemnation now I dread,
    JESUS, and all in Him, is Mine:
Alive in Him, my Living Head,
    And cloath'd in Righteousness Divine,
Bold I approach th'Eternal Throne,   *35*
And claim the Crown, thro' CHRIST, my own.

27. 'attoning' is, of course, a printer's error, although it is continued in
    HSP (1747).

6   IN AFFLICTION

* *Hymns and Sacred Poems* (1739), pp. 144–5.
  Poetical Works, I.128.
  Collection (1780): No. 328.
  Collection (1831): No. 337.
  Collection (1876): No. 337.
  MHB (1904): No. 474.
  MHB (1933): No. 496.

Metre 7: 8.8.8.8
A B A B

1 Eternal Beam of Light Divine,
    Fountain of unexhausted Love,
In whom the FATHER's Glories shine,
    Thro' Earth beneath, and Heav'n above!

2 JESU! the weary Wand'rer's Rest;   *5*
    Give me thy easy Yoke to bear,
With stedfast Patience arm my Breast,
    With spotless Love and lowly Fear.

3 Thankful I take the Cup from Thee,
    Prepar'd and mingled by thy Skill: *10*
Tho' bitter to the Taste it be,
    Pow'rful the wounded Soul to heal.

5. 1831: 'Jesus, the'.

4 Be Thou, O Rock of Ages, nigh:
    So shall each murm'ring Thought be gone,
And Grief, and Fear, and Care shall fly,   *15*
    As Clouds before the Mid-day Sun.

5 Speak to my warring Passions, 'Peace;
    Say to my trembling Heart, 'Be still:
Thy Pow'r my Strength and Fortress is,
    For all Things serve Thy Sov'reign Will.   *20*

6 O Death, where is thy Sting? Where now
    Thy boasted Victory, O Grave?
Who shall contend with GOD: Or Who
    Can hurt whom GOD delights to save?

A MORNING HYMN   7

* *Hymns and Sacred Poems* (1739), pp. 178–9.
  Poetical Works, I.158–9.

Metre 53: 7 7.7 7.7 7.7 7.7 7.7 7
a a b b c c d d e e f f

1 'See the Day-spring from afar
'Usher'd by the Morning-Star!
Haste; to Him who sends the Light,
Hallow the Remains of Night.
Souls, put on your glorious Dress,   *5*
Waking into Righteousness:
Cloath'd with CHRIST aspire to shine,
Radiance He of Light Divine;
Beam of the Eternal Beam,
He in GOD, and GOD in Him!   *10*
Strive we Him in Us to see,
Transcript of the Deity.

2 Burst we then the Bands of Death,
Rais'd by His all-quickning Breath;
Long we to be loos'd from Earth,   *15*
Struggling into second Birth.
Spent at length is Nature's Night;
CHRIST attends to give us Light,
CHRIST attends Himself to give;
GOD we now may see, and live.   *20*
Tho' the Outward Man decay;
Form'd within us Day by Day
Still the Inner Man we view,
CHRIST creating all things New.

3 Turn, O turn us, Lord, again,   *25*
Raiser Thou of Fallen Man!
Sin destroy and Nature's Boast,
Saviour Thou of Spirits Lost!
Thy great Will in Us be done:
Crucified and dead Our own,   *30*
Ours no longer let us be;
Hide us from Ourselves in Thee!
Thou the Life, the Truth, the Way,
Suffer us no more to stray;
Give us, Lord, and ever give   *35*
Thee to know, in Thee to live!

8   HYMN FOR CHRISTMAS-DAY

* *Hymns and Sacred Poems* (1739), pp. 206–8.
MS Richmond Tracts, after *Nativity Hymns* (1745).
Poetical Works, I.183–4.
Hymns and Sacred Poems (Dublin, 1747), pp. 34–5.
Whitefield's *Hymns* (1753): No. 31, pp. 24–5, vv. 1–7, 9.
Madan's *Collection* (1760): No. 8, as Whitefield's *Hymns*.
Pocket Hymn Book (1787): No. 214, vv. 1–7, 9, in doubled verses.
Collection (1831): No. 602, vv. 1 (lines altered), 3–7, 9.
Collection (1876): No. 683, as 1831.
MHB (1904): No. 122, verses doubled, and with the revised opening two lines
    added as refrain, using vv. 1+2, 3+4, 7+9.
MHB (1933): No. 117, as 1904, but using vv. 1+2, 3+4, 6+5.
Hymns A & M (1861): No. 43, vv. 1–6 in three doubled verses; (1875, 1889, 1916,
    1950): No. 60, as 1861; (1904): No. 62, as 1861; Schools edn (1958): No. 37, as
    1861.

                                     Metre 46: 7 7.7 7
                                                 a a b b

1 Hark how all the Welkin rings
  'Glory to the King[1] of Kings,
  'Peace on Earth, and Mercy mild,
  'God and Sinners reconcil'd!

[[1] The 1st edition read 'Kings of Kings', a simple misprint corrected in later editions.]

1–2. Whitefield, Madan, 1787, 1831, &c., *A & M* (1861, &c.—except 1904):

        'Hark! the Herald Angels sing
        Glory to the new-born King!'

When the hymn was added to the 1782 edition of Tate and Brady's *New Version* of the Psalms these two opening lines were also used as a refrain, and the verses were doubled. Both these practices were followed by *A & M*, and by *MHB* (1904, 1933).

    The ill-fated 1904 *A & M* reinstated the original opening lines, though giving Whitefield's opening couplet as an alternative, and using it as a refrain. According to Dr C. S. Phillips (*Hymnody Past and Present* (1937), p. 233): 'The public laughed long and loud: and it is hardly an exaggeration to say that "the welkin" gave the final death-blow to the 1904 book.'

2 Joyful all ye Nations rise,   *5*
  Join the Triumph of the Skies,
  Universal Nature say
  'CHRIST the LORD is born to Day!

3 CHRIST, by highest Heav'n ador'd,
  CHRIST, the Everlasting Lord,   *10*
  Late in Time behold him come,
  Offspring of a Virgin's Womb.

4 Veil'd in Flesh, the Godhead see,
  Hail th'Incarnate Deity!
  Pleas'd as Man with Men t'appear   *15*
  JESUS, our *Immanuel* here!

5 Hail the Heav'nly Prince of Peace!
  Hail the Sun of Righteousness!
  Light and Life to All he brings,
  Ris'n with Healing in his Wings.   *20*

6 Mild he lays his Glory by,
  Born—that Man no more may die,
  Born—to raise the Sons of Earth,
  Born—to give them Second Birth.

7 Come, Desire of Nations, come,   *25*
  Fix in Us thy humble Home,
  Rise, the Woman's Conqu'ring Seed,
  Bruise in Us the Serpent's Head.

6.   Whitefield, Madan, 1787: 'Triumphs'.
7–8. Whitefield: 'Nature rise and worship him,
                 Who is born at Bethlehem.'
       Madan, 1787, 1904, &c.; *A &M* (1861, &c.):
                 'With th'angelic Host proclaim,
                 CHRIST is born in *Bethlehem!*'
12. Whitefield: 'the Virgin's womb'.
15–16. *A &M* (1861, &c.—except 1904); *MHB* (1904):
                 'Pleased as Man with man to dwell,
                 JESUS, our EMMANUEL.'
       A &M (1904), *MHB* (1933):
                 'Pleased as man with men to dwell,
                 Jesus our Immanuel.'
17. 1747, Whitefield, Madan, 1787, 1831, &c., *A &M* (1861, &c.):
                 'Hail the heav'n born Prince of Peace.'
19. 1747: 'and All he brings'; Whitefield: 'around he brings'.
22. Whitefield: 'that Men'.
26. Whitefield: 'thy heav'nly Home'.

8 Now display thy saving Pow'r,
   Ruin'd Nature now restore,   *30*
   Now in Mystic Union join
   Thine to Ours, and Ours to Thine.

9 *Adam*'s Likeness, LORD, efface,
   Stamp thy Image in its Place,
   Second *Adam* from above,   *35*
   Reinstate us in thy Love.

10 Let us Thee, tho' lost, regain,
   Thee, the Life, the Inner Man:
   O! to All Thyself impart,
   Form'd in each Believing Heart.   *40*

33. Whitefield, Madan, 1787, 1831, &c.: 'Adam's likeness now efface'.
34. Madan, 1787: 'thine Image'.
36. Whitefield: 'Work it in us by thy Love.'
38. MS Richmond Tracts: 'Thee, the Life, the Heavenly Man'.

9   HYMN FOR EASTER-DAY

* *Hymns and Sacred Poems* (1739), pp. 209–11.
  MS Richmond Tracts, after *Resurrection Hymns* (1746). See illustration opposite.
  Poetical Works, I.185–6.
  Hymns and Sacred Poems (Dublin, 1747), pp. 37–8.
  Madan's *Collection* (1760): No. 32, vv. 1–6, 10–11.
  Collection (1831): No. 629, vv. 1–5, 11.
  Collection (1876): No. 716, as 1831.
  MHB (1904): No. 170, as 1831.
  MHB (1933): No. 204, as 1831, but conflating vv. 2 & 3, and adding 'Hallelujah'
      at the end of each line.
  Hymns A & M (1950): No. 141, vv. 2–5, 10.

                                              Metre 46: 7 7.7 7
                                                        a a b b

1 'CHRIST the LORD is ris'n to Day,'
   Sons of Men and Angels say,
   Raise your Joys and Triumphs high,
   Sing ye Heav'ns, and Earth reply.

2 Love's Redeeming Work is done,   *5*
   Fought the Fight, the Battle won,
   Lo! our Sun's Eclipse is o'er,
   Lo! He sets in Blood no more.

3 Vain the Stone, the Watch, the Seal;
   CHRIST has burst the Gates of Hell!   *10*
   Death in vain forbids his Rise:
   CHRIST has open'd Paradise!

7. 1831, &c.: 'Lo! the sun's'.
12. MS Richmond Tracts, Madan, 1831, &c.: 'Christ hath open'd'.

14

Hymns for our Lord's
Resurrection.

1. "Christ, the Lord is ris'n to day"
Sons of Men & Angels say,
Raise your Joys & Triumphs high,
Sing ye Heavens, & Earth reply.

2. LOVE's Redeeming Work is done,
Fought the Fight, the Battle won,
Lo! our Sun's Eclipse is o'er,
Lo, He sets in Blood no more!

3. Vain the Stone, the Watch, the Seal;
Christ hath burst the Gates of Hell!
Death in vain forbids his Rise;
Christ hath op'nd Paradise.

4. Lives again our glorious King;
Where, O Death, is now thy Sting?
Once He died our Souls to save;
Where thy Victory, O Grave?

5. Soar we now where Christ has led,
Following our Exalted Head;
Made like Him, like Him we rise;
Ours the Cross, the Grave, the Skies.

6. What tho' once we perish'd all,
Partners of our Parent's Fall,
Second Life we all receive,
In our Heavenly Adam live:

7. Ris'n with Him we upward move,
Still we seek the Things above,
Still pursue, & kiss the Son
Seated on his Father's Throne;

8. Scarce on Earth a Thought bestow,
Dead to all we leave below,
Heaven our Aim & Lord Abode,
Hid our Life with Christ in GOD.

'CHRIST THE LORD IS RIS'N TODAY'
in Charles Wesley's handwriting (see opposite)

4 Lives again our glorious King,
  Where, O Death, is now thy Sting?
  Dying once he All doth save,   *15*
  Where thy Victory, O Grave?

5 Soar we now, where CHRIST has led?
  Following our Exalted Head,
  Made like Him, like Him we rise,
  Ours the Cross—the Grave—the Skies!   *20*

6 What tho' once we perish'd All,
  Partners in our Parent's Fall?
  Second Life we All receive,
  In our Heav'nly *Adam* live.

7 Ris'n with Him, we upward move,   *25*
  Still we seek the Things above,
  Still pursue, and kiss the Son
  Seated on his Father's Throne;

8 Scarce on Earth a Thought bestow,
  Dead to all we leave below,   *30*
  Heav'n our Aim, and lov'd Abode,
  Hid our Life with CHRIST in GOD!

9 Hid; till CHRIST our Life appear,
  Glorious in his Members here:
  Join'd to Him, we then shall shine   *35*
  All Immortal, all Divine!

10 Hail the LORD of Earth and Heav'n!
  Praise to Thee by both be giv'n:
  Thee we greet Triumphant now;
  Hail the Resurrection Thou!   *40*

11 King of Glory, Soul of Bliss,
  Everlasting Life is This,
  Thee to know, thy Pow'r to prove,
  Thus to sing, and thus to love!

15. MS Richmond Tracts, Madan, 1831, &c.: 'Once He died our Souls to
    save:'.
16. 1831, &c.: 'Where's thy victory, boasting grave?'
22. MS Richmond Tracts, Madan: 'Partners of our'.

HYMN FOR ASCENSION-DAY   10

* *Hymns and Sacred Poems* (1739), pp. 211–13.
  MS Richmond Tracts, after *Resurrection Hymns* (1746).
  MS Acts, pp. 5–6: in five verses of 8 lines each.
  Poetical Works, I.187–8.

Metre 46: 7 7.7 7
                a a b b

1 Hail the Day that sees Him rise,
Ravish'd from our wishful Eyes;
CHRIST awhile to Mortals giv'n,
Re-ascends his native Heav'n!

2 There the pompous Triumph waits,   5
'Lift your Heads, Eternal Gates,
'Wide unfold the radiant Scene,
'Take the King of Glory in!

3 Circled round with Angel Powers,
Their Triumphant LORD, and ours,   10
Conqueror over Death and Sin,
Take the King of Glory in!

4 Him tho' highest Heaven receives,
Still he loves the Earth he leaves;
Tho' returning to his Throne,   15
Still he calls Mankind his own.

5 See! He lifts his Hands above!
See! He shews the Prints of Love!
Hark! His gracious Lips bestow
Blessings on his Church below!   20

2. *A & M* (1861, &c.): 'To His Throne above the skies';
    MHB (1904, &c.): 'our wistful eyes'.
3–4. *A & M* (1861, &c.): 'CHRIST, the Lamb for sinners given,
                Enters now the highest heaven.'
5. *A & M* (1861, &c.): 'There for Him high triumph waits'.
6. MS Richmond Tracts: 'y'Eternal'.
11. Whitefield, 1761, 'Conqu'ror o'er Death, Hell, and Sin';
    A & M (1861, &c.): 'He hath conquered death and sin'.
13–14. *A & M* (1861, &c.): 'Lo, the heaven its LORD receives,
                Yet He loves . . .'

6 Still for us his Death he pleads;
  Prevalent, He intercedes;
  Near Himself prepares our Place,
  Harbinger of human Race.

7 Master, (will we ever say)   *25*
  Taken from our Head To-day;
  See thy faithful Servants, see!
  Ever gazing up to Thee.

8 Grant, tho' parted from our Sight,
  High above yon azure Height,   *30*
  Grant our Hearts may thither rise,
  Following Thee beyond the Skies.

9 Ever upward let us move,
  Wafted on the Wings of Love,
  Looking when our LORD shall come,   *35*
  Longing, gasping after Home.

10 There we shall with Thee remain,
  Partners of thy endless Reign,
  There thy Face unclouded see,
  Find our Heav'n of Heav'ns in Thee!   *40*

21-2. MSS, 1746, Whitefield, Madan, 1761:
               'Still for us he intercedes,
               Prevalent his death he pleads';
   A & M (1861, &c.): 'Still for us He intercedes,
               His prevailing death He pleads'.
23.   MS Richmond Tracts, Whitefield, Madan, 1761: 'Next himself'.
24.   *A & M* (1861, &c.): 'He the first-fruits of our race.'
25.   Whitefield: 'Master (may we . . .)'
29.   1933 (transposing opening word from v. 7 to v. 8):
               'Master, parted from our Sight'.
29-30. *A & M* (1861, &c.): 'Lord, though parted from our sight
               Far above the starry height'.
32.   *A & M* (1861, &c.): 'Seeking Thee above the skies.'
33.   Whitefield: 'may we move'.
36.   *A & M* (1950): 'Longing, sighing after home.'
37.   Whitefield: 'There may we'.
38.   MS Richmond Tracts, Whitefield, Madan, 1761, *A & M* (1950):
    'thine endless'.

['ARM OF THE LORD, AWAKE!']   II

* *Hymns and Sacred Poems* (1739), pp. 222-3.
  MS Clarke, pp. 180-1: (as Part II of four parts, in ten verses).
  Hymns and Sacred Poems (1749), I.20-1: (as Part II of four, in ten verses).
  Poetical Works, IV.302-3.
  Hymns for those to whom Christ is all in all (1761): No. 80, in ten halved verses.
  Select Hymns (1761): No. 88.

Collection (1780): No. 375, omitting vv. 2, 3, and presenting the remainder as L.M.
  instead of L.M.D.
Collection (1831): No. 386, as 1780.
Collection (1876): No. 386, as 1780.
MHB (1904): No. 219, as 1870.
MHB (1933): No. 486, as 1780, but omitting also v. 5 of original.

Metre 17: 8.8.8.8.8.8.8.8
A B A B C D C D

Isa. li.9, &c.

1 Arm of the Lord awake, awake!
    Thy own immortal Strength put on.
  With Terror cloath'd the Nations shake,
    And cast thy Foes, in Fury, down.
  As in the antient Days appear!　　　　5
    The Sacred Annals speak thy Fame:
  Be now Omnipotently near,
    Thro' endless Ages still the same.

2 Thy tenfold Vengeance knew to quell,
    And humble haughty *Rahab*'s Pride.　　10
  Groan'd her pale Sons thy Stroke to feel,
    The First-born Victims groan'd and died!
  The wounded Dragon rag'd in vain;
    While bold thine Utmost Plague to brave,
  Madly he dar'd the parted Main　　　15
    And sunk beneath th'o'rewhelming Wave.

3 He sunk; while *Israel*'s chosen Race
    Triumphant urge their wondrous Way.
  Divinely led the Favourites pass,
    Th'Unwatry Deep, and emptied Sea.　　20
  At Distance heap'd on either Hand,
    Yielding a strange unbeaten Road,
  In Chrystal Walls the Waters stand,
    And own the Arm of *Israel*'s GOD!

4 That Arm which is not short'ned now,　25
    Which wants not now the Power to save.
  Still present with thy People Thou
    Bear'st them thro' Life's disparted Wave.
  By Earth and Hell persued in vain,
    To Thee the ransom'd Seed shall come;　30
  Shouting their Heav'nly Sion gain,
    And pass thro' Death triumphant home.

2. MS Clarke, 1749, 1761, 1780, &c.: 'Thine own'.
3. 1780, &c.: 'hell's kingdom shake'.
4. 1761 (*Select Hymns*), 1780, &c.: 'with fury'.
5. 1761 (*Select Hymns*): 'Arise, as in the antient Days'.
8. 1761 (*Select Hymns*), 1780, &c.: 'To endless ages'.
25-6. 1780, &c.: 'Thy arm, Lord, is not shortened now:
        It wants not . . .'.
29. 1780, &c.: 'By death and hell'.

5 The Pain of Life shall there be o're,
   The Anguish and distracting Care;
  There sighing Grief shall weep no more,   *35*
   And Sin shall never enter There!
  Where pure, essential Joy is found
   The LORD's Redeem'd their Heads shall raise,
  With everlasting Gladness crown'd,
   And fill'd with Love, and lost in Praise!   *40*

35. 1761 (*Select Hymns*): 'There, Sighs and Griefs'.

MORNING HYMN   **12**

* *Hymns and Sacred Poems* (1740), pp. 24–5.
  Poetical Works, I.224–5.
  Whitefield's *Hymns* (1753): No. 14, p. 11.
  Collection (1780): No. 150, replacing the first verse with 'O disclose thy lovely face',
    the second verse of another hymn on p. 60 of *Hymns and Sacred Poems* (1740).
  Collection (1831): No. 156, as 1780.
  Collection (1876): No. 963.
  MHB (1904): No. 904.
  MHB (1933): No. 924.
  Hymns A & M (1861), No. 5; (1875, 1889, 1916, 1950), No. 7; (1904), No. 4;
    Schools edn (1958), No. 22.

Metre 47: 7.7.7.7.7 7
a b a b c c

1 CHRIST, whose Glory fills the Skies,
   CHRIST, the true, the only Light,
  Sun of Righteousness, arise,
   Triumph o'er the Shades of Night:
  Day-spring from on High, be near: *5*
  Day-star, in my Heart appear.

2 Dark and Chearless is the Morn
   Unaccompanied by Thee,
  Joyless is the Day's Return,
   Till thy Mercy's Beams I see;   *10*
  Till they Inward Light impart,
  Glad my Eyes, and warm my Heart.

3 Visit then this Soul of mine,
   Pierce the Gloom of Sin, and Grief,
  Fill me, Radiancy Divine,   *15*
   Scatter all my Unbelief,
  More and more Thyself display
  Shining to the Perfect Day.

2. Whitefield: 'true and only'.
6. Whitefield: 'in our Hearts'.
11. 1780, &c.: 'Till thou inward' [actually the 1st edition (1780), has the
    misprint 'thy', which is altered to 'thou' in the 2nd edition (1781)].
11–12. Whitefield: 'Lord thy inward Light impart,
               Glad our eyes and warm each Heart.'
13. Whitefield: 'Visit ev'ry Soul'.
15. Whitefield: 'Fill with'.
16. Whitefield: 'all our'.

19

13 —   BEFORE READING THE SCRIPTURES

* *Hymns and Sacred Poems* (1740), pp. 42–3: the third of a trilogy of prayers to the
    three Persons of the Trinity.
    MS Family, p. 10.
    Poetical Works, I.238–9.
    Whitefield's *Hymns* (1753): No. 28, p. 22.
    Collection (1780): No. 85.
    Collection (1831): No. 87.
    Collection (1876): No. 87.
    MHB (1904): No. 256.
    MHB (1933): No. 305.
    Hymns A & M (1889, 1916), No. 599, omitting v. 3; (1904), No. 399, as 1889.

Metre 1: 8.6.8.6
A B A B

1 Come, HOLY GHOST, our Hearts inspire,
    Let us Thy Influence prove;
Source of the old Prophetick Fire,
    Fountain of Life, and Love.

2 Come HOLY GHOST, (for, mov'd by Thee,   5
    Thy Prophets wrote and spoke:)
Unlock the Truth, Thyself the Key,
    Unseal the Sacred Book.

3 Expand Thy Wings, Prolific Dove,
    Brood o'er our Nature's Night;   10
On our disorder'd Spirits move,
    And let there now be Light.

4 GOD thro' Himself we then shall know,
    If Thou *within us* shine,
And sound, with all Thy Saints below,   15
    The Depths of Love Divine.

2. MS Family, 1780, &c.: 'thine influence'.
4. 1831, &c.: 'Fountain of Light and Love.'
6. MS Family, 1831, &c., *A & M* (1889, &c.): 'The Prophets';
    Whitefield: 'Thy holy Prophets spoke'.
9. MS Family, 1780, &c.: 'celestial Dove'.

14   MAT[T]HEW v. 3, 4, 6

* *Hymns and Sacred Poems* (1740), pp. 65–6.
    Poetical Works, I.258–9.
    Hymns and Spiritual Songs (1753): No. 11, omitting v. 4.
    Collection (1780): No. 130.
    Pocket Hymn Book (1787): No. 65.
    Collection (1831): No. 134.
    Collection (1876): No. 134.
    MHB (1904): No. 310, omitting v. 6.
    MHB (1933): No. 349, as 1904.

Metre 10: 8.8.8.8.8 8
A B A B C C

1 JESU, if still the same Thou art,
   If all Thy Promises are sure,
Set up Thy Kingdom in my Heart,
   And make me rich, for I am poor:
To me be all Thy Treasures given,   5
The Kingdom of an Inward Heaven.

2 Thou hast pronounced the Mourner blest,
   And Lo! for Thee I ever mourn:
I cannot; no! I will not rest,
   Till Thou my only Rest return,   10
Till Thou, the Prince of Peace, appear,
And I receive the Comforter.

3 Where is the Blessedness bestow'd
   On all that hunger after Thee?
I hunger now, I thirst for GOD!   15
   See, the poor, fainting Sinner see,
And satisfy with endless Peace,
And fill me with Thy Righteousness.

4 Ah LORD! ——— if Thou art in that Sigh,
   Then hear Thyself within me pray.   20
Hear in my Heart Thy Spirit's Cry,
   Mark what my lab'ring Soul *would* say,
Answer the deep, unutter'd Groan,
   And shew that Thou and I are One.

5 Shine on Thy Work, disperse the Gloom,   25
   Light in Thy Light I then shall see:
Say to my Soul, 'Thy Light is come,
   'Glory Divine is ris'n on thee,
'Thy Warfare's past, thy Mourning's o'er:
'Look up, for thou shalt weep no more.'   30

6 LORD, I believe the Promise sure,
   And trust Thou wilt not long delay;
Hungry, and sorrowful, and poor,
   Upon Thy Word myself I stay;
Into Thy Hands my All resign,   35
And wait—till All Thou art is mine!

  1. 1831, 1904, 1933: 'Jesus, if'.
  7. 1780, &c.: 'mourners'.
10. 1753, &c.: 'Thou mine only'.
35. 1753 (from 2nd edn, 1754), 1780, &c.: 'Into thine hands'.

15   IN TEMPTATION

* *Hymns and Sacred Poems* (1740), pp. 67–8.
Poetical Works, I.259–60.
Hymns and Spiritual Songs (1753): No. 12, omitting v. 3.
Madan's *Collection* (1760): No. 136, as 1753.
Select Hymns (2nd edn, 1765): No. 144, as 1753.
Pocket Hymn Book (1785): No. 109.
Collection (1831): No. 143, as 1753.
Collection (1876): No. 143, as 1753.
MHB (1904): No. 106, as 1753.
MHB (1933): No. 110, as 1753.
Hymns A & M (1861), No. 179, as 1753; (1875, 1889, 1916, 1950), No. 193, as 1753; (1904), No. 488, as 1753; Schools edn (1958), No. 107, vv. 1, 2, and 5.

Metre 50: 7.7.7.7.7.7.7.7
a b a b c d c d

1 JESU, Lover of my Soul,
    Let me to Thy Bosom fly,
While the nearer Waters roll,
    While the Tempest still is high:
Hide me, O my Saviour, hide,   5
    Till the Storm of Life is past:
Safe into the Haven guide;
    O receive my Soul at last.

2 Other Refuge have I none,
    Hangs my helpless Soul on Thee: 10
Leave, ah! leave me not alone,
    Still support, and comfort me.
All my Trust on Thee is stay'd;
    All my Help from Thee I bring;
Cover my defenceless Head,   15
    With the Shadow of thy Wing.

3 Wilt Thou not regard my Call?
    Wilt Thou not accept my Prayer?
Lo! I sink, I faint, I fall—
    Lo! on Thee I cast my Care: 20
Reach me out Thy gracious Hand!
    While I of Thy Strength receive,
Hoping against Hope I stand,
    Dying, and behold I live!

4 Thou, O CHRIST, art all I want,   25
    More than all in Thee I find:
Raise the Fallen, chear the Faint,
    Heal the Sick, and lead the Blind,
Just, and Holy is Thy Name,
    I am all unrighteousness,   30
False, and full of Sin I am,
    Thou art full of Truth, and Grace.

3. A & M (1861, &c.): 'the gathering waters'.
6. 1831, &c., *A & M* (1861, &c.): 'be past'.
14. Madan: 'mine Help'.
31. Madan: 'Vile and full'.

5 Plenteous Grace with Thee is found,
    Grace to cover all my Sin:
  Let the healing Streams abound,   *35*
    Make, and keep me pure within:
  Thou of Life the Fountain art:
    Freely let me take of Thee,
  Spring Thou up within my Heart,
    Rise to all Eternity!   *40*

34. Madan: 'Grace to pardon';
  A &M (1861, &c.): 'Grace to cleanse from all'.

[HYMN TO THE TRINITY]   16

* *Hymns and Sacred Poems* (1740), pp. 103–4.
  Poetical Works, III.347.
  Hymns to the Trinity (1746): No. 7, printed as 10 10.11 11.
  Hymns for those to whom Christ is all in all (1761): No. 33, as 1746.
  Pocket Hymn Book (1785): No. 87.

Metre 66: 5.5.5.5.6.5.6.5
A B A B C D C D

This appears to be Wesley's first venture into an anapaestic metre.

1 Father of Mankind,
    Be ever ador'd:
  Thy Mercy we find,
    In sending our Lord
  To ransom and bless us: *5*
    Thy Goodness we praise,
  For sending in Jesus
    Salvation by Grace.

2 O Son of his Love,
    Who deignedst to die,   *10*
  Our Curse to remove,
    Our Pardon to buy;
  Accept our Thanksgiving,
    Almighty to save,
  Who openest Heaven,   *15*
    To All that believe.

3 O Spirit of Love,
    Of Health, and of Power,
  Thy Working we prove,
    Thy Grace we adore;   *20*

7–8. Trinity (1746): 'Jesus' Salvation', corrected in later editions.
10. Trinity (1746): 'Who deignest', corrected in later editions to 'deignedst'.
11. 1785: 'Our cause'.

Whose inward Revealing
    Applies our LORD's Blood,
Attesting, and sealing
    Us Children of GOD.

21–4. Trinity (1746) prints these as two lines without extra spacing between 'Revealing' and 'applies', and 'sealing' and 'us', and without capitalizing 'Applies' and 'Us'. The capitals were, however, restored in the 5th and later edns.

17 FOR THE ANNIVERSARY DAY OF ONE'S CONVERSION

* *Hymns and Sacred Poems* (1740), pp. 120–3.
MS Colman 21, p. 3, vv. 7–10, 12–14, 17, 18.
Poetical Works, I.299–301.
Hymns and Spiritual Songs (1753): No. 44, entitled 'Invitation of Sinners to Christ', and comprising vv. 7–13, 15–18.
Collection (1780): No. 1, consisting of vv. 7–10, 12–14, 17, 18.
Pocket Hymn Book (1787): No. 1, as 1780.
Collection (1831): No. 1, consisting of vv. 7–14, 17, 18.
Collection (1876): No. 1, as 1831.
MHB (1904): No. 1, consisting of vv. 7–14.
MHB (1933): No. 1, consisting of vv. 7–9, 11, 10, 14.
Hymns A & M (1889, 1916), No. 522, vv. 7, 9, 11, 12, 8; (1904), No. 501, vv. 7, 9–12, 8; (1950), No. 196, as 1889; Schools edn (1958), No. 109, as 1889.

Metre 1: 8.6.8.6
A B A B

1 Glory to GOD, and Praise, and Love
    Be ever, ever given;
By Saints below, and Saints above,
    The Church in Earth and Heaven.

2 On this glad Day the glorious Sun   *5*
    Of Righteousness arose,
On my benighted Soul he shone,
    And fill'd it with Repose.

3 Sudden expir'd the legal Strife,
    'Twas then I ceas'd to grieve,   *10*
My Second, Real, Living Life
    I then began to live.

4 Then with my *Heart* I first believ'd,
    Believ'd, with Faith Divine,
Power with the Holy Ghost receiv'd   *15*
    To call the Saviour *Mine*.

5 I felt my LORD's Atoning Blood
    Close to *my* Soul applied;
Me, me he lov'd—the Son of GOD
    For *me*, for *me* He died!   *20*

6 I found, and own'd his Promise true,
   Ascertain'd of *my* Part,
My Pardon pass'd in Heaven I *knew*
   When written on my Heart.

7 O for a Thousand Tongues to sing   *25*
   My dear Redeemer's Praise!
The Glories of my GOD and King,
   The Triumphs of his Grace.

8 My gracious Master, and my GOD,
   Assist me to proclaim,   *30*
To spread thro' all the Earth abroad
   The Honours of Thy Name.

9 JESUS the Name that charms our Fears,
   That bids our Sorrows cease;
'Tis Musick in the Sinner's Ears,   *35*
   'Tis Life, and Health, and Peace!

10 He breaks the Power of cancell'd Sin,
   He sets the Prisoner free:
His Blood can make the Foulest clean;
   His Blood avail'd for me.   *40*

11 He speaks; and listening to His Voice,
   New Life the Dead receive,
The mournful, broken Hearts rejoice,
   The humble Poor *believe*.

12 Hear Him ye Deaf, His Praise ye Dumb   *45*
   Your loosen'd Tongues employ,
Ye Blind, behold your Saviour come,
   And leap, ye Lame, for Joy.

13 Look unto Him, ye Nations, own
   Your GOD, ye fallen Race!   *50*
Look, and be sav'd, thro' Faith alone;
   Be justified, by Grace!

14 See all your Sins on JESUS laid;
   The Lamb of GOD was slain,
His Soul was once an Offering made   *55*
   For *every Soul* of Man.

26. MS Colman, 1831, &c.: 'My great Redeemer's';
   A &M (1889, &c., except 1950, 1958): 'my blest Redeemer's'.
31. *A &M* (1889, &c.): 'And spread'.
38. 1753 (from 2nd edn, 1754): 'the Prisoners'.

15 Harlots, and Publicans, and Thieves
   In holy Triumph join!
   Sav'd is the Sinner that believes
   From Crimes as great as Mine.   *60*

16 Murtherers, and all ye hellish Crew,
   Ye Sons of Lust and Pride,
   Believe the Saviour died for you;
   For me the Saviour died.

17 Awake from guilty Nature's Sleep,   *65*
   And CHRIST shall give you Light,
   Cast all your Sins into the Deep,
   And wash the *Ethiop* white.

18 With me, your Chief, you then shall *know*,
   Shall feel your Sins forgiven;   *70*
   Anticipate your Heaven below,
   And own, that Love is Heaven.

62. 1753: 'Blacken'd with lust'.
64. 1753: 'For you'.
65. MS Colman: 'from nature's guilty sleep'.
69. 1753, 1780, &c.: 'ye then'.

18   THE LOVE-FEAST

PART I

There were originally five parts to this poem, each having four stanzas, except the
fifth, which had six. The first four parts were taken over as four hymns into the 1780
Collection, and these four hymns continued in the hymn-book until the revision of
1933, when only the first part was retained, the Love-Feast itself having in the meantime gradually fallen into disuse. (Cf. the following hymn.)

* *Hymns and Sacred Poems* (1740), pp. 181–2.
  MS Colman 21, p. 23.
  Poetical Works, I.350–1.
  Whitefield's *Hymns* (1753): No. 22 in 'Hymns for Society', p. 130, two verses, com-
    prising 1a+2a, 3a+4b.
  Hymns and Spiritual Songs (1753): No. 83.
  Select Hymns (1761): No. 28.
  Collection (1780): No. 505.
  Pocket Hymn Book (1787): No. 240.
  Collection (1831): No. 519.
  Collection (1876): No. 519.
  MHB (1904): No. 740, divided into verses of four lines.
  MHB (1933): No. 748, as 1904.

                              Metre 52: 7 7.7 7.7 7.7 7
                                        a a b b c c d d

1 Come, and let us sweetly join
  CHRIST to praise in Hymns Divine;
  Give we all with one Accord
  Glory to our Common LORD:

Hands, and Hearts, and Voices raise,   *5*
Sing as in the antient Days,
Antedate the Joys above,
Celebrate the Feast of LOVE.

2 Strive we, in Affection strive:
Let the purer Flame revive,   *10*
Such as in the Martyrs glow'd,
Dying Champions for their GOD.
We, like them, may live and love,
Call'd we are their Joys to prove;
Sav'd with them from future Wrath,   *15*
Partners of like pretious Faith.

3 Sing we then in JESU's Name,
Now, as yesterday the same,
One in every Age and Place,
Full for All of Truth and Grace.   *20*
We for CHRIST our Master stand
Lights in a benighted Land;
We our Dying LORD confess,
We are JESU's Witnesses.

4 Witnesses that CHRIST hath died,   *25*
We with Him are crucified:
CHRIST hath burst the Bands of Death,
We His quick'ning Spirit breathe.
CHRIST is now gone up on high,
(Thither all our Wishes fly):   *30*
Sits at GOD's Right-hand above,
There with Him we reign in Love!

19. 1780, &c.: 'every time and place'.
20. Whitefield: 'Full of Love, of Truth, and Grace'.
21. MS Colman: 'May we for our Master stand'.
30. MS Colman: 'There may all our wishes fly'.
Whitefield: 'may our Wishes'.

THE COMMUNION OF SAINTS   19

PART IV

This whole poem formed a companion-piece to the previous one, and was used on similar occasions.

* *Hymns and Sacred Poems* (1740), pp. 194–5.
MS Colman 21, p. 24.
Poetical Works, I.361–2.
Whitefield's *Hymns* (1753): No. 26 in 'Hymns for Society', pp. 133–4, vv. 1, 3, 5.
Hymns and Spiritual Songs (1753): No. 84, Part Four.
Madan's *Collection* (1760): No. 115, omitting vv. 2, 4.
Collection (1780): No. 504, divided into four-lined verses.
Pocket Hymn Book (1787): No. 239, as 1780.

Collection (1831): No. 518, as 1780.
Collection (1876): No. 518, as 1780.
MHB (1904): No. 689, as 1780, but omitting vv. 4 and 5a.
MHB (1933): No. 720, as 1780, but using only vv. 1, 3a, 4a, 5b.

Metre 52: 7 7.7 7.7 7.7 7
a a b b c c d d

1 CHRIST, from whom all Blessings flow,
Perfecting the Saints below,
Hear us, who Thy Nature share,
Who Thy Mystic Body are:
Join us, in One Spirit join,   5
Let us still receive of Thine,
Still for more on Thee we call,
Thee, who fillest All in All.

2 Closer knit to Thee our Head,
Nourish us, O CHRIST, and feed,   10
Let us daily Growth receive,
More and more in JESUS live:
JESU! we Thy Members are,
Cherish us with kindest Care,
Of Thy Flesh, and of Thy Bone: 15
Love, forever love Thine own.

3 Move, and actuate, and guide,
Diverse Gifts to each divide;
Plac'd according to thy Will,
Let us all our Work fulfil,   20
Never from our Office move,
Needful to the Others prove,
Use the Grace on each bestow'd,
Temper'd by the Art of GOD.

4 Sweetly now we all agree,   25
Touch'd with softest Simpathy,
Kindly for each other care:
Every Member feels its Share:
Wounded by the Grief of One,
All the suffering Members groan;   30
Honour'd if one Member is
All partake the common Bliss.

2. MS Colman: 'Perfecting thy saints'.
   Whitefield, Madan: 'Comforting thy Saints'.
13. 1753, 1780, &c.: 'Jesus, we'.
16. MS Colman: 'thy own'.
20. Madan: 'all our Works'.
22. 1780 (from 3rd edn, 1782): 'Needful to each other'.
23. 1780 (from 3rd edn, 1782): 'on all bestowed'.
24. Whitefield: 'Temperd by the blessed God'.
25. MS Colman, 1780, &c.: 'Sweetly may'.
26. 1933: 'loving sympathy'.
28. 1780, &c.: 'feel'.
30. 1780, &c.: 'Now let all the members groan'.

5[1] Many are we now, and One,
 We who JESUS have put on:
 There is neither Bond nor Free,   *35*
 Male nor Female, LORD, in Thee.
 Love, like Death, hath all destroy'd,
 Render'd all Distinctions void:
 Names, and Sects, and Parties fall;
 Thou, O CHRIST, art ALL in ALL!   *40*

   [[1] In the original this stanza is incorrectly numbered 'VI'.]

38. 1780: 'Rendered our distinctions'.

[SUFFICIENT, SOVEREIGN, SAVING GRACE]   20

This poem, like the collection in which it was printed, and like the magazine in whose first volume it was later reprinted, was one of the weapons wielded in Wesley's theological warfare against the extreme Calvinism of his day. Phrases such as 'For *All* he hath the Atonement made' in this and other hymns were not merely general statements of God's love, but Methodist theses for proclamation in song. Nearly all the words and phrases here italicized by Wesley bore such a reference. (These lavish italics were dropped from the later publications noted.)

* *Hymns on God's Everlasting Love* (First Series, 1741), pp. 3–5.
 Poetical Works, III.3–5.
 Arminian Magazine (1778), pp. 430–2.
 Collection (1831): No. 39, vv. 1, 2, 3, 8, 12, 17.
 Collection (1876): No. 39, as 1831.
 MHB (1904): No. 65, vv. 1, 2, 3, 8, 17.
 MHB (1933): No. 75, as 1904.

           Metre 7: 8.8.8.8
              A B A B

1 FATHER, whose *Everlasting Love*
 Thy only Son for Sinners gave,
 Whose Grace *to All* did *freely* move,
 And sent Him down a *World to save;*

2 Help us thy Mercy to extol,   *5*
 Immense, Unfathom'd, Unconfin'd;
 To praise the Lamb who *died for All,*
 The *General Saviour of Mankind.*

3 Thy *Undistinguishing* Regard
 Was cast on *Adam's* fallen Race: *10*
 For All Thou hast in CHRIST prepar'd
 Sufficient, Sovereign, Saving Grace.

4 JESUS hath said, we *All* shall hope;
 Preventing Grace for All is free:
 'And I, if I be lifted up,   *15*
 'I will *draw All Men* unto Me.'

4. 1831, &c.: 'The world'.

         29

5 What Soul those Drawings never knew?
    With whom hath not thy Spirit strove?
  We All *must* own that GOD is True;
    We all *may* feel, that GOD is Love.   *20*

6 *O, all ye Ends of Earth* behold
    The bleeding, All-atoning Lamb!
  Look unto Him for Sinners sold,
    Look and *be sav'd* thro' JESU's Name.

7 Behold the Lamb of GOD, who takes   *25*
    The Sins of All the World away!
  His Pity no Exception makes;
    But All that *will* receive Him, *may.*

8 *A World* He suffer'd to redeem;
    For *All* He hath th'Atonement[1] made: *30*
  For[2] those that *will not come* to Him
    The Ransom of his Life was paid.

9 Their LORD unto *His own* He came;
    His own were who *receiv'd Him not,*
  Denied and trampled on his Name   *35*
    And Blood, by which themselves were bought.

10 Who underfoot their Saviour trod,
    Expos'd *afresh* and *crucified,*
  Who trampled on the SON of GOD,
    For Them, for Them, their Saviour died.   *40*

11 For those who at the Judgment Day
    On Him they pierc'd shall *look* with Pain;
  The Lamb for every *Castaway,*
    For *Every Soul of Man* was slain.

12 Why then, Thou Universal Love,   *45*
    Should any of thy Grace despair?
  To All, to All, Thy Bowels move,
    But straitned in our own We are.

13 'Tis We, the wretched Abjects We,
    Our Sin and Death on Thee translate;   *50*
  We think that Fury is in Thee,
    Horribly think, that GOD is Hate.

[1] The 1st edn has 'Attonement', corrected in the second and subsequent editions.]
[2] The 1st edn has 'Nor', corrected in subsequent editions.]

29. 1831, &c.: 'The world'.
50. Altered in 2nd edn (1756), to 'Our Blasphemies on Thee translate'.

14 'Thou has compell'd the Lost to die;
   'Hast *reprobated* from thy Face;
   'Hast Others sav'd, but them *past by*;   *55*
   'Or mock'd with only [*]*Damning* Grace.'

15 How long, thou jealous GOD, how long
   Shall impious Worms thy Word disprove?
   Thy Justice stain, thy Mercy wrong,
   Deny thy Faithfulness and Love.   *60*

16 Still shall the **Hellish Doctrine** stand?
   And Thee for its dire Author claim?
   No—let it sink at thy Command
   Down to the Pit from whence it came.

17 Arise, O GOD, maintain thy Cause!   *65*
   The Fulness of the Gentiles call:
   Lift up the Standard of thy Cross,
   And All shall own Thou died'st for All.

* *More usually call'd*, Common *Grace*. [In the first edition the * is omitted from the text, but restored in later editions.]

[OUR TITLE TO HEAVEN]   21

In this publication Charles Wesley really masters the 'vulgar' medium of anapaestic verse, which was soon to become so typical of Methodist hymn-singing, and in which a tentative experiment had been made the previous year. (See No. **16**.) Of the eighteen hymns three are in anapaestic 5's and 6's. In later editions this poem was printed in anapaestic 10's and 11's with an internal rhyme.

* *Hymns on God's Everlasting Love* (First Series, 1741), pp. 5–6.
MS Colman 21, p. 4.
Poetical Works, III.6.
Hymns and Sacred Poems (Dublin, 1747): pp. 53–4.
Collection (1780): No. 5, omitting v. 1.
Collection (1831): No. 5, as 1780.
Collection (1876): No. 5, as 1780.
MHB (1904): No. 273, as 1780.
MHB (1933): No. 311, vv. 2, 5 and 3 conflated, 4, 6.

Metre 66: 5.5.5.5.6.5.6.5
A B A B C D C D

1 LORD, not unto me,
   (The Whole I disclaim)
All Glory to Thee
   Thro' JESU[S]'s Name!
Thy Gifts, and thy Graces   *5*
   Pour'd down from above,
Demand all our Praises,
   Our Thanks and our Love?

4. The omitted "s" is inserted in the 2nd and subsequent editions.

2 Thy Faithfulness, LORD,
   Each Moment we find,   *10*
So true to thy Word.
   So Loving, and Kind;
Thy Mercy so tender
   To all the lost Race,
The foulest Offender   *15*
   May turn, and find Grace.

3 The Mercy I feel
   To Others I shew,
I set to my Seal,
   That JESUS is true;   *20*
Ye all may find Favour,
   Who come at his Call:
O! come to my Saviour,
   His Grace is for All.

4 To save what was lost,   *25*
   From Heaven he came:
Come Sinners, and trust
   In JESUS's Name;
He offers you Pardon,
   He bids you 'Be free!   *30*
'If Sin is your Burthen,
   O! Come unto me!

5 O let me commend
   My Saviour to you,
The Publican's Friend,   *35*
   An[d] Advocate too;
For you He is pleading
   His Merits and Death,
With GOD interceeding
   For Sinners beneath.   *40*

6 Then let us submit
   His Grace to receive,
Fall down at his Feet,
   And gladly believe:
We all are forgiven   *45*
   For JESUS's Sake,
Our Title to Heaven
   His Merits we take.

17-18. MHB (1933) replaces these lines by lines *33-4*, but otherwise
          leaves the verse unchanged.
30.   1780 avoids commencing the quotation within the line, and is
          followed by later editions, with or without the use of quotation
          marks.

THE UNIVERSAL LOVE OF CHRIST[1]   **22**

This seems to be Charles Wesley's first publication of a poem in this stirring metre which became one of his favourites. (This is on assumption that this pamphlet was published late in 1741, though it may well have been published in 1742.)

* *Hymns on God's Everlasting Love* (Second Series, 1741-2), pp. 31-3.
MS Colman 21, p. 6, omitting v. 6.
Poetical Works, III.71-3.
Madan's *Collection* (1760): No. 90, vv. 1-4.
Select Hymns (2nd edn, 1765): No. 99.
Arminian Magazine (1778), pp. 191-2.
Collection (1780): No. 33, omitting vv. 6, 8.
Pocket Hymn Book (1787): No. 22, as 1780.
Collection (1831): No. 34, omitting vv. 6, 8, 10.
Collection (1876): No. 34, as 1831.
MHB (1904): No. 99, as 1831.
MHB (1933): No. 114, as 1831.

Metre 25: 6.6.6.6.8 8
A B A B C C

1   Let Earth and Heaven agree,
       Angels and Men be join'd
    To celebrate with me
       The Saviour of Mankind,
    T'adore the All-atoning Lamb,   5
    And bless the Sound of JESU's Name.

2   JESUS, transporting Sound!
       The Joy of Earth and Heaven!
    No other Help is found,
       No other Name is given   10
    By which we can Salvation have:
    But JESUS came the World to save.

3   JESUS, harmonious Name!
       It charms the Hosts above;
    They evermore proclaim,
       And wonder at His Love?   15
    'Tis all their Happiness to gaze,
    'Tis Heaven to see Our JESU's Face.

4   His Name the Sinner hears,
       And is from Sin set free;
    'Tis Musick in His Ears,   20
       'Tis Life, and Victory;
    New Songs do now his Lips employ,
    And Dances his glad Heart for Joy.

[1 This title was given to the reprint in the *Arminian Magazine*.]

9. 1780 (1st edn): 'No other name is found', altered back to 'no other help' in the 2nd edn (1781).

5   Stung by the Scorpion Sin   *25*
      My poor expiring Soul
    The balmy Sound drinks in,
      And is at once made whole,
  See there my LORD upon the Tree!
  I hear, I feel he died for me.   *30*

6   For Me, and All Mankind,
      The Lamb of GOD was slain,
    My Lamb His Life resign'd
      For Every Soul of Man: *35*
  Loving to All, He none pass'd by,
  He would not have One Sinner die.

7   O unexampled Love,
      O All-redeeming Grace!
    How freely didst Thou move
      To save a Fallen Race!   *40*
  What shall I do to make it known
  What Thou for all Mankind hast done!

8   For This alone I breathe
      To spread the Gospel-sound,
    Glad Tidings of Thy Death   *45*
      To all the Nations round;
  Who All *may* feel Thy Blood applied,
  Since All are freely justified.

9   O for a Trumpet-voice
      On all the World to call,   *50*
    To bid their Hearts rejoice
      In Him, who died for All!
  For All my Lord was crucified,
  For All, for All my Saviour died.

10   To serve Thy Blessed Will,   *55*
      Thy Dying Love to praise,
    Thy Counsel to fulfil,
      And minister Thy Grace,
  Freely what I receive to give,
  The Life of Heaven on Earth I live.   *60*

27. 1933, 'The healing sound'.
39. 1765, 1780, &c.: 'How swiftly didst'.
48. MS Colman: 'May all be freely'.

34

PSALM LI.10   **23**

Make me a Clean Heart, O GOD, and renew a right Spirit within me.

* *Hymns and Sacred Poems* (1742), pp. 30–1.
Poetical Works, II.77–8.
Hymns and Spiritual Songs (1753): No. 19.
Madan's *Collection* (1760): No. 3, omitting v. 7.
Select Hymns (2nd edn, 1765): No. 135.
Collection (1780): No. 334.
Pocket Hymn Book (1787): No. 168.
Collection (1831): No. 343.
Collection (1876): No. 343.
MHB (1904): No. 529, vv. 1–4, 8.
MHB (1933): No. 550, as 1904.
Hymns A & M (1889, 1916), No. 549, vv. 1–4, 8; (1904), No. 450, as 1889; (1950),
    No. 325, as 1889; Schools edn (1958), No. 180, as 1889.

Metre 1: 8.6.8.6
ABAB

1 O for an Heart to praise my GOD,
    An Heart from Sin set free!
An Heart that always feels Thy Blood,
    So freely spilt for Me!

2 An Heart resign'd, submissive, meek,   *5*
    My dear Redeemer's Throne,
Where only CHRIST is heard to speak,
    Where JESUS reigns alone.

3 An humble, lowly, contrite Heart,
    Believing, true, and clean,   *10*
Which neither Life nor Death can part
    From him that dwells within.

4 An Heart in Every Thought renew'd,
    And full of Love Divine,
Perfect, and right, and pure and good,   *15*
    A Copy, LORD, of Thine.

5 Thy tender Heart is still the same,
    And melts at Human Woe:
JESU, for Thee distrest I am,
    I want Thy Love to know.   *20*

1, 2, 3, 5, 13. 1780, &c., *A & M* (1889, &c.): 'A heart'.
 3. Madan, 'An Heart that's sprinkled with the Blood';
    A &M (1889, &c.): as Madan, but 'A heart'.
 4. *A &M* (1889, &c.): 'So freely shed'.
 6. 1780, &c., *A &M* (1889, &c., except 1904): 'My great Redeemer's.'
 9. 1780: 'Oh! for a lowly, contrite heart'.
    1831, &c., *A &M* (1889, &c.): 'A humble, lowly'.
14. 1753, Madan, 1765: 'And fill'd with'.
19. 1831, &c.: 'Jesus, for'.

6 My Heart, Thou know'st can never rest,
   Till Thou create my Peace,
Till of my Eden repossest,
   From Self, and Sin I cease.

7 Fruit of Thy gracious Lips, on Me   *25*
   Bestow that Peace unknown,
The Hidden Manna, and the Tree
   Of Life, and the White Stone.

8 Thy Nature, dearest LORD, impart,
   Come quickly from above,   *30*
Write Thy New Name upon my Heart,
   Thy New, Best Name of Love.

24. 1780, &c.: 'From every sin I cease'.
26. 1753, 1765: 'the peace'.
29. 1753, Madan, 1765, 1780, &c., *A & M* (1889, &c.): 'gracious Lord'.

24   THE LII CHAPTER OF ISAIAH
               PART II [vv. 7–10]

* *Hymns and Sacred Poems* (1742), pp. 112–13.
  Poetical Works, II.169–71.
  Hymns on God's Everlasting Love (First series, 1741): p. 33 (last four verses only).
                    Metre 94a: combination of 7 and 66.[1]

1 How beautiful His Feet appear
   High on the Mountain-tops, who brings
Glad Tidings of Salvation near,
   Salvation from the King of Kings!

2 Who publishes the joyful Sound,   *5*
   Proclaims a Peace 'twixt Earth and Heaven,
A Ransom for the Sinner found,
   GOD reconcil'd, and Man forgiven.

3 That says to *Israel*'s Mournful Race,
   Awake, arise, shake off thy Chains,   *10*
Believe the Word of Gospel-Grace,
   Thy GOD, thy great Redeemer reigns.

4 Thy Watchmen shall the Voice lift up,
   Shall sing with gladsome Melody,
Object of all their Joy and Hope,   *15*
   When Eye to Eye their LORD they see.

[1 This device of a change of metre to emphasize the element of song contained in the narrative is similarly used in another paraphrase on Isaiah 44, in *Hymns and Sacred Poems* (1749), using a 'song' already published in *Redemption Hymns* (1747). The same metres are used, but the iambic verses are continued after the close of the anapaestic 'song'. (See *Poetical Works*, IV.297–9.)]

5 Him, Eye to Eye, shall they behold,
 Shall shout to see the Saviour come,
To save a World redeem'd of old,
 To bring the weary Captives home.   *20*

6 Break forth into Joy, Your Comforter sing,
Ye Sinners employ Your All for your King,
Rejoice ye waste Places, Your Saviour proclaim,
Bestow all your Praises, And Lives on His Name.

7 For JESUS the LORD Hath comforted Man,   *25*
The Sinner restor'd; Nor suffer'd in vain,
To bring us to Heaven When rais'd from our Fall,
His Life he hath given A Ransom for All.

8 His Arm he hath bar'd, His Mercy and Grace
Hath Pardon prepar'd For all the Lost Race: *30*
His Uttermost Merit Display'd in our Sight,
We All may inherit, And claim as our Right.

9 The *Gentiles* shall hear The Life-giving Call,
His Grace shall appear, And visit them All:
The Common Salvation To All doth belong,   *35*
To every Nation, And People, and Tongue.

WRESTLING JACOB   **25**

John Wesley's obituary tribute to his brother before the Methodist Conference in 1788 ended thus: 'His least praise was, his talent for poetry: although Dr Watts did not scruple to say, that "that single poem, *Wrestling Jacob*, was worth all the verses he himself had written"' (*Minutes* (1788), p. 5).

* *Hymns and Sacred Poems* (1742), pp. 115–18.
 Poetical Works, II.173–6.
 Hymns and Spiritual Songs (1753): No. 39, in two parts, vv. 1–7, 8–14.
 Collection (1780): No. 136, omitting vv. 5, 7.
 Collection (1831): Nos. 140, 141, as 1780.
 Collection (1876): Nos. 140, 141, as 1780.
 MHB (1904): Nos. 449, 450, as 1780.
 MHB (1933): No. 339, as 1780; also No. 340, an abbreviated version consisting of
  vv. 1, 3, 8, 9.
 Hymns A & M (1904), No. 607, vv. 1–3, 8–9; (1916), No. 774, as 1904; (1950),
  No. 343, as 1904.

Metre 10: 8.8.8.8.8 8
     A B A B C C

1 Come, O Thou Traveller unknown,
 Whom still I hold, but cannot see,
My Company before is gone,
 And I am left alone with Thee,
With Thee all Night I mean to stay,   *5*
And wrestle till the Break of Day.

2 I need not tell Thee who I am,
    My Misery, or Sin declare,
Thyself hast call'd me by my Name,
    Look on Thy Hands, and read it there,   *10*
But who, I ask Thee, who art Thou,
Tell me Thy Name, and tell me now?

3 In vain Thou strugglest to get free,
    I never will unloose my Hold:
Art Thou the Man that died for me?   *15*
    The Secret of Thy Love unfold;
Wrestling I will not let Thee go,
    Till I Thy Name, Thy Nature know.

4 Wilt Thou not yet to me reveal
    Thy new, unutterable Name?   *20*
Tell me, I still beseech Thee, tell,
    To know it Now resolv'd I am;
Wrestling I will not let Thee go,
    Till I Thy Name, Thy Nature know.

5 'Tis all in vain to hold Thy Tongue,   *25*
    Or touch the Hollow of my Thigh:
Though every Sinew be unstrung,
    Out of my Arms Thou shalt not fly;
Wrestling I will not let Thee go,
    Till I Thy Name, Thy Nature know.   *30*

6 What tho' my shrinking Flesh complain,
    And murmur to contend so long,
I rise superior to my Pain,
    When I am weak then I am strong,
And when my All of Strength shall fail,   *35*
I shall with the GOD-man prevail.

7 My Strength is gone, my Nature dies,
    I sink beneath Thy weighty Hand,
Faint to revive, and fall to rise;
    I fall, and yet by Faith I stand,   *40*
I stand, and will not let Thee go,
Till I Thy Name, Thy Nature know.

8. A &M (1904, 1916): 'My misery and sin'.
21. 1753 (from 3rd edn, 1754) omits 'still'.
27–8. 1753: 'Tho every sinew were unstrung,
                Out of my Arms Thou shou'dst not fly'.
35. 1753: 'doth fail'.

8 Yield to me Now—for I am weak;
   But confident in Self-despair:
Speak to my Heart, in Blessings speak,   *45*
   Be conquer'd by my Instant Prayer,
Speak, or Thou never hence shalt move,
And tell me, if Thy Name is LOVE.

9 'Tis Love, 'tis Love! Thou diedst for Me,
   I hear Thy Whisper in my Heart.   *50*
The Morning breaks, the Shadows flee:
   Pure UNIVERSAL LOVE Thou art,
To me, to All Thy Bowels move,
Thy Nature, and Thy Name is LOVE.

10 My Prayer hath Power with GOD; the Grace   *55*
   Unspeakable I now receive,
Thro' Faith I see Thee Face to Face,
   I see Thee Face to Face, and live:
In vain I have not wept, and strove,
Thy Nature, and Thy Name is LOVE.   *60*

11 I know Thee, Saviour, who Thou art,
   JESUS the feeble Sinner's Friend;
Nor wilt Thou with the Night depart,
   But stay, and love me to the End;
Thy Mercies never shall remove,   *65*
Thy Nature, and Thy Name is LOVE.

12 The Sun of Righteousness on Me
   Hath rose with Healing in his Wings,
Wither'd my Nature's Strength; from Thee
   My Soul it's Life and Succour brings,   *70*
My Help is all laid up above;
Thy Nature, and Thy Name is LOVE.

13 Contented now upon my Thigh
   I halt, till Life's short Journey end;
All Helplessness, all Weakness I,   *75*
   On Thee alone for Strength depend,
Nor have I power, from Thee, to move;
Thy Nature, and Thy Name is LOVE.

14 Lame as I am, I take the Prey,
   Hell, Earth, and Sin with Ease o'ercome;   *80*
I leap for Joy, pursue my Way,
   And as a bounding Heart[1] fly home
Thro' all Eternity to prove
Thy Nature, and Thy Name is LOVE.

[¹ Corrected to 'hart' in Errata.]

53. 1904, &c., *A &M* (1904, &c.): 'Thy mercies move'.
68. 1904, &c.: 'Hath risen'.

26   A THANKSGIVING

* *Hymns and Sacred Poems* (1742), p. 119.
  Poetical Works, II.177–8.
  Hymns and Spiritual Songs (1753): No. 50.
  Collection (1780): No. 191.
  Collection (1831): No. 199.
  Collection (1876): No. 199.
  MHB (1904): No. 12.
  MHB (1933): No. 7.

Metre 66: 10 10.11 11
A A B B

1 O Heavenly King, Look down from above,
  Assist us to sing Thy Mercy and Love,
  So sweetly o'reflowing, So plenteous the Store,
  Thou still art bestowing, And giving us more.

2 O GOD of our Life, We hallow Thy Name;   *5*
  Our Business and Strife Is Thee to proclaim;
  Accept our Thanksgiving For Creating Grace,
  The Living the Living Shall shew forth Thy Praise.

3 Our Father and LORD Almighty art Thou;
  Preserv'd by Thy Word, We worship Thee now,   *10*
  The bountiful Donor of All we enjoy,
  Our Tongues to Thine Honour and Lives we employ.

4 But O above All Thy Kindness we praise,
  From Sin and from Thrall Which saves the Lost Race,
  Thy Son Thou hast given A world to redeem,   *15*
  And bring us to Heaven Whose Trust is in Him.

5 Wherefore of Thy LOVE We sing and rejoice
  With Angels above We lift up our Voice;
  Thy LOVE each Believer Shall gladly adore,
  For ever and ever When Time is no more.   *20*

15. 1831, &c.: 'The world'.

27   [GENTLE JESUS]

For notes on the three distinct publications entitled *Hymns for Children*, see introduction to No. 103 below, where it is pointed out that the germ of these publications
was a group of seven hymns in the *Hymns and Sacred Poems* (1742), of which this is
the first. It will be noted that this hymn did not appear in the classic Methodist
hymn-books until the present century, largely because there was no children's
section in those volumes until 1904. It had already become popular in Sunday-
schools, however, and is found in most Methodist Sunday-school hymn-books, from
Joseph Benson's *Hymns for Children* (1806) onward. (It is given as Nos. 32 and 33 in
the supplementary volume 'for younger children'.)

* *Hymns and Sacred Poems* (1742), pp. 194–5.
  Hymns for Children (n.d. c.1746?): No. 1.
  Hymns for Children (1763): No. 69, in two parts of seven verses each, commencing
     the section 'Hymns for the Youngest'.

Hymns for Children (1787): Nos. 21, 22.
Poetical Works, VI.441–2.
MHB (1904): Nos. 879, 880, comprising vv. 1, 2, v. 5 of 'Jesu, gentle, Loving Lamb'
(p. 48 of *HSP* (1742)), 9, 11; 8, 12, 13, 14.
MHB (1933): No. 842, comprising vv. 1, 2, 9, 11; 8, 12, 13, 14.
Hymns A & M (1889, 1916), No. 568, vv. 8–14; (1904), No. 579, vv. 8–11, 13, 14;
(1950), No. 451, in three parts—vv. 1, 2, 7b + 4a; 8, 9, 11; 12–14; Schools edn
(1958), No. 3, vv. 1, 2, and No. 115, vv. 8, 9, 11–14.

Metre 46: 7 7.7 7
a a b b

1 Gentle JESUS, meek and mild,
Look upon a Little Child,
Pity my Simplicity,
Suffer me to come to Thee.

2 Fain I would to Thee be brought,   5
Dearest GOD, forbid it not,
Give me, dearest GOD, a Place
In the Kingdom of Thy Grace.

3 Put Thy Hands upon my Head,
Let me in Thine Arms be stayed,   10
Let me lean upon Thy Breast,
Lull me, lull me, LORD, to Rest.

4 Hold me fast in Thy Embrace,
Let me see Thy smiling Face,
Give me, LORD, Thy Blessing give,   15
Pray for me, and I shall live.

5 I shall live the Simple Life,
Free from Sin's uneasy Strife,
Sweetly ignorant of Ill,
Innocent, and happy still.   20

6 O that I may never know
What the Wicked People do;
Sin is contrary to Thee,
Sin is the Forbidden Tree.

7 Keep me from the great Offence,   25
Guard my helpless Innocence;
Hide me, from all Evil hide,
Self, and Stubborn[n]ess, and Pride.

6. 1904, &c.: 'Gracious Lord, forbid'.
7. A & M (1950, &c.): 'Give me, blessed Lord, a place'.
7–8. 1904, &c.: 'In the kingdom of Thy grace
Give a little child a place.'
10. 1746?: 'in thy Arms'.
13. 1763, 1787, *A & M* (1950): 'thine embrace'.

8 Lamb of GOD, I look to Thee,
   Thou shalt my Example be;
   Thou art gentle, meek, and mild,
   Thou wast once a Little Child.   *30*

9 Fain I would be, as Thou art,
   Give me thy obedient Heart;
   Thou art pitiful and kind,
   Let me have Thy loving Mind.   *35*

10 Meek, and lowly may I be,
   Thou art all Humility;
   Let me to my Betters bow,
   Subject to Thy Parents Thou.   *40*

11 Let me above all fulfil
   GOD my Heavenly Father's Will,
   Never His Good Spirit grieve,
   Only to His Glory live.

12 Thou didst live to GOD alone,   *45*
   Thou didst never seek Thine own;
   Thou Thyself didst never please,
   GOD was all Thy Happiness.

13 Loving JESU, gentle Lamb,
   In Thy gracious Hands I am,   *50*
   Make me, Saviour, what Thou art,
   Live Thyself within my Heart.

14 I shall then shew forth Thy Praise,
   Serve Thee all my happy Days;
   Then the World shall always see   *55*
   CHRIST, the Holy Child, in Me.

49. 1763, 1787, 1904, &c.: 'Loving Jesus'.

28   COME, LORD JESUS!

* *Hymns and Sacred Poems* (1742), pp. 204–6.
  MS Colman 21, p. 41, vv. 1–3, 9–13.
  Poetical Works, II.258–9.
  Hymns and Spiritual Songs (1753): No. 17, vv. 1–3, 9–13.
  Select Hymns (2nd edn, 1765): No. 138, as 1753.
  Collection (1780): No. 157, vv. 1–3, 9–13.
  Pocket Hymn Book (1785): Nos. 44 (vv. 1–3, 9) and 45 (vv. 10–13).
  Collection (1831): No. 163, vv. 1–3, 10–13.
  Collection (1876): No. 163, as 1831.
  MHB (1904): No. 337, vv. 1, 10–13.

Metre 8: 8 8.8 8
A A B B

1 When, dearest LORD, when shall it be,
  That I shall find my All in Thee;
  The Fulness of Thy Promise prove,
  The Seal of Thine Eternal Love!

2 A poor, blind Child I wander here
  If haply I may feel Thee near,
  O dark, dark, dark (I still must say)
  Amidst the Blaze of Gospel-Day.

3 Thee, only Thee I fain would find,
  I cast the World, and Flesh behind,
  Thou, only Thou to me be given
  Of all Thou hast in Earth or Heaven.

4 All Earthly Comforts I disdain,
  They shall not rob me of my Pain,
  Or make me senseless of my Load,
  Or less disconsolate for GOD.

5 Rather let all the Creatures take
  Their Miserable Comforts back,
  With every vain Relief depart,
  And leave me to my Broken Heart.

6 Leave me, my Friends, the Mourner leave,
  For GOD, and not for you I grieve;
  My Weakness, O ye Strong, despise,
  My foolish Ignorance, ye Wise.

7 Let all my Father's Children be
  Still angry, still displeas'd with me,
  Disclaim, dishonour, and disown:
  I would be poor, forlorn, alone.

8 A Child, a Fool, a Thing of nought,
  Abhor'd neglected, and forgot,
  Contemn'd, abandon'd, and distrest
  Till I from Mortal Man have ceas'd.

9 When from the Arm of Flesh set free,
  JESU, my Soul shall fly to Thee:
  JESU, when I have lost my All,
  My Soul shall on Thy Bosom fall.

1. MS Colman, 1753, 1765, 1780, &c.: 'When, gracious Lord'.
34, 35. 1780: 'Jesus'.
36. 1780, 1785: 'I shall upon thy bosom fall'.

10 When Man forsakes, Thou wilt not leave,
 Ready the Outcasts to receive,
 Though all my Simpleness I own,
 And all my Faults to Thee are known.   *40*

11 Ah! wherefore did I ever doubt?
 Thou wilt in no wise cast me out,
 An helpless Soul that comes to Thee
 With only Sin and Misery.

12 LORD, I am sick; my Sickness cure: *45*
 I want; do Thou enrich the Poor:
 Under Thy mighty Hand I stoop,
 O lift the abject Sinner up!

13 LORD, I am blind: be Thou my Sight:
 LORD, I am weak, be Thou my Might: *50*
 An Helper of the Helpless be,
 And let me find my All in Thee.

37. 1753, 1765, 1780, &c.: 'Whom man forsakes'.
43. 1780, 1831, &c.: 'A helpless soul'.

29   BEHOLD THE MAN!

* *Hymns and Sacred Poems* (1742), pp. 264–5.
 Poetical Works, II.323–4.
 Hymns for those to whom Christ is all in all (1761): No. 55.
 Collection (1780): No. 194.
 Pocket Hymn Book (1787): No. 93.
 Collection (1831): No. 202.
 Collection (1876): No. 202
 MHB (1904): No. 363.
 MHB (1933): No. 368.

           Metre 25: 6.6.6.6.8 8
                A B A B C C

1 Arise, my Soul, arise,
  Shake off thy guilty Fears,
 The Bleeding Sacrifice
  In my Behalf appears;
 Before the Throne my Surety stands;   *5*
 My Name is written on His Hands.

2 He ever lives above
  For me to interceed,
 His All-redeeming Love,
  His pretious Blood to plead;   *10*
 His Blood aton'd for All our Race,
 And sprinkles now the Throne of Grace.

3   Five bleeding Wounds He bears,
        Receiv'd on *Calvary;*
     They pour effectual Prayers,   *15*
        They strongly speak for me;
   Forgive him, O forgive, they cry,
   Nor let that Ransom'd Sinner die!

4   The Father hears Him pray,
        His dear Anointed One,
     He cannot turn away   *20*
        The Presence of His Son:
   His Spirit answers to the Blood,
   And tells me, I am born of GOD.

5   My GOD is reconcil'd,   *25*
        His Pard'ning Voice I hear,
     He owns me for His Child,
        I can no longer fear;
   With Confidence I now draw nigh,
   And Father, Abba Father, cry!   *30*

THE WHOLE ARMOUR OF GOD   **30**
Ephesians vi

It is uncertain whether this stirring poem first appeared at the end of the first and second editions of John Wesley's *Character of a Methodist*, both issued in 1742 (it was omitted from the third and later editions), or in an undated broadside, of which there is a copy in the British Museum, placed *c.*1740–9 in a magnificent collection of broadsides. There is only one significant difference between the two versions, however, the use of 'Table' for Altar in the broadside version of stanza 13.

* *The Character of a Methodist* (1742), with title as above.
The Whole Armour of God (n.d.), broadsheet.
MS Thirty, pp. 22–7.
MS Colman 21, pp. 35–6, omitting vv. 9, 10.
Poetical Works, V.40–4.
Hymns and Sacred Poems (1749), Vol. I, No. 140, pp. 236–9.
Select Hymns (1761): No. 131.
Collection (1780): Nos. 258 (vv. 1–4), 259 (vv. 7, 8, 11, 12), and 260 (vv. 13–16).
Pocket Hymn Book (1787): Nos. 123–5, as 1780.
Collection (1831): Nos. 266–8, as 1780.
Collection (1876): Nos. 266–8, as 1780.
MHB (1904): Nos. 433 (vv. 1–4), and 499 (vv. 12, 13, 15, 16).
MHB (1933): Nos. 484 (vv. 1–4), and 541 (vv. 12, 13, 15, 16).
Hymns A & M (1861), No. 181, vv. 1a, 1b, 2a, 16a, 2b followed by a doxology supplied by the compilers; (1875, 1889, 1916), No. 270, as 1861; (1904), No. 437, as 1861; (1950), No. 303, as 1861, but omitting the doxology; Schools edn (1958), No. 173, as 1950.

Metre 31: 6.6.8.6.6.6.8.6
A B A B C D C D

1   Soldiers of CHRIST, arise,
     And put your Armour on,
  Strong in the Strength which GOD supplies
     Thro' his Eternal Son;
     Strong in the LORD of Hosts,
     And in his mighty Power,   *5*
  Who in the Strength of JESUS trusts
     Is more than Conqueror.

2   Stand then in His great Might,
      With all his Strength endu'd,   *10*
    And take, to arm you for the Fight,
      The Panoply of GOD;
      That having all Things done,
      And all your Conflicts past,
    Ye may o'ercome thro' CHRIST alone,   *15*
      And stand entire at last.

3   Stand then against your Foes,
      In close and firm Array,
    Legions of wily Fiends oppose
      Throughout the Evil Day;   *20*
      But meet the Sons of Night,
      But mock their vain Design,
    Arm'd in the Arms of Heavenly Light
      And Righteousness Divine.

4   Leave no Unguarded Place,   *25*
      No Weakness of the Soul,
    Take every Virtue, every Grace,
      And fortify the Whole;
      Indissolubly join'd,
      To Battle all proceed,   *30*
    But arm yourselves with all the Mind
      That was in CHRIST your Head.

5   Let Truth the Girdle be
      That binds your Armour on,
    In Faithful firm Sincerity   *35*
      To JESUS cleave alone;
      Let Faith and Love combine
      To guard your Valiant Breast,
    The Plate be Righteousness Divine,
      Imputed and Imprest.   *40*

6   Still let your Feet be shod,
      Ready His Will to do,
    Ready in all the Ways of GOD
      His Glory to pursue:
      Ruin is spread beneath,   *45*
      The Gospel Greaves put on,
    And safe thro' all the Snares of Death
      To Life eternal run.

11. 1780, &c.: 'But take'.
15–16. A & M (1861, &c., except 1950):

            'Ye may obtain, through Christ alone,
                A crown of joy at last.'

24. 1761, 1780, &c.: 'Of righteousness'.

7   But above all, lay hold
      On FAITH's victorious Shield   *50*
Arm'd with that Adamant and Gold
      Be sure to win the Field;
      If Faith surround your Heart,
      Satan shall be subdu'd
Repell'd his ev'ry Fiery Dart,   *55*
      And quench'd with JESU's Blood.

8   JESUS hath died for You!
      What can his Love withstand?
Believe; hold fast your Shield; and who
      Shall pluck you from His Hand?   *60*
      Believe that JESUS reigns,
      All Power to Him is giv'n,
Believe, 'till freed from Sin's Remains,
      Believe yourselves to Heaven.

9   Your Rock can never shake: *65*
      Hither, He saith, come up!
The Helmet of Salvation take,
      The Confidence of Hope:
      Hope for His Perfect Love,
      Hope for His People's Rest,   *70*
Hope to sit down with CHRIST above
      And share the Marriage Feast.

10   Brandish in Faith 'till then
      The Spirit's two-edg'd Sword,
Hew all the Snares of Fiends and Men   *75*
      In Pieces with the Word;
      'TIS WRITTEN; This applied
      Baffles their Strength and Art;
Spirit and Soul with this divide,
      And Joints and Marrow part.   *80*

11   To keep your Armour bright
      Attend with constant Care,
Still walking in your Captain's Sight,
      And watching unto Prayer;
      Ready for all Alarms,   *85*
      Stedfastly set your Face,
And always exercise your Arms,
      And use your every Grace.

12   Pray, without ceasing pray,
      (Your Captain gives the Word)   *90*
His Summons chearfully obey,
      And call upon the LORD;

72. MS 30: 'And claim the Marriage-feast.'
92. MS 39: 'your Lord'.

To GOD your every Want
In Instant Prayer display,
Pray always; pray, and never faint;   *95*
Pray, without ceasing Pray.

13   In Fellowship; alone
To GOD with Faith draw near,
Approach his Courts, besiege His Throne
With all the Power of Prayer: *100*
Go to His Temple, go,
Nor from His Altar move;
Let every House His Worship know,
And every Heart His Love.

14   To GOD your Spirits dart,   *105*
Your Souls in Words declare,
Or groan, to Him who reads the Heart,
Th'unutterable Prayer.
His Mercy now implore,
And now shew forth His Praise,   *110*
In Shouts, or silent Awe adore
His Miracles of Grace.

15   Pour out your Souls to GOD,
And bow them with your Knees,
And spread your Hearts and Hands abroad   *115*
And pray for *Sion*'s Peace;
Your Guides and Brethren, bear
For ever on your Mind;
Extend the Arms of mighty Prayer
Ingrasping all Mankind.   *120*

16   From Strength to Strength go on,
Wrestle, and fight, and pray,
Tread all the Powers of Darkness down,
And win the well-fought Day;
Still let the Spirit cry   *125*
In all His Soldiers, 'Come'
Till CHRIST the LORD descends from High
And takes the Conqu'rors Home.

95. 1780: 'Pray, always pray, and never faint'.
100. 'Power' seems to be misprint for 'Powers', which is the reading of all other editions noted.
102. Broadsheet: 'Nor from his Table move;'.
112. 1787: 'In miracles'.
115. MS 30: 'And spread your Hands & Hearts abroad'.
120. MS Colman, 1749 and 1761 also have 'Ingrasping', which other editions make into two words.
127. 1831, &c.: 'descend'.

PSALM CXXVI

* *Collection of Psalms and Hymns* (1743), pp. 91–2.
Poetical Works, VIII.241–3.
Collection of Psalms and Hymns for the Lord's Day (1784) (pp. 392–3 in 1788 edn).
Collection (1876): No. 623, vv. 1–4, 6, 7.

Metre 75: 6 6.7.7.7.7
A A b c b c

1   When our redeeming Lord
      Pronounc'd the pard'ning Word,
  Turn'd our Soul's Captivity
    O what sweet Surprize we found!
  Wonder ask'd, 'And can it be!'
    Scarce believ'd the welcome Sound.   5

2   And is it not a Dream?
      And are we sav'd thro' Him?
  Yes, our bounding Heart replied,
    Yes, broke out our joyful Tongue,   10
  Freely we are justify'd;
    This the new, the Gospel song!

3   The Heathen too could see
      Our glorious Liberty:
  All our Foes were forc'd to own,   15
    God for Them hath Wonders wrought:
  Wonders He for us hath done,
    From the House of Bondage brought.

4   To us our gracious God
      His Pard'ning Love hath shew'd,   20
  Now our joyful Souls are free
    From the Guilt and Power of Sin,
  Greater Things we soon shall see,
    We shall soon be pure within.

5   Turn us again, O Lord,   25
      Pronounce the second Word,
  Loose our Hearts, and let us go
    Down the Spirit's fullest Flood,
  Freely to the Fountain flow,
    All be swallow'd up in God.   30

6   Who for thy Coming wait,
      And wail their lost Estate,
  Poor, and sad, and empty still,
    Who for full Redemption weep,
  They shall thy Appearing feel,
    Sow in Tears, in Joy to reap.   35

7 Who Seed immortal bears,
   And wets his Path with Tears,
  Doubtless He shall soon return,
   Bring his Sheaves with vast Increase,   ***40***
  Fully of the Spirit born,
   Perfected in Holiness.

32   TO BE SUNG IN A TUMULT

The troubled months preceding and following the Jacobite Rebellion of 1745 were also months of extreme anti-Methodist persecution, when the followers of the Wesleys were slandered, plundered, and mobbed. In spite of genuine protestations of loyalty to the Crown, Methodists were often dubbed Papists and Jacobites, just as John Wesley was reputed to be the Young Pretender in disguise. This redoubled the fury of the attacks. It is against this background that *Hymns for Times of Trouble and Persecution* was published in 1744. The pamphlet contained 13 'Hymns for Times of Trouble', 16 'Hymns in Time of Persecution', and 4 'Hymns to be sung in a Tumult'. The second edition was enlarged by the addition of 15 'Hymns for Times of Trouble, for the year 1745'. A further pamphlet containing 6 items and entitled *Hymns for Times of Trouble*, appeared some months later.

* *Hymns for Times of Trouble and Persecution* (1744): 'Tumult', No. 1, p. 43.
 Festival Hymns (1746): No. 21, entitled 'The Triumph of Faith', printed in 6
  verses of 8 lines each.
 MS Thirty, p. 202.
 Poetical Works, IV.50–1.
 Whitefield's *Hymns* (1753), No. 50, pp. 41–2, vv. 1, 4–6, as 1746.
 Madan's *Collection* (1760), No. 36, as 1746.
 Select Hymns (1761), No. 121, as 1746.
 Collection (1831), No. 557, omitting v. 3, and adding as v. 6, 'Come, Lord, and
  display', from *Funeral Hymns* (1746), *Poetical Works* VI.195.
 Collection (1876), No. 859, omitting v. 3.
 MHB (1904), No. 388, as 1876.
 MHB (1933), No. 426, omitting vv. 2 & 3; otherwise as 1746.
 Hymns A & M (1916), No. 704, vv. 1, 4–6; (1950), No. 226, as 1916; Schools edn
  (1958), No. 130, as 1916.

           Metre 66: 10 10.11 11
             A A B B

1 Ye Servants of GOD, Your Master proclaim,
 And publish abroad His wonderful Name,
 The Name all-victorious Of JESUS extoll;
 His Kingdom is glorious, And rules over All.

2 The Waves of the Sea Have lift up their Voice,   *5*
 Sore troubled that we In JESUS rejoice;
 The Floods they are roaring, But JESUS is here,
 While we are adoring, He always is near.

3 Men, Devils engage, The Billows arise,
 And horribly rage, And threaten the Skies: *10*
 Their Fury shall never Our Stedfastness shock,
 The weakest Believer Is built on a Rock.

4 God ruleth on High, Almighty to save,
  And still He is nigh, His Presence we have;
  The Great Congregation His Triumphs shall sing,   *15*
  Ascribing Salvation to JESUS our King.

5 Salvation to GOD Who sits on the Throne!
  Let all cry aloud, And honour the SON!
  Our JESUS's Praises The Angels proclaim,
  Fall down on their Faces, And worship the Lamb.   *20*

6 Then let us adore, And give Him His Right,
  All Glory, and Power, And Wisdom, and Might,
  All Honour, and Blessing, With Angels above,
  And Thanks never ceasing, And infinite Love.

15. 2nd edn, 1745, 1746, Whitefield, Madan, 1831, &c., *A & M* (1916, &c.):
    'Triumph'.
19. 1933; *A & M* (1916, &c.): 'The praises of Jesus'.
22. 1831, &c., *A & M* (1916, &c.): 'All wisdom and might'.
23. A & M (1916, &c.): 'And honour and blessing'.

THE TRIUMPH OF FAITH   **33**

This is the first published example of an unusual verse-form which seems to have
originated with Charles Wesley, and to have been imitated hardly at all. In the
undated *Hymns for Times of Trouble* which followed this publication a further batch
of three poems in this metre were given—out of a total of six. Lampe's tune for the
Festival Hymns is still included in the *MHB*, entitled DYING STEPHEN.

* *Hymns for Times of Trouble and Persecution* (2nd edn, 1745), with additional
    hymns 'For the year 1745', of which this is No. 15.
  Poetical Works, IV.79–80.
  Festival Hymns (1746): No. 20, with title as above.
  Whitefield's *Hymns* (1753): No. 19 in 'Hymns for Society', pp. 127–8.
  Madan's *Collection* (1760): No. 30.
  Select Hymns (1761): No. 128.
  Pocket Hymn Book (1785): No. 147.
  Pocket Hymn Book (1787): No. 96.
  Collection (1876): No. 853.
  MHB (1904): No. 386.
  MHB (1933): No. 411, vv. 1, 2, and 4, numbered 1, 3 and 4, with v. 2 supplied
    from *Scripture Hymns* (1762), No. 1313 (*Poetical Works*, X.75).
  Hymns A & M (1916): No. 674.

Metre 36: 7.7.4 4.7.7.7.4 4.7
X AB B A Y CD DC

1 Head of thy Church Triumphant,
  We joyfully adore Thee;
    Till Thou appear,
    Thy Members here
  Shall sing like Those in Glory.   *5*
  We lift our Hearts and Voices
  With blest Anticipation,
    And cry aloud,
    And give to GOD
  The Praise of our Salvation.   *10*

2 While in Affliction's Furnace,
  And passing thro' the Fire,
    Thy Love we praise
    Which knows our Days,
  And ever brings us nigher.   *15*
  We clap our Hands exulting
  In Thine Almighty Favour;
    The Love Divine
    Which made us Thine
  Shall keep us Thine for ever.   *20*

3 Thou dost conduct thy People
  Thro' Torrents of Temptation,
    Nor will we fear,
    While Thou art near,
  The Fire of Tribulation.   *25*
  The World with Sin and Satan
  In vain our March opposes,
    In Thee we shall,
    Break thro' them all
  And sing the Song of *Moses*.   *30*

4 By Faith we see the Glory
  To which Thou shalt restore us,
    The Cross despise
    For that high Prize
  Which Thou hast set before us.   *35*
  And if Thou count us worthy,
  We each, as Dying *Stephen*,
    Shall see Thee stand
    At GOD's Right-Hand
  To take us up to Heaven.   *40*

14. 1761: 'Which knows no Days'.
28. 1746, Whitefield, 1785, 1787: 'By Thee we shall'.
   1876, 1904: 'Through thee'.

34   AN ACT OF DEVOTION

* *A Farther Appeal to Men of Reason and Religion. By John Wesley* (London, **1745**),
   p. (105), with the above title.
MS Colman 21, p. 59.
Poetical Works, V.10–11.
Hymns and Sacred Poems (1749), Vol. I: No. 120, pp. 206–7.
Hymns for those to whom Christ is all in all (1761): No. 87.
Collection (1780): No. 417.
Pocket Hymn Book (1787): No. 212.
Collection (1831): No. 429.
Collection (1876): No. 429.
MHB (1904): No. 594.
MHB (1933): No. 572.

Metre 10: 8.8.8.8.8 8
A B A B C C

1 Behold the Servant of the LORD!
 I wait Thy guiding Hand to feel,
To hear, and keep Thine every Word,
 To prove, and do Thy perfect Will.
Joyful from all my Works to cease,   *5*
Glad to fulfil All Righteousness.

2 Me if Thy Grace vouchsafe to use,
 Meanest of all Thy Creatures me,
The Deed, the Time, the Manner chuse;
 Let all my Fruit be found of Thee,   *10*
Let all my Works in Thee be wrought,
By Thee to full Perfection brought.

3 My every Weak though Good, Design
 O'errule, or change as seems Thee meet,
JESUS, let all the Work be Thine;   *15*
 Thy Work, O Lord, is All-compleat,
And pleasing in Thy Father's Sight;
Thou only hast done All Things right.

4 Here then to Thee Thine own I leave.
 Mould as Thou wilt the passive Clay: *20*
But let me all Thy Stamp receive,
 But let me all Thy Words obey,
Serve with a single Heart and Eye,
And to thy Glory live, and die.

2. MS Colman, 1749, 1761, 1780, &c.: 'thy guiding Eye'.
3. 1780, &c.: 'thy every word'.
5. 1780, &c.: 'from my own works'.
15. 1780, &c.: 'Jesu, let all my work'.
19. 1780, &c.: 'thy own'.
20. 1780, &c.: 'thy passive clay'.

['GOOD TIDINGS']   **35**

Charles Wesley published a dozen or so small hymn-pamphlets, and left others in manuscript. It seems desirable to present one of them *in extenso*. The one selected is *Hymns for the Nativity of our Lord*. It was published (without name, printer, or date) in 1745, and went through at least twenty editions during Wesley's lifetime, and a dozen or more afterwards. A number of the editions, commencing with the second, published by Felix Farley of Bristol in 1745, omitted Hymn 18. This little hymn-book is characteristic in its metrical variety, venturing into fourteen different metres for eighteen hymns. It is also typical in the mixed quality of its verse, about which John Wesley wrote to Charles in 1761: 'Pray tell Brother Sheen I am hugely displeased at his reprinting the Nativity hymns and omitting the very best hymn in the collection, "All glory to God in the sky, &c.". I beg they may never more be printed without it. Omit one or two, and I will thank you. They are *namby-pambical*.'

* *Nativity Hymns* (1745): No. 1.
 Poetical Works, IV.106.

53

Metre 7: 8.8.8.8
ABAB

1 Ye simple Men of Heart sincere,
 Shepherds who watch your Flocks by Night,
Start not to see an Angel near,
 Nor tremble at this glorious Light.

2 An Herald from the Heavenly King   *5*
 I come, your every Fear to chase;
Good Tidings of Great Joy I bring,
 Great Joy to all the Fallen Race!

3 To you is born on this glad Day,
 A Saviour by our Host ador'd,   *10*
Our GOD in *Bethlehem* survey,
 Make Haste to worship CHRIST the LORD.

4 By this the Saviour of Mankind,
 Th'Incarnate GOD shall be display'd,
The Babe ye wrapp'd in Swaths shall find,   *15*
 And humbly in a Manger laid.

36   ['YE HEAVENLY CHOIR']

* *Nativity Hymns* (1745): No. 2.
Poetical Works, IV.107.

           Metre: 66 5.5.5.5.6.5.6.5
              ABABCDCD

1 Ye heavenly Choir,
 Assist me to sing,
And strike the soft Lyre,
 And honour our King:
His mighty Salvation   *5*
 Demands all our Praise,
Our best Adoration,
 And loftiest Lays.

2 All Glory to GOD,
 Who ruleth on high,   *10*
And now hath bestow'd,
 And sent from the Sky
CHRIST JESUS, the Saviour,
 Poor Mortals to bless;
The Pledge of his Favour,   *15*
 The Seal of their Peace.

37   [THE SHEPHERDS' SONG]

* *Nativity Hymns* (1745): No. 3.
Poetical Works, IV.107–8.
Festival Hymns (1746): No. 2, given as five verses of eight lines, with the title
'The Shepherds' Song'.

Metre 58: 8 3 3.6
a b b a

1 Angels speak, let Man give Ear,
    Sent from high,
    They are nigh,
And forbid our Fear.

2 News they bring us of Salvation,   *5*
    Sounds of Joy
    To employ
Every Tongue and Nation.

3 Welcome Tidings! to retrieve us
    From our Fall,   *10*
    Born for All,
CHRIST is born to save us.

4 Born his Creatures to restore,
    Abject Earth
    Sees His Birth,   *15*
Whom the Heavens adore.

5 Wrapt in Swaths th'Immortal Stranger
    Man with Men
    We have seen,
Lying in a Manger.   *20*

6 All to GOD's Free Grace is owing:
    We are his
    Witnesses,
Poor, and nothing knowing.

7 Simple Shepherds Us he raises,   *25*
    Bids us sing
    CHRIST the King,
And shew forth his Praises.

8 We have seen the King of Glory,
    We proclaim   *30*
    CHRIST his Name,
And record his Story.

9 Sing we with the Host of Heaven,
    Reconcil'd
    By a Child   *35*
Who to Us is given.

10 Glory be to GOD the Giver,
    Peace and Love
    From above
Reign on Earth for ever.   *40*

55

38   ['GOD HIMSELF IS BORN']

* *Nativity Hymns* (1745): No. 4.
Poetical Works, IV.108–9.
Collection (1831): No. 607.
Collection (1876): No. 684.
MHB (1904): No. 134.
MHB (1933): No. 134.

Metre 85: 7.6.7.6.7.7.7.6
a B a B c d c D

1 Glory be to GOD on high,
    And Peace on Earth descend;
GOD comes down: He bows the Sky:
    He shews himself our Friend!
GOD th'Invisible *appears*,   5
    GOD the Blest, the Great I AM
Sojourns in this Vale of Tears,
    And JESUS is his Name.

2 Him the Angels all ador'd
    Their Maker and their King: 10
Tidings of their Humbled LORD
    They now to Mortals bring:
Emptied of his Majesty,
    Of His dazling Glories shorn,
Beings Source *begins to* Be,   15
    And GOD himself is BORN!

3 See th'Eternal Son of GOD
    A Mortal Son of Man,
Dwelling in an Earthy Clod
    Whom Heaven cannot contain!   20
Stand amaz'd ye Heavens at This!
    See the LORD of Earth and Skies
Humbled to the Dust He is,
    And in a Manger lies!

4 We the Sons of Men rejoice,   25
    The Prince of Peace proclaim,
With Heaven's Host lift up our Voice,
    And shout *Immanuel*'s Name;
Knees and Hearts to Him we bow;
    Of our Flesh, and of our Bone   30
JESUS is our Brother now,
    And GOD is All our own!

11. 1831: 'their humble Lord'.
19. 1831, &c.: 'an earthly clod'. This reading appears in the 1750 London
    edition; 'earthy' is found in the editions of 1751 and 1756, but from
    1761 'earthly' becomes the normal reading.

['GOD WITH US']   39

* *Nativity Hymns* (1745): No. 5.
Poetical Works, IV.109–10.
Collection (1831): No. 609, omitting v. 3.
Collection (1876): No. 685, as 1831.
MHB (1904): No. 133, as 1831.
MHB (1933): No. 142, as 1831.

Metre 25: 6.6.6.6.8 8
A B A B C C

1 Let Earth and Heaven combine,
   Angels and Men agree
To praise in Songs divine
   Th'Incarnate Deity,
Our GOD contracted to a Span,   5
Incomprehensibly made Man.

2 He laid his Glory by,
   He wrap'd Him in our Clay,
Unmark'd by Human Eye
   The latent Godhead lay;   10
Infant of Days He here became,
And bore the lov'd IMMANUEL's Name.

3 See in that Infant's Face
   The Depths of Deity,
And labour while ye gaze   15
   To sound the Mystery:
In vain; ye Angels gaze no more,
But fall, and silently adore.

4 Unsearchable the Love
   That hath the Saviour brought,   20
The Grace is far above
   Or Men or Angels Thought;
Suffice for Us, that GOD, we know,
Our GOD is manifest below.

5 He deigns in Flesh t'appear,   25
   Widest Extremes to join,
To bring our Vileness near,
   And make us All divine;
And we the Life of GOD shall know,
For GOD is manifest below.   30

Title. This was supplied in the 1831 *Supplement*.
12. 2nd edn (1745) and onwards: 'bore the mild'.

6 Made perfect first in Love,
    And sanctified by Grace,
We shall from Earth remove,
    And see his glorious Face;
His Love shall then be fully shew'd,   *35*
And Man shall be lost in GOD.

35–6. All editions published during Wesley's lifetime appear to be identical with the text. The 1831 *Supplement*, followed by later hymn-books, reads:

'Then shall his love be fully show'd,
And man shall then be lost in God.'

40   ['THE UNIVERSAL SAVIOUR']

This was one of the hymns which John Wesley regarded as 'namby-pambical', and his own copy was so marked as to suggest that verses 3, 4, and 5 should be omitted. (See *Poetical Works*, IV.xii.)

* *Nativity Hymns* (1745): No. 6.
  Poetical Works, IV.110–12.

Metre 36: 7.7.4 4.7
X A B B A D

1 Join all ye joyful Nations
Th'acclaiming Hosts of Heaven!
    This happy Morn
    A Child is born,
To us a Son is given;   *5*
The Messenger and Token
Of GOD's Eternal Favour,
    GOD hath sent down
    To us his Son,
An Universal Saviour!   *10*

2 The wonderful Messias,
The Joy of every Nation,
    JESUS his Name,
    With GOD the same,
The Lord of all Creation: *15*
The Counsellor of Sinners,
Almighty to deliver,
    The Prince of Peace,
    Whose Love's Increase
Shall reign in Man for ever.   *20*

3 Go see the King of Glory,
Discern the Heavenly Stranger,
    So poor and mean,
    His Court an Inn,
His Cradle is a Manger: *25*

Who from his Father's Bosom
But now for Us descended,
 Who built the Skies,
 On Earth he lies,
With only Beasts attended.   *30*

4 Whom all the Angels worship,
Lies hid in Human Nature;
 Incarnate see
 The Deity,
The Infinite Creator!   *35*
See the Stupendous Blessing
Which GOD to us hath given!
 A Child of Man,
 In Length a Span,
Who fills both Earth and Heaven.   *40*

5 Gaze on that Helpless Object
Of endless Adoration!
 Those Infant-Hands
 Shall burst our Bands,
And work out our Salvation;   *45*
Strangle the crooked Serpent,
Destroy his Works for ever,
 And open set
 The Heavenly Gate
To every True Believer.   *50*

6 Till then, thou holy JESUS,
We humbly bow before Thee,
 Our Treasures bring
 To serve our King,
And joyfully adore Thee: *55*
To Thee we gladly render
Whate'er thy Grace hath given,
 Till thou appear
 In Glory here,
And take us up to Heaven.   *60*

['OUR NEWLY-BORN KING']   **41**

* *Nativity Hymns* (1745): No. 7.
Poetical Works, IV.112–13.

Metre 66: 5.5.5.5.6.5.6.5
A B A B C D C D
(published as 10 10.11 11 with internal rhymes)

1 All Glory to GOD, and Peace upon Earth
Be publish'd abroad at JESUS'S Birth;
The Forfeited Favour of Heaven we find
Restor'd in the Saviour and Friend of Mankind.

2 Then let us behold Messias the Lord,   *5*
 By Prophets foretold, by Angels ador'd,
 Our GOD's Incarnation with Angels proclaim,
 And publish Salvation in JESUS's Name.

3 Our newly-born King by Faith we have seen,
 And joyfully sing his Goodness to Men,   *10*
 That all Men may wonder at what we impart,
 And thankfully ponder his Love in their Heart.

4 What mov'd the Most High so greatly to stoop,
 He comes from the Sky Our Souls to lift up;
 That Sinners forgiven, might sinless return   *15*
 To GOD and to Heaven; their Maker is born.

5 IMMANUEL's Love let Sinners confess,
 Who comes from above, to bring us his Peace;
 Let every Believer his Mercy adore,
 And praise him for ever, when Time is no more.   *20*

42   ['MADE FLESH FOR OUR SAKE']

* *Nativity Hymns* (1745): No. 8.
Poetical Works, IV.113–14.
Festival Hymns (1746): No. 3, printed as four verses of eight lines each.

                                        Metre 63: 5 5.5 11
                                                A A B B

1   Away with our Fears!
        The Godhead appears
        In CHRIST Reconcil'd,
 The Father of Mercies in JESUS the Child.

2   He comes from above,   *5*
        In manifest Love,
        The Desire of our Eyes,
 The meek Lamb of GOD, in a Manger he lies.

3   At IMMANUEL's Birth
        What a Triumph on Earth!   *10*
        Yet could it afford
 No better a Place for its Heavenly Lord.

4   The Antient of Days
        To redeem a Lost Race,
        From his Glory comes down,   *15*
 Self-humbled to carry us up to a Crown.

5   Made Flesh for our Sake,
        That we might partake
        The Nature Divine,
 And again in his Image, his Holiness shine;   *20*

8. *Festival:* 'The meek Son of Man'.

6   An Heavenly Birth
        Experience on Earth,
        And rise to his Throne,
  And live with our JESUS eternally One.

7   Then let us believe,   *25*
        And gladly receive
        The Tidings they bring,
  Who publish to Sinners their Saviour and King.

8   And while we are here,
        Our King shall appear,   *30*
        His Spirit impart,
  And form his full Image of Love in our Heart.

32. Festival: 'his whole Image'.

['THE GIFT UNSPEAKABLE']   **43**

* *Nativity Hymns* (1745): No. 9.
  Poetical Works, IV.114–15.
  Festival Hymns (1746): No. 1.
  Select Hymns (1761): No. 13, omitting v. 2.
  Pocket Hymn Book (1785): No. 129.

Metre 31: 6.6.8.6 D
        A B A B

1 Father, our Hearts we lift
    Up to thy Gracious Throne,
  And bless Thee for the precious Gift
    Of thine Incarnate Son;
    The Gift unspeakable   *5*
    We thankfully receive,
  And to the World thy Goodness tell,
    And to thy Glory live.

2 JESUS, the holy Child,
    Doth by his Birth declare,   *10*
  That GOD and Man are reconcil'd,
    And One in Him we are.
    Salvation thro' his Name
    To all Mankind is given,
  And loud his Infant-Cries proclaim   *15*
    A Peace 'twixt Earth and Heaven.

3 A Peace on Earth He brings,
    Which never more shall end:
  The Lord of Hosts, the King of Kings,
    Declares Himself our Friend,   *20*

18. 1761: 'That never'.
20. 1761: 'Proclaims Himself'.

Assumes our Flesh and Blood,
That we his Sp'rit[1] may gain,
The everlasting Son of GOD,
The mortal Son of Man.

4   His Kingdom from above   *25*
    He doth to us impart,
And pure Benevolence and Love
    O'erflow the faithful Heart:
Chang'd in a Moment we
    The sweet Attraction find,   *30*
With open Arms of Charity
    Embracing all Mankind.

5   O might they all receive
    The new-born Prince of Peace,
And meekly in his Spirit live,   *35*
    And in his Love increase!
Till He convey us home,
    Cry every Soul aloud,
Come, Thou Desire of Nations come,
    And take us all to GOD!   *40*

[1 This elision of the first 'i' in Spirit is essential to the proper scansion of much of Charles Wesley's verse. It continued to be spelt as in the text throughout most of his lifetime, but the London edition of 1777 and later editions read 'Spirit'. This word remains the most awkward in Charles Wesley's hymns for modern congregations, particularly as no indication is given as to whether it should be pronounced as one or two syllables. In the *Festival Hymns* the word is printed 'Spir't'.]

23. 1761: 'The eternal Son'.

44   ['DEAR DESIRE OF EVERY NATION']

* *Nativity Hymns* (1745): No. 10.
  Poetical Works, IV.116.
  Madan's *Collection* (1760): No. 118.
  Collection (1876): No. 688.
  MHB (1904): No. 198, divided into four verses.
  MHB (1933): No. 242, as 1904.
  Hymns A & M (1916): No. 640, as 1904; (1950), No. 54, as 1904.
                        Metre 56: 8.7.8.7.8.7.8.7
                                 a b a b c d c d

1 Come Thou long-expected JESUS,
    Born to set thy people free,
From our Fears and Sins relieve us,
    Let us find our Rest in Thee:
Israel's Strength and Consolation,   *5*
    Hope of all the Earth Thou art,
Dear Desire of every Nation,
    Joy of every longing Heart.

3. Madan, 1876, &c., *A & M* (1916, &c.): 'release us'. Most editions during Wesley's lifetime have 'relieve', but 'release' appears in the London editions for 1777 and 1787.

2 Born thy People to deliver,
    Born a Child and yet a King,   *10*
Born to reign in Us for ever,
    Now thy gracious Kingdom bring;
By thine own eternal Spirit
    Rule in all our Hearts alone,
By thine all-sufficient Merit   *15*
    Raise us to thy glorious Throne.

13, 15. A & M (1916, &c.): 'By Thy'.

['THE LIGHT OF THE GENTILES']   **45**

* *Nativity Hymns* (1745): No. 11.
  Poetical Works, IV.116–17.
  Collection (1831): No. 606.
  Collection (1876): No. 687.
  MHB (1904): No. 199.
  MHB (1933): No. 261.

                  Metre 56: 8.7.8.7.8.7.8.7
                        a b a b c d c d

1 Light of those whose dreary Dwelling
    Borders on the Shades of Death,
Come, and by thy Love's revealing
    Dissipate the Clouds beneath:
The new Heaven and Earth's Creator,   *5*
    In our deepest Darkness rise,
Scattering all the Night of Nature,
    Pouring Eye-sight on our Eyes.

2 Still we wait for thy Appearing,
    Life and Joy thy Beams impart,   *10*
Chasing all our Fears, and chearing
    Every poor benighted Heart.
Come, and manifest the Favour
    GOD hath for our ransom'd Race;
Come, thou universal Saviour,   *15*
    Come, and bring the Gospel-Grace.

3 Save us in thy great Compassion,
    O Thou mild pacific Prince,
Give the Knowledge of Salvation,
    Give the Pardon of our Sins;   *20*
By thine all-redeeming Merit
    Every burden'd Soul release,
Every weary wandring Spirit
    Guide into thy perfect Peace.

 3. 1831: 'love revealing'.
21. 1831, &c.: 'all-restoring merit'. This reading appeared in the 2nd
    edn of 1745, and remained the normal one throughout Wesley's
    lifetime.

46 ['ARTLESS MELODY']

* *Nativity Hymns* (1745): No. 12.
Poetical Works, IV.117–18.

Metre 46: 7 7.7 7
a a b b

1 Sing, ye ransom'd Nations, sing
 Praises to our new-born King,
 Son of Man our Maker is,
 Lord of Hosts and Prince of Peace.

2 Lo! He lays his Glory by,   5
 Emptied of his Majesty!
 See the GOD who all Things made,
 Humbly in a Manger laid.

3 Cast we off our needless Fear,
 Boldly to his Cratch draw near,   10
 JESUS is our Flesh and Bone,
 GOD-WITH-US is all our own.

4 Let us then with Angels gaze
 On our new-born Monarch's Face,
 With the Quire Celestial join'd,   15
 Shout the Saviour of Mankind.

5 Son of Man, will he despise
 Man's well-meaning Sacrifice?
 No; with condescending Grace
 He accepts his Creature's Praise.   20

6 Will his Majesty disdain
 The poor Shepherd's simple Strain?
 No; for Israel's Shepherd He
 Loves their artless Melody.

7 He will not refuse the Song   25
 Of the stammering Infant's Tongue,
 Babes He hears humanely mild,
 Once Himself a little Child.

8 Let us then our Prince proclaim,
 Humbly chant *Immanuel*'s Name,   30
 Publish at his wondrous Birth
 Praise in Heaven and Peace on Earth:

9 Triumph in our Saviour's Love,
 Till He takes us up above,
 All his Majesty displays,   35
 Shews us all his Glorious Face.

['ANGELS AND ARCHANGELS']   47

* *Nativity Hymns* (1745): No. 13.
Poetical Works, IV.118–19.

Metre 10: 8.8.8.8.8 8
A B A B C C

1 Let Angels and Archangels sing
    The wonderful *Immanuel*'s Name,
  Adore with us our new-born King,
    And still the joyful News proclaim,
  All Earth and Heaven be ever join'd   5
  To praise the Saviour of Mankind.

2 The everlasting GOD comes down
    To sojourn with the Sons of Men;
  Without his Majesty or Crown,
    The great INVISIBLE is seen: 10
  Of all his dazling Glories shorn
  The everlasting GOD is born!

3 Angels, behold that Infant's Face,
    With rapt'rous Awe the Godhead own:
  'Tis all your Heaven on Him to gaze,   15
    And cast your Crowns before his Throne;
  Tho' now He on his Footstool lies,
  Ye know He built both Earth and Skies.

4 By Him into Existence brought,
    Ye sang the All-creating Word;   20
  Ye heard Him call our World from nought:
    Again, in Honour of your Lord,
  Ye Morning-Stars your Hymns employ,
  And shout, ye Sons of GOD, for joy.

['O ASTONISHING GRACE!']   48

* *Nativity Hymns* (1745): No. 14.
Poetical Works, IV.119–20.

Metre 63: 5 5.5 11
A A B B

1   O Astonishing Grace,
      That the Reprobate Race
      Should be so reconcil'd!
  What a Wonder of Wonders that GOD is a Child!

2   The Creator of all,   5
      To repair our sad Fall,
      From his Heav'n stoops down,
  Lays hold of our Nature, and joins to his own.

3   Our *Immanuel* came,
      The whole World to redeem,
      And Incarnated shew'd   10
  That Man may again be united to GOD!

4   And shall we not hope,
      After GOD to wake up,
      His Nature to know?   *15*
His Nature is sinless Perfection below.

5   To this Heavenly Prize,
      By Faith let us rise
      To his Image ascend,
Apprehended of GOD let us GOD apprehend.   *20*

49   ['INCARNATED IN ME']

* *Nativity Hymns* (1745): No. 15.
MS Thirty, pp. 42–3.
Poetical Works, IV.120–2.

               Metre 4: 8 8.6.8 8.6
                    A A B C C B

1 All-wise, all-good, almighty Lord,
  JESUS, by highest Heaven ador'd,
    E'er Time its Course began,
  How did thy glorious Mercy stoop
  To take the fallen Nature up,   *5*
    When Thou thyself wert Man?

2 Th'Eternal GOD from Heav'n came down,
  The King of Glory dropp'd his Crown,
    And veil'd his Majesty,
  Empty'd of all but Love He came;   *10*
  JESUS, I call Thee by the Name
    Thy Pity bore for me.

3 O holy Child, still let thy Birth
  Bring Peace to us poor Worms of Earth,
    And Praise to GOD on high!   *15*
  Come, Thou who didst my Flesh assume,
  Now to the abject Sinner come,
    And in a Manger lie.

4 Didst Thou not in thy Person join
  The Natures Human and Divine,   *20*
    That GOD and Man might be
  Henceforth inseparably One?
  Haste then, and make thy Nature known
    Incarnated in me.

                      e
11–12. MS 30: 'Jesus, I call Thee by th~~at~~ Name
            ~~Which~~ ~~Thou~~ ~~hast~~ ~~born~~ for me.   Thy goodness bore'
14. MS 30: 'to a poor Worm of Earth'.
20. MS 30: 'The Human Nature and'.

5 In my weak sinful Flesh appear,   *25*
   O GOD, be manifested here,
     Peace, Righteousness, and Joy,
   Thy Kingdom, Lord, set up within
   My faithful Heart, and all my Sin,
     The Devil's Works destroy.   *30*

6 I long thy Coming to confess
   The mystic Power of Godliness,
     The Life Divine to prove,
   The Fulness of thy Life to know,
   Redeem'd from all my Sins below,   *35*
     And perfected in Love.

7 O CHRIST, my Hope, make known in me
   The great, the glorious Mystery,
     The hidden Life impart:
   Come, thou Desire of Nations, come,   *40*
   Form'd in a spotless Virgin's Womb,
     A pure believing Heart.

8 Come quickly, dearest Lord, that I
   May own, tho' Antichrist deny,
     Thy Incarnation's Power,   *45*
   May cry, a Witness to my Lord,
   'Come in my Flesh is CHRIST, the Word,
     And I can sin no more!'

31. MS 30: 'I long thy Power'.
35. MS 30: 'my Sin below'.

['A WONDER OF GRACE']   **50**

From this hymn John Wesley would have omitted verses 4–6, 10, 11, 13, 14. (See
Poetical Works, IV.xii.)

* *Nativity Hymns* (1745): No. 16.
  Poetical Works, IV.122–3.

                                  Metre 61: 5 5 11
                                          A A A

1   O Mercy Divine
        How couldst Thou incline
    My GOD to become such an Infant as *mine!*

2   What a Wonder of Grace!
        The Antient of Days   *5*
    Is found in the Likeness of *Adam*'s frail Race.

3   He comes from on high,
        Who fashion'd the Sky,
    And meekly vouchsafes in a Manger to lie.

4 Our GOD ever blest   *10*
  With Oxen doth rest,
Is nurst by his Creature and hangs at the Breast.

5 So Heavenly-mild
  His Innocence smil'd,
No wonder the Mother should worship the Child. *15*

6 The Angels she knew
  Had worshipp'd him too,
And still they confess Adoration his Due.

7 On JESUS's Face,
  With eager Amaze,   *20*
And Pleasure extatic the Cherubim gaze.

9[1] Their newly-born King,
  Transported they sing,
And Heav'n and Earth with the Triumph doth ring.

10 The Shepherds behold   *25*
  Him promis'd of old,
By Angels attended, by Prophets foretold.

11 The wise Men adore,
  And bring him their Store,
The Rich are permitted to follow the Poor. *30*

12 To the Inn they repair,
  To see the young Heir:
The Inn is a Palace; for JESUS is there!

13 Who now would be great,
  And not rather wait   *35*
On JESUS their Lord in his humble Estate?

14 Like him would I be,
  My Master I see
In a Stable; a Stable shall satisfy me.

15 With Him I reside: *40*
  The Manger shall hide
Mine Honour: the Manger shall bury my Pride.

16 And here will I lie,
  Till rais'd up on high
With Him on the Cross I recover the Sky. *45*

[1 The incorrect numbering of verses 8–15 was put right in the 2nd edition.]

Hymns for the Nativity (1745)

['WHERE IS HE?']   51

* *Nativity Hymns* (1745): No. 17.
  Poetical Works, IV.123–4.

Metre 7: 8.8.8.8
A B A B

1 Where is the holy Heav'n-born Child,
  Heir of the everlasting Throne,
Who Heav'n and Earth hath reconcil'd,
  And GOD and Man rejoin'd in One?

2 Shall we of earthly Kings enquire,   5
  To Courts or Palaces repair?
The Nation's Hope, the World's Desire,
  Alas! we cannot find Him there.

3 Shall Learning shew the Sinner's Friend,
  Or Scribes a Sight of CHRIST afford?   10
Us to his Natal Place they send,
  But never go to see their Lord.

4 We search the Outward Church in vain,
  They cannot Him we seek declare,
They have not found the Son of Man,   15
  Or known the sacred Name they bear.

5 Then let us turn no more aside,
  But use the Light Himself imparts,
His Spirit is our surest Guide,
  His Spirit glimmering in our Hearts.   20

6 Drawn by his Grace we come from far,
  And fix on Heaven our wishful Eyes,
That Ray divine, that orient Star
  Directs us where the Infant lies.

7 See there! the new born Saviour see,   25
  By Faith discern the great I AM;
'Tis He! the Eternal GOD! 'tis He
  That bears the mild *Immanuel*'s Name.

8 The Prince of Peace on Earth is found,
  The Child is born, the Son is given;   30
Tell it to all the Nations round,
  JEHOVAH is come down from Heaven!

9 JEHOVAH is come down to raise
  His dying Creatures from their Fall,
And all may now receive the Grace   35
  Which brings eternal Life to all.

10 Lord, *We* receive the Grace and Thee,
 With Joy unspeakable receive,
 And rise Thine open Face to see,
 And one with GOD for ever live.

40

52   [PRINCE OF PEACE]

* *Nativity Hymns* (1745): No. 18.
 MS Colman 21, p. 58, omitting v. 4.
 Poetical Works, IV.125–6.
 Collection (1780): No. 211.
 Pocket Hymn Book (1785): No. 181.
 Pocket Hymn Book (1787): No. 104.
 Collection (1831): No. 220.
 Collection (1876): No. 220.
 MHB (1904): No. 979, omitting v. 5.
 MHB (1933): No. 902, as 1904.

Metre 68: 8.8.8.8.8.8.8.8
A B A B C D C D

1 All Glory to GOD in the Sky,
 And Peace upon Earth be restor'd!
 O JESUS, exalted on high,
 Appear our omnipotent Lord:
 Who meanly in *Bethlehem* born,
 Didst stoop to redeem a lost Race,
 Once more to thy Creature return,
 And reign in thy Kingdom of Grace.

5

2 When Thou in our Flesh didst appear,
 All Nature acknowledg'd thy Birth;
 Arose the acceptable Year,
 And Heaven was open'd on Earth:
 Receiving its Lord from above,
 The World was *united* to bless
 The Giver of Concord and Love,
 The Prince and the Author of Peace.

10

15

3 O wouldst Thou again be made known,
 Again in thy Spirit descend,
 And set up in each of thine own,
 A Kingdom that never shall end!

20

5. MS Colman: 'Who meekly in'.
7. 'Creature' was probably a misprint for 'Creatures', which from 1764
 became the normal reading.
 MS Colman: 'Once more in thy Sp[irit] return'.
12. 1780 (1st edn): 'open'; corrected to 'opened' in 2nd edn (1781).
13. MS Colman: 'Receiving their Lord'.
14. MS Colman: 'All earth was united'.
18. 1780: 'Again in the spirit'.

Thou only art able to bless,
    And make the glad Nations obey,
And bid the dire Enmity cease,
    And bow the whole World to thy Sway.

4 Come then to thy Servants again,   *25*
    Who long thy Appearing to know,
Thy quiet and peaceable Reign
    In Mercy establish below:
All Sorrow before Thee shall fly,
    And Anger and Hatred be o'er,   *30*
And Envy and Malice shall die,
    And Discord afflict us no more.

5 No horrid Alarm of War
    Shall break our Eternal Repose;
No sound of the Trumpet is there,   *35*
    Where JESUS's Spirit o'erflows:
Appeas'd by the Charms of thy Grace
    We all shall in Amity join,
And kindly each other embrace,
    And love with a Passion like Thine.   *40*

22. MS Colman: 'To make'.
33. 'Alarm' seems to have been an error for 'Alarum'. The 4th Bristol
    edition of 1750 rectifies the metre by reading 'No horrid Alarm of
    dread War', but Cock's London edition of the same year read
    'Alarum', which became normal, and was confirmed by the 1780
    Collection. MS Colman has 'alarum'.
37. MS Colman: 'Allur[ed] by the charms'.

ON THE CRUCIFIXION   **53**

* *Hymns on the Lord's Supper* (1745): No. 20.
  Festival Hymns (1746): No. 5.
  Madan's *Collection* (1760), pp. 152–3.
  Select Hymns (1761): No. 125.
  Poetical Works, III.228–9.
  Collection (1831): No. 548.
  Collection (1876): No. 900.
  MHB (1904): No. 731, omitting v. 4.
  MHB (1933): No. 181, as 1904.

Metre 86: 7.6.7.6.7.8.7.6
a B a B c D c D

1   Lamb of GOD, whose Bleeding Love
        We thus recall to Mind,
    Send the Answer from above,
        And let us Mercy find;
    Think on us, who think on Thee   *5*
    And every struggling Soul release:
        O remember *Calvary*,
        And bid us go in Peace.

1. 1904, &c.: 'whose dying love'.
2. 1761, 'We now'.

2   By thine Agonizing Pain,
       And Bloody Sweat, we pray,   *10*
    By thy Dying Love to Man,
       Take all our Sins away;
       Burst our Bonds, and set us free,
    From all Iniquity release:
       O remember *Calvary*,   *15*
       And bid us go in Peace.

3   Let thy Blood, by Faith applied
       The Sinner's Pardon seal,
    Speak us freely Justified,
       And all our Sickness heal: *20*
    By thy Passion on the Tree
    Let all our Griefs and Troubles cease:
       O remember *Calvary*,
       And bid us go in Peace.

4   Never will we hence depart,   *25*
       Till Thou our Wants relieve,
    Write Forgiveness on our Heart,
       And all thine Image give:
    Still our Souls shall cry to Thee
    Till perfected in Holiness: *30*
       O remember *Calvary*,
       And bid us go in Peace.

10. 1933: 'And sweat of blood'.
25. Madan: 'Never let us hence depart'.
27. 2nd edn (1747), Madan: 'in our Heart'.
29. Madan: 'May our Souls still cry to Thee'.
30. 1746: 'Till all renew'd in Holiness:'.

54   [GOD OF UNEXAMPLED GRACE]

* *Hymns on the Lord's Supper* (1745): No. 21.
  Poetical Works, III.229–31.
  Madan's *Collection* (1760), pp. 159–60: vv. 1–3, 9.
  Select Hymns (1761): No. 122 (vv. 1–3) and 123 (vv. 4–9).
  Collection (1831): Nos. 621 (vv. 1–3) and 552 (vv. 4–9).
  Collection (1876): No. 701 (vv. 1–3).
  MHB (1933): No. 191, as 1876.

                      Metre 85: 7.6.7.6.7.7.7.6
                           a B a B c d c D

1 GOD of unexampled Grace,
     Redeemer of Mankind,
  Matter of eternal Praise
     We in thy Passion find:
  Still our choicest Strains we bring,   *5*
     Still the joyful Theme pursue,
  Thee the Friend of Sinners sing
     Whose Love is ever new.

2 Endless Scenes of Wonder rise
  With that mysterious Tree,   *10*
Crucified before our Eyes
  Where we our Maker see:
Jesus, Lord, what hast Thou done!
  Publish we the Death Divine,
Stop, and gaze, and fall, and own   *15*
  Was never Love like Thine!

3 Never Love nor Sorrow was
  Like that my Jesus show'd;
See Him stretch'd on yonder Cross
  And crush'd beneath our Load!   *20*
Now discern the Deity,
  Now his heavenly Birth declare!
Faith cries out 'Tis He, 'tis He,
  My God that suffers there!

4 Jesus drinks the bitter Cup;   *25*
  The Wine-press treads alone,
Tears the Graves and Mountains up
  By his expiring Groan:
Lo! the Powers of Heaven He shakes;
  Nature in Convulsions lies,   *30*
Earth's profoundest Centre quakes,
  The great *Jehovah* dies!

5 Dies the glorious Cause of All,
  The true Eternal *Pan*,
Falls to raise us from our Fall,   *35*
  To ransom sinful Man:
Well may *Sol* withdraw his Light,
  With the Sufferer sympathize,
Leave the World in sudden Night,
  While his Creator dies.   *40*

6 Well may Heaven be cloath'd with black
  And solemn Sackcloth wear,
Jesu's Agony partake
  The Hour of Darkness share:
Mourn th'astonied Hosts above,   *45*
  Silence saddens all the Skies,
Kindler of Seraphick Love
  The God of Angels dies.

18. Madan: 'our Jesus'.
    1831, &c.: 'my Saviour'.
40. 1831: 'While the Creator'.
42. 'sackcloth' from 5th edn (1762).
45. 'astonished' from 9th edn (1786).

73

7 O my GOD, he dies for me,
   I feel the mortal Smart!   *50*
See Him hanging on the Tree ——
   A Sight that breaks my Heart!
O that all to Thee might turn!
   Sinners ye may love him too,
Look on Him ye pierc'd, and mourn   *55*
   For One who bled for You.

8 Weep o'er your Desire and Hope
   With Tears of humblest Love;
Sing, for JESUS is gone up,
   And reigns enthron'd above!   *60*
Lives our Head, to die no more:
   Power is all to JESUS given,
Worship'd as He was before
   Th'immortal King of Heaven.

9 LORD, we bless Thee for thy Grace,   *65*
   And Truth which never fail,
Hastning to behold thy Face
   Without a dimming Veil:
We shall see our Heavenly King,
   All thy Glorious Love proclaim,   *70*
Help the Angel-quires to sing
   Our dear triumphant Lamb.

55   [HIS PRESENCE MAKES THE FEAST]
* *Hymns on the Lord's Supper* (1745): No. 81.
Poetical Works, III.273–4.
MHB (1933): No. 761, in verses of four lines, comprising 1a, 2a, 2b, 3a, 3b.
                 Metre 31: 6.6.8.6.6.8.6
                          A B A B C D C D

1   JESU, we Thus obey
       Thy last and kindest Word,
   Here in thine own Appointed Way
       We come to meet our LORD;
   The Way Thou hast Injoin'd   *5*
       Thou wilt therein appear:
   We come with Confidence to find
       Thy special Presence here.

2   Our Hearts we open wide
       To make the Saviour room: *10*
   And lo! the Lamb, the Crucified,
       The Sinner's Friend is come!

1. MHB (1933): 'Jesus, we thus obey'.
4. MHB (1933): 'to meet Thee, Lord'.

His Presence makes the Feast,
And now our Bosoms feel
The Glory not to be exprest,   *15*
The Joy unspeakable.

3   With pure celestial Bliss
    He doth our Spirits chear,
His House of Banquetting is This,
    And He hath brought us here: *20*
He doth his Servants feed
With Manna from above,
His Banner over us is spread,
His everlasting Love.

4   He bids us drink and eat   *25*
    Imperishable Food,
He gives his Flesh to be our Meat
And bids us drink his Blood:
Whate'er th'Almighty Can
To pardon'd Sinners give,   *30*
The Fulness of our GOD made Man
We here with CHRIST receive.

All the following are in *MHB* (1933):
13. 'Thy presence'.
14. 'Now let our spirits feel'.
17. 'With high and heavenly bliss'.
18. 'Thou dost our'.
19. 'Thy house'.
20. 'And Thou'.
21. 'Now let our souls be fed'.
23. 'And over us Thy banner spread'.
24. 'Of everlasting love'.

[LIFE-GIVING FOOD]   **56**

* *Hymns on the Lord's Supper* (1745): No. 92.
  Poetical Works, III.282–3.
  Select Hymns (1761): No. 6, vv. 1–3, 5, 6, 8–12.

                                                        Metre 63: 5 5.5 11
                                                                  A A B B

1   Ah tell us no more
    The Spirit and Power
    Of JESUS our GOD
Is not to be found in this Life-giving Food!

2   Did JESUS ordain   *5*
    His Supper in vain,
    And furnish a Feast
For none but his earliest Servants to taste?

4. *Select Hymns* (1761): 'the life-giving'.

3   Nay, but this is his Will
     (We know it and feel)   *10*
     That *we* should partake
    The Banquet for All He so freely did make.

4   In rapturous Bliss
     He bids us do This,
     The Joy it imparts   *15*
    Hath witness'd his gracious Design in our Hearts.

5   'Tis GOD we believe,
     Who cannot deceive,
     The Witness of GOD
    Is present, and speaks in the Mystical Blood.   *20*

6   Receiving the Bread
     On JESUS we feed,
     It doth not appear
    His Manner of working; but JESUS is here!

7   With Bread from above,   *25*
     With Comfort and Love
     Our Spirit he fills,
    And all his unspeakable Goodness reveals.

8   O that all Men would haste
     To the Spiritual Feast,   *30*
     At JESUS's Word
    Do This, and be fed with the Love of our LORD!

9   True Light of Mankind
     Shine into their Mind,
     And clearly reveal   *35*
    Thy perfect and good and acceptable Will.

10   Bring near the glad Day
     When all shall obey
     Thy dying Request,
    And eat of thy Supper, and lean on thy Breast.   *40*

11   To all Men impart
     One Way and one Heart,
     Thy People be shewn
    All righteous and sinless and perfect in One.

All the following are in *Select Hymns* (1761):
24. 'The Manner'.
30. 'To this'.
32. 'of their Lord!'
44. 'All righteous, and spotless'.

12   Then, then let us see   *45*
        Thy Glory, and be
        Caught up in the Air
    This Heavenly Supper in Heaven to share.

[VICTIM DIVINE]   **57**

* *Hymns on the Lord's Supper* (1745): No. 116.
  Poetical Works, III.301–2.
  Collection (1831): No. 551.
  Collection (1876): No. 902.
  MHB (1904): No. 727, vv. 1, 2, 5.
  MHB (1933): No. 771, as 1904.
  Hymns A & M (1889, 1916), No. 556, omitting v. 3; (1904), No. 276, as 1889.

Metre 10: 8.8.8.8.8 8
A B A B C C

1 Victim Divine, thy Grace we claim
    While thus thy precious Death we shew,
  Once offer'd up a spotless Lamb
    In thy great Temple here below,
  Thou didst for All Mankind atone,   *5*
  And standest now before the Throne.

2 Thou standest in the Holiest Place,
    As now for guilty Sinners Slain,
  Thy Blood of Sprinkling speaks, and prays
    All-prevalent for helpless Man,   *10*
  Thy Blood is still our Ransom found,
  And spreads Salvation all around.

3 The Smoke of thy Atonement here
    Darken'd the Sun and rent the Vail,
  Made the New Way to Heaven appear,   *15*
    And shew'd the great Invisible:
  Well pleas'd in Thee our GOD look'd down,
  And call'd his Rebels to a Crown.

4 He still respects thy Sacrifice,
    It's Savour Sweet doth always please,
  The Offering smoaks thro' Earth and Skies,   *20*
    Diffusing Life and Joy and Peace,
  To these thy lower Courts it comes,
  And fills them with Divine Perfumes.

  9. 1831, &c.: 'The blood'.
12. 1831, &c.: 'And speaks Salvation'. [This emendation first appeared
    in the 7th edn (1776).]
18. 1831: 'And calls'.
19. *A & M* (1889, &c.): 'God still respects'.

5 We need not now go up to Heaven 25
    To bring the long-sought Saviour down,
Thou art to All already given:
    Thou dost ev'n Now thy Banquet crown,
To every faithful Soul appear,
And shew thy Real Presence here. 30

27. *A & M* (1889, &c.): 'Thou art to all that seek Thee given'.

58   CONCERNING THE SACRIFICE OF OUR PERSONS

* *Hymns on the Lord's Supper* (1745): No. 155.
  MS Colman 21, p. 34.
  Poetical Works, III.333–4.
  Madan's *Collection* (1760): No. 141, vv. 1, 3, 4, 6 (entitled 'Self-Dedication').
  Select Hymns (1761): No. 102, vv. 1, 3, 4, 6.
  Collection (1780): No. 418.
  Pocket Hymn Book (1787): No. 215.
  Collection (1831): No. 430.
  Collection (1876): No. 430.
  MHB (1904): No. 562.
  MHB (1933): No. 574.
  Hymns A & M (1889, 1916): No. 636, omitting v. 2; (1904), No. 615, as 1889.

Metre 47: 7.7.7.7.7 7
a b a b c c

1 FATHER, SON, and HOLY GHOST,
    One in Three, and Three in One,
As by the celestial Host
    Let thy Will on Earth be done;
Praise by All to Thee be given, 5
Glorious LORD of Earth and Heaven!

2 Vilest of the fallen Race,
    Lo! I answer to thy Call,
Meanest Vessel of thy Grace,
    (Grace divinely free for All) 10
Lo, I come to do thy Will,
All thy Counsel to fulfil.

3 If so poor a Worm as I
    May to thy great Glory live,
All my Actions sanctify, 15
    All my Words and Thoughts receive:
Claim me, for thy Service, claim
All I have, and all I am.

5. MS Colman: 'Praise by Sons of'.
7. MS Colman, 1780, &c.: 'the sinful race'.
13. *A & M* (1889, &c.): 'If a sinner such as I'.

4 Take my Soul and Body's Powers,
    Take my Mem'ry, Mind, and Will,   *20*
  All my Goods, and all my Hours,
    All I know, and all I feel,
  All I think, and speak, and do;
  Take my Heart—but make it new.

5 Now, O GOD, thine own I am,   *25*
    Now I give Thee back thy own,
  Freedom, Friends, and Health, and Fame,
    Consecrate to Thee alone;
  Thine I live, thrice happy I,
  Happier still for Thine I die.   *30*

6 FATHER, SON, and HOLY GHOST,
    One in Three, and Three in One,
  As by the celestial Host,
    Let thy Will on Earth be done;
  Praise by All to Thee be given,   *35*
  Glorious LORD of Earth and Heaven.

21. Madan: 'mine Hours'.
23. MS Colman, 1780, &c., *A & M* (1889, &c.): 'or speak, or do'.
24. Madan: 'mine Heart'.
25. *A & M* (1889, &c.): 'O my God';
    1780, 1787: 'thy own'.
26. *A & M* (1889, &c.): 'Let me give Thee back Thine own'.
29. *A & M* (1889, &c.): 'Thine to live'.
30. MS Colman, 1780, &c., *A & M* (1889, &c.): 'if thine I die'. (In spite of
    John Wesley's emendation for the *Collection*, the original reading
    continued to appear in *Hymns on the Lord's Supper*.)

REJOICE EVERMORE   **59**

J. F. Lampe composed a tune especially for this hymn (*Festival Hymns*, No. 8),
and Lampe's master Handel also set the words to music. The hymn was published in
various collections, as will be seen from the authorities quoted below. Yet it remained
comparatively little known to Methodists generally until it was adopted by the
Collection of 1876. There is little doubt that Handel's tune, discovered by Samuel
Wesley in the Fitzwilliam Library, Cambridge, in 1826, had much to do with its
subsequent popularity, even though its effect was somewhat belated. Under its title
'GOPSAL' (from the home of the librettist of the *Messiah*) this tune is still wedded to
the hymn in Methodist worship.

* *Hymns for our Lord's Resurrection* (1746): No. 8.
  MS Thirty, pp. 196–7: to which the above title is given.
  MS Gwynne, pp. (24–5): entitled, 'A Hymn on the Resurrection'.
  Poetical Works, IV.140–1.
  Festival Hymns (1746): No. 8.
  Whitefield's *Hymns* (1753): No. 20 in 'Hymns for Society', pp. 128–9, vv. 1–4, 6.
  Madan's *Collection* (1760): No. 9.
  Select Hymns (1761): No. 101.
  Pocket Hymn Book (1785): No. 94.
  Collection (1876): No. 729.

MHB (1904): No. 213.
MHB (1933): No. 247.
Hymns A & M (1868), No. 296, vv. 1–4; (1875, 1889, 1916), No. 202, as 1868;
(1904), No. 346, as 1868; (1950), No. 216, as 1868; Schools edn (1958): No. 122,
as 1868.

Metre 25: 6.6.6.6.8 8
ABABCC

1   Rejoice, the LORD is King!
     Your LORD and King adore,
     Mortals, give Thanks, and sing,
     And triumph evermore;
    Lift up your Heart, lift up your Voice,   *5*
    Rejoice, again, I say, Rejoice.

2   JESUS the Saviour reigns,
     The GOD of Truth and Love,
     When He had purg'd our Stains,
     He took his Seat above: *10*
    Lift up your Heart, lift up your Voice,
    Rejoice, again, I say, rejoice.

3   His Kingdom cannot fail,
     He rules o'er Earth and Heaven;
     The Keys of Death and Hell   *15*
     Are to our JESUS given:
    Lift up your Heart, lift up your Voice,
    Rejoice, again, I say, Rejoice.

4   He sits at GOD's Right-hand,
     Till all his Foes submit,   *20*
     And bow to his Command,
     And fall beneath his Feet.
    Lift up your Heart, lift up your Voice,
    Rejoice, again, I say, Rejoice.

5   He all his Foes shall quell,   *25*
     Shall all our Sins destroy,
     And every Bosom swell
     With pure Seraphic Joy;
    Lift up your Heart, lift up your Voice,
    Rejoice, again, I say, rejoice.   *30*

5, 11, 17, 23, 29. Madan: 'Lift up your Hearts', except that v. 2 has
    'Heart'—apparently a misprint.
25, 27. MSS: 'He all our Foes shall quell . . .
         And every Bosom fill'.
    MS Gwynne has 'Quell' over an erasure, presumably 'kill'.
    Festival : 'He all his Foes shall kill . . .
         And every Bosom fill'.
28. MS 30: 'With everlasting Joy'.

[N.B. All later editions of *Resurrection Hymns* seem to follow the first; MS Thirty
and *Festival Hymns* represent earlier versions.]

6   Rejoice in Glorious Hope,
       JESUS the Judge shall come;
     And take his Servants up
       To their Eternal Home:
We soon shall hear th'archangel's Voice,   *35*
The Trump of GOD shall sound, Rejoice.

[THE SPIRIT IS COME]   **60**

* *Hymns of Petition and Thanksgiving for the Promise of the Father* (1746): No. 32.
Poetical Works, IV.203–4.
Select Hymns (1761): No. 8, omitting v. 4.
Collection (1876): No. 760.
MHB (1904): No. 239, vv. 1–3, 5, printed as eight verses.
MHB (1933): No. 278, as 1904.

Metre 64: 5 5.5 11.5 5.5 11
A A B B C C D D

1   Away with our Fears,
     Our Troubles and Tears!
     The SPIRIT is come,
The Witness of JESUS Return'd to his Home:
     The Pledge of our LORD   *5*
     To his Heaven restor'd,
     Is sent from the Sky,
And tells us our Head is exalted on high.

2   Our Advocate there
     By his Blood and his Prayer   *10*
     The Gift hath obtain'd,
For Us he hath pray'd, and the Comforter gain'd:
     Our Glorified Head
     His Spirit hath shed
     With his People to stay,   *15*
And never again will He take Him away.

3   Our Heavenly Guide
     With us shall abide;
     His Comforts impart,
And set up his Kingdom of LOVE in the Heart: *20*
     The Heart that Believes
     His Kingdom receives,
     His Power and his Peace,
His Life, and his Joy's everlasting Increase.

19. 1761: 'His Comfort'.
20. 1761: 'in our Heart'.

4   The Presence Divine   *25*
      Doth inwardly shine,
      The *Schechinah* rests
On all our Assemblies, and glows in our Breasts.
      By Day and by Night
      The Pillar of Light   *30*
      Our Steps shall attend,
And convoy us safe to our Prosperous End.

5   Then let us rejoice
      In Heart and in Voice,
      Our Leader pursue,   *35*
And shout as we travel the Wilderness thro';
      With the Spirit remove
      To Sion above,
      Triumphant arise
And walk in our GOD, 'till we fly to the Skies.   *40*

27–8. 1876:   'The Shechinah shall rest
        On all our assemblies, and glow in our breast:'.
38. 1761: 'To the Sion'.
40. 1761, 1876, &c.: 'walk with our God'.

61   INVITATION TO SINNERS

The *Hymns on the Great Festivals, and other Occasions,* published in 1746, is one of the rarest yet one of the most important volumes in Methodist hymnological study. It contains the first group of original tunes specifically written for Methodist hymns. They were composed by John Frederic Lampe, compatriot and friend of Handel. He had been converted from deism through reading John Wesley's *Earnest Appeal* (1743), but his real affinity seems to have been with Charles Wesley. Although far too florid for modern congregations, the tunes were popularized by the Wesleys, references to them being given in *Redemption Hymns* and *Graces*. The volume reached a second edition in 1753.

Festival Hymns is also important in showing the basic metres which Methodists were expected to sing at this time—no fewer than twenty-two, and seven more if one counts the simple metres for whose doubled forms only tunes were given. These metres are as follow: Nos. 4, 5, 8, 10, 13, 16, 26, 32, 33, 37, 47, 50, 52 (two tunes), 57, 60, 63, 65, 67 (two tunes), 71, 75, 79a, 87.

Although it seems likely that Lampe published the volume on his own financial responsibility, he had access to Charles Wesley's manuscripts, as well as to his published works. Seven of the poems had not so far been published: of these, three later appeared in *Hymns and Sacred Poems* (1749), three in *Funeral Hymns* [1746?], and one does not appear in Wesley's *Poetical Works*, both Osborn and Green having apparently confused it with other hymns having the same opening line.

[See further W. H. S. *Proc.* III.237–9, J. T. Lightwood's *Methodist Music of the Eighteenth Century*, pp. 21–3, and *Dictionary of National Biography*, under 'Lampe, John Frederic, (1703?–1751)'.]

* *Festival Hymns* (1746): No. 4, entitled 'On the Crucifixion'.
MS Cheshunt, pp. 116–18: in 14 halved verses.
MS Clarke, pp. 134–5: as MS Cheshunt, but entitled 'Hymns for the Justified. I'.
MS Colman 21, p. 8.
Poetical Works, IV.371–2.
Hymns and Sacred Poems (1749), Vol. I: No. 42, pp. 87–8, entitled 'Invitation to Sinners'.
Madan's *Collection* (1760): No. 21, omitting v. 4.

Metre 62: 5 5 11.5 5 11
A A A B B B

1   All ye that pass by,
      To JESUS draw nigh;
To you is it Nothing that JESUS should die?
      Your Ransom and Peace,
      Your Surety He is: *5*
Come, see if there ever was Sorrow like His!

2   For what you have done
      His Blood must atone;
The Father hath punish'd for you his dear Son.
      The Lord, in the Day   *10*
      Of his Anger, did lay
Our Sins on the Lamb; and He bore them away.

3   He answer'd for All:
      O come at his Call,
And low at his Cross with Astonishment fall.   *15*
      But lift up your eyes
      At JESUS's Cries;
Impassive, He suffers; Immortal, He dies.

4   He dies to atone
      For Sins not his own: *20*
Your Debt He hath paid, and your Work He hath done.
      Ye all may receive
      The Peace He did leave,
Who made Intercession, *My Father, forgive!*

9. 1904: 'hath stricken'.
12. MSS Clarke, Colman, 1749, 1761, 1785, &c.: 'Your sins'.
                        Cross
15. MS Cheshunt: 'at his ~~Feet~~';
    1761: 'his Feet'.
                  Immortal He
18. MS Clarke: '~~and Infinite~~ dies'.
21. MS Cheshunt: 'Our Debt . . . our Work';
            Your   yr
    MS Clarke: "~~Our~~ Debt . . . ~~our~~ Work'.
24. MSS: 'He made Intercession'.

5   For you and for me   *25*
       He pray'd on the Tree:
   The Pray'r is accepted, the Sinner is free.
       The Sinner am I,
       Who on JESUS rely,
   And come for the Pardon GOD cannot deny.   *30*

6   My Pardon I claim,
       For a Sinner I am,
   A Sinner believing on JESUS's Name.
       He purchas'd the Grace
       Which now I embrace: *35*
   O Father, Thou know'st He hath dy'd in my Place.

7   His Death is my Plea;
       My Advocate see,
   And hear the Blood speak, that hath answer'd for me.
       Acquitted I was,   *40*
       When he bled on the Cross;
   And by losing His Life, He hath carry'd my Cause.

28. 1831, &c.: 'That sinner'.
       God
30. MSS: 'He cannot deny';
    1904: 'God will not deny'.
33. MSS, 1749, 1785, &c.: 'believing in Jesus's name'.
40. 1876, &c.: 'My ransom He was'.
41. MS Colman, 1761: 'When he hung'.

62   THE INVITATION

* *Festival Hymns* (1746): No. 18.
  MS Cheshunt, pp. 86–7.
  MS Clarke, pp. 98–100.
  MS Colman 21, p. 4, varying the order of the lines thus: 25–6, 31–2, 29–30, 27–8,
    33–4, 35–6.
  Poetical Works, V.63–4.
  Hymns and Sacred Poems (1749), I.259–60: No. 155.
  Whitefield's *Hymns* (1753): No. 6, pp. 4–5, vv. 1–4, 6.
  Madan's *Collection* (1760): No. 6, vv. 1–4, 6.
  Select Hymns (1761): No. 69.
  Collection (1780): No. 9.
  Pocket Hymn Book (1785): No. 3.
  Pocket Hymn Book (1787): No. 7.

Title. This is used only in *Festival Hymns*. The MSS, followed by *Hymns
    and Sacred Poems* (1749), give Luke 14[17] as a title—'Come, for all
    things are now ready'. Madan gives 'Invitation*', his footnote giving
    an incorrect reference: '* Luke xiv.16.'

Hymns on the Great Festivals (1746)

Collection (1831): No. 9.
Collection (1876): No. 9.
MHB (1904): Nos. 275 (vv. 1–5) and 276 (vv. 6–10).
MHB (1933): Nos. 326 (vv. 1–5) and 325 (vv. 6–10).

Metre 8: 8 8.8 8
A A B B

1 Sinners, obey the Gospel-Word;
  Haste to the Supper of my LORD;
  Be wise to know your gracious Day;
  All Things are ready; come away!

2 Ready the Father is to own   *5*
  And kiss his late-returning Son;
  Ready the loving Saviour stands,
  And spreads for you his bleeding Hands.

3 Ready the Spirit of his Love
  Just now the Stony to remove;   *10*
  T'apply and witness with the Blood,
  And wash and seal the Sons of GOD.

4 Ready for you the Angels wait,
  To triumph in your blest Estate;
  Turning[1] their Harps, they long to praise   *15*
  The Wonder of redeeming Grace.

5 The Father, Son, and Holy Ghost
  Is ready with Their shining Host;
  All Heaven is ready, to resound
  The Dead's alive, the Lost is found!   *20*

[1 That this is a misprint is confirmed by the fact that the MSS and later editions have 'tuning'.]

2. Whitefield, Madan: 'our Lord'.
7. MSS, 1749, 1761, 1780, &c.: 'your loving Saviour'.
10. Whitefield, Madan: 'the stony Heart to move'.
    1933: 'the hardness to remove'.
12. Whitefield, Madan: 'seal you Sons of God'.
16. MSS, 1749, Whitefield, Madan, 1761, 1780, &c.: 'The wonders'.
18. The italicizing of the ungrammatical 'Is' in order to show that the
    plural subject is really a unity, a feature frequent in Wesley's
    poems, is omitted from all later editions. *MHB* (1904), followed by
    that of 1933, smooths out the purposeful awkwardness still further
    by changing 'their' (contrasting with 'is') to 'the'.

6 Come then, ye Sinners, to your LORD,
To Happiness in CHRIST restor'd,
His proffer'd Benefits embrace,
The Plenitude of Gospel-Grace.

7 A Pardon written with His Blood,   *25*
The Favour and the Peace of GOD,
The seeing Eye, the feeling Sense,
The mystic Joy of Penitence;

8 The Godly Grief, the pleasing Smart,
The Meltings of a broken Heart,   *30*
The Tears that speak your Sins forgiv'n,
The Sighs that waft your Soul to Heav'n.

9 The guiltless Shame, the sweet Distress,
Th'unutterable Tenderness,
The genuine meek Humility,   *35*
The Wonder, why such Love to me!

10 Th' o'erwhelming Pow'r of saving Grace,
The Sight that veils the Seraph's Face,
The speechless Awe that dares not move,
And all the silent Heaven of Love!   *40*

21. 1904, &c.: 'O come, ye sinners'.
22. MSS, 1749, 1761, 1780, &c.: 'In Christ to paradise restored'.
23. 1785: 'The proffer'd benefits'.
25. MSS: 'A Pardon seal'd with sacred Blood'.
28. MSS, 1749, 1761, 1780, &c.: 'mystic joys'.
31. 1749, 1761, 1780, &c.: 'tears that tell'.
32. MS Cheshunt, 1780, &c.: 'your souls'.

63   DESIRING TO LOVE

* *Festival Hymns* (1746): No. 19.
  MS Thirty, pp. 6–7.
  MS Colman 21, p. 61, omitting vv. 5, 7.
  Poetical Works, IV.341–2.
  Hymns and Sacred Poems (1749), I.58–9: No. 23.
  Whitefield's *Hymns* (1753): No. 86, p. 68, vv. 1, 3, 4, 7.
  Madan's *Collection* (1760): No. 41, vv. 1, 3, 4, 7.
  Select Hymns (1761): No. 105.
  Collection (1780): No. 141, omitting vv. 5 and 7.
  Pocket Hymn Book (1787): No. 70, as 1780.
  Collection (1831): No. 147, omitting vv. 5–7.
  Collection (1876): No. 147, omitting v. 7.
  MHB (1904): No. 416, as 1831.
  MHB (1933): No. 434, as 1831.
  Hymns A & M (1861): No. 199, vv. 1–4; (1875, 1889, 1916, 1950): No. 195, as
  1861.

Metre 4: 8 8.6.8 8.6
A A B C C B

1 O Love Divine, how sweet Thou art!
  When shall I find my longing Heart
    All taken up by Thee?
  I thirst, I faint, and die, to prove
  The Greatness of redeeming Love,   5
    The Love of CHRIST to me.

2 Stronger his Love, than Death or Hell;
  Its Riches are unsearchable:
    The first-born Sons of Light
  Desire in vain its Depth to see;   10
  They cannot reach the Mystery,
    The Length, and Breadth, and Height.

3 GOD only knows the Love of GOD.
  O that it now were shed abroad
    In this poor stony Heart!   15
  For Love I sigh, for Love I pine:
  This only Portion, LORD, be mine,
    Be mine this Better Part!

4 O that I could for ever sit,
  With *Mary*, at the Master's Feet!   20
    Be this my Happy Choice!
  My only Care, Delight, and Bliss,
  My Joy, my Heav'n on Earth be this,
    To hear the Bridegroom's Voice.

  2.   MS 30, 1749, 1761, 1780, &c., *A & M* (1861, &c.—except 1950): 'my
        willing Heart';
        Whitefield, Madan: 'When shall we find our longing Hearts'.
  4.   MS 30, 1749, 1761: 'I thirst, and faint, and die to prove';
        Whitefield, Madan: 'O make me pant, and thirst to prove';
        1780, &c., *A & M* (1861, &c.—except 1950): 'I thirst, I faint, I die
        to prove'.
  7.   1780 (1st edn): 'Stronger is love';
        1780 (2nd edn, 1781), &c.: 'Stronger his love'.
10.   1780, &c., *A & M* (1861, &c.—except 1950): 'its depths'.
14.   1761: 'was shed'.
15.   Whitefield, Madan: 'In each poor'.
16.   Whitefield, Madan: 'For Love I'd sigh, for Love I'd pine'.
18.   MS 30: 'Give *me* the Better Part'.
19.   Whitefield, Madan: 'O that we could'.
        A & M (1861, &c.): 'For ever would I take my seat'.
20.   MS 30: 'With Mary at the Saviour's feet';
        1904, &c.: 'Like Mary'.
21–3. Whitefield, Madan: 'our happy', 'Our only', 'Our Joy, our Heav'n'.

5 O that with humbled *Peter* I   *25*
   Could weep, believe, and thrice reply,
     My Faithfulness to prove!
   Thou know'st, for all to Thee is known,
   Thou know'st, O LORD, and Thou alone,
     Thou know'st, that Thee I love.   *30*

6 O that I could, with favour'd *John*,
   Recline my weary Head upon
     The dear Redeemer's Breast!
   From Care, and Sin, and Sorrow free,
   Give me, O LORD, to find in Thee   *35*
     My everlasting Rest.

7 Thy only Love do I require,
   Nothing on Earth beneath desire,
     Nothing in Heaven above:
   Let Earth and Heaven, and all Things go,   *40*
   Give me thine only Love to know,
     Give me thine only Love.

33. 1876: 'The great Redeemer's breast'.
37. Whitefield, Madan: 'may we require'.
40. MS 30: 'Let Heav'n, and Earth, & all Things go'.
     Whitefield, Madan: 'Let Earth and all its Trifles go'.
41–2. MS 30, 1749: 'thy only Love'.
     Whitefield, Madan: 'Give us, O Lord, thy Love to know,
                        Give us thy precious Love.'

64   ON THE CORPSE OF A BELIEVER

This hymn has achieved some little renown as the typical example of what some regard as a morbid preoccupation with death in early Methodism, and others as a triumphant faith illustrating the saying: 'The Methodists die well.' It was frequently reprinted in America as the work of George Whitefield. Commenting on its omission from the 1876 *Collection* G. J. Stevenson remarked: 'It had many admirers, and a few stern opponents' (*MHB Illustrated*, p. 62). Strangely enough it was the *Funeral Hymns* which popularized the rollicking anapaestic 8's among the Methodists, with seven examples out of sixteen hymns. (Single examples occur also in *Whitsunday Hymns* and in the *Graces*, both issued about the same time.) 'Rejoice for a brother deceased', which is perhaps the more typical death-triumph of the Methodist Revival, and which is still in use, is in the same metre, and first appeared in the same collection of *Funeral Hymns*.

   The genesis of this hymn, and perhaps also of 'Rejoice for a brother deceased', may possibly be traced to the triumphant death of a Cardiff Methodist on 13th August 1744. The preaching service on the morning following his death is thus described in Charles Wesley's *Journal*: 'We had prayed last night with joy full of glory for our departing brother, just while he gave up his spirit,—as I pray God I may give up mine. This morning I expounded that last best triumph of faith, "I have fought a good fight", &c. . . . We sang a song of victory for our deceased friend; then went to the house, and rejoiced, and gave thanks; and rejoiced again with singing over him. The spirit, at its departure, had left marks of its happiness on the clay. No sight upon earth, in my eyes, is half so lovely.'

* *Festival Hymns* (1746): No. 22.
  Funeral Hymns [1746?]: No. 5, entitled 'On the Sight of a Corpse'.
  MS Death (c) [Funeral Hymns], pp. 109–10: 'corrected'.
  MS Gwynne, pp. 23–4.
  Poetical Works, VI.193–5.
  Madan's *Collection* (1760): No. 131, entitled 'On the Death of a Believer'.
  Select Hymns (1761): No. 103.
  Collection (1780): No. 47.
  Pocket Hymn Book (1787): No. 33.
  Collection (1831): No. 48.

Metre 68: 8.8.8.8.8.8.8.8
A B A B C D C D

1 Ah! lovely Appearance of Death!
   No Sight upon Earth is so fair:
Not all the gay Pageants that breathe
   Can with a dead Body compare.
With solemn Delight I survey   5
   The Corpse, when the Spirit is fled,
In love with the beautiful Clay,
   And longing to lie in its stead.

2 How blest is our Brother, bereft
   Of all that could burthen his Mind!   10
How easy the Soul, that hath left
   This wearisom Body behind!
Of Evil incapable thou,
   Whose Relicks with Envy I see;
No longer in Misery now,   15
   No longer a Sinner like me.

3 This Earth is affected no more
   With Sickness, or shaken with Pain:
The War in the Members is o'er,
   And never shall vex him again: 20
No Anger hence forward, or Shame,
   Shall redden this Innocent Clay;
Extinct is the Animal Flame,
   And Passion is vanish'd away.

2. 1780, &c.: 'What sight'.
4. Madan: 'this dead Body'.
5. MS Death: 'Delighted, and awed I survey'.
6. MS Death: 'when a spirit'.
10. MS Death: 'Of all that incumbred'.
15. MS Death: 'With envy whose relics I see'.
17–32. MS Death has as v.3 lines 25–8, 21–4, while lines 17–20 and 29–32
     are omitted.
22. MS Death: 'his innocent'.

4 This languishing Head is at rest,   *25*
   Its Thinking and Aching are o'er;
This quiet immoveable Breast
   Is heav'd by Affliction no more:
This Heart is no longer the Seat
   Of Trouble and torturing Pain,   *30*
It ceases to flutter and beat,
   It never shall flutter again.

5 The Lids he so seldom could close,
   By Sorrow forbidden to sleep,
Seal'd up in eternal Repose,   *35*
   Have strangely forgotten to weep:
The Fountains can yield no Supplies,
   These Hollows from Water are free,
The Tears are all wip'd from these Eyes,
   And Evil they never shall see.   *40*

6 To mourn and to suffer is mine,
   While bound in a Prison I breathe,
And still for Deliverance pine,
   And press to the Issues of Death:
What now with my Tears I bedew,   *45*
   O might I this Moment become,
My Spirit created anew,
   My Flesh be consign'd to the Tomb!

25, 27, 29. MS Gwynne, *Funeral Hymns*, 1761: 'The languishing', 'The
   quiet', 'The heart'.
27.   MS Death: 'insensible breast'.
34.   MS Death: 'Tho weary, forbidden'.
37–8. MS Death: 'The springs can afford no supplies,
          By Mercy's almighty decree'.
39.   MS Gwynne: 'from those Eyes'.
40.   MS Death: 'And sorrow they'.
41–3. MS Death: 'To sorrow and suffer is mine,
          While bound in a dungeon I breathe,
          For speedy deliverance pine'.
46.   MS Death: 'My soul be created anew'.
48.   MS Gwynne: 'to a Tomb.'

65   REJOICE FOR A BROTHER DECEASED

This was one of the author's favourite hymns, and in his old age he would often repeat
the third verse. Cf. introduction to No. **64.**

* *Funeral Hymns* [1746?]: No. 2.
  Poetical Works, VI.189–90.
  Collection (1780): No. 48.
  Pocket Hymn Book (1787): No. 36.
  Collection (1831): No. 49.
  Collection (1876): No. 49.
  MHB (1904): No. 831.
  MHB (1933): No. 973.

Graces [1746?]

Metre 68: 8.8.8.8.8.8.8.8
A B A B C D C D

1 Rejoice for a Brother deceas'd,
   (Our Loss is his infinite Gain)
A Soul out of Prison releas'd,
   And freed from its bodily Chain:
With Songs let us follow his Flight,   5
   And mount with his Spirit above,
Escap'd to the Mansions of Light,
   And Lodg'd in the Eden of Love.

2 Our Brother the Haven hath gain'd,
   Outflying the Tempest and Wind,   10
His Rest He hath sooner obtain'd,
   And left his Companions behind;
Still toss'd on a Sea of Distress,
   Hard toiling to make the Blest Shore,
Where all is Assurance and Peace,   15
   And Sorrow and Sin are no more.

3 There all the Ship's Company meet,
   Who sail'd with the Saviour beneath,
With Shouting each other they greet,
   And triumph o'er Trouble and Death: 20
The Voyage of Life's at an End,
   The mortal Affliction is past,
The Age that in Heaven they spend
   For ever and ever shall last.

4. 1831: 'And free from'.

[THE BOUNTEOUS GOD]   **66**

* *Graces* [1746?]: No. 13, 'To—*Angels speak, let Man*, &c., Hymn 2.'[1]
MS Family, pp. 15–16, where it is numbered 'VIII' among the Graces.
Poetical Works, III.364–5.

Metre 59: 8.3 3.6.8.3 3.6
a b b a c d d c

1 Glory, Love, and Praise, and Honour
     For our Food
     Now bestow'd
Render we the Donor,
Bounteous GOD, we now confess Thee,   5
     GOD who thus
     Blessest us,
Meet it is to bless Thee.

[[1] I.e. tune No. 2 in *Hymns on the Great Festivals, and other Occasions* (1746).]

2 Knows the Ox his Master's Stable,
  And shall we   *10*
   Not know Thee,
  Nourish'd at thy Table?
Yes, of all good Gifts the Giver
  Thee we own,
   Thee alone   *15*
  Magnify for ever.

67   [THANKFUL FOR OUR EVERY BLESSING]

* *Graces* [1746?]: No. 17, 'To—*Angels speak, let Men give Ear*, Hymn 2.'[1]
 MS Family, p. 17: No. 17 of 'Graces'.
 Poetical Works, III.367.
 Madan's *Collection* (1760): No. 151, one of the 'Sacramental Hymns', divided into
  four verses.

             Metre 59: 8.3 3.6.8.3 3.6
                 a b b a c d d c

1 Thankful for our every Blessing
  Let us sing
   CHRIST the Spring,
  Never, never ceasing.
Source of all our Gifts and Graces   *5*
  CHRIST we own,
   CHRIST alone
  Calls for all our Praises.

2 He dispels our Sin and Sadness,
  Life imparts,   *10*
   Chears our Hearts,
  Fills with Food and Gladness.
Who Himself for all hath given
  Us He feeds,
   Us He leads   *15*
  To a Feast in Heaven.

[1 I.e. tune No. 2 in *Hymns on the Great Festivals, and other Occasions* (1746).]

 4. This line is in error set back in the printed *Graces* to the same position
  as lines *2* and *3*, while lines *8, 12,* and *16* are printed 'full out' as
  line *1*. Charles Wesley himself, in MS Family, begins lines *4, 8, 12,*
  and *16* in a position intermediate between lines *1* and *2* (as given
  above).
 13. Madan: 'He Himself for us hath given'.

68 THANKSGIVING FOR THE SUCCESS OF THE GOSPEL

Charles Wesley's *Journal* for Monday 11th August 1746 opens: 'I expressed the
gratitude of my heart in the following thanksgiving:—
     "All thanks be to God . . . &c." '
His journal-letter to his brother John, completed the following week-end, transcribed
the complete poem, to which was given the title 'After Preaching the Gospel in

Cornwall, 1746'. This same letter gives something of the background for the poem—
a series of heart-warming gatherings in various centres, with a computed 12,000
(later reduced to 10,000) gathered in Gwenap Pit on Sunday evening, 10th August,
to whom Charles Wesley preached for nearly two hours with great effect, leading to a
great outpouring of the Holy Spirit in the Society Meeting which followed.

* *Redemption Hymns* (1747): No. 3.
　MS letter to John Wesley, 17th August 1746 (Colman Collection, at Methodist Book
　　Room, London).
　MS Colman 21, p. 55, omitting v. 4.
　Poetical Works, IV.210–12.
　Hymns for those to whom Christ is all in all (1761): No. 65, omitting v. 4.
　Collection (1780): No. 210, as 1761.
　Collection (1831): No. 219, as 1761.
　Collection (1876): No. 219, as 1761.
　MHB (1904): No. 217, omitting v. 4 and conflating vv. 7 and 8.
　MHB (1933): No. 262, as 1904.

Metre 64:　5　5.5　11.5　5.5　11
　　　　　　　　A AB B C C D D

1　All Thanks be to GOD,
　　Who scatters abroad
　　Throughout every Place,
　By the least of his Servants his Savour of Grace!
　　Who the Victory gave,　　　　　　　　　　　　5
　　The Praise let Him have
　　For the Work He hath done,
　All Honour and Glory to JESUS alone.

2　Our Conquering LORD
　　Hath prosper'd the Word,　　　　　　　　　　10
　　Hath made it prevail,
　And mightily shaken the Kingdom of Hell:
　　His Arm he hath bar'd,
　　And a People prepar'd,
　　His Glory to shew,　　　　　　　　　　　　15
　And witness the Power of his Passion below.

3　He hath open'd a Door
　　To the Penitent Poor,
　　And rescu'd from Sin,
　And admitted the Harlots and Publicans in:　　20
　　They have heard the glad Sound,
　　They have Liberty found
　　Thro' the Blood of the Lamb,
　And plentiful Parson in JESUS's Name.

4　The Opposers admire　　　　　　　　　　　25
　　The Hammer and Fire,
　　Which alll things o'ercomes,　　[sic]
　And breaks the hard Rocks, and the Mountains consumes.
　　With quiet Amaze
　　They listen and gaze,　　　　　　　　　　30
　　And their Weapons resign,
　Constrain'd to acknowledge—The Work is Divine!

10. 1761, 1780, &c.: 'his word'.

5   And shall *we* not sing
Our Saviour and King?
Thy Witnesses, we   35
With Rapture ascribe our Salvation to Thee.
Thou JESUS hast bless'd,
And Believers encreas'd,
Who thankfully own
We are freely forgiven thro' Mercy alone.   40

6   The[1] Spirit revives
His Work in our Lives,
His Wonders of Grace
So mightily wrought in the Primitive Days.
O that all Men might know   45
Thy Tokens below,
Our Saviour confess,
And embrace the glad Tidings of Pardon and Peace!

7   Thou Saviour of All,
Effectually call   50
The Sinners that stray;
And O! let a Nation be born in a Day.
Thy Sign let them see,
And flow unto Thee
For the Oil and the Wine,   55
For the blissful Assurance of Favour Divine.

8   Our Heathenish Land
Beneath thy Command
In Mercy receive,
And make us a Pattern to all that Believe: 60
Then, then let it spread
Thy Knowledge and Dread,
Till the Earth is o'er-flow'd,
And the Universe fill'd with the Glory of GOD.

[¹ This is corrected to 'Thy Spirit' in the errata.]

41. MS Colman: 'Thy Spirit'.
1780, &c.: 'His Spirit'.

69   [LOVE DIVINE, ALL LOVES EXCELLING]

Although this hymn seems to have originated as a spiritual parody of 'Fairest Isle', Wesley himself originally suggested that it should be sung 'To—*Jesu, shew us thy Salvation*', i.e. to Lampe's tune No. 9 in *Festival Hymns*. Dr Alan Kay has pointed out that Purcell's famous music (slightly varied) was used as the setting for the hymn in *Select Hymns with Tunes Annext* (1761)—the tune-book itself being known as *Sacred Melody*—and in *Sacred Harmony* (Green's *Wesley Bibliography*, No. 358). In each case it is entitled 'Westminster', being numbered 'Hymn 128' in *Sacred Melody*, and 'Hymn 118' in *Sacred Harmony*. The *School Hymn-book of the Methodist Church* of 1949 also sets the hymn to Purcell's music.

* *Redemption Hymns* (1747): No. 9.
MS Thirty, pp. 135–6.
MS Colman 21, p. 56.
Poetical Works, IV.219–20.

Madan's *Collection* (1760): No. 49.
Hymns for those to whom Christ is all in all (1761): No. 67, omitting v. 2.
Select Hymns (1761): No. 128 (incorrectly numbered 127 in the words section).
Collection (1780): No. 374, as 1761, *Hymns . . . Christ . . . all.*
Pocket Hymn Book (1787): No. 186, as 1780.
Collection (1831): No. 385, as 1780.
Collection (1876): No. 385, as 1780.
MHB (1904): No. 426, as 1780.
MHB (1933): No. 431, as 1780.
Hymns A & M (1889, 1916), No. 520, omitting v. 2 and dividing into six halved
    verses; (1904), No. 497, as 1889; (1950), No. 205, as 1889, but in three verses;
    Schools edn (1958), No. 118, as 1889.

Metre 56: 8.7.8.7.8.7.8.7
a b a b c d c d

1 Love Divine, all Loves excelling,
      Joy of Heaven to Earth come down,
   Fix in us thy humble Dwelling,
      All thy faithful Mercies crown;
   JESU, Thou art all Compassion,   5
      Pure unbounded Love Thou art,
   Visit us with thy Salvation,
      Enter every trembling Heart.

2 Breathe, O breathe thy loving Spirit
      Into every troubled Breast,   10
   Let us all in Thee inherit,
      Let us find that Second Rest:
   Take away our Power of sinning,[1]
      Alpha and Omega be,
   End of Faith as its Beginning,   15
      Set our Hearts at Liberty.

[1 It was this line particularly which impelled John Wesley and others to omit the
second verse from their hymn-books, since it implies an extreme view of Christian
perfection—a subject on which Charles Wesley himself was very scathing in some of
his later poems. The Rev John Fletcher of Madeley suggested its alteration to 'Take
away the love of sinning', pertinently asking: 'Can God take away from us our
power of sinning without taking away our power of free obedience?']

1. Madan: 'all Love excelling'.
2. 1780, &c., insert a comma after 'Heaven', thus making 'to earth come
    down' a prayer instead of a declaration of faith. MS 30 and editions
    up to the 9th in 1776 do not have this comma, which is first added
    in the 10th edition (London, 1779).
3. Madan: 'thine humble Dwelling'.
5. Madan: 'Jesus! Thou'.
6. MS 30: 'Love, unbounded Love'.
12. MS 30: 'the Second Rest';
    Madan: 'thy promis'd Rest'.
13. Later editions (2nd (1747) to 10th (1779) and that of 1788) print
    'Power' in italics;
    Madan: 'the Pow'r'.

3 Come, Almighty to deliver,
  Let us all thy Life receive,
Suddenly return, and never,
  Never more thy Temples leave.   *20*
Thee we would be always blessing,
  Serve Thee as thy Hosts above.
Pray, and praise Thee without ceasing,
  Glory in thy perfect Love.

4 Finish then thy New Creation,   *25*
  Pure and sinless let us be,
Let us see thy great Salvation,
  Perfectly restor'd in Thee;
Chang'd from Glory into Glory,
  Till in Heaven we take our Place,   *30*
Till we cast our Crowns before Thee,
  Lost in Wonder, Love, and Praise.

18. 1780, &c., *A & M* (1889, &c.): 'Let us all thy grace receive'. The 1788
  edition retains 'life'.
20. MS 30 shows that the original reading was 'temple', to which the 's'
  was later added.
22. MS 30: 'the Hosts above';
  Madan: 'thine Hosts above'.
24. MS 30: 'thy Dying Love';
  Madan: 'thy previous Love'.
26. Madan: 'Pure, unspotted may we be'.
  1780, &c., *A & M* (1889, &c.): 'Pure and spotless let us be'. The 1788
  edition of *Redemption Hymns* retains 'sinless'.
28. Madan: 'restor'd by Thee'.
29. MS 30: 'Glory unto Glory'.
31. MS 30: 'Sing, & cast our'.

70   PROV. III.13, &c.

* *Redemption Hymns* (1747): No. 18 (Misprinted 'XXIII' in the 1st edn. Tune
  suggested, 'To—*Sinners, obey the Gospel-Word*'.)
MS Thirty, pp. 163–4.
Poetical Works, IV.234–5.
Select Hymns (1761): No. 70.
Collection (1780): No. 14, vv. 1–3, 6, 7, 9.
Pocket Hymn Book (1787): No. 11, as 1780.
Collection (1831): No. 14, as 1780.
Collection (1876): No. 14, as 1780, title 'Prov. iii.13–18'.
MHB (1904): No. 295, as 1780.
MHB (1933): No. 360, as 1780.

Metre 8: 8 8.8 8
A A B B

1 Happy the Man, who finds the Grace,
  The Blessing of GOD's Chosen Race,
  The Wisdom coming from above,
  The Faith that sweetly works by Love.

1. 1761, 1780, &c.: 'the man that finds'.

2 Happy beyond Description He
   Who knows *The Saviour died for me,*
   The Gift unspeakable obtains,
   And Heav'nly Understanding gains.

3 Wisdom Divine! Who tells the Price
   Of Wisdom's costly Merchandize!
   Wisdom to Silver we prefer,
   And Gold is Dross, compar'd to Her.

4 Better she is than richest Mines,
   All earthly Treasures she outshines,
   Her Value above Rubies is,
   And precious Pearls are vile to This.

5 Whate'er thy Heart can wish is Poor
   To Wisdom's all-sufficient Store:
   Pleasure, and Fame, and Health, and Friends,
   She all created Good transcends.

6 Her Hands are fill'd with Length of Days,
   True Riches, and Immortal Praise,
   Riches of CHRIST on All bestow'd,
   And Honour, that descends from GOD.

7 To purest Joys She All invites,
   Chaste, holy, spiritual Delights:
   Her Ways are Ways of Pleasantness,
   And all her flowery Paths are Peace.

8 He finds, who Wisdom apprehends,
   A Life begun that never ends,
   The Tree of Life Divine She is,
   Set in the midst of Paradise.

9 Happy the Man who Wisdom gains,
   Thrice happy who his Guest retains,
   He owns, and shall for ever own
   Wisdom, and CHRIST, and Heaven are One.

30. MS 30: 'A Life of God that never ends'.
32. MS 30: 'Fixt in the Midst'.

AT MEETING OF FRIENDS

71

* *Redemption Hymns* (1747): No. 32.
  MS Colman 21, p. 24.
  Poetical Works, IV.252–3.
  Hymns for those to whom Christ is all in all (1761): No. 72.
  Collection (1831): No. 500, in halved verses.
  Collection (1876): No. 500, as 1831.
  MHB (1904): No. 681, as 1831.
  MHB (1933): No. 745, as 1831.

Metre 5: 8.6.8.6.8.6.8.6
A B A B C D C D

To—*When all thy Mercies, O my God.*

1 All Praise to our Redeeming Lord,
   Who joins us by his Grace,
And bids us, Each to Each restor'd,
   Together seek his Face.
He bids us build each other up,   5
   And gather'd into One;
To our high Calling's glorious Hope
   We Hand in Hand go on.

2 The Gift which He on One bestows
   We all delight to prove,   10
The Grace thro' every Vessel flows
   In purest Streams of Love.
E'en now we speak, and think the same,
   And cordially agree,
Concentred all thro' JESUS' Name   15
   In perfect Harmony.

3 We all partake the Joy of One,
   The Common Peace we feel,
A Peace to Sensual Minds unknown,
   A Joy unspeakable.   20
And if our Fellowship below
   In JESUS be so sweet,
What Height of Rapture shall we know,
   When round his Throne we meet.

13. 1761, 1831, &c.: 'Ev'n now we think, and speak'.
23. 1831, &c.: 'What heights'. ('Height' continued to appear in the editions
   published during Wesley's lifetime.)

72   THE GREAT SUPPER

Luke xiv.16–24

* *Redemption Hymns* (1747): No. 50.
MS Cheshunt, pp. 40–3.
MS Clarke, pp. 43–6: on which was based *The Great Supper . . . By the Rev. Charles
   Wesley,* published by James Nichols in 1842.
Poetical Works, IV.274–7.
Madan's *Collection* (1760): No. 22, vv. 1, 4, 6 + 8 + 3 conflated, 12, 14, 22–4.
Collection (1780): No. 2, vv. 1, 2, 12, 14, 19–22, 24.
Pocket Hymn Book (1787): No. 2, as 1780.
Collection (1831): No. 2, as 1780.
Collection (1876): No. 2, as 1780.
MHB (1904): No. 270, vv. 1, 2, 12, 21, 22, 24.
MHB (1933): No. 323, vv. 1, 2, 12, 21, 24.

Metre 8: 8 8.8 8
A A B B

To—*Awake,* Jerusalem, *awake.*

1 Come, Sinners, to the Gospel-Feast,
Let every Soul be JESU's Guest,
You need not One be left behind,
For GOD hath bidden all Mankind.

2 Sent by my LORD, on You I call,   *5*
The Invitation is to All:
Come all the World: Come, Sinner, Thou,
All Things in CHRIST are ready now.

3 JESUS to you his Fulness brings,
A Feast of Marrow, and fat Things:
All, all in CHRIST is freely given,   *10*
Pardon, and Holiness, and Heaven.

4 Do not begin to make Excuse,
Ah! do not you his Grace refuse;
Your worldly Cares and Pleasures leave,   *15*
And take what JESUS hath to give.

5 Your Grounds forsake, your Oxen quit,
Your every Earthly Thought forget,
Seek not the Comforts of this Life,
Nor sell your Saviour for a Wife.   *20*

6 'Have me excus'd' why will ye say?
Why will ye for Damnation pray?
Have you excus'd—from Joy and Peace!
Have you excus'd—from Happiness!

7 Excus'd from Coming to a Feast!   *25*
Excus'd from being JESU's Guest!
From knowing *Now* your Sins forgiven,
From tasting *Here* the Joys of Heaven!

11. MSS: 'are freely'.
12. MSS: 'Pardon, & Happiness, & Heaven.'
14–16. Madan: 'Ah! do not ye his Grace refuse;
　　　　　This World's vain cares and Lusts forsake,
　　　　　What JESUS freely gives ye, take.'
15. MSS: 'worldly Care, &'.
20. MSS: 'Nor lose your Saviour—for a Wife.'
21, 30, 11–12. Thus conflated by Madan in his v. 3:
　　　　　'Have me excus'd, why will ye say,
　　　　　From Health, and Life, and Liberty,
　　　　　From all that is in JESUS giv'n,
　　　　　From Pardon, Holiness, and Heav'n!'
27–8. MSS: 'From knowing here [Clarke, *'here'*] your . . .
　　　　　From tasting Now the . . .'

8 Excus'd, alas! why would ye be
  From Health, and Life, and Liberty,   *30*
  From entring into Glorious Rest,
  From leaning on your Saviour's Breast.

9 Yet must I, LORD, to Thee complain,
  The World have made thy Offers vain,
  Too Busy, or too Happy They,   *35*
  They will not, LORD, thy Call obey.

10 Go then, my angry Master said,
  Since These on all my Mercies tread,
  Invite the Rich and Great no more,
  But preach my Gospel to the Poor.   *40*

11 Confer not Thou with Flesh and Blood,
  Go quickly forth, invite the Crowd,
  Search every Lane, and every Street,
  And bring in all the Souls you meet.

12 Come then ye Souls, by Sin opprest,   *45*
  Ye restless Wanderers after Rest,
  Ye Poor, and Maim'd, and Halt, and Blind,
  In CHRIST an hearty Welcome find.

13 Sinners my gracious LORD receives,
  Harlots, and Publicans, and Thieves,   *50*
  Drunkards, and all the hellish Crew,
  I have a Message now to You.

14 Come, and partake the Gospel-Feast,
  Be sav'd from Sin, in JESUS rest,
  O taste the Goodness of our GOD,   *55*
  And eat his Flesh, and drink his Blood.

15 'Tis done; my All-redeeming LORD,
  I have gone forth, and preach'd thy Word,
  The Sinners to thy Feast are come,
  And yet, O Saviour, there is Room.   *60*

34.   MSS: 'Thine offers'.
45.   1780, &c.: 'Come all ye souls'.
48.   1780, 1st edn, 'From Christ' altered back to 'In Christ' in 2nd,
      1781, and later editions.
      1780, &c.: 'a hearty welcome'.
55.   1780, &c.: 'of your God'.
60.   MSS: 'And yet, O Jesus'.

16 Go then, my Lord, again injoin'd,
   And other wand'ring Sinners find,
   Go to the Hedges, and Highways,
   And offer All my pard'ning Grace.

17 The Worst unto my Supper press,   *65*
   Monsters of daring Wickedness,
   Tell them my Grace for All is free,
   They cannot be too bad for Me.

18 Tell them their Sins are all forgiven,
   Tell every Creature under Heaven,   *70*
   I died to save them from All Sin,
   And force the Vagrants to come in.

19 Ye vagrant Souls, on You I call,
   (O that my Voice could reach you All)
   Ye all are freely Justified,   *75*
   Ye All may live, for GOD hath died.

20 My Message as from GOD receive,
   Ye all may come to CHRIST, and live,
   O let his Love your Hearts constrain,
   Nor suffer Him to die in vain.   *80*

21 His Love is mighty to compel,
   His conqu'ring Love consent to feel,
   Yield to his Love's resistless Power,
   And fight against your GOD no more.

22 See Him set forth before your Eyes,   *85*
   Behold the Bleeding Sacrifice,
   His offer'd Love make haste t'embrace,
   And freely now be sav'd by Grace.

23 Ye who believe his Record true,
   Shall sup with Him, and He with you: *90*
   Come to the Feast; be sav'd from Sin,
   For JESUS waits to take you in.

68. MSS: 'too Lost for me.'
71. MSS: 'from their Sin'.
72. MSS: 'And force the Rebels'.
75. 1831, 1876: 'Ye all may now be justified'.
                                consent to
82. MS Clarke: 'ye ~~sinners~~, feel'.
86–7. 1780, &c.: 'That precious, bleeding sacrifice!
                  His offered benefits embrace'.
87. Madan: 'make haste, embrace'.

24 This is the Time, no more delay,
 This is the Acceptable Day,
 Come in, this Moment, at his Call,   *95*
 And live for Him who died for All.

94. Madan: 'This is the glorious Gospel-day'.
   1780 (1st and 2nd edns only), 1787: 'your acceptable day'.
   1933: 'This is the Lord's accepted day'.

73   [RAPTUROUS HEIGHT]

* *Hymns and Sacred Poems* (1749), I.123–5: No. 65 (Part I only of No. 15 of 'Hymns
 for One fallen from Grace').
 MS Occasional, pp. 6–7 (Part I of poem entitled 'The Backslider').
 Poetical Works, IV.408–9.
 Pocket Hymn Book (1787): No. 80.
 Collection (1876): No. 807, vv. 1, 2, 4, 7.
 MHB (1904): No. 382, as 1876.
 MHB (1933): No. 407, as 1876.

           Metre 65: 5 5.9.5 5.9
               A A B C C B

1 How happy are They
  Who the Saviour obey,
 And have laid up their Treasure above,
  Tongue cannot express
  The sweet Comfort, and Peace   *5*
 Of a Soul in its earliest Love.

2 That Comfort was Mine,
  When the Favour Divine
 I first found in the Blood of the Lamb;
  When my Heart it believ'd,   *10*
  What a Joy it receiv'd,
 What a Heaven in JESUS his Name!

3 'Twas an Heaven below
  My Saviour to know;
 The Angels could do Nothing more   *15*
  Than fall at his Feet,
  And the Story repeat,
 And the Lover of Sinners adore.

4 JESUS all the Day long
  Was my Joy and my Song;
 O that All his Salvation may see!   *20*
  He hath lov'd me, I cried,
  He hath suffer'd, and died,
 To redeem such a Rebel as me.

11. MS Occ., 1787: 'I receiv'd'.
12. MS Occ.: 'What an Heaven';
  MS Occ., 1787, 1876, &c.: 'Jesus's Name.'
14. MS Occ.: 'My Jesus'.
21. MS Occ., 1787: 'might see!'

5   On the Wings of his Love   *25*
      I was carried above
   All Sin, and Temptation, and Pain;
      I could not believe
      That I ever should grieve,
   That I ever should suffer again.   *30*

6   I rode on the Sky
      (Freely justified I!)
   Nor envied *Elijah* his Seat;
      My Soul mounted higher
      In a Chariot of Fire,   *35*
   And the Moon it was under my Feet.

7   O the rapturous Height
      Of that holy Delight,
   Which I felt in the Life-giving Blood!
      Of my Saviour possest   *40*
      I was perfectly blest,
   As if fill'd with the Fulness of GOD.

35. MS Occ.: 'In her Chariot'.
38. 1876, &c.: 'Of the holy'.

AFTER A RECOVERY   **74**

* *Hymns and Sacred Poems* (1749), I.162–4: No. 92 (No. 5 of eight hymns under the
    same title).
   Poetical Works, IV.445–7.
   Collection (1780): No. 207, vv. 9, 11–18.
   Collection (1831): No. 216, as 1780.
   Collection (1876): No. 216, as 1780.
   MHB (1904): No. 66, vv. 11–15, 17.
   MHB (1933): No. 77, as 1904.

                  Metre 1: 8.6.8.6
                       A B A B

1   O what an evil Heart have I,
      So cold, and hard, and blind,
   With Sin so ready to comply,
      And cast my GOD behind!

2   So apt his Mercy to forget,   *5*
      So soon dissolv'd in Ease,
   So false, so full of all Deceit,
      And desperate Wickedness!

3   Long have I murmur'd to be clean,
      From all Iniquity,   *10*
   But knew not that I lov'd my Sin,
      And would not be set free.

4 Oft when the pleasing Ill drew nigh,
    And GOD fore-shew'd my Fall,
I would not from Temptation fly,   *15*
    Or heed the Spirit's Call.

5 His warning Voice I would not mind,
    But turn'd mine Ear away,
And lingring stood, 'till Sin should find
    And seize its willing Prey.   *20*

6 Oft have I ask'd for Help, afraid
    Lest GOD my Voice should hear,
While with deceitful Lips *I said*
    Th'Abominable Prayer.

7 Oft, when He would not let me yield,   *25*
    But stopt me by his Grace,
I rag'd from Sin to be with-held,
    And burst from his Embrace.

8 When after each foul sinful Fall,
    I would have All given up,   *30*
He would not let me give up All,
    But forc'd me still to hope.

9 Infinite, unexhausted Love!
    JESUS and Love are One:
If still to me thy Bowels move,   *35*
    They are restrain'd to None.

10 If me, ev'n me Thou yet canst spare,
    Fury is not in Thee;
For All thy tender Mercies are,
    If Mercy is for me.   *40*

11 What shall I do my GOD to love,
    My loving GOD to praise!
The Length, and Breadth, and Height to prove,
    And Depth of Sovereign Grace!

12 Thy Sovereign Grace to All extends,   *45*
    Immense and unconfin'd,
From Age to Age it never ends,
    It reaches All Mankind.

13 Throughout the World its Breadth is known,
    Wide as Infinity,   *50*
So wide, it never pass'd by One,
    Or it had pass'd by me.

14 My Trespass is grown up to Heaven,
  But far above the Skies,
  In CHRIST abundantly forgiven   *55*
  I see thy Mercies rise.

15 The Depth of All-redeeming Love
  What Angel-Tongue can tell!
  O may I to the utmost prove
  The Gift unspeakable!   *60*

16 Deeper than Hell, it pluck'd me thence,
  Deeper than Inbred Sin,
  JESUS his Love my Heart shall cleanse,
  When JESUS enters in.

17 Come quickly then, my LORD, and take   *65*
  Possession of Thine own,
  My longing Heart vouchsafe to make
  Thine everlasting Throne.

18 Assert thy Claim, receive thy Right,
  Come quickly from above,   *70*
  And *sink* me to Perfection's Height,
  The *Depth* of Humble Love.

53. 1780, &c.: 'was grown up'.
63. 1780, &c.: 'Jesus's love'.
65. 1780, &c.: 'Come quickly, gracious Lord,'.
69. 1780, &c.: 'maintain thy right'.

[MY GOD, I AM THINE] *75*

* *Hymns and Sacred Poems* (1749), I.219–20: No. 128.
MS Cheshunt, pp. 118–19.
MS Clarke, p. 136.
MS Colman 21, p. 35.
Poetical Works, V.24.
Hymns for those to whom Christ is all in all (1761): No. 87.
Select Hymns (1761): No. 2.
Collection (1780): No. 197, printed in three verses, 11 11.11 11.
Collection (1831): No. 205, as 1780.
Collection (1876): No. 205.
MHB (1904): No. 368, printed in three verses 5 5 11.5 5 11.
MHB (1933): No. 406, as 1904.

Metre 61: 5 5 11
A A A

1   My GOD, I am thine,
    What a Comfort divine,
  What a Blessing to know that my JESUS is mine!

  2. MS Clarke: 'What Comfort'.
     MS Cheshunt: 'a' added afterwards by Charles Wesley.

2 In the Heavenly Lamb
  Thrice happy I am;   *5*
My Heart it doth dance to the Sound of thy Name.

3 True Pleasures abound
  In the rapturous Sound;
And whoever hath found it hath Paradise found.

4 My JESUS to know,   *10*
  And feel his Blood flow,
'Tis Life Everlasting, 'tis Heaven below.

5 Yet onward I haste
  To the Heavenly Feast;
That, that is the Fulness: but This is the Taste. *15*

6 And this I shall prove,
  'Till with Joy I remove
To the Heaven of Heavens of JESUS's Love.

4. MSS Cheshunt, Clarke: 'In Thee my dear Lamb'.
               it doth dance
6. MSS Cheshunt, Clarke: '~~And dances~~ my Heart ⋏ to'.
  1761 (*Select Hymns*), 1780 (1st edn): 'And my heart doth rejoice at
   the sound';
  1780, from 2nd edn (1781), &c.: 'And my heart it doth dance at'.
  MS Colman: 'My heart it doth dance at the sound'.
7–9. Missing from MS Cheshunt, but added in MS Clarke, commencing
  line *9*, 'Whoever hath found'.
11. MS Cheshunt: 'And to feel'.
18. 1761 (*Select Hymns*), 1780, &c.: 'in Jesus's love'.

76   [THY MIGHTY NAME]

* *Hymns and Sacred Poems* (1749), I.245–6: No. 143.
 Poetical Works, V.50.
 Hymns for those to whom Christ is all in all (1761): No. 91.
 Select Hymns (1761): No. 114.
 Collection (1780): No. 201.
 Collection (1831): No. 209.
 Collection (1876): No. 209.
 MHB (1904): No. 107.
 MHB (1933): No. 98.

           Metre 10: 8.8.8.8.8 8
              A B A B C C

1 Thou hidden Source of calm Repose,
 Thou all-sufficient Love Divine,
My Help, and Refuge from my Foes,
 Secure I am, if Thou art mine,
And lo! from Sin, and Grief, and Shame *5*
I hide me, JESUS, in thy Name.

2 Thy might If Name Salvation is,
   And keeps my happy Soul above,
Comfort it brings, and Power, and Peace,
   And Joy, and everlasting Love: *10*
To me with thy dear Name are given
Pardon, and Holiness, and Heaven.

3 JESU, my All in All Thou art,
   My Rest in Toil, my Ease in Pain,
The Med'cine of my broken Heart,   *15*
   In War my Peace, in Loss my Gain,
My Smile beneath the Tyrant's Frown,
In Shame my Glory, and my Crown.

4 In Want my plentiful Supply,
   In Weakness my Almighty Power,   *20*
In Bonds my perfect Liberty,
   My Light in *Satan*'s darkest Hour,
In Grief my Joy unspeakable,
My Life in Death, my Heaven in Hell.

BEFORE WORK   77

* *Hymns and Sacred Poems* (1749), I.247: No. 145.
MS Colman 21, p. 36, omitting v. 3.
Poetical Works, V.50–1.
Hymns for those to whom Christ is all in all (1761): No. 94, omitting v. 3.
Collection (1780): No. 315, as 1761.
Collection (1831): No. 324, as 1780.
Collection (1876): No. 324, as 1780.
MHB (1904): No. 586, as 1780.
MHB (1933): No. 590, as 1780.
Hymns A & M (1861): No. 6, vv. 1, 2, 4–6 and a doxology; (1875, 1889, 1916):
   No. 8, vv. 1, 2, 4–6; (1904): No. 6, as 1875; (1950): No. 336, as 1875; Schools
   edn (1958): No. 188, as 1875.

Metre 7: 8.8.8.8
A B A B

1 Forth in thy Name, O LORD, I go,
   My daily Labour to pursue,
Thee, only Thee resolv'd to know
   In all I think, or speak, or do.

2 The Task thy Wisdom hath assign'd   *5*
   O let me chearfully fulfil,
In all my Works thy Presence find,
   And prove thine acceptable Will.

5. 1780: 'has assigned'.
8. 1780, &c.: 'thy acceptable will';
   A & M (1861, &c.): 'Thy good and perfect will.'

3 Preserve me from my Calling's Snare,
 And hide my simple Heart above,   *10*
Above the Thorns of Choaking Care,
 The gilded Baits of Worldly Love.

4 Thee may I set at my Right-hand,
 Whose Eyes mine inmost Substance see,
And labour on at thy Command,   *15*
 And offer all my Works to Thee.

5 Give me to bear thy Easy Yoke,
 And every Moment watch and pray,
And still to Things Eternal look,
 And hasten to thy Glorious Day.   *20*

6 For Thee delightfully employ
 Whate'er thy bounteous Grace hath given,
And run my Course with even Joy,
 And closely walk with Thee to Heaven.

14. 1780, &c., *A & M* (1861, &c.): 'my inmost substance'.
21. A & M (1861): 'Fain would I still for Thee employ'.

78   FOR A PREACHER OF THE GOSPEL

* *Hymns and Sacred Poems* (1749), I.300–1: No. 188—the last of a group of twelve
 'Hymns for a Preacher of the Gospel'.
 Poetical Works, V.105–6.
 Hymns for those to whom Christ is all in all (1761): No. 97, vv. 3–8.
 Collection (1780): No. 421, vv. 3–7 only.
 Collection (1831): No. 433, as 1780.
 Collection (1876): No. 433, as 1780.
 MHB (1904): No. 563, as 1780.
 MHB (1933): No. 390, vv. 3, 5–7.

Metre 10: 8.8.8.8.8 8
A B A B C C

1 O that I was as heretofore
 When first sent forth in JESU's Name
I rush'd thro' every open Door,
 And cried to All, 'Behold the Lamb!
Seiz'd the poor trembling Slaves of Sin,   *5*
And forc'd the Outcasts to come in.

2 The GOD who kills, and makes alive,
 To me the quickning Power impart,
Thy Grace restore, thy Work revive,
 Retouch my Lips, renew my Heart,   *10*
Forth with a fresh Commission send,
And all thy Servants Steps attend.

3 Give me the Faith which can remove,
   And sink the Mountain to a Plain,
 Give me the Child-like praying Love,   15
   That longs to build thine House again;
 The Love which once my Heart o'erpower'd,
 And all my simple Soul devour'd.

4 I want an even strong Desire,
   I want a calmly-fervent Zeal,   20
 To save poor Souls out of the Fire,
   To snatch them from the Verge of Hell,
 And turn them to the Pardning GOD,
 And quench the Brands in JESU's Blood.

5 I wou'd the pretious Time redeem,   25
   And longer live for This alone
 To spend, and to be spent for Them
   Who ha^ve not yet my Saviour known,
 Fully on These my Mission prove,
 And only breathe, to breathe thy Love.   30

6 My Talents, Gifts, and Graces, LORD,
   Into thy blessed Hands receive,
 And let me live to preach thy Word,
   And let me for thy Glory live,
 My every sacred Moment spend   35
 In publishing the Sinner's Friend.

7 Inlarge, inflame, and fill my Heart
   With boundless Charity Divine,
 So shall I all my Strength exert,
   And love Them with a Zeal like Thine,   40
 And lead them to thine open Side,
 The Sheep, for whom their Shepherd died.

8 Or if, to serve thy Church and Thee
   Myself be offer'd up at last,
 My Soul brought thro' the Purple Sea   45
   With Those beneath the Altar cast
 Shall claim the Palm to Martyrs given,
 And mount the highest Throne in Heaven.

14. 1780: 'the mountains'.
16. 1780, &c.: 'Which longs . . . thy house'.
17–18. 1780, &c.: 'Thy love let it my heart o'erpower,
               And all my simple soul devour.'
23. 1780, &c.: 'a pardoning God'.
34. 1780, &c.: 'to thy glory'.
41. 1780, &c.: 'thy open side'.

79   AFTER PREACHING TO THE
NEWCASTLE COLLIERS

In the related Cheshunt and Clarke MS volumes this poem is included with two others 'Written at Leaving ye Staffordshire Colliers', as was No. 118 in the *Hymns and Sacred Poems*, which is here grouped with 'See how great a flame'. It seems likely that it was actually written for the coalminers in Staffordshire, probably in 1743 or 1744, and taken up with enthusiasm by those in Newcastle. In either case it may well have been suggested by the glow of the colliery fires, lighting up the night skies.

* *Hymns and Sacred Poems* (1749), I.315–16: No. 199—the last of four hymns with this title.
MS Cheshunt, p. 51.
MS Clarke, pp. 57–8.
MS Thirty, pp. 210–11.
Poetical Works, V.120–1.
Hymns for those to whom Christ is all in all (1761): No. 98.
Collection (1780): No. 209.
Collection (1831): No. 218.
Collection (1876): No. 218.
MHB (1904): No. 218.
MHB (1933): No. 263.

Metre 50: 7.7.7.7.7.7.7.7
a b a b c d c d

1 See how great a Flame aspires,
    Kindled by a Spark of Grace!
JESU's Love the Nations fires,
    Sets the Kingdoms on a Blaze.
To bring Fire on Earth he came;   5
    Kindled in some Hearts it is;
O that All might catch the Flame,
    All partake the Glorious Bliss!

2 When He first the Work begun,
    Small and feeble was his Day;   10
Now the Word doth swiftly run,
    Now it wins its widening Way,
More and more it spreads, and grows,
    Ever mighty to prevail,
Sin's strong-holds it now o'erthrows,   15
    Shakes the trembling Gates of Hell.

3 Sons of GOD, your Saviour praise,
    He the Door hath open'd wide,
He hath giv'n the Word of Grace;
    JESU's Word is glorified: 20

7. MS 30: 'all may catch'.
8. MS 30: 'common bliss.'
12. MS Cheshunt: 'larger Way';
            widening
    MS Clarke: ~~larger~~ way'.
15. MS 30: 'it overthrows'.

JESUS Mighty to redeem,
   He alone the Work hath wrought,
Worthy is the Work of Him,
   Him who spake a World from Nought.

4 Saw ye not the Cloud arise   *25*
   Little as an Human Hand?
Now it spreads along the Skies,
   Hangs o'er all the thirsty Land!
Lo! the Promise of a Shower
   Drops already from above;   *30*
But the LORD shall shortly pour
   All the Spirit of his Love.

26. 1780, &c.: 'a human hand.'
28. MS 30: 'Now it covers all the Land.'
31. MS 30, 1780, &c.: 'will shortly'.

[THE BEATIFIC SIGHT]   **80**

* *Hymns and Sacred Poems* (1749), II.29–31: No. 22.
MS Colman 21, p. 38, omitting v. 3.
Poetical Works, V.168–9.
Madan's *Collection* (1760): No. 129, vv. 1, 3–6.
Hymns for those to whom Christ is all in all (1761): No. 104.
Select Hymns (2nd edn, 1765): No. 141.
Collection (1780): No. 324, omitting v. 3.
Pocket Hymn Book (1787): No. 160, as 1780.
Collection (1831): No. 333, as 1780.
Collection (1876): No. 333, as 1780.
MHB (1904): No. 471, vv. 1, 2, 4–6.
MHB (1933): No. 487, as 1780.

Metre 4: 8 8.6.8 8.6
A A B C C B

1 Come on, my Partners in Distress,
My Comrades thro' the Wilderness,
   Who still your Bodies feel,
A while forget your Griefs, and Fears,
And look beyond the Vale of Tears   *5*
   To that celestial Hill.

2 Beyond the Bounds of Time, and Space,
Look forward to that happy Place,
   The Saints secure Abode,
On Faith's strong Eagle Pinions rise,   *10*
And force your Passage to the Skies,
   And scale the Mount of GOD.

5. 1761, 1780, &c.: 'this vale'.
8. 1780, &c.: 'that heavenly place';
   1787 retains 'heavenly'.

3 See, where the Lamb in Glory stands,
  Incircled with his radiant Bands,
    And join th'Angelic Powers,   *15*
For all that Height of glorious Bliss
Our everlasting Portion is,
    And all that Heaven is Ours.

4 Who suffer for our Master here,
  We shall before his Face appear,   *20*
    And by his Side sit down:
To Patient Faith the Prize is sure,
And all, that to the End endure
    The Cross, shall wear the Crown.

5 Thrice blessed bliss inspiring Hope!   *25*
  It lifts the fainting Spirits up,
    It brings to life the Dead:
Our Conflicts here shall soon be past,
And you and I ascend at last
    Triumphant with our Head.   *30*

6 That great Mysterious Deity
  We soon with open Face shall see:
    The Beatific Sight
Shall fill the Heavenly Courts with Praise,
And wide diffuse the golden Blaze   *35*
    Of Everlasting Light.

7 The Father shining on his Throne,
  The glorious co-eternal Son,
    The Spirit one and seven,
Conspire our Rapture to compleat,   *40*
And lo! we fall before his Feet,
    And Silence heightens Heaven.

8 In Hope of that Extatic Pause,
  JESUS, we now sustain thy Cross,
    And at thy Footstool fall,   *45*
'Till Thou our hidden Life reveal,
'Till Thou our ravish'd Spirits fill,
    And GOD is All in All.

19. MS Colman, 1780, &c.: 'Who suffer with'.
23. Madan: 'And those that'.
25. 1761, 1780: 'Thrice blessed bliss, inspiring hope'.
    1831, &c.: 'Thrice blessed, bliss-inspiring hope'.
34. 1780, from 3rd edn, 1782, &c.: 'Shall fill heaven's sounding courts
    with praise';
    1787 retains the original line.
41. 1780 (1st and 2nd edns only), 1787: 'before thy feet'.
44. 1780, 1787: 'Jesu'.

112

FOR ONE DEPARTING 81

* *Hymns and Sacred Poems* (1749), II.75: No. 55.
Poetical Works, V.216.
Select Hymns (1761): No. 66, divided into four verses.
Pocket Hymn Book (1785): No. 198, as 1761.
Pocket Hymn Book (1787): No. 34, as 1761.
Collection (1831): No. 725, as 1761.
Collection (1876): No. 922, as 1761.
MHB (1904): No. 832, as 1761.

Metre 56: 8.7.8.7.8.7.8.7
a b a b c d c d

1 Happy Soul, thy Days are ended,
　　All thy mourning Days below:
Go, by Angel-Guards attended,
　　To the Sight of JESUS go!
Waiting to receive thy Spirit,　　　　　　　5
　　Lo! the Saviour stands above,
Shews the Purchase of his Merit,
　　Reaches out the Crown of Love.

2 Struggle thro' thy latest Passion
　　To thy dear Redeemer's Breast,　　　　10
To his uttermost Salvation,
　　To his Everlasting Rest:
For the Joy He sets before Thee,
　　Bear a momentary Pain,
Die, to live the Life of Glory,　　　　　　15
　　Suffer, with thy LORD to reign.

4. 1787: 'to the light'.
9. 1785: 'the latest passion'.

[MEET AND RIGHT IT IS TO SING] 82

* *Hymns and Sacred Poems* (1749), II.136–7: No. 97. 'Hymn XIV' of a series of
　　nineteen 'Hymns for the Watch-Night', a selection from which was published
　　separately under that title.
Poetical Works, V.279–80.
Hymns for the Watch-Night (n.d.): No. 8.
MS Colman 21, p. 38.
Hymns for those to whom Christ is all in all (1761): No. 111.
Collection (1780): No. 212.
Collection (1831): No. 221.
Collection (1876): No. 221.
MHB (1904): No. 11.
MHB (1933): No. 17.

Metre 85: 7.6.7.6.7.7.7.6
a B a B c d c D

1 Meet and right it is to sing
  At every Time and Place
Glory to our Heavenly King,
  The GOD of Truth and Grace:
Join we then with sweet accord,   5
  All in one Thanksgiving join,
Holy, holy, holy, LORD,
  Eternal Praise be Thine!

2 Thee the first-born Sons of Light
  In choral Symphonies   10
Praise by Day, Day without Night,
  And never, never cease:
Angels, and Archangels all
  Sing the Mystic Three in One,
Sing, and stop, and gaze, and fall   15
  O'erwhelm'd before thy Throne.

3 Vyeing with that happy Quire
  Who chaunt thy Praise above,
We on Eagles Wings aspire,
  The Wings of Faith and Love: 20
Thee they sing with Glory crown'd,
  We extol the slaughter'd Lamb,
Lower if our Voices sound,
  Our Subject is the same.

4 Father, GOD, thy Love we praise,   25
  Which gave thy Son to die,
JESUS full of Truth and Grace
  Alike we glorify,
Spirit, Comforter Divine,
  Praise by All to Thee be given,   30
'Till we in full Chorus join,
  And Earth is turn'd to Heaven.

2. 1780, &c.: 'In every time'.
3. 1780 (3rd edn, 1782): 'the heavenly King'.

83   INNOCENT DIVERSIONS

The Watchnight Service seems to have been commenced by the Wesleys as a counter-attraction to the ale-house roistering to which the Kingswood miners were addicted on Saturday nights. Prayer, praise, and preaching sometimes went on until 'a little beyond the noon of night'. In the early years these services were held once a month while the moon was nearly full, so as to avoid inconvenience, danger, and scandal for the late travellers.

* *Hymns and Sacred Poems* (1749), II.140–1: No. 100, being 'Hymn XVII' of 'Hymns for the Watch-Night'.
Poetical Works, V.282–4.
Hymns for the Watch-Night (n.d.): No. 9, without the title.

Metre 64: 5 5.5 11.5 5.5 11
A A B B C C D D

1   Come let us anew
      Our Pleasures pursue:
      For *Christian* Delight
The Day is too short; let us borrow the Night.
      In sanctify'd Joy   5
      Each Moment employ,
      To JESUS's Praise,
And spend, and be spent in the Triumph of Grace.

2   The Slaves of Excess,
      Their Senses to please   10
      Whole Nights can bestow,
And on in a Circle of Riot they go:
      Poor Prodigals, They
      The Night into Day
      By Revellings turn,   15
And all the Restraints of Sobriety scorn.

3   The Drunkards proclaim
      At Midnight their Shame,
      Their Sacrifice bring,
And loud to the Praise of *their* Master they sing: 20
      The Hellish Desires
      Which *Satan* inspires,
      In Sonnets they breathe,
And shouting descend to the Mansions of Death.

4   The Civiller Croud,   25
      In Theatres proud,
      Acknowledge his Power,
And *Satan* in Nightly Assemblies adore:
      To the Masque and the Ball
      They fly at his Call;   30
      Or in Pleasures excel,
And chaunt in a Grove* to the Harpers of Hell.[1]

---

* *Ranelagh's Gardens, Vaux-Hall, &c.*
[1 This line was brought up against Wesley when in later years his own son Charles became a musician. He faced the challenge boldly, and in February, 1769, read out a public proclamation on the subject, containing the following passage: 'How can I call musicians harpers of hell, yet breed my Son a Musician? I answer, there are Heavenly as well as Hellish Harpers. . . . Therefore the term is too general & liable to be misunderstood. For which reason I have altered it long ago; as you will find, if that hymn is ever reprinted.' It was reprinted, many times, in the *Watchnight Hymns*, but Charles Wesley's emendation did not appear.]

24. *Watch-Night:* 'to the Regions of Death'.

5 And shall we not sing
   Our Master and King
   While Men are at rest,   *35*
 With JESUS admitted at Midnight to feast?
   Here only we may
   With Innocence stay,
   The Enjoyment improve,
 And abide at the Banquet of JESUS's Love.   *40*

6 In Him is bestow'd
   The Spiritual Food,
   The Manna Divine,
 And JESUS's Love is far better than Wine:
   With Joy we receive   *45*
   The Blessing, and give
   By Day and by Night,
 All Thanks to the Source of our endless Delight.

7 Our Concert of Praise
   To JESUS we raise,   *50*
   And all the Night long
 Continue the New Evangelical Song:
   We dance to the Fame
   Of JESUS's Name,
   The Joy it imparts   *55*
 Is Heaven begun in our Musical Hearts.

8 Thus, thus we bestow
   Our Moments below,
   And singing remove,
 With all the Redeem'd to the *Sion* above: *60*
   There, there shall we stand
   With our Harps in our Hand,
   Interrupted no more,
 And eternally sing, and rejoice, and adore.

61. Watch-Night: 'there we shall stand'.

THE TRUE USE OF MUSICK 84

Writing in 1859, the Rev John Kirk (*Charles Wesley, the Poet of Methodism*, pp. 44–6) reported a tradition that Charles Wesley was interrupted during an open-air service in a sea-port by a company of half-drunken sailors. As he began to sing a hymn they struck up 'one of their lewd songs called "Nancy Dawson".' Charles Wesley mastered the tune and metre, and at the following service got the people to sing new words to the sailors' tune. Mr George Barratt in his *Recollections of Methodism . . . in . . . Lincoln* (1866) published a similar story as told to him over fifty years earlier by 'an old soldier' who had supposedly been present on the occasion, though in this narrative the sailors have been transformed to soldiers, and Charles to John Wesley, and there are a few slight errors in the memorization of the words by either Barratt or his informant. Something of the kind probably did happen, however, and it is tempting to think that it may have been during Charles Wesley's visit to Plymouth in June 1746, when 'an whole army of soldiers and sailors stood behind [him] shouting and blaspheming', so that he stayed a few days extra in order to quieten the opposition. Wesley's verses were first published in 1749.

Which 'Nancy Dawson' was the heroine of this 'lewd song', however? The famous dancer of that name, about whom George Alexander Stevens composed his 'Ballad of Nancy Dawson', did not dance her way to fame until 1759, performing her captivating horn-pipe in Gay's *Beggar's Opera* at the Covent Garden Theatre. Stevens wrote the ballad to this same horn-pipe tune, and it still remains a favourite melody (in slightly varied form) as 'Here we go round the mulberry bush'. There was another Nancy Dawson, however, who lived at Portsmouth toward the end of the previous century. She apparently kept a house of ill fame, and the sailors sang a ribald song about her. Could the arm of coincidence stretch far enough for the song about the Portsmouth Nancy Dawson to be to the same tune later made more respectable, not only by Charles Wesley, but by the dancer of that name? Certainly a catchy horn-pipe tune would be quite likely for the sailors' 'lewd song'. (Inquiries at Portsmouth have failed to elicit any details about this earlier Nancy Dawson.)

Certainly Charles Wesley's poem, as published in *Hymns and Sacred Poems* (1749), is in a most unusual metre for him, though having experimented with it he did not completely discard it (see 'Jesus, to Thee I would look up', No. **130**). The basic structure is an emphatic and rapid opening '*One-two-three*', followed by trochaic feet. Some years later, however, Charles Wesley re-wrote the poem, adding a syllable to every other line. This has the effect of making it far easier to scan the verses as double long metre with an iambic beat, though there remain so many examples of the choriambus or reversed accent at the beginning of the lines that there is still the urge to scan the first foot as a dactyl. This revised version was published in a periodical early in 1769, but did not appear in a more permanent publication. Both versions are here given.

84A   THE TRUE USE OF MUSICK

* *Hymns and Sacred Poems* (1749), II.253–4, No. 189.
MS Occasional, pp. 74–6.
Poetical Works, V.397–8.

Metre 60: 8.7.8.7.8.7.8.7
a b a b c d c d

1 Listed into the Cause of Sin,
    Why should a Good be Evil?
Musick, alas! too long has been
    Prest to obey the Devil:
Drunken, or lewd, or light the Lay   *5*
    Flow'd to the Soul's Undoing,
Widen'd, and strew'd with Flowers the Way
    Down to Eternal Ruin.

2 Who on the Part of GOD will rise,
    Innocent Sound recover,   *10*
Fly on the Prey, and take the Prize,
    Plunder the Carnal Lover,
Strip him of every moving Strain,
    Every melting Measure,
Musick in Virtue's Cause retain,   *15*
    Rescue the Holy Pleasure?

3 Come let us try if JESU's Love
    Will not as well inspire us:
This is the Theme of Those above,
    This upon Earth shall fire us.   *20*
Say, if your Hearts are tun'd to sing,
    Is there a Subject greater?
Harmony all its Strains may bring,
    JESUS's Name is sweeter.

4 JESUS the Soul of Musick is;   *25*
    His is the Noblest Passion:
JESUS's Name is Joy and Peace,
    Happiness and Salvation:
JESUS's Name the Dead can raise,
    Shew us our Sins forgiven,   *30*
Fill us with all the Life of Grace,
    Carry us up to Heaven.

4. MS Occas. underlines 'Prest' to emphasize the fact of its being a pun
    likely to appeal to soldiers and sailors, for whom the press-gang
    was an all too common experience.
16. MS Occas.: 'the Noble Pleasure.'
20. MS Occas.: 'sh[oul]d fire us.'

THE TRUE USE OF MUSIC   **84**B

* Newspaper cutting, in MS 339 at the Methodist Book Room, London. From evidence on the verso this was published about the end of February 1769, but extensive inquiries have failed to establish the actual periodical. MS Patriotism: Misc., pp. 9–10.

Metre 17: 8.8.8.8.8.8.8.8
ABABCDCD

1 Listed into the cause of sin
   Why should a good in evil end?
Music alas, too long has been
   Prest to obey the roaring fiend.
Drunken, or lewd, or light the lay,   *5*
   To thoughtless souls destructive flow'd,
Widen'd and smooth'd the downward way,
   And strew'd with flowers th'infernal road.

2 Who on the part of God wil[l] rise,
   Restorers of instructive song;   *10*
Fly on the prey and take the prize,
   And spoil the gay Egyptian throng?
Who will the powers of sound redeem
   Music in virtue's cause retain,
Give Harmony its proper theme,   *15*
   And vie with the celestial train?

3 Come let us try if Jesus' love
   Will not its votaries inspire:
The subject this, of those above,
   This upon earth the saints should fire: *20*
Say, if your hearts be turn'd to sing,
   What theme like this you[r] songs can claim?
Harmony all its stores may bring,
   Not half so sweet as Jesus Name.

4 His name the soul of Music is,   *25*
   And captivates the virgin's pure:
His name is health and joy and bliss,
   His name doth every evil cure:
Jesus's name the dead can raise,
   Can ascertain our sins forgiven;   *30*
And fill with all the life of grace,
   And bear our raptur'd souls to heaven.

5. MS: 'Drunken, or light, or lewd the lay'.
10. MS: 'Restorer of'.
21. MS: 'be tuned to sing'; the 'turn'd' of the printed version is almost certainly a misprint.
22. MS: 'your songs'.
27. MS has 'joy, & ~~peace~~, bliss'.
29. MS: 'Jesus his Name'.

84A (*cont.*)

5 Who hath a Right like Us to sing,
　　Us whom his Mercy raises?
　Merry our Hearts, for CHRIST is King,　　　　　　　　*35*
　　Chearful are all our Faces:
　Who of his Love doth once partake
　　He evermore rejoices:
　Melody in our Hearts we make,
　　Melody with our Voices.　　　　　　　　　　　　*40*

6 He that a sprinkled Conscience hath,
　　He that in GOD is merry,
　Let him sing Psalms, the Spirit saith,
　　Joyful, and never weary,
　Offer the Sacrifice of Praise,　　　　　　　　　　*45*
　　Hearty, and never ceasing,
　Spiritual Songs and Anthems raise,
　　Honour, and Thanks, and Blessing.

7 Then let us in his Praises join,
　　Triumph in his Salvation,　　　　　　　　　　　*50*
　Glory ascribe to Love Divine,
　　Worship, and Adoration:
　Heaven already is begun,
　　Open'd in Each Believer;
　Only believe, and still sing on,　　　　　　　　　*55*
　　Heaven is Ours forever.

40. MS Occas.: 'Echoing to our Voices.'
51. MS Occas.: 'to Grace Divine'.

84B (*cont.*)

5 Who hath a right like us to sing,
   Us whom his pardoning mercy chears?
Merry the heart where Christ is King,   *35*
   And in the brighten'd face appears:
Who of his pardoning love partake
   Are call'd for ever to rejoice:
Melody in our hearts we make,
   Return'd by every echoing voice.   *40*

6 He that a sprinkled conscience knows,
   The mirth divine, the mystic peace,
The joy that from believing flows,
   Let him in psalms and hymns confess,
Offer the sacrifice of praise,   *45*
   Praise ardent, cordial, constant, pure,
And triumph in harmonious lays,
   While endless ages shall endure.

7 Then let us in the triumph join,
   Responsive to the harps above,   *50*
Glory ascribe to grace divine,
   Worship, and majesty, and love:
We feel our future bliss begun,
   We taste by faith the heavenly powers:
Believe, rejoice, and still sing on,   *55*
   And heaven eternally is ours!

35. MS: 'Merry the heart, for Christ is King'.

85 [AT PARTING OF CHRISTIAN FRIENDS]

Although this hymn was used in a general way, 'For the Society Parting', there is little doubt that it was sung whenever Methodist preachers left these shores as missionaries, and for over a century it has been the traditional 'rolling-off' hymn for the missionaries leaving Richmond College.

* *Hymns and Sacred Poems* (1749), II.317–19: No. 233, Part I, being No. 43 of 'Hymns for Christian Friends', and headed 'At Parting'.
MS Colman 21, p. 30.
Poetical Works, V.462–3.
Collection (1780): No. 521, divided into twelve verses.
Pocket Hymn Book (1785): Nos. 211, 212, vv. 1–3, 4–6 divided into twelve verses, heading a section 'For the Society Parting'.
Pocket Hymn Book (1787): No. 248, as 1780.
Collection (1831): No. 535.
Collection (1876): No. 535.
MHB (1904): No. 792, vv. 1–4 divided into eight verses.
MHB (1933): No. 807, as 1904.

Metre 31: 6.6.8.6.6.6.8.6
ABABCDCD

1 And let our Bodies part,
To different Climes repair,
Inseparably join'd in Heart
The Friends of JESUS are:
JESUS the Corner-Stone,   5
Did first our Souls unite;
And still He holds, and keeps us One,
Who walk with Him in White.

2 Then let us still proceed
In JESU's Work below,   10
And following our Triumphant Head,
To farther Conquests go;
The Vineyard of the LORD
Before his Labourers lies;
And lo! we see the vast Reward   15
That waits us in the Skies.

3 O let our Heart, and Mind
Continually ascend,
That Haven of Repose to find,
Where all our Labours end,   20

6. 1780, &c.: 'our hearts'.
7. 1780, &c.: 'And still he keeps our spirits one'.
9. 1780, &c.: 'O let us still proceed'.
13. 1780, &c.: 'of their Lord'.
16. 1780, &c.: 'Which waits'.
20. 1780, 1st edn: 'When all our labours end', altered back in 2nd edn (1781) to 'Where all'.

Where all our Grief is o'er,
Our Suffering, and our Pain:
Who meet on that Eternal Shore
Shall never part again.

4   O happy, happy Place,   *25*
Where Saints and Angels meet!
There we shall see each others Face,
And all our Brethren greet,
The Church of the first-born,
We shall with them be blest,   *30*
And crown'd with endless Joy return
To our eternal Rest.

5   With Joy we shall behold
In yonder blest Abode
The Patriarchs and Prophets old,   *35*
And all the Saints of GOD;
Abraham and *Isaac* there,
And *Jacob* shall receive
The Followers of their Faith and Prayer,
Who now in Bodies live.   *40*

6   We shall our Time beneath
Live out in chearful Hope,
And fearless pass the Vale of Death,
And gain the Mountain-top:
To gather home his own   *45*
GOD shall his Angels send,
And bid our Bliss on Earth begun
In endless Triumphs end.

21. 1780, 1st edn: 'When all our toils are o'er'.
     1780, (2nd edn, 1781), &c.: 'Where all our toils are o'er'.
26. 1780, 1787: 'When saints'.
48. 1780, 1785, 1787: 'In deathless triumphs end.'
     1831, &c.: 'In deathless triumph end.'

AT MEETING OF FRIENDS   **86**

This hymn was placed by John Wesley as the opening hymn of Part V, Section I, of his famous *Collection*—'For the Society . . . At meeting'. Ever since John Wesley's later years it has been the opening hymn for the sessions of the Methodist Conference.

* *Hymns and Sacred Poems* (1749), II.321–2: No. 236, being No. 46 in 'Hymns for
    Christian Friends'.
MS Thirty, pp. [237–8], with title as given.
MS Colman 21, p. 24.
Poetical Works, V.466–7.
Collection (1780): No. 466, omitting v. 4.
Collection (1831): No. 478, as 1780.
Collection (1876): No. 478, as 1780.
MHB (1904): No. 785, as 1780, in 6 half-verses.
MHB (1933): No. 709, as 1904.

Metre 31: 6.6.8.6.6.6.8.6
A B A B C D C D

1   And are we yet alive,
      And see Each other's Face?
  Glory, and Thanks to JESUS give
      For his Almighty Grace:
      Preserv'd by Power Divine   5
      To full Salvation here,
  Again in JESU's Praise we join,
      And in his Sight appear.

2   What Troubles have we seen,
      What mighty Conflicts past,   10
  Fightings without, and Fears within,
      Since we assembled last!
      Yet out of all the LORD
      Hath b[r]ought us by his Love,[1]
  And still he doth his Help afford,   15
      And hide our Life above.

3   Then let us make our Boast
      Of his Redeeming Power,
  Which saves us to the uttermost,
      'Till we can sin no more: 20
      Let us take up the Cross,
      'Till we the Crown obtain,
  And gladly reckon all Things loss,
      So we may JESUS gain.

4   JESUS, to Thee we bow,   25
      And for thy Coming wait:
  Give us for Good some Token Now
      In our imperfect State;
      Apply the Hallowing Word,
      Tell Each who looks for Thee,   30
  Thou shalt be perfect as thy LORD,
      Thou shalt be all like me!

[[1] The misprint 'bought' for 'brought' is noted in the Errata at the end.]

3. 1780, &c.: 'Glory and praise'.
4. 1780, &c.: 'For his redeeming grace'.
10. 1780, &c.: 'What conflicts have we past'.
13. 1780, &c.: 'But out of all'.
16. 1831, &c.: 'And hides'.

87   ['MY LORD AND MY GOD!']

* *Hymns and Sacred Poems* (1749), II.324–5: No. 239, being No. 49 of 'Hymns for
  Christian Friends'.
  MS Thirty, pp. 71–2, entitled 'At meeting Friends'.
  MS Colman 21, p. 30.
  Poetical Works, V.469–70.

Metre 1: 8.6.8.6
ABAB

1 See, JESU, thy Disciples see,
   The promis'd Blessing give,
Met in thy Name, we look to Thee,
   Expecting to receive.

2 Thee we expect our faithful LORD,   *5*
   Who in thy Name are join'd,
We wait, according to thy Word,
   Thee in the midst to find.

3 With us Thou art assembled here,
   But O Thyself reveal,   *10*
Son of the Living GOD, appear,
   Let us thy Presence feel.

4 Breathe on us, LORD, in this our Day,
   And these dry Bones shall live,
Speak Peace into our Hearts, and say   *15*
   The HOLY GHOST receive.

5 Whom now we seek O might we meet!
   JESUS the Crucified,
Shew us thy bleeding Hands and Feet,
   Thou who for us hast died.   *20*

6 Cause us thy Record to receive,
   Speak, and the Tokens shew,
'O be not faithless, but believe
   In me, who died for You.'

7 LORD, I believe for me, ev'n me   *25*
   Thy Wounds were open'd wide,
I see the Prints, I more than see
   Thy Feet, thy Hands, thy Side.

8 I cannot fear, I cannot doubt,
   I feel the sprinkled Blood: *30*
Let every Soul with me cry out
   Thou art my LORD, my GOD!

1. 1831: 'See, Jesus'.
17. 1780, &c.: 'O may we meet'.
       wo
20. MS 30: 'If Thou for us hast died'.
21. 1780, &c.: 'the record'.
       e
27. MS 30: 'I see thy Prints'.
28. MS 30: 'Thy ever-streaming Side.'

125

88   [OUR LIFE IS A DREAM]

* *Hymns for New Year's Day* (1750): No. 5.
  Poetical Works, VI.14.
  Madan's *Collection* (1760): No. 88.
  Select Hymns (1761): No. 7.
  Collection (1780): No. 45.
  Pocket Hymn Book (1787): No. 32.
  Collection (1831): No. 46, in 6 halved verses.
  Collection (1876): No. 47, as 1831.
  MHB (1904): No. 930, as 1831.
  MHB (1933): No. 956, as 1831.

Metre 64: 5 5.5 11.5 5.5 11
A A B B C C D D

1   Come, let us anew
     Our Journey pursue,
     Roll round with the year,
     And never stand still, 'till the Master appear;
     His adorable will   *5*
     Let us gladly fulfil,
     And our talents improve
     By the patience of hope, and the labour of love.

2   Our life is a Dream,
     Our time as a stream   *10*
     Glides swiftly away,
     And the fugitive moment refuses to stay,
     The Arrow is flown,
     The moment is gone,
     The millennial year   *15*
     Rushes on to our view, and Eternity's here!

3   O that each in the day
     Of His coming might say
     'I have fought my way thro',
     'I have finish'd the work thou didst give me to do!   *20*
     O that each from his LORD
     May receive the glad word,
     'Well and faithfully done,
     'Enter into my joy, and sit down on my throne!

17. Madan: 'And that each', corrected in Errata to 'O that'.
18. Madan, 1761, 1780, &c.: 'may say'.

89   [ANOTHER VARIOUS YEAR]

* *Hymns for New Year's Day* (1750): No. 7.
  Poetical Works, VI.16.
  Pocket Hymn Book (1785): No. 94.
  Pocket Hymn Book (1787): No. 100.
  Collection (1831): No. 712, with 6 halved verses.
  Collection (1876): No. 979, as 1831.
  MHB (1904): No. 931, as 1831.
  MHB (1933): No. 959, as 1831, but omitting v. 3b.

Metre 5: 8.6.8.6.8.6.8.6
A B A B C D C D

1 Sing to the great JEHOVAH's praise!
 All praise to Him belongs,
Who kindly lengthens out our days,
 Demands our choicest songs:
Whose Providence has brought us thro'   5
 Another various year,
We all with vows and anthems new
 Before our GOD appear.

2 Father, thy mercies past we own,
 Thy still-continued care,   10
To Thee presenting thro' thy Son
 Whate'er we have, or are.
Our lips and lives shall gladly shew
 The wonders of thy love,
While on in JESU's steps we go   15
 To see thy face above.

3 Our residue of days or hours
 Thine, wholly thine shall be,
And all our consecrated powers
 A sacrifice to Thee;   20
'Till JESUS in the clouds appear
 To Saints on earth forgiven,
And bring the grand Sabbatic year,
 The Jubilee of Heaven.

[EARTHQUAKE, PLAGUE, AND SWORD]   **90**

In June 1755 hostilities broke out between England and France in America, and sovereigns and diplomats were unsuccessfully attempting to stave off the threatened major conflict which we know as the 'Seven Years War'. An actual French invasion of England was feared. Details were gradually coming through about the terrible earthquake at Lisbon on 1st November 1755, when tens of thousands were killed. A severe cattle plague was still raging in Britain and Western Europe, and in ten years about three million cattle were lost. There had been a series of poor harvests—though a worse was to follow. Altogether it was a gloomy and somewhat frightening time. Small wonder that even intelligent people seriously debated whether the end of the world was close at hand—though they discouraged the efforts of many to set a date to the event. Friday, 6th February 1756, was proclaimed a National Fast Day. Nearly all work ceased, and the churches were thronged. It was against this background, and particularly for this occasion, that Charles Wesley prepared his collection of seventeen *Hymns for the Year 1756*, published simultaneously in Bristol and Dublin. He also reprinted his *Hymns for Times of Trouble and Persecution* and the two parts of *Hymns occasioned by the Earthquake*, to which were added poems referring to the Lisbon disaster and to the troubles in America.

* *Hymns for the Year 1756*: No. 16.
 Poetical Works, VI.94–5.
 Collection (1780): No. 60.
 Pocket Hymn Book (1787): No. 44.
 Collection (1831): No. 61.
 Collection (1876): No. 61.

Metre 86: 7.6.7.6.7.8.7.6
a B a B c D c D

1 Stand th'Omnipotent Decree,
  JEHOVAH's Will be done!
 Nature's End we wait to see,
  And hear her final Groan:
 Let this Earth dissolve, and blend   *5*
In Death the Wicked and the Just,
 Let those pondrous Orbs descend,
  And grind us into Dust.

2 Rests secure the righteous Man,
  At his Redeemer's Beck   *10*
 Sure t'emerge, and rise again
  And mount above the Wreck.
 Lo! the heavenly Spirit towers,
Like Flames, o'er Nature's funeral Pyre,
 Triumphs in immortal Powers,   *15*
  And claps his Wings of Fire.

3 Nothing hath the Just to lose
  By Worlds on Worlds destroy'd:
 Far beneath his Feet he views
  With Smiles the flaming Void: *20*
 Sees this Universe renew'd,
The grand millennial Reign begun,
 Shouts with all the Sons of GOD
  Around th'Eternal Throne.

4 Resting in this glorious Hope   *25*
  To be at last restor'd,
 Yield we now our Bodies up
  To Earthquake, Plague, or Sword;
 List'ning for the call Divine,
The latest Trumpet of the Seven,   *30*
 Soon our Soul and Dust shall join,
  And both fly up to Heaven.

22. 1787: 'millennial year'.

91   [NATURE'S FINAL HOUR]

* *Hymns for the Year 1756*: No. 17.
MS Wesley Family Letters, IV.77 (At Methodist Book Room, London), vv. 1–3, 5,
 numbered 1–4, in letter to wife (22nd Dec. 1755).
Poetical Works, VI.95–6.
Collection (1780): No. 61.
Collection (1831): No. 62.
Collection (1876): No. 62.

Metre 4: 8 8.6.8 8.6
A A B C C B

1 How happy are the little Flock,
  Who safe beneath their Guardian Rock
    In all Commotions rest!
  When Wars and Tumult's Waves run high,
  Unmov'd above the Storm they lie,
    They lodge in JESU'S Breast.   5

2 Such Happiness, O LORD, have we,
  By Mercy gather'd into Thee,
    Before the Floods descend:
  And while the bursting Cloud comes down,   10
  We mark the vengeful Day begun,
    And calmly wait the End.

3 The Plague, and Dearth, and Din of War
  Our SAVIOUR'S swift approach declare,
    And bid our Hearts arise: 15
  Earth's Basis shook confirms our Hope,
  Its Cities fall but lifts us up,
    To meet Thee in the Skies.

4 Thy Tokens we with Joy confess,
  The War proclaims the Prince of Peace,   20
    The Earthquake speaks thy Power,
  The Famine all thy Fulness brings,
  The Plague presents thy healing Wings,
    And Nature's final Hour.

5 Whatever Ill the World befall,   25
  A Pledge of endless Good we call,
    A Sign of JESUS near:
  His Chariot will not long delay:
  We hear the rumbling Wheels, and pray
    Triumphant LORD, appear.   30

  4. MS: 'War's and Tumult's'.
 11. MS: 'They mark'.
 13. MS: 'The Dearth, & Plague, & Din'.
 14. MS: 'sure approach'.
 17. MS: 'Her cities' Fall'.
 18. MS: 'To meet Him'.
 25. 1780, &c.: 'Whatever ills'.
 26. MS: 'A Token of his Day we call'.
 30. MS: 'Appear, great God, appear!'

6 Appear with Clouds on *Sion*'s Hill,
  Thy Word and Mystery to fulfil,
    Thy Confessors t'approve,
  Thy Members on thy Throne to place,
  And stamp thy Name on every Face   *35*
    In glorious heavenly Love.

32. 1780 (1st & 2nd edns): 'The word and mystery fulfil'.
    1780 (3rd edn, 1782): 'Thy word and mystery fulfil'.
    1831: 'The word and mystery to fulfil'.
    1876: 'Thy word and mystery to fulfil'.

92   THY KINGDOM COME!

The lengthy discussion of this hymn in Julian's *Dictionary of Hymnology* shows that John Cennick published a hymn in this metre in 1752, commencing 'Lo! He cometh, countless trumpets', and that in his 1760 *Collection* Martin Madan presented a cento from the two hymns, Madan's version coming into more general use than either of the originals. The position is complicated by the fact that Thomas Olivers also wrote a hymn in this same metre, with similar sentiments and phraseology.

Wesley's hymn is really the second of a trilogy of hymns in this metre; they are preceded by two other hymns under the same title.

* *Hymns of Intercession for all Mankind* (1758): No. 39.
  Poetical Works, VI.143–4.
  Madan's *Collection* (1760): No. 42, entitled 'The Second Advent. Rev. i.7', using
    vv. 1, 2, 4 as vv. 1, 2, 6 of his cento.
  Select Hymns (2nd edn, 1765): No. 139.
  Pocket Hymn Book (1787): No. 41.
  Collection (1831): No. 66.
  Collection (1876): No. 66.
  MHB (1904): No. 200.
  MHB (1933): No. 264.
  Hymns A & M (1861): No. 39; (1875, 1889, 1916, 1950): No. 51; (1904): No. 52,
    including 2 vv. from Cennick.

                        Metre 54: 8.7.8.7.4.7
                                a b a b x b

1 Lo! He comes with clouds discending,
  Once for favour'd sinners slain!
Thousand, thousand saints attending,
  Swell the triumph of his train:
    Hallelujah,   *5*
GOD appears, on earth to reign!

2 Every eye shall now behold Him
  Rob'd in dreadful majesty,
Those who set at nought and sold Him,
  Pierc'd, and nail'd Him to the tree,   *10*
    Deeply wailing
  Shall the true Messiah see.

1. *A & M* (1861): 'in clouds descending' [the spelling 'discending' is
    amended to 'descending' in all later editions].
6. Madan: 'Hallelujah! Amen!';
    A & M (1861, &c., except 1950): 'Christ appears on earth again';
    A & M (1950): 'Christ appears on earth to reign'.

3 The dear tokens of his passion
　Still his dazling body bears,
Cause of endless exultation　　　　　　　　　　　*15*
　To his ransom'd worshippers;
　　With what rapture
　Gaze we on those glorious scars!

4 Yea, amen! let all adore Thee
　High on thine eternal throne　　　　　　　　　*20*
Saviour, take the power and glory
　Claim the kingdom for thine own:
　　JAH, JEHOVAH,
　Everlasting GOD, come down.

13. A & M (1861, &c.): 'Those dear tokens'.
20. 1831, &c.: 'thy eternal'.
22. A & M (1861): 'the kingdoms'.
23. 1933: 'Hallelujah'.
23–4. Madan (using the closing two lines from Cennick's hymn):
　　'O come quickly!/Hallelujah! Come, LORD, come!'
　A & M (1861): 'O come quickly!/Alleluia! Amen.'
　A & M (1875, &c.): 'Alleluia!/Thou shalt reign, and Thou alone.'

[ONE CHURCH, ABOVE, BENEATH] 　　　　**93**

* *Funeral Hymns* (1759): No. 1.
MS Richmond, p. 157: last verse added later.
MS Six, pp. 23–4.
Poetical Works, VI.215–16.
Pocket Hymn Book (1785): No. 13.
Collection (1831): No. 735.
Collection (1876): No. 949.
MHB (1904): No. 805.
MHB (1933): No. 824, conflating vv. 3 & 4 (3a+4b).
Hymns A & M (1861): No. 169, vv. 1b, 2a, 2b, 3a, and 5b, in five halved verses;
　(1875, 1889, 1916): No. 221, as 1861; (1904): No. 387, as 1861; (1950): No. 272,
　as 1861, and No. 628, vv. 1a, 4b; Schools edn (1958): No. 158, as 1861.
　　　　　　　　　　　　　Metre 5: 8.6.8.6.8.6.8.6
　　　　　　　　　　　　　A B A B C D C D

1 Come let us join our Friends above
　That have obtain'd the prize,
And on the eagle-wings of love
　To joy celestial rise;
Let all the Saints terrestrial sing　　　　　　　　*5*
　With those to glory gone,
For all the servants of our King
　In earth and heaven are one.

2. MS Richmond: 'Who have'.
4. 1831, &c.: 'To joys'.
5–6. A & M (1861, &c.): 'Let saints on earth in concert sing
　　　　　　　　　　With those whose work is done;'
　Dr W. H. Frere, the editor of the 1909 Historical Edition of *A & M*,
　says that these alterations appeared first in Murray's *Hymnal*.
8. A & M (1861, &c., except 1904): 'In heaven and earth are one.'
　A & M (1904): 'Both quick and dead are one.'

2 One family we dwell in Him,
   One Church above, beneath,   *10*
Tho' now divided by the stream,
   The narrow stream of death:
One Army of the living GOD,
   To his command we bow:
Part of his host hath cross'd the flood,   *15*
   And part is crossing *now*.

3 Ten thousand to their endless home
   This solemn moment fly,
And we are to the margin come,
   And we expect to die: *20*
His militant, embodied host
   With wishful looks we stand,
And long to see that happy coast,
   And reach that heavenly land.

4 Our old companions in distress   *25*
   We haste again to see,
And eager long for *our* release
   And full felicity:
Ev'n now by faith we join our hands
   With those that went before,   *30*
And greet the blood-besprinkled bands
   On the eternal shore.

5 Our spirits too shall quickly join,
   Like theirs, with glory crown'd,
And shout to see our Captain's sign,   *35*
   To hear his trumpet sound:

15. MS Richmond, 1831, &c.: 'his host have cross'd';
     A & M (1861, &c.): 'the host have crossed'.
16. 1831, &c., *A & M* (1861, &c.): 'are crossing'.
17–20. A & M (1861, &c.): 'E'en now to their eternal home
               There pass some spirits blest;
            While others to the margin come,
               Waiting their call to rest.'
22. 1904: 'with wistful looks'.
24. MS Richmond: 'And grasp';
     1785, &c.: 'the heavenly land'.
27. MS Richmond: 'eager look'.
30. MS Richmond: 'blood-besprinkled' added later in blank space left
     for such an insertion;
     MS Six: 'And ~~greet . . .~~'; '~~grasp clasp~~ greet' in margin.
31. A & M (1950): 'Our Captain's ransomed bands'.

O that we now might grasp our guide,
  O that the word were given!
Come Lord of hosts the waves divide,
  And land us all in heaven.   *40*

37–40. A & M (1861, &c.): 'Jesu, be Thou our constant Guide.
              Then, when the word is given,
           Bid Jordan's narrow stream divide,
             And bring us safe to heaven.'

   [For *40*, *A & M* (1904) reads: 'And show the path to heaven.']

['OUR PROVIDENTIAL WAY']   **94**

* *Scripture Hymns* (1762), I.42–3: O.T. 133.
  Scripture Hymns (1794), I.39: O.T. 125.
  Poetical Works, IX.43.
  Collection (1780): No. 317.
  Pocket Hymn Book (1787): No. 153.
  Collection (1831): No. 326.
  Collection (1876): No. 326.
  MHB (1904): No. 611.
  MHB (1933): No. 608.

                             Metre 10: 8.8.8.8.8 8
                                     A B A B C C

*The Lord went before them by day in a pillar of a cloud, to lead them the way, and by night
in a pillar of fire, to give them light: to go by day and night.*—[Exodus] xiii.21.

1 Captain of Israel's host, and Guide
  Of all who seek that land above,
Beneath thy shadow we abide,
  The cloud of thy protecting love,
Our strength thy grace, our rule thy word,   *5*
Our end, the glory of the LORD.

2 By thine unerring Spirit led,
  We shall not in the desart stray,
The light of man's direction need,
  Or miss our providential way,   *10*
As far from danger as from fear,
While Love, Almighty Love, is near.

  2. 1780, 1831, &c.: 'the land above'.
  7. 1780, 1787: 'thy unerring spirit'.
  9. John Wesley's copy of *Scripture Hymns* (1762) has his note, 'Yes—
     J.W.'
    1780, &c.: 'We shall not full direction need'.
10. 1831, &c.: 'Nor miss'.

[DIVINE PROVIDENCE]   **95**

* *Scripture Hymns* (1762), I.53–4: O.T. 169–171.
  Scripture Hymns (1794), I.48–9: O.T. 157, vv. 3–4.
  Poetical Works, IX.55.
  Arminian Magazine (1779 [May]), pp. 271–2: Nos. 168, 170–2.

Collection (1780): No. 241, in 6 halved verses.
Pocket Hymn Book (1787): No. 120, as 1780.
Collection (1831): No. 250, as 1780.
Collection (1876): No. 250, as 1780.
MHB (1904): No. 67, as 1780.
MHB (1933): No. 49, as 1780.

Metre 5: 8.6.8.6.8.6.8.6
A B A B C D C D

[*And the Lord passed by before* (Moses), *and proclaimed, The Lord, The Lord God, merciful and gracious, long-suffering, and abundant in goodness and truth.*—Exodus xxxiv.6.]

169. *Gracious, long-suffering*—xxxiv.6

Thy causeless unexhausted love,
  Unmerited and free,
Delights our evil to remove,
  And help our misery;
Thou waitest to be gracious still,   5
  Thou dost with sinners bear,
That sav'd, we may thy goodness feel,
  And all thy grace declare.

170. *Abundant in goodness*—xxxiv.6

Thy goodness and thy truth to me,
  To every soul abound,   10
A vast unfathomable sea,
  Where all our thoughts are drown'd;
Its streams the whole creation reach,
  So plenteous is the store,
Enough for all, enough for each,   15
  Enough for evermore.

171. *Abundant in truth*—xxxiv.6

Faithful, O LORD, thy mercies are,
  A rock that cannot move,
A thousand promises declare
  Thy constancy of love: 20
Throughout the universe it reigns
  Unalterably sure,
And while the truth of GOD remains,
  The goodness must endure.

1. 1780 (from 2nd edn 1781), 1831, &c.: 'Thy ceaseless'.
24. 1779: 'Thy goodness'.

96   [INEXTINGUISHABLE BLAZE]

* *Scripture Hymns* (1762), I.57: O.T. 183.
  Scripture Hymns (1794), I.52: O.T. 165.
  Poetical Works, IX.58–9.
  Arminian Magazine (1779 [August]), p. 439.
  Collection (1780): No. 318, subdivided into four halved verses.

Metre 17: 8.8.8.8.8.8.8.8
ABABCDCD

The fire shall ever be burning upon the altar, it shall never go out.—[Leviticus] vi.13.

1 O Thou who camest from above,
　The pure, celestial fire t'impart,
Kindle a flame of sacred love
　On the mean altar of my heart;
There let it for thy glory burn　　　　　　　　　　*5*
　With inextinguishable blaze,
And trembling to it's Source return,
　In humble prayer, and fervent praise.

2 *Jesus*, confirm my heart's desire
　To work, and speak, and think for thee,　　　　　*10*
Still let me guard the holy fire,
　And still stir up thy gift in me,
Ready for all thy perfect will
　My acts of faith and love repeat,
'Till death thy endless mercies seal,　　　　　　　*15*
　And make my sacrifice compleat.

2. *A & M* (1904, &c.): 'The fire celestial to impart'.
6. 1779: 'unextinguishable';
　　A & M (1904): 'With ever-bright, undying blaze'. (Cf. p. xviii above.)
8. 1780, 1785, 1787: 'In humble love'.
9. 1780, 1785, 1787: 'Jesu, confirm'.
12. *A & M* (1904, &c.): 'the gift'.
13. *A & M* (1904, &c.): 'Still let me prove Thy perfect will'.
16. 1780, &c. (except 1794), *A & M* (1904, &c.): 'the sacrifice complete.'

[A CHARGE TO KEEP]　　　　　　　　　　　　**97**

Metre 31: 6.6.8.6.6.6.8.6
A B A B C D C D

Keep the charge of the LORD, *that ye die not.*—[Leviticus] viii.35.

1   A charge to keep I have,
    A GOD to glorify,
A never-dying soul to save,
    And fit it for the sky;
    To serve the present age,   5
    My calling to fulfil:
O may it all my powers engage
    To do my Master's will!

2   Arm me with jealous care,
    As in thy sight to live,   10
And O! thy servant, LORD, prepare
    A strict account to give:
    Help me to watch and pray,
    And on thyself rely,
Assur'd, if I my trust betray,   15
    I shall for ever die.

12. A & M (1904, &c.): 'A good account'.
15–16. A & M (1904, &c.): 'And let me ne'er my trust betray,
                But press to realms on high.'

98   [THE PRIESTLY BLESSING]

* *Scripture Hymns* (1762), I.62–3: O.T. 200, 201, 202.
  Scripture Hymn (1794), I.57–8: O.T. 177, combined into one poem.
  Poetical Works IX.65.
  Arminian Magazine, 1779 (June), pp. 327–8.
  Pocket Hymn Book (1785): No. 91, divided into six verses.
  Pocket Hymn Book (1787): No. 121, as 1785.
  Collection (1831): No. 252, as 1785.
  Collection (1876): No. 252, as 1785.
  MHB (1904): No. 354, as 1785.
  MHB (1933): No. 378, as 1785, but omitting vv. 1 and 2, i.e. v. 1 of the original.

Metre 5: 8.6.8.6.8.6.8.6
A B A B C D C D

200. *The* LORD *bless thee and keep thee.*—[Numbers] vi.24.

Come, Father, Son, and Holy-Ghost,
    One GOD in persons three,
Bring back the heavenly blessing, lost
    By all mankind, and me:
Thy favour, and thy nature too   5
    To me, to all restore,
Forgive, and after GOD renew,
    And keep us evermore.

201. *The LORD make his face shine upon thee, and be gracious*
    unto thee.—vi.25.

> Eternal Sun of righteousness,
>   Display thy beams divine,   *10*
> And cause the glory of thy face
>   Upon my heart to shine;
> Light in thy light O may I see,
>   Thy grace and mercy prove,
> Reviv'd, and chear'd, and blest by thee,   *15*
>   The GOD of pard'ning love.

202. *The LORD lift up his countenance upon thee, and*
    give thee peace.—vi.26.

> Lift up thy countenance serene,
>   And let thy happy child
> Behold without a cloud between
>   The Godhead reconcil'd: *20*
> That all-comprizing peace bestow
>   On me thro' grace forgiven,
> The joys of holiness below,
>   And then the joys of heaven.

11. 1785, &c. (except 1794): 'the glories'.

[CONSECRATION]   **99**

* *Scripture Hymns* (1762), I.194: O.T. 621.
  Scripture Hymns (1794), I.175: O.T. 562.
  Poetical Works, IX.203.
  Collection (1780): No. 414, in two halved verses.
  Pocket Hymn Book (1787): No. 202, as 1780.
  Collection (1831): No. 426, as 1780.
  Collection (1876): No. 426, as 1780.
  MHB (1904): No. 561, as 1780
  MHB (1933): No. 594, as 1780.

Metre 31: 6.6.8.6.6.6.8.6
A B A B C D C D

Who is willing to consecrate his service this day unto the LORD?—[1 Chronicles] xxix.5.

> LORD, in the strength of grace,
>   With a glad heart and free
> Myself, my residue of days,
>   I consecrate to thee;
> Thy ransom'd servant I   *5*
>   Restore to thee thine own,
> And from this moment live, or die,
>   To serve my GOD alone.

6. 1780, &c. (except 1794): 'thy own'.

100 [MY ONLY WISDOM]

* *Scripture Hymns* (1762), I.241: O.T. 757.
  Scripture Hymns (1794), I.216: O.T. 691.
  Poetical Works, IX.260.
  Collection (1780): No. 311.
  Pocket Hymn Book (1787): No. 148.
  Collection (1831): No. 320.
  Collection (1876): No. 320.
  MHB (1904): No. 582.
  MHB (1933): No. 576.

Metre 4: 8 8.6.8 8.6
A A B C C B

Behold, the fear of the LORD, *that is wisdom, and to depart from evil is understanding.*—
[Job] xxviii.28.

1 Be it my only wisdom here
　To serve the LORD with filial fear,
　　With loving gratitude;
　Superior sense may I display
　By shunning every evil way,   *5*
　　And walking in the good.

2 O may I still from sin depart;
　A wise and understanding heart,
　　Jesus, to me be given,
　And let me thro' thy Spirit know   *10*
　To glorify my GOD below,
　　And find my way to heaven.

101 [THAT HAPPIEST PLACE]

* *Scripture Hymns* (1762), I.294–5: O.T. 931.
  Scripture Hymns (1794), I.263–4: O.T. 864.
  Poetical Works, IX.362–3.
  Select Hymns (2nd edn, 1765): No. 145.
  Arminian Magazine (1780 [July]), pp. 399–400.
  Collection (1831): No. 228.
  Collection (1876): No. 228.
  MHB (1904): No. 423.
  MHB (1933): No. 457.

Metre 68: 8.8.8.8.8.8.8.8
A B A B C D C D

*Tell me, O thou whom my soul loveth, where thou feedest, where thou makest thy flock to
rest at noon.*—[Song of Solomon] i.7.

1 Thou Shepherd of *Israel*, and mine,
　The joy and desire of my heart,
　For closer communion I pine,
　　I long to reside where thou art;
　The pasture I languish to find   *5*
　　Where all who their Shepherd obey,
　Are fed, on thy bosom reclin'd,
　　Are skreen'd from the heat of the day.

8. 1831, &c.: 'And screened'.

2 Ah, shew me that happiest place,
   That place of thy people's abode,   *10*
Where saints in an extasy gaze,
   And hang on a crucified GOD:
Thy love for a sinner declare,
   Thy passion and death on the tree,
My spirit to *Calvary* bear,   *15*
   To suffer, and triumph, with thee.

3 'Tis there with the lambs of thy flock,
   There only I covet to rest,
To lie at the foot of the Rock,
   Or rise to be hid in thy breast;   *20*
'Tis there I would always abide,
   And never a moment depart,
Conceal'd in the clift of thy side,
   Eternally held in thy heart.

10. 1831, &c.: 'The place'.
23. 1780 corrects to 'cleft', and is followed by later editions.

[ALPHA AND OMEGA]   102

* *Scripture Hymns* (1762), II.414: N.T. 826.
  Scripture Hymns (1796), II.343–4: N.T. 773.
  Poetical Works, XIII.221.
  Collection (1876): No. 674.
  MHB (1904): No. 121.
  MHB (1933): No. 105.

               Metre 24: 6 6 . 6 6 . 6 6
                      A A B B C C

I am Alpha and Omega, the first and the last.—[Revelation] i.11.

1 Jesus, the first and last,
  On thee my soul is cast:
Thou didst thy work begin
  By blotting out my sin;
Thou wilt the root remove,   *5*
  And perfect me in love.

2 Yet when the work is done,
  The work is but begun:
Partaker of thy grace,
  I long to see thy face: *10*
The first I prove below,
  The last I die to know.

[GOD OF ALL-CREATING GRACE]   103

A group of seven 'Hymns for Children' were included in the *Hymns and Sacred Poems*
of 1742, including 'Gentle Jesus' [No. **27** in this volume q.v.]. Shortly thereafter
Charles Wesley seems to have published a twelve-page tract under this same title
and containing five of the seven hymns of 1742, together with two other hymns each

from the *Collection of Psalms and Hymns* of 1741 and the *Hymns and Sacred Poems* of 1740; the tract closed with some simple guides to the devotional life. Green listed this as No. 99 in his *Wesley Bibliography*, without having seen a copy, and later doubted whether it was actually published by the Wesleys. [For a study of this see *Proceedings* of the Wesley Historical Society, XXXI: 81–5.] The volume of 1763 contains exactly 100 hymns, some of them divided into parts (as is 'Gentle Jesus'), with six of the 1742 group opening a section entitled 'Hymns for the Youngest'. The title-page of later editions bore the additional words, 'and others of riper years'. Actually many of the poems would certainly not be recommended by modern educationists for the use of children, and in particular there is a frequent preoccupation with death, due partly to the high child mortality of the time and the lack of any strong contemporary desire to shield children from contact with death, but also to the sometimes morbid strain in Charles Wesley himself. From this larger volume forty-four hymns were selected (by which of the brothers is uncertain), and published under the same title in 1787. A later edition of this abridgement (which was all that Richard Green had seen, and which he therefore numbered 414), contained the following preface by John Wesley, paying tribute to his brother's approach to children's verse:

'To the Reader:
There are two ways of writing or speaking to children: the one is, to let ourselves down to them; the other, to lift them up to us. Dr Watts has wrote on the former way, and has succeeded admirably well, speaking to children as children, and leaving them as he found them. The following Hymns are written on the other plan: they contain strong and manly sense, yet expressed in such plain and easy language as even children may understand. But when they do understand them, they will be children no longer, only in years and in stature.
    March 27th, 1790.'

* *Hymns for Children* (1763): No. 18.
   Poetical Works, VI.387–8.
   Collection (1780): No. 223.
   Collection (1831): No. 233.
   Collection (1876): No. 233.
   MHB (1904): No. 77.

Metre 52: 7 7.7 7.7 7.7 7
             a a b b c c d d

1 Happy man whom GOD doth aid!
  GOD our soul, and body made,
  GOD on us in gracious showers
  Blessings every moment pours;
  Compasses with angel-bands,   5
  Bids them bear us in their hands:
  Parents, friends, 'twas GOD bestow'd,
  Life, and all descends from GOD.

2 He this flowery carpet spread,
  Made the earth on which we tread,   10
  GOD refreshes in the air,
  Covers with the cloaths we wear,
  Feeds us in the food we eat,
  Cheers us by the light and heat,
  Makes the sun on us to shine;   15
  All our blessings are divine.

  2. 1780, &c.: 'souls and bodies'.
  13. 1780, &c.: 'Feeds us with'.
  14. 1780, &c.: 'his light'.
  15. 1780 (from 2nd edn, 1781), &c.: 'his sun'.

3 Give Him then, and always give
  Thanks for all that we receive:
Man we for his kindness love,
How much more our GOD above?   *20*
Worthy Thou, our heavenly LORD,
  To be honour'd, and ador'd,
GOD of all-creating grace,
Take the everlasting praise.

17. 1780, &c.: 'ever give'.

[IN THE MORNING OF LIFE]   **104**

* *Hymns for Children* (1763): No. 39.
MS Clarke, pp. 140–1: in thirteen half-verses, not including lines 37–9.
MS Richmond, pp. 47–8, as MS Clarke.
Poetical Works, VI.405–7.

Metre 62: 5 5 11.5 5 11
A A A B B B

1   O SAVIOUR of all,
    We come at thy call,
In the morning of life at thy feet do we fall.
    Thy mercy is free;
    Our helplessness see,   *5*
And let little children be brought unto Thee.

2   To us the love shew
    Who nothing do know,
For of such is the kingdom of heaven below:
    O give us thy grace   *10*
    In our earliest days,
And let us grow up to thy honour and praise.

3   But rather than live
    Thy goodness to grieve,
Back into thy hands we our spirits would give: *15*
    O take us away
    In the morn of our day,
And let us no longer in misery stay.

                do
3. MS Clarke: 'T~~ill reed in thy Arms~~ at thy Feet ~~will~~ we'.
       In the morning of Life
5. MS Clarke: Helplessness
       'Our Innocence see'.
12. MSS Clarke, Richmond: 'thy Glory & Praise'.
       Thy Goodness
14. MS Clarke: '~~Our Saviour~~ to grieve'.
17. MSS Clarke, Richmond: 'In the Dawn of our Day'.
       in Misery
18. MS Clarke: '~~from Happiness~~ stay'.

4 If now we remove,
   Thy pity and love   *20*
  Will certainly take us to heaven above:
    With Thee we shall dwell,
    Who hast lov'd us so well:
  For O, wilt Thou send little children to hell?

5 We need not come there,   *25*
   But at death may repair
  To heaven, and heavenly happiness share:
    Us mercy shall raise
    To that happy place,
  And we shall behold with our angels thy face. *30*

6 They now are our guard,
   And ready prepar'd
  To carry us hence to our glorious reward:
    E'er long it shall be;
    We are ransom'd by Thee,   *35*
  And we our all-loving Redeemer shall see.

7 Our bodies are thine
   Our souls we resign
  To be wholly employ'd in the service divine,
    Our spirits we give   *40*
    For Thee to receive:
  O who would not die, with his Saviour to live!

24. MSS Clarke, Richmond:
    'For sure there are no little Children in Hell.'
25–27. MS Clarke has the following as verse 9 (i.e. lines *25–7*) and the
  present lines *25–7* are numbered '~~10~~'. This tentative verse 9 was
  later refashioned to become verse 10:
    '9. ~~Thine Arms shall embrace~~
     ~~Us, who pray for thy Grace~~
    ~~And we shall behold, with our Angels, thy Face.~~
    ~~10.~~ We need not be there
     But die & repair . . .'
  This version of lines *25–6* was followed by MS Richmond.
          Thy
28–9. MS Clarke: '~~Us his~~ mercy shall raise
      Us To that happy place'.
  MS Richmond: 'Us his mercy shall raise
      To that blessed Place'.
35. MS Clarke: 'And we even we'.

AT THE OPENING OF A SCHOOL IN KINGSWOOD   105

Kingswood, near Bristol, was the scene of John Wesley's most famous experiment in education. A school for the children of the colliers had been opened in 1739, but the great venture was the opening of one to give a more advanced education of the 'public school' type, but with a stricter régime and a more evangelical atmosphere than most. (Cf. No. 107.) It is almost certainly for this later school that this poem was written. Kingswood School was removed in 1852 to Lansdowne Hill, Bath.

* *Hymns for Children* (1763): No. 40.
Poetical Works, VI.407–8.

Metre 10: 8.8.8.8.8 8
A B A B C C

1 Come Father, Son, and Holy-Ghost,
   To whom we for our children cry,
The good desir'd and wanted most
   Out of thy richest grace supply,
The sacred discipline be given   5
To train, and bring them up for heaven.

2 Answer on them that end of all
   Our cares, and pains, and studies here,
On them, recover'd from their fall,
   Stampt with the humble character,   10
Rais'd by the nurture of the LORD,
To all their paradise restor'd.

3 Error and ignorance remove,
   Their blindness both of heart and mind,
Give them the wisdom from above,   15
   Spotless, and peaceable, and kind,
In knowledge pure their mind renew,
And store with thoughts divinely true.

4 Learning's redundant part and vain
   Be here cut off, and cast aside: 20
But let them, LORD, the substance gain,
   In every solid truth abide,
Swiftly acquire, and ne'er forego
The knowledge fit for man to know.

5 Unite the pair so long disjoin'd,   25
   Knowledge and vital piety,
Learning and holiness combin'd,
   And truth and love let all men see
In these whom up to Thee we give,
Thine, wholly thine to die and live.   30

6 Father, accept them in thy Son
   And ever by thy Spirit guide,
Thy wisdom in their lives be shewn,
   Thy name confess'd and glorified,
Thy power and love diffus'd abroad,   35
'Till all our earth is fill'd with GOD.

106   FOR THE LORD'S DAY

* *Hymns for Children* (1763): No. 61.
Poetical Works, VI.429–30.
Collection (1876): No. 953.
MHB (1933): No. 661.

Metre 15: 8 8.8 8.8 8
A A B B C C

1 Come, let us with our LORD arise,
 Our LORD who made both earth and skies,
 Who died to save the world He made,
 And rose triumphant from the dead;
 He rose, the Prince of life and peace,   *5*
 And stamp'd the day forever his.

2 This is the day the LORD hath made,
 That all may see his power display'd,
 May feel his resurrection's power,
 And rise again, to fall no more,   *10*
 In perfect righteousness renew'd,
 And fill'd with all the life of GOD.

3 Then let us render Him his own,
 With solemn prayer approach his throne,
 With meekness hear the gospel word,   *15*
 With thanks his dying love record,
 Our joyful hearts and voices raise,
 And fill his courts with songs of praise.

4 Honour and praise to JESUS pay
 Throughout his consecrated day,   *20*
 Be all in JESU's praise employ'd,
 Nor leave a single moment void,
 With utmost care the time improve,
 And only breathe his praise and love.

 8. 1876, &c.: 'his love displayed'.
 14. 1876, &c.: 'the throne'.

107   BEFORE, OR IN THEIR WORK

[Particularly at Kingswood School, near Bristol.]

As noted above (introduction to No. **105**) the régime at Wesley's Kingswood School
was stricter than at most public schools. One of his famous *dicta* occurs in the original
rules: 'We have no play-days . . . neither do we allow any time for play on any day.
He that plays when he is a child will play when he is a man.' The basic alternatives to
sleeping, eating, studying, and worshipping, were walking and working.

* *Hymns for Children* (1763): No. 66.
Poetical Works, VI.434–5.

1   Let heathenish boys
      In their pastimes rejoice,
  And be foolishly happy at play;
      Overstock'd if *they* are,
      We have nothing to spare,   *5*
  Not a moment to trifle away.

2   Our minds to unbend,
      We need not offend,
  Or our Saviour by idleness grieve:
      Whatsoever we do,   *10*
      Our end is in view,
  And to JESUS his glory we live.

3   Recreation of mind
      We in exercise find,
  And our bodily strength is renew'd: *15*
      New employment is ease,
      And our pleasure, to please,
  By our labour a merciful GOD.

4   Our hearts and our hands
      He justly demands,   *20*
  And both to our LORD we resign,
      Overpaid, if He smile
      On our innocent toil,
  And accept as a service divine.

5   In our useful employ   *25*
      We his blessing injoy,
  Whither clearing or digging the ground,
      With songs we proclaim
      Our Immanuel's name,
  And our angels attend to the sound.   *30*

6   The meadow and field
      True pleasure doth yield,
  When to either with JESUS we go:
      Or a paradise find,
      Like the Head of mankind,   *35*
  And our pains on a garden bestow.

7   Howsoever employ'd,
      In the presence of GOD,
  We our forfeited Eden regain,
      And delightfully rise   *40*
      To our LORD in the skies,
  In his fulness of glory to reign.

108   [A CHILD'S DOXOLOGY]

* *Hymns for Children* (1763): No. 99.
  Hymns for Children (1787): No. 44.
  Poetical Works, VI.464–5.

                                          Metre 49: 7 7.7 7.7 7
                                                   a a b b c c

1 Praise the Father for his love,
  CHRIST He sent us from above;
  Publish the Redeemer's praise,
  Bless the Spirit of his grace;
  He reveals the trinity,   5
  Three in one, and one in three.

2 Glory be to GOD alone,
  One in three, and three in one,
  GOD from whom all blessings spring
  Every child of *Adam* sing,   10
  Praise Him all ye heavenly host,
  Father, Son, and Holy-Ghost.

109   [THE DAYSPRING FROM ON HIGH]

* MS Luke, pp. 20–1.
  Poetical Works, XI.114–15.
  Collection (1831): No. 608, entitled 'Christ the Light of the World'.
  Collection (1876): No. 686.
  MHB (1904): No. 137.
  MHB (1933): No. 135.

                                          Metre 10: 8.8.8.8.8 8
                                                   A B A B C C

Through the tender mercy of our God, whereby the day-spring from on high hath visited us.—[Luke 1] v. 78.

1 Stupendous height of heavenly love,
      Of pitying tenderness Divine!
  It brought the Saviour from above,
      It caus'd the Springing Day to shine,
  The Sun of righteousness t'appear,   5
  And gild our gloomy hemisphere.

2 God did in Christ himself reveal
      To chase our darkness by his light,
  Our sin and ignorance dispel,
      Direct our wand'ring feet aright,   10
  And bring our souls with pardon blest
  To realms of everlasting rest.

3 Come then, O Lord, the light impart,
   The faith that bids our terrors cease,
 Into thy love direct my heart,   *15*
   Into thy way of perfect peace,
 And chear my soul of death afraid,
 And guide me thro' the dreadful shade.

4 Answer thy mercy's whole design,
   My God incarnated for me,   *20*
 My spirit make thy radiant shrine,
   My Light and full Salvation be,
 And thro' the dreary vale unknown
 Conduct me to thy dazling throne.

13. 1831, &c.: 'thy light impart'.
15. 1831, &c.: 'direct our heart'.
17, 18. 1831, &c.: 'And cheer the souls . . . And guide them'.
23. 1831, &c.: 'And through the shades of death'.

THE COLLIERS' HYMN   **110**

* *Family Hymns* (1767): No. 124.
MS Richmond, pp. 60–1, set out in 8-lined verses.
Poetical Works, VII.148–9.

Metre 59: 8.3 3.6.8.3 3.6
           a b b a c d d c

1 Teacher, Friend of foolish sinners,
   Take the praise of thy grace
 From us young beginners.
 Struck with loving admiration
   Hear us tell Of thy zeal   *5*
 For our soul's salvation.

2 Foes to God and unforgiven
   Once we were, Distant far,
 Far as hell from heaven:
 But we have thro' Thee found favour,   *10*
   Brought to God By thy blood,
 O Thou precious Saviour.

3 Thou hast in the weak and feeble
   Power display'd, Call'd and made
 Us thy favourite people:
 Us the vulgar, and obscure   *15*
   Thou dost own; Us unknown,
 Ignorant and poor.

147

4 Simple folk and undiscerning,
    Nothing we Know but Thee,   *20*
  Love is all our learning:
We with loving hearts adore thee,
    This our deep Scholarship,
  This is all our glory.

5 Thou, we know, hast died to save us,   *25*
    We are thine, Love Divine,
  Thou who bought'st shalt have us:
Taught and led by thy good Spirit
    We shall soon Share thy throne,
  All thy joys inherit.   *30*

6 Here is knowledge rare, and hidden
    From the wise, Who despise
  All our inward Eden;
Thou to us the truth hast given,
    We in Thee, (Happy we!)   *35*
  Know the way to heaven.

III   [WILL GOD APPEAR TO ME?]

Dr W. F. Moulton (W.H.S. *Proc.* I.26–7) chooses this hymn as an illustration of 'the extent to which the words of Scripture are embedded in the Wesley hymns', tracing references to no fewer than fifty verses of Scripture. Cf. J. W. Waterhouse, *The Bible in Charles Wesley's Hymns*, pp. 14–16.

* *Family Hymns* (1767): No. 161.
  Poetical Works, VII.194–5.
  Collection (1780): No. 124.
  Pocket Hymn Book (1785): No. 47.
  Pocket Hymn Book (1787): No. 64.
  Collection (1831): No. 128.
  Collection (1876): No. 128.
  MHB (1904): No. 151.
  MHB (1933): No. 172, omitting vv. 6, 7.

Metre 1: 8.6.8.6
A B A B

1 With glorious clouds incompast round
    Whom angels dimly see,
Will the Unsearchable be found,
    Or God appear to me?

2 Will He forsake his throne above,   *5*
    Himself to worms impart?
Answer thou Man of grief and love,
    And speak into my heart.

6. 1934: 'Himself to me impart'.
8. 1780, &c.: 'speak it to'.

3 In manifested love explain
    Thy wonderful design,   *10*
What meant the suffering Son of man,
    The streaming blood divine?

4 Didst thou not in our flesh appear,
    And live and die below,
That I may now perceive thee near,   *15*
    And my Redeemer know?

5 Come then, and to my soul reveal
    The heights and depths of grace,
Those wounds which all my sorrows heal,
    That dear disfigur'd face.   *20*

6 Before my eyes of faith confest
    Stand forth a slaughter'd Lamb,
And wrap me in thy crimson vest,
    And tell me all thy name.

7 Jehovah in thy person show,   *25*
    Jehovah crucified,
And then the pard'ning God I know,
    And feel the blood applied:

8 I view the Lamb in his own light
    Whom angels dimly see,   *30*
And gaze transported at the sight
    Thro' all eternity.

15. 1787: 'That I might now'.
19. 1780, &c.: 'The wounds'.
32. 1780, 1785, 1787, 1831: 'To all eternity'.

[DRUDGERY DIVINE]   112

* MS Miscellaneous Hymns, pp. 274–5: No. 2 of 'Hymns for Some called to earn their
  bread'.
MS Charles Wesley, Vol. IV, folio 74, at Methodist Book Room, London.

Metre 64: 5 5.5 11.5 5.5 11
A A B B C C D D

1   Come, let us away,
    And his summons obey,
    Who justly demands
The sweat of our brows, and the work of our hands;
    His acceptable will   *5*
    Let us gladly fulfil,
    And rejoice in the Lord
Whose service on earth is our present reward.

  6. CW. IV: 'With pleasure fulfil'.

2   None on earth can conceive
      How happy we live   *10*
      Who our labour pursue,
    And do unto the Lord whatsoever we do:
      Whene'er with a smile
      He repays all our toil,
      Of his favor possest   *15*
    We an earnest obtain of our heavenly rest.

3   While earning our bread,
      On the mercy we feed
      Of a God reconcil'd,
    The Father of mercies in Jesus the Child;   *20*
      While he deigns to approve
      Our service of love,
      At his glory we aim,
    And present our oblations in Jesus's Name.

4   O Father, impart   *25*
      His grace to my heart,
      To the heart of my friends,
    And companions in toil, till our pilgrimage ends,
      Till our work is all done,
      And receiv'd to thy throne   *30*
      Our Redeemer we see,
    And inherit our fulness of heaven in Thee.

14. CW. IV: 'He or'epays'.
               the
18. CW. IV: 'On ~~his~~ mercy'.
32. CW. IV: 'our heaven of heavens in Thee.'

PART TWO

SACRED POEMS

This poem, in Charles Wesley's favourite metre, was almost certainly written as he was on the verge of his brief and unhappy ministry in Georgia—though the clue in verse 1 ('the bosom of the deep') might fit almost equally well his return from Georgia. His letters to James Hutton on 28th November 1735 (while they were held up at Cowes), and to 'Varanese' on 5th February 1736 (as the *Simmonds* lay off the coast of Georgia) are both filled with the same desperate searching for either spiritual or physical release from life's doubts and darkness. Dr George Osborn points out that in some editions the hymn was entitled 'A Midnight Hymn for one under the Law', but that in [John] Wesley's copy of the 5th edition this was altered to 'A Midnight Hymn for one convinced of Sin'. John Wesley's emendations subtly change the whole character of the hymn.

* *Hymns and Sacred Poems* (1739): pp. 55–7.
   Poetical Works, I.49–51.
   Collection (1780): No. 148, vv. 3–6.
   Collection (1831): No. 154, as 1780.
   Collection (1876): No. 154, as 1780.

Metre 10: 8.8.8.8.8 8
A B A B C C

1 While Midnight Shades the Earth o'erspread,
   And veil the Bosom of the Deep,
Nature reclines her weary Head,
   And Care respires and Sorrows sleep:
My Soul still aims at Nobler Rest,   5
Aspiring to her Saviour's Breast.

2 Aid me, ye hov'ring Spirits near,
   Angels and Ministers of Grace;
Who ever, while you guard us here,
   Behold your Heav'nly Father's Face!   10
Gently my raptur'd Soul convey
To Regions of Eternal Day.

3 Fain would I leave this Earth below,
   Of Pain and Sin the dark Abode;
Where shadowy Joy, or solid Woe   15
   Allures, or tears me from my GOD:
Doubtful and Insecure of Bliss,
Since Death alone confirms me His.[1]

4 Till then, to Sorrow born I sigh,
   And gasp, and languish after Home;   20
Upward I send my streaming Eye,
   Expecting till the Bridegroom come:
Come quickly, Lord! Thy own receive,
Now let me see thy Face, and live.

[1 MS Note by John Wesley: 'No'. See *Poetical Works*, I.50 note.]

13. 1780, &c.: 'Fain would I leave the world below'.
18. 1780, &c.: 'Since faith alone'.

5 Absent from Thee, my exil'd Soul   *25*
   Deep in a Fleshly Dungeon groans;
Around me Clouds of Darkness roll,
   And lab'ring Silence speaks my Moans:
Come quickly, Lord! Thy Face display,
And look my Midnight into Day.   *30*

6 Error and Sin, and Death are o'er
   If Thou reverse the Creature's Doom;
Sad, *Rachel* weeps her Loss no more,
   If Thou the GOD, the Saviour come:
Of Thee possest, in Thee we prove   *35*
The Light, the Life, the Heav'n of Love.

30. 1780, &c.: 'And look my darkness'.
31. 1780, &c.: 'Sorrow, and sin, and death'.
33. 1780 (1st edn): 'Lord, Rachael weeps'.
    1780 (2nd edn, 1781), &c.: 'Sad Rachael weeps'.

114   AFTER A RECOVERY FROM SICKNESS

It seems likely, as Thomas Jackson claims (*Life of the Rev. Charles Wesley*, I.119–24), that this poem was written at Oxford during March 1738, shortly after the author had 'been within the jaws of death' with pleurisy, which forbade his projected return to Georgia. On 23rd March he wrote to James Hutton: 'I am now walking about my Room & may venture out of it in a few days unless prevented by a Relapse. The Doctor tells me he expected at his second visit to have found me Dead, that I must lay asside the Thoughts for Georgia for sometime at least unless I would run upon certain Death.' In his 'extreme pain' Wesley asked Peter Böhler to pray with him, and that the illness was a step onward in Wesley's spiritual progress is hinted at in Böhler's own account—'I prayed with him for the salvation of his soul and body.' Actually, of course, it was not until his later illness in London, in May, that Charles Wesley experienced fully that spiritual release and certainty, the longing for which is expressed in this poem.

* *Hymns and Sacred Poems* (1739), pp. 82–4.
  Poetical Works, I.74–6.

                                Metre 7: 8.8.8.8
                                        A B A B

1 And live I yet by Pow'r Divine?
   And have I still my Course to run?
Again brought back in its Decline
   The Shadow of my parting Sun?

2 Wondring I ask, Is This the Breast   *5*
   Struggling so late and torn with Pain!
The Eyes that upward look'd for Rest,
   And dropt their weary Lids again!

3 The recent Horrors still appear:
   O may they never cease to awe!   *10*
Still be the King of Terrors near,
   Whom late in all his Pomp I saw.

4 Torture and Sin prepar'd his Way,
  And pointed to a yawning Tomb!
  Darkness behind eclips'd the Day,   15
  And check'd my forward Hopes of Home.

5 My feeble Flesh refus'd to bear
  Its strong redoubled Agonies:
  When Mercy heard my speechless Pray'r,
  And saw me faintly gasp for Ease.   20

6 JESUS to my Deliv'rance flew,
  Where sunk in mortal Pangs I lay:
  Pale Death his Ancient Conqu'ror knew,
  And trembled, and ungrasp'd his Prey!

7 The Fever turn'd its backward Course,   25
  Arrested by Almighty Pow'r;
  Sudden expir'd its Fiery Force,
  And Anguish gnaw'd my Side no more.

8 GOD of my Life, what just Return
  Can sinful Dust and Ashes give?   30
  I only Live my Sin to mourn,
  To love my GOD I only Live!

9 To Thee, benign and saving Pow'r
  I consecrate my lengthen'd Days;
  While mark'd with Blessings, ev'ry Hour   35
  Shall speak thy co-extended Praise.

10 How shall I teach the World to love,
  Unchang'd myself, unloos'd my Tongue?
  Give me the Pow'r of Faith to prove,
  And Mercy shall be all my Song.   40

11 Be All my Added Life employ'd
  Thy Image in my Soul to see:
  Fill with Thyself the Mighty Void;
  Enlarge my Heart to compass Thee!

12 O give me, Saviour, give me more!   45
  Thy Mercies to my Soul reveal:
  Alas! I *see* their endless Store,
  Yet O! I cannot, cannot *feel*!

13 The Blessing of thy Love bestow:
  For This my Cries shall never fail;   50
  Wrestling I will not let Thee go,
  I will not, till my Suit prevail.

14 I'll weary Thee with my Complaint;
 Here at thy Feet for ever lie,
With longing sick, with groaning faint: *55*
 O give me Love, or else I die!

15 Without this best, divinest Grace
 'Tis Death, 'tis worse than Death to live;
'Tis Hell to want thy Blissful Face,
 And Saints in Thee their Heav'n receive.   *60*

16 Come then, my Hope, my Life, my Lord,
 And fix in me thy lasting Home!
Be mindful of thy gracious Word,
 Thou with thy promis'd Father, come!

17 Prepare, and then possess my Heart,   *65*
 O take me, seize me from above:
Thee Do I love, for GOD Thou art;
 Thee Do I feel, for GOD is Love!

67–8. It is pure conjecture, but the last two lines are so at variance with
the remainder of the poem that I make the suggestion that Charles
Wesley originally wrote 'Thee would I love . . . feel', and substituted
the word 'Do' when preparing the poem for publication after his
conversion.

115   LOOKING UNTO JESUS

The chief significance of this and the following hymn is that they appear to represent
the introduction into English of a metre borrowed from the German of the Moravian
hymn-book. It became one of the favourite metres of John Cennick, whose best-
known example is 'Ere I sleep, for every favour'. It should be remembered, however,
that although Cennick's first volume of hymns did not appear until 1740, Charles
Wesley had corrected them for the press as early as July 1739, and it seems at least
possible that the urge for writing in this metre came as much from Cennick as from
the *Gesangbuch*. Wesley has two examples in the 1740 volume, this one in the first
part, and 'Praise be to the Father given' in the second part.

* *Hymns and Sacred Poems* (1740), pp. 22–4.
 Poetical Works, I.223–4.

               Metre 58: 8.3 3.6
                  a b b a

1 GOD of Love, incline thine Ear!
  Christ my King,
  Haste and bring
 Thy Salvation near.

2 Thee my restless Soul requires;   *5*
  Restless till
  Thou fulfill
 All its large Desires.

3 Only thou to me be given;
  Thou be mine,
  I resign
 All in Earth and Heaven.   *10*

4 JESUS, come, my Sickness cure;
  Shew thine Art,
  Cleanse a Heart   *15*
 Full of Thoughts impure.

5 Painfully it now aspires
  To be free,
  Full of Thee,
 Full of hallow'd Fires.   *20*

6 Lo, I tread on Deaths and Snares,
  Sinking still
  Into Ill,
 Plung'd in Griefs and Cares.

7 When, O when wilt Thou appear?   *25*
  O draw nigh!
  Say, 'Tis I;
 And I will not fear.

8 Hasten, hasten the glad Hour,
  Come and be   *30*
  Unto me
 Health, and Love, and Power.

9 CHRIST, my Life, my Inward Heaven,
  Thro' the whole
  Of my Soul   *35*
 Spread thy Little Leaven.

10 Make me to the End endure;
  Let me feel
  Love the Seal:
 Love shall make it sure.   *40*

11 Love, thine Image Love restore:
  Let me love,
  Hence remove,
 And be seen no more.

116   HYMN TO THE TRINITY

(See intro. to No. **115**.)

* *Hymns and Sacred Poems* (1740), pp. 101–2.
  Hymns to the Trinity (1746): No. 4.
  Poetical Works, III.346.
  Madan's *Collection* (1760): No. 46.
  Select Hymns (1761): No. 9.

Metre 58: 8.3 3.6
a b b a

1 Praise be to the Father given;
    CHRIST He gave
    Us to save,
  Now the Heirs of Heaven.

2 Pay we equal Adoration   5
    To the Son:
    He alone
  Wrought out our Salvation.

3 Glory to th'Eternal Spirit!
    Us He seals,   10
    CHRIST reveals,
  And applies his Merit.

4 Worship, Honour, Thanks, and Blessing,
    One and Three,
    Give we Thee,   15
  Never, never ceasing.

117   THE HORRIBLE DECREE

The *Hymns on God's Everlasting Love* were published as a counterblast to extreme
Calvinism, and this particular poem was one of the most effective weapons in the
theological warfare. The words employed by Wesley for its title occur frequently
throughout his anti-Calvinist poems. They come from Calvin's *Institutes*, Book III,
chapter xxxiii, sect. 7: 'How is it that the fall of Adam involves so many nations,
with their infant children, in eternal death without remedy, unless that it so seemed
meet to God?... The decree, I admit, is dreadful (*Decretum quidem horribile fateor*);
and yet it is impossible to deny that God foreknew what the end of man was to be
before He made him, and foreknew because He had so ordained by His decree'
(Beveridge's translation, quoted by Dr Osborn in Wesley's *Poetical Works*, III.xviii).

* *Hymns on God's Everlasting Love* (First Series, 1741), pp. 33–6.
  Poetical Works, III.34–8.

Metre 31: 6.6.8.6.6.6.8.6
A B A B C D C D

1   Ah! gentle gracious Dove,
       And art Thou griev'd in me,
     That Sinners should restrain thy Love,
       And say, 'It is not free:
       'It is not free for *All*:   5
       'The *Most*, Thou *passest by*,
     'And mockest with a fruitless Call
       'Whom Thou hast doom'd to die.

2   They think Thee *not sincere*
    In giving Each His Day,
'Thou only draw'st the Sinner near   10
    'To cast him quite away,
    To aggravate his Sin,
    His sure Damnation Seal:
Thou shew'st him Heaven, and say'st, go in—   15
    And thrust's him into Hell.

3   O **Horrible Decree**
    Worthy of whence it came!
Forgive their hellish Blasphemy
    Who charge it on the Lamb:
    Whose Pity him inclin'd   20
    To leave his Throne above,
The Friend, and Saviour of Mankind,
    The GOD of Grace, and Love.

4   O gracious, loving LORD;   25
    I feel thy Bowels yearn;
For those who slight the Gospel-Word
    I share in thy Concern:
    How art Thou griev'd to be
    By ransom'd Worms withstood!   30
How dost Thou bleed afresh to see
    Them trample on thy Blood!

5   To limit Thee they dare,
    Blaspheme Thee to thy Face,
Deny their Fellow-Worms a Share
    In thy redeeming Grace: 35
    All for their own they take,
    Thy righteousness engross,
Of none Effect to most they make
    The Merits of thy Cross.   40

6   Sinners, abhor the Fiend,
    His *other* Gospel hear,
The GOD of Truth did not intend
    The Thing his Words declare,
    He offers Grace to All,
    Which most cannot embrace   45
Mock'd with an ineffectual Call
    And insufficient Grace.

7   *The righteous GOD consign'd*
    Them over to their Doom,
And sent the Saviour of Mankind   50
    To damn them from the Womb;

159

> *To damn for falling short,*
> *Of what they could not do,*
> *For not believing the Report*   55
> *Of that which was not true.*

8   *The* GOD *of Love* pass'd by
> *The most of those that fell,*
> *Ordain'd poor Reprobates to die,*
> *And forc'd them into Hell.*   60
> *He did not do the deed*
> (Some have more mildly rav'd,)
> *He did not* damn *them—but decreed*
> *They never should be saved.*

9   He did not Them bereave   65
> Of Life, or stop their Breath,
> *His Grace He only would not give,*
> *And starv'd their Souls to Death.*
> Satanick Sophistry!
> But still All-gracious GOD,   70
> They charge the Sinner's Death on Thee,
> Who bought'st him with thy Blood.

10   They think with Shrieks and Cries
> To please the LORD of Hosts,
> And offer Thee, in Sacrifice   75
> Millions of slaughter'd Ghosts:
> With New-born Babes they fill
> The dire infernal Shade,
> *For such* they say, *was thy Great Will,*
> *Before the World was made.*   80

11   How long, O GOD, how long
> Shall Satan's Rage proceed!
> Wilt Thou not soon avenge the Wrong,
> And crush the Serpent's Head!
> Surely Thou shalt at last   85
> Bruise him beneath our Feet:
> The Devil, and his Doctrine cast
> Into the burning Pit.

12   Arise, O GOD, arise,
> Thy glorious Truth maintain,   90
> Hold forth the Bloody Sacrifice
> For every Sinner slain!
> Defend thy Mercy's Cause,
> Thy Grace divinely free,
> Lift up the Standard of thy Cross,   95
> Draw all Men unto Thee.

13 O vindicate thy Grace
  Which every Soul may prove,
 Us in thy Arms of Love embrace,
  Of everlasting Love.   *100*
  Give the pure Gospel-Word,
  Thy Preachers multiply,
 Let All confess their Common LORD,
  And dare for Him to die.

14 My Life I here present,   *105*
  My Heart's last Drop of Blood,
 O let it all be freely spent
  In Proof that Thou art Good,
  Art Good to all that breathe,
  Who All may Pardon have: *110*
 Thou willest not the Sinner's Death,
  But all the World *wouldst* save.

15 O take me at my Word,
  But arm me with thy Power,
 Then call me forth to suffer, LORD,
  To meet the fiery Hour: *115*
  In Death will I proclaim
  That all *may* hear thy Call,
 And clap my Hands amidst the Flame,
  And Shout—HE DIED FOR ALL.   *120*

PSALM LXXX   **118**

(Adapted to the Church of England)

* *Collection of Psalms and Hymns* (1743), pp. 14–17.
MS Cheshunt, pp. 72–5.
MS Clarke, pp 80–4.
Poetical Works, VIII.161–5.
Collection of Psalms and Hymns for the Lord's Day (1784) (pp. 339–40 in the 1788
 edn), in two parts comprising vv. 1–4, and 18, 25–7.

Metre 7: 8.8.8.8
ABAB

1 Shepherd of Souls, the Great, the Good,
 Who leadest *Israel* like a Sheep,
 Present to guard, and give them Food,
  And kindly in thy Bosom keep;

      Israel
2. MS Clarke: 'leadest ~~Joseph~~'.

2 Hear thy afflicted People's Prayer,   5
   Arise out of thy holy Place,
 Stir up thy Strength, thine Arm make bare,
   And vindicate thy chosen Race.

3 Haste to our help, thou GOD of Love,
   Supreme Almighty King of Kings,   10
 Descend all-glorious from above,
   Come flying on the Cherubs Wings.

4 Turn us again, O Lord, and shew
   The Brightness of thy lovely Face,
 So shall we all be Saints below,   15
   And sav'd, and perfected in Grace.

5 O Lord of Hosts, O GOD of Grace,
   How long shall thy fierce Anger burn
 Against Thine own peculiar Race
   Who ever pray Thee to return!   20

6 Thou giv'st us plenteous Draughts of Tears,
   With Tears Thou dost thy People feed,
 We sorrow, till thy Face appears,
   Affliction is our Daily Bread.

              vindicate thy Chosen
  8. MS Clarke: 'And ~~magnify thy saving~~ Grace'; MS Cheshunt retains
     'Chosen Grace'.
13–16. MSS Clarke and Cheshunt both contain 28 verses in all, and the
     divergence between the manuscript and published versions com-
     mences here. In the MSS these two verses follow verse 3:

          '4 Turn us again, Thou God of Might,
             The Brightness of thy Face display,
           So shall we walk with Thee in Light,
             As Children of the Perfect Day.

           5 We all shall be thro' Faith made whole,
             If Thou the Healing Grace impart,
           Thy Love shall hallow every Soul,
             And take up every sinless Heart.'

The printed verse 4 is similar to the MS verse 4; in effect, however, it
is an earlier insertion (with the alteration of one word) of the printed
verse 8, which is again repeated as the final verse of the poem.
This insertion in place of the MS verses 4 and 5 involves a net loss
of one verse, so that the printed verse 5 is the MS verse 6, and so
on to the end, where the printed verse 27 is the MS verse 28.

162

7 A Strife we are to All around,   *25*
     By vile intestine Vipers torn,
  Our bitter Hous[e]hold Foes abound,
     And laugh our ~~Fallen~~ Church to scorn.

8 Turn us again, O God, and shew
     The Brightness of thy lovely Face,   *30*
  So shall we all be Saints below,
     And sav'd, and perfected in Grace.

9 Surely, O Lord, we once were Thine,
     (Thou hast for Us thy Wonders wrought)
  A generous and right noble Vine,   *35*
     When newly out of *Egypt* brought.

10 Thou didst the Heathen Stock expel,
     And chase them from their quiet Home,
  Druids, and all the Brood of Hell,
     And Monks of Anti christian *Rome*.   *40*

11 Planted by thine Almighty Hand,
     Watred with Blood, the Vine took Root,
  And spread thoughout the happy Land,
     And fill'd the Earth with golden Fruit.

12 The Hills were cover'd with her Shade,   *45*
     Her branchy Arms extending wide
  Their fair luxuriant Honours spread,
     And flourish'd as the Cedar's Pride.

13 Her Boughs she stretch'd from Sea to Sea,
     And reach'd to frozen *Scotia's* shore,   *50*
  (They once rever'd the Hierarchy,
     And bless'd the Mitre's Sacred Power).

14 Why then hast Thou abhor'd Thine own,
     And cast thy pleasant Plant away:
  Broke down her Hedge, her Fence o'erthrown,   *55*
     And left her to the Beasts of Prey?

15 All that go by pluck off her Grapes,
     Our *Sion* of her Children spoil,
  And Error in ten thousand Shapes
     Would every gracious Soul beguile.   *60*

32. MS Clarke: 'And ~~wholly~~ sav'd'.
43. MSS: 'And spread thro' all'.
46. MSS: 'Her Branching Arms extended wide'.

16 The Boar out of the *German* Wood[1]
   Tears up her Roots with baleful Power;
 The Lion roaring for his Food,
   And all the Forest Beasts devour.

17 Deists, and Sectaries agree,   *65*
   And *Calvin* and *Socinus* join
 To spoil the Apostolic Tree
   And Root and Branch destroy the Vine.

18 Turn Thee again, O Lord our GOD,
   Look down with Pity from above,   *70*
 O lay aside thy vengeful Rod,
   And visit us in pard'ning Love.

19 The Vineyard which thine own right Hand
   Hath planted in these Nations see;
 The Branch that rose at thy Command   *75*
   And yielded Gracious Fruit to Thee:

20 'Tis now cut down, and burnt with Fire.
   Arm of the Lord, awake, awake,
 Visit thy Foes in righteous Ire,
   Vengeance on all thy Haters take.   *80*

21 Look on them with thy flaming Eyes,
   The sin-consuming Virtue dart;
 And bid our fallen Church arise,
   And make us after thy own Heart.

22 To us our Nursing-Fathers raise,   *85*
   Thy Grace be on the Great bestow'd,
 And let the King shew forth thy praise,
   And rise to build the House of GOD.

23 Thou hast ordain'd the Powers that be:
   Strengthen thy Delegate below;   *90*
 He bears the Rule deriv'd from Thee,
   O let him All thine Image shew.

[¹ The Moravians.]

65–9. This verse is omitted from the 1748 and subsequent editions, and
   the following verses are renumbered accordingly.
72. MSS: 'with pard'ning Love.'
88. MSS: 'And gladly build'.

24 Support him with thy guardian Hand,
    Thy royal Grace be seen in Him,
  King of a re-converted Land   *95*
    In goodness as in Power supreme.

25 So will we not from thee go back,
    If Thou our ruin'd Church restore,
  No, never more will we forsake,
    No, never will we grieve thee more.   *100*

26 Revive, O GOD of Power, revive
    Thy Work in our degenerate Days,
  O let us by thy Mercy live,
    And all our Lives shall speak thy Praise.

27 Turn us again, O Lord, and shew   *105*
    The Brightness of thy lovely Face,
  So shall we all be Saints below,
    And sav'd, and perfected in Grace.

94. MS Clarke: 'Let all thy Mind';
                Thy Royal grace
  MS Cheshunt: 'Let all thy mind'.
98. Collection (1784): 'If thou our fallen souls restore'.

PSALM VIII   **119**

* *Collection of Psalms and Hymns* (1743), pp. 66–7.
  Poetical Works, VIII.15–17.

                         Metre 85: 7.6.7.6.7.7.7.6
                             a B a B c d c D

1 Sovereign, Everlasting Lord,
    How excellent thy Name!
  Held in Being by thy Word,
    Thee all Thy Works proclaim:
  Thro' this Earth thy Glories shine,   *5*
    Thro' those dazling Worlds above,
  All confess the Source Divine,
    Th'Almighty God of Love.

2 Thou, the God of Power and Grace
    Whom highest Heavens adore,   *10*
  Callest Babes to sing thy Praise,
    And manifest thy Power:
  Lo! they in thy Strength go on,
    Lo! on all thy Foes they tread,
  Cast the dire Accuser down,   *15*
    And bruise the Serpent's Head.

3 Yet when I survey the Skies
   And Planets as they roll,
Wonder dims my aching Eyes,
   And swallows up my Soul;   *20*
Moon and Stars so wide display,
   Chaunt their Maker's Praise so loud,
Poor insufferable Day,
   And draw me up to God!

4 What is Man, that Thou, O Lord,   *25*
   Hast such Respect to Him!
Comes from Heaven th'incarnate Word,
   His Creature to redeem:
Wherefore would'st Thou stoop so low?
   Who the Mystery shall explain?   *30*
God is Flesh, and lives below,
   And dies for wretched Man.

5 Jesus, his Redeemer dies,
   The Sinner to restore,
Falls that Man again may rise,   *35*
   And stand as heretofore;
Foremost of created Things,
   Head of all thy Works he stood,
Nearest the great King of Kings,
   And *little less than* God![1]   *40*

6 Him with glorious Majesty
   Thy Grace vouchsaf'd to crown,
Transcript of the One in Three,
   He in Thine Image shone:
All thy Works for Him were made,   *45*
   All did to his Sway submit,
Fishes, Birds, and Beasts obey'd,
   And bow'd beneath his Feet.

7 Sovereign, everlasting Lord,
   How excellent thy Name,   *50*
Held in Being by thy Word
   Thee all thy Works proclaim:
Thro' this Earth thy Glories shine,
   Thro' those dazling Worlds above,
All confess the Source Divine,   *55*
   Th'Almighty God of Love.

[1 In the 3rd (1744) and later editions, perhaps in reply to criticisms that the Bible said 'little lower than *the angels*', the following footnote was added: 'So it is in the Hebrew.']

UNIVERSAL R[EDEMPTIO]N   **120**

* MS Thirty, p. 124.

Metre 7: 8.8.8.8
A B A B

1 O All-embracing Love Divine
    O All-illuminating Light,
Throughout the World victorious shine
    Victorious or'e the Shades of Night.

2 The Smoak that issues from the Pit,   *5*
    And darkens Heavens All-chearing Face,
Scatter; & bruise beneath our Feet
    The bold Blasphemer of Thy Grace.

3 Let him blaspheme Thy Grace no more,
Or ~~And~~ mock us while he calls it free,   *10*
Silence his reprobating Roar,
    Cancel his Horrible Decree.

              -ist
4 Drive the Old <u>Fatal</u> ~~Foe~~ to Hell,
    Nor longer let him Refuge take
In Kirk,[a] or School,[b] or Mosque,[c] or Cell,[d]   *15*
    Not ev'n in his own Leman-Lake.[e]

5 Spare the poor Advocates for Sin,
    But let their Master's Kingdom fall,
Destroy the Frogs, the Spirits unclean
    That croak 'Thou didst not die for all.'   *20*

[a] Of Scotland.   [b] of Zeno, ye heathen Philosopher.   [c] Of Mahomet the Impostor.
    [d] of Dominick the Popish Friar—All Predestinarians.   of Geneva.

FROM THE GERMAN   **121–2**

It will be recognized immediately by those who have given any study to the unsolved literary problem of the differentiation of the poetry of John and Charles Wesley that the title 'From the German' for any poem by Charles Wesley threatens to undermine any possibility of such differentiation. Dr Henry Bett, in *The Hymns of Methodism*, has produced by careful research canons of judgement which have in principle been generally accepted. They are based, however, on the assumption that Charles Wesley knew no German, and therefore never translated from that language. Thus any Wesley hymns translated from the Herrnhut *Gesangbuch* or other German source must *ipso facto* be ascribed to John.

From the evidence furnished by Charles Wesley's manuscript hymn-books it is clear that he either did have at least a sufficient smattering of German to enable him to do some translating for himself, or that he transcribed into volumes of what seem otherwise to be his own verses some of his brother's, and was even bold enough to correct them!

This is not the place to enter into a full discussion of the problem, but the basic facts may be stated. It is true that while the Wesley brothers crossed over to Georgia Charles did not see as much of the Moravians as John, and that while John was learning German he (as a newly-ordained minister) was preparing sermons. Nor in Georgia did he come into contact with the Moravians very much. When he wrote to Count Zinzendorf in 1737 it was in Latin, the common language of scholarship, and they conversed in Latin (as did John and the Count). But the subject of Charles's conversations with Zinzendorf was a proposed visit to Germany, which he would hardly attempt without at least a smattering of German. Indeed a basic knowledge seems to have been picked up *via* his elder brother's enthusiasm on board the *Simmonds*. John Wesley, always the leader, would remain the spokesman as well as the more fluent of the two, and we believe that to his hand can be ascribed nearly all, if not quite all of the translations 'from the German'. The very sentences which Dr Bett quoted from John Wesley's Sermon 117, however, in order to prove that John was the translator, can also be used to prove that Charles could speak German, and was therefore a potential translator: 'My brother and I, in our voyage to America, became acquainted with the (so-called) Moravian Brethren . . . Every day *we conversed* with them, and consulted them on all occasions. *I translated* many of their hymns . . .' [The italics are mine.] Cf. Introduction, pp. lviii–lix.

121   THE LIFE OF FAITH

This poem is a free paraphrase of No. 762 in *Das Gesang-Buch der Gemeine in Herrn-Huth* (1737). It is by Wolfgang Christoph Dessler (1660–1722), is founded on Canticles 8.5, and commences: '*Wie wohl ist mir, O Freund der seelen!*' A much more literal (and therefore much clumsier) translation is given in the *Collection of Hymns . . . for the Use of . . . the Brethren's Church* (1754), No. 621.

* *Collection of Moral and Sacred Poems* (1744), III.273–5.
  MS Clarke, pp. 197–8, headed 'From the German'.
  MS Cheshunt, pp. 196–8, indexed as 'From ye German. O how happy am I here',
    but actually torn out.
  Poetical Works, III.167–8.
  Hymns for those to whom Christ is all in all (1761): No. 133.

Metre 47: 7.7.7.7.7 7
a b a b c c

1 O how happy am I here,
   How beyond Expression blest,
When I feel my JESUS near,
   When in JESU's Love I rest,
Peace, and Joy, and Heaven, I prove,   5
Heaven on Earth in JESU's Love.

2 Nothing else but Love I know,
   Worldly Joys and Sorrows end,
Man may rage, my feeble Foe,
   Thou, O JESUS, art my Friend: 10
Man may smile; I trust in Thee:
Thou art all in all to me.

3 Thou my faithful Friend[1] and true
   Reachest out thy gracious Hand:
What can Men or Devils do   15
   While by Faith in Thee I stand?
Stand immoveably secure,
Love hath made my Footsteps sure.

[[1] The *Errata* at the end of Vol. III corrects the misprint 'Freind' to 'Friend'.]

  6. MS Clarke: 'is' is written over 'in'.
  9. 1761: 'Men may'.
                   Men or Devils
15. MS Clarke: 'What can ~~Human Malice~~ do'.

4 Satan stirs a Tempest up,
   Calm I wait till all is past;   *20*
See the Anchor of my Hope
   On the Rock of Ages cast!
Never can that Anchor fail,
Entred now within the Veil.

5 Shouldst Thou o'er the Desart lead,   *25*
   Will me farther Griefs to know,
After Thee with steady Tread
   Leaning on thy Love I'd go,
Drink the Fountain from above,
Eat the Manna of thy Love.   *30*

6 O how wonderful thy Ways!
   All in Love begin and end:
Whom Thy Mercy means to raise
   First thy Justice bids descend,
Sink into themselves, and rise   *35*
Glorious all above the Skies.

7 There I shall my Lot receive,
   Soon as from the Flesh I fly,
Happy in thy Love I live,
   Happier in Thy Love I die;   *40*
Lo! the Prospect opens fair!
I shall soon be harbour'd there.

8 Light of Life, to Thee I haste,
   Glad to quit this dark Abode,
On thy Truth and Mercy cast,   *45*
   Longing to be lost in GOD,
Ready at thy Call to say,
Lo! I come, I come away!

                 wait
20. MS Clarke: 'Calm I ~~rest~~ till'.
          See the Anchor of my
21. MS Clarke: '~~I have now my stedfast~~ Hope'.
24. MS Clarke: 'Enter'd ~~deep~~ within the Vail.'
               now
        O how wonderful
31. MS Clarke: '~~Wonderful are all~~ thy Ways!'
32. MS Clarke: 'All in Love & Mercy end;'
34. MS Clarke: 'First ~~Them~~ thy Justice'.
37–54. MS Clarke: in a smaller hand (still Charles Wesley's), as if squeez-
    ing the verses in, or writing them at a later date.
39. MS Clarke: 'Happy in thy Love I die:'.

9 Ministerial Spirits come,
  Spread your golden Wings for me,   *50*
Waft me to my Heavenly Home,
  Land me in Eternity,
Bear me to my Glorious Rest,
Take me to my Saviour's Breast.

                    golden
50. MS Clarke: '~~Angels~~, spread yr Wings for me'.
54. MS Clarke: 'me' omitted.

122   THE LIFE OF FAITH. Part II.

Although given as 'Part II' of 'The Life of Faith', this is an independent poem in a
different metre. Like the former part it is a free paraphrase of a German hymn,
this time apparently by Christian Friedrich Richter (1676–1711). It begins '*Zeuch hin
mein Geist, in Jesu blut und wunden*', and is given as No. 753 in the *Gesangbuch*
(1737), a translation appearing as No. 633 in the 1754 Moravian Hymn Book. Actually
Wesley concentrates mainly on the first half of the poem, and particularly on verse
three, though there are reminiscences of later verses. Perhaps it should be added
that this 'Blood and Wounds' school of hymn-writing was far from popular with
John Wesley, and it is strange that he was ready to include this example in his *Moral
and Sacred Poems*.

* *Collection of Moral and Sacred Poems* (1744), III.275–8.
  MS Cheshunt, pp. 199–201: headed 'Another' (i.e. 'From the German').
  MS Clarke, pp. 199–201: headed 'Another', as MS Cheshunt.
  Poetical Works, III.168–71.
  Hymns for those to whom Christ is all in all (1761): No. 134.

                       Metre 4: 8 8.6.8 8.6
                         A A B C C B

1 Melt happy Soul, in JESU's Blood,
  Sink down into the Wounds of GOD,
    And there forever dwell:
  I now have found my Rest again,
  The Spring of Life, the Balm of Pain   *5*
    In JESU's Wounds I feel.

2 Thirsty so long, and weak and faint,
  I here enjoy whate'er I want,
    The sweet refreshing Tide
  Brings Life and Peace to dying Souls;   *10*
  And still the gushing Comfort rolls
    From JESU's wounded Side.

3 Swift as the panting Hart I fly,
  I find the Fountain always nigh,
    And Heavenly Sweetness prove,   *15*
  Pardon, and Power, and Joy, and Peace,
  And pure Delight, and Perfect Bliss,
    And everlasting Love.

6. MSS: 'In Jesus' Blood'.
             I find ye Fountain always nigh
14. MS Clarke: '~~I drink, and yet am ever dry,~~';
    MS Cheshunt: 'And find'.

4 The World can no Refreshment give:
  Shall I its deadly Draughts receive,   20
    Scoup'd from the Hellish Lake?
  Nay, but I turn to the pure Flood,
  Which issues from the Throne of GOD,
    And living Water take.

5 Soon as I taste the liquid Life,   25
  Sorrow expires, and Pain, and Strife,
    And Suffering is no more:
  My inmost Soul refresh'd I feel,
  And fill'd with Joy unspeakable
    The bleeding Lamb adore.   30

6 I now the broken Cisterns leave;
  My all of Good from GOD receive,
    And drink the crystal Stream:
  The crystal Stream doth freely flow
  Thro' Hearts which only JESUS know,   35
    And ever pant for Him.

7 JESUS alone can I require,
  No Mixture of impure Desire
    Shall in my Bosom move:
  I fix on Him my single Eye,   40
  His Love shall all my Wants supply,
    His All-sufficient Love.

8 How vast the Happiness I feel,
  When JESUS doth Himself reveal,
    And His pure Love impart,   45
  Holy Delight, and Heavenly Hope,
  And everlasting Joy springs up
    And overflows my Heart.

9 He pours his Spirit into my Soul,
  The thirsty Land becomes a Pool,   50
    I taste the unknown Peace
  Such as the World will not believe;
  No carnal Heart can e'er conceive
    Th'unutterable Bliss.

    Scoup'd
21. MS Clarke: '~~Brought~~ from'.
    Nay, but I turn to
22. MS Clarke: '~~I turn me to~~ ye pure Flood'.
    Cisterns
31. MS Clarke: 'Broken ~~Fountain~~'.
35. MSS: 'And only pant'.
47. 1761: 'spring up', apparently a misprint.
48. MSS: 'And bubbles in my'.

10 Light in thy only Light I see,   *55*
　Thee, and Myself I know thro' Thee,
　　Myself a sinful Clod,
　A worthless worm without a Name,
　A burning Brand pluck'd from the Flame,
　　And quench'd in JESU's Blood.   *60*

11 The Light of thy Redeeming Love,
　Like Sun-beams darted from above
　　Doth all my Sins display,
　Countless as dancing Motes, and small;
　But O! the Love that shews them all,   *65*
　　Shall chase them all away.

12 The Sun of Righteousness shall rise,
　Thy Glory streaming from the Skies,
　　Shall in my Soul appear;
　I know the cloudless Day shall shine,   *70*
　And then my Soul is all-divine,
　　And I am Perfect here.

67–72. MS Clarke: in later hand (still Charles Wesley) and much smaller,
　　though there is plenty of room on the page.
　　　　　　　　　　　　　　　　Cloudless
70. MS Clarke: 'the ~~Perfect~~ *Day'.*
72. MS Clarke: 'And I am ~~Sinless~~ *here'.*
　　　　　　　　　　　　　　　　Perfect

123　　　　　　　FOR A DYING FRIEND

Moral and Sacred Poems (1744): III.278–9.
MS Richmond Tracts; after *Funeral Hymns*, entitled 'For a Dying Believer'.
Poetical Works, III.171–2.
　　　　　　　　　　　　　　　　　　　Metre 45: 7.7.7.7
　　　　　　　　　　　　　　　　　　　　　　a b a b

1 Happy Soul, depart in Peace,
　　Leave awhile thy Friends below,
　JESUS speaks the kind Release,
　　Go, to JESU's Bosom go!

2 Hark, He calls his Exile home   *5*
　　(Joyfully the Call obey)
　Come up hither, quickly come,
　　Rise, my Love, and come away.

3 'I have thy Salvation wrought,
　　I did for thy Guilt atone,   *10*
　Thou art mine, so dearly bought,
　　Thee I challenge for my own.

4 'I ev'n I have purg'd thy Sin,
　　Have for Thee a Place prepar'd;
　Heaven is open, Enter in,   *15*
　　Find in me thy great Reward.

5 'Thee the Purchase of my Blood,
  Thee my Servant, Child, and Bride,
Thee I claim, thy LORD and GOD,
  Who for Thee have liv'd and died.   *20*

6 'Come, thro the dark Valley come!
  Do not I thy Spirit stay?
Fear no Evil, hasten home,
  Rise, my Love, and come away!

20. MS: 'Who for Thee, for Thee have died.'

[THAT LAST TREMENDOUS AGONY]   124

Hymns on the Lord's Supper (1745): No. 6.
Poetical Works, III.220.

                                     Metre 15: 8 8.8 8.8 8
                                               A A B B C C

1 Ah give me, LORD, my Sins to mourn,
My Sins which have thy Body torn,
Give me with broken Heart to see
Thy last tremendous Agony,
To weep o'er an expiring GOD,   *5*
And mix my Sorrow with thy Blood.

2 O could I gain the Mountain's Height,
And look upon that piteous Sight!
O that with *Salem*'s Daughters I
Might stand and see my Saviour die,   *10*
Smite on my Breast and inly mourn,
But never from thy Cross return!

[DEAR, EXPIRING LOVE]   125

This is the first example of this mixed metre in its earlier form. Wesley published
two more examples in *Redemption Hymns* (1747), and one in *Hymns and Sacred Poems*
(1749). In this latter publication he added six examples in which the rhyming pattern
of the closing quatrain was altered from BCBC to BCCB, thus linking by rhyme lines
which were already linked by syllabic length. An early manuscript example of this
form is given as item 237. Wesley discarded the original experimental form for this
variant, of which he published 22 examples, and left about 40 in manuscript.

* *Hymns on the Lord's Supper* (1745): No. 80.
  Festival Hymns (1746): No. 14.
  Poetical Works, III.272.

                                     Metre 79a: 8 7.6.8.8.6
                                                A a B C C B

1 With Pity, LORD, a Sinner see
  Weary of thy Ways and Thee:
    Forgive my fond Despair
A Blessing in the Means to find,
My Struggling to throw off the Care   *5*
    And cast them all behind.

  3. Festival: 'my rash Despair'.

2 Long have I groan'd thy Grace to gain,
   Suffer'd on but all in vain:
     An Age of mournful Years
  I waited for thy passing by,   *10*
  And lost my Prayers, and Sighs, and Tears,
     And never found Thee nigh.

3 Thou wouldst not let me go away;
   Still Thou forcest me to stay.
     O might the Secret Power   *15*
  Which will not with its Captive part,
  Nail to the Posts of Mercy's Door
     My poor unstable Heart.

4 The Nails that fixt Thee to the Tree
   Only They can fasten me:
     The Death thou didst endure   *20*
  For me let it effectual prove:
  Thy Love alone my Soul can cure,
     Thy dear expiring Love.

5 Now in the Means the Grace impart,   *25*
   Whisper Peace into my Heart;
     Appear the Justifier
  Of all who to thy Wounds would fly,
  And let me have my One Desire
     And see thy Face, and die.   *30*

24. Festival: 'Thy balmy bleeding Love.'
30. Festival: 'To taste thy Love, and die.'

126   [ON THE ASCENSION]

* *Hymns for Ascension Day* (1746): No. 4.
  Festival Hymns (1746): No. 12.
  Poetical Works, IV.157–8.

                          Metre 13: 8 8.8.8 8.8
                               A A B C C B

1 Hail, JESUS, hail, our Great High-Priest,
  Enter'd into thy Glorious Rest,
    That Holy Happy Place above!
  Thou hast the Conquest more than gain'd,
  The Everlasting Bliss obtain'd   *5*
    For all who trust thy Dying Love.

3–6. Festival: 'That Holy Blissful Place above;
                  The Conquest Thou hast more than gain'd,
                  The Heavenly Happiness obtain'd
                    For all that trust thy Dying Love.'

2 The Blood of Goats and Bullocks slain
  Could never purge our guilty Stain,
    Could never for our Sins atone;
  But Thou thine own most precious Blood   *10*
  Hast spilt to quench the Wrath of GOD,
    Hast sav'd us by thy Blood alone.

3 Shed on the Altar of thy Cross,
  Thy Blood to GOD presented was
    Thro' the Eternal Spirit's Power: *15*
  Thou didst a spotless Victim, bleed,
  That We from Sin and Suffering freed
    Might live to GOD, and sin no more.

4 That We the Promise might receive,
  Might soon with Thee in Glory live,   *20*
    Thou stand'st before thy Father now!
  For us Thou dost in Heaven appear,
  Our Surety, Head, and Harbinger,
    Our Saviour to the utmost Thou.

5 Not without Blood,—Thou pray'st above: *25*
  The Marks of thy Expiring Love
    GOD on thy Hands ingraven sees!
  He hears thy Blood for Mercy cry,
  And sends his Spirit from the Sky,
    And seals our Everlasting Peace.   *30*

6 Thankful we now the Earnest take,
  The Pledge Thou wilt at last come back
    And openly thy Servants own;
  To Us, who long to see Thee here,
  Thou shalt a second Time appear,   *35*
    And bear us to thy Glorious Throne.

[THE UNIVERSAL SOUL]   **127**

* *Hymns of Petition and Thanksgiving for the Promise of the Father* (1746): No. 28.
Poetical Works, IV.198–9.
Pocket Hymn Book (1785): No. 80.

Metre 13: 8 8.8.8 8.8
A A B C C B

1 Author of every Work Divine
  Who dost thro' both Creations shine,
    The GOD of Nature and of Grace,
  Thy glorious Steps in all we see,
  And Wisdom attribute to Thee,   *5*
    And Power, and Majesty, and Praise.

2 Thou didst thy mighty Wings outspread,
  And brooding o'er the Chaos, shed
    Thy Life into th'impregn'd Abyss,
  The Vital Principle infuse,   *10*
  And out of Nothing's Womb produce
    The Earth and Heaven, and all that Is.

3 That All-informing Breath Thou art
  Who dost Continued Life impart,
    And bidst the World persist to Be: *15*
  Garnish'd by Thee yon azure Sky
  And all those beauteous Orbs on high
    Depend in Golden Chains from Thee.

4 Thou dost create the Earth anew,
  (Its Maker and Preserver too)   *20*
    By thine Almighty Arm sustain;
  Nature *perceives* thy secret Force,
  And still holds on her even Course,
    And owns thy Providential Reign.

5 Thou art the *Universal* Soul,   *25*
  The Plastick Power that fills the whole,
    And governs Earth, Air, Sea, and Sky,
  The Creatures all, thy Breath receive,
  And who by thy Inspiring live,
    Without thy Inspiration die.   *30*

6 Spirit immense, Eternal Mind,
  Thou on the Souls of lost Mankind
    Dost with benignest Influence move,
  Pleas'd to restore the ruin'd Race,
  And new-create a World of Grace   *35*
    In all the Image of thy Love.

18. 1785: 'Descend in golden chains'.

128   FOR A PERSON CALLED FORTH
            TO BEAR HIS TESTIMONY

Edmund Gibson, the learned Bishop of London, in his charge to the clergy of his
diocese published in 1747, called them to the task of 'arming and fortifying their
people against the Moravians or Methodists, and their doctrines.' In a printed reply
John Wesley defended both Methodist practice and Methodist doctrine, and appended
this poem by his brother, in which the basic preaching of the Methodists is set forth.

* *A Letter to the Right Reverend the Lord Bishop of London*, by John Wesley (London,
    1747: Green 103). Poem appended, with no title. Another edn (Dublin, 1748)
    supplies the title 'For a Preacher of the Gospel'. The so-called 2nd edn (Bristol,
    1749) gives the title as above.

Hymns and Sacred Poems (1749), the last item (No. 209) in Vol. I, pp. 330–2,
   with title as above.
Poetical Works, V.134–8.
Hymns for those to whom Christ is all in all (1761): No. 100, vv. 5–9.
Collection (1780): Nos. 427 (vv. 5–7) and 428 (vv. 8–9).
Pocket Hymn Book (1785): No. 164, vv. 5–7.
Collection (1831): Nos. 439, 440, as 1780.
Collection (1876): Nos. 439, 440, as 1780
MHB (1904): No. 595, vv. 8, 9.
MHB (1933): No. 584, as 1904.

Metre 22: 8 8.8.8 8.8 D
A A B C C B

1 O Thou, who at thy Creature's Bar
  Thy glorious Godhead didst declare,
    A true and good Confession make;
  Come in thy Spirit from above,
  And arm me with thy faithful Love,   5
    For thy own Truth and Mercy's Sake.
  Call'd forth by thee, thou know'st, I am,
  Thy Truth and Mercy to proclaim,
    Thy Godhead, and eternal Power,
  The Man whom GOD his Fellow owns,   10
  Whom Angel-Powers, Dominions, Thrones,
    Thro' all Eternity adore.

2 Thee high-inthron'd above all Height,
  Thee GOD of GOD, and Light of Light
    I come undaunted to confess,   15
  With GOD essentially the same,
  JEHOVAH, JAH, the Great I AM,
    The Lord of Hosts, the Prince of Peace:
  The Sovereign everlasting LORD,
  The glorious Unbeginning WORD,   20
    The Son of GOD, the Son of Man,
  GOD over Heaven and Earth supreme,
  Made Flesh thy Creature to redeem,
    For me incarnated, and slain.

3 Slain for a sinful World and me,   25
  Our Surety hung upon the Tree;
    Thy Body bore our guilty Load:
  My Lamb for Sin an Offering made,
  The Debt of all Mankind hath paid,
    And bought, and sprinkled us with Blood.   30
  That Blood applied by Faith I feel,
  And come its Healing Power to tell,
    Through which I know my Sins forgiv'n;
  A Witness I, that all may find
  The Peace deserv'd for all Mankind,   35
    And walk with GOD, my GOD, to Heaven.

4 I come, to testify the Grace
  My Lord obtain'd for all our Race,
    Enough ten thousand Worlds to save:
  Salvation is in JESU's Name,   *40*
  Which every Soul of Man may claim,
    And all that seek, the Grace shall find:
  Salvation from the Power of Sin,
  Salvation from the Root within,
    Salvation into perfect Love,   *45*
  (Thy Grace to all hath brought it near)
  An uttermost Salvation here,
    Salvation up to Heaven above.

5 Thy Power, and saving Grace to shew,
  A Warfare at thy Charge I go,   *50*
    Strong in the LORD, and thy great Might,
  Gladly take up the hallow'd Cross,
  And suffering all Things for thy Cause,
    Beneath that bloody Banner fight.
  A Spectacle to Fiends and Men,   *55*
  To all their fierce or cool Disdain,
    With calmest Pity I submit,
  Determin'd nought to know beside
  My JESUS, and him crucify'd,
    I tread the World beneath my Feet.   *60*

6 Superior to their Smile, or Frown,
  On all their Goods my Soul looks down,
    Their Pleasures, Wealth, and Pomp, and State:
  The Man who dares their GOD despise,
  The CHRISTIAN, he alone is wise,   *65*
    The CHRISTIAN, he alone is great!
  O GOD, let all my Life declare
  How happy all thy Servants are,
    How far above these earthly Things,
  How pure, when wash'd in JESUS' Blood,   *70*
  How intimately one with GOD,
    An Heav'n-born Race of Priests and Kings!

7 For this alone I live below,
  The Power of Godliness to shew,
    The Wonders wrought by JESUS' Name: *75*

42. *HSP* (1749): 'shall have'. The 1748 and 1749 edns of the *Letter* retain
    the unrhyming 'find'.
49. 1780, &c.: 'saving truth'.
54. 1780, &c. (except 1785): 'thy bloody banner'.
63. 1780, &c.: 'power, and state'.
64. *HSP* (1749), &c.: 'the man that dares'.

O that I may but faithful prove,
Witness to all thy pard'ning Love,
  And point them to th'atoning Lamb!
Let me to every Creature cry,
(The Poor, and Rich, the Low, and High,)   *80*
  Believe, and feel thy Sins forgiven:
Damn'd, till by JESUS sav'd, thou art,
Till JESUS Blood hath wash'd thy Heart,
  Thou can'st not find the Gate of Heaven.

8 Thou, JESUS, thou my Breast inspire,   *85*
  And touch my Lips with hallow'd Fire,
    And loose a stammering Infant's Tongue,
  Prepare the Vessel of thy Grace,
  Adorn me with the Robes of Praise,
    And Mercy shall be all my Song.   *90*
  Mercy for those who know not GOD,
  Mercy for all, in JESUS' Blood,
    Mercy, which Earth and Heaven transcends,
  Love that o'erwhelms the Saints in Light,
  The Length and Breadth, and Depth, and Height   *95*
    Of Love Divine, which never ends.

9 A faithful Witness of thy Grace,
  Long may I fill th'allotted Space,
    And answer all thy great Design,
  Walk in the Works by thee prepar'd,   *100*
  And find annex'd the sure Reward,
    The Crown of Righteousness divine.
  When I have liv'd to thee alone,
  Pronounce the welcome Word *well done*,
    And let me take my Place above,   *105*
  Enter into my Master's Joy,
  And all Eternity imploy
    In Praise, and Exstacy, and Love.

76. 1780, &c.: 'O that I might'.
85. *HSP* (1749), &c.: 'Thou, Jesu'.
91. *HSP* (1749), 1761: 'Mercy for those that';
    1780, &c.: 'Mercy for all who'.
93. *HSP* (1749), &c.: 'Mercy that earth'.
98. 1780, &c.: 'Well may I fill'.
101. *HSP* (1749), &c.: 'the vast reward'.

WAITING FOR REDEMPTION   129

* MS Cheshunt, p. 124.
MS Clarke, p. 142.
Poetical Works, XIII.245.

Metre 69: 11 11.11 11
A A B B

1 Brim full of all Evil, & void of all good,
   Heavy laden w[i]th Guilt, & o'erwhelm'd w[i]th the Load,
   At Jesus's Feet a meer Sinner I lie,
   A Sinner at Jesus's Feet cannot die.

2 Sick of every Disease yt a Spirit can know,   5
   I out of myself for a Remedy go;
   The Remedy gushes from Jesus's Side,
   And my Soul sh[al]l be heal'd w[he]n ye Blood is applied.

1. Charles Wesley's index to MS Clarke gives the first line as 'Replete with
   all Evil', while the text itself has 'Brimfull' (as one word).

130   IN TEMPTATION

* MS Cheshunt, pp. 215–16.
  MS Richmond, p. 49.
  Poetical Works, XIII.253.

Metre 60: 8.7.8.7.8.7.8.7
a b a b c d c d

1 Jesus, to Thee I would look up,
   Tost in a Storm of Passion,
   Thou art the Anchor of my Hope,
   Thou art my strong Salvation:
   Pity and save a Soul, distrest   5
   Till I the Port recover;
   O that I in thy Wounds might rest,
   Till all the Storm is over.

2 Great is the Storm that works within,
   Jesus his Grace is greater: 10
   Thou art above the Power of Sin,
   Thou art the GOD of Nature:
   Speak: & at thy supream Command
   Trouble & Sin shall leave me.
   Stir up thy Strength, stretch out thine Hand,   15
   Say 'It is I', and save me.

3 Give me this Hour thy Help to find,
   Shew me thy great Salvation,
   So will I call on All Mankind
   In loving Admiration,   20
   O what a Man, a GOD, is This!
   Nature is still'd before Him,
   Lo! at his Word the Winds & Seas
   Suddenly calm'd adore Him.

15. MS Richmond: 'thy H[an]d'.
19. MS Richmond: 'cry to all Mankind'.
22. MS Richmond: 'is still'.

A HYMN AT THE SACRAMENT

* *A Hymn at the Sacrament* (c. 1746) (12mo, pp. 4).
MS Richmond, pp. 64–5, given as five 8-lined verses.
MS Miscellaneous Hymns, pp. 198–200: No. 3 of eight 'Sacramental Hymns'.
Poetical Works, VIII.441–3.
Collection (1876): No. 910, vv.1–4, 6, 7, 9, 10.

Metre 46: 7 7.7 7
a a b b

1 God of Truth and Power and Grace,
  Drawn by Thee to seek thy Face,
  Lo! I in thy Courts appear,
  Humbly come to meet Thee here;

2 Trembling at thine Altar stand,   *5*
  Lift to Heaven my Heart and Hand,
  Of thy promis'd Strength secure
  All my Sins I now abjure.

3 All my Promises renew,
  All my Wickedness eschew,   *10*
  Chiefly that I call'd my own,
  Now I hate, renounce, disown.

4 Never more will I commit,
  Follow, or be led by it;
  Only grant[1] the Grace I claim,   *15*
  Arm my Soul with Jesus' Name.

5 Sure I am, Thou able art
  To confirm my feeble Heart;
  Yes, Thou wilt from Sin defend,
  Make me faithful to the End.   *20*

6 Sure I am, it is thy Will,
  I shou'd never yield to Ill,
  Never lose thy gracious Power,
  Never sin or grieve Thee more.

7 What doth then my Hopes prevent?   *25*
  Lord, Thou stay'st for my Consent;
  My Consent thro' Grace I give,
  Promise in thy Fear to live.

8 Kept by all-sufficient Grace,
  I will not to Sin give place,   *30*
  I my Bosom Sin abjure,
  Jesus' Blood shall keep me pure.

[1 The misprint 'great' is thus corrected by hand.]

19. MS Richmond: 'Canst from my own sin defend'.
25. MS Misc.: 'What then doth my hopes prevent?'

9 Father, Son, and Holy Ghost,
   Present with thy Angel Host,
   While I at thine Altar bow,   *35*
   Witness to the Solemn Vow!

10 Now admit my bold Appeal,
   Now affix thy Spirit's Seal,
   Now the Power from high be given,
   Register the Oath in Heaven.   *40*

35. 1876: 'thy altar'.

132   MODERN CHRISTIANITY

* MS Richmond, pp. 70–1.

                                        Metre 10: 8.8.8.8.8 8
                                                  A B A B C C

1 How vainly do the Heathen strive
   To falsify our Master's Word,
  Who teach us We may godly live,
     Yet never suffer for our Lord,
  In antient Times the Fact allow,   *5*
  But say The World is *Christian* Now.

2 Christian the World of Drunkards is,
     The World of Whoremongers & Thieves,
  The Slaves of foul & fair Excess,
     Whoe'er the Christian Rite receives,   *10*
  Led from the Font at Satan's Will,
  Haters of Christ, & Christians still.

3 The Devilish, & the sensual Crowd,
     Who as brute Beasts their Lusts obey,
  Lovers of Pleasure more than GOD   *15*
     Who dance, & curse, & fight, & play,
  Monsters of Vice, our Nature's Shame,
  All Hell assumes the Christian Name.

4 Yet still when Antichrist prevails,
     And Satan sits in Moses Chair,   *20*
  The Gospel-Truths are idle Tales,
     No Cross, no Holy Ghost is there,
  The Heathen World will Christian seem,
  And bid us take the Rule from Them.

5 The Temple of the Lord are We,   *25*
     (The Synagogue of Satan th cry)
  We need not persecuted be
     Or cruelly ourselves deny:
  Come see, ye Fools, who sigh & grieve,
  How much at Ease we Christians live.   *30*

6 We are the Men—of Wealth & State,
    Of Pomp, & Fashionable Ease,
Honour, & Power, & Pleasure wait
    The silken Sons of downy Peace,
And lo! we glide secure & even   35
Down a broad flowry Way—to Heav[e]n.

7 While House to House, & Field to Field,
    And Living we to Living join
The gazing Crowd obeysance yield
    And praise the slick & smooth Divine   40
Who saves them all the Madman's Care,
The Drudgery of Faith, & Prayer.

8 No fanciful Enthusiasts we
    To look for Inspiration here,
To dream from Sin to be set free   45
    Or hope to *feel* the Spirit near,
Or *know* our Sins on Earth forgiven,
Or madly give up all for Heaven!

[FORGIVENESS OR VINDICTIVE PRIDE?]   133

This searching analysis of his own sincerity in forgiving his enemies was apparently written in 1748, when he was facing obstacles to his proposed marriage to Sally Gwynne.

* MS Richmond, pp. 99–100.

Metre 10: 8.8.8.8.8 8
ABABCC

1 Try me, O Lord, & search my Heart,
    Nor let me my own Soul deceive,
Tell me, Omniscient as Thou art,
    Do I indeed my Foes forgive,
As GOD in Grace divinely free,   5
Hath for thy sake forgiven me!

2 Is it for thy dear sake alone
    My most injurious Foes I love?
Or aim I at my own Renown,
    And mimick what I must approve,   10
While by a specious show I hide
The Baseness of vindictive Pride.

3 It speaks a weak ignoble Soul
    Injurious Evil to return:
But do I, Lord, my Wrath controul,   15
    With-held by honourable Scorn,
And skilfully my Sore conceal
Too proud to tell the Pain I feel.

4 I am not now condemn'd within,
  Or conscious of the Ill I fear,   *20*
Pure of the Unforgiving Sin,
  Thou knowst *I think* myself sincere:
But make me, Jesus, as Thou art,
But bless me with a simple Heart.

5 O could I view them with *thine* eyes   *25*
  Thine eyes, before they close in death,
Embrace my mortal enemies
  And bless them with my latest breath,
And die, that they may live forgiven,
May follow, whom they send, to heaven.   *30*

134   [JACOB'S LADDER]

* MS Richmond, pp. 105–6, with title 'Sacrament-Hymn'.

Metre 31: 6.6.8.6.6.6.8.6
A B A B C D C D

1   How dreadful is the Place
     Where GOD appoints to meet
Sinners that humbly seek his Face,
     And tremble at his Feet,
     Where to th'Assembled Crowd   *5*
     His Promis'd Grace is given:
This is the solemn House of GOD,
     This is the Gate of Heaven!

2   His Ordinance Divine
     He now vouchsafes to own,   *10*
Blessings herein & Duties join,
     And GOD & Man is One:
     The Sacramental Rite
     Which Jesus Love commands
Heaven & Earth by Faith t'unite   *15*
     Like Jacob's Ladder stands.

3   On this mysterious ~~Rite~~ Tree
     Where our Redeemer hung
Descending & ascending see
     The bright Angelick Throng!   *20*
     They fill the hallow'd Place
     While we his Death record,
And lost in silent wonder gaze
     On our redeeming Lord   expir-

4   By Jesus Cross sustain'd   *25*
     Our souls to Heaven aspire,
Blessings by Jesus Cross descend
     And raise our raptures higher.

184

The Ministers of Grace
Swift to our succour move, 30
Our Guardians fill the middle space
And GOD appears above!

5 He calls us to the skies,
And lo! we spurn the ground,
Light on the sacred Ladder rise, 35
And gain the topmost Round,
~~The~~ Of Everlasting Life
The glorious Pledge is given;
Another Step shall end the Strife,
And lodge us all in Heaven! 40

THE BEATITUDES 135
Matt. v.3–12

* *Hymns and Sacred Poems* (1749), I.35–40: No. 8.
  MS Cheshunt, pp. 155–60, in hand of amanuensis, but numbered and corrected by
  Charles Wesley.
  Poetical Works, IV.317–22.

Metre 96: Trochaic 7's

Who believes the Tidings? Who
Witnesses that GOD is true?
Sees his Sins and Follies more
Than the Sands upon the Shore;
Sees his Works with Evil fraught, 5
All his Life a constant Blot;
Sees his Heart of Virtue void,
Alien from the Life of GOD;
Tastes in every tainted Breath
Pride, and Self, and Sin, and Death! 10

Who, ah, who deserves to feel
Never-ending Pains in Hell?
Conscious owns the just Desert
Of his Life, and of his Heart?
Trembling views his long-sought Hire, 15
Vengeance of Eternal Fire?
Who hath fruitless Toil bestow'd
To appease the Wrath of GOD?
Vain is all thy Toil and Care,
Vain all Nature's Treasures are, 20
More to buy One Soul it cost,
More to save a Spirit lost.

12. MS: 'of Hell.'
21. MS: ''twill cost'.

What then wilt thou, Canst thou do?
Canst thou form thyself anew?
Canst thou cleanse a filthy Heart,   *25*
Life to the Dead Soul impart?
Canst Thou thy lost Powers restore,
Rise, go forth, and Sin no more?

Never, never can it be,
GOD alone can set Thee free!   *30*
GOD alone the Work hath done,
Fought the Fight, the Battle won:
GOD alone the Price hath paid,
All thy Sins on Him were laid.
Happy Soul, from Guilt set free,   *35*
JESUS died for Thee, for Thee!
JESUS does for Thee atone,
Points Thee to th'Eternal Crown,
Speaks to Thee the Kingdom given,
Kingdom of an Inward Heaven,   *40*
Glorious Joy, unutter'd Peace,
All victorious Righteousness.

Why then do thy Fears return?
Yet again why dost thou mourn?
Whence the Clouds that round thee roll?   *45*
Whence the Doubts that tear thy Soul?
Why are all thy Comforts fled?
'Sin revives, and I am dead.'
Dead alas! thou art within,
Still remains the Inbred Sin,   *50*
Dead within thou surely art,
Still unclean remains thy Heart;
Pride and Self are still behind,
Still the earthly Carnal Mind,
The untam'd rebellious Will,   *55*
Foe to Good, inslav'd to Ill;
Still the Nature unrenew'd,
Alien from the Life of GOD.

Mourn awhile for GOD thy Rest,
GOD will soon pronounce Thee blest,   *60*
Soon the Comforter will come,
Fix in Thee his constant Home,
With thy Heart his Witness bear
Strong, and permanent, and clear:

25. MS: 'a spotted Heart'.

All thy Griefs shall then be gone,   *65*
Doubt, and Fear no more be known,
Holy Love thy Heart possess,
Silent Joy, and stedfast Peace,
Peace that never can decay,
Joy that none can take away.   *70*

 Happy Soul, as Silver tried,
Silver seven Times purified,
Love hath broke the Rock of Stone,
All thy Hardness melted down,
Wrath, and Pride, and Hatred cease,   *75*
All thy Heart is Gentleness.
Let the Waves around thee rise,
Let the Tempest threat the Skies,
Calm Thou ever art within,
All unruffled, all serene: *80*
Thy sure Anchor cannot fail,
Enter'd now within the Veil;
Glad this Earth thou canst resign:
The New Heavens and Earth are Thine.

 Why then heave again thy Sighs,   *85*
Heir of all in Earth and Skies?
Still thou feel'st the Root within,
Bitter Root of Inbred Sin;
Nature still in Thee hath Part,
Unrenew'd is still thy Heart,   *90*
Still thy Heart is unrenew'd,
Alien from the Life of GOD:
Hence with secret earnest Moans,
Deep unutterable Groans,
Day and Night thy ceaseless Cries   *95*
To the Mercy Seat arise;
'Come, Thou holy GOD and true!
'Come, and my whole Heart renew;
'Take me now, possess me whole,
'Form the Saviour in my Soul,   *100*
'In my Heart thy Name reveal,
'Stamp me with thy Spirit's Seal,
'Change my Nature into Thine,
'In me thy whole Image shine:
'Bow thine Ear, in Mercy bow,   *105*
'Fill me with thy Fulness now.
Happy Soul, thy Suit is won,
As Thou wilt it shall be done.

69. MS: 'shall decay'.
   all
98. MS: '& my ~~whole~~ Heart'; corrected by Wesley.

187

Happy Soul, who now renew'd,
GOD in Thee, and Thou in GOD,　　　　　　　　　*110*
Only feel'st within thee move
Tenderness, Compassion, Love,
Love immense, and unconfin'd,
Love to All of Humankind,
Love, which willeth All should live,　　　　　　*115*
Love, which All to All would give,
Love, that over All prevails,
Love, that never, never fails:
Stand secure, for Thou shalt prove
All th'Eternity of Love.　　　　　　　　　　　*120*

Happy Soul, from Self and Sin
Clean, ev'n as thy LORD is clean,
GOD hath made thy Footsteps sure,
Purified as He is pure.
GOD thou dost in all Things see;　　　　　　　*125*
GOD is All in All to Thee;
Heaven above, and Earth abroad,
All to Thee is full of GOD.

Happy Soul, whose Active Love
Emulates the Blest above,　　　　　　　　　　*130*
In thy every Action seen,
Sparkling from the Soul within:
Thou to every Sufferer nigh,
Hearest, not in vain, the Cry
Of the Widow in Distress,　　　　　　　　　　*135*
Of the Poor and Fatherless!
Rayment Thou to all that need,
To the Hungry deal'st thy Bread,
To the Sick Thou giv'st Relief,
Sooth'st the hapless Prisoner's Grief,　　　　　*140*
The weak Hands thou liftest up,
Bid'st the helpless Mourners hope,
Giv'st to Those in Darkness Light,
Guid'st the weary Wanderer right,
Break'st the roaring Lion's Teeth,　　　　　　*145*
Sav'st the Sinner's Soul from Death;
Happy Thou, for GOD doth own
Thee, his well beloved Son.

Let the Sons of *Belial* rage,
Let all Hell its Powers engage,　　　　　　　　*150*

125. MS: 'God in all things dost thou see'.
129. MS: 'Happy Thou whose'.
142. MS: 'helpless Mourner'.
150. MS: 'its Power engage'.

Brand with Infamy thy Name,
Put Thee to an open Shame;
Let Earth's Comforts be with-drawn,
Parents, Kindred, Friends be gone;
Naked didst Thou hither come?　　155
Naked let them send thee home:
Happy, O thrice happy Thou,
Seal'd unto Redemption now!
Let thy Soul with Transport swell
Glorious and Unspeakable;　　160
All in Earth Thou well hast given,
GOD is thy Reward in Heaven.

151. MS: 'Cast as Evil out thy Name'.
159. MS: 'with Transports swell'.
161. MS: 'All in Earth well hast Thou given'.

FOR ONE CONVINC'D OF UNBELIEF　**136**

* *Hymns and Sacred Poems* (1749), I.45–6: No. 13, the fifth of ten hymns under the
　same general title.
　Poetical Works, IV.328–9.

Metre 33: 6.6.6.6.4 4.6.4 4.6
A B A B C C D E E D

1 What Tongue alas! can tell
　The Trouble and the Grief,
The Shame and Fear I feel,
　In hopeless Unbelief!
　　In ceaseless Groans　　5
　　My Soul bemoans
　　Its perfect Misery:
　　Thou Pardning GOD,
　　Remove my Load,
　　Or at thy Feet I die.　　10

2 Why should I longer live
　In Unavailing Pain?
Thy Will is not to grieve
　The helpless Sons of Men:
　　Send from above　　15
　　Thy Saving Love,
　　And take me up on high,
　　Thou Pard'ning GOD,
　　Remove my Load,
　　Or at thy Feet I die.　　20

3 What shall a Sinner say
　Thy Pity to incline?
In JESU's Name I pray
　Forgive this Soul of mine,

189

For JESUS' Sake   *25*
    Compassion take,
And freely justify,
    Thou Pardning GOD,
    Remove my Load,
Or at thy Feet I die.   *30*

4 Father of Mercies hear,
    In Answer to my Moan,
Thy helpless Mourner chear,
    And give me to thy Son;
    'Till Thou restore   *35*
    My Peace and Power,
This shall be all my Cry,
    Thou Pardning GOD,
    Remove my Load,
Or at thy Feet I die.   *40*

34. Possibly a misprint for 'And give to me', although the second edition
    (1755) retains the original phrase.

137   [MATCHLESS GRACE]

* *Hymns and Sacred Poems* (1749), I.253–5: No. 151; No. 39 of 'Hymns for
    Believers'.
    Poetical Works, V.58–9.

                                                        Metre 73: 4 4.6.7.5
                                                                A A B a b

1   O Love Unknown!
        GOD's Only Son,
All Earth and Heaven's Desire
        Leaves for me his glorious Throne,
Doth for me expire.   *5*

2   See, Sinners, see
        He dies for me,
For You his Life He pours!
        Blessings rain from yonder Tree
In eternal Showers.   *10*

3   Come catch the Blood,
        And Life of GOD,
And lose your guilty Fears,
        Rise, releas'd from all your Load,
JESUS' Cross appears!   *15*

4   Break Hearts of Stone
        To hear Him groan,
To hear his Dying Prayer,
        Father, look with Pity down,
And my Murtherers spare.   *20*

5   He prays, and cries!
      He bleeds, and dies!
  Appeas'd by sacred Gore
    God accepts his Sacrifice,
  Man is Curst no more.   *25*

6   O matchless Grace!
      The Prince of Peace
  Th'Immortal King of Heav'n
    Suffers in his Murtherers Place,
  And we are all forgiven.   *30*

30. It may be that this last line, the solitary variation from the basic
    pattern of this metre form, suggested the experiment of a poem
    with this as the basic closing line, such as No. **138**. Indeed this line
    not only suggests the closing 6-syllable iambic of the following poem
    (taking 'forgiven' on the analogy of 'Heav'n' as having two syllables
    only) but also the variant 7-syllable iambic with a feminine ending,
    if 'forgiven' is pronounced with three syllables.

[SAVIOUR OF THE DYING THIEF]   **138**

* *Hymns and Sacred Poems* (1749), I.254–5: No. 152; No. 40 of 'Hymns for
    Believers'.
    Poetical Works, V.59–60.

Metre 73a: 4 4.6.7.6
A A B a B

1   O that I cou'd
      Cast all my Load
  Of Guilt and Grief and Care
    On the Sin-atoning God,
  Who hangs expiring there!   *5*

2   O that my Mind
      On Him reclin'd,
  'Till all these Storms are o'er,
    Might abiding Comfort find,
  And disbelieve no more!   *10*

Metre: This is not only a variant of No. 73, in which the last line is iambic
    instead of trochaic. It seems most probable that to Wesley it
    was a variant of No. 74—4 4.7.7.7—the long vowels ending the
    third and fifth lines of each verse being taken as diphthongs, and
    so making the six syllables into seven. (In the poem which follows
    this in *Hymns and Sacred Poems*, and which is in the same basic
    metre, three of the thirteen verses have third and fifth lines of
    seven clear syllables with feminine endings, while the remainder
    end in either diphthongs or long syllables which might be pronounced
    as diphthongs.) It might equally well, therefore, be designated No.
    74a. Cf. Nos. **137, 182**.

3   Thou slaughter'd Lamb,
     If Thine I am,
  Fulfil my Heart's Desire,
    Blow the Spark into a Flame,
  And set me all on Fire.   *15*

4   Look from the Tree,
     As when for me
  Thou didst the Death endure:
    Let thy Blood the Med'cine be,
  And all my Sickness cure.   *20*

5   Pity my Grief,
     And *look* Relief,
  The worst of Sinners spare;
    Saviour of the Dying Thief,
  Regard my latest Prayer.   *25*

6   Regard *thy own*,
     Repeat *'Tis done*,
  Declare my Sins forgiven,
    Ransom'd by thy mortal Groan
  Receive me up to Heaven.   *30*

139   EPITAPH ON MRS SUSANNA WESLEY

On Sunday 1st August 1742, John Wesley's *Journal* records: 'Almost an innumerable company of people being gathered together, about five in the afternoon I committed to the earth the body of my mother.' This was in Bunhill Fields, resting-place of 100,000 Nonconformists, and her headstone pointed out that, good Anglican though she was, she was the child of a famous Nonconformist—'Here lies the Body of Mrs Susannah Wesley, the youngest and last surviving daughter of Dr Samuel Annesley'. She had died on 23rd July just across the way at John Wesley's Foundery Chapel. Although both John Wesley's *Journal* and the headstone used the spelling 'Susannah', Charles followed his mother's own practice of omitting the 'h'.

* *Hymns and Sacred Poems* (1749), I.282: No. 175.
  John Wesley's *Journal*, Part 5 (1749) [Green, 120], p. 57.
  Poetical Works, V.86.
  MS Cheshunt, p. 80.
  MS Clarke, p. 91.

Metre 8: 8 8.8 8
        A A B B

1 In sure and stedfast Hope to rise,
  And claim her Mansion in the Skies,
  A *Christian* here her Flesh laid down,
  The Cross exchanging for the Crown.

Title. MSS Cheshunt, Clarke: 'Epitaph./ For Mrs Susanna Wesley.'
  4. *Journal:* 'a Crown'.

2 True Daughter of Affliction she,   *5*
  Enur'd to Pain and Misery,
  Mourn'd a long Night of Griefs and Fears,
  A Legal Night of Seventy Years.[1]

3 The Father then reveal'd his Son,
  Him in the broken Bread made known,   *10*
  She knew, and felt her Sins forgiven,
  And found the Earnest of *her* Heaven.

4 Meet for the Fellowship above,
  She heard the Call, 'Arise, my Love:
  I come, her Dying Looks replied,   *15*
  And Lamb-like as her LORD she died!

[[1] Mrs Wesley was 73 when she died, and whilst receiving Holy Communion in 1739 had experienced an assurance of her own acceptance with God. Her son seems to have been guilty of exaggeration, however, in speaking of her previous religion as 'a legal night'.]

12. MSS Cheshunt, Clarke: 'And long'd for all her Inward Heaven'; in
    MS Clarke the first six words are erased.

THE TRIAL OF FAITH   140

* *Hymns and Sacred Poems* (1749), II.11–12: No. 7, the seventh of eleven under the
    general title given above.
  Poetical Works, V.149–51.

                                            Metre 10: 8.8.8.8.8 8
                                                      A B A B C C

1 And did my LORD on Earth endure
    Sorrow, and Hardship, and Distress,
  That I might sit me down secure,
    And rest in self-indulgent Ease,
  His delicate Disciple I   *5*
  Like Him might neither live, nor die!

2 Master, I have not learnt Thee so:
    Thy Yoke, and Burthen I receive,
  Resolve in all thy Steps to go,
    And bless the Cross by which I live,   *10*
  And curse the Wisdom from beneath,
  That strives to rob me of thy Death.

3 Thy holy Will be done, not mine,
    Be suffer'd all thy holy Will:
  I dare not, LORD, the Cross decline,   *15*
    I will not *lose* the slightest Ill,
  Or lay the heaviest Burthen down,
  The richest *Jewel* of my Crown.

4 Sorrow is solid Joy, and Pain
  Is pure Delight, endur'd for Thee,   *20*
Reproach and Loss are glorious Gain,
  And Death is Immortality;
And who for Thee their All have given,
Have nobly barter'd Earth for Heaven.

5 Saved is the Life for JESUS lost,   *25*
  Hidden from Earth, but found in GOD,
To suffer is to triumph most,
  The highest Gift on Man bestow'd,
Seal of my sure Election This,
Seal of mine everlasting Bliss.   *30*

6 The Touchstone, and the Proof of Grace,
  The Standard of Perfection here,
The Measure of my Heavenly Place,
  When CHRIST and all his Saints appear,
The Mark Divine, by JESUS Art   *35*
Imprinted on my faithful Heart.

7 O might it deeper sink (but give
  Me Strength thy strongest Love to bear)
Fain would I die with Thee to live,
  Fain would I all thy Passion share;   *40*
To me thy Thorny Crown be given
On Earth, thy glorious Crown in Heaven.

141   THE MARKS OF FAITH

* *Hymns and Sacred Poems* (1749), II.220–2: No. 161, being the first of five poems in
   the same metre and under the same title.
Poetical Works, V.363–5.
Hymns for those to whom Christ is all in all (1761): No. 116.
Collection (1780): No. 93, vv. 1–3, 6–8, altered to SMD by the addition of two
   syllables in the third line and the omission of two in the fifth. By these simple
   but skilfully effected changes John Wesley transformed a 'sacred poem' into a
   stirring hymn.
Collection (1831): No. 96, as 1780.
Collection (1876): No. 96, as 1780.
MHB (1904): No. 359, as 1780, but given in half-verses, using only vv. 1, 2, 6, 8.
MHB (1933): No. 377, as 1904, but using vv. 1–3, 6b, 8a.

Metre 32: 6.6.6.6.8.6.8.6
A B A B C D C D

1   How can a Sinner *know*
           His Sins on Earth forgiven?
         How can my Saviour, shew
           My Name inscrib'd in Heaven?[1]

[¹ The opening lines of the poem are taken up by the closing lines of the second
poem on the same theme, 'How shall a Slave releast', *q.v.*, No. 142.]

3. 1780, &c.: 'How can my gracious Saviour show'.

What we ourselves have felt, and seen,   *5*
  With Confidence we tell,
And publish to the Sons of Men
  The Signs Infallible.

2   We who in CHRIST believe
      That He for us hath died,   *10*
    His unknown Peace receive,
      And feel his Blood applied:
Exults for Joy our rising Soul,
  Disburthen'd of her Load,
And swells, unutterably full   *15*
  Of Glory, and of GOD.

3   His Love, surpassing far
      The Love of all beneath
    We find within, and dare
      The pointless Darts of Death: *20*
Stronger than Death, or Sin, or Hell
  The mystic Power we prove,
And Conquerors of the World we dwell
  In Heaven, who dwell in Love.

4   The *Pledge* of Future Bliss   *25*
      He now to us imparts,
    His gracious Spirit is
      The *Earnest* in our Hearts:
We antedate the Joys above,
  We taste th'Eternal Powers,   *30*
And *know* that all those Heights of Love,
  And all those Heavens are Ours.

5   'Till He our Life reveal,
      We rest in CHRIST secure:
    His Spirit is *The Seal*,   *35*
      Which made our Pardon sure:
Our Sins his Blood hath blotted out,
  And sign'd our Soul's Release:
And can we of his Favour doubt,
  Whose Blood declares us His?   *40*

5. 1780, &c.: omit 'ourselves'.
11. 1780, &c.: 'We all his unknown peace receive'.
13. 1780, &c.: omit 'for Joy'.
19. 1780, &c.: 'We find within our hearts, and dare'.
21. 1780 (2nd edn, 1781), &c.: 'Stronger than death and hell';
    1st edn., 1780, reads 'or hell'.

6   We by his Spirit prove,
       And know the Things of GOD,
     The Things which of his Love
     He hath on us bestow'd:
Our GOD to Us his Spirit gave,   45
     And dwells in Us, we *know*,
The Witness in ourselves we have,
     And all his Fruits we shew.

7   The meek and lowly Heart,
       Which in our Saviour was,   50
     He doth to us impart,
     And signs us with his Cross:
Our Nature's Course is turn'd, our Mind
     Transform'd in all its Powers,
And both the Witnesses are join'd,   55
     The Spirit of GOD with Ours.

8   Whate'er our Pardning LORD
       Commands, we gladly do,
     And guided by his Word,
     We all his Steps pursue: 60
His Glory is our sole Design,
     We live our GOD to please,
And rise with Filial Fear Divine
     To perfect Holiness.

43. 1780, &c.: 'The things which freely of his love'.
45. 1780, &c.: 'His spirit to us he gave'.
48. 1780: 'And all his fruit';
    1831, &c.: 'And all its fruits'.
50. 1780, &c.: 'That in our'.
51. 1780, &c.: 'To us his spirit does impart';
    1831, &c.: 'To us his spirit doth impart'.
53. 1780 (2nd edn, 1781), &c.: 'Our nature's turned, our mind';
    1st edn, 1780, 'our course is turned'.
59. 1780, &c.: 'And guided by his sacred word'.
61. 1780, &c.: 'His glory our design'.

142   [IS MY PARDON SURE?]

One of the chief charges levelled against the early Methodists was that of 'enthusiasm'.
One of the main reasons for making that charge was the Methodist claim that you
could experience 'assurance'—you could *know* that your sins were forgiven by God,
instead of piously hoping that it might be so. Charles Wesley here meets the critic's
argument by the method of *reductio ad absurdum*.

* *Hymns and Sacred Poems* (1749), II.222–4: No. 162, the second of five poems in this
    metre under the title 'The Marks of Faith'.
Poetical Works, V.365–7.
Pocket Hymn Book (1785): No. 17, omitting v. 3.

Metre 32: 6.6.6.6.8.6.8.6
ABABCDCD

1 How shall a Slave releast
   From his oppressive Chain
  Distinguish Ease, and Rest
   From Weariness, and Pain?
Can He his Burthen borne away   *5*
 Infallibly *perceive?*
Or I before the Judgment-Day
 My pardon'd Sin believe?

2 Redeem'd from all his Woes,
   Out of his Dungeon freed,   *10*
  Ask, how the Prisoner knows
   That He is free indeed!
How can He tell the Gloom of Night
 From the Meridian Blaze?
Or I discern the Glorious Light,   *15*
 That streams from JESU's Face?

3 The gasping Patient lies
   In Agony of Pain!
  But see Him light arise,
   Restor'd to Health again!   *20*
And doth He *certainly* receive,
 The Knowledge of his Cure!
And am I *Conscious* that I live?
 And is my Pardon sure?

4 A Wretch for Years consign'd   *25*
   To hopeless Misery,
  The happy Change *must* find,
   From all his Pain set free:
And must not I the Difference know
 Of Joy, and anxious Grief,   *30*
Of Grace, and Sin, of Weal, and Woe,
 Of Faith, and Unbelief?

5 Yes, LORD, I now perceive,
   And bless Thee for the Grace,
  Thro' which redeem'd I live   *35*
   To see thy smiling Face:
Alive I am, who once was dead,
 And freely Justified;
I *know* thy Blood for me was shed,
 I feel it *now* applied.   *40*

6   By Sin no longer bound,
      The Prisoner is set free,
    The Lost again is found
      In Paradise, in Thee:
In Darkness, Chains, and Death I was,   *45*
    But lo! to Life restor'd,
Into thy wondrous Light I pass,
    The Freeman of the LORD.

7   In Comfort, Power, and Peace
      Thy Favour, LORD, I prove,   *50*
    In Faith, and Joy's Increase,
      And self-abasing Love:
Thou dost my pardon'd Sin reveal,
    My Life, and Heart renew;
The Pledge, the Witness, and the Seal   *55*
    Confirm the Record true.

8   The Spirit of my GOD
      Hath certified Him Mine,
    And all the Tokens shew'd
      Infallible, Divine: *60*
Hereby the pardon'd Sinner knows[1]
    His Sins on Earth forgiven,
And thus my faithful Saviour *shews*
    My Name inscrib'd in Heaven.

[1 The closing half of v. 8 takes up the opening lines of the preceding poem on the same theme—'How can a sinner know', *q.v.*, No. **141**.]

60. 1785: 'Infallibly divine'.

143   [TWO SOULS THAT WOULD BE ONE]

This is one of the many poems which Charles Wesley wrote during his courtship of Sarah Gwynne. Originally written on a loose sheet with two others, it was the first of 27 poems transcribed into a manuscript volume (MS Friendship I), from which they were again transcribed, with alterations and additions, into a little volume entitled 'Hymns Sacred to Friendship' (MS Friendship II). From this they were published in the *Hymns and Sacred Poems* of 1749. For its use in Methodist worship generally John Wesley disguised the personal nature of this, as of others of Charles Wesley's love poems, by little touches such as changing 'both' to 'all'.

* *Hymns and Sacred Poems* (1749), II.274–5: No. 199, No. 9 of 'Hymns for Christian Friends'.
  MS in Wesley Family Letters I (Methodist Book Room, London), p. 45, 'To—The Lord my Pasture shall prepare'.
  MS Friendship I, pp. 11–12. Tune as in MS Letters.
  MS Friendship II, p. 9. Tune as in MS Letters.
  Poetical Works, V.418–19.

Collection (1780): No. 499.
Collection (1831): No. 513.
Collection (1876): No. 513.
MHB (1933): Verses No. 45, v. 4 only.

Metre 15: 8 8.8 8.8 8
A A B B C C

1 JESUS, with kindest Pity see
  Two Souls that would be One in Thee,
  If now Accepted in thy Sight,
  Thou dost our upright Hearts unite,
  Allow us, while on Earth to prove,   *5*
  The noblest Joys of Heavenly Love.

2 Before thy glorious Eyes we spread
  The wish which doth from Thee proceed,
  Our Love from Earthly Dross refine,
  Holy, Angelical, Divine   *10*
  Thee let it its great Author shew,
  And back to the pure Fountain flow.

3 A Drop of that unbounded Sea
  O GOD, resorb it into Thee,
  While both our Souls with restless Strife   *15*
  Spring up into Eternal Life,
  And lost in endless Raptures prove
  Thy whole Immensity of Love.

1. 1780: 'Jesu, with';
    MS Letters: 'with kind compassion'.
2. 1780, &c.: 'The souls';
    MS Letters: 'who wd'.
4. MS Letters: 'Our childlike simple Hearts unite';
               Thou dost
    MS Friendship I: 'Our simple ~~childlike~~ Hearts';
    MS Friendship II: 'Thou dost our simple Hearts'.
5. MS Letters: 'And grant us while';
           Allow
    MS Friendship I: '~~And grant~~ us while';
    MS Friendship II: 'Allow us';
    1780, &c.: 'even on earth'.
11. MSS: 'O let it its';
    1831, &c.: 'Thee its great Author let it show'.
14. 1780, &c.: 'O Lord, resorb';
    MS Letters: 'absorb it'.
15. 1780, &c.: 'While all'.
17. MSS Friendship I, II: 'rapture'.
18. 1780 (1st edn): 'The whole', corrected to 'Thy whole' in 2nd edn (1781).

4 A Spark of that Etherial Fire,
　Still let it to its Source aspire,　　　　　　　　　　　20
　To Thee in every Wish return,
　Intensely for thy Glory burn,
　With both our Souls fly up to Thee,
　And blaze thro' all Eternity!

20. MS Letters: 'Still may it'.
21. MS Letters: 'To Heaven in'.
21–2. MS Letters reverses order.
23. 1780, &c.: 'While all our souls'.

144　　　　　　　　　[KINDRED SPIRITS]

* *Hymns and Sacred Poems* (1749), I.279–80: No. 203, No. 13 of 'Hymns for Christian
　　Friends'.
　MS Friendship I, pp. 19–20.
　MS Friendship II, pp. 14–15.
　MS Colman 21, pp. 28–9, but p. 28 is missing.
　Poetical Works, V.422–3.
　Select Hymns (1761): No. 100.
　Collection (1780): No. 496, omitting v. 7.
　Pocket Hymn Book (1787): No. 238, as 1780.
　Collection (1831): No. 510, as 1780.
　Collection (1876): No. 510, as 1780.
　MHB (1904): No. 692, as 1780.
　MHB (1933): No. 716, omitting vv. 3, 7.

　　　　　　　　　　　　　　　　Metre 25: 6.6.6.6.8 8
　　　　　　　　　　　　　　　　　　　　A B A B C C

1　Thou GOD of Truth and Love,
　　We seek thy Perfect Way,
　Ready thy Choice t'approve,
　　Thy Providence t'obey,
　Enter into thy wise Design,　　　　　　　　　　　5
　And sweetly lose our Will in Thine.

2　Why hast Thou cast our Lot
　　In the same Age and Place,
　Or why together brought
　　To see Each other's Face,　　　　　　　　　　　10
　To join with softest Sympathy,
　And mix our friendly Souls in Thee?

Title. This hymn is given as 'IV' in MS Friendship I, and as 'Hymn
　　VIII' in MS Friendship II. Both MSS suggest the tune 'Arise, my
　　Soul, arise'.
4. 1780 (1st & 2nd edns only), 1787: 'The Providence obey'.
9. 1780, &c.: 'And why'.
11. Friendship I: 'To join in Sym with softest Sympathy';
　　1904, &c.: 'To join with loving sympathy'.

3   Didst Thou not make us One,
      That Both might One remain,
    Together travel one,   15
      And bear each other's Pain,
'Till Both Thine utmost Goodness prove,
And rise renew'd in perfect Love.

4   Surely Thou didst unite
      Our kindred Spirits here,
    That Both hereafter might   20
      Before thy Throne appear,
Meet at the Marriage of the Lamb,
And all thy Glorious Love proclaim.

5   Then let us ever bear   25
      The blessed End in view,
    And join with mutual Care
      To fight our Passage thro',
And kindly help Each other on,
'Till Both receive the Starry Crown.   30

6   O might thy Spirit seal
      Our Souls unto That Day,
    With all thy Fulness fill,
      And then transport away,
Away to our Eternal Rest,   35
Away to our Redeemer's Breast.

7   There, only there we shall
      Fulfil thy great Design,
    And in thy Praise with all
      Our Elder Brethren join,   40
And hymn in Songs which never end
Our Heavenly Everlasting Friend.

14. 1780 (1st & 2nd), 1787: 'That all might';
    1780 (3rd edn, 1782), &c.: 'That we might one remain'.
17. Friendship I: 'Till both thy';
    1780, &c.: 'Till all thy'.
21. 1780, &c.: 'That all hereafter might'.
30. 1780, &c.: 'Till all receive'.
31. 1780, &c.: 'O may thy'.
41. Friendship I: 'Songs w[hi]ch ne'er shall end';
    Friendship II: 'Songs yt ne'er shall end'.

[TWO ARE BETTER FAR THAN ONE]   145

This love poem, written during Charles Wesley's courtship of Sally Gwynne, was first sent to her as part of a letter written from Cork on 17th September 1748. He was on the point of setting out for Dublin and thus back to England. The phrases in verse 4 —'interposing oceans roll', 'reaching hearts across the flood'—thus have a particular personal reference which unfitted them for more general congregational use, and the

verse was therefore omitted by John Wesley; at the same time phrases in other
verses were made more general.

* *Hymns and Sacred Poems* (1749), II.309–10: No. 227, being No. 37 of 'Hymns for
Christian Friends'.
MS Letter to Sally Gwynne, 17th September (1748), in volume 'Charles Wesley's
Letters II', p. 49, at Methodist Book Room, London.
MS Friendship I, pp. 59–60, 'To—Lamb of God, whose bleeding Love'.
MS Friendship II, pp. 44–5, tune as Friendship I.
MS Colman 21, p. 22.
Poetical Works, V.452–4.
Collection (1780): No. 475, omitting v. 4.
Pocket Hymn Book (1787): No. 227, as 1780.
Collection (1831): No. 487, as 1780.
Collection (1876): No. 487, as 1780.

Metre 85: 7.6.7.6.7.7.7.6
a B a B c d c D

1 Two are Better far than One
  For Counsel, and for Fight:
How can One be warm alone,
  Or serve his GOD aright?
Join we then our Hearts and Hands,   5
  Each to Love provoke his Friend,
Run the Way of His Commands,
  And keep them to the End.

2 Woe to Him, whose Spirits droop,
  To Him, who falls alone!   10
He has none to lift him up,
  And help his Weakness on:
Happier We Each other keep,
  We Each other's Burthen bear;
Never *need* our Footsteps slip,   15
  Upheld by Mutual Prayer.

3 Who of Twain hath made us One
  Maintains our Unity,
JESUS is the Corner-stone,
  In whom we All agree;   20
Servants of our Common LORD,
  Sweetly of one Heart and Mind,
Who can break a Threefold Cord,
  Or part whom GOD hath join'd?

2. MS Letter, 1780, &c.: 'For Counsel or for'.
6. MS Letter: 'Haste my S[iste]r, D[aughte]r, Friend';
  MS Friendship I: 'Haste my D[aughter], S[ister], F[riend]';
  MS Friendship II: 'Rise my Partner, Bro[the]r, Friend'.
8. 1780, &c.: 'And keep it'.
12. MS Letter: 'Or help';
  1780, &c.: 'To help'.
14. 1780, &c.: 'burdens'.
17. 1780: 'has made'.
20. MS Letter: 'we Both agree'.
21. 1780, &c.: 'one common Lord'.

4 Breath[e]s as in us Both One Soul,   25
   When most distinct in Place,
Interposing Oceans roll,
   Nor hinder our Embrace;
Each as on *his* Mountain stands,
   Reaching Hearts across the Flood,   30
Join our Hearts, if not our Hands,
   And sing the Pardning GOD.

5 O that All with Us might prove
   The Fellowship of Saints!
Find supplied in JESU's Love   35
   What every Member wants!
Gain we our high Calling's Prize,
   Feel our Sins thro' CHRIST forgiven,
Rise, to all his Image rise,
   And meet our Head in Heaven.   40

30. MS Letter: 'Reach our Hearts across'.
37. 1780, &c.: 'Grasp we'.
38. MS Letter, Friendship I, II: 'in Christ forgiven';
   1780, &c.: 'on earth forgiven'.
39. 1780, &c.: 'Rise, in his whole image rise'.

CATHOLICK LOVE   146

* *Catholick Spirit. A Sermon on 2 Kings x.15. By John Wesley* (1755), pp. 29–31, signed
  'C.W.'.
Poetical Works, VI.71–2.

               Metre 10: 8.8.8.8.8 8
                    A B A B C C

1 Weary of all this wordy Strife,
   These Notions, Forms and Modes, and Names,
To Thee, the Way, the Truth, the Life,
   Whose Love my simple Heart inflames,
Divinely taught, at last I fly   5
With Thee, and Thine, to live, and die.

2 Forth from the midst of *Babel* brought,
   Parties and Sects I cast behind,
Inlarg'd my Heart, and free my Thought,
   Where'er the latent Truth I find,   10
The latent Truth with Joy to own,
And bow to JESUS' Name alone,

3 Redeem'd by thine almighty Grace,
   I taste my glorious Liberty,
With open Arms the World embrace,   15
   But *cleave* to those who cleave to Thee,
But only in thy Saints *delight*
Who walk with GOD in purest White.

4 One with the little Flock I rest,
   The Members sound who hold the Head,   *20*
The chosen Few, with Pardon blest,
   And by th'anointing Spirit led
Into the Mind that was in Thee,
Into the Depths of Deity.

5 My Brethren, Friends, and Kinsmen these,   *25*
   Who do my heavenly Father's Will,
Who *aim* at perfect Holiness,
   And all thy Counsels to fulfil,
Athirst to be whate'er Thou art,
And love their GOD with all their Heart.   *30*

6 For these, howe'er in Flesh disjoin'd,
   Where'er dispers'd o'er Earth abroad,
Unfeign'd, unbounded Love I find,
   And constant as the Life of GOD:
Fountain of Life, from thence it sprung,   *35*
As pure, as even, and as strong,

7 Join'd to the hidden Church unknown,
   In this sure Bond of Perfectness,
Obscurely safe, I dwell alone,
   And glory in th'uniting Grace,   *40*
To me, to each Believer giv'n,
To all thy Saints in Earth and Heav'n.

147   ON CHRISTMAS DAY

* MS Festivals: No. 8.

Metre 42: 10 10.10 10.10 10.10 10
      A A B B C C D D

Favour & Peace on Earth & Praise in Heaven!
To us a Son is born, a Child is given!
~~Jehovah~~ To day Jehovah lays aside his Crown,
To day the Saviour of the World comes down,
God over all supream, who all things made,   *5*
Cloath'd with our Flesh, & in a Manger laid,
Is ~~As~~ on this happy Morn to Mortals given:
Favour & Peace on Earth, & Praise in Heaven!

148   [BRUISER OF THE SERPENT'S HEAD]

* *Scripture Hymns* (1762): O.T. 22 (I.9).
  Scripture Hymns (1794): O.T. 21 (I.10).
  Poetical Works, IX.7.

Metre 19: 8 8.8 8.8.8.8.8
A A B B C D C D

It shall bruise thy head.—[Genesis] iii.15.

Awake, the woman's heavenly Seed,
Thou Bruiser of the serpent's head,
Redeem thy creature from his fall,
And crush the fiend that crush'd us all,
That author of our total ill,   5
   That poisoner of the human mind,
Whom in our inmost souls we feel,
   Destroy him out of all mankind.

[THE ORACLES DIVINE]   149

Frequently in his *Short Hymns on Select Passages of the Holy Scriptures* Charles
Wesley presented a series of short hymns, on consecutive verses of Scripture, which
were written in the same metre and actually formed parts of a larger whole. Later
John Wesley extracted some of these from their context in order to provide congregational hymns, of which the following is an example. The six separate hymns are
presented as they appear in the first edition. John Wesley took the last four 'hymns'
(based on a single verse) to form one unit, which was thus printed in the second
edition of the *Scripture Hymns*.

* *Scripture Hymns* (1762): O.T. Nos. 287–92 (I.91–3).
  Scripture Hymns (1794): O.T. Nos. 256–8 (containing the last four verses, 289–92)
    (I.83–4).
  Poetical Works, IX.94–5.
  Collection (1780): No. 319 (containing 289–92 only).
  Pocket Hymn Book (1787): No. 155, as 1780.
  Collection (1831): No. 328, as 1780.
  Collection (1876): No. 328, as 1780.
  MHB (1904): No. 264, as 1780.
  MHB (1933): No. 310, as 1780.

Metre 10: 8.8.8.8.8 8
A B A B C C

287. *These words which I command thee, shall be in thy*
        heart.—[Deuteronomy] vi.6.

The table of my heart prepare,
   (Such power belongs to thee alone)
And write, O GOD, thy precepts there,
   To shew thou still canst write in stone,
So shall my pure obedience prove   5
All things are possible to love.

288. *Thou shalt teach them diligently unto thy children.*
        —[Deuteronomy] vi.7.

Father, instruct my docile heart,
   Apt to instruct I then shall be,
I then shall all thy words impart,
   And teach (as taught myself by thee)   10
My children in their earliest days,
To know, and live the life of grace.

289. *Thou shalt talk of them, when thou sittest in thy
house.*—[Deuteronomy] vi.7.

When quiet in my house I sit,
  Thy book be my companion still,
My joy thy sayings to repeat,   *15*
  Talk o'er the records of thy will,
And search the oracles divine,
'Till every heart-felt word is mine.

290. *And when thou walkest by the way.*—[Deuteronomy] vi.7.

O might the gracious words divine
  Subject of all my converse be,   *20*
So would the LORD his follower join,
  And walk, and talk himself with me,
So would my heart his presence prove,
And burn with everlasting love.

291. *And when thou liest down.*—[Deuteronomy] vi.7.

Oft as I lay me down to rest,   *25*
  O may the reconciling word
Sweetly compose my weary breast,
  While on the bosom of my LORD
I sink in blissful dreams away,
And visions of eternal day.   *30*

292. *And when thou risest up.*—[Deuteronomy] vi.7.

Rising to sing my Saviour's praise,
Thee may I publish all day long,
And let thy precious word of grace
  Flow from my heart, and fill my tongue,
Fill all my life with purest love,   *35*
And join me to thy church above.

18. 1780, 1787, 1831, &c.: 'be mine.'
19. 1780, 1787, 1831, &c.: 'O may'.
21. 1780, 1787, 1831, &c.: 'So will'.
23. 1780, 1787, 1831, &c.: 'So shall'.
36. 1831, &c.: 'to the church above'.

150   [THE PROMISED LAND]

* *Scripture Hymns* (1762): O.T. 352 (I.113–14).
  Scripture Hymns (1794): O.T. 314 (I.102).
  Poetical Works, IX.118.

                   Metre 91: 7 8.7 7.7 7.8 7
                         a A b b c c D d
Moses went up to the top of Pisgah.—[Deuteronomy] xxxiv.1.

Rapt to *Pisgah*'s top, I stand,
And more than see the promis'd land!
Flows the word in milky rills,
Honey from the Rock distils;

Fountains pure of life arise,   5
Flowers, and trees of Paradise;
And heavenly joys on earth I prove:
Heaven on earth is *Jesu*'s love!

[THE JOY OF THE LORD]   151

* *Scripture Hymns* (1762): O.T. 687 (I.215–16).
  Scripture Hymns (1794): O.T. 623 (I.194).
  Poetical Works, IX.225.

Metre 9: 8 8.8 8 8
A A B B B

The joy of the LORD is your strength.—[Nehemiah] viii.10.

This is the joy my soul desires,
The joy my Saviour's love inspires,
Which brings the power that sets me free, ⎞
Power to renounce whate'er is *me*;   ⎟
Power to sell all, and purchase thee.   ⎠   5

[EVIL]   152

* *Scripture Hymns* (1762): O.T. 709 (I.223).
  Scripture Hymns (1794): O.T. 644 (I.200).
  Poetical Works, IX.231.

Metre 77: 7 7.7 7.8 8
a a b b C C

Shall we receive good at the hand of God, and shall we not receive evil?—[Job] ii.10.

Patiently receiv'd from thee,
Evil cannot evil be:
Evil is by evil heal'd;
Evil is but good conceal'd,
And thro' the virtue of thy blood   5
Shall turn to our eternal good.

['O THAT I KNEW WHERE I MIGHT FIND HIM']   153

* *Scripture Hymns* (1762): O.T. 754 (I.240).
  Scripture Hymns (1794): O.T. 688 (I.215).
  Poetical Works, IX.257.

Metre 23: 6.6.6.6
A B A B

O that I knew where I might find him.—[Job] xxiii.3.

Where but on yonder tree?
Or if too rich thou art,
  Sink into poverty,
And find him in thine heart.

154 [THE FURNACE OF DISTRESS]

* *Scripture Hymns* (1762): O.T. 755 (I.241).
  Scripture Hymns (1794): O.T. 689 (I.215).
  Poetical Works, IX.259.

Metre 82: 7.7.7.7.7 8 8
a b a b c C C

When he hath tried me, I shall come forth as gold.—[Job] xxiii.10.

Try me then, and try me still
 In the furnace of distress,
By my own, and others ill,
 By the hidings of thy face;
Yet will I the promise hold   5
Which *Jesus* to my heart hath told,
I shall at last come forth as gold.

155 [SAVE ME]

* *Scripture Hymns* (1762): O.T. 788 (I.253).
  Scripture Hymns (1794): O.T. 722 (I.227–8).
  Poetical Works, IX.275.

Metre 51: 7.7.7.7.7 7.7 7
a b a b c c d d

In thee have I put my trust; save me.—[Psalm] vii.1.

Save me, gracious LORD, for why?
 I believe thou canst, and wilt:
I on thee alone rely;
 Purge, and wash out all my guilt:
Thee for holiness I trust;   5
Make whom thou accountest just:
Thou for me to heaven art gone;
Come, and take me to thy throne.

156 [THE LORD IS KING]

* *Scripture Hymns* (1762): O.T. 847 (I.269).
  Scripture Hymns (1794): O.T. 781 (I.241–2).
  Poetical Works, IX.317.

Metre 3: 4 4.6.4 4.6
A A B C C B

The LORD is king.—[Psalm] xcvii.1.

The LORD is king,
 Rejoice and sing;
My LORD and king thou art,
 Thy Spirit reigns,
 Thy love maintains   5
Its sway within my heart.

[POVERTY AND RICHES]   157

* *Scripture Hymns* (1762): O.T. 917 (I.288).
Scripture Hymns (1794): O.T. 850 (I.259).
Poetical Works, IX.355.

Metre 90: 7 7.7 8.7 7.8 8
a a b B c c D D

Give me neither poverty nor riches.—[Proverbs] xxx.8.

Thou to me, O GOD, hast sent,
Food, and raiment, and content;
Yet for farther grace I sue,
For poverty, and riches too:
　Both, and both at once, I want: 5
　Poverty of spirit grant,
And fill me, Father, from above
With all the riches of thy love.

[THE VOICE OF MY BELOVED!]   158

The first two verses of this series of three seem to have been written during the same rural retirement at Chertsey in April 1751, which gave birth to a number of others based on popular ballads. (See introduction to No. **247.**) In this particular case Charles Wesley wrote in the 12mo volume in which it was inscribed the original upon which it was based, and then the draft of the opening four lines, all in Byrom's shorthand. Then he transcribed the two verses in longhand, and ten years later included them, with an additional verse, in the *Scripture Hymns*. His model ran thus:

How brisk the breath of morning blows,
How sweet the fragrance of the rose,
What lovely verdure crowns the fields
What pure delight the prospect yields.
　Here the shepherd blithe and gay
　Pipes his rural roundelay.

[This ballad is not listed among the 18,000 entries in the *Song Index* and its supplement, by Miss M. E. Sears.]

* *Scripture Hymns* (1762): O.T. 935–7 (I.295–6).
Scripture Hymns (1794): O.T. 867–9 (I.265).
MS Richmond, pp. (151–2) (first two verses only).
Poetical Works, IX.363–4.
Select Hymns (2nd edn, 1765): Nos. 148 (934–5) and 149 (936).
Pocket Hymn Book (1787): No. 204 (Nos. 934–5).

Metre 80: 8 8.8 8.7 7
A A B B c c

934. *The voice of my beloved!*—[Song of Solomon] ii.8.

The voice of my Beloved sounds,
While o'er the mountain-tops he bounds,
He flies exulting o'er the hills,
And all my soul with transport fills!
　Gently doth he chide my stay   5
　'Rise, my love, and come away.'

3. MS Richmond (shorthand draft) has 'He comes exulting'.
4. MS Richmond (shorthand draft and longhand copy) has 'with rapture fills.'

935. *Lo, the winter is past, the rain is gone, &c.*—[Song of Solomon] ii.11.

The scatter'd clouds are fled at last,
The rain is gone, the winter past,
The lovely vernal flowers appear,
The warbling quire enchant our ear: *10*
　　Now with sweetly pensive moan
　　Cooes the turtle-dove alone.

936. *My beloved is mine, and I am his.*—[Song of Solomon] ii.16.

Jesus my love, my life, my peace,
Jesus is mine, and I am his,
His bride, his dear-bought property,   *15*
Who lov'd, and gave himself for me,
　　Joy, and glory of my soul,
　　While eternal ages roll!

　　　　　　　　　　　　　　　invite
10. MS Richmond: 'The feathered Quires enchant our ear,'.

11. In the Richmond MS 'Now' is written in substitution for an erased word beginning 'Th'. The *Scripture Hymns* (1762) actually print lines *11–12* full out, and lines *7–10* indented; in the 1794 edition all six lines are printed full out.

12 In the Richmond MS 'Cooes' is underlined, which means that Wesley intended seeking an alternative word.

159　　　　　　[HEAVENLY INSTINCT]

* *Scripture Hymns* (1762): O.T. 1128 (I.376).
　Scripture Hymns (1794): O.T. 1034 (I.335).
　Poetical Works, IX.454.

　　　　　　　　　　　　　　Metre 17: 8.8.8.8.8.8.8.8
　　　　　　　　　　　　　　　　　　　A B A B C D C D

Who are these that fly as a cloud, and as the doves to their windows?—[Isaiah] lx.8.

Who, what are these, that as a cloud
　Swiftly divide the darkned sky,
Like flocking doves, a countless croud,
　Like doves which to their windows fly!
Weary of wandring after rest,   *5*
　Lo, to the ark, the church, they come,
And housing in their Saviour's breast
　Haste by an heavenly instinct home.

160　　　　　[THE MYSTERY OF INCARNATION]

* *Scripture Hymns* (1762): O.T. 1231 (II.32).
　Scripture Hymns (1796): O.T. 1122 (II.26).
　Poetical Works, X.41.

　　　　　　　　　　　　　　Metre 86: 7.6.7.6.7.8.7.6
　　　　　　　　　　　　　　　　　　　a B a B c D c D

A woman shall compass a man.—[Jeremiah] xxxi.22.

When He did our flesh assume
    That everlasting Man,
Mary held Him in her womb
    Whom heaven could not contain!
Who the mystery can believe?   5
Incomprehensible thou art;
    Yet we still by faith conceive,
      And bear thee in our heart.

[PRAYER]   **161**

* MS Matthew, pp. 47–8.
Poetical Works, X.177.

Metre 10: 8.8.8.8.8 8
           A B A B C C

When ye pray, use not vain repetitions.—[Matthew 6] v. 7.

1 Prayer is the language of the heart,
    By humble faith to Heaven addrest,
Above the studied rules of art,
    And more in groans than words exprest,
Groans by the wrestling Spirit bestow'd,   5
Groans which affect the heart of God.

2 Father, the prayer Thou dost require
    Thro' Jesus I present to Thee,
In vehemence of inflam'd desire,
    In faith's resign'd simplicity,   *10*
In hope thy promis'd grace to prove,
In speechless eloquence of love.

[BUILT ON CHRIST THE ROCK]   **162**

* MS Matthew, 78–9.
  Scripture Hymns (1762): N.T. 96 (II.150), v. 1 only.
  Scripture Hymns (1796): N.T. 85 (II.126), v. 1 only.
  Poetical Works, X.206.
  Arminian Magazine, 1781 (May), p. 288, v. 1 only.

Metre 85: 7.6.7.6.7.7.7.6
           a B a B c d c D

*Whosoever heareth these sayings and doth them I will liken him unto a wise man which
built his house upon a rock, &c.*—[Matthew 7] v. 24, 25.

1 Let the rain descend, the floud
    And vehement wind assail,
Built on an eternal God
    The house can never fail:

Text: Scripture Hymns head the poem: '*It fell not, for it was founded upon
    a Rock.*—vii.25.'
3. *Scripture Hymns, Arm. Mag.:* 'Built on the'.

Built on Christ the Rock it stands: 5
Stablish'd in obedience sure,
Man who keeps his God's commands,
    Shall as his God endure.

2 Who on Jesus' love rely,
    And keep His word of grace,   10
We the rain and storm defy,
    And flouds of wickedness:
Troubles pouring from above,
Men and fiends, like flouds and wind
Never can the house remove,   15
    The soul on Christ reclin'd.

163   ['WHAT MANNER OF MAN IS THIS?']

* *Scripture Hymns* (1762): N.T. 109 (II.153).
  Scripture Hymns (1796): N.T. 95 (II.128).
  MS Matthew, p. 92.
  Poetical Works, X.217.

Metre 26: 6 6.6 6.8 8
A A B B C C

What manner of man is this?—[Matthew] viii.27.

What kind of man is this,
Obey'd by winds and seas,
Whose powerful word controuls
The tempest in our souls!
A Man, who built both earth and sky,   5
A Man, whose name is God most-high!

164A   [MERCY, NOT SACRIFICE]

* *Scripture Hymns* (1762): N.T. 114 (II.154).
  Scripture Hymns (1796): N.T. 100 (II.129).
  Poetical Works, X.223–4.

Metre 18: 8.8.8.8.8 8.8 8
A B A B C C D D

Go ye, and learn what that meaneth, I will have mercy, and not sacrifice.—[Matthew]
ix.12.

To whom should thy disciples go,
    Of whom should they be taught, but thee?
Thy Spirit must thy meaning shew;
    O might he shew it now to me!
Blessings thou dost to sinners *give*,   5
Not sacrifice from us *receive*:
Thy grace to all doth freely move,
Thy favourite attribute is love.

In MS Matthew (p. 100) Charles Wesley rewrote this poem thus:

164B

Metre 10: 8.8.8.8.8 8
A B A B C C

1 To whom should thy disciples go,
   Of whom should they be taught, but Thee?
Thy Spirit doth thy meaning show:
   O might He shew it now to me,
And give my heart to understand   *5*
The new, the old, supremé command.

2 Blessings Thou dost to sinners give,
   Not sacrifice from us require;
Thou wil'st that we should still receive,
   Should after all thy mind aspire.   *10*
And moulded in thine image prove
Thy first, great attribute is Love.

[A WICKED PRIEST]   165

* MS Matthew, p. 112.

Metre 10: 8.8.8.8.8 8
A B A B C C

And Judas Iscariot who also betrayed him, [Matthew 10] v. 4.

1 The wisdom of our Lord would chuse
   A traitor by the fiend possest,
That none the guiltless may accuse,
   Or stumbling at a wicked priest,
Deny the Ministerial call,   *5*
And dare for one to censure all.

2 Whate'er the messenger he sends,
   He gives the efficacious grace:
The word and sacrament depends
   On Christ for its assur'd success,   *10*
Whate'er of good on earth is done
Christ doth it all, and Christ alone.

[SIGNS OF THE SAVIOUR]   166

* *Scripture Hymns* (1762): N.T. 134 (II.160).
Scripture Hymns (1796): N.T. 120 (II.133–4).
MS Matthew, pp. 128–9.
Poetical Works, X.245.

Metre 88: 7 7.7 7.7 7.7 8
a a b b c c d D

Art thou He that should come, or do we look for another?—[Matthew] xi.3.

Give me, Lord, if thou art He,
Deaf to hear, and blind to see,
Lame, to walk in all thy ways,
Dead, to live the life of grace;
Bid my leprosy depart,   5
Preach thyself into my heart;
Satisfied, when thou art given,
I seek no more in earth or heaven.

2. MS Matthew: 'Deaf, to hear, and blind, to see'.

167   [LEARN OF ME]

* *Scripture Hymns* (1762): N.T. 143 (II.162).
 Scripture Hymns (1796): N.T. 129 (II.135).
 Poetical Works, X.255.

Metre 48: 7 7.7.7.7.7
a a b c b c

Learn of me.—[Matthew] xi.29.

LORD, I fain would learn of thee
Meekness and humility;
In thy gentleness of mind
 In thy lowliness of heart
Rest mine inmost soul shall find,   5
 Rest that never can depart.

168   [HE ANSWERED NOTHING]

* *Scripture Hymns* (1762): N.T. 262 (II.194).
 Scripture Hymns (1796): N.T. 245 (II.163).
 Poetical Works, X.419.

Metre 29: 6 6.6 6.6 6.8 8
A A B B C C D D

He answered nothing.—[Matthew] xxvii.12.

Speechless the Saviour stood
Beneath my guilty load,
He answer'd not, for I
Have nothing to reply:
But when condemn'd and dumb   5
I before God become,
His mouth is open'd then for me,
His blood proclaims the sinner free.

169   [NUNC DIMITTIS]

* MS Luke, pp. 32–3.

Metre 35: 7.6.7.6.7.6.7.6
A B A B C D C D

Lord, now lettest thou thy servant depart in peace, &c.—[Luke 2] v. 29–32.

1 Father, since Thou permittest
    A weary soul's release,
And for thy presence fittest,
    I now depart in peace.
With joyful consolation   5
    I out of life depart
For I have seen Salvation,
    Have felt Him in my heart.

2 Thine image & thy favor
    With Jesus is restor'd,   10
And shewing me my Sav[iou]r,
    Thou hast perform'd thy word,
Hast recompens'd my patience
    With Jesus Xt, design'd
Thy Blessing to the nations,   15
    Thy Gift to all mankind.

3 Jesus thine Heir Anointed
    The common Sav[iou]r is,
Light of the world appointed,
    And Israel's glorious bliss: 20
Illumin'd by his Spirit
    I find my way to Thee,
And die, O Lord, t'inherit
    The joys prepar'd for me.

[AMBITION'S UTMOST HEIGHT]   **170**

Although Charles Wesley believed in the possibility of achieving the spiritual condition of 'Christian perfection' or 'perfect love', and continually prayed for it, he became very disgusted with the many unworthy claimants to that grace. He believed that his brother John was much too credulous about those who claimed that they had obtained this 'second blessing', and pointed out that it could not exist together with pride, especially pride in the experience itself.

* MS Luke, pp. 51–2.

Metre 4: 8 8.6.8 8.6
A A B C C B

He set him on a pinnacle of the temple.—[Luke 4] v. 9.

1 Ah, wretched souls, who lifted up
    By Satan to the temple's top,
        The highest, holiest place,
Look down with scorn on all below,
Your own superior virtue *show*,   5
        Your own consummate grace!

2 Whom God exalts, he humbles too:
    But devilish pride hath blinded you
        Who your perfection boast:
The fiend hath set you up on high,   10
And casts you down in sin to die,
        To die forever lost.

215

3 While ye on ruin's verge ye stand,
  Beneath Jehovah's mighty hand
    Your towering selves abase;   15
  Cast yourselves down at Jesus' word,
  Own, ye vile worms, before the Lord
    Your utter sinfulness.

4 Crawl on the earth, nor ever more
  At Satan's instigation soar   20
    Above the clouds to sit;
  Humility your whole delight,
  And your ambition's utmost height
    To weep at Jesus' feet.

171   [FORGIVENESS]

* *Scripture Hymns* (1762): N.T. 327 (II.215).
  Scripture Hymns (1796): N.T. 306 (II.181–2).
  MS Luke, pp. 86–7.
  Poetical Works, XI.155–6.
  Collection (1876): No. 830, vv. 1, 2, 4.

Metre 10: 8.8.8.8.8 8
A B A B C C

Forgive, and ye shall be forgiven.—[Luke] vi.37.

1 Forgive my foes? it cannot be:
    My foes with cordial love embrace?
  Fast bound in sin and misery,
    Unsav'd, unchang'd by hallowing grace,
  Throughout my fallen soul I feel   5
  With man this is impossible.

2 Great Searcher of the mazy heart,
    A thought from thee I would not hide,
  I cannot draw th'envenom'd dart,
    Or quench this hell of wrath and pride,   10
  Jesus, till I thy Spirit receive,
  Thou know'st, I never can forgive.

3 Come, Lord, and tame the tiger's force,
    Arrest the whirlwind in my will,
  Turn back the torrent's rapid course,   15
    And bid the headlong sun stand still,
  The rock dissolve, the mountain move,
  And melt my hatred into love.

4 Root out the wrath thou dost restrain;
    And when I have my Saviour's mind,   20
  I cannot render pain for pain,
    I cannot speak a word unkind,
  An angry thought I cannot know,
  Or count mine injurer my foe.

[THE MISSION OF CHRIST] 172

* MS Luke, p. 99.

Metre 17: 8.8.8.8.8.8.8.8
A B A B C D C D

The blind see, the lame walk, &c.—[Luke 7] v. 22.

On us, O Christ, thy mission prove,
  Thy full authority to heal,
The blindness of our hearts remove,
  The lameness of our feeble will,
Open our faith's obedient ear,   5
  Our filthy, leprous nature cure,
Call us out of the sepulchre,
  And preach Perfection to the poor.

[DAVID'S SON, AND SOVEREIGN LORD] 173

* MS Luke, pp. 293–4.

Metre 75: 6 6.7.7.7.7
A A b c b c

David therefore calleth him Lord; how is he then his Son?—[Luke 20] v. 44.

1   In Jesus Christ we see
      The depths of deity,
Compound strange of God and man,
    Creature and Creator join'd!
Who the myst'ry can explain   5
    Fathom the eternal Mind?

2   Lowliness meets in Him
      With majesty supreme,
Poor, dependant, and unknown,
    Scorn'd on earth, by heaven ador'd,
David's uncreated Son,   10
    David's Son, and sovereign Lord.

3   Wisdom and Power Divine
      Unfold his love's design,
Bid us stedfastly believe,
    God became the Son of man,   15
That we may this life retrieve,
    Sons of God with Jesus reign.

4   Lord, we with joy confess
      The myst'ry of thy grace:
God and man because Thou art,   20
    God and man shall still agree;
God and man no more shall part,
    One in all thy saints, and me.

174   [BLIND I FOLLOW ON]

* *Scripture Hymns* (1762): N.T. 436 (II.252).
Omitted from *Scripture Hymns* (1796).
MS John, p. 146.
Poetical Works, XI.419.

Metre 94: 7 7.7 7.7 7.8 8 8
a a b b c c D D D

He that followeth Me, shall not walk in darkness.—[John] viii.12.

Jesus, I believe in thee,
Yet my way I cannot see,
Yet I cannot see thy face,
Dark, and dead, and comfortless:
But if blind I follow on,   5
Trusting in thy word alone,
I cannot long in darkness stay,
The darkness must be chas'd away,
And turn'd into the perfect day.

6. MS. John alters to 'Feeling for the God unknown'.
8. MS. John alters to 'It must at last be chas'd away'.

175   ['I AM THE DOOR']

* *Scripture Hymns* (1762): N.T. 440 (II.253).
Scripture Hymns (1796): N.T. 411 (II.212).
(MS John (p. 194) uses this as the basis for verse two of a poem in three verses in the
metre 8 8.6D, No. 4. *Poetical Works* (XI.458) publishes this complete poem, but
omits the original verse[1]).

Metre 84: 6 6.7 7.6.8 8.6
A A b b C D D C

I am the door: by me, if any man enter in, he shall be saved.—[John] x.9.

Then I may happy be,
I enter in by thee:
Thro' thine interceding blood
Free access I have to God,
His dear adopted son: 5
The blood shall all my wants supply,
And bear me up beyond the sky
To that eternal throne.

[1] The verse as re-shaped for this later poem runs thus:

Through Thee and Thine atoning blood
I come with free access to God,
His dear adopted son:
Thy blood shall all my wants supply,
And bear me up beyond the sky
To that eternal throne.

[NATURE'S NIGHT] **176**

* MS John, pp. 251–2.
Poetical Works, XI.495–6.

Metre 17: 8.8.8.8.8.8.8.8
A B A B C D C D

He hath blinded their eyes, and hardened their hearts; that they should not see, &c.—
[John 12] v. 40.

He offer'd them sufficient light
   Which when they could, but would not see,
He left them in their nature's night,
   Their unbelief's obscurity:
He offer'd them his soft'ning grace,   5
               scorn'd to
And when its power they ~~would not~~ feel
Forsook the sick self-harden'd race
Who would not suffer him to heal.

[I HAVE CHOSEN YOU] **177**

* *Scripture Hymns* (1762): N.T. 471 (II.261).
Scripture Hymns (1796): N.T. 442 (II.219).
Poetical Works, XII.27–8.
MS John, p. 313, with a varied ending.

Metre 76: 7.7.7.7.8 8
a b a b C C

Ye have not chosen Me, but I have chosen you.—[John] xv.16.

   Thee we never could have chose,
      Dead in sins and trespasses:
   But thou hast redeem'd thy foes,
      Bought the universal peace,
That all our ransom'd race might prove   5
The sweetness of electing love.

5–6. MS John omits these two lines, and by substituting the following
   makes a stanza of the more normal metre 50:
         That our whole apostate kind,
           Might receive thee from above,
         Call'd our common Lord to find
           Sav'd by free electing love.

[BEARING WITNESS] **178**

* *Scripture Hymns* (1762): N.T. 474 (II.262).
Scripture Hymns (1796): N.T. 445 (II.219–20).
MS John, pp. 320–1.
Poetical Works, XII.33.

Metre 27: 6.6.6.6.6.6.6.6
A B A B C D C D

And ye also shall bear witness, because ye have been with me from the beginning.—
[John] xv.27.

Thy weak disciple I,
    Jesus, for years have been:
Thee let me testify
    The Truth, that frees from sin,
The Wisdom from above,   5
    The Life to mortals given,
The Power of perfect Love,
    The Way to God in heaven.

179   [THE ATONEMENT]
* MS John, p. 398.

Metre 10: 8.8.8.8.8 8
A B A B C C

Behold, I bring him forth to you, that ye may know that I find no fault in him.—[John 19]
v. 4.

1 If the just God himself consent
    That thou should'st be entreated so,
Thou must deserve the punishment
    For crimes which Pilate doth not know,
The crimes which only God can find,   5
The crimes of me, & all mankind.

2 Thee, innocent in deed & thought,
    Th'unrighteous judge is forc'd to clear;
Yet burthen'd with another's fault
    Thou bear'st the sinner's character,   10
And suffer'st, guiltless, on the tree,
That God may find no fault in me.

180   [RABBONI!]
* MS John, pp. 426-7.
Poetical Works, XII.104-5.

Metre 80: 8 8.8 8.7 7
A A B B c c

Jesus saith unto her, Mary: She turned herself & saith unto him, Rabboni, which is to say,
Master.—[John 20] v. 16.

1 It is the voice of my Belov'd,
My fears are fled, my griefs remov'd,
He calls a sinner by his name,
And He is mine, & his I am!
    Jesus, by a word made known   5
    Thee my gracious Lord I own.

2 My gracious Lord, I know, Thou art,
The lawful Master of my heart,
I feel thy resurrection's power,
And joyful at thy feet adore;   10
    ~~Here~~ Now
    ~~Yes~~; I only live to prove
    Thou art God, & God is Love.

[THE HAPPY SHORE]   **181**

* MS John, p. 443.
Poetical Works, XII.115.

Metre 79: 8 7.6.8 8.6
     A a B C C B

But when the morning was now come, Jesus stood on the shore.—[John 21] v. 4.

1 See a rough draught of human life!
    All is one continued strife,
      Fatigue, & misery!
A night of perilous distress,
Without relief, without success,   5
      We tempt the stormy sea.

2 But when the dreary hour is o're,
    Jesus on the happy shore
      Shall satisfy our need,
Shall bless us with the sight of God,   10
      imperishable
And with ~~the true celestial~~ food
      raptured spirits
    Our ~~souls for ever~~ feed.

['FEED MY SHEEP']   **182**

* MS John, pp. 455–6.

Metre 74: 4 4.7.7.7
     A A B a B

[*Feed my lambs: feed my sheep.*—(John 21) vv. 15, 16.]

II

1   Words cannot prove
      That Thee I love
My soul's eternal Lover;
    Actions must the doubt remove,
And all my soul discover.   5

2   Fill'd may I be
      With charity
And carry in my bosom
    The dear lambs redeem'd by thee,
And rather die than lose 'em.   10

3   By pangs extreme
      Thou didst redeem
The flock of thine election:
    Let me give this proof supreme
Of my unfeign'd affection.   15

4   ~~Arm'd with thy mind~~
    ~~I come resign'd~~

    By thee renew'd
    Thou Shepherd good
I can thy cross endure,
    Strive resisting unto blood
With love divinely pure.   *20*

5   Arm'd with thy mind
    I come resign'd
A rival of thy passion,
    Lose my life with joy, to find
The God of my salvation.   *25*

6   Now, dearest Lord,
    Let fire or sword
My soul & body sever,
    Give me but that parting word,
'I love my God for ever!'   *30*

16. Apparently in error, Charles Wesley commenced verse 4 with the first two lines of verse 5, and then struck them out to write 'By thee renew'd', &c.

183   [DIVINE EPITOME]

* MS Acts, p. 24.
Poetical Works, XII.147.

Metre 79: 8 7.6.8 8.6
A a B C C B

Whosoever shall call on the name of the Lord, shall be saved.—[Acts 2] v. 21.

1 In this divine epitome,
    Father, we thy goodness see,
      Who kindly dost declare
The way thro' which to heaven we go,
And all our duty here below   *5*
      Summ'd up in faith and prayer.

2 Father, the promis'd bliss I claim,
    Thee invoke in Jesus' name;
      For Jesus' sake forgive,
Save me from sin, and earth & hell,
Stamp with thy hallowing Spirit's seal,   *10*
      And to thy throne receive.

[THE CRUCIFIED IS KING]   **184**

* MS Acts, p. 553.
MS *Scriptural Hymns* (1783), p. 9.
Poetical Works, XII.150–1.

Metre 12: 8.8.8.8.10 12
A B A B C C

*Let all the house of Israel know assuredly, that God hath made that same Jesus whom ye
have crucified, both Lord and Christ.*—[Acts] 2.36. ˙

1   Let the whole house of Israel know
        Jehovah hath extol'd his Son,
     That Jesus crucified below
        Who laid the general ransom down,
His Father hath supremely magnified,   *5*
And raised him up to sit in triumph at his side.

2   All power He to the Man hath given,
        That ye may surely know and praise
     The glorious Lord of earth & heaven
        Sublime in majesty and grace,   *10*
Him Prophet, Priest, and King with rapture own,
And shout your God restor'd to his eternal throne.

3   Jesus, if Thou the faith impart,
        Assur'd we of thy Godhead are,
     We find Thee praying in our heart,   *15*
        We hear our heavenly Teacher there,
Thy partners in celestial places sit,
And reign with the Most-high—adoring at thy feet!

12.   MS Scriptural Hymns: 'And shout our God return'd'.

[JESUS' MEANEST WITNESSES]   **185**

* MS Acts, pp. 62–3.
Poetical Works, XII.174.

Metre 86: 7.6.7.6.7.8.7.6
a B a B c D c D

*When they perceived that they were unlearned & ignorant men, they marvelled, and they
took knowledge of them, that they had been with Jesus.*—[Acts 4] v. 13.

1   Weakness still with ignorance
        And poverty combin'd
     Triumph or'e the boasted sense
        And wisdom of mankind,
Grandeur, wealth, & power subdue,   *5*
        ' self maintains
For Jesus ~~undertakes~~ our cause,
        Jesus, who the world or'ethrew
        While bleeding on his cross.

2   Men in every age are seen
        By grace Divine employ'd,   *10*
    Simple, rude, unletter'd men,
        And only taught of God:
    Sent into the world we go,
  And gather souls on every side,
        Nothing else resolv'd to know   *15*
        But Jesus crucified.

3   Let the great & wise confess
        From whence our boldness flows,
    Jesus' meanest witnesses
        We cannot dread our foes;   *20*
    Men who have with Jesus been,
  And at his mouth receiv'd his word,
        Conquerors of the world & sin
        We only fear the Lord.

186   [JESUS' WITNESSES]

* MS Acts, pp. 72–3.

                       Metre 34: 6.6.8.6.6.6.8.6 D
                         A B A B C D C D

And with great power gave the Apostles witness of the resurrection of the Lord Jesus
—[Acts 4] v. 33.

1   Where is that ancient power
    Which did the Lord reveal,
  And spake him more than conqueror
    Or'e death, & earth, & hell!
    While men by Jesus chose   *5*
    Were bold to testify
  He died to pay our debt, and rose
    To ~~clear us from~~ the sky: / fit us for
    He rose himself, to raise
    His creatures from their fall,   *10*
  He sits at God's right-hand, & prays,
    Demanding life for all:
    The Spirit of life he gives
    In sinners hearts to dwell;
      still   ~~still who~~
  And <u>he</u> who hears with faith, receives   ~~hears~~   *15*
    This Gift unspeakable.

2   Our record is the same,
    Our testimony's sure,
        ~~you~~ day
  The gospel we to ~~do~~ / proclaim
    Shall evermore endure: *20*

Who minister the word
Are Jesus' witnesses,
And still we preach our risen Lord,
The Prince of life & peace:
High on his Father's throne   25
Forgiveness to confer,
He sends the promis'd Blessing down,
Th'abiding Comforter!
His power, & peace, & love
Our cancel'd sin attest,   30
And heaven is open'd from above
In every faithful breast.

[HEALING FOR THE MULTITUDE]   187

* MS Acts, p. 83.
Poetical Works, XII.186–7.

Metre 64: 5 5.5 11.5 5.5 11
A A B B C C D D

*There came a multitude out of the cities round about unto Jerusalem, bringing sick folk,
and them which were vexed with unclean spirits: and they were healed every one.—*
[Acts 5] v. 16.

1 When the gospel of grace
   Is proclaim'd in our days,
         all
   From ~~the~~ places around
What a multitude flock to the life-giving sound!
   To the church they repair;   5
   For Jesus is there
   In his virtue to heal,
And ready his love in their hearts to reveal.

2 The desperate crowd
   With infirmities bow'd,   10
   Sick of every sin,
         vex'd
And ~~possest~~ with a legion of spirits unclean
   The Physician attend,
   And his goodness commend,
   Who his patients relieves,   15
And a pardon to all the incurable gives.

[DEACONS' ORDERS]   188

Like his brother John, Charles Wesley was a keen student of the Apostolic Church,
and anxious that there should be a revival of 'primitive Christianity'. Again like his
brother, he seems to have been convinced (probably by Lord King's *Primitive Church*
and Stillingfleet's *Irenicum*) that bishops and presbyters were essentially of the same
order, and that normally the congregation also were intimately concerned in the choice

of clergy. He refused, however, to follow Stillingfleet (and John Wesley himself) in taking the further step that 'in cases of necessity' presbyters could ordain without authorization by a bishop.

In this poem and Nos. **189** and **198** we find Charles Wesley speaking of presbyteral ordination and using respectively the terms 'priest', 'presbyter', and 'elder'—yet with no mention at all of 'bishop', unless one takes as such the phrase 'Apostolic hands' in this one poem.

* MS Acts, pp. 100–1.

Metre 10: 8.8.8.8.8 8
A B A B C C

*Wherefore, brethren, look out among you seven men of honest report, full of the holy Ghost,
and wisdom, whom we may appoint over this business.*—[Acts 6] v. 3.

1 O that with ancient harmony
   Pastors & flock might still combine,
In choice of officers agree,
   Of servants for the work divine,
Pursue the Apostolic plan;   5
The church present, the priest ordain!

2 The people should look out & find
   Not children weak, but solid men,
Whose judgment & experience join'd
   Throughout their spotless life is seen,   10
Men from among themselves alone,
Whose truth and ways to all are known.

3 Not of a blemish'd character
   The sacred candidates should be,
But irreproachably sincere   15
   Adorn'd with genuine piety,
Fill'd by the Spirit of holiness,
And led by him in all their ways.

4 But piety cannot suffice,
   Unless both gifts & graces meet;   20
The deacons should be grave & wise,
   Prudent, deliberate, and discreet,
Appointed, when their trial's past,
By Apostolic hands at last.

5 Ordain'd to long laborious pain,   25
   They then their one great work fulfil,
Tend the poor sinsick souls of men,
   Exert their utmost strength & skill
Themselves the least & meanest call,
Servants & ministers of all.   30

[APOSTOLIC ORDINATION]   189

(See Introduction to No. **188**.)

* MS Acts, p. 103.

Metre 86: 7.6.7.6.7.8.7.6
a B a B c D c D

*Whom they set before the Apostles: and when they had prayed, they laid their hands on
them.—[Acts 6] v. 6.*

Each presents the officers,
    And makes the choice his own;
All unite in faithful prayers
    To bring the Spirit down:
Presbyters their hands impose,   5
The whole collected Church approve,
But the Grace Ordaining flows
    From our High-priest above!

[STRANGE DISPENSATION]   190

* MS Acts, pp. 202–3.
Poetical Works, XII.251.

Metre 66: 5.5.5.5.6.5.6.5
A B A B C D C D

*And they of the circumcision which believed were astonished, because that on the Gentiles
also was poured out the gift of the Holy Ghost.—[Acts 10] v. 46.*

1 Ye Jews of our days,
    Who heathens reject,
Confining the grace
    Of Christ to a sect,
His strange dispensation   5
    Of mercy adore
While gospel-salvation
    Is preach'd to the poor.

2 The sinners unclean
    Are wash'd in his blood,   10
The outcasts of men
    Accepted with God,
Thro' Jesus his merit
    They pardon receive,
And fill'd with the Spirit   15
    Of holiness live.

[WITHSTANDING GOD]   191

* MS Acts, pp. 213–14.

Metre 17: 8.8.8.8.8.8.8.8
A B A B C D C D

*Forasmuch then as God gave them the like gift as he did unto us, what was I, that I could
withstand God?—[Acts 11] v. 17.*

1 And what are we, who still withstand
    Our God, & thwart his Spirit's design,
Impose the yoke of man's command
    On souls that know the grace Divine?
          oft
Whom God receives we ~~dare~~ reject,   5
    Part of the church invisible
We force into a separate sect,
    And dare exclude them from our pale.

2 New terms of fellowship we frame,
   <u>And modes</u> & forms, & orders new,   ~~Fashions~~   10
And absolute obedience claim
    To rules the Scriptures never knew:
More we invent; th'important stress
    (a)   (b)   (c)
    On buttons, caps, & ruffles lay,
      they
As ~~those~~ of our religious dress,   15
    ~~Alone could find the heavenly way~~.
    Were surely sav'd, & only They.

3 Thus let us God withstand no more,
    No more usurp the Saviour's right,
But bow to true religion's power,
    And honour all the sons of light.   20
Into our hearts and church receive
    As
  ~~The~~ saints begotten from above
Who e'er in our dear Lord believe,
    And live by faith which works by love.

    (a) the Friends.
    (b) the Moravians.
    (c) the Methodists.

16. The final version is also given in shorthand in the margin.

192   [NO CAUSE OF DEATH]
* MS Acts, p. 253.

Metre 7: 8.8.8.8
          A B A B

They found no cause of death in him.—[Acts 13] v. 28.

    No cause of death, no slightest blame
           human
      In Christ the ~~mortal~~ judge could find,
    But God in that ~~unspotted~~ Lamb   unblemish'd
      Beheld the sins of all mankind!

[NOVELTIES] **193**

* MS Acts, pp. 344–5.
Poetical Works, XII.338–9.

Metre 26: 6 6.6 6.8 8
A A B B C C

*All the Athenians spent their time in nothing else, but either to tell or to hear some new
thing.*—[Acts 17] v. 21.

1   Modern Athenians, hear
    Your worthless character,
    Unprofitable men,
    Who seem to live—in vain,
  Dissolv'd in Academic ease,   *5*
  In learn'd luxurious idleness.

2   In worse than childish play
    Ye lounge your time away;
    Your talents misemploy'd,
    Your life an useless void,   *10*
  As God who did your being give
  Design'd you for yourselves to live.

3   Inquisitive to know
    The triffling things below,
    The things ye will not learn,   *15*
       ~~must~~ pretious
  Which ~~may your~~ souls concern,
  Insure your real happiness,
  And seal your everlasting peace.

4   Yet here your curious pride
    Is never satisfied,   *20*
    Who restlessly pursue
    On earth amazements new,
  Till gasping out your idle breath
  Ye feel the novelties *beneath !*

[THE POISON OF A SLANDEROUS TONGUE] **194**

* MS Acts, pp. 536–7.

Metre 10: 8.8.8.8.8 8
A B A B C C

*He shook off the beast into the fire, and felt no harm. Howbeit they looked when he should
have swollen, or fallen down dead.*—[Acts 28] v. 5, 6.

1 Our Christian savages expect
    That by the hellish viper stung
  We soon shall feel the dire effect,
    The poison of a slanderous tongue,
  And gasp our last infected breath,   *5*
  And die the everlasting death.

2 But lo, the tooth of calumny
   Calm & unmov'd we still abide,
From nature's fretful passion free,
   Hasty revenge & swelling pride;   *10*
Men
~~They~~ cannot their own spirit impart,
Or taint a pure, believing heart.

3 Ourselves with Jesus' mind we arm,
   And our envenom'd foes confound,   ~~most ven'~~
Defy their sharpest words to harm,   ~~-mous~~   *15*
   Or once inflict the slightest wound,
While all the power of faith we prove
In meek invulnerable love.

4 Let Satan still their tongues employ,
   The vipers fasten'd on our fame,
The deadly things can not annoy,   *20*
   Shook off at last into the flame:
But O, they never can expire,
The worms in that infernal fire!

195   **[ST PAUL IN ROME]**

* MS Acts, pp. 550–1.
Poetical Works, XII.455–6.

                        Metre 32: 6.6.6.6.8.6.8.6
                                 A B A B C D C D

*And Paul dwelt two whole years in his own hired house, and received all that came in
unto him, Preaching the kingdom of God, and teaching those things which concern the
Lord Jesus, with all confidence, no man forbidding him.*—[Acts 28] v. 30, 31.

1   Gifts to the saints at Rome
       He long had wish'd t'impart;
     And now the time is come
       For uttering all his heart,
For publishing to rich & poor   *5*
   The kingdom from above,
The joy that always shall endure,
   The power of Jesus love.

2   Jesus, & Him alone
       The Saviour he proclaims,   *10*
     The God & Man makes known,
       ~~By all his glorious~~ names
       His offices and
~~His life and death for sinners here~~
His doctrine, life, and wonders here,
   His suffering and his rise,
His mission of the Comforter,   *15*
   And reign above the skies.

3 The door which Christ displays
  Nor men nor fiends can close,
 Or stop the course of grace
  That thro' his vessel flows;   *20*
The chosen Vessel of his Lord
 Must his whole counsel show,
And ~~freely deal~~ that royal word bold disperse
 Which builds his church below.

4 Not in a lower sphere   *25*
  Of narrower good ~~confin'd~~ he moves
 Ordain'd to minister
  To all whom Jesus loves,
Apostle of the ransom'd race
 He preaches unconfin'd,   *30*
    in
In every age ~~and~~ every place
 ~~And~~ *writes* to all mankind.
 He

[THE FOOLISHNESS OF PREACHING] **196**

* *Scripture Hymns* (1762): N.T. 545 (II.288).
 Scripture Hymns (1796): N.T. 515 (II.242–3).
 Poetical Works, XIII.22–3.

Metre 10: 8.8.8.8.8 8
ABABCC

It pleased God by the foolishness of preaching to save them that believe.—1 Cor. i.21.

1 The foolishness of preaching hear,
 Sinners the strange report believe,
Your God did once on earth appear,
 And died that all mankind might live,
Redeem'd, and reconcil'd to God,   *5*
Thro' simple faith in *Jesu*'s blood.

2 Believe, and sav'd this moment be
 From sin, the guilt, the power, the pain;
Believe, and full salvation see,
 Who still your precious faith retain; *10*
Be faithful unto death, and rise
To claim your thrones above the skies.

6. 1796: 'Thro living faith'.

[THE ACCEPTED TIME] **197**

* *Scripture Hymns* (1762): N.T. 581 (II.301).
 Scripture Hymns (1796): N.T. 550 (II.252–3).
 Poetical Works, XIII.50.

Metre 87: 7.7.7.7.7.6.7.6
aBaBcdcd

Now is the accepted time; now is the day of salvation.—[2 Corinthians] vi.2.

Now the season is of love
  And heavenly visitation!
Sinners, know the time, and prove
  The day of your salvation:
All may now in *Christ* retrieve   5
  God the Father's favour,
Claim the Holy Ghost, and live
  Priests and kings forever!

198   [THE CHRISTIAN PRIEST]

The threat of unauthorized ordination was a black cloud on Charles Wesley's horizon
for half a lifetime. (See Nos. **188, 255.**) It is quite understandable that this poem was
omitted from the second edition of the *Scripture Hymns* in 1796, when the type of
Methodism which Charles Wesley feared had become an established fact.

* *Scripture Hymns* (1762): N.T. 685 (II.351).
  Poetical Works, XIII.129.

Metre 13: 8 8.8.8 8.8
A A B C C B

No man taketh this honour unto himself, but he that is called of God, as was Aaron.—
[Hebrews] v. 4.

1 Impower'd thro' *Moses* hallowing hands,
  Aaron before the altar stands,
    The consecrated priest of God!
JESUS *his* officers ordains:
And thus the *Christian* priest obtains   5
    The gift by elders hands bestow'd.

2 Ye that uncall'd the power assume,
  Expect the rebels fearful doom;
    The pit its mouth hath open'd wide
For *Jesu's* sacrilegious foes!   10
Repent before its mouth it close
    On all the hard'ned sons of pride.

199   [HOPE IS THE ANCHOR]

* *Scripture Hymns* (1762): N.T. 695 (II.356–7).
  Scripture Hymns (1796): N.T. 647 (II.294).
  Poetical Works, XIII.135.

Metre 20: 8 8.8 8.8 8.8 8
A A B B C C D D

Which hope we have as an anchor of the soul.—[Hebrews] vi.19.

Let the winds blow, and billows roll,
Hope is the anchor of the soul:
  But can I by so slight a tie,
  An unseen hope, on God rely?
Stedfast and sure it cannot fail,   5
It enters deep within the veil,
  It fastens on a land unknown,
  And moors me to my Father's throne!

['FREE FROM SIN'S EGYPTIAN YOKE']   **200**

* *Scripture Hymns* (1762): N.T. 716 (II.368).
Scripture Hymns (1796): N.T. 667 (II.304).
Poetical Works, XIII.151.

Metre 83: 6.6.6.6.7 7. 8 8
A B A B c c D D

By faith he forsook Egypt.—[Hebrews] xi.27.

> I too have done the same;
> Yet not, O Lord, to me,
> The praise be to thy name,
> Which set the captive free:
> Free from sin's *Egyptian* yoke,   *5*
> To th'Invisible I look,
> And see my great Redeemer stand,
> My Leader to the heavenly land.

[LOOK AND LIVE]   **201**

* *Scripture Hymns* (1762): N.T. 718 (II.369–70).
Scripture Hymns (1796): N.T. 669 (II.305).
Poetical Works, XIII.152–3.

Metre 46: 7 7.7 7
a a b b

Looking unto Jesus, the author and finisher of our faith.—[Hebrews] xii.2.

1 O that I could look to thee,
  Jesus, lifted up for me,
  Me a wounded Israelite,
  Me expiring in thy sight!

2 Guilt the serpent's sting I feel,   *5*
  Anguish inconceivable,
  Bleeding, gasping on the ground,
  Dying of the poisonous wound.

3 But with a believing eye
  If I can my Lord espy,   *10*
  Hanging on the sacred pole,
  I, ev'n I, shall be made whole.

4 Give me now to find thee near,
  Now as crucified appear;
  Life is thro' thy wounds alone,   *15*
  Mine to heal, display thine own.

[NEVER MORE TO SIN]   **202**

* *Scripture Hymns* (1762): N.T. 792 (II.400).
Scripture Hymns (1796): N.T. 740 (II.332).
Poetical Works, XIII.203.

Metre 16: 8.8.8.8.8 8 8
A B A B C C C

Whosoever abideth in Him, sinneth not.—[1 John] iii.6.

What never, never more to sin!
　When shall I so abide in thee?
Open thine heart and take me in,
　Plunge in the depths of Deity
A soul that to thy bosom flies   5
From sin: possest of this high prize,
I ask no other paradise.

203　　　　　　　[REVELATION]

* *Scripture Hymns* (1762): N.T. 820 (II.410).
　Scripture Hymns (1796): N.T. 767 (II.340–1).
　Poetical Works, XIII.218.

Metre 54: 8.7.8.7.4.7
a b a b x b

The Revelation of Jesus Christ.—Rev. i.1.

1 See, ye heirs of sure salvation,
　　Jesu's most majestic grace,
　At his final revelation,
　　While he pompously displays
　　　All his glories,   5
　All the Godhead in his face!

2 From the mystic volume hearing
　　How his kingdom is restor'd,
　Look ye for his last appearing:
　　True to his prophetic word,   10
　　　Lo, he cometh!
　Go ye forth to meet your Lord.

3 To his royal Proclamation
　　Manifested here, attend,
　In his state of exaltation   15
　　While he doth with clouds descend,
　　　Brings the kingdom,
　Gives the joy that ne'er shall end.

4 Power is all to *Jesus* given:
　　All his foes must fall before   20
　The great King of earth and heaven,
　　When he takes his royal power!
　　　Now assume it,
　Jesus, reign for evermore!

[SILENCE IN HEAVEN]   204

* *Scripture Hymns* (1762): N.T. 852 (II.426).
  Scripture Hymns (1796): N.T. 799 (II.354).
  Poetical Works, XIII.234.

Metre 30: 6.6.8.6
ABAB

There was silence in heaven.—[Revelation] viii.1.

What doth that silence mean?
  Can man or angel shew?
Away this noisy world between,
  And let me die to know!

FOR A WOMAN IN TRAVAIL   205

* *Family Hymns* (1767): No. 56.
  Poetical Works, VII.63–4.

Metre 55: 8.7.8.7.7 7
abab c c

1 Jesus, help! no longer tarry,
    Hasten to redeem thine own:
  Son of God, and son of Mary,
    Answering to thy creature's groan,
  Now omnipotently near,   5
  Prince of life in death appear.

2 Save her by thy righteous merit
    From the just reward of sin:
  By the travail of thy Spirit,
    Bring the timely succours in;   10
  By thy passion on the tree
  Save a soul that gasps to Thee.

3 Soften, sanctify the anguish,
    Sad memorial of her fall;
  Let her on thy bosom languish,   15
    Till thou bring her safe thro' all,
  Ransom'd from th'extreme distress,
  Bid her live—in perfect peace.

4 God of her compleat salvation,
    Heal, and bid her body rise,   20
  Let her soul with exultation
    Mount to thee beyond the skies,
  Happy as thy saints above,
  Lost in her Redeemer's love.

206 FOR ONE RETIRED INTO THE COUNTRY

This poem, like Nos. **158** and **247**, was probably composed in April 1751, while Wesley was spending a week at St Anne's Hill, near Chertsey.

* *Family Hymns* (1767): No. 149.
  MS Richmond, pp. 146–7: headed 'To—Hail, charming Grotto, still Retreat'. (This ballad is not listed among the 18,000 entries in the *Song Index* and its Supplement, by Miss M. E. Sears.)
  Poetical Works, VII.179–80.

Metre 4: 8 8.6.8 8.6
A A B C C B

1 Hence, lying world, with all thy care,
  With all thy shews of good or fair,
    Of beautiful or great!
  Stand with thy slighted charms aloof,
  Nor dare invade my peaceful roof,   5
    Or trouble my retreat.

2 Far from thy mad fantastic ways,
  I here have found a resting place
    Of poor wayfaring men:
  Calm as the hermit in his grot,
  I here enjoy my happy lot,   10
    And solid pleasures gain.

3 Along the hill or dewy mead
  In sweet forgetfulness I tread,
    Or wander thro' the grove,   15
  As Adam in his native seat,
  In all his works my God I meet
    The object of my love.

4 I see his beauty in the flower;
  To shade my walks, and deck my bower,   20
    His love and wisdom join:
  Him in the feather'd quire I hear,
  And own, while all my soul is ear,
    The music is divine!

            sacred
  5. MS: 'peaceful roof'.
  8. MS: 'Lodging-place'.
            solid
 12. MS: 'And real pleasures'.
            native
 16. MS: 'blisful seat'.
            own
 23. MS: 'And cry,'.

5 In yon unbounded plain I see   *25*
  A sketch of his immensity
    Who spans these ample skies,
  Whose presence makes the happy place,
  And opens in the wilderness
    A blooming paradise.   *30*

6 O would he now himself impart,
  And fix the Eden in my Heart
    The sense of sin forgiven,
  How should I then throw off my load,
  And walk delightfully with God,   *35*
    And follow Christ to heaven!

30. MS: 'An earthly Paradice.'
32. MS: 'And plant the Eden'.
     my
34. MS: '~~the~~ load'.
     And walk ~~unblameable~~—delightfully
35. MS: '~~Of irksom Life and walk~~ with GOD'.

[THY SERVANT STILL]   **207**

From about 1756 Charles Wesley took a far less active part in the administrative life of the Methodist societies. Ill-health and family cares were partly responsible, but the main deterrent was disagreement with his brother John, particularly over the question of separation from the Church of England, which Charles felt was being hastened by the increasing ambition of the preachers, and their demands to administer the sacraments. He remained a faithful pastor and preacher to the end, however.

* *Family Hymns* (1767): No. 151.
  Poetical Works, VII.181–3.

                                Metre 4: 8 8.6.8 8.6
                                     A A B C C B

1 My God and Lord, thy counsel shew,
  What wouldst thou have thy servant do
    Before I hence depart?
  How shall I serve thy church, and where?
  The thing, the time, the means declare,   *5*
    And teach my listning heart.

2 Thrust out from Them I serv'd so long,
  I dare not strive against the wrong,
    But silently resign
  The charge I never *could* forsake,   *10*
  And give my dearest children back
    Into the hands divine.

3 Where first I preach'd the word of grace,
  If now I have no longer place,
    By my own flesh unknown,   *15*
  Thy secret Hand in all I see,
  Thy will be done, whate'er it be,
    Thy welcome will be done.

4 Free for whate'er thy love ordains,
  I offer up my life's remains   *20*
    To be for Thee employ'd:
My little strength can little do,
Yet would I in thy service true,
    Devote it all to God.

5 Wilt Thou not, Lord, my offer take?   *25*
  Canst Thou in helpless age forsake
    The creature of thy will?
My strength is spent in the best cause:
Thy zealous messenger I was;
    I am thy servant still.   *30*

6 Master, be Thou my might, my mouth,
  And send me forth to north or south,
    To farthest east or west;
Be Thou my Guide to worlds unknown:
Rest to my flesh I covet none,   *35*
    But give my spirit rest.

7 My rest on earth to toil for Thee,
  My whole delight and business be
    To minister thy word,
For Thee immortal souls to win,   *40*
And make the wretched slaves of sin
    The freemen of my Lord.

8 Witness and messenger of peace
  I only languish to decrease
    In trumpeting thy name,   *45*
I only live to preach thy death,
And publish with my latest breath
    The glories of the Lamb.

208   GLORIA PATRI, &c.

* *Family Hymns* (1767): No. 166.
  Poetical Works, VII.200.

                        Metre 21: 8 8.10 12.8 8.10 12
                                A A B B C C D D

1   Glory to the Paternal God,
      To Jesus lavish of his blood,
    God over all supreme in power and grace,
And God the Holy Ghost with equal ardors praise.
        Sing all on earth like those on high;   *5*
        Let saints and angels magnify
      One undivided God in persons three,
And lengthen out the song to all eternity!

['ONE GLORIOUS GOD'] 209

* *Family Hymns* (1767): No. 166: II.
Poetical Works, VII.200.

Metre 14: 8 8.8.8 8.12
A A B C C B

2   Thankful the Father's grace we own;
Jehovah's Fellow and his Son,
   With God the Holy Ghost adore,
One glorious God in persons three,
All honour we ascribe to Thee,   *5*
As always was, and is, and shall be evermore!

[ONE LAWGIVER IN THREE] 210

* *Hymns on the Trinity* (1767): No. 114, Section, 'The Trinity in Unity'.
Poetical Works, VII.284.

Metre 86: 7.6.7.6.7.8.7.6
a B a B c D c D

Rom. vii.25. I myself serve the LAW of GOD.
Gal. vi.2. Fulfil the LAW of CHRIST.
Rom. viii.2. The LAW of the Spirit of life.
Jam. iv.12. There is ONE LAWGIVER who is able to save and to destroy.

1   We the Father's law receive,
   The law of Christ fulfil,
Keep the Spirit's law, and live
   According to his will;
Live to make the mystery known,   *5*
And testify, from sin set free,
   God our Lawgiver is One,
   But One in Persons Three.

2   Shall we then with sin comply,
   Against our God rebel,   *10*
His authority defy
   Who can destroy in hell?
He that doth to sin give way,
The glorious Trinity offends,
   Treasures up against that day   *15*
   The wrath which never ends.

[TRIUNE TRUTH] 211

* *Hymns on the Trinity* (1767): No. 120, Section, 'The Trinity in Unity'.
Poetical Works, VII.287-8.

Metre 32: 6.6.6.6.8.6.8.6
A B A B C D C D

John vii.28. He that sent Me is TRUE.
Rev. iii.7. These things saith He that is TRUE, He that hath the key of David.
1 *John* v.6. The Spirit is TRUTH.

Who sent the Son is true;
    True is the Son that came;
    True is the Spirit too,
      Conferr'd in Jesus' name:
The Father, Son, and Holy Ghost   5
    Essential Truth we own,
And prostrate with his heavenly host
    Adore the Three in One.

212   [WITNESSES THREE]

* *Hymns on the Trinity* (1767): Section 'Hymns and Prayers to the Trinity', No. 4.
  Poetical Works, VII.302.

Metre 62: 5 5 11.5 5 11
A A A B B B

To—*All ye that pass by.*

1   Three Persons there are
      Their record who bear,
And Jehovah in heavenly places declare:
    But in Father, and Son,
    And Spirit made known,   5
The Witnesses Three are essentially One.

2   Full credence we give,
      And exult to believe
What our reason in vain would aspire to conceive:
    Not *against*, but *above*   10
    Our reason we prove
Three Persons reveal'd in the essence of love.

3   The Father alone
      Very God will we own,
Very God will we worship the Spirit and Son: 15
    Each Person is He,
    Whom believing we see,
And Jehovah adore in the wonderful Three.

4   No distinction we find
      Of will or of mind   20
In the Maker, Inspirer, and Friend of mankind;
    But one God we proclaim
    In nature and name
Indivisibly One, and for ever the same.

213   [WITH MY DEAR LORD TO LIVE]

* *Preparation for Death* (1772): No. 12.
  Source *51* (*and* 97) MS Death (a): No. 12.
  Poetical Works, VII.364.

Metre 28: 6 6.6 6.6 6.6 6
A A B B C C D D

1 Thee, Saviour, I confess
  Omnipotent in grace:
  True I account thee, Lord,
  And faithful to thy word:
  Freely thou wilt confer   *5*
  Whate'er we ask in prayer,
  And readier art to give
  Than sinners to receive.

2 Ere with my lips I pray,
  Thou know'st what I would say: *10*
  Might I be found of thee
  In peace and purity,
  And then my spirit give
  With my dear Lord to live:
  Safe on that happy shore,   *15*
  I could desire no more.

[MY LATEST WISH]   **214**

* MS Death (a): No. 60.

Metre 7: 8.8.8.8
A B A B

1 O Thou, to whom all hearts are known,
      My latest wish, my one desire
  Breath'd in the Spirit of thy Son
      Accept, and grant what I require:

2 Pardon for my offences past,   *5*
      Grace for a few good days to come,
  Love, the sure pledge of heaven at last,
      And a smooth passage to the tomb.

[HIDE ME, O MY SAVIOUR, HIDE!]   **215**

* MS Death (a): No. 74.
Poetical Works, VII.418–9.

Metre 52: 7 7.7 7.7 7.7 7
a a b b c c d d

1 Far from passion, and from pride,
  Hide me, by Thy presence hide
  From the world's outrageous wrongs,
  From the angry strife of tongues,
  From the malice of the fiend,   *5*
  From the woes that never end,
  From the memory of ill,
  From myself, and all I feel.

2 Poor, unnotic'd, and unknown
  Let me dwell with Thee alone,   *10*
  Dwell in safety and in peace,
  Cease from sin, for ever cease:
  Or, if grief with life must last,
  Let me wail my follies past,
  Live my follies to lament,   *15*
  Die a pardon'd penitent.

3 Dying every mournful day,
  Let me at Thy footstool pray,
  Drink Thy indignation's cup,
  Fill my penal measure up: *20*
  Then Thy servant, Lord, dismiss
  With a reconciling kiss,
  Binding up my broken heart
  Bid me then in peace depart.

20. Works: 'my mournful measure'.

216   [TAKE THIS EVIL ALL AWAY]

* MS Death (b) ['Hymns for Love']: No. 11, p. 54.
Poetical Works, VIII.364–5.

                                        Metre 49: 7 7.7 7.7 7
                                                  a a b b c c

1 Full of sin, and void of Thee,
  Lord, my real state I see,
  Ask according to Thy will
  Thou Thy own desire fulfil
  Take this evil all away,   *5*
  Give the good for which I pray.

2 Granting my incessant suit
  Sin destroy both branch and root,
  All the unregenerate mind,
  All my heart to sin inclin'd,   *10*
  All my bent to sin remove,
  Cast it out by purest love.

3 Purest love, and joy, and peace,
  Everlasting righteousness,
  All the good with Christ bestow'd,   *15*
  All the plentitude of God,
  Bring into my new-born soul,
  Consecrate, and fill the whole.

4 Nothing more can I desire,
  Nothing less will I require,
  God supreme for ever blest   *20*
  Come, and in thy temple rest,
  Father, Son, and Spirit come,
  Seal me thine eternal home.

[GLORIOUS HOLINESS]   **217**

* MS Death (b) ['Hymns for Love']: No. 16, p. 61.
Poetical Works, VIII.370.

Metre 35: 7.6.7.6.7.6.7.6
ABABCDCD

1 Jesus, my soul aspires
    By faith to compass Thee,
With infinite desires
    To grasp Immensity:
Of all in earth and heaven   *5*
    I nothing want beside,
But when my God is given
    My soul is satisfied.

2 Thy nature pure partaking,
    To Thee in spirit join'd,   *10*
And in Thine image waking,
    The true delight I find:
The God of my salvation
    If Thou in me appear,
With bless'd anticipation   *15*
    I see, and taste Thee here.

3 Yet still my Lord possessing,
    For more of heaven I pray,
I want the final blessing
    In that most joyful day,   *20*
The intimate fruition
    Of glorious Holiness,
The full, eternal vision
    Of my Redeemer's face.

4 Come then in all thy glory,   *25*
    The saints triumphant King,
Of all things transitory
    The flaming period bring:
And lo, out of the burning
    On angels wings I fly,   *30*
And meet my Lord returning,
    And grasp Him in the sky!

[THY SERVANT READY TO DEPART]   **218**

* MS Death (b) ['Hymns for Love']: No. 32, p. 79.
Poetical Works, VIII.384–5.

Metre 7: 8.8.8.8
abab

1 Thy servant ready to depart,
    Jesus, to Thee for help I cry;
The virtue of thy Name exert,
    Or saved so long, in sin I die.

2 Preserv'd by my redeeming Lord   *5*
   In twice ten thousand conflicts past,
Unless thy help Thou still afford,
   I faint, and perish in the last.

3 If thro' thy strength I have run well,
   And almost won the doubtful race,   *10*
Most sensibly my want I feel
   Of more, of persevering grace.

4 The countless storms of life brought thro',
   If Thou refuse my heart's desire,
Justly forsook, the land I view,   *15*
   And shipwreck'd in the port expire.

5 I cannot to the end endure,
   Unless the patience Thou bestow,
And make my latest footsteps sure,
   And with me thro' the valley go: *20*

6 But, jealous of myself, I hope
   Thou wilt my Guide and Keeper be,
My weak, defective faith fill up,
   And to the end remember me.

7 Throughout my life of death afraid,   *25*
   Yet, Lord, in Thee I still confide;
On Thee my trembling soul is stay'd,
   Who hast for me both lived and died:

8 Thou wilt, I stedfastly believe,
   My Saviour to the utmost prove,   *30*
And to thyself in death receive
   The purchase of thy dying love.

219   A DEPARTING MINISTER'S PRAYER

* *Arminian Magazine* (1780), pp. 453–4 (August number).
MS Death (a): No. 78, pp. 41–2.
Poetical Works, VII.420–1.

Metre 4: 8 8.6.8 8.6
                            A A B C C B

Shepherd of souls, the great, the good,
Who on thy servant's side hast stood,
   And blessed my ministry,
Ready my prospered course to end,
I to thy guardian love commend   *5*
   The flock received from Thee.

Beneath thy wings, their sure defence,
Protected by Omnipotence,
 Thy most distinguished care;
The lambs and sheep of England's fold   *10*
Now in thy book of life inrolled
 Preserve for ever there.

Our Church a thousand-fold increase,
With every gospel blessing bless,
 And o'er the earth disperse,   *15*
Till every heart thy kingdom own,
Till thou art feared, confessed and known,
 Throughout the universe.

In hope of that thrice happy day,
To quit this tenement of clay   *20*
 Thy summons I receive;
For when I lay my body down,
Thy work shall still be carried on,
 And God for ever live.

The Spirit's residue is thine: *25*
Fit instruments for thy design,
 Dispensers of thy grace,
(If some like salt. their savour lose)
Thou canst from other stones produce,
 And nobler vessels raise.   *30*

Come then, thy servant to release,
And suffered to depart in peace,
 Without a lingering sigh;
In all the confidence of hope,
I now ascend the mountain-top   *35*
 I get me up and die!

11. MS: 'in the book'.
19. MS: 'that most joyful day'.
26. MS: 'of Thy design'.
36. MS: 'And get me up'.

[SO IMPOTENT MY CARNAL MIND]   **220**

* MS Scriptural Hymns (1783): O.T., pp. 51–2.
Poetical Works, IX.296–7.

           Metre 11: 8.8.8.8.8 10
               A B A B C C

*Innumerable troubles are come about me; my sins have taken such hold on me, that I am
not able to look up, &c.*—[Psalm] 40.15 [actually, v. 12].

1   Troubles and sins, a countless crowd,
      Beyond conception multiplied,
    Have long this abject spirit bow'd
      And hemm'd me in on every side,
    Forbad my weakness to look up,   *5*
And seem'd to quench my last faint spark of hope.

2   So strongly to all sin inclin'd,
      So fast by vile affections held,
    So impotent my carnal mind,
      I yield constrain'd, or'epower'd I yield,   *10*
    No longer strug[g]le in the snare
But sinks my heart or'ewhelm'd with sad despair.

221   [SING WE MERRILY TO GOD]

This poem might have been intended as a straightforward composition in trochaic 7's, yet it seems more likely that Wesley intended the dactylic trip of the keyword 'merrily' to operate in the second foot of each line.

* MS Scriptural Hymns (1783): O.T., p. 60.
Poetical Works, IX.312.

Metre 50: 7.7.7.7.7.7.7.7
a b a b c d c d

Sing ye merrily unto God our strength, make a cheerful noise unto the God of Jacob.—
[Psalm] 81.1.

Sing we merrily to God,
    We the creatures of his grace,
We the purchase of his blood
    Only live to sing and praise,
Make we then a chearful noise,   *5*
    Every child of Adam join'd
Share the universal joys,
    Shout the Friend of all mankind.

222   [THE LEAVEN OF SPIRITUAL PRIDE]

* MS Scriptural Hymns (1783): N.T., pp. 38–9.

Metre 10: 8.8.8.8.8 8
A B A B C C

Your glorying is not good: know ye not that a little leaven leaveneth the whole lump?—
[1 Corinthians] 5.6.

1 Who glory in your ripest grace,
    Your holiest, purest, perfect love,
Yourselves ye ignorantly praise,
    Yourselves abundantly disprove,
Nor can by folly's fig-leaves hide   *5*
Your glaring nakedness of pride.

2 Impatient to be disbeliev'd,
  Is it for God alone ye speak?
Self-confident, and self-deceiv'd,
  Your own applause ye blindly seek,   *10*
When humble, not in heart, but word,
Ye seem to glory in the Lord.

3 The smallest spark of self-respect
  Of self-esteem, conceal'd within,
Doth all your boasted gifts infect,   *15*
  And turns your graces into sin:
Self-love and vanity the leaven
Which lifts your swelling souls to heaven.

4 While there in fancied pomp ye reign,
  Fond nature's pride in secret spreads,   *20*
With visions turns your heated brain,
  With gilded rays adorns your heads,
Till sunk at once ye lose your light,
Ye lose your souls in endless night.

['WHATEVER IS, IS BEST'][1]   **223**

* MS Scriptural Hymns (1783): N.T., p. 73.
Poetical Works, XIII.81–2.

Metre 2: 4 4.6.8.6
A AB A B

Be careful for nothing.—[Philippians] 4.6.

1   Most gracious Lord,
        Thy kindest word
    I joyfully obey,
Hold fast my confidence restor'd,
    And cast my sins away.   *5*

2   No longer I
        Lament and sigh
    With guilty fear opprest,
To me who on thy love rely
    Whatever is, is best.   *10*

3   In each event
        The kind intent
    Of Love divine I see,
And mixt with joyful thanks present
    My humble prayers to Thee.   *15*

[1 The title, taken from the poem itself, is Wesley's version of the famous phrase popularised by Alexander Pope (one of his favourite poets): 'Whatever is, is right.' Wesley's phrase has been used by a modern verse-writer, Ella Wheeler Wilcox. Wesley's use, however, avoids fatalism on the one hand, and anaemic resignation on the other.]

4   Then let thy peace
        My heart possess;
    By thy unspotted mind,
Preserve in perfect quietness
    A soul to Jesus join'd.   *20*

5   In Spirit one
        With Christ thy Son
    Henceforth his life I live,
Till Jesus claim me for his own,
    And to his arms receive.   *25*

224   [SPRINKLED FROM AN EVIL CONSCIENCE]

* MS Scriptural Hymns (1783): N.T., pp. 97–8.
Poetical Works, XIII.144–5.

                Metre 4: 8 8.6.8 8.6
                       A A B C C B

Having our hearts sprinkled from an evil conscience.—[Hebrews] 10.22.

1 Conscious of all that I have done,
  Of evils to the world unknown,
    My punishment I feel,
  Driven out from my Creator's face,
  A vagrant Cain, in every place   *5*
    I carry my own hell.

2 Remembrance shakes her whip severe,
  His scorpion whip of guilty fear,
    Of sad remorse and shame;
  But from myself I cannot fly,   *10*
  Or find one drop of comfort nigh
    To cool this scorching flame.

3 Jesus, my only Hope Thou art;
  Sprinkle thy blood upon my heart,
    And make its troubles cease: *15*
  Thy blood the wounded conscience heals,
  Thy blood the sinner's pardon seals,
    And bids me die in peace.

4 Faith in thy blood if Thou bestow,
  The sting of guilt no more I know,   *20*
    The self-tormenting mind;
  I plunge me in th'oblivious floud,
  I wash away my sinful load,
    And leave myself behind.

5 Help then my desperate unbelief,   *25*
  Appear, to end my sin and grief,
    With all thy wounds confest,
  Thy love on Calvary display,
  And bear my ransom'd soul away
    To that eternal Rest.   *30*

[WE MERRILY SING]   **225**

* MS Scriptural Hymns (1783): N.T., p. 109.

Metre 72: 7.7.5 5.8
X A B B A

Is any merry? let him sing psalms.—[James] 5.13.

1 In the Belov'd accepted,
  For Jesus' sake forgiven,
    At the word of a King
    We merrily sing
  The Delight of earth and heaven.   *5*

2 Triumphant in his favor,
  With joyful acclamation
    We thankfully raise
    A full Anthem of praise
  To the God of our salvation.   *10*

[THE SINNER'S FRIEND]   **226**

* MS Scriptural Hymns (1783): N.T., p. 110.

Metre 57: 8.7.8.7.7 7.8 8
a b a b c c d d

Christ suffered, that he might bring us to God.—[1 Peter] 3.18.

  Jesus, purge our foul transgression
    In the fountain of thy blood,
  By thy powerful intercession
    Bring me to my gracious God:
  Sinner's Friend, I humbly claim   *5*
  Pardon, glory in thy name,
  Pardon now, thy passion's wages,
  Glory thro' eternal ages.

[FOR THE SELF-RIGHTEOUS]   **227**

* MS Miscellaneous Hymns, pp. 180–1: as No. 16 in 'Hymns of Intercession'.
MS Intercession: No. 16.

Metre 10: 8.8.8.8.8 8
A B A B C C

1 Saviour, Thou readst what is in man,
  Thine eyes his inmost substance see:
  Wrapt up in forms and shadows vain
    He cannot hide himself from Thee,
  Who knowst his deep, serpentine art,   *5*
  And all the windings of his heart.

2 Ev'n now thy searching eye perceives
 Thy fugitives among the trees,
Veiling their shame with virtuous leaves,
 (The fig-leaves of self-righteousness)   *10*
Willing themselves to justify,
And Thee with thy own gifts to buy.

3 Tear from them, Lord, their figleaves tear,
 Themselves let the deceivers know,
Wretched, & poor, & blind, & bare,   *15*
 Consign'd to everlasting woe,
Unless thy mercy step between,
And freely save them from their sin.

4 Stop Thou their mouths, confound their pride,
 Their souls to endless woe condemn;   *20*
Then point them to thine open side,
 Then plunge them in that purple stream,
Which only can for sin atone,
And wafts the Pardon'd to thy throne.

12. MS Intercession: 'And God with his own gifts'.
21. MS Intercession: 'that open side'.
24. MS Intercession: 'And waft'.

228   FOR THE PRETENDERS TO PERFECTION

* MS Miscellaneous Hymns, pp. 183–4: as No. 18 in 'Hymns of Intercession'.
MS Intercession, No. 18.

           Metre 10: 8.8.8.8.8 8
                A B A B C C

1 Arise, Thou jealous God, arise,
 Whose word doth soul & body part,
Look with thy all-discerning eyes,
 And sound the most deceitful heart
Of Those, whom erring men approve   *5*
As witnesses of perfect love.

2 Thou knowst, the fiend hath set them up,
 Hath on the sacred Summit placed,
That falling from their towering hope,
 From highest heaven to hell debased,   *10*
Their souls may prove his wretched thrall,
And stumble thousands by their fall.

Title. MS Intercession: 'For the ~~false~~ Pretenders to Perfections.'
 2. MS Intercession: 'soul & spirit'.
 6. MS Intercession: 'False witnesses'.

3 Ah, do not, Lord, the tempted leave
   A prey to Luciferian pride,
Ah do not let the foe deceive   15
   The souls for whom thyself has died,
Or shake our faith who dare profess
Our faith in finish'd holiness.   hope of

4 Whoever stands or falls, the word
   The one Foundation must endure,   20
Sure is the promise of our Lord,
   The oath divine hath made it sure,
And *we*, when Christ the power imparts,
Shall love our God with all our hearts.

5 Now, Saviour, now our hearts prepare   25
   Thy gracious fulness to receive;
But pluck our brethren from the snare,
   Beguil'd like vain, aspiring Eve,
Deliverance to the captives send,
And let the strong Delusion end.   30

6 Gently into the valley lead,
   And give them then themselves to know,
Till to themselves intirely dead
   Their grace they by their *silence show*,
Thee only good, & perfect *call*,   35
And sink, and into nothing fall.

18. MS Intercession: 'in perfect holiness.'
21. MS Intercession: 'True is' and 'Sure' in margin.

[THE PENITENT THIEF]   229

The 'Holy Club' at Oxford made prison-visitation one of their important services to the community, and from the outset of his ministry in England Charles Wesley devoted much time and effort to the pastoral care of criminals. As the climax to his successful labours as an unofficial chaplain to a group of men awaiting execution in July 1738, he conducted a service at Tyburn, singing hymns by his father and Isaac Watts, and had the joy of seeing the criminals penitent and converted, so that he could say: 'That hour under the gallows was the most blessed hour of my life.'

These labours continued to the end of his ministry, and he wrote a number of hymn-prayers in simple metres specifically for use by the unfortunates executed so lavishly and so publicly throughout the eighteenth century. Indeed his ministry at executions was undoubtedly one factor, however minor, in rousing public conscience against such spectacles, and on the occasion for which this particular poem was apparently written the *Gentleman's Magazine* reported with some shame: '*Thursday* 28 [April 1785]. This day a most lamentable spectacle was exhibited to an innumerable multitude of their wretched fraternity, who were assembled from all quarters on the occasion, viz. Nineteen of their fellow-labourers hanged up like dogs, for crimes

251

committed against the laws of their country, which no punishment will prevent, while common-strumpets are permitted, at all hours, and in all places, to stroll the streets, to entice youth, to initiate them in vice, and deprave their morals.'

* *Prayers for Condemned Malefactors* (1785): No. 6.
  MS Miscellaneous Hymns, pp. 97–8.
  Poetical Works, VIII.343.

Metre 1: 8.6.8.6
A B A B

1 Return'd into thy kingdom, Lord,
　For good remember me,
And tell a penitent restor'd,
　I soon shall be with thee.

2 The offering of a broken heart　　　　　　　　5
　Thou never wilt despise,
But while my soul and body part,
　Accept the sacrifice.

3 My spirit humbly I commend,
　To thy redeeming care,　　　　　　　　　　10
My last important moments spend
　In penitence and prayer.

4 And if I may not testify
　On earth my sins forgiven,
Yet, I, the poorest outcast I　　　　　　　　15
　May praise thy love in heaven.*

* These prayers were answered, Thur. April 28, 1785, on nineteen malefactors, who all died penitent. Not unto me, O Lord; not unto me! [This footnote appears only in MS Misc. Hymns.]

230　　　　　TAKE AWAY ALL INIQUITY

Dr George Osborn, in a footnote in *Poetical Works*, VIII.431, speaks of this as 'not improbably his last *written* poem'. Actually the manuscript from which the verses are now published is in such a firm hand that one might have expected a somewhat earlier date. He himself may have prepared a revised text nearer his death, or his brother John may have been responsible for the alterations.

* CW. MSS I (q), xxii, at the Methodist Book Room, London.
  Arminian Magazine, 1788 (August), p. 446, with the prefatory note: 'The following Verses were written by the late Rev. Charles Wesley, a little before his Death. Hosea. iv. 2.'
  Poetical Works, VIII.431–2.

Metre 15: 8 8.8 8.8 8
A A B B C C

Take away all iniquity, and give good. Hosea 14 [v. 2].

1 How long, how often shall I pray
Take all iniquity away,
And give the comprehensive good,
Purchas'd by my Redeemer's blood,
Concupiscence, and pride remove,   *5*
And fill my soul with humble love.

2 I take the words prescrib'd to me
And offer thy own prayer to Thee,
Thy kingdom come to root out sin,
And perfect holiness bring in,   *10*
And swallow up my will in thine,
And human change into divine.

3 So shall I render Thee thine own,
And tell the wonders Thou hast done,
The power and faithfulness declare   *15*
Of God, who hears and answers prayer,
And sing the riches of thy grace,
And spend my latest breath in praise.

4 O that the joyful hour were come
Which calls thy ransom'd Servant home,   *20*
Unites me to the Church above
Where angels chant the song of love,
And saints eternally proclaim
The glories of the heavenly Lamb!

3–4. *Arm. Mag.*: 'And give the plenitude of good,
                The blessing bought by Jesu's blood'.
 6. *A.M.*: 'And fill me, Lord,'.
7–8. *A.M.*: 'Again I take the words to me
              Prescribed, and offer them to Thee'.
17. *A.M.*: 'Extol the riches'.
19. *A.M.*: 'was come'.
20. *A.M.*: 'ready servant'.

PART THREE

MISCELLANEOUS POEMS

The earliest extant lines of verse in Charles Wesley's hand are preserved in his earliest extant letter, written from Oxford to his brother John, who had temporarily returned to Epworth in order to serve as curate to their father. John's previous letter had conveyed 'that plaguy piece of news' that he might not return to Oxford, being 'settled for life—at least for years'. Not only would Charles thus miss the benefits of comparative affluence and comfort conferred by his brother's Fellowship of Lincoln: even the literary dalliance with Bob Kirkham's sisters and their friends Mary Pendarves and Anne Granville would lose much of its attraction. (It was Anne Granville who wrote to John Wesley about his brother Charles on 1st December 1731: 'Is not Araspes' hymn quite charming?'—our first reference to his hymn-writing, though the hymn itself seems to have disappeared, or at least to have become merged indistinguishably with those published later.)

When I first published the following lines in 1948 (*Charles Wesley as revealed by his letters*, p. 9) I believed them to be his own composition. I now discover that he was quoting (somewhat imperfectly) from a poem which seems clearly to be the work of his brother John, and only the second line is in fact original. This gives point to a later phrase in Charles's letter: 'You'l pardon my turning your own Words upon you.' The complete poem is to be found in John Wesley's 'Miscellany Verses'. Charles Wesley has mentally extracted four unrelated couplets from his brother's poem, replaced one line, and both rearranged and varied the others.

* Letter to John Wesley, 20th January, 1727/8, Colman Collection, at the Methodist Book Room, London.

John Wesley's 'Miscellany Verses', pp. 39–43, Colman Collection, at the Methodist Book Room, London.

Metre 98: Iambic 10's

'Nor yet from my dim Eyes THY form retires.'!
(The cold empty starving Grate before me makes me add ye
following disconsolate Line.)
   Nor cheering image of thine absent Fires.
           Hinxy's
No longer now on Horrel's airy Van,
With Thee shall I admire the subject Plain,
Or where the Sight in neighbouring Shades is lost,   5
Or where the lengthned Prospect widens most;
While or ye tunefull Poet's (something) song,
Or Truths Divine flow'd easy from thy Tongue.

3. 'Horrel' is a plantation of beech-trees on the crest of a hill to the south of Stanton, where Kirkham's father was rector. 'Hinksey Hill' is two miles south of Oxford.

The relevant lines in John Wesley's poem are the following:

(82–3) 'Nor yet from my dim Eyes Thy Form retire's,
     Fain would they mix with Thine their soften'd Fires,'
(90–1) 'Ah no! No more on Horrel's airy Van
     With Thee must I admire the subject Plain;'
(67–8) 'Where, or the Sight in neighb'ring Shades is lost
     Or the extended Prospect widen's most.'
(94–5) 'While or ye Sprightly Poet's tunefull Song
     Or Truths Divine flow easy from thy Tongue.'

232 [WOMAN AND WAR]

The Rev. Henry Moore (1751–1844), converted in Dublin in 1777, came to London as a Methodist preacher in 1784 to serve as John Wesley's companion and amanuensis. He was also for some years a close friend of Charles Wesley, and his *Life of the Rev. John Wesley* throws a good deal of light on the younger brother. In particular Moore speaks of Charles Wesley's 'complete knowledge of the classic writers, and his high relish for their beauties', marvelling at the mastery that had come through much initial drudgery under his elder brother Samuel at Westminster School. Charles did not parade his classical knowledge, but occasionally it slipped out. Moore relates the following incident: 'One day, after having talked on religious subjects for some time, he broke out,—"Come, I'll give you two hundred lines of Virgil." He began, and it was Virgil indeed. I question if the great poet was ever more honoured. The prosody was as truly Roman as the language.' [Moore's *Wesley*, II.369.] From the closing sentence it seems that Wesley actually recited his own translation into English verse of Virgil's Latin—though he could doubtless have recited the original just as well! (On one occasion he is said to have endeavoured to submerge a tirade of Mrs John Wesley's by reciting the sixth book of the *Aeneid*. See F. Luke Wiseman's *Charles Wesley*, p. 200.) It is Moore who preserves one of John Wesley's reminiscences of his younger brother at Oxford, blundering about short-sightedly and absent-mindedly, intent on nothing else but versifying [Moore's *Wesley*, II.368–9]. What was he versifying? And where are the results?

It is my own belief that having come under the spell of the Latin and Greek poets at Westminster, and having had to translate passages into English verse as a normal part of the educational routine of that day, he realized that he had a gift for versifying, which he developed at Oxford. He probably filled several volumes with versifications of purple passages from the major classical poets—in much the same way as he was later to compose his *Short Hymns on Selected Passages of the Holy Scriptures*. Most, probably all, would be (in both traditional and contemporary mode) in decasyllabic couplets, often with a closing alexandrine. It seems very likely that these volumes were for some reason among the mass of worldly writings destroyed by the Rev. John Pawson in 1797, along with John Wesley's annotated copy of Shakespeare. (If not, there is still a chance of their coming to light.) Of the thousands of lines which I believe him to have written in this way only 33 survive. They were preserved by Henry Moore, who gives five separate poems, with no indication of their source. Actually two come from neighbouring passages in Horace's *Satires*, and three from a group of 35 lines of the first book of Ovid's *Metamorphoses*. Moore speaks of giving 'some specimens from his translations of the most admired Classics', and (if I interpret his mind aright), he dipped into the original volumes, or into transcripts of some extracts made earlier, at two different sections, and printed the two little groups that caught his eye as typical examples of the whole. This is conjecture, of course, but the composition of such a corpus of translations from the classics explains much of Wesley's future success, as well as the classical mould in which it was formed. We already have sufficient proof that Charles Wesley did not leap forth as a ready-made poet immediately after his conversion: rather his genius was transmuted to a nobler subject and a more lyrical medium.

* The following example, from Moore's *Wesley* (II.366) translates Horace's *Satires*, I.iii.107–10.

Metre 98: Iambic 10's

Fuit ante Helenam mulier[1] teterrima belli
Causa: Sed ignotis perierunt mortibus omnes[2]
Quos Venerem incertam rapientes, more ferarum,
Viribus editior caedebat, ut in grege taurus.

Full many a war has been for woman wag'd,
Ere half the world in Helen's cause engag'd;

[1, 2 Wesley may well have been quoting his Latin from a slightly faulty memory. For '*mulier*' Horace wrote '*cunnus*', and for '*omnes*' he wrote '*illi*'.]

But unrecorded in historic verse,
Obscurely died those savage ravishers:
Who, like brute beasts, the female bore away,   5
Till some superior brute re-seiz'd the prey.
As a wild bull, his rival bull o'erthrown,
Claims the whole subject-herd, and reigns alone.

[DEGENERATE HUMANITY]   **233**

* H. Moore's *Life of . . . John Wesley*, II.367.
This is a translation from Ovid's *Metamorphoses*, Book I, lines 144, 148–50, treated
as a unit.

Metre 98a: Iambic 10's

Vivitur ex rapto: Non hospes ab hospite tutus:
Filius ante diem patrios inquirit in annos;
Victa jacet pietas; et virgo caede madentes,
Ultima coelestum terras Astraea reliquit.

They live by rapine. The unwary guest
Is poison'd at the inhospitable feast.
The son, impatient for his father's death,
Numbers his years, and longs to stop his breath;
Extinguish'd all regard to God and man: 5
And Justice, last of the celestial train,
Spurns the earth drench'd in blood, and flies to heaven again.

A PRAYER FOR HIS MAJESTY KING GEORGE   **234**

* *Hymns for Times of Trouble and Persecution* (1744), pp. 19–20, 'Trouble': 11.
Poetical Works, IV.22–3.

Metre 75: 6 6.7.7.7.7
A A b c b c

1   Immortal Potentate,
       Whose Sov'reign Will is Fate,
Own the King we have from Thee,
   Bless the Man of thy Right-hand,
Crown Him with thy Majesty,   5
   Let Him in Thine Image stand.

2   Him for thy Glory's Sake,
       Thy faithful Subject make:
Pour the Unction from above,
   All the Gifts divine impart,   10
Make Him happy in thy Love,
   Make Him after thine own Heart.

3   His sacred Life defend,
       And save him to the End:
Guard from all impending Harms,   15
   O Almighty King of Kings;
Keep Him in thy Mercy's Arms,
   Wrap Him in thy Mercy's Wings.

4   Defeat, confound, oppress
        The Troublers of his Peace: *20*
  Blast their every vain Design;
        Stablish Thou his quiet Throne;
  Tell his Foes This Soul is mine,
        Touch not Mine Anointed One:

5   Preserve a Life so dear,   *25*
        And long detain Him here:
  Late his spotless Soul receive
        To thy Palace in the Skies;
  Bid him late in Glory live,
        Live the Life that never dies.   *30*

235   FOR HIS MAJESTY KING GEORGE

        As sung at Mr Wesley's Room in the Horsefair, Bristol.

Later historians recognized that 6th December 1745 was the turning-point of the
Young Pretender's ill-fated venture, but danger was still far from being averted, and
it was by no means certain even in the early weeks of 1746 that he had actually shot
his bolt. This poem shows Wesley setting the Methodists to loyal song and prayer on
their sovereign's behalf. It was probably first sung on Wednesday 18th December,
which had been declared a public fast day.

* *Bristol Journal* (28th December 1745).
    A Word in Season: or, Advice to an Englishman (3rd edn, n.d., but probably early
    1746), printed in four 8-line verses.
    Poetical Works, IV.81-2.

                                                        Metre 30: 6.6.8.6
                                                                   A B A B

1   Immortal King of Kings
        Whose Favour or whose frown,
  Monarchs and states to honour brings
        Or turns them upside down.

2   To Thee in danger's hour   *5*
        We for our Sovereign cry,
  Protect him by thy gracious power
        And set him up on high.

3   Not by a mighty host
        Can he deliver'd be;   *10*
  Let others in their numbers trust,
        We look, O Lord, to thee.

4   Help to thy Servant send,
        And strengthen from above,
  And still thy Minister defend   *15*
        By thine Almighty Love.

5   The Spirit of thy Grace
    And Heavenly unction shed
And hosts of guardian angels place
    Around his sacred head.   *20*

6   Confound whoe'er oppose
    Or force them to retire,
Be Thou a tower against his foes,
    Be Thou a wall of fire.

7   O bring him out of all   *25*
    His *sanctified* distress
And by His name thy servant call,
    And fill him with thy peace.

8   Shew him, Almighty Lord
    That thou *his* Saviour art,   *30*
And speak the soul converting word,
    My son, give me thy heart.

18. Word: 'Thy heavenly unction'.

[THE VICTORY AT CULLODEN]   **236**

John Wesley's *Journal* for Thursday 9th October 1746 announced: 'The day of
Public Thanksgiving for the victory at Culloden was to us a day of solemn joy.'
The battle which ended the Stuart threat to the throne had been fought on 16th April,
though the Young Pretender did not escape from Scotland until September. The
Gentleman's Magazine had this to report about 9th October: 'Being appointed for a
publick thanksgiving for the total reduction of the rebels, it was observ'd by a great
resort to the publick places of worship, extraordinary illuminations at night, and all
other marks of joy, justly due on so happy an event.' Charles Wesley composed seven
hymns for the occasion, of which we give the second.

* *Hymns for the Public Thanksgiving-Day* (October 9, 1746): No. 2 [from the Bristol
    edition—identical with London edition, except that the latter has verses
    numbered '1.', '2.' &c.].
    Poetical Works, IV.95–6.

                                                Metre 15: 8 8.8 8.8 8
                                                          A A B B C C

1 Thanks be to GOD, the GOD of Power,
    Who shelter'd us in Danger's Hour,
    The GOD of Truth, who heard the Prayer,
    Let all his Faithfulness declare,
    Who sent us Succours from above,   *5*
    Let all adore the GOD of Love.

2 GOD sitting on his holy Seat
    Compels the Heathen to submit,
    The Grashoppers of Earth he sees,
    And mocks their prosp'rous Wickedness,   *10*
    Frustrates their Counsels with a Frown,
    And turns their *Babels* upside down.

3 His Eye observ'd the dark Design,
  To blast our rightful Monarch's Line,
  The Scheme in Satan's *Conclave* laid,   *15*
  Improv'd by *Rome*'s unerring Head,
  To gaul us with their Yoke abhor'd,
  And plant *their* Faith with Fire and Sword.

4 He saw the Serpent's Egg break forth,
  The Cloud arising in the North,   *20*
  He let the *slighted* Mischief spread,
  And hang in Thunder o'er our Head;
  And while we scorn'd our abject Foes,
  The Drop into a Torrent rose.

5 Lur'd by the grateful Scent of Blood,   *25*
  The Vultur[e]s hasten'd to their Food,
  The Aliens urg'd their rapid Way,
  Resolv'd to die, or win the Day;
  Madly resolv'd their Doom to brave,
  And gain *a Kingdom or a Grave*.   *30*

6 Swell'd to an Host, the daring Few
  Thro' ours as waving Lightning flew,
  Rush'd on with *unresisted* Power,
  And scal'd the Wall, and storm'd the Tower,
  While GOD *seem'd* pleas'd their Cause to bless,   *35*
  And curs'd them with a short Success.

7 Drunk with the bold aspiring Hope,
  Behold them march triumphant up,
  Of Conquest fatally secure,
  They vow to make our Ruin sure,   *40*
  And shout around our threatened Towers,
  '*The Day, the Crown, and all is ours*!'

8 Who was it then dispers'd the Snare,
  And choak'd those ravening Dogs of War?
  JEHOVAH curb'd their furious Speed,   *45*
  JEHOVAH sent the panick Dread,
  And damp'd and fill'd them with Dismay,
  And scar'd the Vultur[e]s from their Prey.

9 His hidden Power controll'd the Foe,
  And said, 'No farther shalt thou go.'   *50*
  His Bridle in their Mouths they found,
  And fled subdu'd without a Wound,
  (As Stubble by the Whirlwind driven)
  They fled before the Frown of Heaven.

10 Thanks be to GOD, the GOD of Power,   55
   Who shelter'd us in Danger's Hour,
   The GOD of Truth, who heard the Prayer,
   Let all his Faithfulness declare,
   Who sent Deliverance from above,
   Let all adore the GOD of Love!   60

WRITTEN IN D[UBLI]N   237

John Wesley first visited Dublin, the jumping-off point for all his evangelism in
Ireland, on 9th August 1747. Speedily realizing both the opportunities and the dif-
ficulties, he sent urgent messages for Charles to come and take over, and it was upon
the shoulders of the younger brother that much of the responsibility rested for steering
the infant societies through dissensions and persecutions. Throughout that winter he
faced troubles in plenty, and a number of his poems throw light on his promising yet
perilous experiences: 'For the Roman Catholicks in Ireland', 'Thanksgiving for the
Success of the Gospel in Ireland', 'After our Deliverance at Athlone', and 'Occasioned
by an Irish Judge's Sentencing me to Transportation'. This unfinished poem is the
precipitate from one of those many occasions when persecution seemed bound to end
in death. This is one of the earliest examples of what became his standard variant of
metre 79a. (See item **125**.)

* MS Richmond, pp. 67–8.
   MS Occasional, pp. 77–8, with note 'To—With pity, Lord, &c.' and '6.' at end for
   unwritten additional verse.
                                              Metre 79: 8 7.6.8 8.6
                                                      A a B C C B

1 Far from my Native Land remov'd
   Far from all I priz'd & Lov'd,
      In a black Wilderness,
   I ask my Soul, What dost Thou here,
   Thou poor afflicted Sojourner,   5
      This Earth is not thy Place.

2 Nothing beneath my Heart commands,
      Hope & I have shaken hands,
         And parted long ago.
   Inur'd to Pain, & Shame, & Grief,   10
   I ask, I look for no Relief,
      For no Delight below.

3 Happy, forever happy I,
      Suffer'd to escape, & fly
         To that eternal Shore   15
   Where all the Storms of Life are past,
   And Exiles find their Home at last,
      And Losers weep no more.

4 Come then, ye threatning Sons of Rome
      Kindly to my Rescue come,
         And set my Spirit free,   20
   Nor tremble at th'Avenger near
   No Justice is for Christians here,
      For slaughter'd Sheep—or me.

   3. MS Occas.: 'bleak Wilderness'.

5 An Outcast for my Master's sake   *25*
     Haste, ye Ruffian Band to take
     This mournful Life of mine;
  A Life by Sin & Sorrow stain'd,
  A Life, w[hi]ch I have long disdain'd,
     And languish'd to resign.   *30*

25. MS Occas.: 'An Outlaw'.

238   [PUREST PASSION]

Charles Wesley's courtship of Sarah Gwynne of Garth, Brecon, was even more a
succession of emotional crises, uncertainties and raptures than is normal in such
processes. In his case this inevitably involved several series of poems, scores of them,
some of which were transcribed by him into little volumes and became treasured
family heirlooms, though they were not (for the most part) published. (See Nos.
78–83 in the *Sources*.) To begin with, there was a serious discrepancy in the ages of
the two lovers. When at last the relationship of spiritual instructor and pupil was
transformed into a more intimate one, during the summer of 1748, Charles Wesley
was forty and Sally Gwynne twenty-one. Far more serious (for Sally's parents at any
rate) was his lack of financial prospect. This was partly overcome by the firm arrangements upon which they insisted about securing his own share in the expected profits
of the Wesleys' joint publications, and also by the independent publication in 1749
of two volumes of *Hymns and Sacred Poems*. More important still, to Charles Wesley
at least, was the uncertainty whether this proposed marriage was in fact the will of
God, to be used for the spiritual enrichment of both partners, and for the increase of
their usefulness in His work. With a few minor complications thrown in for good
measure, the year preceding their wedding on 8th April 1749 was for Charles Wesley
a succession of desert wanderings in search of advice, comfort, and hope, a few minor
peaks of elation, and many deep chasms of despair.

* MS Deliberative Hymns, pp. 5–6.
  MS Occasional Hymns, pp. 53–4.

                                                    Metre 58 : 8.3 3.6
                                                              a b b a
'To the Tune of—Jesus, Lord, in pity hear us.'

1 Christ, my Life, my Only Treasure,
     Thou alone
     Mould Thine own,
  After thy Good pleasure.

                              direct
2 Thou, who paidst my Price ~~shalt have~~ me!   *5*
     Thine I am,
     Holy Lamb,
  Save, and always save me.

3 Order Thou my whole Condition,
     Chuse my State,   *10*
     Fix my Fate
  By thy wise Decision.

5. MS Occas.: 'shalt have me'.

Dec. 18, 1748.

PROPOSALS

For Printing by SUBSCRIPTION,

TWO VOLUMES

OF

Hymns and Sacred Poems.

By CHARLES WESLEY, M. A.
Student of *Chrift-Church Oxford.*

CONDITIONS.

I. EACH Volume will contain upward of 300 Pages in large Duodecimo.

II. The Price of the Two Volumes will be 5*s.* half to be paid down, the reft on the Delivery of the Books, in Quires.

III. The whole Work is ready for the Prefs, and will be Printed immediately.

IV. Bookfellers fubfcribing for fix Copies, will have a feventh Gratis.

SUBSCRIPTIONS are taken in by *T. Trye*, near *Gray's-Inn Gate, Holbourn*; and at the *Foundry* in *Upper-Moor-Fields, London*:—In *Newcaftle upon Tyne*, by *R. Akenhead*:—In *Briftol*, by *Felix Farley*, in *Caftle-Green*; *J. Wilfon*, Bookfeller, in *Wine-ftreet*.

The SUBSCRIBERS are defired to fend th———

Dec. 24. 1748

Received of [...]

the Sum of Two Shillings and Six-Pence, for the Subfcription of Two Volumes of Hymns, which I promife to deliver on the Payment of Two Shillings and Six-Pence more.

Wesley

PROPOSALS FOR
*HYMNS AND SACRED
POEMS* (1749)
*on which Charles Wesley
noted his betrothed as his first
subscriber (see opposite)*

4 From all Earthly Expectation
      Set me free,
      Seize for Thee
  All my Strength of Passion.   *15*

5 Into absolute Subjection
      Be it brought,
      Every Thought,
  Every fond Affection.   *20*

6 That which most my Soul requires
      For thy sake
      Hold it back
  Purge my Best Desires.

7 Keep from me thy loveliest Creature,   *25*
      Till I prove
      JESUS' Love
  Infinitely sweeter;

8 Till with purest Passion panting
      Cries my Heart   *30*
      'Where Thou art
  'Nothing more is wanting.'

9 Blest with thine Abiding Spirit,
      Fully blest
      Now I rest,   *35*
  All in Thee inherit.

10 Heaven is now with Jesus given;
      Christ in me,
      Thou shalt be
  Mine Eternal Heaven.   *40*

33. MS Occas.: 'thy Abiding Spirit'.
36. MS Occas.: 'All in One inherit.   Thee'.
40. MS Occas.: 'My Eternal'.

[DREAM OF HOPE]   **239**

* MS Deliberative Hymns, p. 23.
  MS Occasional Hymns, p. 19.

                                          Metre 7: 8.8.8.8
                                                   A B A B

1 Thou righteous GOD, whose Plague I bear,
    Whose Plague I from my Youth have borne,
  Shut up in Temporal Despair,
    Ordain'd to suffer, & to mourn;

2 If now I had forgot to grieve,   *5*
   As every Penal Storm were or'e,
Forgive, the Senseless Wretch forgive,
   And all my Chastisement restore.

3 Asham'd of having hop'd for Rest,
   Or ask'd for Comfort here below,   *10*
Lo! I revoke the rash Request,
   And sink again in desp'rate Woe.

4 Submissive to the Stroke again
   I bow my faint devoted Head.
Till Thou discharge the latest Pain,   *15*
   And write me free among the Dead.

5 Ah! what have I to do with Peace,
   Or Converse sweet, or Social Love?
From Man, & all his Help, I cease,
   From Earth, & all her Goods remove: *20*

6 Waking out of my Dream of Hope
   I see the fond Delusion end,
And give the whole Creation up,
   And live and die—without a Friend.
                                        Q?

End: MS Occasional Hymns omits the 'Q?'.

240   [A FEW UNRUFFLED DAYS?]

This unfinished poem was sent in a letter to Sally Gwynne, dated 'L[ondo]n. Tues.
Nt.' It was probably written on 20th December 1748, shortly after the combined
judgements of the Rev. Vincent Perronet, whom he visited at Shoreham on the 19th,
and of Mrs Blackwell and Mrs Dewal, of Lewisham, whom he saw on the 20th, all
concurring with that of his brother John, had at last convinced him that the proposed
marriage was a worthy project, and that it was likely to take place.

* MS Wesley Family Letters, IV.48, at Methodist Book Room, London.
                                        Metre 31: 6.6.8.6.6.6.8.6
                                                   A B A B C D C D

1   And is there Hope for me
      In Life's distracting Maze,
   And shall I live on Earth to see
      A few unruffled Days?
      A Man of Sorrows I   *5*
      A Sufferer from the Womb,
   Twas all my Hope in Peace to die,
      And rest within my Tomb.

2   How then can I conceive
      A Good for me design'd   *10*
   The greatest God Himself could give
      The Parent of Mankind?

A good by Sovereign Love
To sinless Adam given
His joyous Paradise t'improve,   *15*
And turn his Earth to Heaven.

3   God of unbounded Grace,
If yet Thou wilt bestow
On me the Vilest of the Race
Thy choicest Gift below;   *20*
My drooping Heart prepare
The Blessing to receive
And bid the Child of sad Despair
With Confidence Believe.

4   My new & strange Distress   *25*
To Thee I simply own,
Inur'd to Pain I start from Peace
And dread a *Good* unknown :
My Heart Thou seest it ache
Its dearest Wish t'obtain   *30*
And kno[we]st my Fear of measuring back
My steps to Earth again.

5   Assure my trembling ~~Heart~~ Soul
Of the decisive Will
My endless Doubts & Fears controul,   *35*
And bid my Heart be still:
Regard thy Servant's Call
And shed thy Love abroad
The Sign Infallible that all
My Works are wrought in God.   *40*

6   Thou, Lord, direct my Ways,
On all my Counsels shine
And lead by thine unerring Grace
This feeble Soul of mine;
Thy Pardning Love reveal   *45*
In Proof of thy Decree,
And stamp Her with thy Spirit's Seal,
The Friend *design[e]d* for me.

7   With stedfast Faith & Love
Let me thy Creature take   *50*
As a good Angel from above,
Sent down for Jesus sake.
Not to inthrall my Will
Not to put out my Eyes
But fix my Heart & fire my Zeal   *55*
And lift me to the Skies.

8 I have not time to finish: Your Heart will say
  Amen to a Prayer in w[hi]ch yourself are so nearly
  concerned . . . Ln. Tues.Nt.

241   [MY FAMILY]

After their marriage on 8th April 1749, a brief honeymoon, and months of separation, Charles and Sally Wesley eventually set up their home in Charles Street, Bristol, on 1st September 1749. They signalized their beginning of household duties by what Charles Wesley called his '*first* Family Hymn'.

* *Charles Wesley's Journal* (edn, Jackson), II.65.
    Transcript by Thomas Marriott of letter by Charles Wesley to Ebenezer Black-
    well, 4th September 1749 (at Richmond College, Surrey). Cf. *Methodist Magazine*
    (1848), pp. 638–9, and W.H.S. *Proceedings*, XXII.154.
Poetical Works, VIII.401–2.

Metre 85: 7.6.7.6.7.7.7.6
a B a B c d c D

God of faithful Abraham, hear
  His feeble son and thine,
In thy glorious power appear,
  And bless my just design:
Lo! I come to serve thy will,   *5*
  All thy blessed will to prove;
Fired with patriarchal zeal,
  And pure primeval love.

Me and mine I fain would give
  A sacrifice to Thee,   *10*
By the ancient model live,
  The true simplicity;
Walk as in my Maker's sight,
  Free from wordly guile and care,
Praise my innocent delight,   *15*
  And all my business prayer.

Whom to me thy goodness lends
  Till life's last gasp is o'er,
Servants, relatives, and friends,
  I promise to restore;   *20*
All shall on thy side appear,
  All shall in thy service join,
Principled with godly fear,
  And worshippers divine.

Them, as much as lies in me,   *25*
  I will through grace persuade,
Seize, and turn their souls to Thee
  For whom their souls were made;
Bring them to th' atoning blood,
  (Blood that speaks a world forgiven,)   *30*
Make them serious, wise, and good,
  And train them up for heaven.

[SACRED HORROR] 242

On 8th February 1750, between 12 noon and 1 p.m., an earthquake was felt through-out London, Westminster, and the home counties. Many houses were damaged, and the event provided much matter for conversation and newspaper articles. A month later, on Tuesday 8th March, a far more serious and prolonged shock was felt throughout the same area. Many people were awakened. The good Methodists were in the middle of their early morning preaching service in the Foundery, which shook so violently that they expected it to fall on their heads. Charles Wesley, who was conducting the service, immediately cried out: 'Therefore will we not fear, though the earth be removed and the hills be carried into the midst of the sea; for the Lord of hosts is with us. . . .' He followed the event up with a published sermon entitled *The Cause and Cure of Earthquakes* (the cure being repentance), and with two little collections of hymns, which were reprinted after the Lisbon earthquake of 1755.

* *Hymns occasioned by the Earthquake*, 8th March 1750, Part 1: No. 2.
Poetical Works, VI.20–1.

Metre 86: 7.6.7.6.7.8.7.6
a B a B c D c D

1 GOD of glorious majesty,
　Whose judgments are abroad,
Pierce and turn our hearts to thee
　With sacred horror aw'd;
All this drowsy land awake,　　　　　　　　　　5
　And by the thunder of thy power
Shake, our inmost spirits shake,
　And let us sleep no more.

2 Rising in thy dreadful might
　The wicked to rebuke,　　　　　　　　　　　　10
Thou hast with unwonted fright
　Our sleeping bodies shook;
Earth did to her center quake,
　Convulsive pangs her bowels tore;
Shake, our inmost spirits shake,　　　　　　　15
　And let us sleep no more.

3 E'er the threatned ruin come,
　A general terror dart,
Send the keen conviction home
　To every thoughtless heart;　　　　　　　　20
Shake us out of *Satan*'s hands,
　Burst open every prison door,
Rouse and loose us from our bands,
　And bid us sin no more.

4 Jesus, Lord, to whom we cry,　　　　　　　25
　The true repentance give,
Give us at thy feet to lie,
　And tremble and believe;
On the Rock of ages place
　Our souls till all the wrath is o'er,　　　　30
Ground and stablish us in grace,
　And bid us sin no more.

243 [DIRE PORTENTS]

* Hymns occasioned by the Earthquake, 8th March 1750, Part. 1: No. 5.
Poetical Works, VI.24–5.

Metre 10: 8.8.8.8.8 8
A B A B C C

1 From whence these dire portents around,
    That strike us with unwonted fear!
Why do these earthquakes rock the ground,
    And threaten our destruction near?
Ye prophets smooth the cause explain,   *5*
And lull us to repose again.

2 Or water swelling for a vent,
    Or air impatient to get free,
Or fire within earth's intrails pent;
    Yet all are order'd Lord, by thee;   *10*
The elements obey thy nod,
And nature vindicates her GOD.

3 The pillars of the earth are thine,
    And thou hast set the world thereon;
They at thy sovereign word incline,   *15*
    The center trembles at thy frown,
The everlasting mountains bow,
And GOD is in the earthquake *now*!

4 Now, Lord, to shake our guilty land,
    Thou dost in indignation rise,   *20*
We see, we see thy lifted hand,
    Made bare a nation to chastise,
Whom neither plagues nor mercies move
To fear thy wrath or court thy love.

5 Therefore the earth beneath us reels,   *25*
    And staggers like our drunken men,
The earth the mournful cause reveals,
    And groans our burthen to sustain;
Ordain'd our evils to deplore,
And fall with us to rise no more.   *30*

15. Hymns, 2nd edn (1756): 'They at thy threatning Look incline'.

244 HYMN FOR APRIL 8, 1750

On Tuesday 3rd April 1750, writing from London, Charles Wesley sent the following
poem to his wife, who was staying with her parents in Ludlow while her husband
was busied on his preaching rounds. There is little but the poem in the letter, together with the introductory words: 'I have barely time to transcribe an hymn for
April 8, if we live so long, & commend you to the tender mercies of God in Xt Jesus!'
This was their first wedding anniversary. I am indebted to Professor Benjamin

Boyce for pointing out that the two opening lines, which Wesley had quoted in the diary entry for his wedding day, are quoted from George Herbert's 'Virtue'. This poem, indeed, was a favourite with the Wesleys; an adaptation appeared in *Hymns and Sacred Poems* (1739), and a simple reprint in *Select Parts of Mr Herbert's Poems* (1773).

* MS Richmond, pp. 123–4, with the shorthand note 'transcribed'.
   Wesley Family Letters, I.48 (Charles Wesley to his wife, 3rd April 1750), at the Methodist Book Room, London.

Metre 7: 8.8.8.8
A B A B

1 Sweet Day, so cool, so calm, so bright
   The Bridal of the earth & sky!
I see with joy thy chearing light,
   And lift my heart to things on high.

2 To Him my grateful heart I lift,   *5*
   Who did my guardian Angel send
Inrich'd me with an heavenly gift
   And bless'd me with a bosom-friend.

3 The mountains at his presence flow'd,
   His Providence the bar remov'd,   *10*
His grace my other soul bestow'd,
   And join'd me to his well-belov'd.

4 Twas GOD alone who join'd our hands,
   Who join'd us first in mind & heart,
In love's indissoluble bands   *15*
   W[hi]ch neither life nor death can p[ar]t.

5 GOD of eternal power & grace
   I bow my soul before thy throne,
I only breathe to breathe thy praise,
   I live & die to thee alone.   *20*

6 My more than life to thee I give,
   My more than friend to thee restore,
When summon'd with thyself to live,
   And fall, & silently adore.

7 Yet if thy gracious will consent   *25*
   To spare her yet another year,
With joy I grasp whom GOD hath lent,
   And clasp her to my bosom *here*.

All the following are in the Letter:
  5. 'My grateful heart to Him I lift'.   *6.* 'Who did the guardian'.
10. 'the Bars remov'd'.   *11.* 'my Better Soul'.
15. 'By love's'.   *19.* 'I only live to sing thy praise'.
25. 'Yet if thy ~~blessed~~ welcome will consent'.
27. 'With joy I take whom thou hast lent'.

271

8 Her in the arms of faith I bring,
    And place before thy glorious throne   *30*
Receive her, O thou heavenly king,
    And save whom thou hast call'd thine own.

9 Thy choicest blessing from above,
    Thy strongest consolations send,
And let her know thy perfect love,   *35*
    And freely talk with GOD her friend.

10 Keep up the intercourse between
    Our souls, our kindred souls & thee,
And fix our eye on things unseen,
    The glories or eternity.   *40*

11 O let us steadily pursue
    With strength combin'd the heavenly prize,
And kindled by the nearer view,
    Together both invade the skies.

12 The crown with holy violence seize,   *45*
    The perfect grace to conquerors giv'n
And rise renew'd in righteousness,
    And keep the marriage-feast in heaven.

33. 'The choicest'.
35. 'thine utmost love'.
36. 'And truly talk'.
38. 'our souls, our gasping souls'.
42. 'th'immortal Prize'.
46. 'The starry crown to'.
48. 'To share the'.

245   ON THE BIRTH-DAY OF A FRIEND

* *Family Hymns* (1767): No. 165.
    MS Richmond, pp. 2–4, where it is the second of two with this title; the added
       date 'Oct. 12' shows that it was written for his wife, probably in the first, or
       at least the early years of their marriage.
    Poetical Works, VII.198–200.
    Collection (1780): No. 478.
    Pocket Hymn Book (1787): No. 228.
    Collection (1831): No. 491.
    Collection (1876): No. 491.

Metre 65: 5 5.9.5 5.9
A A B C C B

1   Come away to the skies,
      My beloved arise,
And rejoice on the day thou wast born,

3. 1780, &c.: 'rejoice in the day'.

On the festival day
Come exulting away,   *5*
To thy heavenly country return.

2   We have laid up our love
     And treasure above,
Though our bodies continue below;
     The redeem'd of the Lord   *10*
     We remember his word,
And with singing to Sion we go.

3   With singing we praise
     The original grace
By our heavenly Father bestow'd,   *15*
     Our being receive
     From his bounty, and live
To the honour and glory of God.

4   For thy glory we Are,
     Created to share   *20*
Both the nature and kingdom divine:
     Created again,
     That our souls may remain
In time and eternity thine.

5   With thanks we approve   *25*
     The design of thy love
Which hath join'd us, in Jesus his name,
     So united in heart,
     That we never can part,
Till we meet at the feast of the Lamb.   *30*

6   There, there at his seat
     We shall suddenly meet,
And be parted in body no more,
     We shall sing to our lyres
     With the heavenly quires,   *35*
And our Saviour in glory adore.

4. 1780 (from 3rd edn, 1782), &c.: 'On this festival day'.
6. 1780, &c.: 'And with singing to Sion return.'
12. 1780, &c.: 'singing to paradise go.'
23. 1780 (1st edn): 'Your souls may remain' corrected to original in 2nd
     edn (1781).
25. MS: 'With Joy we approve'.
27. MS, 1780, &c.: 'In Jesus's Name'.
31. 1780, &c.: 'at his feet'.

273

7   Hallelujah we sing
    To our Father and King,
And his rapturous praises repeat;
    To the Lamb that was slain   *40*
    Hallelujah again
Sing all heaven, and fall at his feet.

8   In assurance of hope
    We to Jesus look up,
Till his banner unfurl'd in the air   *45*
    From our grave we doth see,
    And cry out IT IS HE,
And fly up to acknowledge him there!

39. MS: 'rapturous Glory repeat'.
46. MS: 'we both see'—'doth' is obviously a misprint;
      1780 (1st and 2nd edns): 'From our graves we do see';
      1780 (3rd, 1782), &c.: 'From our graves we shall see'.

246   [ON JOHN WESLEY'S MARRIAGE]

In spite of their differences in age and temperament, John and Charles Wesley were
the closest and the warmest friends. The first serious breach was when Charles (from
the worthiest of motives) intervened to prevent John's marriage to Grace Murray.
Little more than a year later, in February 1751, John Wesley made an even worse
mistake in marrying Mrs Mary Vazeille, and—contrary to their agreement—he did
not inform his brother of his intention. Two manuscript poems in the Richmond
volume reflect the deep wound thus inflicted:

> My Friend with me to live & die
>   Before thy altar sworn,
> Is like a summer's brook past by
>   And never shall return.

Charles believed that this blow fell partly because of his near-adoration of his elder
brother, from which God intended thus to save him:

> [I] fondly made my friend my God,
>   And sought my all from Him . . .
> The stream of creature-love dried up,
>   I still the Fountain see,
> And all my Joy, & all my Hope,
>   And all my Heav'n in Thee.

The strange thing is that under the immediate impact of the shattering blow there
is no hint that Charles found any compensation in the fact that he had himself
gained a new friend through his own marriage.

* MS Richmond, pp. (142)–3.

Metre 1: 8.6.8.6
A B A B

1 Ah woe is me, a man of woe,
    A mourner from the womb,
  I see my Lot and softly go
    Lamenting to the tomb.

2 In calm despair I bow my head,   *5*
    The heavenly Loan restore,
For O! my latest Hope is dead,
    And Friendship is no more.

3 Too happy in His Love I was,
    I was—but I submit!   *10*
Irreparable is the Loss,
    The Ruin is compleat.

4 O could I to the Desart fly
    Till pain with life sh[oul]d end,
And ah! my *faithless Bro[the]r* cry   *15*
    And ah! my faithless Friend.

5 The dearest Sharer of my heart,
    Ah! whither is he fled!
My Friend, whom death c[oul]d never p[ar]t,
    To me is doubly dead.   *20*

6 In simple innocency drest
    The soft Ephesian's charms
Have caught him from my honest breast
    To her bewitching Arms.

7 My other Self, but more belov'd   *25*
    In youth, in manhood tried
        30
Faithful for 4̶0̶ winters prov'd
    Is ravish'd from my side.

8 O what a mighty Loss is mine!
    The anguish who can tell,   *30*
The more than anguish to resign
    A Soul I lov'd so well!

9 But shall a sinful man complain
    Or murmur at the Rod?
I yield, I yield him back again   *35*
    Into the Arms of God.

10 There let me find him in that day
    When all the Saints ascend,
And lo! I weep my life away,
    For my Departed Friend.   *40*

[THE PEACEFUL SHADE]   **247**

In April 1751, still suffering from the shock of his brother's unheralded wedding to
Mrs Vazeille, Charles Wesley retired for a week to the home of Mrs Colvil and Miss
Degge on St Anne's Hill, Chertsey. His *Journal*, under date 9th April, states that the
time was spent chiefly in 'reading, singing, and prayer'. The singing seems to have
included a number of contemporary ballads, to which Wesley wrote his own words,

some of them simple appreciations of rural life, others more specifically religious in tone. 'The Peaceful Shade' is an example of the first class, and 'Pastures Green' of the second, which was found suitable for inclusion in his *Scripture Hymns*. Cf. No. **158**.

Both these poems were described as set 'To—Let me wander, not unseen'. This is the ballad composed by Handel in his '*Songs in L'Allegro ed Il Penseroso*' (1740), pp. 22–3, in the key of F, in a smooth swaying 12/8 measure modelled on the Siciliano dance mode. The words are adapted from Milton's *L'Allegro*, lines 57–8, 63–8, and are given thus by Handel to be 'Sung by Mr Beard':

> Let me Wander, not unseen
> by Hedgerow Elms, on Hillocks Green,
> There the Plowman near at Hand
> Whistles o'er the furrow'd Land,
> There the plowman near at Hand
> Whistles o'er the Furrow'd Land.
> And the Milkmaid Singeth Blithe;
> And the mower whets his scythe;
> and every Shepherd tells his Tale
> under the Hawthorn, in the Dale,
> And every Shepherd tells his Tale
> under the Hawthorn, in the Dale.

The song became very popular and was included in various collections, while the air was used for other songs, as for 'My Dolly' in 'Love in a Village' (1762).
[N.B.—The following two poems have been set out according to Charles Wesley's normal practice, although in fact MS Richmond uses no indenting, and in the *Scripture Hymns* all but the second and eighth lines are indented. In Handel's original the words are interlined with the music.]

* MS Richmond, p. (148).

Metre 92: 7 8.7 7.7 7.8 8
a A b b c c D D

> Hide me in the peaceful shade
> For lonely Contemplation made,
> Where the Birds on every tree
> Whistle artless melody,
> Where the River glides so slow,   5
> Where the Landscape swells below,
> And every soul may muse its fill
> Under the Side of S[t. Anne's] Hill.

248   **[PASTURES GREEN]**

* MS Richmond, p. (148).
Scripture Hymns (1762): O.T. 795 (I.255).
Scripture Hymns (1794): O.T. 729 (I.299).
Poetical Works, IX.281.

Metre 92: 7 8.7 7.7 7.8 8
a A b b c c D D

> Bear me to the sacred Scene,
> The silent Streams & pastures green.
> There the chrystal waters shine,
> Springing up with Life divine,
> There the Flock of Israel feed,   5
> Guided by their Shepherd's Tread,
> And every sheep delights to hide
> Under the Tree where Jesus died!

3, 5. *Scripture Hymns*: 'Where the'.

[FOR PREACHERS IN CONFERENCE]   **249**

In 1751 John Wesley asked his brother Charles to tour England for the specific purpose of 'purging the preachers', that is of discovering how far the lay preachers were men of good character and suitable gifts, and of dispensing with those who proved unworthy. Charles Wesley took his task very seriously. He suggested some basic rules for the choice and employment of the preachers, yet tried to avoid undue rigidity in their application to the preachers already serving. He summoned a conference of the chief preachers in the Leeds area for 11th–12th September, which was attended by two other clergymen, William Grimshaw and John Milner. In his manuscript journal of the tour, sent in letters to John, he described how this Conference commenced with 'Part of an Hymn'—the twelve verses given below. After this exercise in self-examination, Charles Wesley led in prayer and went on 'to speak of the qualifications, work, & trials of a preacher'.

* Charles Wesley MSS IV.26, at the Methodist Book Room, London.
 MS Preachers Extraordinary, pp. 1–3.
 MS Miscellaneous Hymns, pp. 109–11, as the first of thirteen 'Hymns for Preachers'.
 Poetical Works, VIII.404–5.

Metre 1: 8.6.8.6
ABAB

1 Arise, thou jealous GOD, arise,
   Thy sifting Power exert,
 Look thro' us with thy flaming eyes,
   And search out every Heart.

2 Our inmost Souls thy Spirit knows,   *5*
   And let him now display
 Whom Thou hast for thy Glory chose,
   And purge the rest away.

3 Th'Apostles false far off remove,
   The faithful Labourers own,   *10*
 And give *us* each himself to prove,
   And know as he is known.

4 Do *I* presume to preach thy word
   By Thee uncall'd unsent?
 Am *I* the Servant of the Lord,   *15*
   Or Satan's Instrument?

5 Is this, great God, my single Aim,
   Thine, wholly Thine to be;
 To serve thy Will, declare thy Name,
   And gather Souls for Thee?   *20*

6 To labour in my Master's Cause,
   Thy Grace to testify,
 And spread the Victory of thy Cross,
   And on thy Cross to die?

7 I once *unfeignedly believ'd*   *25*
   Myself sent forth by Thee:
 But have I *kept* the Grace rec[eive]d,
   In simple Poverty?

8 Still do I for thy Kingdom pant
   Till all its Coming prove,   *30*
   And Nothing seek, & Nothing want
   But more of Jesu's Love?

9 If still I in thy Grace abide,
   My Call confirm & clear,
   And into thy whole Counsel guide   *35*
   Thy poorest Messenger.

10 Unite my heart to All yt bear
   The Burthen of the Lord,
   And let our spotless Lives declare
   The Virtue of thy Word.   *40*

11 One Soul into us all inspire,
   And let it strongly move
   In fervent Flames of calm Desire
   To glorify thy Love.

12 O may we in thy Love agree   *45*
   To make its Sweetness known,
   Thy Love the Bond of Union be,
   And perfect us in One.

42.   MSS Preachers, Misc. Hymns: 'let us strongly'.
43.   MSS Preachers, Misc. Hymns: 'pure desire'.
45–6. MSS Preachers, Misc. Hymns: 'And while we cordially agree.
                         To make thy goodness known'

250   PRAYER FOR AN UNBORN CHILD

Charles Wesley was a man built for family life, and the great difference in age between himself and his wife increased rather than lessened his attachment to her and their children. The coming of their first-born son in 1752 was an event deeply charged with emotion, particularly as they had been saddened by a previous miscarriage. Charles Wesley's feelings found vent in prayer-poems for the unborn child and for the mother-to-be. The birth brought forth more poems, and the joys and anxieties of infancy still more. When the child (christened 'John Wesley' after his uncle) was little more than a year old both he and his mother contracted small-pox. Mrs Wesley recovered, but was so marked that the nineteen years' difference between her husband and herself was no longer noticeable. Little Jackie died. It was a shattering blow to them both, and perhaps particularly to Charles Wesley, who had so far held his emotions in check, alike from a natural reserve, from a fear of spoiling the child, and from an exaggerated dread of giving him the worship which should be reserved for his Creator. A series of eight poems on the child's death were published (their personal origin only partly disguised) in *Funeral Hymns* (1759). Others were left in manuscript. The date of young Jackie's death continued to be a black-letter day in his diary long years after the longed-for family had become a reality. Although Charles Wesley wrote many poems about other children and other events, the death of his first-born son probably meant more to him than any other domestic happening. The poetic expression of his grief, however, is softened (and, some might feel, almost stultified) by a characteristic restraint.

* MS Miscellaneous Hymns, p. 71.

Metre 79: 8 7.6.8 8.6
A a B C C B

1 Fountain of life and happiness,
　Jesus sent the world to bless,
　　With true felicity,
　My infant yet unborn receive,
　And let it for thy glory live　　　　5
　　A sacrifice to Thee.

2 Before it sees this outward light,
　Claim it, Saviour, as thy right,
　　Thy purchas'd Creature claim,
　Before it draws *this* tainted air,
　Adopt for thy peculiar care,　　　　10
　　And mark it with thy Name.

PRAYER FOR A SICK CHILD　　　**251**

MS Miscellaneous Hymns, pp. 71–2.

Metre 46: 7 7.7 7
a a b b

1 God of love, incline thine ear,
　Hear a cry of grief and fear,
　Hear an anxious Parent's cry,
　Help, before my Isaac die.

2 All my comfort in distress,　　　　5
　All my earthly happiness,
　Spare him still, the precious Loan;
　Is he not my only Son?

3 Whom I did from Thee obtain
　Must I give him back again?　　　　10
　Can I with the blessing part?
　Lord, Thou know'st a Mother's heart:

4 All its passionate excess,
　All its yearning tenderness,
　Nature's soft infirmity　　　　15
　Is it not a drop from Thee?

5 For thy own compassion's sake,
　Give me then my Darling back
　Rais'd as from the dead, to praise,
　Love, and serve Thee all his days.　　20

6 Speak, and at the powerful word,
　Lo, the witness for his Lord,
　Monument of grace divine,
　Isaac lives, for ever thine!

252   ON THE DEATH OF A CHILD[1]

* *Funeral Hymns* (1759): No. 20.
Poetical Works, VI.252–3.

Metre 10: 8.8.8.8.8 8
ABABCC

1 Dead! dead! the Child I lov'd so well!
    Transported to the world above!
I need no more my heart conceal:
    I never dar'd indulge my love:
But may I not indulge my grief,   5
And seek in tears a sad relief?

2 Mine earthly happiness is fled,
    His mother's joy, his father's hope,
(O had I dy'd in *Isaac*'s stead!)
    He *should* have liv'd, my age's prop,   10
He should have clos'd his father's eyes,
And follow'd me to paradise.

3 But hath not heaven, who first bestow'd,
    A right to take his gifts away?
I bow me to the sovereign GOD,   15
    Who snatch'd him from the evil day!
Yet nature *will* repeat her moan,
And fondly cry, 'My son, my son!'

4 Turn from him, turn, officious thought!
    Officious thought presents again   20
The thousand little acts he wrought,
    Which wound my heart with soothing pain:
His looks, his winning gestures rise,
His waving hands, and laughing eyes!

5 Those waving hands no more shall move,   25
    Those laughing eyes shall smile no more:
He cannot now engage our love,
    With sweet insinuating power
Our weak unguarded hearts insnare,
And rival his Creator there.   30

6 From us, as we from him, secure,
    Caught to his heavenly Father's breast,
He waits, till we the bliss insure,
    From all these stormy sorrows rest,
And see him with our Angel stand,   35
To waft, and welcome us to land.

[1 There seems not the slightest doubt that this, like the other seven poems in this series, were written on the death of his own first-born. The clues all point in that direction—'He justly claims the first-born son' (21.6); 'The mother left, the child He took' (21.15—both were ill of small-pox); 'Hath singled out our only son' (26.5).]

WRITTEN JANUARY 7, 1768   **253**

* MS Miscellaneous Hymns, pp. 73–4.
Poetical Works, VIII.409–10.

Metre 93: 7 8.7 8.7 8.8 8
a A b B c C D D

1   Solemn, memorable day
That snatch'd my darling Son[1] away,
   Calm I welcome thy return
Which summons me again to mourn,
   After a sad length of years   *5*
To pour again my selfish tears,
To bleed with undiminish'd smart,
And feel the recent wound of heart.

2   Time may gently bring relief,
Assuage, or cure a common grief,   *10*
   I no end of sorrow see,
Till harbour'd in eternity:
   Then, my God, and not before
My penal woes shall all be o're,
And gloomy sorrow flee away   *15*
At the first dawn of endless day.

3   Now accepting my distress,
I suffer out my evil days,
   Softly toward the tomb I tread,
Myself lamenting, not the dead;   *20*
   Till my Life in death appears,
And Jesus, banishing my fears,
Chears by the beauties of his Face
O'rewhelms me with the glorious Blaze.

[[1] Charles Wesley notes, 'John I', i.e. his first-born, who died 7th January 1754.]

FOR A WOMAN NEAR THE TIME OF HER TRAVAIL   **254**

In his *Hymns for the Use of Families* Charles Wesley inserted no fewer than eleven under the title used above. Six of these, including that given below, were transcribed by Charles Wesley's wife into a much-thumbed little note-book which she obviously used for her devotions during her frequent pregnancies. One more is added in the hand of Charles Wesley, together with a prayer in verse 'For a Sick Child'. The actual occasion of this particular poem is fairly clear. It seems to have been written as she was awaiting the birth of Martha Maria in the summer of 1755, and the first three verses are introduced thus: 'Take an imperfect Hymn just as it came to my mind—'.

* *Family Hymns* (1767): No. 53.
MS Letter (? 17th May 1755), Emory University, Georgia. (First three verses only.)
MS Travail: No. 6.
Poetical Works, VII.60–1.

Metre 85: 7.6.7.6.7.7.7.6
a B a B c d c D

1 Lord, I magnify thy power,
   Thy love and faithfulness,
Kept to my appointed hour
   In safety and in peace:

Let thy providential care 5
    Still my sure protection be,
'Till a living child I bear,
    A sacrifice to Thee.

2 Who so near the birth hast brought,
    (Since I on Thee rely) 10
Tell me, Saviour, wilt thou not
    Thy farther help supply?
Whisper to my list'ning soul,
    Wilt thou not my strength renew,
Nature's fears and pangs controul, 15
    And bring thy handmaid thro'?

3 Father, in the name I pray
    Of thine incarnate Love,
Humbly ask, that as my day
    My suffering strength may prove: 20
When my sorrows most increase,
    Let thy strongest joys be given;
Jesus come *with* my distress,
    And agony is heaven.

4 Father, Son, and Holy Ghost, 25
    For good remember me,
Me whom Thou hast caus'd to trust
    For more than life in Thee:
With me in the fire remain,
    'Till like burnish'd gold I shine, 30
Meet, thro' consecrated pain,
    To see the Face Divine.

    8. MSS Letter, Travail: 'And give it back to Thee.'
  13. MS. Letter: 'S̶p̶e̶a̶k̶ ̶i̶t̶ Whisper'.
  15. MS Travail: 'Pains Controul'.
  18. MSS Letter, Travail: 'Of thy'.
  20. MSS Letter, Travail: 'My passive strength'.
  28. MS Travail: 'on Thee'.

255   [A SHORT-LIVED FLOWER]

On 25th July 1755, Charles Wesley's second child died, a girl, christened Martha Maria only a few weeks earlier. Once again the mother's pregnancy, the birth, the days and nights of sickness, and the death, were the occasions for 'hymns', some to be published later for devotional use by other parents. The loss of this second child heightened the tragedy of the death of their first-born son eighteen months earlier.

* *Family Hymns* (1767): No. 73 [actually 72, since there is no No. 71].
  Poetical Works, VII.82–4.

Title. Charles Wesley entitled the poem 'On her Death', the previous one having been 'For a sick Child'.

Metre 47: 7.7.7.7.7 7
a b a b c c

1 Lovely-fair, but breathless clay,
   Whither is thy tenant gone?
Would the soul no longer stay
   Prisoner in a world unknown?
Surfeited with life and pain,   *5*
Is she fled to heaven again?

2 Wherefore did she visit earth,
   Earth so suddenly to leave,
Gaul'd and burthen'd from the birth,
   Only born to cry and grieve?   *10*
What was all her life below?
One sad month of fruitless woe.

3 Count we now our mournful gains,
   We who call'd the child our own:
Lo, she pays her mother's pains   *15*
   With her last expiring groan:
Mocking all his fond desires,
Lo, her father's Hope expires!

4 Thus her parents grief she chears,
   Transient as a short-liv'd flower,   *20*
Scarcely seen she disappears,
   Blooms, and withers in an hour,
Thus our former loss supplies,
Thus our *promis'd* Comfort dies!

5 But shall sinful man complain   *25*
   Stript by the Divine decree?
Dares our impious grief arraign
   Heaven's tremendous Majesty?
Rather let us meekly own
All is right which God hath done.   *30*

6 God hath answer'd all our prayers,
   Mended after his own will,
Number'd with salvation's heirs
   Her whose happy change we *feel*,
Her whose bliss rebukes our sighs,   *35*
Bids us follow to the skies.

7 God, t'enhance her joy above,
   Gave her a few painful days,
Object of his richest love,
   Vessel of his choicest grace,   *40*
Bad her suffer with his Son,
Die to claim an earlier throne.

8 Best for her so soon to die:
   Best for us how can it be?
   Let our bleeding hearts reply,   *45*
     Torn from all, O Lord, but Thee,
To thy righteous will subdued,
Panting for the sovereign good.

9 Let them pant, and never rest
   'Till thy peace our sorrows heal,   *50*
Troubled be our aching breast
   'Till the balm of love we feel,
Love, which every want supplies,
Love of One that never dies.

10 Might we, Lord, thy love attain!   *55*
   Cure of every evil this,
This would turn our loss to gain,
   Turn our misery into bliss,
Love our Eden here would prove,
Love would make our heaven above.   *60*

256   AN EPISTLE TO THE REVEREND MR GEORGE
       WHITEFIELD: WRITTEN IN THE YEAR MDCCLV

John and Charles Wesley, together with George Whitefield, were the acknowledged leaders of the Methodist Revival. Alike members of the 'Holy Club' at Oxford, and ordained clergymen of the Church of England, their close friendship continued till death, and they often spoke of themselves as a 'threefold cord'. Even their strong theological differences strained their friendship only for a time, even though the Arminian Wesleys and the Calvinist Whitefield no longer found it practicable to work together as one team.

In 1755 Charles Wesley prepared for publication 'Epistles / To Moravians, Pre-destinarians, and Methodists / By a Clergyman of the Church of England'. It contained eight epistles, comprising 1920 lines in decasyllabic couplets. Their general tendency was to deplore any breach with the Church of England, even though acknowledging the spiritual good that had been done by the Moravians and the Calvinist wing of the Revival. Only that to his brother John was published at the time, and is given as No. **257** of the present volume. The *Epistle to Whitefield* rejoiced that after their doctrinal estrangement the Wesleys and Whitefield were once more united. John Wesley had written in his *Journal* for 5th November 1755: 'Mr Whitefield called upon me. Disputings are now no more; we love one another, and join hand in hand to promote the cause of our common Master.' This *Epistle* was not published until after Whitefield's death.

* *Epistle to Whitefield* (1771).
MS Epistles, pp. 45–51, entitled 'An Epistle to the Revd. Mr. G. Whitefield, 1755'.
Poetical Works, VI.67–72.

                    Metre 98a: Iambic 10's with closing 12's

Come on, my WHITEFIELD! (since the strife is past,
And friends at first are friends again at last)
Our hands, and hearts, and counsels let us join
In mutual league, t'advance the work Divine,
Our one contention now, our single aim,   5
To pluck poor souls as brands out of the flame;
To spread the victory of that bloody cross,
And gasp our latest breath in the Redeemer's cause.

Too long, alas! we gave to Satan place,
When party-zeal put on an angel's face,   *10*
Too long we list'ned to the couz'ning fiend,
Whose trumpet sounded, 'For the faith contend!'
With hasty blindfold rage, in error's night,
How did we with our fellow-soldiers fight!
We could not then our father's children know,   *15*
But each mistook his brother for his foe.
'Foes to the truth, can you in conscience spare?
'Tear them, (the tempter cry'd) in pieces, tear!'
So thick the darkness, so confus'd the noise,
We took the stranger's for the Shepherd's voice;   *20*
Rash nature wav'd the controversial sword,
On fire to fight the battles of the LORD,
Fraternal love from every breast was driv'n,
And bleeding Charity return'd to heaven.

The SAVIOUR saw our strife with pitying eye,   *25*
And cast a look that made the shadows fly:
Soon as the day-spring in his presence shone,
We found the two fierce armies were but one;
Common our hope, and family, and name,
Our arms, our Captain, and our crown the same,   *30*
Inlisted all beneath IMMANUEL's sign,
And purchas'd every soul with precious blood divine.

Then let us cordially again embrace,
Nor e'er infringe the league of gospel-grace;
Let us in JESUS' name to battle go,   *35*
And turn our arms against the common foe;
Fight side by side beneath our Captain's eye,   ⎫
Chase the Philistines, on their shoulders fly,   ⎬
And, more than conquerors, in the harness die. ⎭

For whether I am born to 'blush above,'   *40*
On earth suspicious of electing love,
Or you, o'erwhelm'd with honourable shame,
To shout the universal SAVIOUR's Name,
It matters not; if, all our conflicts past,
Before the great white throne we meet at last: *45*
Our only care, while sojourning below,
Our real Faith by real Love to show:
To blast the aliens' hope, and let them see
How friends of jarring sentiments agree:
Not in a party's narrow banks confin'd,   *50*
Not by a sameness of opinions join'd,
But cemented with the Redeemer's blood,
And bound together in the heart of GOD.

       e'er   Gospel
34. MS: 'Nor ~~ever more~~ infringe the League of ⁄ Grace:'.
53. MS: 'And bound ~~forever~~'; and 'together' on opposite page.

Can we forget from whence our union came,
When first we simply met in JESUS' name?   *55*
The name mysterious of the GOD UNKNOWN,
Whose secret love allur'd, and drew us on
Thro' a long, lonely, legal wilderness,
To find the promis'd land of gospel peace.
True yoke-fellows, we then agreed to draw   *60*
Th'intolerable burden of the Law,
And jointly lab'ring on with zealous strife,
Strengthen'd each other's hands to work *for* Life:
To turn against the world our steady face,
And, valiant for the truth, enjoy disgrace.   *65*

Then, when we serv'd our GOD thro' fear alone,
Our views, our studies, and our hearts were one;
No smallest difference damp'd the social flame:
In MOSES' school we thought, and spake the same:
And must we, now in CHRIST, with shame confess,   *70*
Our love was greater when our light was less?
When darkly thro' a glass with servile awe,
We first the spiritual commandment saw,
Could we not then, our mutual love to show,
Thro' fire and water for each other go?   *75*
We could:—we did:—In a strange land I stood,
And beckon'd thee to cross th'Atlantic flood:[1]
With true affection wing'd, thy ready mind,
Left country, fame, and ease, and friends behind,
And, eager all heav'n's counsels to explore,   *80*
Flew thro' the watry world and grasp'd the shore.

Nor did I linger, at my friend's desire,
To tempt the furnace, and abide the fire:[2]
When suddenly sent forth, from the high-ways
I call'd poor outcasts to the feast of grace;   *85*
Urg'd to pursue the work by thee begun,
Thro' good and ill report I still rush'd on,
Nor felt the fire of popular applause,
Nor fear'd the tort'ring flame in such a glorious cause.

[1 Charles Wesley wrote to Whitefield immediately on his return from Georgia in December 1736, saying that he was 'come over to procure labourers', and a letter from John Wesley a few days later confirmed this call. There is no extant letter to confirm that Charles Wesley had written along these lines to Whitefield while still in Georgia, however, as the poem suggests. (Cf. Tyerman's *Whitefield*, I.60.)]

[2 It is well known that upon Whitefield's challenge and following his example John Wesley commenced 'field-preaching' at Bristol on 2nd April 1739. Charles Wesley's first venture seems to have been on 29th May, in a field near Broadoaks, where he preached to about 500 on 'Repent, for the kingdom of heaven is at hand', and 'returned to the house rejoicing'. Again Whitefield's was the controlling example and influence.]

Ah! wherefore did we ever seem to part,   *90*
Or clash in sentiment, while one in heart?
What dire device did the old Serpent find,
To put asunder those whom GOD had join'd?
From folly and self-love Opinion rose,
To sever friends who never yet were foes;   *95*
To baffle and divert our noblest aim,
Confound our pride, and cover us with shame;
To make us blush beneath her short-liv'd pow'r,
And glad the world with one triumphant hour.

But lo! the snare is broke, the captive's freed,   *100*
By Faith on all the hostile powers we tread,
And crush thro' JESUS' strength the Serpent's head,
JESUS hath cast the curst Accuser down,
Hath rooted up the tares by Satan sown:
Kindled anew the never-dying flame,   *105*
And re-baptiz'd our souls into his Name.
Soon as the virtue of his Name we feel,
The storm of strife subsides, the sea is still,
All nature bows to his benign command,
And two are one in his Almighty hand.   *110*
One in his hand, O may we still remain,
Fast bound with love's indissoluble chain;
(That adamant which time and death defies,
That golden chain which draws us to the skies!)
His love the tie that binds us to his throne,   *115*
His love the bond that perfects us in one;
His love (let all the ground of friendship see)
His only love constrains our hearts t'agree,
And gives the rivet of Eternity!

100. MS: 'the Captives freed'.
109. MS: 'his supream Command'.
     Tie   binds
115. MS: 'His Love the ~~Bond~~ that ~~ties~~ us to his Throne'.
118. MS: 'His Love alone'.

AN EPISTLE TO THE REVEREND MR JOHN WESLEY **257**

At the Methodist Conference of 1755, held in Leeds, two related subjects of epochal importance were warmly debated for three days—whether lay preachers should administer the Sacraments, and whether Methodism should separate from the Church of England. On both questions Charles Wesley had the strongest convictions, and attended the Conference in fighting mood. After long preliminary discussions with his brother, Charles was sure that John was hovering on the brink of ordaining the Methodist preachers, and thus clearly putting himself in the wrong with the Anglican Church and demonstrating that Methodism was a sect. Eventually the Conference arrived at what was in effect a compromise, 'that (whether it was *lawful* or not) it was in no ways *expedient*'. Charles Wesley wrote home to his wife: 'I left the Brethren in Conference; but had quite enough of them first. Yet I don't repent my Trouble. . . . All agreed not to separate. So the Wound is healed—slightly.' Later in the same letter, written from Rotherham on 9th May, he informed Mrs Wesley: 'I have delivered my own Soul in this Society & exhorted them to continue stedfast in Fellowship with the Ch. of E. The same Exhortation I hope to leave with every Society throughout the Land.' Soon Charles Wesley had ready another weapon in defence of Methodism's alliance with the Church of England—an open letter in verse to his brother John. Before the end of the month it was published, read to crowded congregations, and despatched to various parts of the country. In the first instance William Strahan printed an edition of 3,000, but by the end of May Charles Wesley had ordered and paid for another thousand.

John Wesley's reaction to the Epistle is somewhat difficult to assess. It contained no direct and obvious attack on him, yet the challenge was implicit in the fact of publication, and in the disguised sting at the end. His letters to Charles during the following month seem a little more curt than usual, and one of them hinted that separation might be necessary after all, since the Bishop of London could excommunicate a preacher for not having a licence—'We have no time to trifle!'

* *An Epistle to the Reverend Mr John Wesley, by Charles Wesley, Presbyter of the Church of England* (1755).
MS Epistles, pp. 89–107. [See No. **256.**]
Poetical Works, VI.53–64.

Metre 98: Iambic 10's

My first and last unalienable Friend,
A Brother's Thoughts with due Regard attend,
A Brother, still *as thy own Soul belov'd*,
Who speak to learn, and write to be reprov'd:
Far from the factious undiscerning Crowd,   5
Distrest I fly to Thee, and *think aloud;*
I tell Thee, wise and faithful as Thou art,
The Fears and Sorrows of a burthen'd Heart,
The Workings of (a blind or heav'nly?) Zeal,
And all my *Fondness for the Church* I tell,   10
The Church whose Cause I serve, whose Faith approve,
Whose Altars reverence, and whose Name I love.

But does she still exist in more than Sound?
The Church—alas, where is she to be found?
Not in the Men, however *dignified*,   15
Who *would* her Creeds repeal, her Laws deride,
Her Prayers expunge, her Articles disown,
And thrust the Filial Godhead from his Throne.
Vainest of all their antichristian Plea,
Who cry *The Temple of the Lord are We!*   20
'We have the Church, nor will we quit our hold—'
Their hold of what? the Altar? or the Gold?
The Altar Theirs, who will not light the Fire,
Who spurn the Labour, but accept the Hire,
Who not for Souls, but their own Bodies care,   25
And leave to Underlings the Task of Pray'r?
As justly might our christen'd Heathen claim,
Thieves, Drunkards, Whoremongers, the sacred Name;

5. MS: 'The <u>curious</u> undiscerning', with 'factious' added on opposite page.

Or Rabble-rout succeed in their Endeavour
With *High Church and Sacheverell for ever!*   30
As *Arians* be for Orthodox allow'd,
For Saints the Sensual, Covetous, and Proud,
And Satan's Synagogue for the true Church of God. }

Then let the zealous *Orthodox* appear,
And challenge the contested Character: 35
Those, who renounce the whole Dissenting Tribe,
Creeds, Articles, and Liturgy subscribe;
Their Parish-Church who never once have mist,
At Schism ~~can~~[1] rail, and hate a *Methodist;*
'The Company of faithful Souls' are These,   40
Who strive to 'stablish their own Righteousness,
But count the Faith Divine a Madman's Dream?
Howe'er they to Themselves may Pillars seem,
Of Christ, and of his Church they make no Part:
They never knew the Saviour in their Heart.   45

But Those who in their Heart have Jesus known, }
Believers, justified by Faith alone, }
Shall we not Them *the* faithful People own? }
In whom the Power of Godliness is seen,
Must we not grant The Methodists *The Men?*   50
No: tho' we granted them from Schism free,
From wild enthusiastic Heresy,
From ev'ry wilful Crime, and moral Blot,
Yet still the Methodists *The Church* are not:
A single Faculty is not the Soul,   55
A Limb the Body, or a Part the Whole.

Whom then, when ev'ry vain Pretender's cast,
With Truth may we account The Church at last?
'All who have felt, deliver'd from above,
'The holy Faith that works by humble Love,   60
'All that in pure religious Worship join,
'Led by the Spirit, and the Word divine,
'Duly the Christian Mysteries partake,
'And bow to Governors for Conscience sake:'
In These *the Church of England* I descry,   65
And vow with *these alone* to live and die.

[1 This correction is made in contemporary ink in all the copies seen.]

39. MS: 'At Schism rail'.
41. MS: 'That strive'.
60. MS: 'The <u>heavenly</u> Faith, yt works by <u>holy</u> Love', and 'holy
    humble' on opposite page.
63. MS: '~~All~~ Duely the'.

Yet while I warmly for her Faith contend,
Shall I her Blots and Blemishes defend?
Inventions *added* in a fatal Hour,
Human Appendages of Pomp and Power,   *70*
Whatever shines in outward Grandeur great,
I give it up—*a Creature of the State!*
Wide of the Church, as Hell from Heav'n is wide,
The Blaze of Riches, and the Glare of Pride,
The vain Desire to be intitled *Lord*,   *75*
The worldly Kingdom, and the princely Sword.

But should the bold usurping Spirit dare
Still higher climb, and sit in Moses' chair,
Power o'er my Faith and Conscience to maintain,
Shall I submit, and suffer it to reign?   *80*
Call it *the Church*, and Darkness put for Light,
Falshood with Truth confound, and Wrong with Right?
No: I dispute the Evil's haughty Claim,
The Spirit of the World be still its Name,
Whatever call'd by Man 'tis purely Evil,   *85*
'Tis Babel, Antichrist, and Pope, and Devil!

Nor wou'd I e'er disgrace the Church's Cause
By penal Edicts, and compulsive Laws,
(Should wicked Powers, as formerly, prevail
T'exclude her choicest Children from her Pale)   *90*
Or force my Brethren in her Forms to join,
As every Jot and Tittle were divine,
As all her Orders on the Mount were given,
And copied from the Hierarchy of Heaven.
Let Others for the Shape and Colour fight   *95*
Of Garments short or long, or black or white;
Or fairly match'd, in furious Battle join
For and against the Sponsors and the Sign;
Copes, Hoods, and Surplices *the Church* miscall,
And fiercely run their Heads against *the Wall*;   *100*
Far different Care is mine; o'er Earth to see
Diffus'd her true essential Piety,
To see her lift again her languid Head,
Her lovely Face from ev'ry Wrinkle freed,
Clad in the simple, pure, primeval Dress,   *105*
And beauteous with internal Holiness,
Wash'd by the Spirit and the Word from Sin,
Fair without Spot, and glorious all within.

71. MS: 'in ~~earthly~~ Grandeur', and 'outward' on opposite page.
75. MS: 'to be ~~saluted~~ Lord', and 'intitled' opposite.
83. MS: 'No: I ~~deny~~', and 'dispute' opposite.
92. MS: 'As every Rite & ~~Usage~~ were Divine', with 'Rubric' opposite.

Alas! how distant now, how desolate,
Our fallen Zion, in her captive State!   *110*
Deserted by her Friends, and laugh'd to Scorn,
By inbred Foes, and bosom Vipers torn.
With Grief I mark their rancorous Despight,
With Horror hear the clam'rous *Edomite*;
'Down with her to the Ground, who fiercely cries,   *115*
'No more to lift her Head, no more to rise!
'Down with her to the Pit, to Tophet doom
'A Church emerging from the Dregs of *Rome*!
'Can there in such a Church Salvation be?
'Can any Good come out of Popery?   *120*
Ye moderate Dissenters—come, and see!

See us, when from the Papal Fire we came,
Ye frozen Sects, and warm you at the Flame,
Where for the Truth our Host of Martyrs stood,
And clapp'd their Hands, and seal'd it with their Blood!   *125*
Behold Elijah's fiery Steeds appear,
Discern the Chariot of our Israel near!
That flaming Car, for whom doth it come down?
The Spouse of Christ?—Or whore of Babylon?
For Martyrs, by the Scarlet Whore pursu'd   *130*
Thro' Racks and Fires, into the Arms of GOD.
These are the Church of Christ, by Torture driv'n
To Thrones triumphant with their Friends in Heav'n;
The Church of Christ (let all the Nations own),
The Church of Christ *and England*—is but One!   *135*

Yet vainly of our Ancestors we boast,
We who their Faith and Purity have lost,
Degenerate Branches from a noble Seed,
Corrupt, apostatiz'd, and doubly dead:
Will GOD in such a Church his Work revive!   *140*
It cannot be that these dry Bones should live.

But who to teach Almighty Grace shall dare
How far to suffer, and how long to spare?
Shall Man's bold Hand our Candlestick remove,
Or cut us off from our Redeemer's Love?   *145*
Shall Man presume to say, 'There is no Hope:
'GOD *must* forsake, for *We* have giv'n her up:
'To save a Church so near the Gates of Hell,
'This is a thing—with GOD impossible!'

110. MS: 'Our captive Zion in her fallen State!'
       their
113. MS: 'her rancorous'.
132. MS: 'The Church of Christ are These, by Tortures driven'.
148. MS: 'To raise a Church', and 'save' opposite.

And yet this thing impossible *is* done,   **150**
The Lord *hath* made his Power and Mercy known,
Strangely reviv'd our long forgotten Hope,
And brought out of their Graves his People up.
Soon as we prophesied in Jesus' Name,
The Noise, the Shaking, and the Spirit came!   **155**
The Bones spontaneous to each other cleav'd,   ⎫
The Dead in Sin his powerful Word receiv'd,   ⎬
And felt the quickning Breath of GOD, and liv'd. ⎭
Dead Souls to all the Life of Faith restor'd,
(The House of Israel now) confess the Lord,   **160**
His People and his Church, out of their Graves
They rise, and testify that Jesus saves,
That Jesus gives the multiplied Increase,
While One becomes a thousand Witnesses.

Nor can it seem to Souls already freed   **165**
Incredible, that GOD should wake the dead,
Should farther still exert his saving Power,
And call, and quicken twice ten thousand more,
Till our whole Church a mighty Host becomes,
And owns the Lord, the Opener of their Tombs.   **170**

Servant of GOD, my Yokefellow and Friend,
If GOD by *us* to the *dry Bones* could send,
By *us* out of their Graves his People raise,
By *us* display the Wonders of his Grace,
Why should we doubt his Zeal to carry on   **175**
By abler Instruments the Work begun,
To build our Temple that in Ruins lay,
And reconvert a Nation in a Day,
To bring our Sion forth, as Gold refin'd,   ⎫
With all his Saints in closest union join'd   ⎬   **180**
A Friend, a Nursing-mother to Mankind? ⎭

Surely the Time is come, for GOD to rise,
And turn upon our Church his glorious Eyes,
To shew her all the Riches of his Grace,
And make her throughout all the Earth a Praise: **185**
For O! his Servants think upon her Stones,
And in their Hearts his pleading Spirit groans;
It pitieth them to see her in the Dust,
Her Lamp extinguish'd, and her Gospel lost:
Lost—till the Lord, the great Restorer came,   **190**
Extinguish'd—till his Breath reviv'd the Flame;
His Arm descending lifted up the Sign,
His Light appearing bad her *rise and shine,*

152. MS: 'our long-extinguish'd Hope'.

Bad her glad Children bless the heavenly Ray,
And shout the Prospect of a Gospel-day.   *195*

   Meanest and least of all her Sons, may I
Unite with theirs my Faith and Sympathy!
Meanest, and least—yet can I never rest,
Or quench the Flame enkindled in my Breast:
Whether a Spark of Nature's fond Desire,   *200*
That warms my Heart, and sets my Soul on fire,
Or a pure Ray from yon bright Throne above,
That melts my yearning Bowels into Love;
Even as Life, it still remains the same,
My fervent Zeal for our Jerusalem;   *205*
Stronger than Death, and permanent as true,
And purer Love, it *seems*, than Nature ever knew.

   For her, whom her Apostate Sons despise,
I offer up my Life in Sacrifice,
My Life in cherishing a Parent spend,   *210*
Fond of my Charge, and faithful to the End:
Not by the Bonds of sordid Interest ty'd,
Not gain'd by Wealth or Honours to her Side,
But by a *double Birth* her Servant born:
Vile for her sake, expos'd to general Scorn,   *215*
Thrust out as from her Pale, I gladly roam,
Banish'd myself, to bring her Wanderers home.
While the lost sheep of Israel's House I seek,

   By Bigots branded for a Schismatick,
By real Schismaticks disown'd, decry'd,   *220*
As a blind Bigot on the Church's Side:
Yet well-content, so I my Love may shew,
My friendly Love, to be esteem'd her Foe,
Foe to her Order, Governours, and Rules:
The Song of Drunkards, and the Sport of Fools;   *225*
Or, what my Soul doth as Hell-fire reject,
A Pope—*a Count*[2]—and Leader of a Sect.

   Partner of my Reproach, who justly claim
The larger Portion of the glorious Shame,
My Pattern in the Work and Cause divine,   *230*
Say is thy Heart as *bigoted* as mine?

[2 The most scathing of the eight 'Epistles' prepared by Charles Wesley for the press at this period was one 'To the Rt. Hon. & Rt. Revd. C[ount] Z[inzendorf]'. The very title reflects his scorn at what he deemed Zinzendorf's hypocritical humility, as leader of the revived Moravian Church.]

201, 203. MS: 'Wch warms', 'Wch melts'.
222–3. MS: 'Yet well-content (so I my Love may shew
        My friendliest Love) to be esteem'd her Foe'.

Wilt Thou with me in the Old Church remain,
And share her Weal or Woe, her Loss or Gain,
Spend in her Service thy last Drop of Blood,
And die—to build the Temple of our GOD?   235

   Thy Answer is in more than Words exprest,
I read it thro' the Window in thy Breast:
In every Action of thy Life I see
Thy faithful Love, and filial Piety.
To save a sinking Church, Thou dost not spare   240
Thyself, but lavish all thy Life for Her:
For Sion sake Thou wilt not hold thy Peace,
That she may grow, impatient to decrease,
To rush into thy Grave, that she may rise,
And mount with all her Children to the Skies.   245

  · What then remains for us on Earth to do,
But labour on with Jesus in our View,
Who bids us kindly for his Patients care,
Calls us the Burthen of his Church to bear,
To feed his Flock, and nothing seek beside,   250
And nothing know, but Jesus crucify'd.

   When first sent forth to minister the Word,
Say, did we preach ourselves, or Christ the Lord?
Was it our Aim Disciples to collect,
To raise a Party, or to found a Sect?   255
No; but to spread the Power of Jesus' Name,
Repair the Walls of our Jerusalem,
Revive the Piety of antient Days,
And fill the Earth with our Redeemer's Praise.

   Still let us steadily pursue our End,   260
And only for the Faith divine contend,
Superior to the Charms of Power and Fame,
Persist thro' Life, invariably the same:
And if indulg'd our Heart's Desire to see,
Jerusalem in full Prosperity,   265
To pristine Faith, and Purity restor'd;
How shall we bless our good redeeming Lord,
Gladly into his Hands our Children give,
Securely in their Mother's Bosom live,
With calm Delight accept our late Release,   270
Resign our Charge to GOD, and then depart in peace!

235. MS: 'And ~~long~~ die—'.
248. MS: 'for his Hous[e]hold care'.
                his
268. MS: 'Gladly into ~~our~~ Hands'.
269. MS: 'Bosom leave,'.
270. MS: '~~With Confidence~~ accept', and 'With calm Delight' opposite.

ON INNOCENTS' DAY   **258**

* MS Festivals: No. 10.

Metre 42: 10 10.10 10.10 10.10 10
A A B B C C D D

We blame the Savage King whose Cruel Word
Gave up his Subjects Children to the Sword,
We praise our *doting* selves, who every Hour
Yield our own Babes to the Destroyer's Power:
Which to poor Innocents doth heavier prove   5
The Tyrant's Hatred, or the Parents' Love?
His Fury on their slaughter'd Bodies fell,
Our Fondness sends their pamper'd souls to Hell.

ON THE KING'S BIRTHDAY   **259**

This poem, one of a group of commemorative poems apparently prepared for a
public occasion in Bristol, seems to have been written in the 1750's, before the death
of George II in 1760.

* MS Festivals: No. 4.

Metre 43: 10 10.10 10.10 10.10 12
A A B B C C D D

With Joy we see th'auspicious Day return,
When Heaven on Brittain smil'd, and George was born!
                    Fate
Born for the General Good, by ~~Heav'n~~ design'd
A Parent, King, a Patron of Mankind!
Long may He bless the Nations with his Sway,   5
See the calm Sunset of his glorious Day
With golden Beams thro' all th'Horison shine,
And late return to Heaven in Majesty Divine!

ON THE PRINCE OF WALES   **260**

Apparently written for the future George III, during the 1750's. [See No. **259**.]
* MS Festivals: No. 7.

Metre 43: 10 10.10 10.10 10.10 12
A A B B C C D D

Hail happy Prince, in whom combin'd we see
Imperial State, and mild Humanity!
~~Let every Virtue~~ In Thee let every Virtue still be join'd,
To constitute the Darling of Mankind:
And when your Royal Greatness shall supply   5
The Throne of GEORGE, translated to the Sky,
With equal Mercy may You use your Power,
And leave a Race of Kings, till Time shall be no more.

261   FOR THE KING OF PRUSSIA

While the forty prayer-hymns in *Hymns of Intercession* cover, in *Prayer Book* phrase, 'all sorts and conditions of men', their content is greatly influenced by the national situation at the time. They were published, and seem for the most part to have been written, during the opening years of the Seven Years' War. Newcastle's ministry had been replaced by Pitt's, whose unpopularity with the king led to a three-months' 'caretaker' Government, and then to an uneasy coalition between Pitt and Newcastle. At first little but failure seemed to meet Pitt's imaginative and seemingly too-bold strategy for containing French ambitions by supporting Frederick the Great, who was hemmed in by the armies of France, Austria and Russia. In June 1757 came news of Frederick's crushing defeat at Kolin, and in July the terrible story of the Black Hole of Calcutta. September brought news of a succession of failures, in America, on the coast of France, and particularly in Germany, where the Duke of Cumberland's expeditionary force had capitulated, and left Frederick single-handed. It was probably in September or October that Charles Wesley wrote No. 12, 'For the King of Prussia', while Nos. 13 and 14 were almost certainly written after Frederick's spectacular victory at Rossbach. Charles Wesley regarded Frederick the Great as 'a second Cyrus', and saw much more than Pitt's diplomacy at work in the Seven Years War.

> *Hymns of Intercession for all Mankind* (1758): No. 12.
> *Poetical Works*, VI.121–2.

Metre 10: 8.8.8.8.8 8
A B A B C C

1 Head over all in earth and skies,
    Immortal Potentate, appear,
While men and fiends against them rise,
    Be mindful of thy members here,
Nor let thy changeless promise fail,   5
Nor let th'infernal gates prevail.

2 By Thee if rightful Monarchs reign,
    If all things bow to thy command,
Thy power, to strengthen and sustain,
    Be on the Man of thy right-hand;   10
Arm him with thine and Gideon's sword
To fight the battles of the LORD.

3 The Champion of Religion pure,
    To fall the last, He stands alone:
His foes have made his ruin sure,   15
    And spoil'd his life, and seiz'd his throne,
Thy Church with Him in hope o'erpower'd,
And all thine heritage devour'd.

4 But is th'almighty GOD restrain'd
    To save by many or by few?   20
Almighty GOD, lay to thine hand,
    For now—He knows not what to do—*
Push'd to the last extremity,
He sinks—He lifts his eyes to Thee!

* Written before the Battle of Ros[s]bach, Nov. 5. [1757].

5 Arm of the LORD, awake, awake,   *25*
  Thine own resistless strength put on,
Preserve him for thine Israel's sake,
  To make thy power, and mercy known,
Thy Church t'exalt, thy foes to shame,
And spread thro' earth thy Saving Name.   *30*

[A SECOND CYRUS]   **262**

This poem seems to have been written soon after Frederick II of Prussia routed the French at the Battle of Rossbach, and before the news had come through of his victory over the Austrians at Leuthen on 5th December.

* *Hymns of Intercession for all Mankind* (1758): No. 13.
  Poetical Works, VI.122–3.

Metre 10: 8.8.8.8.8 8
A B A B C C

1 While yet we call, the prayer is seal'd,
  Thou answerest 'here am I to save!'
Thou hast thy faithful word fulfill'd,
  Thy sovereign Nod the victory gave,
Whate'er subservient causes join,   *5*
O King of kings, the work is thine.

2 Thee let thy prosperous Servant own
  Sole Author of his strange success,
Who liftest up, and castest down,
  But dost with all thy blessings bless   *10*
The man that in his Maker trusts,
And glories in the LORD of hosts.

3 Rais'd up thro' Thee the righteous man,
  Call to thy foot, and girt by Thee,
Bid him a Second Cyrus, reign,   *15*
  And execute thy whole decree;
Kings to his sword as dust bestow,
As driven stubble to his bow.

4 Whom thou dost for thy glory chuse,
  Arm, and uphold with thy right-hand: *20*
The loins of hostile Monarchs loose,
  Nations subdue to his command,
While nought his rapid course can stay,
Nor earth, nor hell obstruct his way.

5 Before thy chosen Servant go,   *25*
  Thine utmost counsel to fulfil,
And when his work is done below,
  And when he hath perform'd thy will,
Turn on him, LORD, thy Son embrace,
And shew him all thy glorious Face.   *30*

297

263   [FOR 'FREDERICK THE GREAT']

Wesley's mental attitude toward Frederick II of Prussia underwent a subtle change as his succession of victories brought the kind of praise that might easily turn a despotic head. Nevertheless he still remained for Wesley the 'Christian hero'.

Hymns of Intercession for all Mankind (1758): No. 14.
Poetical Works, VI.123–4.

Metre 10: 8.8.8.8.8 8
A B A B C C

1 Still in the arms of faith and prayer,
    (The prayer that shuts and opens heaven)
  Thy Champion to thy throne we bear;
    To Him the farther grace be given;
  Sav'd from his foes, persist to bless,   5
  And save him from his own success.

2 While distant climes resound his name,
    And raise his glory to the skies,
  O might he all the praise disclaim,
    Little, and mean in his own eyes,   10
  And prostrate in the dust submit
  To lay his lawrels at thy feet.

3 Far from his generous bosom chase
    That cruel insolence of power,
  Which tramples on the human race,   15
    Restless to have, and conquer more,
  While bold above the clouds t'ascend,
  The Hero sinks into a Fiend.

4 Thou by the Christian Hero stand,
    And guard the Issues of his heart,   20
  Let mercy all his powers command,
    Mercy his inmost soul convert,
  MERCY, which came from Heaven, to find
  To die for—him, and all mankind.

5 The sword, which he reluctant drew,   25
    O may he soon rejoice to sheath,
  And rendring Thee the glory due,
    Sole Arbiter of life and death,
  His Saviour, and the World's confess,
  And triumph in eternal peace.   30

264   [DANGER'S DARKEST HOUR]

The summer months of 1759 were punctuated, not only by news of French successes in the Seven Years War, but by a genuine threat of invasion of the coasts of England, for which three hundred flat-bottomed boats were being constructed in the French ports. The facts were inflated by rumours, including the report which spread around London on 7th July that the French had actually landed. In the event the French fleet suffered a series of defeats, and the invasion was never attempted. For weeks, however, the country was in a state approaching panic, and on 5th July Charles Wesley wrote from London to his wife in Bristol: 'No power less than that which defeated the Spanish Armada will rescue England now. You will see my thoughts (but not mine only) in a penny hymn book I shall publish against our Fast.' (This was a Methodist occasion, not a National Fast Day.)

These hymns were re-issued during the invasion scare of 1779 (cf. No. 297).

* *Hymns on the Expected Invasion*, (1759): No. 1.
CW. MSS. I: (q) ii, at the Methodist Book Room, London.
Poetical Works, VI.149–50.

Metre 34: 6.6.8.6.6.6.8.6.D
A B A B C D C D

I.

Let GOD, the mighty GOD,
  The Lord of hosts arise,
With terror clad, with strength endued,
  And rent, and bow the skies!
  Call'd down by faithful prayer,   5
  Saviour, appear below,
Thine hand lift up, thine arm make bare,
  And quell thy church's foe.

Our refuge in distress,
  In danger's darkest hour,   10
Appear as in the antient days
  With full redeeming power;
  That thy redeem'd may sing
  In glad triumphant strains,
The Lord is GOD, the Lord is King,   15
  The Lord for ever reigns!

II.

We with our ears have heard,
  Our fathers us have told
The work that in their days appear'd,
  And in the times of old;   20
  The mighty wonders wrought
  By Heaven in their defence,
When Jacob's GOD for Britain fought,
  And chas'd th'invaders hence.

Vainly INVINCIBLE   25
  Their fleets the seas did hide,
And doom'd our sires to death and hell,
  And Israel's GOD defied:
  But with his wind He blew,
  But with his waves He rose,   30
And dash'd, and scatter'd, and o'erthrew,
  And swallow'd up his foes.

6. MS: 'Saviour, *appear* below'.
7. MS: 'Thy hand ... thy arm'.
22. MS: 'in our defence'.

III.

Jesus, Jehovah, Lord,
  Thy wonted aid we claim;
Not trusting in our bow or sword,   *35*
  But in thy saving Name:
Thy Name the mighty tower,
  From whence our foes we see
Ready our country to devour,
  Without a nod from thee.   *40*

Thou wilt not give us up
  A prey unto their teeth,
But blast their aim, confound their hope,
  Their league with hell and death;
With *such* deliverance bless   *45*
  Whom Thou hast chose for thine,
That we, and Europe, may confess
  The work is all divine!

47. MS: 'That Brittain's Sons may now confess'.

265   THANKSGIVING DAY

On Saturday 26th October a proclamation was issued for a public thanksgiving to be observed throughout England and Wales on Thursday 29th November. The worst fears of invasion had gone, and the tide of war had turned. The preamble to the proclamation stated: 'We do most devoutly and thankfully acknowledge the great goodness and mercy of Almighty God, who hath afforded us protection and assistance in the just war, in which . . . we are now engaged; and hath given such signal successes to our arms both by sea and land; particularly by the defeat of the French army in Canada, and the taking of Quebec; and who hath most seasonably granted us at this time an uncommon plentiful harvest.'

The pamphlet which Wesley issued for this occasion consisted of eight poems on twelve octavo pages, paged continuously with the *Invasion Hymns*. The day after Thanksgiving Day arrived news of Admiral Hawke's decisive victory over the French fleet in Quiberon Bay, upon which Wesley issued a continuation of his pamphlet, a further twelve pages, containing Hymns 9 to 15, once more emphasizing his general theme:

'Thy love hath our protection been;
  Thy love, and not the sea between,
    Forbad our foes to pass:
Our watry walls had nought avail'd,
Our wooden walls themselves had fail'd,
    Without our WALL OF BRASS.'

Not all the populace, however, upheld Wesley's point of view, which is the main point of the following poem.

* *Hymns to be used on the Thanksgiving-Day, Nov. 29, 1759, and after it*, No. 2.
Poetical Works, VI.164–6.

1 But ah! what means this frantick Noise!
  Do These, good GOD, to Thee rejoice,
    Whose ecchoing shouts we hear!
  A beastly Bacchanalian Crowd!
  Whose oaths prophane, and curses loud   *5*
    Torment the sober ear!

2 With foul and riotous excess,
  With surfeiting and drunkenness
    They *magnify* thy name,
  With vauntings proud, and impious jest,   *10*
  (The horrors of Belshazzar's Feast)
    They glory in their Shame.

3 The rich to thy dread Courts repair,
  And offering up their formal Prayer
    As incense to the skies,   *15*
  With SPORTS they close the *hallow'd* day,
  Their promis'd vows to Satan pay,
    An hellish Sacrifice!

4 But do ye thus the LORD requite,
  (While Britain's Host goes forth to fight,)   *20*
    Or thus his help engage!
  Ah! foolish Souls, who still declare
  Your hatred against GOD, and war
    With your Defender wage!

5 Ye rob Britannia of her Shield,   *25*
  JEHOVAH, by *your Thanks* compel'd
    To join the vanquish'd Side:
  Ye force him to exalt the Foe,
  To lay our lofty Nation low,
    And scourge us for our pride.   *30*

6 Yet, O most patient GOD, forbear
  The Wretches who thy anger dare,
    And court th'Invader's Sword;
  Rather regard the faithfull seed,
  Who to the *Opening Seal* give heed,   *35*
    And tremble at thy Word.

7 *We* do not dream the danger *past!*
  The first may soon become the last,
    Unless thine Hand we see
  Extended o're the Nations now,   *40*
  And humbly to thy judgments bow,
    And ask our lives from Thee.

301

8 Our lives are in our Maker's hand;
  And 'till thy mind we understand,
    Thine utmost counsel prove,   *45*
  O let us in the Spirit groan,
  Father, thy will on earth be done,
    As in the Courts above!

266   [A CHARNEL OF DRY BONES]

The greatest single cause of tension within Methodism, and particularly between
John and Charles Wesley, was the possibility—which at times seemed the inevit-
ability—of the Methodists developing from a reforming society within the Church of
England to a sect completely separated from it. The danger was present and realized
from the beginning, but it became acute after the turn of the century. Charles
Wesley complained that many of the Methodist preachers were ambitious to become
Dissenting ministers, and that John Wesley too readily gave way to their pleas.
In his *Epistle* [No. 257] Charles had challenged his brother to declare himself. In
spite of some natural annoyance and some conscientious hesitancy, John Wesley
did support Charles' campaign, and even agreed 'to write a treatise to confirm the
Methodists in the Church'. This promise was fulfilled in his *Reasons against a Separation from the Church of England*, which appeared in 1758 at the end of a volume
entitled *A Preservative against unsettled notions in religion*. It could not be expected
that a volume of 250 pages would get into as many hands as would a twopenny
pamphlet, and Charles Wesley himself seems to have been responsible for ensuring
that his brother's declarations reached a wider public. In 1760 he issued the *Reasons*
separately, supported by his own endorsement, and particularly by seven hymns
which are introduced thus:
  'I have subjoined the Hymns for the Lay-Preachers; still farther to secure this
End, *to cut off all Jealousy and Suspicion from our Friends, or Hope from our Enemies,
of our having any Design of ever Separating from the Church.*'

* *Reasons against a Separation* (1760): No. 5.
  MS Preachers: No. 5.
  MS Preachers Extraordinary: No. 10.
  MS Miscellaneous Hymns, pp. 123–5: No. 10 of 'Hymns for Preachers'.
  Poetical Works, VI.104–5.

                                   Metre 10: 8.8.8.8.8 8
                                             A B A B C C

1 JESU, thy waiting servants see
    Assembled here with one accord,
  Ready to be sent forth by Thee,
    To preach, when Thou shalt give, the word:
  Now, Lord, our work, our province shew,   *5*
  For lo! we come, thy will to do.

2 O what a scene attracts our eyes!
    What multitudes of lifeless souls!
  An open vale before us lies,
    A place of graves, a place of skulls,   *10*
  The desolate house of England's sons,
  A Church—a charnel of dry bones!

1. MSS P. Extra. and Misc.: 'Jesus, thy'.
7. MS Preachers: 'salutes our eyes'.
                    lifeless
8. MS Preachers: 'of ~~senseless~~ souls'.
11. MS Misc.: 'desolate church of'.
12. MS P. Extra.: 'A Church? A Charnel'.

3 The slaves of pride, ambition, lust,
  Our broken pale, alas, receives!
The world into the temple thrust,   *15*
  And make our Church a den of thieves,
Her grief, her burthen, and her shame,
Yet all assume the Church's name.

4 Her desolate state too well we know,
  But neither hate her, nor despise: *20*
Our bosoms bleed, our tears o'erflow;
  We view her, Saviour, with thine eyes,
(O might she know in this her day!)
And still we weep, and still we pray.

5 We pray that these dry bones may live: *25*
  We see the answer of our prayer!
Thou dost a thousand tokens give,
  That England's Church is still thy care,
Ten thousand witnesses appear,
Ten thousand proofs, that GOD is here!   *30*

6 Here then, O GOD, vouchsafe to dwell,
  And mercy on our Sion shew;
Her inbred enemies expel,
  Avenge her of her hellish foe;
Cause on her wastes thy face to shine,   *35*
And comfort her with light divine.

7 O Light of life, thy spirit shed,
  In all his chearing, quick'ning power:
Thy word that rais'd *us* from the dead,
  Can raise ten thousand, thousand more,   *40*
Can bring them up from nature's grave,
And the whole house of Israel save.

14. MS Preachers: 'Our broken Fence & Pale receives'.
16. MS P. Extra.: 'And make God's house'.
18. MS Preachers: 'They all assume'.
22. MS P. Extra.: 'with thy Eyes'.
                                        them
41. MS P. Extra.: 'Can bring ~~us~~ up'.

THE PREACHER'S PRAYER FOR THE FLOCK   **267**

Reasons against a Separation (1760): No. 7.
MS Preachers Extraordinary: No. 5.
MS Miscellaneous Hymns, pp. 115–17.
Poetical Works, VI.107–8.

Metre 4: 8 8.6.8 8.6
A A B C C B

1 Shepherd of souls, the great, the good,
For the dear purchase of thy blood
   To Thee in faith we pray:
The lambs and sheep of England's fold,
Now in thy book of life inroll'd,   *5*
   Preserve unto that day.

2 Whom Thou by us hast gather'd in,
Defend the little flock from sin,
   From error's paths secure:
Stay with them, Lord, when we depart,   *10*
And guard the issues of their heart,
   And keep their conscience pure.

3 Soon as their guides are taken home,
We know the grievous wolves will come,
   Determin'd not to spare;   *15*
The stragglers from thy wounded side,
The Wolves will into Sects divide,
   And into parties tear.

4 Ev'n of ourselves shall men arise,
With words perverse and soothing lies,   *20*
   Our children to beset,
Disciples for themselves to make,
And draw, for filthy lucre's sake,
   The sheep into their net.

5 What then can their protection be?   *25*
The virtue that proceeds from Thee,
   The power of humble love:
The strength of all-sufficient grace,
Receiv'd in thine appointed ways,
   Can land them safe above.   *30*

6 Now, Saviour, cloath them with thy power,
And arm their souls against that hour
   With faith invincible,
Teach them to wield the spirit's sword,
And mighty in the written word   *35*
   To chase both earth and hell.

10. MS P. Extra.: 'till we depart'.
19. MSS P. Extra., Misc.: 'will men arise'.
23. The 1760 edition actually has 'And, draw for', a misprint corrected in
    later editions.
30. MSS P. Extra., Misc.: 'Shall land them'.
34. MSS P. Extra., Misc.: 'thy Spirit's sword'.

7 When I from all my burthens freed,
  Am number'd with the peaceful dead,
    In everlasting rest,
  Pity the sheep I leave behind,   *40*
  My GOD, unutterably kind,
    And lodge them in thy breast.

8 Ah! never suffer them to leave
  The Church, where thou art pleas'd to give
    Such tokens of thy grace!   *45*
  Confirm them in their calling here,
  Till ripe by holiest love t'appear
    Before thy glorious face.

9 Whom I into thy hands commend,
  Wilt Thou not keep them to the end,
    Thou infinite in love?   *50*
  Assure me, Lord, it shall be so,
  And let my quiet spirit go
    To join the Church above.

10 Sion, my first, my latest care,   *55*
   The burthen of my dying prayer,
     Now in thine arms I see;
   And sick on earth of seeing more,
   I hasten home, my GOD t'adore
     Thro' all eternity.   *60*

             keep
50. MS Misc.: 'Wilt thou not ~~love~~ them'.

[SEEKING THE PRIESTHOOD]   **268**

This is one of several poems in which Charles Wesley castigated what he felt was the undue ambition of the Methodist preachers who sought a higher status for themselves. It earned his brother's displeasure, and was omitted from the second edition.

* *Scripture Hymns* (1762): O.T. 239 (I.76).
  Poetical Works, IX.79.

                Metre 20: 8 8.8 8.8 8.8 8
                        A A B B C C D D
And seek ye the priesthood also?—[Numbers] xvi.10.

  Rais'd from the people's lowest lees,[1]
  Guard, LORD, thy preaching witnesses,
  Nor let their pride the honour claim
  Of sealing covenants in thy Name:
  Rather than suffer them to dare   *5*
  Usurp the priestly character,
  Save from the arrogant offence,
  And snatch them uncorrupted hence.

    [[1] In his own copy John Wesley added the note, 'Query? J.W.']

269   [ON WORLDLY BISHOPS]

* MS Luke, pp. 294–5.
Poetical Works, XI.273–4 (extract only).

Metre 22: 8 8.8.8 8.8 D
A A B C C B

Beware of the scribes, which desire to walk in long robes, &c.—[Luke 20] v. 46, 47.

1 Alas, for us, who need beware
   Of men, that sit in Moses' chair,
     And should to heaven the people guide!
   Men with the pomp of office clad,
   In robes pontifical array'd,   *5*
     But stain'd with avarice and pride:
   They love to be prefer'd, ador'd,
   Affect the state and stile of *lord*,
     And shine magnificently great:
   They for precedency contend,   *10*
   And on ambition's scale ascend
     Hard-labouring for the highest seat.

2 The church they call their proper care,
   The temple of the Lord they are,
     Abusers of their legal power;   *15*
   Greedy the church's goods to seize,
   Their wealth they without end increase,
     And the poor Widow's house devour.
   O what a change they soon shall know,
   When torn away by death, they go   *20*
     Reluctant from their splendid feasts,
   Condemn'd in hottest flames to dwell,
   And find the spacious courts of hell
     Pav'd with the skulls of Christian Priests!*

                    * A saying of Chrysostom.

270   [SCHOOL FOR YOUNG LADIES]

* *Hymns for Children* (1763): No. 67, Part II.
Poetical Works, VI.437–8.

Metre 4: 8 8.6.8 8.6
A A B C C B

1 See from the world's politest school
   The goddess rise, mankind to rule,
     As born for her alone!
   Unclogg'd by thought, she issues forth,
   And justly conscious of her worth,   *5*
     Ascends her gaudy throne.

2 With lust of fame and pleasure fir'd,
   The virgin shines caress'd, admir'd,
     And idoliz'd by all:
   Obedient to her dread command,   *10*
   Around her throne the votaries stand,
     Or at her footstool fall.

3 Prostrate before the idol's shrine,
They celebrate her charms divine,
  Her beauty's awful power,   *15*
By brutal appetite inspir'd,
By passion urg'd, by Satan hir'd,
  To damn whom they adore.

4 Eager she drinks their praises in,
Repeats the heaven-invading sin,   *20*
  And seems with gods to dwell,
Triumphant, 'till her hour is past,
And quite undeified at last
  The sinner sinks to hell.

ON BEING DESIRED TO WRITE AN EPITAPH 271
FOR MR JAMES HERVEY

The Rev. James Hervey (1714–58) was one of the 'Holy Club' at Oxford, grateful for the inspiration he had received from the Methodists, even though he did not remain in active co-operation with them. His flowery prose-poems such as *Meditations among the Tombs* became extremely popular and remunerative. Toward the end of his life he was converted to Calvinism, and his *Theron and Aspasio* propagated the doctrine of imputed righteousness. John Wesley criticized this work, and Hervey was preparing a reply when he died. On his deathbed he directed that the incomplete and unrevised manuscript should be destroyed, but his brother William felt that it should be published—with a sole eye to financial gain, according to his detractors. He handed over the preparation of the manuscript to an extreme Calvinist, William Cudworth. The resultant *Eleven Letters* (published in 1765) were felt by John Wesley's friends to be tantamount to a forgery, and it is hardly to be wondered that Charles Wesley later refused to compose an epitaph for Hervey (possibly for his collected *Works*), though he had written two moving poems on his death.

* MS Patriotism: Misc., p. 23.
  Poetical Works, VIII.443 (incorrectly divided into four verses, as was the transcript in Jackson's *Charles Wesley*, II.159).
                    Metre 41: 10.10.10.10.10.10.10.10
                             A B A B C D C D

Or'ereach'd, impel'd by a sly Gnostick's Art
  To stab his Father, Guide, & faithful Friend,
W[oul]d pious Hervey act th'Accuser's part,
  And *cou[l]d* a life like his in malice end?
No: by redeeming Love the snare is broke,   *5*
  In death his rash ingratitude he blames,
Desires, and *wills* the evil to revoke,
  And dooms th'unfinish'd Libel to the flames.

W[h]o then for filthy gain betray'd his trust,
  And show'd a kinsman's fault in open light?   *10*
Let *Him* adorn the Monumental Bust,
  Th'Encomium fair in brass or marble write:
Of if they need a nobler Trophy raise,
  As long as Theron and Aspasio live,
Let Madan, or Romaine record his praise,[1]   *15*
  Enough that Wesley's Brother *can forgive*!

[1 Martin Madan and William Romaine both belonged to the Calvinistic wing of the Evangelical Revival.]

272   HYMN FOR PEACE
OCCASIONED BY SOME PUBLIC TROUBLES. FEB. 1766

On 22nd March 1765 was passed the Stamp Act, by which a stamp was to be affixed
to all legal documents in the colonies, in order to assist Great Britain's revenue.
There was an immediate outcry in America, accompanied by rioting, and the Act
continued to be the target for party controversy in England itself. On Friday 21st February William Pitt hobbled to the House of Commons on crutches in order to plead for its
repeal. Although his plea was successful, its sting was left by a statutory declaration
of the absolute supremacy of Parliament over the colonies, whether represented or
not. This was the spark which smouldered for years until it was fanned into the flame
of war. This poem represents Charles Wesley's answer to those who insist that a
Christian must have nothing whatever to do with politics.

* Miscellaneous Hymns, pp. 153–4.

Metre 4: 8 8.6.8 8.6
A A B C C B

1 While blackning clouds o'respread the sky,
  And discord's turbid waves run high,
    Are Christians free from care?
  Conscious our life is hid above,
  Yet still we must our Country love,   5
    And all her troubles share.

2 Tis not for us to rule the state,
  Or mingle in their high debate
    When Princes disagree:
  Jehovah in their council stands,   10
  And (for the Cause is in thy hands)
    We leave it, Lord, to Thee.

3 Excus'd, our privilege we own,
  We blame, arraign, and censure none
    That at the helm appear,   15
  But quietly our souls possess,
  Who worship Thee, the Prince of peace,
    Who God and Cesar fear.

4 Yet danger national requires,
  And draws out all our heart's desires   20
    For their prosperity;
  Thy Church the common burthen feels,
  Their present, and approaching ills
    With Jesus eyes we see.

5 With Jesus sympathy we cry,   25
  Father of all, in trouble nigh
    Stir up thy helping power,
  Their violence curb, controul their rage,
  Nor let them war intestine wage,
    Each other to devour.   30

6 By whom Thou wilt the rescue send,
　But bid their fierce contentions end,
　　But suddenly suppress
And scatter who in war delight,
And by thy Providential might　　　　　　　　　　　*35*
　Restore the public peace.

273

The following four light-hearted effusions are presented as samples of how Charles Wesley unbent to compose nursery rhymes for his children—almost certainly with their help. No poetic merit is claimed for them, but they undoubtedly amused the children!

* MS Nursery, p. 2.

GLEE[1]

Metre 16a: 8 8.8 8.8 8 8
A A B B C C C

There are, by fond Mamma supplied,
Six reasons against Sammi's Ride:
Because a different Turn he takes,
Because his back, or finger aches;
Because tis wet, because tis dry; ⎫　　　　　　　*5*
Because it may be by & by　　　 ⎬
Or any other reason why.　　　　⎭

[1] The original idea for these two glees apparently comes from Dean Aldrich's 'Five reasons we should drink', whose last two lines are practically identical with those of Wesley's first. It was a translation of a Latin epigram, and appeared in Playford's *Banquet of Music* (1689). John Wesley also had written an imitation in 1748, when the Ireland packet-boat was delayed at Holyhead:
　There are, unless my memory fail,
　Five causes why we should not sail:
　The fog is thick; the wind is high;
　It rains; or may do by-and-by;
　Or—any other reason why.
John Wesley's *Journal* (Standard Edn), III.335.

ANOTHER　　　　　　　　　　　　　　　　　**274**

Metre 16a: 8 8.8 8.8 8 8
A A B B C C C

There are, as idle gossips talk,
Five Obstacles to Tommi's walk;
Because the wind may chance to blow,
Because it rain'd a week ago;
Because tis cold; because tis hot; ⎫　　　　　　　*5*
Because Mamma a fright has got;　⎬
Because he ails—she knows not what. ⎭

EXTEMPORE—ON DERDHAM DOWNS　　　　**275**

* MS Nursery, p. 3.
　CW. MSS I. (p) viii, at the Methodist Book Room, London: vv. 1–3 only.

Title: The title is taken from MSS. I. That in Nursery reads simply 'Derdham Downs'. The area was to the NW of Bristol and was usually spelt 'Durdham'.

Metre 65: 5 5.9.5 5.9
A A B C C B

1   Alack & alack!
      The Clouds are so black
And my Coat is so flimsy & thin,
      If we farther ride on
      The rain will come down   5
And wet little Sam to the skin.

2   But to clear up the doubt,
      The Sun is broke out,
And says, We may do as we will:
      So before the next shower   10
      Or'e the Downs let us scour
Or gallop away to the Hill.

3   Gallop on my grey Nag,
      As fleet as a Stag,
            rudders
Or a Ship with her ~~streamers~~ & sails;   15
      Or (Mamma to afright)
      As ~~nimble and light~~ skittish & light
As a Goat—on the mountains of Wales.

4   How rapid the course
      Of my swift-flying Horse!   20
I have got the Poetical Beast,
      And on Pegasus I
      Leap over the sky—
Or leap over the Severn at least!

14. MSS I: 'As swift'.
15. MSS I: 'her streamers & sails'.
17. MSS I: 'As nimble & light'.

276   [A] N[EW] T[ESTAMENT MNEMONIC]

This mnemonic on a loose scrap of paper was probably prepared by Charles Wesley to help his children to remember the books of the New Testament. That it was done in a great hurry and not revised is suggested by the unnecessary irregularity, which could have been avoided by reading line 3 as 'Cor. Galat. Eph. Philipp. Colō.' or line 4 as 'Thess. Tim. Tit. and Philemo.'

* MS CW. IV.81 (Methodist Book Room, London).

Metre 81: 8 8.7 8.8 8
A A b B C C

Matthew, and Mark, and Luke, and John:
The Acts, and Romans follow on:
Cor. Galat. Eph. Phipp. Colō.
Thess. Tim. and Tit. and Philemo:
Heb. James and Peter, John and Jude,   5
With Revelation to conclude.

[THE SEEDS OF HARMONY]   **277**

Charles Wesley's younger son Samuel wrote in his *Autobiography*: 'My father was extremely fond of music, and in the early part of life, I believe, performed a little on the flute. . . . He had a most accurate ear for time. . . . He had not a vocal talent, but could join in a hymn or simple melody tolerably well in tune. . . . My father used to say of my brother and me, "The boys have music by the mother's side," meaning that *he* had no claim to any of the talent which she certainly possessed.' [Quoted in J. T. Lightwood's *Samuel Wesley, Musician*, pp. 14–15.] It must be remembered that Samuel Wesley's recollections are of his father's later years—he was born when his father was 58. Nevertheless Charles Wesley's musical urges undoubtedly outstripped his talents.

* MS Festivals, transcribed by the editor from Charles Wesley's shorthand jottings
   thereon, and therefore in part conjectural.

Metre 44: 8 8.8 10.10 8.8.6.10.10
A A B B C C D E D E

Who would not wish to have the skill
Of tuning instruments at will?
Ye powers who guide my actions, tell
Why I, in whom the seeds of music dwell,
Who most its power and excellence admire,   *5*
Whose very breast itself a lyre
Was never taught the happy art
Of modulating sounds
And can no more in concert share a part
Than the wild roe that o'er the mountain bounds.   *10*

Title: This comes from Charles Wesley's account of Samuel, transmitted
to Daines Barrington. See No. **293**.

WRITTEN IN HANDEL'S LESSONS   **278**

* MS Patriotism: Misc., p. 5.

Metre 8: 8 8.8 8
A A B B

Here all the mystic Powers of Sound,
The Soul of Harmony is found,
It's perfect Character receives,
And Handel dead for ever lives!

ODE ON HANDEL'S BIRTHDAY   **279**
S. MATTHIAS' DAY, FEBR. 24

According to the *Dictionary of National Biography* Handel was actually born on 23rd February 1685, but was *baptized* on the 24th, St Matthias' Day. Charles Wesley, at least, continued to show his admiration for Handel on the 24th, particularly after his own second musical son, Samuel, was born on that day in 1766.

* MS, Dr E. T. Clark Collection, Lake Junaluska, N.C., U.S.A.

Metre 78: 7.8.8.8.8 12
a B A B C C

Hail the bright auspicious Day
That gave Immortal Handel birth
Let every moment glide away
In solemn joy~~ful~~ and sacred mirth
Let every Soul like his aspire   *5*
And catch a glowing spark of pure etherial fire.

280   AN APOLOGY FOR THE ENEMIES TO MUSIC

Charles Wesley experienced much opposition when he showed himself ready to foster the musical ambitions of his sons, and even arranged professional concerts in his own home. The main criticism was puritanical in origin, apt to sweep aside all except Church music as of the devil.

* MS Patriotism: Misc., p. 11.
  Poetical Works, VIII.444.

Metre 98a: Iambic 10's, with closing 12

> Men of true piety, they know not why,
> Music with all its sacred powers decry,
> Music itself (not its abuse) condemn,
> For good or bad is just the same to Them.
> But let them know, They quite mistake the Case,   5
> Defect of nature for excess of grace:
> And, while they reprobate th'harmonious Art, ⎫
> Blam'd, we excuse, and candidly assert   ⎬
> The fault is in their ear, not in their upright heart. ⎭

281   MODERN MUSIC

Young Charles Wesley, a musical prodigy of eleven, was committed by his father to the care of Joseph Kelway (died 1782), a famous performer on the organ and harpsichord, and a notable extemporizer admired by Handel himself. Kelway, like Charles Wesley, was conservative in his musical tastes, and on 21st September 1769 told his pupil: 'My dear, let not the world debauch you. Some decry music for being old. They may as well object to an antique statue, or painting. But B——, A——, and G——, have cut the throat of music; true music is lost.' Neither father nor son nor Kelway himself, however, dreamed how much riches was to accrue to musical appreciation by that much-feared innovation, the pianoforte, and by other modernities and extravagances which were associated with it.

* MS Patriotism: Misc., pp. 6–7.

Metre 95: Iambic 6's

> G[iardini]¹, B[ach]², and all
> Their followers, great and small,
> Have cut Old Music's throat,
> And mangled every Note;
> Their superficial pains   5
> Have dash'd out all his brains:*
> And now we doat upon
> A lifeless sceleton,
> The empty sound at most,
> The Squeak of Music's Ghost.   10

Or. Have quite beat out his brains.
[¹ This is almost certainly the identification of 'G——'. Felice de Giardini (1716–96) was a brilliant violinist who was very popular in London, renowned for his extravagant extempore cadenzas.]
[² It seems most likely that Wesley was thinking here (as was almost certainly Kelway) of Johann Christian Bach (1735–82), who was popularizing the pianoforte in England.]

WRITTEN IN THE YEAR 1770. MARCH 22   **282**

John Wilkes (1727–97) was a notorious *roué* long before expulsion from Parliament for seditious libel made him the focal point of revolutionary tendencies in Great Britain. While still an outlaw he secured re-election as the Member of Parliament for Middlesex, his supporters going to the poll on 28th March 1768 with the cry: 'Wilkes and Liberty!' After his election he surrendered to his outlawry and was committed to the King's Bench prison, from which he conducted a continuous campaign against the Government. On 4th February 1769 he was again expelled from his membership of the House of Commons, was speedily re-elected by the Middlesex electors, and on 17th February was declared by the House to be incapable of election. This arbitrary decision led to the annulling of two subsequent returns and the declaration of his defeated opponent as Member. Wilkes found several champions, including 'Junius', and was the centre of important constitutional issues. John Horne (later Horne Tooke, 1736–1812), an ordained clergyman, said that he was ready to 'dye his black coat red' in support of Wilkes, and early in 1769 founded a 'Society for supporting the Bill of Rights', which raised over £17,000 to discharge Wilkes's many debts. The tempo of events quickened toward the date when Wilkes was released from prison, 17th April 1770. A month earlier, on 14th March, the City of London, having petitioned the King in vain, presented its first 'Remonstrance' to him, calling for the dissolution of Parliament, and setting off a new train of controversy. On 19th March 'Junius' wrote to the *Public Advertiser* a letter which ended thus: 'The time is come, when the body of the English people must assert their own cause: Conscious of their strength, and animated by a sense of their duty, they will not surrender their birthright to Ministers, Parliaments, or Kings. . . . His [Majesty] will find at last . . . that it is not his interest to support either Ministry or Parliament, at the hazard of a breach with the collective body of his subjects.—That he is the King of a free people, is indeed his greatest glory. That he may long continue the King of a free people, is the second wish that animates my heart. The first is, THAT THE PEOPLE MAY BE FREE. JUNIUS.'

Charles Wesley could not but resent this attack on the Crown, quite apart from the difficulty that he found in finding anything praiseworthy in the dissolute hero of the day. His emotions came to a boil in the spring of 1770, resulting in a group of poems of which we present four.

When this first poem was written Junius's attack on the Crown had just appeared, and was being hotly debated. The Lord Mayor of London arranged a great banquet at the Mansion House for a large company of leading Members of Parliament. Loyal toasts were drunk, interspersed with music, but the main items seemed to be toasts strengthening the attack on the Crown, such as, 'May the violator of the right of election and petition against grievances be confounded'. A footnote in the *Gentleman's Magazine* account of the occasion adds: 'Several persons had their windows broken at night by the mob, for not illuminating their houses.'

* MS Patriotism: Misc., pp. 27–8.

Metre 97a: Iambic 8's and 9's

Huzza for Wilkes and liberty!
The Rabble are already free
Free from the Bridle in their jaws,
Free from the dread of penal laws;
Free to pull down the wicked Courtiers,   5
Free to support the good Supporters,[1]
Their friends to guard, their foes to chase,
And curse, and spit in George's face.

What tho' the Quiet in the land
Our freedom cannot understand,   10
But think Mob-government is ever ill,
Whether for Wilkes, or for Sacheveril,

[1 i.e. 'Supporters of the Bill of Rights'.]

Their Maxim is by Us denied
Who have the Rabble on our side,
And shout with the triumphant Croud   *15*
'The People's is the Voice of God!'

   The voice of god, we all agree,
Of an infernal Deity
Which cries to Majesty, Prevent
Y[ou]r doom; dissolve the Parliament,   *20*
Y[ou]r foes embrace, your friends disown,
Or, Sire, we pluck you from your throne,
'And, to your family's confusion,
'Effect a Second Revolution,
'Th'Authority *we lent* revoke,   *25*
'Unking—and bring you to the block!'

283   EPIGRAM

* MS Patriotism: Misc., p. 29.

Metre 17: 8.8.8.8.8.8.8.8
A B A B C D C D

Voters of Middlesex forbear
   O're your rejected Friend to grieve,
And find a Candidate as rare,
   As meet a Representative:
Beggars ye soon can qualify,   *5*
   Can Patriots from the gallows fetch,
Since then the Court Jack Wilkes sets by
   Assert your right, & chuse Jack Ketch![1]

[1 The notorious hangman, who died in 1686, but who remained the symbol of the barbarous executioner.]

284   ADVICE TO THE CITY

* MS Patriotism: Misc., pp. 29–32.

Metre 97a: Iambic 8's and 9's

Ye zealous Citizens of London,
Keep up your Mob, or ye are undone,
To truth if prejudice submits,
And party-fools retrieve their wits,
If Faction shrinks with ebbing tides,   *5*
And Anarchy at last subsides,
If George his resolution stand to
Or pays your zeal with Quo warranto![1]

[1 i.e. 'By what authority?']

Y[ou]r zeal, as ancient Story sings,
Was always pestilent to Kings: *10*
Your spirit still the Mob engages,
The same in this, as former, ages,
'When all the Prentices in town
'Rose up, to cry the Bishops down,'²
When cobling Quacks turnd State-physicians   *15*
With humble—riotous—petitions,
With arms their Sovereign Lord assaulted,
Into a *glorious* King exalted,
Blasting by their infernal breath,
And fairly worrying him to death.   *20*

Ye brave *associated* Supporters,
Sworn enemies to Scots and Courtiers,
Muster, and bring your forces on,
Headed by patriotic Vaughan:³
Or if your Chairman in disgrace   )   *25*
Hides for a while his modest face   }
Let bolder Wilkes supply his place   )

Fired with the thought, ev'n now I see
The reign of Wilkes and liberty,
Anticipate the festal season,   *30*
And hail him marching out of prison!
The Shrieves in honourable state
Receive him at the Marshal's gate:
Intrepid Horne who breaks our fetters,
Close follower of the Martyr Peters,⁴   *35*
Who his black Coat, for England's good,
Vows to die red in hostile blood,
With all the swell of Roman pride
Appears at the great Patriot's side!

[² Wesley seems to be adapting or misquoting lines 529–30 in Part I, Canto II of Butler's *Hudibras*, whose freely varying 8's and 9's ('Hudibrastics') he employs for this poem. The 'Grand Remonstrance' had been presented to Charles I on 1st December 1641, and Pym and his fellows were striving to undermine the king's power by the Root and Branch Bill to abolish the Bishops. The city mob took up the cause of 'King Pym', assaulting the Bishops in Palace Yard on 27th December. These events, leading to the Civil War, 1642–6, and the execution of Charles, seemed to Wesley a close parallel to the events of his own day. Butler wrote:
    'And make all cries about the town
    Join throats to cry the bishops down.']
[³ Samuel Vaughan, 'an eminent merchant, and an active supporter of the bill of rights', had offered a bribe through the Lord Mayor of London to the First Lord of the Treasury, the Duke of Grafton, in order to secure for his son the position of Clerk of the Crown in Jamaica. The matter was brought before Lord Chief Justice Mansfield and the Court of King's Bench, and provided plenty of interesting material both for 'Junius' and other writers in the periodicals.]
[⁴ Rev. Hugh Peters (1598–1660), who was tried and executed for his part in bringing about the death of Charles I.]

He comes, the conquering Hero comes,   *40*
Who tyrants to destruction dooms,
Sublime, illustrious from afar!
No vulgar beasts may draw his car,
But choicest of the Scarlet Train,
Six venerable Aldermen   *45*
Their shoulders & *long ears* submit
To drag him thro' the crouded street.
Mob shouts, increas'd to half a million,
And meek Maccauley[5] rides postilion!

Whom shall the many-headed Brute,   *50*
With their fierce Driver, first salute?
Ambitious to deserve the gallows,
March on, ye Patriots, to the palace,
Lead your audacious Legions nigher,
Provoke, and dare the Troops to fire,[6]   *55*
And to your King again present
His choice of death, or banishment.

But can ye hope by means like these
To heal the Nation's grievances?
And must the reformation spring   *60*
From insults on a gracious King?
Your rights licentious be maintain'd
By sacred Majesty prophan'd?
By poisoning a distracted nation,
By Regicide, or Abdication?   *65*
Sooner let Horne be dubb'd a martyr,
And factious London lose her charter,
Sooner be wicked Wilkes forgot,
Or stinking, like his memory, rot,
And your whole Mob, both low & high-born,   *70*
Conclude your glorious Course at Tyburn!

[5 Mrs Catharine Macaulay (1731–91), historian and controversialist, described by Boswell as 'a great Republican'. Cf. introduction to No. **291**.]
[6 An allusion to the 'massacre' in St George's Fields on 10th May 1768, when the mob around the prison where Wilkes was incarcerated was fired on by a detachment of foot guards after the reading of the Riot Act. Several people were killed.]

285   THE CITY REMONSTRANCE

* MS Patriotism: Misc., p. 32.

Metre 100: Anapaestic 13's

We y[ou]r Majesty's dutiful subjects & Leiges,
To exhibit our skill in political Seiges,
Our Remonstrance present—May it please or displease you,
For our aim is To worry, & bully, & teize you,

And by impotent threats of a new Revolution, ⎱   5
Of your own, & y[ou]r Family's utter confusion, ⎰
To frighten you into a Mad Dissolution. ⎰

. . . .

. . . .

Desunt caetera[1]

[[1] 'The remainder is missing.']

AN ELEGY ON THE LATE   **286**
REVEREND GEORGE WHITEFIELD, M.A.,
WHO DIED SEPTEMBER 30, 1770,
IN THE 56TH YEAR OF HIS AGE

The Rev. George Whitefield (1714–70) was the preacher *par excellence* of the Evangelical Revival, a man of passionate evangelism, great histrionic talent, and a tremendous voice. He did not, however, share John Wesley's talent for shepherding his converts. Although it was against Whitefield that the approbrious title 'Methodist' was most furiously hurled in the early days of the revival, because of the strong theological differences between him and the Wesleys few of his converts became Methodists in the modern sense—members of 'the Society of the People called Methodists'. He was, however, the forerunner and inspirer of the Wesleys in 'field-preaching'.

Whitefield died, burnt out with unremitting labours, in Newburyport, Massachusetts, and was buried at his own desire in the Presbyterian Meeting House there. Thus in his death was symbolized the fact that a large and fruitful part of his ministry was fulfilled outside his own country and outside his own Anglican Church. Following hard on the Wesleys' footsteps to Georgia, he had founded an Orphan House near Savannah, maintaining it by preaching and by prayer. This continued one of the focal points of his ministry, and remains to this day, one of the oldest orphanages in America.

Of the 536 lines of the original poem just under half are here reproduced.

* *An Elegy on the late Reverend George Whitefield*, 1771.
  Poetical Works, VII.423–42.

                                    Metre 98a: Iambic 10's, with closing 12's

And is my Whitefield entred into rest,
With sudden death, with sudden glory blest?
Left for a few sad moments here behind,
I bear his image on my faithful mind;
To future times the fair example tell   5
Of One who lived, of One who died, so well,
Pay the last office of fraternal love,
And then embrace my happier Friend above.

  O Thou who didst, in our degenerate days,
This chosen Vessel for thy glory raise,   10
My heart with my Companion's zeal inspire,
And touch *my* lips with the celestial fire,
That while thy servant's labours I record,
Sinners may see, and magnify his Lord,
Bow to the saving Name, and thankful own   15
The good on earth perform'd is wrought by God alone. . . .

Can I the memorable day forget, 50
When first we by divine appointment met?
Where undisturb'd the thoughtful student roves,
In search of truth, thro' Academic groves,
A modest, pensive youth, who mus'd alone,
Industrious the frequented path to shun, 55
An Israelite without disguise or art
I saw, I loved, and clasp'd him to my heart,
A stranger as my bosom-friend carest,
And unawares receiv'd an angel-guest. . . .

Moved by the Holy Ghost to minister,
And serve his altar, in the house of prayer,
Though long resolv'd for GOD alone to live 110
The outward call he trembled to receive,
Shrunk from the awful charge, so well prepar'd,
The gift by Apostolic hands confer'd,
And cried, with deep unfeign'd humility,
Send, LORD, by whom Thou wilt, but send not me. 115

Yet soon he bows before the will Divine
Clearly demonstrating its own design,
Call'd by a Prelate good,[1] no more delays
T'accept with awe the consecrating Grace,
And offers up, thro' the Redeemer's blood, 120
His body, spirit, soul, a sacrifice to GOD.

He now begins, from every weight set free,
To make full trial of his ministry,
Breaks forth on every side, and runs, and flies,
Like kindling flames that from the stubble rise, 125
Where'er the Ministerial Spirit leads,
From house to house the heavenly fire he spreads,
Ranges thro' all the city-lanes and streets,
And seizes every prodigal he meets.

Who shall the will and work divine oppose? 130
His strength with his increasing labour grows:
Workman and work th'Almighty hath prepar'd,
And sent of GOD, the servant must be heard,
Rush thro' the opening door, on sinners call,
Proclaim the truth, and offer CHRIST to all. 135

'Sound an alarm, the gospel-trumpet blow,
'Let all their time of visitation know;
'The Saviour comes! (you hear his herald cry)
'Go forth and meet the Friend of sinners nigh!'

[1 Whitefield was ordained by Martin Benson, Bishop of Gloucester (1689–1752), as deacon on 20th June 1736, and as priest on 14th January 1739.]

Rous'd from the sleep of death, a countless croud,   *140*
(Whose hearts like trees before the wind are bow'd,
As a thick cloud, that darkens all the sky,
As flocking doves, that to their windows fly,)
Press to the hallow'd courts, with eager strife,
Catch the convincing word, and hear for life.   *145*
Parties and sects their endless feuds forget
And fall, and tremble at the preacher's feet,
Prick'd at the heart, with one consent inquire
What must we do t'escape the never-dying fire? . . .

But lo! an ampler field appears in view,
And calls his champion forth to conquests new:
Nor toils, nor dangers can his zeal repress,
Nor crouds detain him by his own success: *165*
In vain his children tempt him to delay,
With prayers and tears invite his longer stay,
Or ask, as sharers of his weal or woe,
To earth's remotest bounds with him to go:
He leaves them all behind at JESUS' word,   *170*
He finds them all again in his beloved LORD.

See, where he flies! as if by Heaven design'd,
T'awake and draw our whole apostate kind!
He takes the eagle's with the morning's wings,
To other worlds the great salvation brings,   *175*
As sent, with joyful news of sins forgiven,
To every ransom'd soul on this side heaven!

With ready mind th'Americans receive
Their angel-friend, and his report believe,
So soon the servant's heavenly call they find,   *180*
So soon they hear the Master's feet behind:
He comes—to wound, and heal! At his descent
The mountains flow, the rocky hearts are rent;
Numbers acknowledging their gracious day
Turn to the LORD, and cast their sins away,   *185*
And faint and sink, beneath their guilty load,
Into the arms of a forgiving GOD.
His Son reveal'd, they now exult to know,
And after a despis'd Redeemer go,
In all the works prepar'd their faith to prove,   *190*
In patient hope, and fervency of love.

How blest the messenger whom JESUS owns,
How swift with the commission'd word he runs!
The sacred fire shut up within his breast
Breaks out again, the weary cannot rest,   *195*

Cannot consent his feeble flesh to spare,
But rushes on, JEHOVAH's harbinger:
His one delightful work, and stedfast aim
To pluck poor souls as brands out of the flame,
To scatter the good seed on every side,   *200*
To spread the knowledge of the Crucified,
From a small spark a mighty fire to raise,
And fill the continent with JESUS praise. . . .

The man of GOD, whom GOD delights t'approve
In his great labours of Parental love,
Love of the little ones—for these he cares,   *215*
The lambs, the orphans, in his bosom bears;
Knowing in whom he trusts, provides a place,
And spreads a table in the wilderness,
A father of the fatherless, supplies
Their daily wants—with manna from the skies,   *220*
In answer to his prayer so strangely given,
His fervent prayer of faith that opens heaven. . . .

More grace is on the humble man bestow'd,   *245*
More work on him that loves to work for GOD;
By whose supreme decree, and kind command
He now returns, to bless his native land,
(Nor dreads the threatnings of the watry[2] deep,
Or all its storms, with JESUS in the ship)   *250*
To see how the belov'd disciples fare,
Fruits of his toil, and children of his prayer,
A second gospel-benefit t'impart,
And comfort, and confirm the faithful heart. . . .
Renews his strength, renews his prosperous toil
In every corner of our favour'd isle,
And publishes salvation to the poor,   *275*
And spreads the joyous news from shore to shore.

For when the rich a proffer'd CHRIST reject,
And spurn the preacher with his odious sect,
Out of their temples cast, he strait obeys,
Goes forth to all the hedges and high-ways,   *280*
Arrests the most abandon'd slaves of sin,
And forces the poor vagrants to come in,
To share the feast for famish'd souls design'd,
And fill the house inlarg'd for all the sinful kind.

How beauteous on the mountain-tops appear   *285*
The feet of GOD's auspicious Messenger,
Who brings good tidings of a world forgiven,
Who publishes a peace 'twixt earth and heaven,
And cries to Zion, He that purg'd thy stains,
Thy SAVIOUR-GOD and KING for ever reigns!   *290*

[2 All copies seen are corrected in a contemporary hand from 'watry' to 'wintry'.]

Soon as he thus lifts up his trumpet-voice,
Attentive thousands tremble, or rejoice:
Who faithfully the welcome truth receive,
Rejoice, and closer to their SAVIOUR cleave:
Poor christless sinners, wounded by the word *295*
(Lively and sharper than a two-edg'd sword,
Spirit and soul almighty to divide) ⎫
Drop, like autumnal leaves, on every side, ⎬
Lamenting after Him they crucified! ⎭
While GOD inspires the comfort, or the dread, *300*
Wider, and wider still the cry is spread,
Till all perceive the influence from above.
O'rewhelm'd with grief, or swallow'd up in love.

What multitudes repent, and then believe,
When GOD doth utterance to the preacher give! *305*
Whether he speaks the words of sober sense,
Or pours a flood of artless eloquence,
Ransacks the foul apostate creature's breast,
And shews the man half devil, and half beast;
Or warmly pleads his dear Redeemer's cause; *310*
Or pity on the poor and needy draws:
'The Deist scarce from offering can with-hold,
'And misers wonder they should part with gold:'³
Opposers struck the powerful word admire
In speechless awe, the hammer and the fire, *315*
While WHITEFIELD melts the stubborn rocks, or breaks,
In consolation, or in thunder speaks,
From strength to strength, our young Apostle, goes,
Pours like a torrent, and the land o'erflows,
Resistless wins his way with rapid zeal, *320*
Turns the world upside down, and shakes the gates of hell! . . .

Betwixt the mountain and the multitude,
His life was spent in prayer and doing good:
To search the sacred leaves, his soul's delight,
And pray them o're and o're by day and night, *370*
To wrestle on for faith, and faith's increase,
To follow after peace and holiness,
At JESUS feet to catch the quickning word,
And into nothing sink before his LORD.

Though long by following multitudes admir'd, *375*
No party for himself he e'er desir'd,
His one desire to make the SAVIOUR known,
To magnify the name of CHRIST alone:

[³ It is well known that Benjamin Franklin, employed as Whitefield's printer, had made up his mind not to contribute to the Orphan House scheme. On hearing him preach, however, he 'began to soften', and thought he would give some copper; then decided to make it silver; and at the end, 'emptied [his] pocket into the collector's dish, gold and all'.]

If others strove who should the greatest be,
No lover of pre-eminence was he,   *380*
Nor envied those his LORD vouchsaf'd to bless,
But joy'd in theirs as in his own success,
His friends in honour to himself prefer'd,
And least of all in his own eyes appear'd.

When crouds for counsel or relief applied,   *385*
No surly rustic he, with cruel pride
To bid the sorrowful intruders wait,
Or send the suppliants weeping from his gate;
But ever listning to the wretch's call,
Courteous, and mild, and pitiful to all.   *390*
No prophet smooth to men of high estate,
No servile flatterer of the rich or great,
Their faults he dared with freedom to reprove,
The honest freedom of respectful love,
And sweetly forc'd their consciences to own   *395*
He sought not theirs, but them, for JESUS sake alone. . . .

Single his eye, transparently sincere   *405*
His upright heart did in his words appear,
His chearful heart did in his visage shine;
A man of true simplicity divine,
Not always as the serpent wise, yet love
Preserv'd him always harmless as the dove: *410*
Or if into mistake thro' haste he fell,
He shew'd what others labour to conceal;
Convinc'd, no palliating excuses sought,
But freely own'd his error, or his fault,
Nor fear'd the triumph of ungenerous foes,   *415*
Who humbler from his fall, and stronger rose.

When Satan strove the brethren to divide,
And turn their zeal to—who is on my side?
One moment warm'd with controversial fire,
He felt the spark as suddenly expire,   *420*
He felt reviv'd the pure etherial flame,
The love for all that bow'd to JESUS name,
Nor ever more would for opinions fight
With men whose life, like his, was in the right.
His soul disdain'd to serve the selfish ends   *425*
Of zealots, fierce against his bosom-friends,
(Who urg'd him with his bosom-friends to part,
Might sooner tear the fibres from his heart)
He now the wiles of the accuser knew,
And cast him down, and his strong-holds o'rethrew,   *430*
With each partition-wall by men design'd
To put asunder those whom GOD had join'd.

How have we heard his generous zeal exclaim,
And load with just reproach the bigot's name!
The men by sameness of opinion tied,   *435*
Who their own party love, and none beside;
Or like the Romish sect infallible,
Secure themselves, and send the rest to hell!
Impartial, as unfeign'd, his love o'erflow'd
To all, but chiefly to the house of GOD;   *440*
To those who thought his sentiments amiss—
O that their hearts were half as right as his,
Within no narrow party-banks confin'd,
But open, and inlarg'd to all mankind!

Lover of all mankind, his life he gave,   *445*
Christ to exalt, and precious souls to save:
Nor age, nor sickness could abate his zeal,
To feed the flock, and serve the Master's will.
Though spent with pain, and toils that never ceas'd,
He labour'd on, nor ask'd to be releas'd;   *450*
Though daily waiting for the welcome word,
Longing to be dissolv'd, and meet his LORD,
Yet still he strangely lived, by means unknown,
In deaths immortal, till his work was done,
And wish'd, for CHRIST his latest breath to spend,   *451*
That life and labour might together end. . . .

THE SPEECH OF PONIATOWSKI, KING OF POLAND, 1771   **287**

The early 1770's were troubled times for Poland, with Civil War and then partition.
On 3rd November 1771 an apparently successful attempt was made to assassinate
the king, Stanislaus Poniatowski. Though wounded he escaped, largely through the
help of the leader of the assassins, who was later strangled in contravention of the
king's orders that no harm should come to him. The trial of the assassins did not take
place until 1773. In the *Gentleman's Magazine* for August that year appeared the
following account, which Wesley would almost certainly have read: 'Thursday 26. By
advices this day received in the foreign press, it is said, that whilst the Chamber was
sitting, at Warsaw, on the trial of the Regicides, his Polish Majesty came into the
Court, and, being seated on the Throne, interceded in the most pathetic manner,
not only for the life of the man who saved him, and brought him back, but for all the
others, representing them as the innocent victims of the infamous projects of their
superiors, and being obliged to obey, at the risk of their lives, the orders of their
Commanders.'

* MS Patriotism: Misc., p. 26.

Metre 98: Iambic 10's

Ye Nations hear! A Monarch great & good
Pleads for the Parricides, w[h]o spilt his blood,
The Judges prays their sentence to suspend
And let their King his Murtherers defend:
'They thought it right their Leaders to obey,   *5*
'A Tyrant, & their Country's Foe to slay,
'Mercy extend to Them that dying I
'With confidence may thus for mercy cry
'Father, for Jesus sake, the sinner save,
'Forgiving me, as I my Foes forgave!   *10*

288   ON THE DEATH OF CHARLES WORGAN, AGED 17 OR 18

Dr John Worgan, famous organist (1724–90), was a friend of Charles Wesley, and tutor to that musical prodigy, his son Charles (1757–1834). The young man here commemorated was probably one of Dr Worgan's sons.

* MS C. Wesley's Letters, IV.78, 1 page 4to (Methodist Book Room, London).
MS 339, 1 page 4to (Methodist Book Room, London).
MS Death (b) [Hymns for Love], p. 72.
Poetical Works, VI.365.

Metre 47: 7.7.7.7.7 7
a b a b c c

1 Blooming Innocent, adieu!
   Lovely, transitory Flower,
Faded is thy youthful hue,
   Ended is thy morning hour!
Death hath seal'd thy sleeping eyes,—   5
      now
Open'd ~~them~~—in paradise!

2 Ravish'd hence by Sovereign LOVE,
   Wing'd with empyrean fire,
Soars thy soul to realms above,
            immortal
   Mingles with the ~~Angel~~ quire   10
Hears the Music of the Spheres,
      ~~Angelic~~   heavenly
All the ~~heavenly~~ ⋀ Harpers hears.

       Happy
3 ~~Heavenly~~ Harmonist, to Thee
   Sovereign LOVE assigns a Place,
Crowns thy spotless purity,   15
   Decks thy head with brighter rays,
Bids thee join the Virgin throng,
Chant th'inimitable Song.

4 Passing thro' this mortal Vale,
   Lo, we after Thee aspire,   20
Where Thou dost their triumphs swell,
   Raise their highest raptures higher;
Sing the glorious One in Three,
Shout thro' all eternity.

Title. 'Mr' added by MS Death; 'aged 17 or 18' omitted by MSS 339, Death.
  1. MSS 339, Death: 'Blooming Innocence'.
  5. MSS 339, Death: 'Death hath closed'.
  6. MS 339: 'Opend now—in';
              ing
       MS Death: 'Open'~~d~~ ~~now~~ them'.
  9. MSS 339, Death: 'to joys above'.
  10. MS Death: 'Mingled with'.
  12. MSS 339, Death: 'All those heavenly harpers'.
  18. MS 339 adds '(Rev.14)'.
  19. MSS 339, Death: 'Hast'ning thro' this'.
  21. MS Death: 'their triumph'.

AN EPISTLE TO DR LUDLOW **289**

The origin of the following verses is somewhat obscure, just as there is also some uncertainty about their authorship. The most likely occasion prompting them seems to have been a musical festival held in the Bristol Cathedral on Thursday 31st March 1774. It was arranged for the benefit of the Infirmary, and the profits handed over amounted to £100. After a morning service during which selections from Handel's music were rendered, there was a special evening performance of Handel's Messiah by 91 performers, the tickets for which were 5s. 3d. It was announced that during the evening performance 'Master Charles Wesley (by particular desire) will perform a Concerto on the organ'. Apparently, however, young Samuel Wesley had been asked to deputize for his elder brother, who had another engagement, but was unexpectedly able to appear after all.

It is uncertain whether the disappointed young Samuel composed the verses himself, either unaided or with the help of his father, or whether in fact Charles Wesley composed them in the name of his son. The basic extant manuscript, however, is in the hand of Charles Wesley. In spite of assertions to the contrary, the 'Letters MS' does not appear to be in the hand of Samuel Wesley. The 'Emory MS' is more like that of his sister Sarah, though ending '1775. Saml Wesley'. In this as in other details, Clarke's *Family* followed the 'Emory MS'. Stevenson's *Wesley Family* and Lightwood's *Samuel Wesley* followed the 'Letters MS', but introduced other variants. Stevenson stated that he possessed the 1775 original in the hand of the father, and a 1777 copy in the hand of the son. Other copies may well be extant.

The title is variously given. The 'Letters MS' has 'An Epistle to his much respected Friend Dr Ludlow: By Master Saml. Wesley'. The 'Emory MS' has the title 'To Dr Ludlow' preceded by the note: 'A Copy of Verses by Saml. Wesley younger son of the Revd Mr C. Wesley occasioned by his Brother C. Wesley Junr being chose[n] to Play a solo on a Violin before the Corporation of Bristol and some business calling him from Bristol about the time, Saml Wesley was chose[n] in his Room but in the meantime C. Wesley return'd and Saml was set aside.' Clarke also has 'To Dr Ludlow'. Stevenson has 'A Serio-Comic Epistle, addressed to Dr Ludlow, of Bristol, by Samuel Wesley'. Lightwood, claiming to give 'the original version', and presumably the original title, has 'A Serio-Comic Epistle in Verse addressed to Dr Ludlow of Bristol by Samuel Wesley on being advertised, *as a child*, to play before the Worshipful the Mayor and Corporation at a City Feast, and afterwards declined.' The 'Pryor MS' has 'Lines written by Mastr S. Wesley then eight years old . . .'

The Dr Abraham Ludlow to whom the poem is addressed was surgeon at the Bristol Infirmary. He was elected to that position in 1767 at the age of thirty, and died at the home of his married daughter in Bristol in 1807.

---

* Nursery MS, pp. 3–5.
 Letters of Wesley Family, I.62 (Methodist Book Room, London).
 Emory MS (Emory University, Atlanta, Georgia).
 Pryor MS, a transcript from memory by Mrs Pryor for the Rev. J. Gaulter, early
  19th century (Wesley's Chapel, City Road, London).
 A. Clarke's *Wesley Family* (1844), II.373–4.
 G. J. Stevenson's *Wesley Family* (1876), pp. 499–500.
 J. T. Lightwood's *Samuel Wesley, Musician* (1937), pp. 38–40.

Metre 6: 8.7.8.7
A B A B

1 To you, dear Doctor, I appeal,
   To all the Tuneful City.
  Am I not used extremely ill
   By Musical Committee?

2. Letters, Stevenson, Lightwood: 'the learned city.'
   Letters adds a note: '* The City of Bristol: where he was advertised
     to play, at the Oratorio, before the Corporation, but was afterwards
     refused on account of his age; being about Eight years old.'

4. Stevenson, Lightwood: 'By the Musical Committee?'

2 Why tis enough to make one wild— 5
   They court, and then refuse me,
They Advertize and call me Child,
   And as a Child they use me.

3 Excusing their contempt, they say
   (Which more inflames my passion) 10
I am not grave enough to play
   Before the Corporation.

4 To the sweet City-waits altho'
   I may not hold a candle,
I question if their Worships know 15
   The Odds t'wixt me and Handel.

5 'A Child of 8 years old' I ~~own~~ grant,
   Must be both light & giddy,
The Solidness of Burgum[1] want
   The Steadiness of Liddy:[2] 20

6 Yet quick perhaps as other folks
   I can assign a reason,
And keep my time as well as Stokes[3]
   And come as much in season.

[1 Henry Burgum, patron of the arts, Handel enthusiast, and friend of the Wesleys —a pewterer by trade. He was treasurer for the festival.]
[2 Thomas Lediard, another organizer of the festival, and a friend of the Wesleys.]
[3 Possibly Thomas Stokes, a lawyer, who was linked with the Wesleys, as were other members of the Stokes family at Bristol. Emory MS notes: 'Remarkable for bad time.']

8. Emory, Pryor, Clarke: 'like a child'.
9–12. Given as v. 7 by Stevenson, and v. 5 by Lightwood.
13–16. Given as v. 8 by Stevenson, and v. 6 by Lightwood.
13. Letters: 'their sweet City Waits';
   Stevenson, Lightwood: 'these sweet City waits'.
17–18. Stevenson, Lightwood:
         'That I'm a child I freely grant,
           Playful, and somewhat giddy'.
18. Pryor; 'May be'. Letters: 'I am but light, and giddy'.
19–20. Pryor: 'The steadiness of Burgan want
          The gravity of Laddie';
   Stevenson, Lightwood:
         'The judgment of a Burgum want,
          The gravity of Liddy'.
21. Pryor: 'But quick'.
21–3. Stevenson, Lightwood:
        'But still in that I see nor rhyme,
          Nor any other reason,
        Since I [Lightwood, 'Sure I'] perhaps can keep my time'.
23. Emory, Clarke: 'as well as Holks'.

7 With Bristol-Organists not yet   25
    I come in competition:
    But let them know I wou'd be great
    I do not want ambition;

8 Spirit I do not want, or will
    Upon a just occasion,   30
    To make the rash Despisers feel
    My weight of indignation.

            twill
9 Tread on a worm, he'll turn again:
    And shall not I resent it?
    Who gave the sore affront, in vain   35
    They wou'd with tears repent it.

        shall, sir, appease my Rage
10 Nothing ~~mine anger shall assuage~~
    At their uncouth demeanor,
    Unless they prudently assuage
    Mine anger with—A Steyner.[4]   40

[[4] A violin made by the famous Tyrolese violin-makers, the Stainers.]

25–8. Omitted by Pryor, Lightwood.
26. Letters: 'I stand in competition'.
27. Letters: 'Like them you know I would be great'.
    Emory, Clarke, Stevenson: 'Yet let them know'.
28. Letters: 'And do not want'.
29–32. Omitted by Pryor, Lightwood.
29. Letters: 'nor Will'.
33–6. Omitted by Stevenson, Lightwood.
33. Letters, Emory, Pryor, Clarke: 'The trodden Worm will turn again'.
37–8. Letters, Stevenson, Lightwood:
        'Nothing shall e'er appease my Rage,
          At their unjust demeanour'.
    Emory, Pryor, Clarke:
        'Still will I fret, and fume, and rage,
          And keener wax, and keener'.

TO MISS DAVIS   **290**

Miss Cecilia Davies (1750?–1836) was one of the most popular vocalists of the eighteenth century. In the late 1760's she commenced singing to the accompaniment of her elder sister Marianne's performances on Benjamin Franklin's 'armonica'. Shortly afterwards the family toured in Austria and then in Italy, where Cecilia Davies was a great success, and was known as '*L'Inglesina*'—she was, in fact, the first Englishwoman to appear on the Italian stage. After an interval of a few years in England during the 1770's she returned to Italy, fell on evil times, was rescued from poverty and enabled to return to England, where she spent her declining years in obscurity, illness, and poverty. Wesley probably wrote this poem during her first interval in England, while she was still thoroughly Italianized, and eager to return to Italy.

* MS, loose sheet, Lamplough Collection (Methodist Book Room, London).

Metre 89: 7 7.7 7.7 7.8 8
a a b b c c D D

Gentle Inglisina, say,
Can the smooth Italian Lay
Nature's ruggedness remove,
Soften Britons into love?
Yes: if the stocks & stones draw near,   5
Thy inchanting Voice to hear
And all the Savages agree
In praise of harmony & Thee!

291   WRITTEN AFTER PASSING BY WHITEHALL

In 1775 Charles Wesley was revising the manuscript of his brother's *Concise History of England*, published in four volumes the following year. On 29th December he wrote to John: 'I must continue to plead for my Namesake . . . "He was rigorously just—but wanting in sincerity". . . . Such a Drawback from his good Character will exceedingly grieve more than me; as much as it will please the Patriots & Republicans. At such a time as this especially when it is the fashion to "blacken the Tyrant". You & I shd. not join in the popular cry, but rather go—contra Torrentem. Let Mac-cauley & Co. call the K.'s Murther "This great Act of National Justice." . . . Let not your hand be upon him or mine.' In the final revision the sentence stood: 'He was rigorously just; but is supposed to have been wanting in sincerity.'
As the attacks on George III increased in virulence, Charles Wesley continually compared them with those on his favourite Charles I, and this poem inspired by the place of execution was almost certainly written at some time in the 1770's.

* MS Patriotism: Misc., pp. 2–3.
Poetical Works, VIII.445.

Metre 98: Iambic 10's

Unhappy Charles, mistaken, and misled,
In error by a wretched Father bred,
By flattery nurst, and disciplin'd to stray,
As born a Monarch for despotic sway;
Push'd on by Churchmen's interested Zeal,   5
Or'erul'd by Relatives belov'd too well:
What shall I say? with partial fondness aim
To palliate faults Thou didst thyself condemn?
Or in the spirit of these furious times
Blacken thy memory with fictitious crimes?   10
No: let me rather blame thy course begun, ⎫
Admire the glories of thy setting Sun,   ⎬
And virtues worthy a Celestial Crown.   ⎭

Convinc'd of every error in thy reign,
Thy upright soul renounc'd them all; in vain!   15
Resolv'd to make the Laws thy constant Guide,
(And every heighten'd wrong *was* rectified)
Rejoic'd to bid the Cause of discord cease,
And lay the Basis sure of public peace.

But fruitless all a righteous Monarch's pains,   *20*
If God to plague our guilty land ordains,
Suffers his foes their fatal choice to feel,
Cries 'havock', and lets slip the dogs of hell.
The Champion fierce of violated laws[1]
His sword in prosperous rebellion draws,   *25*
And scorning all the laws of man & God,
Imbrues his ruffian hands in sacred blood,
Holds up the Martyr's, as a Traitor's, head,
And glories in the dire infernal deed!

[[1] Oliver Cromwell.]

[THE GOOD-HEARTED GOSSIP]   **292**

The subject of this lighthearted poem is still unidentified, but 'Jimmy R—' was obviously a jovial, good-hearted young 'man about town', who seems to have dabbled in art. One wonders whether the artist John Russell had a brother called James who might fit the bill, though if so he does not appear in Wesley's references to the family.

* MS Patriotism: Misc., pp. 36–7.

Metre 67: 6 6.6 6.6 6.6 6
A A B B C C D D

Vitiis nemo sine nascitur, optimus ille
Qui minimis urgitur.[1] Hor[ace].

Come, prick up your ears,
Jimmy R—— appears,
In all haste to produce
His budget of news,
To sing or to say   *5*
What he learnt at the play,
And retail the bons mots
Of theatrical beaux.

With what glee he declares
The pranks of the players!   *10*
With what pleasure repeats
The Actresses feats!
Or if chancing to stray
They slip out of the way,
He transmits their renown   *15*
To be hawk'd thro the town.

Whene'er he thinks fit
With his delicate wit
His friends to or'epower,
His words we devour,   *20*
While by elegant chat
And similies pat
He delights us—or stuns
With a torrent of puns.

[[1] No one is born without faults, and the best man is he who is beset by the least faults.]

329

But the Punster's vain boast   *25*
In the Painter is lost,
In a goodness of heart
Surpassing his art:
His worth we receive,
His foibles forgive,   *30*
And true Piety own
In the Dutiful Son.

293   ON S[AMUEL] W[ESLEY]

The Honourable Daines Barrington, famous man of letters, was greatly impressed
by the musical sons of Charles Wesley, Charles (1757–1834) and Samuel (1766–1837).
He first heard Samuel toward the end of 1775. In 1781 he published an account of the
two musical prodigies both in the *Philosophical Transactions* and in his own *Miscel-
lanies*. In recounting the beginnings of Samuel's musical career for the benefit of
Barrington Charles Wesley wrote: 'The seeds of harmony did not spring up in him
quite so early as in his brother; for he was three years old before he aimed at a tune.
His first were, "God save great George our King", Fischer's Minuet, and such like,
mostly picked up from the street-organs.'

* MS Patriotism: Misc., pp. 7–8.

Metre 98a: Iambic 10's with closing 12

Sam for his three first years the Secret kept,
While in his heart the Seed of Music slept,
Till Charles's Chissel by a carnal Stroke
Brought forth the Statue latent in the block:
Like Memnon then, he caught the Solar Fire,   *5*
And breath'd spontaneous to Apollo's lyre,
With nature's ease th'Harmonious Summit won
The envious, and the gazing Croud outrun,
Left all the rest behind, & seizd on—Barrington.†

† al. Mornington. [Another admirer of the young Wesleys, and a regular attender at
the concerts in Marylebone, was the Earl of Mornington.]

294   THE MAN OF FASHION

* MS Patriotism: Misc., pp. 37–8.
Poetical Works, VIII.479–80.

Metre 97a: Iambic 8's & 9's

What is a modern Man of fashion?
A man of taste, and dissipation,
A busy man, without employment,
A happy man, without injoyment;
W[h]o squanders all his time and treasures   *5*
On empty joys, and tast[e]less pleasures,
Visits, attendance, and attention,
And courtly arts too low to mention.
In sleep, and dress, and sport, and play
He throws his worthless life away;   *10*
Has no Opinions of his own,
But takes from leading beaux the ton;

Born to be flatter'd, and to flatter,
The most important *thing* in nature,
Wrapt up in self-sufficient pride,   *15*
With his own virtues satisfied.
With a disdainful smile or frown
He on the riffraff croud looks down,
The World polite, his friends and He—
And all the rest are—Nobody!   *20*

 Taught by the Great his smiles to sell
And how to write, and how to spell,
The Great his Oracles he makes,
Copies their vices and mistakes,
Custom pursues, his only Rule,   *25*
And lives an Ape, and dies a Fool!

 'But say, thou criticizing clown,
'(If thou canst pull the Ladies down)
'What is a Woman nicely bred,
'In every step by fashion led?   *30*
The proverb makes us understand her,
What's sauce for Goose is sauce for gander:
From which I rightly reason thus,
What's sauce for Gander is for Goose—
But here I for my faults atone,   *35*
By letting the fair Sex alone.

ADDRESS TO THE CALVINISTS   295

The *Arminian Magazine* was founded by John Wesley specifically to combat the
teaching 'that *God is* not *loving to every man*, that *his mercy is* not *over all his works*:
and consequently, that *Christ did* not *die for all*, but for one in ten, for the Elect only'.
To this end he included a number of poems, particularly from the *Hymns on God's
Everlasting Love* of a generation earlier. There are a number of other poems, like the
one here given, which were not published in any other Wesley publication, but cannot
be traced to any other author, and seem almost certainly to be the work of Charles
Wesley. [After this poem had been prepared for the Press a fragment of it was discovered in the handwriting of Charles Wesley, a confirmation of his authorship.]

* *Arminian Magazine*, 1778 [August], pp. 383–4.

Metre 97: Iambic 8's

God has, you say, a two-fold Will,
One to Preserve, and one to Kill:
That in his Word to All reveal'd,
This from the Reprobate conceal'd:
That would have All the Fallen kind   *5*
Repentance and Salvation find;
To Hell's inevitable pains,
This the far greater part ordains;
Compell'd to Sin by his Decree,
And Damn'd from all Eternity.   *10*

His written Will to All displays
Offers of Life and pard'ning Grace:
His secret doth this Life deny
To most, yet asks, 'Why will ye die?'
His *seeming* Will their good pretends,   *15*
His *real* their damnation sends;
Makes the devoted victims fit,
And thrusts them down into the pit.

'Tis thus, O God, they picture Thee,
Thy Justice and Sincerity;   *20*
Thy Truth which never can remove,
Thy bowels of unbounded Love:
Thy freedom of Redeeming Grace,
'With-held from almost all the Race,
'Made for Apollyon to devour,   *25*
'In honour of thy Sovereign Power!'

Ye weak, mistaken Worms, believe
Your God, who never can deceive;
Believe his word sincerely meant,
Whose Oath confirms his kind intent: *30*
Believe his Tears: believe his Blood:
Both for a World of Sinners flow'd;
For those who nail'd Him to the Tree,   ⎱
For those who forg'd *the dire Decree*,   ⎰
For ev'ry Reprobate—and me!   ⎱   *35*

296   AFTER READING MR HILL'S REMARKS
          AND FARRAGO DOUBLE DISTILLED

The theological warfare in which Charles Wesley had been engaged in the early
years of the Revival flared up again in the 1770's. The chief Calvinist pamphleteer
was Sir Richard Hill, and the Arminian champion was the Rev John Fletcher of
Madeley. Hill's *Friendly Remarks occasioned by the Spirit and Doctrines contained in
the Rev Mr Fletcher's . . . Second Check to Antinomianism* was published in 1772.
Though mainly directed against Fletcher and John Wesley, Charles also came in for
some castigation, and his *Hymns on God's Everlasting Love* were referred to as 'certain
godly lampoons of famous memory'. *Logica Wesleiensis: or the Farrago Double
Distilled*, published the following year, was designed to show that John Wesley con-
tradicted himself in his various publications, thus following up Hill's *Review of all the
Doctrines taught by the Rev Mr John Wesley*, of 1772. Again Charles Wesley is drawn
in, and the *Hymns on God's Everlasting Love* are described as 'that shocking medley of
gross misrepresentation'.

* *Arminian Magazine* (1778, September), p. 430.
  MS Patriotism: Misc., p. 24.
  Poetical Works, VIII.446.

                                        Metre 98: Iambic 10's

Why do the zealots of *Geneva* rage,
And fiercest war with an old prophet wage?
Why doth their Chief with blackest slanders load
An hoary servant of the living God?

Sincerely hate, affectedly contemn,   5
'Because he contradicts himself—not them.'
Let W[esley] then, a different method try,
Himself gainsay, his own Report deny;
Evade, or contradict the General Call,
And teach, 'The Saviour did *not* die for all.'   10
This Contradiction openly confest,
Would cancel and atone for all the rest.

5. MS Patriotism: '*Sincerely* hate, *affectedly* contemn?'
7. MS Patriotism: 'Let Wesley then a wiser method try'.
12. MS Patriotism: 'Woud cover, and atone'.

WRITTEN AFTER A FALL   297

Riding horseback over treacherous roads between London and Bristol, and even around those cities, Charles Wesley could hardly avoid occasional accidents. They seem to have become more numerous, as well as more serious, as he became older. In 1772 he wrote to Joseph Benson, 'I have lately escaped death or maiming by a fall', though a week later he was 'almost recovered of [his] bruises'. After a fall at Bristol in his seventieth year, 'while quietly walking' his horse, he vowed: 'NB. I shall never more ride that Beast.' On 25th November he had a bad fall in London, blaming it on the fact that his horse had 'been almost starved at the Foundery', and believing that another fall might be his last. On Saturday the 28th he wrote: 'A fall I had on Wednesday night brought ye breath out of my body. But my work is not quite done. Tomorrow's service may scatter the pains in my side.' It was probably on this occasion, as he was nearing his seventieth birthday, that he wrote the following poem.

* MS Miscellaneous Hymns, p. 92.

Metre 1: 8.6.8.6
A B A B

1 Let fools, and infidels revere
   And bow to Fortune's shrine,
No chance, or accident is here,
   But Providence divine.

2 Thou, Lord, hast suffer'd me to fall,   5
   That I again may prove
My worthless hairs are numbred all,
   My life secur'd above.

3 Thankful the token I receive
   Of greater things to come,   10
And trust, thy love will never leave,
   But bring me safely home.

4 For when I fall into the grave,
   I only fall to rise,
Whom Thou dost to the utmost save   15
   And bear above the skies.

298   PRAYER FOR [A] MURTHERER J.H.
          AT HIS EXECUTION APRIL 19, 1779

The Rev James Hackman (1752–79) had been ordained only a few weeks when he murdered Miss Martha Ray, mistress of the fourth Earl of Sandwich, for whom he had a hopeless passion. He then attempted to commit suicide. His trial at Old Bailey before Mr Justice Blackstone furnishes one of Burke's *Celebrated Trials*. Dr Johnson, hearing from Boswell (who travelled with Hackman to Tyburn) that he prayed for the mercy of heaven, said, 'in a solemn fervid tone, "I hope he *shall* find mercy".'

* MS Death (c) [Funeral Hymns], p. 82.
Poetical Works, VIII.352–3.

Metre 10: 8.8.8.8.8 8
A B A B C C

1 Jesus, was ever love like thine!
    Jesus, remember Calvary!
Who didst thy precious life resign,
    Who didst, expiring on the tree,
Pity the men that nail'd thee there   *5*
And save them by thy dying prayer.

2 A Ruffian drench'd in guiltless blood
    Thy utmost strength of grace requires:
From all the righteous wrath of God
    From inextinguishable fires   *10*
Redeem him at this dreadful hour,
Thou Infinite in saving power!

3 The one unpardonable sin
    Great God, if he hath never done,
We ask that blood to wash him clean,   *15*
    Which did for murtherers atone;
Wash'd in that blood his soul require,
And save him—save him—as by fire!

Title. In original, 'Prayer for her Murtherer . . .'.

299   WRITTEN SEPT. 9, 1779, WHEN THE COMBINED
          FLEETS OF FRANCE AND SPAIN WERE IN THE CHANNEL

On 9th July 1779 a Royal Proclamation prophesied an imminent invasion of England by the united fleets of France and Spain. Arrangements were made to evacuate the coastal areas; a special bill came before Parliament for impressing into the Armed Forces men normally exempt; a score of volunteer regiments were being mustered; John Wesley sponsored a plan prepared by Captain Webb for enrolling and training Methodist volunteers. During August the fleets entered the English Channel, while England waited tensely, and the Government and Admiral Sir Charles Hardy dithered. For over a fortnight an attack on Plymouth seemed imminent, and on 3rd September Hardy withdrew to Spithead. Eventually the combined enemy fleet, far superior in numbers, but dejected, disease-ridden, and battered by easterly gales, gave up the venture, and by the middle of September they had retired to Brest, another Invincible Armada conquered by non-human forces.

* Miscellaneous Hymns, pp. 239–40.

Metre 31: 6.6.8.6.6.6.8.6
A B A B C D C D

334

1   Supreme, Almighty Lord,
     To whom in Christ we pray,
Tempests and storms fulfil thy word,
     And winds and seas obey;
     Thee King of kings we own,   *5*
     Thee Lord of hosts confess,
And from thine outstretch'd Arm alone
     Expect our whole success.

2   To save the faithful race
     From Rome and Satan near,   *10*
Appear as in the ancient days,
     On Britain's side appear;
     Thy wondrous works renew'd
     Let us exult to see,
And Fleets invincible subdued   *15*
     By one great word from Thee.

3 ~~Thou know'st the hellish aim~~
     Of our inveterate Foe,
Who Britain's rebel sons inflame
     Their country to or'ethrow: *20*
     Defend the righteous cause,
     Thy needful help afford,
While urg'd, our injur'd nation draws
     The slow, defensive sword.

                   compact
4   Dissolve their ~~counsel~~ dire,   *25*
     Nor let their Counsel stand
Who vow to waste with sword and fire
     Our whole, devoted land:
     To lay their malice low,
     To end their furious boast,   *30*
Blow with thy wind tempestuous, blow
     And scatter all their host.

5   By many, or by few
     Thou art not bound to save,
Whose arm th'Egyptian host or'ethrew,   *35*
     By the or'ewhelming wave:
     Extend that arm once more,
     And by a whirlwind driven
Compel our vanquish'd foes t'adore
     The Lord of earth and heaven.   *40*

41 ff. Charles Wesley wrote at least one more stanza, but in binding this
       particular volume omitted a page, so that only the first two lines
       and the catchword leading to the third survive:
            '6 So shall our lives declare
              The Power who safety brings
                      /The'

300   FOR SOME OF THE PREACHERS
WRITTEN IN 1779

Charles Wesley had long been troubled about what seemed undue ambition among some of the itinerant preachers. Things came to a head in the autumn of 1779, when Alexander McNab, stationed in Bath, refused to recognize the authority of an Irish clergyman, the Rev. Edward Smyth, whom John Wesley had invited to preach on the Sunday evenings that he was in Bath. Charles Wesley believed that he had actually uncovered a widespread and determined conspiracy against John Wesley's authority, of which this was the first blow. Yet he was sure that McNab's attitude was not shared by the majority of the preachers, who were fervently though perhaps humbly making up for the shortage of evangelical clergy.

* MS Preachers Extraordinary, pp. 20–3.
  MS Charles Wesley, Vol. IV, folios 72 & 73 (a fair copy of 72), 'Written Oct. 10. 1779' (Methodist Book Room, London).
  MS Miscellaneous Hymns, pp. 128–31, 'For Several of the Method[is]t Preachers. Written Oct. 10, 1779'.

Metre 4: 8 8.6.8 8.6
A A B C C B

1 Lord over all, thy people hear
  For every favour'd messenger
    Whom Thou hast own[e]d for thine,
  For every chosen instrument
  Without our rules or orders sent   5
    To serve the cause divine.

2 Sent forth they were to prophesy,
  Their lack of service to supply
    Who sit in Moses chair,
  But love the world, and seek their own,   10
  Neglect their ministry, and shun
    The gospel to declare.

3 Because the prophets held their peace
  The stones, thy quicken'd witnesses,
    Cried out on every side,   15
  In streets, and houses, and high-ways
  They spread the news of pardning grace,
    They preach'd the Crucified.

4 Their doctrine sinsick spirits heal'd,
  The Lord himself their mission seal'd   20
    By daily signs from heaven,
  Blind souls their inward sight receiv'd,
  The dead were rais'd, the poor believ'd,
    And felt their sins forgiven.

12. MS CW.IV.73: 'They Gospel'.
13. MS Misc.: 'hold their peace'.
                              quicken'd
14. MS CW.IV.72: 'thy ~~living~~ witnesses'.
                    Their doctrine sinsick spirits
19. MS CW.IV.72: '~~Distemper'd souls their doctrine~~ heal'd'.
21. MSS CW.IV.72, 73: 'With miracles from heaven'.
22. MS CW.IV.72: 'The blind to God their'.

5 By ceaseless toils of humble love   25
   Thy serv[an]ts sought their faith t'approve,
     They spake, and liv'd the word,
   Simple & poor, despis'd of men,
   They liv'd immortal souls to gain,
     And glorify their Lord.   30

6 With tears we own, They *did* run well!
   But where is now their fervent zeal,
     Their meek humility,
   Their upright heart, their single eye,
   Their vows the Lord to magnify   35
     And live, and die for Thee?

7 The love of ease, and earthly things
   The pride from which contention springs,
     The fond desire of praise,
   Have imperceptibly stole in,   40
   Brought back the old besetting sin,
     And poison'd all their grace.

8 They now preeminence affect
   Eager to form the rising Sect,
     Some better thing to gain: 45
   Like hireling priests, they serve for hire,
   And thro' ambition blind, aspire
     Without the cross to reign.

9 The flock they w[oul]d in pieces tear,
   That each may seize the largest share,   50
     May feed himself alone:
   'Come, see my zeal' at first they cried,
   But now they ask 'W[h]o's on my side
     Will make my cause his own?'

10 The men w[h]o have their savour lost   55
   Themselves ag[ains]t the branches boast,
     And dignities despise:
   Their greedy hopes the flock devour,
   As all were left within their power
     To glut their avarice.   60

               fervent
32. MS CW.IV.73: 'their ~~former~~ zeal'.
33. MS CW.IV.72: 'Their deep humility';
    MS CW.IV.73: 'Their meek humility'.
               serve
46. MS CW.IV.72: 'they pant for'.
            with   n vain
47. MS CW.IV.72: 'And ~~all~~ ambitio~~usly~~ aspire';
               thro'
    MS CW.IV.73: 'And ~~with~~ ambition blind'.
53. MSS CW.IV.72, 73, Misc.: 'Who on';

337

11 But O thou Shepherd great & good,
   The sheep redeem'd by thy own blood
      Into thine arms receive;
   If still with England's Church Thou art
   True pastors after thy own heart   65
      To thy own people give.

12 Thy flock out of their hands redeem
   Who of their own importance dream
      As God had need of man:
   Send whom Thou wilt, in mercy send,   70
   Thy cause and gospel to defend,
      Thy glory to maintain.

13 And O their faithful hearts inflame
   With love of our Jerusalem
      Thy Church Establish'd here: 75
   Still may they cry, & never ~~cease~~ rest:
   Till Glory, in thy face exprest,
      Throughout our land appear:

14 Till Thee, the Glory of the Lord,
   In truth and righteousness restor'd   80
      All flesh together see,
   Salute Thee on thy great white throne
   And sink in speechless raptures down
      For ever lost in Thee.

63. MS CW.IV.72: 'thy arms'.
                       of their own importance dream
68. MS CW.IV.72: 'Who ~~seek~~ themselves, ~~themselves esteem~~'.
76. MSS CW.IV.72, 73: 'never rest'.
82. MS CW.IV.72: 'And hail thee on'.

301   PARTY LOYALTY

Written in the year 1780

Charles Wesley was even more attached to Church and King than his brother John,
and was constantly distressed at the political attacks on George III. This poem was
probably written shortly after 6th April 1780, when John Dunning secured the passage of his famous resolution: 'That the influence of the Crown has increased, is
increasing, and ought to be diminished.'

* *Arminian Magazine*, 1781 (June), p. 340, using the last line of the poem as title.
  CW. MSS I (p) xiii, with title as above (Methodist Book Room, London).
  MS Patriotism, pp. 45–6, with title as above.
  Poetical Works, VIII.447–8.

Metre 97: Iambic 8's

The First and Second *George* were wise,
And understood a Faction's price;
Little account of those they made,
That from mere principle obeyed,
But purchased with an annual bribe   5
The votes of the Dissenting Tribe;
Who served with flaming zeal and hearty,
The Heads of their own favoured Party.

Why are they changed to *George* the Third,
And never give him a good word?   10
His rebels why do they embrace,
And spit in a mild Monarch's face!
'Because he slights his Father's friends,
And the three kingdoms comprehends,
All Sects and Parties reconciles,   15
Alike on Whig and Tory smiles:
Aims at impossibilities,
And studies friends and foes to please;
Because our pensions he withdraws,
And if he starve the good, old Cause,   20
And if he nothing more advance—
No longer pipe, no longer dance!'

8. MS Patriotism: 'The Heads'.
     MSS I, Patriotism, 'fav'rite Party.'
18. MSS I, Patriotism: 'studies all the world to please'.

WRITTEN ON THURSDAY, JUNE 8, 1780   **302**

Quis cladem illius noctis, quis funera fando explicit.—Virg.

In 1778 Sir George Savile had secured the passage of a Bill mitigating the harsh legislation against Roman Catholics. Immediately a 'Protestant Association' was formed in order to render the Relief Act worthless. Controversy raged, in which John Wesley was involved, for he had written to the *Public Advertiser* commending the *Appeal* published by the Protestant Association. On 29th May 1780 Lord George Gordon, the President of the Association, held a mass meeting, when plans were put forward for a march of at least 20,000 men from St George's Fields to the Houses of Parliament to demand the repeal of the Relief Act. When the petition was presented on 2nd June its consideration was deferred, and the crowd of 100,000 got out of hand. For some days brawling, pillaging, and assault were let loose, with the leaders of the Association powerless to control the evil spirit which they had conjured up. Literally hundreds of people lay dead in the gutters of the city, killed by the gin which they had sucked up from the staved casks out of plundered distilleries. Not only Roman Catholic churches and other property, but scores of other buildings were destroyed, and Wesley's newly erected chapel in City Road had a very narrow escape. John Wesley himself was in the north of England, Charles being left in charge of affairs in London. Even on 8th June, although the worst fury had subsided, Charles Wesley wrote to his daughter Sally, who was away, 'Matters here are in a dreadful situation', so that Mrs Wesley and young Sam were being evacuated. His letter on the 12th said: 'The roaring of the Waves is ceased: but it, the Agitation, continues.' In that same letter he enclosed one of his poems on the Gordon Riots, written on 8th June. It was probably a little later in the month that he wrote the four cantos of *The Protestant*

Association, and the associated satires, the 'Address to the City', 'Advice to the City', and 'Second Address to the City'. In these he lashed both the passion of the mob and the pusillanimity of the magistrates.

* *Hymns written in the Time of the Tumults* (1780): No. 3.
MS Charles Wesley's Letters, II.42 (Methodist Book Room, London).
Poetical Works, VIII.267–8.

Metre 8: 8 8 . 8 8
A A B B

1 Saviour, thou dost their threatnings see
  Who rage against our king and thee,
  Nor know, thy bridle in their jaws
  Restrains the friends of Satan's cause.

2 As in religion's cause they join,   5
  And blasphemously call it thine,
  The cause of persecuting zeal,
  Of treason, anarchy, and hell.

3 See, where th'impetuous Waster comes,
  Like legion rushing from the tombs;   10
  Like stormy seas, that toss and roar,
  And foam, and lash the trembling shore!

4 Havock, th'infernal leader cries!
  Havock, th'associate host replies!
  The rabble shouts—the torrent pours—   15
  The city sinks—the flame devours!

5 A general consternation spreads,
  While furious crouds ride o'er our heads;
  Tremble the powers thou didst ordain,
  And rulers bear the sword in vain!   20

6 Our arm of flesh entirely fails,
  The many-headed beast prevails;
  Conspiracy the state o'returns,
  Gallia exults—and London burns!

7 Arm of the Lord, awake, put on   25
  Thy strength, and cast Apollyon down,
  Jesus, against the murtherers rise,
  And blast them with thy flaming eyes:

Title. This is in the MS only.
7–8. MS: 'The Cause of blind fanatic zeal,
          Rebellion, anarchy, & hell.'
13–14. MS: 'HAVOCK—th'infernal Leader cries!
          HAVOCK—th'*Associate* Host replies!'
25. MS: 'Arm of the Lord, awake, ~~arise~~, put on'.

8 Forbid the flood our land t'o'erflow,
  Tell it—thou shalt no farther go;   *30*
  My will be done, my word obey'd,
  And here let thy proud waves be stay'd!

31–2. MS: 'Thy will be done, thy word obey'd,
          And here let it's proud Waves be stay'd!'

WRITTEN AFTER THE CONFERENCE IN AUG. 1780   **303**
THE LAST WHICH THE WRITER WAS PRESENT AT

For years Charles Wesley had fought a losing battle against the forces within Methodism which were making for separation from the Church of England. The question of
ordaining the preachers was again to be brought up at the Conference of 1780, and
therefore John Wesley invited his brother to be present. At first Charles declined the
invitation, both on the grounds of his being unable to control his temper on such a
question, and because in any case he could do no good. Actually he did attend, but
kept in the background, as 'some sort of check to the independents'. It was his
intention not to attend another Conference because he felt that he could not stay the
tide of events. In fact, however, he *did* attend the Conference of 1786, when it seemed
that John Wesley was prepared to restrict the ministerial powers of the ordained
preachers to America and Scotland; that Conference, which was indeed his last, also
resisted and overcame a determined attempt to secure the ordination of a preacher
for Yorkshire, which would have implied separation.

* MS Miscellaneous Hymns, pp. 134–5.
  Poetical Works, VIII.416–17.

                                                    Metre 4: 8 8.6.8 8.6
                                                             A A B C C B

1 Why should I longer, Lord, contend,
  My last, important moments spend
    In buffetting the air,
  In warning those who will not see,
  But rest in blind security,   *5*
    And rush into the snare!

2 Prophet of ills why shoud I live,
  Or by my sad forebodings grieve
    Whom I can serve no more?
  I only can their loss bewail   *10*
  Till life's exhausted sorrows fail,
    And the last pang is o're.

3 Here then I quietly resign
  Into those gracious hands divine
    Whom I receiv'd from Thee,   *15*
  My brethren and companions dear,
  And finish with a parting tear
    My useless ministry.

4 Detatch'd from every creature now
  I humbly at thy footstool bow,   *20*
    Accepting my release,
  Till Thou the promis'd grace bestow,
  Salvation to thy Servant show,
    And bid me die in peace.

304 [A SAD DISTRACTED LAND]

On 20th January 1782 the following proclamation was issued: 'GEORGE R. We, taking into our most serious consideration the just and necessary hostilities in which we are engaged, and the unnatural rebellion carrying on in some of our provinces and colonies in North America, and putting our trust in Almighty God, that he will vouchsafe a special blessing on our arms both by sea and land, have resolved, and do, by and with the advice of our privy-council, hereby command, that a public Fast and Humiliation be observed throughout that part of our kingdom of Great Britain called England, our Dominion of Wales, and Town of Berwick upon Tweed, upon Friday the 8th day of February next. . . .' (A similar General Fast for Scotland was arranged for the 7th.) Charles Wesley speedily produced a 24-page collection of fifteen hymns for the occasion. He followed it up with two similar pamphlets under the title *Hymns for the Nation in 1782*, containing respectively nine and eight hymns. During the same year there were also published three varying compilations from these three original collections.

* *Hymns for the National Fast, Feb. 8, 1782*: No. 13.
  Poetical Works, VIII.332–4.

Metre 31: 6.6.8.6.6.6.8.6
A B A B C D C D

1   Jesus, thy flaming eyes
      Full on the wicked dart,
  Who in Rebellion's Cause arise,
      And take the murtherer's part,
      Their bloody path pursue,   *5*
      A Congress from beneath
  A daring, dark, and desperate Crew,
      In league with Hell and Death.

2   Possest of lawless power,
      Of absolute command,   *10*
  The beasts with iron teeth devour
      A sad distracted land:
      Traitors with Gaul combin'd,
      Their cruel sway maintain,
  The scum and refuse of mankind   *15*
      As sovereign lords they reign.

3   Their heart, O Lord, thou know'st,
      Elated with success,
  Who triumph now, and make their boast
      Of prosperous wickedness;   *20*
      Who blasphemously claim
      Divine authority,
  As acting treasons in thy name,
      And countenanced by Thee.

4   How long, O God, how long,   *25*
      Wilt Thou their crimes pass by,
  And suffer their oppressive wrong,
      Who all thy plagues defy?
      Blast the aspiring Fiend,
      Avenge us of the foe,   *30*
  Confound his sworn Allies, and end
      Their Empire at a blow.

5   So shall Thy people sing
        The Power that sets us free,
    The Arm that doth deliverance bring   *35*
        From hellish tyranny;
        The same in heart and mind
        With loyal Britons prove,
    In strictest bonds fraternal join'd,
        In everlasting love.   *40*

6   Then, when the work is done
        Which fiends in vain withstand,
    America and Britain, One
        In thy all-healing Hand,
        The Lord's Redeem'd shall come,   *45*
        And crown'd with joy arise
    To Sion's heights, their long-sought home,
        Their Country in the skies!

[THE NEW WORLD]   **305**

* *Hymns for the Nation, in 1782*: No. 11.
  Poetical Works, VIII.299–300.
  Collection ((1831): No. 703, vv. 1, 3–5.
  Collection (1876): No. 730, vv. 1, 3, 4.
                    Metre 94b: Varied, Nos. 85 & 86

1 Saviour, whom our hearts adore,
    To bless our earth again,
  Now assume thy royal power
    And o'er the Nations reign:
  Christ, the world's Desire and Hope,   *5*
    Pow'r compleat to thee is given,
  Set the last great empire up,
    Eternal God of heaven.

2 When thy foes are swept away,
    And meet their righteous doom,   *10*
  Then thy Deity display,
    And let thy kingdom come:
  Then in the New World appear,
    In lands where thou wast never known,
  There th'Imperial standard rear,   *15*
    And fix thy fav'rite throne.

3 Where they all thy laws have spurn'd,
    Thy holiest Name profan'd,
  Where the ruin'd earth hath mourn'd,
    With blood of millions slain: *20*

  8. 1831, &c.: 'Eternal Lord'.
18. 1876: 'Where they thy name profane'.
19. 1831, &c.: 'ruin'd world'.

343

Open there th'ethereal scene,
  Claim the savage race for thine,
There thy endless reign begin
  With majesty divine.

4 Universal Saviour, Thou   *25*
  Wilt all thy creatures bless,
Every knee to Thee shall bow,
  And every tongue confess:
None shall in thy mount destroy;
  War shall then be learnt no more,   *30*
Saints shall their great King enjoy
  And all mankind adore.

5 Then, according to thy word,
  Salvation is reveal'd;
With thy glorious knowledge, Lord,   *35*
  The new-made earth is fill'd:
Then we sound the mystery,
  The depths and heights of Godhead prove,
Swallow'd up in mercy's sea,
  For ever lost in Love.   *40*

22. 1831, &c.: 'Claim the heathen tribes'.
23. 1831, &c.: 'the endless'.

306   WRITTEN ON A LATE DECLARATION OF LORD C——
THAT THE CONQUEST OF AMERICA BY FIRE AND SWORD
IS NOT TO BE ACCOMPLISHED

Like many of his fellow countrymen in all times, Charles Wesley did not like the way
in which the war was being conducted. He had many scathing things to say about
Sir William Howe (1729–1814), Commander-in-Chief in America from 1775 to 24th
May 1778. Nor did Wesley approve of Howe's successor, Sir Henry Clinton (1738–95),
nor of Clinton's second-in-command, Charles, Earl Cornwallis (1738–1805). Before
the war Cornwallis had pleaded for more sympathetic treatment of the Americans,
yet reluctantly took up command and loyally and efficiently carried out his duties,
even though he and Clinton were at loggerheads. That he surrendered at Yorktown
on 19th October 1781 (the virtual end of active hostilities) was through no mis-
management of his own, though there were plenty to blame him, including Clinton—
and, apparently, Wesley. He had constantly endeavoured to conciliate the Americans
as the only means of lasting victory, and he had also urged that hostilities could only
be waged successfully on a very limited front. Clinton proffered his resignation in
May 1781, and in February 1782 (a month after Cornwallis landed in England),
Sir Guy Carleton (1724–1808) was appointed Commander-in-Chief. He fulfilled all
Charles Wesley's hopes, though not in the way that Wesley expected: he did help to
bring peace, but by conciliating, not conquering, the Americans.

* *Arminian Magazine*, 1782 (September), pp. 501–2.
  CW.I MSS (c), with the eight verses numbered (Methodist Book Room, London).
  MS Patriotism, pp. 47–9.
  Poetical Works, VIII.482–4.

Title. MS Patr.: 'Written on a Declaration of Lord C——'s, that "the
              Conquest of America by sword and fire is not to be
              accomplished".'
       MS CW.I also omits 'late' and adds the inverted commas, but
       retains the order 'fire and sword'.

Metre 15: 8 8.8 8.8 8
A A B B C C

1   True is the Patriotic word,
    'We never can by fire and sword
    The fierce Americans subdue;'
    If we our General's steps pursue,
    His own allies who tears and rends,   5
    And turns his sword against his friends.

2   The loyal if he first invite[1]
    For Britain and its King to fight,
    Promise to succour and protect;
    He then abandons to neglect,   10
    Or draws them in an easy prey
    For their inveterate foes to slay.

3   Poor credulous slaves if he allure,
    By flattering hopes of refuge sure,
    Their cruel tyrants to desert;   15
    He then with an unfeeling heart
    Leaves them, who on his faith rely,
    By hunger or disease to die.

4   Thousands who unconsumed remain,
    He drives out of his camp again;   20
    (While trusting in his treacherous words,)
    Gives up the victims to their lords,
    To punish in the lingering fire,
    By varied torments to expire.

5   Such faithful Leaders we allow   25
    Fit to succeed immortal H—e,
    Who fierce Americans subdued,

[1 MS Patriotism adds the footnote, 'At Hillsborough', i.e. Hillsboro, North Carolina. On 20th February 1781 Cornwallis issued a proclamation from Hillsborough inviting 'all such faithfull and loyal subjects to repair without loss of time, with their arms and ten days' provisions, to the Royal Standard now erected at Hillsborough, where they will meet with the most friendly reception. . . .']

1. MS Patr.: 'True is the Noble Patriot's word'.
5–6. MS Patr.: 'His sword against his friends who turns,
           And spoils, and plunders them, and burns.'
    MS CW.I: 'Against his friends his sword who turns,
           And spoils, and plunders them, and burns.'
18. MSS: 'By famine, and disease to die.'
20. MSS: 'He thrusts'.
21. MSS: 'And, while they trust his treacherous words'.
22. MSS: 'Gives up'.
23. MSS: 'To perish'.
24. MS Patr.: 'By varied tortures'.
26. MS Patr.: 'immortal Howe'.

And conquer'd them whene'er he would;
Too generous to pursue his blow,
Or trample on a vanquished foe.   *30*

6   His vanquished foe full oft he reared,
And kindly their despondence cheered:
Too brave to take them by surprise,
He saw their straits with pitying eyes;
And put them out of all their pain,   *35*
And gave them back their towns again.

7   Such Generals never can aspire
Rebels to quell with sword and fire;
But without fire, another can
Accomplish it—an honest man,   *40*
Who truth and public faith approves,
And more than life his country loves.

8   A man for this great end designed
Our Nation now expects to find,
By providential Love bestowed,   *45*
Whose object is Britannia's good,
Britannia's peace his only aim!
And *Carlton* is the Patriot's Name.

28.   MS Patr.: 'conquer'd them—whene'er'.
29.   MS CW.I: 'the blow'.
37.   MSS: 'Such Leaders'.
40.   MS CW.I: 'another honest Man'.
41.   MSS: 'Who truth and righteousness approves'.
42.   MSS: 'more than gold'.
44.   MSS: 'We now at last expect to find'.

307   WRITTEN ON A LATE VOTE FEBR. 22, 1782

On Friday 22nd February 1782 General Henry Seymour Conway (1721–95), who had
been consistently opposed to the war with the Americans, moved in the House of
Commons an address to the king, urging his ministers 'not to pursue any longer the
impracticable object of reducing his Majesty's revolted Colonies, by force, to their
allegiance, by a war on the continent of America'. Horace Walpole described the
effect of the speech as 'incredible'—on a division the Government was left with a
majority of only one.

* MS Patriotism, p. 50.
  CW.MSS I (o) 6a (Methodist Book Room, London).
                                         Metre 99: Anapaestic 11's, 12's

How furiously now do the Patriots strive,
And on to the brink of the Precipice drive!
'No longer oppose: let the Rebels alone:
'Give up the dispute, and the business is done:
'Our Commanders may then with impunity rest,   *5*
'The matter be hush'd, and Inquiry supprest,

                  drive
      2. MS CW.I: 'strive'.

346

'While the men who so well understood peculation,
'And grew fat on the spoils of a sacrific'd nation,
'Their own villanies charge on their Rivals in pow'r,
'Given up for the Popular Beast to devour.   10

'Then a fig for the old Constitution and laws,
'Set aside by the Rump, & Republican Cause,
'Then in spite of a titular, obstinate King,
'To justice we all the Delinquents shall bring;
'Or set an impertinent Monarch aside,   15
'The inheritance seize, & the kingdom divide,
'Our zealous, unlimited liberty prove,
'And demonstrate how dearly our Country we love.

'Shall the war be abandon'd, or still carried on?
(Now we come to the Point, and the day is our own)   20
'Shall Britain exist as a Nation, or not?
'It exists by a single, unfortunate Vote:

                                        our lies
'But if numbers of Votes we cou[l]d gain by ~~surprize~~,
'Over-reach half a senate, & put out their eyes,
'We shall surely prevail, if we bravely persist,   25
'The whole Parliament conquer, & do as we list.

23. MS CW.I: 'surprize'.

A MOTION OF THE MINORITY   **308**

This poem may relate to the vote of 22nd February 1782, which almost forced the seeking of peace terms with the American colonists. (See No. **307.**) Certainly the background is similar.

* *Arminian Magazine*, 1782 (March), p. 167.
MS Patriotism, p. 46.
Poetical Works, VIII.480.

                              Metre 99: Anapaestic, 11's, 12's

Agreed! let it be as the Patriots hope,
To their Friends let us give all America up:
Let the Rebels be lords, and the Loyalists swing,
For loving Old England, and serving their King:
Be the Westerly Isles the next easy prize,   5
Which Geneva bestows on her Popish allies:
The East Indies must then unavoidably fall,
And dominion at sea be transferred to the Gaul.

Here's an end of the Story, and end of the Dance,
By GREAT Britain becoming—a Province to France!   10

5–6. MS Patriotism:
          'Let the Westernly Isles be the next easy Prize
          Wch Congress bestows on their Popish Allies:'.

309 WRITTEN AFTER THE NEXT VOTE

On Wednesday 27th February 1782 General Conway moved to the attack again. He taunted some who had voted in favour of continuing the war—yet confessed in private their desire for peace—with 'the gift of tongues—double tongues'. This time his motion to end the war with America passed without a division. The Government was overthrown, and Lord North forced to resign, much to Charles Wesley's dismay. In the subsequent Rockingham coalition Conway became commander-in-chief, with a seat on the Cabinet.

* MS Patriotism, pp. 51–2.
   CW.MSS I (o), pp. 8–9 (Methodist Book Room, London).

Metre 70: 11 11.11 11.11 11
   A A B B C C

Come away to the chase! the Republican Pack
With a rabble of Livery-men all at their back,
Have started the Stag; & resolve to press on
Till the blood-thirsty hellhounds have hunted him down,
And worried to death, without mercy or pity,   5
To make a magnificent Feast for the City.

The City so famed for their exquisite taste
In the present, as well as the century past,
At their annual⟨Club who so greedily feed,   ⟨ Jan. 30[1]
And to Turtle itself prefer a Calf's head,   10
Shall be treated again with the Cannibal's food,
And royally drunk at a banquet of blood.

So thy promise and vow w[h]o triumphantly sing
For their victory over their Country & King:
Their King they have conquer'd, & routed his friends,   15
In pursuit of their own diabolical ends.
By hard strug[g]ling and lying their purpose attain'd,
And by Treason—at last, a Majority gain'd!

With what madness & rage do they now lay about 'em,
The old ministers threaten, & rage, till they out 'em!   20
'But the worst of them all, for whose horrible crime
'His blood shall atone, is the Minister Prime!'
In billingsgate language, & highwayman's phrase,
They command him, to *stand and deliver*—his Place.

[1 30th January was the anniversary of the execution of King Charles I, and on that day until well into the eighteenth century the Calves' Head Club met to feast in derision of Charles, and to drink the toast 'to those worthy patriots who killed the tyrant'.]

2. MS CW.I omits 'all'.
            greedi
9. MS CW.I: 'eagerly'.

Our soldiers abroad they forbid to oppose,   25
Or molest, or annoy their innocent foes,
But tamely to give all the Loyalists up
To the Rebels, or French, to the Sword, or the Rope,
To keep out of harm's way, & their weapons lay down,
Till the Mob has secur'd their Republican Crown.   30

But true Englishmen hope, yt the Nation or'ereach'd
Will recover their wits, & awake unbewitch'd,
Then the Traitors at home, & the Agents of France
Will finish their course with a sorrowful dance,
Then we all shall unite in defence of our King,   35
And the Rebels at last, and the Patriots, swing!

        they
25. MS CW.I: 'to̶'.

[WRECKERS OF THE REALM]   310

Like many before and since, Charles Wesley looked upon the American War as caused largely by the self-seeking yet clumsy machinations of politicians, rather than the result of deep-seated national needs. Relatively free from selfish ambitions himself, he found it difficult to keep his temper with demagogues and dictators. This poem, like many similar ones, was probably written shortly after the overthrow of Lord North's ministry early in 1782.

* MS Patriotism, pp. 59–60.
  Poetical Works, VIII.480–2, omitting verses 9 and 10.

                      Metre 10: 8.8.8.8.8 8
                             A B A B C C

Non tali auxilio, nec defensoribus istis
Tempus eget. Virg.[1]

1 What hope of safety for our Realm,
   From men who by destruction thrive,
By violence seize the shatter'd Helm,
   And madly let the Vessel drive,
Till dash'd against the rocks it break   5
And then they gather up the wreck.

2 Makers of wrecks, a desperate race
   Who treason and rebellion love,
Who spit in a mild Monarch's face,
   Can they the public ills remove,   10
Or plung'd themselves in depths of vice,
Assist our sinking State to rise?

3 Proud, profligate, to evil sold,
   Their Country's curse, reproach, & shame,
Their lust of power, and thirst of gold   15
   Cloaking beneath the patriot's name,
Shall These our liberties defend,
Shall These, who caus'd, our troubles end?

[1 The occasion does not call for such help, nor for your kind of 'protectors'.]

349

4 Who their own Countrymen destroy'd,
   Kindled & fed Rebellion's fire,   *20*
And all their hellish arts employ'd
   To raise the civil discord higher,
Will These restore our happiness
Or give us back a lasting peace?

5 Order and government they scorn,   *25*
   Forbid the slighted laws to reign,
And while their injur'd King they spurn,
   The Rabble's Majesty maintain,
Those abject instruments of ill,
Those tools of every tyrant's will.   *30*

6 First for themselves the Patriots care,
   And each sincerely seeks his own,
Eager the public spoils to share,
   (Now they have pull'd their Rivals down)
And all into their hands to seize,   *35*
The mead of prosperous wickedness.

7 Thro' avarice and ambition blind,
   Their schemes, bewilder'd, they pursue,
Grasping at that they cannot find,
   Still undetermin'd what to do,   *40*
Till some superior Fiend appear,
And claim the Sovereign Character.

8 Daring as Charles' spurious brood,
   Harden[e]d as W[il]k[e]s in wickedness,
As dissolute as F[ox] and lewd,   *45*
   Worthy of the Protector's place,
Worthy the Place by right his own
When Cromwell fills a burning throne.

9 Such is the crooked Statesman's hire,
   The Traitors who their Country sell,   *50*
Or in Rebellion's Cause expire,
   They claim the hottest place in hell,
Unless the Saviour interpose,
To snatch them from eternal woes.

10 Saviour, the human Fiends convince,   *55*
   Persuade them from their sins to part,
And when they cast away their sins,
   And turn to Thee with all their heart,
O let them all thy love receive,
And saved, with us, for ever live!   *60*

THE ASSOCIATORS 311

The 1780's saw the phenomenal growth of plans for an 'Association', supposedly of 'the people', which should dictate to the Crown and Government. They took their cue from revolutionaries both in America and Ireland. Almost inevitably the genuine grievances were almost forgotten as the Association became a political tool in the hands of men like Fox. (See H. Butterfield: *George III, Lord North, and the People, 1779–80*.)

* MS Patriotism, pp. 61–2.

Metre 97: Iambic 8's

Nec lex est justior ulla
Quam necis artificis arte perire suâ. Ovid.[1]

Once on a time, a gallant Ship
Was sailing on th'Atlantic deep,
A gang of Transports in the hold
Confin'd, to desperation bold,
And madly bent to break their chain,   5
Their freedom, and the Helm to gain;
Had long their hands in secret ply'd,
And in the bottom bored a wide
Tremendous hole—alarm'd the Crew
Swift to their boat, escaping, flew: 10
(But none unlocks the fetter'd slaves,
But none the Self-destroyers saves.)
The sea pour'd in, as well it might,
The vessel fill'd, and sunk outright,
But sunk with all its wicked freight,   15
And whirl'd the Felons to their fate.

So in our days a Gang we see
Link'd in a dark Conspiracy,
The Vessel of the State to make
A sure, but profitable, wreck,   20
That while the waves our Ship or'ewhelm,
Themselves may seize, and rule the Helm;
Nor do the desperate Wretches dream
The foundring Ship will bury Them.

Must not HE sink in the abyss   25
The shackled slave of every vice,
Unless some friendly hand unlocks
The Fetters of felonious F[ox]?
Must not his Comrades share his fate,
Opprest by their own guilty weight,   30
By avarice, lust, ambition, pride,
And plunge in the avenging tide?
Can the Associators shun
The mischiefs their own hands have done?

[1 Nor is there any clearer justice than that the contriver of murder shall perish by his own plot.]

Can the assassin band emerge,   *35*
When Britain sinks beneath the Surge?
Or claim the empire of the main,
Or kings by our destruction reign?

  You that survive the wreck, attend
The Patriot-plan, and mark the end!   *40*
Tho' oft the Wicked here we see
Triumphant in their villany,
Their wickedness, or soon or late,
Shall surely fall on their own pate,
And sink them with their plots profound   *45*
In bottomless perdition drown'd.

312   THE PATRIOTS KING

Much against the personal desires of King George III, the American colonies had in
effect been surrendered by the demand of the Commons in February 1782 for peace
negotiations. Both in the appointment and policy of the new ministry under Rockingham and Shelburne he was further humiliated, particularly by somewhat niggling
attempts to reduce the royal household expenditure, as part of a determined attack
on the power of the Crown. Charles Wesley saw in these measures a repetition of the
attack on the Divine Right of Kings which culminated in the execution of Charles I.

* MS Patriotism, pp. 69–70.

Metre 71: 11 11.11 11.11 11.11 11
A A B B C C D D

The doctrine is old, and obsolete too,
That subjects shou[l]d render to Cesar his due:
The things w[hi]ch are his, are his own proper right;
But right must give way to oppression & might:
Prescription & laws, constitution & charters   *5*
Are all swallow'd up by an army of Tartars,
Who have conquer'd the nation, the mob, & the House,
So for Country & King they care not a louse.

The patriot-clans, by treason unawed,
Dispoil'd him at first of his empire abroad,   *10*
And now the Republican Harpies are come,
To strip him of all his dominions at home:
In so lavish a King they cannot confide
For himself & a family large to provide,
So Hibernian Pity the Faction engages   *15*
Both his children & Him to put out at board-wages.

T'were Madness, they cry, in a Monarch to trust
W[h]o wou[l]d trample Americans brave in the dust,
(If his absolute will he were suffer'd to have)
And free Britons at last by his Tories inslave;   *20*
Within proper bounds t'was high time to reduce him;
But first for our own private purposes use him.
To bully, and threaten, to humble and tame,
Till he gives us a grant of whatever we claim.

Our freedom & rights we can never secure   25
If we leave him a single Prerogative sure,
If the load of our slanders we rashly remove,
And suffer his subjects their Monarch to love:
But we still must cajole, & throw dust in their eyes,
That they still may oppose him & hate & despise,   30
And be ready to act whatsoever we say
And implicitly all our commands to obey.

We allow him at present, a pitiful thing,
To make use of the name & the stile of a King,
But the slave of the people must always confess   35
Tis Ours to set up, or pull down, as we please:
For howe'er we permit him to reign for an hour,
We shall give him to know our unlimited power,
To rob, and abuse, to insult him and mock
Or command him—to lay down his head on a block.   40

THE AMERICAN REFUGEES   313

Among the sufferers from the American war were dispossessed people loyal to the Crown yet for various reasons not in the armed forces. Many of these gathered in New York. Others found their way back to England. In neither place were they really welcome, and many endured great hardships. In May 1779 Lord North secured £60,000 for the relief of American refugees in Great Britain. Their numbers and their plight increased during the peace negotiations in 1782, and after the actual Treaty of Paris in 1783. This problem provided plentiful material for Parliamentary debate and public conversation. Charles Wesley was unhesitating in his affirmation that their homeland should support them generously.

* MS Patriotism, pp. 73–4.
MS American, No. 3 in 'Written in 1782'.

Metre 4: 8 8.6.8 8.6
A A B C C B

1 So be it then! if God's decree
  Ordains, or suffers it to be
    For wisest ends unknown,
  The land from which our Fathers came
  Our native soil we see, and claim   5
    The country for our own.

2 From dire Rebellion's rage we fled,
  (Proscrib'd and singled out to bleed)
    And left our all behind,
  Wanderers and Emigrants once more,   10
  On Britain's hospitable shore
    A sanctuary to find.

3 But who with open arms receives
  The poor, the loyal fugitives,
    Or generous pity shows?   15
  The Great will not incline their ear,
  The Happy cannot stop to hear
    The annals of our woes.

4 When all are patriots, not one
   Will make the sufferer's cause his own,   *20*
      Or succour one distress;
   Zealous for liberty and right,
   Humane, they cast out of their sight
      The sons of wretchedness.

5 We who for All a table spread,   *25*
   Are forced to beg our bitter bread,
      Which when we scarce obtain,
   The scanty meal, the short relief,
   Is, to inhance our pining grief,
      Snatch'd from our mouth again.   *30*

6 But if the aids of life we need,
   And want a place to lay our head,
      The latest boon we crave
   Our gracious King will not deny,
   Our Country will a spot supply   *35*
      And hide us in the grave.

35. MS American: 'the spot'.

314   FOR THE LOYAL AMERICANS

* *Hymns for the Nation, in 1782*, No. 2.
Poetical Works, VIII.284–6.

                   Metre 10: 8.8.8.8.8 8
                      A B A B C C

1 Father of everlasting love,
   The only refuge of despair,
   Thy bowels toward th'afflicted move,
      And now thou hear'st the mournful prayer
   We for our helpless Brethren breathe,   *5*
   Who pant within the jaws of death.

2 The men who dared their King revere,
   And faithful to their Oaths abide,
   Midst perjur'd Hypocrites sincere,
      Harass'd, oppress'd on every side;   *10*
   Gaul'd by the Tyrant's iron yoke,
   By Britain's faithless sons forsook.

3 Our patriot Chiefs betray'd their trust,
   To serve their own infernal ends,
   The Slaves of avarice and lust,   *15*
      Sparing their foes, they spoil'd their friends;
   Basely repaid their loyal zeal,
   And left them—to the Murtherer's will.

4 As sheep appointed to be slain,
    The victims of fidelity,
To man they look for help in vain;   *20*
    But shall they look in vain to Thee,
God over all, who canst subdue
The hearts which mercy never knew.

5 Ev'n now thou canst disarm their rage,   *25*
    (If so thy gracious will intends)
The wrath implacable asswage,
    The malice of remorseless fiends:
Mercy at last compell'd to show,
And let the hopeless captives go.   *30*

6 Yet if our Brethren's doom be seal'd,
    And for superior joys design'd,
They have their glorious course fulfill'd;
    To souls beneath the altar join'd,
Their guiltless blood hath found a tongue,   *35*
And every drop exclaims—'How long?'

7 O earth, conceal not thou their blood
    Which loud as Zechariah's cries!
O God, Thou just, avenging God,
    Behold them with thy flaming eyes,   *40*
And blast, and utterly consume
Those Murtherers of *fanatic* Rome.

8 Till then, thou bidst thy servants rest,
    Who suffer'd death for conscience sake,
And wait to rise completely blest,
    The general triumph to partake,   *45*
To see the righteous Judge come down,
And boldly claim the Martyr's crown.

WRITTEN ON THE PEACE, 1783   **315**

Charles Wesley, like many of his contemporaries, resented the Peace Treaty signed in Paris on 3rd September 1783 which ended the War of American Independence. He showed his resentment in four poems, of which we give the first.

* MS Patriotism, pp. 93–5.
  MS Peace, 1783.

Metre 4: 8 8.6.8 8.6
A A B C C B

1 Tremendous God, thy hand we see!
    Permitted by thy just decree,
        The woeful day is come!
    Kept off by a few righteous men
    Suspended by their prayers in vain,   *5*
        We meet our fearful doom.

2 Allur'd and bought with Gallic gold,
  Our statesmen have their Country sold,
    While, deaf to Misery's cries,
  Innocent millions they compel   *10*
  Oppression's iron yoke to feel,
    Or fall a sacrifice.

3 Nations* who did in Treaties trust
  They leave, perfidious and unjust,
    To fierce fanatic zeal,   *15*
  To men athirst for guiltless blood,
  Who send, as offerings worthy God,
    Poor Savages to hell.

4 They force their Country to receive
  A Peace which only Hell could give   *20*
    Which deadly feuds creates,
  Murders, and massacres, and wars;
  A peace which loyalty abhors
    And each true Briton hates.

5 A peace, whose evils know no bounds,   *25*
  Which mercy, truth, and justice wounds
    Our nation's curse and shame.
  Brands us, as long as time shall be,
  Or'ewhelms with loads of infamy
    And sinks the British name.   *30*

6 A peace which never coud have been,
  But as the Punishment of sin,
    Of riot in excess,
  Of foul concupiscence and pride,
  Of crimes the great disdain to hide,   *35*
    Of general wickedness.

7 Lost to all sense of shame or fear,
  We neither God nor man revere;
    All ranks and orders join
  To fill our sinful measure up   *40*
  And claim th'intoxicating cup
    Of bitter wrath divine.

  '* The Six Indian Nations'.

7. MS Peace: 'by Gallic gold'.
20. MS Peace: 'A peace which only Fiends coud give'.
23–4. MS Peace: 'Peace which Humanity abhors
            And every Briton hates.'
34. MS Peace: 'Of falshood, cruelty, and pride'.
37–8. MS Peace: 'Lost to all sense of shame and fear,
            Who neither God . . .'.

8 Yet unconcern'd the Many meet
  Their doom, and rush into the pit
    By human fiends prepar'd   45
  Those instruments of public ill
  Reserv'd the utmost wrath to feel
    And gain a full reward.

9 When God awakes, the vengeful God,
  And inquisition makes for blood,   50
    Will he not call to mind
  Those Pests of our afflicted race,
  And turn them into their own place
    The Murtherers of mankind.

10 Yet then, O God, thy church shall see   55
  A gracious difference made by Thee
    In favor of thine own,
  Preserv'd by thy redeeming love,
  And safe with Christ their Head above
    On an eternal throne.   60

49.   MS Peace: 'the righteous God'.
53.   MS Peace: 'And thrust them down to their own place'.
58–60. MS Peace: 'Preserv'd by thy redeeming ~~grace~~, love
              And safe in Christ their Life above
              On thy eternal throne.'

AMERICAN INDEPENDENCY   316

With Charles Wesley's disgust at the (apparently) unnecessary loss of 'our American
colonies' went a deep resentment at the associated undermining of the powers of the
British monarchy.
* MS Patriotism, pp. 99–102.

Metre 97a: Iambic 8's and 9's

  What harm, if Ministers agree
To rebel-independancy,
Or British Senators consent
To what we never can prevent?
We never *can* prevent it now?   5
But *could* we not? inquire of H[owe],[1]
Who had the Yankies at his mercy
So oft, and drove them arsey-versy,
Yet still permitted to take breath,
And snatch'd them from the jaws of death: 10
Subdue them finally he cou[l]d not,
And reason good—because he *wou[l]d* not
Who only fought for double pay,
A trust accepting—to betray.

[1 General William Howe, (1729–1814).]

Or let his warlike Brother[2] own   *15*
What with his Fleet he *might* have done,
Block'd all their harbours up, and seiz'd,
Or burnt their ships, whene'er he pleas'd,
Their raggamuffin host compel'd,
Their Chief without a stroke to yield,   *20*
Reduc'd to desperate condition,
And starv'd into intire submission.

Ask Will, why he refus'd to join
And save the resolute Burgoigne,
Marching (his rival to betray)   *25*
Three thousand miles another way?
Right glad and happy then was he
To mock at his calamity:
And then with treacherous design
To spare his friends at Brandywine.   *30*

Or let Monsieur sincerely say
Cou[l]d we have kept America,
And forc'd the rebels to submit—
'No: for ye ne'er intended it:
'Your generals ne'er in earnest fought,   *35*
'Or a decisive victory sought;
'To trust their friends with arms afraid,
'Lest Loyalists themselves shou[l]d aid,
'And crush their foes, and mar the plots
'Of spurious, English Patriots.   *40*

Our Patriots here, a restless Party,
For their Allies abroad so hearty
Might safely promise and foretell
America invincible,
While all in the conspiracy   *45*
Determin[e]d—It shall never be
That Britain shou[l]d obtain her ends
And triumph or'e Rebellion's friends.

Oft when the Cause appear'd as lost
And ready to give up the ghost,   *50*
By some political manouvre
They help'd their Partners to recover,
The last, expiring spark of war
Reviv'd, and snatch'd them from despair:
Till headlong and precipitate   *55*
C[ornwalli]s rush'd upon his fate:[3]

[2 Richard Viscount Howe (1726–99), later Earl Howe and Admiral of the Fleet.]
[3 Wesley is a little harsh on Lord Cornwallis, whose surrender at Yorktown in
1781 was not caused by rashness—at least not his own.]

Yielding at once without a stroke,
And passing, tame, beneath the yoke,
He *begd* the haughty Foe to spare
His sutlers, and his tools of war,   *60*
But left the Loyalists to feel
The mercy of those Fiends from hell.

Wou[l]d faction's sons neglect th'occasion
Of subjecting both King and nation?
Furious they rise with one consent,   *65*
And seize the helm of government
They vote, of sovereign power possest,
The ruinous war at once supprest,
And all who dare their plans oppose
Declare their King's and Country's foes: *70*
Loyalists must the strife give o're,
The soldiers must contend no more,
But from America withdraw,
And congress give to Britain law,
And traitors force us all t'agree   *75*
To Rebel-Independancy.

PART II

O what a scene before us lies,
When Britons use their open eyes!
Britons employ them now and see
Your weak, dismembred Monarchy,   *100*
Your shatter'd State behold, and mourn
Into a thousand parties torn;
Your King diminish'd and betray'd,
And shrunk into a Royal shade;
Your Country sold by his own sons,   *105*
And dying with convulsive groans;
Your brethren for their loyal zeal
Abandon'd to the murtherer's will;
Your Provinces Rebellion's prey,
Renounc'd, and vilely cast away   *110*
(Kingdoms that countless millions cost)
And public Faith for ever lost!

See the brave men of British race,
Our nation's glory, and disgrace,
Commanded to stand forth in fight,   *115*
T'assert their King's and Country's Right,
Promis'd by both protection sure,
And in our plighted faith secure;

105. Charles Wesley's daughter Sally has altered 'his own sons' to 'Briton's
    sons'.

Yet while to Us for help they look,
Disown'd, disfranchis'd, and forsook,   120
Their Country's gratitude to prove,
And perish for their faithful love,
To spread thro' earth the British name,
And brand us with eternal shame.

   See, how the bold, rapacious Great   125
Their Rivals, and their King intreat!
They strip him of his wealth and power,
That patriots may both devour,
They load him with indignities,
And threaten all his realms to seize,   130
Who gave the larger half away
In spite, and lost America.
Yet no concern they feel or pain
For thousands, and ten thousand slain,
Yet no remorse the ruffians know   135
For millions plung'd in hopeless woe:
The ruffians, wallowing in excess,
And glorying in their wickedness,
By no account hereafter awed,
Injoy the wrath, and curse of God.   140

PART III

How strange a sight at court appears!
A Congress of first ministers,
Each other who in pieces tear,
Ingag'd in an intestin[e] war,
And to the brink of ruin bring   145
Themselves, their Country, and their King
Furious the shatter'd helm to seize
And rule their Ruler as they please.

   He hears their insolent demands
'Give up your power into our hands: 150
'The Power executive are we
'And absolute is our decree:
'Either from us receive the law,
'Or, Sire, to Hanover withdraw,
'Tamely submit to Abdication   155
'(Unless you chuse Decapitation)
'And vacant leave the throne, nor fear
'We soon shall find a Successor.
'Either the Youth so wise and good,
'Or one of Charles's spurious brood,   160
'Perhaps we may permit a while
'To bear, for form, the Regal style,
'Till we have perfected our Plan,
'As high and mighty States to reign,

'And following Congress's example   *165*
'On Kings and Monarchy to trample
'And our dear Independant Cub lick
'Into the Shape of a Republic.

FOR THE PRIME MINISTER   **317**

Although Charles Wesley believed that Christians were exempt from party politics, he himself was a Tory by temperament, and found himself strongly supporting most of the measures of Lord North, who was Prime Minister from 1770 until his resignation in March 1782. North's failure to subdue the American colonies had led to constant attacks on him. There followed the brief ministries of Rockingham and Shelburne, the Coalition ministry of North and Fox, and then, from December 1783 until 1801, the first ministry of William Pitt the younger. Although this poem was supposedly written for any Prime Minister of England, it was probably written originally during North's later months, and subtly altered after his resignation.

* MS Intercession, No. [20]. (A figure '4' at the end shows that Wesley originally
     intended to continue the poem.)
  MS Miscellaneous Hymns, pp. 185–6, being No. 20 of 'Hymns of Intercession'.

Metre 10: 8.8.8.8.8 8
A B A B C C

1 Father, we praise thy guardian Care,
    Which hath on Us a Man bestow'd
(Brittania's Refuge in despair)
    A Man to seek our Nation's Good,
Resolv'd our sinking Land to save,   *5*
Or rush into his Country's Grave.

2 His Talents take into thy Hand,
    And bless them for the Public Weal,
His Spirit bow to thy Command,
    His Heart with heavenly Fervor fill   *10*
And fix the Patriot's noblest Aim,
To act for GOD in Jesus Name.

3 As One whom Heaven delights to bless
    As Daniel prosperous and wise,
Restorer of true righteousness   *15*
    By Him, by Him, let Jacob rise,
Virtue revisit Albion's Coast,
And Piety for ages lost.

1–3. MS Misc.: 'O that we coud obtain by prayer
            A Man by special grace bestow'd
          Britannia's refuge in despair'.

[WITCHES]   **318**

* MS Scriptural Hymns (1783), p. 7.
 Poetical Works, IX.52.

Metre 8: 8 8.8 8
A A B B

Thou shalt not suffer a witch to live. [Exodus] 22.18.

'Thou shalt not suffer her to live,'
But Deists can a Witch reprieve,
And all our Senators reply
'Thou shalt not suffer her to die.'

2. Orig. 'a Witch retrieve'.
3. Alternative in margin: 'And Britain's Senators reply'.

319 THE PIANOFORTE
WRITTEN IN THE YEAR 1783

The pianoforte was introduced into England during the second half of the eighteenth
century, and the first public performance on the instrument was apparently given at
Covent Garden in 1767. It was popularized by 'the English Bach', Johann Christian
(1735–82), eighteenth child of Johann Sebastian Bach. Unfortunately it was pub-
licized as the rival of the harpsichord and organ from the beginning, instead of as an
additional instrument, and so the musical world took sides. Charles Wesley makes his
own position quite clear!

* MS Patriotism: Misc., pp. 13–15.
  MS CW Letters, IV.92 (Methodist Book Room, London).

Metre 98: Iambic 10's

Our Connoisseurs their plausive voices raise,
And dwell on the Piano-Forte's praise.
More brilliant (if we simply take their word)
More sweet than any tinkling Harpsichord,
While soothing Softness and Expression meet   5
To make the Contrast, and the joy compleat.
To strike our fascinated ears and eyes
And take our Sense and Reason by surprize.

'Tis thus the men whose dictates we obey,
Their taste, and their Authority display,   10
Command us humbly in their steps to move,
Damn what they damn, & praise what they approve.
With Faith implicit, and with blind esteem,
To own—All Music is ingross'd by Them.

So the Nation whose capricious law   15
Keeps the whole fashionable world in awe,
Nor to Italian Airs their ear incline,
Nor to the noblest Harmony divine,
But as the Sum of Excellence propose
Their own sweet Sonnets—warbled thro' the Nose!   20

Yet skilful Masters of the tuneful string,
(Masters who teach the Harpsichord to—*sing*)
Tell us of Music's powers a different story,
And rob Piano-Forte of its glory;
Assuring us, if uncontroul'd by Fashion   25
We hear, and judge without exaggeration,

362

The Merit of the favourite instrument,
And all its Use and musical intent,
By the discerning Few is understood
'To hide bad Players, & to spoil the Good.'   *30*

Second Part

What cannot Fashion do? with magic ease
It makes the dull Piano-forte please,
Bids us a triffling Instrument admire,
As far superior to Apollo's Lyre:
Loud as a spanking Warming-pan its tone,   *35*
Delicious as the thrilling Bagpipe's Drone.
Organs and Harpsichords it sweeps away
And reigns alone, triumphant for a day:
The Great acknowledge its inchanting power
The echoing multitude of course adore: *40*
Ev'n Those who *real* Music dared esteem
Caught for a while, are carried down the stream,
O'er all her slaves while Fashion domineers,
And Midas lends them his sagacious Ears!

Shou'd Fashion singling out (if that cou[l]d be)   *45*
A poorer tool of modern harmony
The sanction of her approbation give;
The world polite her dictates wou'd receive,
The list'ning Herd wou'd fall with awe profound
And die transported at a JEWS-HARP's Sound!   *50*

36. MS IV.92: 'Delicious, thrilling as the Bagpipe's drone'.
45. MS IV.92: '(if that can be)'.

WRITTEN MARCH 4 : 1784   **320**

Dr Samuel Johnson claimed that Charles James Fox 'divided the kingdom with
Caesar; so that it was a doubt whether the nation should be ruled by the sceptre of
George III or the tongue of Fox'. This grim struggle for power reached its climax
during the opening months of 1784, after the impossible coalition between Lord
North and Fox had been succeeded by the first ministry of William Pitt the Younger.
Pitt joined forces with the King, and Fox's popularity gradually waned, accompanied
by a rash of private intrigues and public lampoons. There was little doubt where
John or Charles Wesley would find themselves in a contest involving the sovereignty
of the Crown. Charles Wesley's extreme bitterness against Fox was fed by a combination of things, however—Fox's determined efforts to undermine the royal power,
his support of the American colonists' claim for independence, the immoralities of his
private life, and his corruption of the future king. Such was Wesley's anger that he
was even ready to castigate Fox's attempt to reform the finances of the Indian
government.

On 1st March 1784 Fox secured the passage of another in his series of addresses
from the Commons to the Crown, claiming the right to advise on any exercise of the
royal prerogative. On the 14th the King's reply was read, in which he said that he
was ready to listen to their advice at any time, and then to act for the welfare of his

people, whereupon Fox called for a debate upon the answer the following Monday. All the time, however, Fox's majorities were dwindling, and the end was in sight.

* MS Charles Wesley's Letters, IV.92, a transcript in a later hand. (Methodist Book Room, London.)

Metre 8: 8 8.8 8
AABB

1 Why boastest Thou thy baleful power,
Agent of Satan for an hour?
As Senates must thy Nod obey,
And Kings be subject to thy sway;

2 As all the high-born slaves of vice   5
Were sworn with Thee to fall or rise;
As all the nation's Scum were join'd,
T'exalt the Vilest of mankind.

3 Use them a while thy hopes to crown
And turn thy Country upside down,   10
Rais'd up in these flagitious times
To scourge us by thy bolder crimes.

4 Eat drink and play, and take thine ease,
The wealth of Asian Plunderers seize,
Seize as thy own the Public Store   15
And waste it all, and grasp for more.

5 Supporter of rebellion's cause,
Go, trample on our rights and laws,
Our King degrade, our Prince pervert,
And mould him after thy own heart.   20

6 Prosperous in ill, at nothing stop,
Make haste to fill thy measure up,
Thy powers exert, thy talents show,
As far as human guile can go.

7 Thy Ethiop-Soul, as black as night,   25
May reach ambition's utmost height,
Defy thy foes to pluck thee thence,
And laugh at sleeping Providence.

8 Yet shall thy jaws the Bridle feel,
Thy nose the Hook invisible,   30
Yet are thy fatal limits set,
And Vengeance holds thee in its Net.

9 Thy deeds shall soon in judgments rise---
Thy treasons and conspiracies,
And sad America o'erflow'd   35
With torrents of fraternal blood.

10 Thy deeds can never be forgot,
   Thy sure destruction slumbers not;
   The day shall suddenly reveal,
   Thy League with Death—& France & Hell.   *40*

11 Hell from beneath is moved to meet
   Thy soul in wickedness compleat,
   Thy sinful Excellence to own,
   Most worthy of a burning throne.

12 Thy guilt and merits infinite   *45*
   Lay claim to the Sulphureous pit
   Keep up the flame with fresh supplies,
   And feed the worm that never dies.

[PERFECT WICKEDNESS]   **321**

This page bears three epigrams on the politician most detested by Charles Wesley—Charles James Fox. As in the poem 'Written March 4:1784' the villain of the piece is not named, so here the name is only given in typical eighteenth-century fashion, as 'F——'. Charles Wesley's daughter Sally has made things more difficult still by pasting a sheet of plain paper over this page, but it is possible to read the original against the light.

* MS Patriotism, p. (108).

                Metre 98: Iambic 10's

Clodius, inspir'd with fierce inveterate hate,
With furious faction shook his Roman state,
His Country to destroy was the design
Of daring, dark, atrocious Catiline,
But both assassins meet in F—— alone   *5*
And perfect wickedness is all his own.

[LEGION]   **322**
Metre 98: Iambic 10's

Hear, Britons, hear, and tremble at the Rod,
The Scourge vindictive of an angry God,
The public crimes commission'd to chastise
Behold in F—— no single fiend arise
While Legion in her multitude doth reign   *5*
Satan and Belial share the *people's man*
Malice and pride with lewd intemperance meet
And make th'infernal character compleat.

[THE RABBLE'S MAN]   **323**
Metre 15: 8 8.8 8.8 8
AABBCC

Does he assume the name in vain
Who calls himself *the rabble's man*?
The rabble's man he surely is,
If Justice may her Debtor seize
And F—— his debt at Tyburn pay   *5*
And make *the Rabble's Holiday*!*

* Commonly called Hanging day.

324 [ON HIS SON BECOMING A ROMAN CATHOLIC]

One of the most shattering blows in the later life of Charles Wesley was the occasion when he was informed that his son Samuel had become a Roman Catholic. This was in 1784, when Samuel was eighteen. The broken-hearted father wrote a series of thirteen poems on the occasion. Parts of the one here given he scored out, but his daughter Sally added her transcript to the manuscript, as 'Made out thro the Blots'.

* MS Samuel Wesley, R.C., No. 3, pp. 3–4.
Poetical Works, VIII.422–3.

Metre 4: 8 8.6.8 8.6
A A B C C B

1 Farewell [my all of earthly hope,]
  My n[ature's stay, my age's prop,]
     Irrevocably gone!
  Submissive to the will divine
  I acquiesce, and make it mine;   5
     I offer up my Son.

2 But give I God a sacrifice
  That costs me nought? my gushing eyes
     The answer sad express,
  My gushing eyes and troubled heart   10
  Which bleeds with its belov'd to part
     Which breaks thro fond excess.

3 Yet since he from my heart is torn,
  Patient, resign'd, I calmly mourn
     The darling snatch'd away: 15
  Father, with Thee thy own I leave;
  Into thy mercy's arms receive,
     And keep him to that day.

4 [Keep (for I nothing else desire)
  The bush unburnt amidst the fire   20
     And freely I resign
  My Child for a few moments lent
  (My Child no longer!) I consent
     To see his face no more.]

5 [Receive me! and accept my pain!   25
  Nor let him view my parting scene
     Or catch my parting breath!
  Nor let the hast'ner of my end
  Th'unconscious Parricide attend
     To trouble me in death!]¹   30

[¹ The bitterness of the initial days softened; Samuel continued to live with his parents, and on his deathbed Charles Wesley said to Samuel: 'I shall bless God to all eternity that ever you was born; I am persuaded I shall.' It was not until after his father's death that Samuel Wesley forsook the Roman Catholic faith.]

6 But hear my agonizing prayer
  And O, preserve him, and prepare
    To meet me in the skies
  When thron'd in Bliss the Lamb appears,
  Repairs my loss and wipes the tears   *35*
    For ever from my eyes!

EPIGRAM   **325**

The year 1784 marked an epoch in Methodism. Not only did John Wesley secure legal
continuity for his societies by the Deed of Declaration; on 1st and 2nd September of
that year, in semi-secrecy, he ordained three preachers to serve the Methodists in
America. Their leader was Dr Thomas Coke, already a priest of the Church of England,
whom Wesley ordained as 'superintendent'—a term thinly disguising his function of
bishop. John Wesley believed that he had reason and expediency on his side, but
Charles Wesley was aghast. Charles quoted the dictum of his old schoolfellow, Lord
Mansfield—'Ordination is Separation'. Both his letters and his verses show how
bitterly he resented, not only the fact that he had been kept in ignorance of this step,
but the reason behind the secrecy, namely that he would thus be prevented from
interfering in what was so obviously a serious breach with the Church of England.

The Charles Wesley kept a small manuscript notebook (herein known as 'MS Ordinations') in which the opening words are a quotation from William Chillingworth's
Religion of Protestants, p. 272: 'That a Pretence of Reformation will acquit no man
from Schism, we grant very willingly, and therefore say I that it concerns every man
who separates from any Church-Communion, *even as much as his Salvation is worth* to
look most carefully to it, that the Cause of his Separation be just & necessary.'
There follow ten numbered poems written on the occasion, together with John
Wesley's *apologia* for ordaining, dated Bristol, 10th September 1784, Charles Wesley's
letter to Dr Samuel Chandler, dated 28th April 1785, and other documents, including
a number relating to the consecration of Bishop Seabury for service in the United
States of America.

The only generally known poems from this collection are the first and fifth, both
entitled 'Epigram', and both in the same metre, so that they have sometimes been
associated as a single poem.

* MS Ordinations, No. [1].
MS Samuel Wesley, p. 2, which uses 'Wesley' and 'Coke' for 'W-' and 'C'.

Metre 1: 8.6.8.6
A B A B

W—— himself and friends betrays,
  By his ~~own~~ good sense forsook,
While suddenly his hands he lays
  On the hot head of C——:

Yet *we* at least shou'd spare the weak,   5
  His weak Co-evals *We*,
Nor blame an hoary Schismatic,
  A Saint of Eighty-three![1]

[1 At the time of the first ordinations John Wesley was actually only eighty-one,
but when this booklet was completed he was in fact eighty-three.]

3. Sam. W, 'When suddenly'.

326 EPIGRAM

* MS Ordinations, No. [5].   Metre 1: 8.6.8.6
                                                      A B A B

So easily are Bishops made
   By man's, or woman's whim?
W—— his hands on C—— hath laid,
   But who laid hands on Him?

Hands on himself he laid, and *took*   5
   An Apostolic Chair:
And then ordain'd his Creature C——
   His Heir and Successor.

Episcopalians, now no more
   With Presbyterians fight,   10
But give your needless Contest o're,
   'Whose Ordination's right?'

It matters not, if Both are One,
   Or different in degree,
For lo! ye see ~~in Prelate~~ John   contain'd in   15
   The whole Presbytery!

327 LEADER OF A SECT

* MS Ordinations, No. 3.   Metre 38: 10.10.10.10
                                                    A B A B

1 And is it come to this? and has the Man
   On whose Integrity our Church relied,
Betray'd his trust, render'd our boastings vain,
   And fal'n a Victim to ambitious Pride?

2 Whose seal so long her Hierarchy maintain'd,   5
   Her humble Presbyter, her duteous Son*
Call'd an High-priest, & by Himself Ordain'd,
   He glorifies himself, & mounts a Throne.
                     claims

3 Ah! where are all his Promises and Vows
   To spend, & to be spent for Sion's Good,   10
To gather the lost sheep of Israel's house,
   The Outcasts bought by his Redeemer's bl[oo]d?

4 W[h]o won for God the wandring Souls of men,
   Subjecting multitudes to Xt's command,
He shuts his eyes, & scatters them again,   15
   And spreads a thous[an]d Sects throughout the land.

* His usual Signature was E.A.P.J. [The first three letters clearly stand for 'Ecclesiae Anglicanae Presbyter', 'Presbyter of the Church of England'. The 'J' could stand for 'Johannes' or 'John' but for the fact that his two clerical brothers used the same designation. It might represent 'jure' (lawfully) or 'juratus' (sworn), though there are other possibilities.]

5 The great Restorer of Religion pure
   Ah! why sh[oul]d he a meaner style affect
His friends, his principles in death abjure
   Head of a
   ~~Founder of~~ Kirks, & Leader of a Sect?   *20*

6 His Charge, departing to the Wolf he leaves
   (For Who so fit to keep the Flock as He?)
And to that fawning Beast unwary gives
          great
'His power, & seat, & ~~much~~ authority.'

7 W[ha]t e'er of weak, or human in his Plan,   *25*
       built
Wood, stubble, hay ~~heap'd~~ on the Solid Base,
(His own by-laws, his own inventions vain)
     furious
He leaves his ~~headlong~~ Successor to raze.

8 Secure he now the sacred Pale o'releaps,
   (Tau[gh]t by audacious C—— to slight the guilt)   *30*
And with that Besom of destruction sweeps
   The Babylon w[hi]ch his own hands had built.

9 How is the Mighty fallen from his height,
   His weapons scatter'd, & his buckler lost!
Ah! tell it not in Gath, nor cause delight   *35*
   And triumph in the proud Philistine Host.

10 Publish it not in Askelon, to make
   The world exult in his disastrous End!
Rather let every soul my Grief partake,
   And ah! my Father, cry, & ah my Friend!   *40*
     Brother

11 The pious Mantle or'e his Dotage spread,
   W[i]th silent tears his shameful Fall deplore,
And let him sink, forgot, among the dead
   And mention his unhappy name no more.

[A SELF-ORDAINED BISHOP]   **328**

* MS Ordinations, No. 7.

Metre 37: 10 10 10
A A A

1 Who can the odd Phenomenon explain?
A Bishop new, who doth himself ordain,
And hands extends beyond th'Atlantic main?

2 Sends his intrepid Suffragan before,
   To found (for Presbyterians to adore)   5
   His Church *Episcopal* at Baltimore!

3 Tis done! the deed adventurous is done!
   The sword is drawn, the civil war begun,
   And John at last has pass'd the Rubicon!

4 A troop of Jeroboam's priests appears   10
                life
   For, after a long ~~length~~ of fourscore years,
   Poor John had Rehoboam's Counsellers.

5 But you who censure his ductility,
   His hoary hairs with *my* compas[sio]n see,
   And own—Twas Age yt made the breach, not He.   15

329   [ON BISHOP COKE]

Arrived in America, Dr Coke summoned the American Methodist preachers, and in Baltimore on Christmas Eve 1784 they agreed to form themselves into an episcopal church, unanimously electing Coke and Francis Asbury as their first Bishops. Asbury was ordained on successive days as deacon, elder, and superintendent. On 27th December, the day of his ordination as superintendent or bishop, Coke preached a sermon, from Revelation 3.7–11, in which he defended the ordination which had just taken place, and went on to describe the spiritual qualities of a true Christian bishop. In the course of defending the ordination he claimed that most (not all) of the Anglican churches in America had previously been 'filled with the parasites and bottle-companions of the rich and the great', who were 'faithful abettors of the ruling powers'. By the Revolution, however, 'these intolerable fetters are now struck off, and the antichristian union which before subsisted between Church and State, is broken asunder'. 'One happy consequence' of the Revolution, he maintained, was 'the expulsion of most of those hirelings', to supply whose place the Methodist preachers had been called, and were now ordained. He also stated that the majority of Methodists in Britain were in favour of separation from the Church of England, but were restrained by deference to the Wesleys. Coke's sermon was later published in England (the dedication being dated Baltimore, March 1, 1785). It was immediately attacked (apparently by Charles Wesley himself) in *Strictures on Dr Coke's Ordination Sermon preached at Baltimore, in the State of Maryland, in December 1784*, in which the writer castigated Coke for condemning the British constitution, vilifying his Anglican brethren, and contradicting the Wesleys' declarations of loyalty to the Church of England. It was probably about the same time that Charles Wesley penned the following lines.

* MS Ordinations, No. 4.

                          Metre 40: 10.10.10.10.11 13
                               A B A B C C

   Happy America, whose ruinous wars,
      Direful calamities, & loss extreme,
   One single man, (above man's height) repairs,
      In rank sublime, in dignity supreme:
   To gain a C[oke] is 'ample Compensation,   5
   For half a million slain, and general Desolation!*

   * Witness himself in his Ordination Sermon at Baltimore 1784. [Although Wesley's reference to 'dignity supreme' contains a satirical glance at Coke's description of the final characteristic of a true bishop, his seriousness or dignity, the phrases in the last two lines are not (as might be thought) quotations, but Wesley's own elaboration from Coke's words about the 'happy consequence' of the Revolution.]

[TRUE YOKEFELLOWS] **330**

Charles Wesley's abhorrence of his brother's ordinations did not make a final breach between the two men. Bitterness was in fact overcome by pity and a recourse to prayer. In yet another notebook Charles Wesley transcribed both John Wesley's *apologia* of 10th September 1784 and the quotation from Chillingworth (see above, No. **325**), and appended nine poems on the ordinations. Whether these included any of those in 'MS Ordinations' it is now impossible to say, nor indeed which of the two compilations was penned first, for in 'MS Brothers' only the following poem remains.

* MS Brothers, No. 9.

Metre 97: Iambic 8's

IX

Happy the days, when Charles and John
By nature and by grace were One
The same in office as in name,
Their judgment and their will the same:
True Yokefellows, they join'd to draw   5
The galling burthen of the Law,
And urg'd with unremitting strife
Each other on, to work for life:
Chearful beneath the Legal Load,
Joyful to do imperfect good,   10
And all the Lord's commands t'obey,
Before they knew in Christ The Way.

In infancy their hopes and fears,
In youth, and in their riper years,
Their hearts were to each other known   15
Attun'd in perfect Unison.
No private End, no selfish art
Did then the faithful Brothers part,
No flatterer the Friends divide,
Who each from each coud nothing hide.   20
Neither injoyd' a good alone,
Or calld' what he possess'd his own,
Their good supream with humble zeal
To know, and do the Master's will.

To both at once their Lord reveald'   25
His counsel from the Wise conceald'
His will to chuse the weak and base
And save a much-lovd' world by grace.
To the highways and hedges sent
They both with one Commission went,   30
Zealous immortal souls to win,
And force the Vagrants to come in.
He bad[e] them first for England care,
               th
And to her Church the true declare

To love his own Jerusalem,   *35*
To spend, and to be spent for Them,
Outcasts of men, a thoughtless ~~Croud~~ Herd,
Who sinning on with conscience sear'd,
Rush'd down the steep, by Satan driven,
As far from God, as hell from heaven.   *40*

 Jesus, who sent them out by pairs,
Prosper'd his gospel-messengers,
HE their united labours bless'd,
Their flock abundantly increas'd,
Increas'd their word-begotten Sons,   *45*
And preachers rais'd from stocks & stones.

 But rais'd out of the people's lees,[1]
Raw, inexperiencd' Novices,
They soon their low Estate forgot,
And of themselves too highly thought,   *50*
While the ambitious Fiend stole in,
And poisoning them with his own sin,
Used as his Agents to inspire
With lofty thoughts their flatter'd Sire.

 They urg'd the Elder Presbyter   *55*
Himself a Bishop to declare,
And then to answer their demands,
By laying on his hasty hands;
The mighty Babel to erect,
And found a new Dissenting Sect,   *60*
His Mother-Church to rend, disclaim,
And brand the Party with his Name.
But for a length of years he stood,
By a whole Army unsubdued,
By friendship kept, refus'd to yield,   *65*
And all their fiery Darts repeld',
And check'd the Madness for a space
Of Corah's[2] bold, rebellious race,
Who heard, like Eli's sons unmov'd,
His words, too tenderly reprov'd,   *70*
'In vain you tempt me to do ill
'For separate I never will [—]
'Will never with my Brother break,
'Will never die a Schismatick!'

[1 Cf. No. 268.]
[2 i.e. Korah, who demanded priestly power from Moses and Aaron. See Numbers xvii. John Wesley's own later rebuke to his ambitious preachers was frequently called 'The Korah Sermon', though its title was 'The Ministerial Office.' (See his *Works*, 4th edn, VII.273–281.)]

O had he died *before* that day,   75
When W—— did himself betray
Did boldly on himself confer
The Apostolic Character!
O that we both had took our flight
Together to the realms of light,   80
Together yielded up our breath,
In life united, and in death!
Leaving an honest Name behind,
We then assur'd that Rest to find
Had past the valley undismay'd,   85
Nor fear'd to meet a Father's shade,[3]
A Cloud of Witnesses inrolld'
In heaven, the sheep of England's fold,
A noble host of Martyrs too
Who faithful unto death, and true,   90
Spent their last breath for Sion's good,
And strove resisting unto blood.

God of unbounded power and grace,
Whose pleasure is to save and bless,
At whose omnipotent Decree   95
Things most impossible shall be,
Who only, cancelling our sin,
Canst make it as it neer had been;
Thine energy of love exert
And change thy favour'd Servant's heart,   100
Thy own prevailing Plea we plead [—]
In ignorance he did the Deed,
The Deed with endless mischiefs fraught,
Alas, he did he knew not what.
Pity the Blind who went astray   105
And turn'd the Lame out of the way;
Whom still Thou dost vouchsafe to own—
Undo the evil he hath done,
Incline him humbly to revoke
The fatal Step his haste hath took,   110
And his true heart again shall be
Turn'd back to England's Church and Thee.

Stir up thy faithful people, Lord,
To urge their suit with one accord,
And rescue thro' the Strength of prayer   115
Their Father, Guide, and Minister.
His prayers for us have reachd' thy throne,
And brought us many a blessing down:

[³ This passage (like much of the poem) is reminiscent of Charles Wesley's letter to his brother of 14th August 1785: 'Go to your grave in peace: at least suffer me to go first, before this Ruin is under your hand. So much, I think, you owe to my Father . . . let us leave behind us the name and character of honest men.']

Thy blessings all on Him be shed;
With glory crown his reverend head[;]   *120*
Found in the way of righteousness
There let him stay, and die in peace:
Let all the children of his prayers,
Seals of his Ministerial cares,
To Him by his Redeemer given,   *125*
Compose his Crown of joy in Heaven!

331   LUNARDI FOR EVER!

                              An Air for Three Voices

Neither John nor Charles Wesley was in London on 15th September 1784 when
Vincenzo Lunardi (1759–1806) made his famous ascent in a hydrogen-filled balloon
thirty-two feet in diameter. But among the 200,000 spectators there must have been
many of their followers, especially since the event took place from the Honourable
Artillery Company's ground in Moorfields, just across the way from Wesley's Chapel
in the City Road. Charles Wesley, however, caught some of the public excitement on
the occasion, perhaps from members of his own family, though he obviously regarded
the event as a mere curiosity rather than as a serious foreshadowing of aeronautical
progress.

* MS Patriotism: Misc., p. 35.

                                                Metre 99: Iambic 11's and 12's

From the Poets we learn, yt an Artist of Greece
On pinions of wax, flew over the seas;
And as bold an attempt we were tau[gh]t to admire,
When we saw with our eyes the Italian High-flyer;
But when next he ascends in his airy baloon,   *5*
If himself he excels, & flies over the moon,
All Europe shall ring of an action so hardy
And the world shall be fill'd with the fame of Lunardi!

                         CHORUS

            Lunardi for ever!
            Sing a Hero so clever,
            So brave and victorious,
            So happy and glorious,
            Sing a Hero so clever
            Lunardi for ever!

332   EPITAPH [FOR MRS HORTON]

Mrs Mary Horton, wife of John Horton, one of John Wesley's executors, died 4th
May 1786, aged thirty-four, and was buried in City Road burial-ground, London.
She was the daughter of Henry Durbin, one of the stalwarts of Bristol Methodism.
Charles Wesley wrote a lengthy poem on her death, as well as this epitaph.

* CW. MSS I. (q), xxiv. (Methodist Book Room, London).
  MS 'On the Death of Mrs Horton, May 4.1786', Didsbury College, Bristol.
  MS Henderson, p. (1).
  Poetical Works, VIII.437.

Metre 39: 10 10.10 10.10 12
A A B B C C

A meek and lowly Follower of the Lamb,
She more than conquer'd all in Jesus Name,
Wash'd in his blood, & kept her garments white,
And blameless walk'd in her Redeemer's sight,
Till fill'd with love, she fainted on his breast,   5
And found ~~in Jesus~~ arms her everlasting Rest!
  within his

[REST, HAPPY SAINT]   333

The *Gentleman's Magazine* for December 1786 contained the following obituary
notice under date 29th November: 'In Fetter-lane, in his 59th year, the rev. Mr La
Trobe, who succeeded the late worthy Mr Gambold as archbishop of the Moravians.'
During that very summer Charles Wesley had been in correspondence with Benjamin
La Trobe about the possibility of the Moravians uniting with the Church of England,
within which the Methodists were still nominally a society. Like Peter Böhler and the
other early Moravians buried in the Moravian burying ground, Chelsea, La Trobe had
no elaborate wording on the flat stone covering his grave. Charles Wesley, however,
seems to have written a poetical tribute to him which was eventually used for his
own tombstone. Dr John Whitehead, the physician of his later months, thus writes
of his death: 'He died March 29, 1788, aged seventy-nine years and three months;[1]
and was buried, April 5, in Marybone church-yard, at his own desire. The pall was
supported by eight Clergymen of the Church of England. On his tomb-stone[2] are the
following lines, written by himself on the death of one of his friends: they could not
be more aptly applied to any person than to Mr Charles Wesley.'

* John Whitehead: *Life of the . . . Rev. Charles Wesley*, 1793, I.370.
 Poetical Works, VIII.438.

Metre 20: 8 8.8 8.8 8.8 8
A A B B C C D D

With poverty of spirit bless'd,
Rest, happy Saint, in Jesus rest;
A Sinner sav'd, through grace forgiv'n,
Redeem'd from earth to reign in heav'n!
Thy labours of unwearied love,   5
By thee forgot, are crown'd above;
Crown'd, through the mercy of thy Lord,
With a free, full, immense reward!

[1 Whitehead was mistakenly accepting Charles Wesley's birth as 18th December
1708, instead of 1707. (See W. H. S. *Proc.* XXI.25–6.)]
[2 Replaced by the present obelisk in the middle years of the nineteenth century.]

[IN AGE AND FEEBLENESS EXTREAM]   334

Dr Whitehead speaks thus of Charles Wesley's last days, and of his last poem:
'I visited him several times in his last sickness, and his body was indeed reduced to
the most extreme state of weakness. He possessed that state of mind which he had
been always pleased to see in others—unaffected humility, and holy resignation to
the will of God. He had no transports of joy, but solid hope and unshaken confidence
in Christ, which kept his mind in perfect peace. A few days before his death he com
posed the following lines. Having been silent and quiet for some time, he called Mrs
Wesley to him, and bid her write as he dictated.' Mrs Wesley herself headed the copy

in her hymn-book thus: 'The following lines I wrote from Mr Charles Wesley's repeating, a few days before he departed ys. Life.' To Mrs Jones she wrote a little more fully: 'I shall add a few lines w[hi]ch my good Partner desir[e]d me to transcribe when he came in faint & drooping f[ro]m taking an airing in a Coach, a few days before his End.'

Charles's daughter Sally sent a circumstantial account of her father's death to John Wesley, and a week or two later seems to have asked whether she had at the same time sent this poem. Wesley replied: 'You did not send me those verses before. They were very proper to be his last, as being worthy of one bought by the blood of the Lamb and just going forth to meet Him!' In preparing them for publication only a few months before his own death he added the note: 'The last lines composed by the Rev. Charles Wesley, M.A., a little before he went hence, which he dictated to his Wife, but could scarcely articulate.'

* MS Fonmon Letters, National Library of Wales, in undated letter from Mrs Charles Wesley to Mrs Robert Jones of Fonmon.
  MS in handwriting of Mrs Charles Wesley preserved in her hymn-book (Facsimile in brochure describing the Dublin celebration of the bi-centenary of Charles Wesley's birth).
  Arminian Magazine, 1790 (December), p. 672.
  John Whitehead, *Life of the ... Rev. Charles Wesley* (1793), I.369.
  Poetical Works, VIII.432.
  Collection (1876): No. 918, entitled 'A Last Wish'.
  MHB (1904): No. 821.
  MHB (1933): Verses, No. 47.

Metre 15: 8 8.8 8.8 8
A A B B C C

In age & feebleness extream,
Who shall a helpless worm Redeem?
Jesus, my only Hope thou art,
Strength of my failing flesh and Heart,
O could I catch a smile from Thee,   5
And drop into Eternity!

2. Whitehead: 'sinful worm'.
3. *Arm. Mag., Works*, 1876, 1933: 'Jesus!'
5. Whitehead: 'O! could I catch a smile'.
   Arm. Mag., Works: 'Oh! could I catch one smile'.
   1876, &c.: 'O could I catch one smile'.

335   [AN ELEGIAC ODE]

As a pendant to all that has been said and exemplified on Charles Wesley's metrical inventiveness I give a draft composition discovered after this volume reached the page-proof stage, a salutary warning that it is impossible to say the last word about anything. This poem was written upon the death of some unnamed Christian about whose identity it is idle to speculate. The manuscript is on two sides of a quarto sheet of laid paper, and I am unable to date it more precisely than to state that it appears to come from the last quarter of Charles Wesley's life.

At first it seemed that this manuscript contained a series of separate compositions on the same theme, chiefly of interest because they included some hitherto unrecorded stanza-forms. Closer study, however, made it clear that Wesley intended these separate units to form a poetical whole displaying a progression of thought. It is, indeed, an ode, so far a unique example in the writings of Charles Wesley, despite the

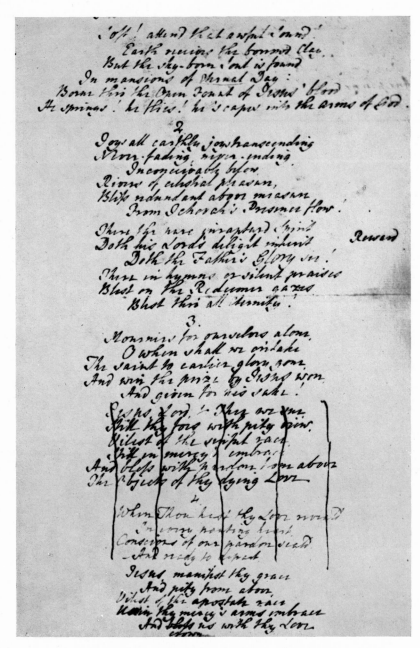

CHARLES WESLEY'S MANUSCRIPT OF AN ELEGIAC ODE

(see pages 376–8)

title of No. 279, which consists of one stanza only, although this stanza is similar to the opening and closing stanzas of the present composition.

The opening stanza announces that the saint's body is buried in the earth, but his soul has escaped to heaven. The second stanza takes up this theme of heaven, in the first part outlining the joys of heaven in a cascade of rapturous phrases, and in the second elaborating the closing statement of the first part that these joys spring from the presence of God. In the third stanza Wesley returns to the mourners on earth, again in a two-part stanza: in the first part the mourners long for the joys experienced by the saint, and in the second they realize that they are sinners unworthy of heaven, and therefore pray for the pardon offered by Christ. The closing stanza, a close counterpart of the opening one, claims that this pardon is in fact the preparation for the life of heaven, so that having received it the mourners will be reunited with the dead saint in the presence of God. Thus the wheel comes full circle. Wesley's original draft of 3b and 4a, later erased, reveals this same progression of thought, though not the same symmetry of stanzaic structure. To achieve greater regularity he discarded the original second part of the third stanza for another modelled on the first part, though this was framed so clumsily that he would surely have wished to revise the third and fourth lines if he had ever published the poem.

See illustration opposite.

* Hendrix MSS, Duke University

Metre 94c: Varied, Nos. 78a, 55a, 74a, (77, 85? or 86?), 74a, and 78b.

1   Soft! attend that awful Sound!
         Earth receives the borrow'd Clay,
      But the sky-born Soul is found
      In mansions of Eternal Day:
    Borne thro' the Open Fount of Jesus' blood   5
He springs! he flies! he 'scapes into the arms of God!

2   Joys all earthly joys transcending
      Never-fading, never-ending,
        Inconceivable below,
      Rivers of celestial pleasure,   10
      Bliss redundant above measure
        From Jehovah's Presence flow!

      There the pure inraptur'd Spirit
      Doth his Lord's delight inherit   Reward[1]
        Doth the Father's Glory see!   15
      There in hymns or silent praises
      Blest on the Redeemer gazes
        Blest thro' all Eternity!

3   Mourners for ourselves alone,
        O when shall we or'etake   20
    The saint to earlier glory gone,
    And win the prize by Jesus won,
      And given for his sake!

[1 'Reward' in the margin is obviously an alternative for 'delight'.]

<pre>
        Jesus, Lord, to Thee we sue,   23a
        Still thy foes with pity view,
        Vilest of the sinful race,
        Still in mercy's [arms]² embrace
   And bless with pardon from above
   The Objects of thy dying Love.   23f

4   When Thou hast thy Love reveal'd
           In every panting heart,
        Conscious of our pardon seal'd,
           And ready to depart,   23j

        Jesus, manifest thy grace
           And pity from above,   25
        Vilest of the apostate race
        Us in thy mercy's arms embrace²
           And ̶b̶l̶e̶s̶s̶ us with thy Love.
                  crown
</pre>

[4]   Happy in thy love reveal'd
            ̶D̶i̶f̶f̶u̶s̶'̶d̶ ̶t̶h̶r̶o̶u̶g̶h̶o̶u̶t̶ ̶t̶h̶e̶ ̶h̶e̶a̶r̶t̶,   To the expanded heart,   30
          Conscious of our pardon seal'd,
     And thus made ready to depart
   Our souls to that triumphant soul unite
   And plunge in the full blaze of Everlasting Light.

[² There is a gap in the MS between 'mercy's' and 'embrace', but lines *23c, 23d* are obviously the prototypes of lines *26–7*, where 'mercy's arms' occurs.]

PRINCIPAL SOURCES OF CHARLES WESLEY'S VERSE

THIS does not set out to be a complete bibliography of Charles Wesley's verse, either published or even manuscript. Hymns and poems from his pen appeared in well over a hundred volumes and pamphlets during his lifetime, and that figure has been multiplied since. The manuscript sources, with their drafts and duplicates, their mutilated volumes and their divorced fragments, are probably richer and more complicated than for any other poet. In the case of the printed sources only the chief works used in this volume are listed, although as a matter of fact these do include almost all the major items. In the case of manuscripts, while the chief sources actually quoted form the bulk of the items listed, it has been felt desirable to describe the few other major sources which have not been used for this particular volume. There has been no attempt to do this, however, in the case of the many manuscripts of small single poems, or fragmentary groups. References in the text to non-listed works and to a score or more of manuscripts of single poems will serve as a reminder of the submerged depths of documentation beneath what is here presented.

The arrangement is chronological, in two sections—printed, and manuscript sources. A number (in a type distinctive from that used for the poems themselves) is assigned to each source, and an alphabetical index to these sources is added for ready consultation.

After a brief description of each source there follows a list of the items in which that particular source is here transcribed or collated.

'21*'—An asterisk added after a number indicates that in the introduction to that item there is a note on the source.

'(21*)'—An asterisked number within parentheses indicates a note at that reference, though the source itself is not used. In the case of the manuscript sources the location is indicated.

PRINTED SOURCES

Normally first editions only are listed, though in many cases there were later editions.

'(G.15)'—Items included in Richard Green's *Wesley Bibliography* are noted as '(G.15)' &c. All the works were published anonymously unless the contrary is stated.

1. *Hymns and Sacred Poems* (London, 1739). (G.15; by J. & C. Wesley; 139 unnumbered items by various unnamed authors, but mainly original or adaptations from George Herbert and others.) **Nos. 1–11, 113–14.**
2. *Hymns and Sacred Poems* (London, 1740). (G.19; by J. & C. Wesley; 105 unnumbered items, all original or adaptations by the Wesleys.) **Nos. 12–19, 115–16.** Cf. p. xlii.
3. *Hymns on God's Everlasting Love* (Bristol, 1741). (G.31; 18 items.) **Nos. 20*, 21, 24, 117*.** Cf. p. lv.
4. *Hymns on God's Everlasting Love* (London, 1741–2?). (G.32; 28 items.) **No. 22.** Cf. p. lv.

5. *The Character of a Methodist* (Bristol, 1742). (G.34; by John Wesley; appended to the 1st and 2nd editions only is 'The Whole Armour of God'.) **No. 30***.

6. *The Whole Armour of God* (n.p., n.d.). (Broadsheet, British Museum, 1871.e.9 (205).) **No. 30***.

7. *Hymns and Sacred Poems* (Bristol, 1742). (G.40; by J. & C. Wesley; 161 original unnumbered items.) **Nos. 23–9.** Cf. pp. xlii, lii.

8. *Collection of Psalms and Hymns* (2nd edn, 'enlarged', London, 1743). (G.30; by J. & C. Wesley; 1st edn (1741), by J. Wesley, included many non-Wesleyan items, some of which were dropped from the 2nd edn, to which many by Charles Wesley were added; 130 items.) **Nos. 31, 118–19.**

9. *Collection of Moral and Sacred Poems* (Bristol, 1744). (G.58; 3 vols by J. Wesley; at the end of Vol. III are 17 items 'by the Revd Mr John and Charles Wesley'.) **Nos. 121–3.**

10. *Hymns for Times of Trouble and Persecution* (London, 1744). (G.59; 3 separately numbered parts, with a total of 33 items; to the 2nd edn were added 15 items 'For the year 1745'.) **Nos. 32*, 33, (90*), 234.**

11. *Hymns for Times of Trouble* (n.p., n.d.; 1745?). (G.60; 6 items.) **No. (32*).** Cf. p. liii.

12. *A Hymn at the Sacrament* (n.p., n.d.; 1745?). (G.61.) **No. 131.**

13. *A Farther Appeal to Men of Reason and Religion* (London, 1745). (G.63; by J. Wesley, with appended hymn.) **No. 34.**

14. *Hymns on the Lord's Supper* (Bristol, 1745). (G.83; by J. & C. Wesley; 166 items.) **Nos. 53–8, 124–5.**

15. *Hymns for the Nativity of our Lord* (n.p., n.d.; 1745). (G.84; 18 items, reprinted in full as a sample of the many hymn-pamphlets published by Charles Wesley.) **Nos. 35*–52.**

16. *Hymns for our Lord's Resurrection* (London, 1746). (G.90; 16 items.) **No. 59.**

17. *Hymns for Ascension Day* (Bristol, 1746). (G.91; 7 items.) **No. 126.**

18. *Hymns of Petition and Thanksgiving for the Promise of the Father* (Bristol, 1746). (G.92; 32 items; drop-title, 'Hymns for Whit-Sunday'.) **Nos. 60, 127.** Cf. **No. 64.**

19. *Gloria Patri, &c., or Hymns to the Trinity* (London, 1746). (G.93; 24 items.) **Nos. 16, 116.**

20. *Hymns on the Great Festivals, and other occasions* (London, 1746). (G.94; 24 items, with tunes by J. F. Lampe.) **Nos. 10, 32–3, 37, 42–3, 53, 59, 61*–4, 125–6.**

21. *Hymns for the Public Thanksgiving-Day, October 9, 1746* (London, 1746). (G.95; 7 items.) **No. 236.**

22. *Funeral Hymns* (n.p., n.d.; 1746?). (G.96; 16 items.) **Nos. 64–5.**

23. *Graces before Meat* (n.p., n.d.; 1746?). (G.98; 26 items.) **Nos. 66–7.** Cf. **No. 64.**

24. *Hymns for Children* (n.p., n.d.; 1746?). (G.99; 9 items.) **Nos. 27, (103*).**

25. *A Letter to the Right Reverend the Lord Bishop of London* (London, 1747). (G.103; by J. Wesley, with appended poem.) **No. 128*.**

26. *Hymns for those that seek and those that have Redemption in the Blood of Jesus Christ* (London, 1747). (G.105; 52 items.) **Nos. 68–72.** Cf. **No. 24.**

27. *Hymns and Sacred Poems* (Dublin, 1747). (G.106; 37 items, all but 3 from Source *1*, the exceptions being from Sources *3, 7,* and *8.*) **Nos. 2, 5, 8–10, 21.**

28. *Hymns and Sacred Poems* (Bristol, 1749). (G.138; 2 vols, 'By Charles Wesley, M.A., Student of Christ-Church, Oxford'; published by subscription, largely in order to underwrite his marriage that year to Sarah Gwynne; 209 numbered items in Vol. I, and 266 in Vol. II.) **Nos. 11, 30, 34, 61–3, 73–87, 128, 135–45.** Cf. **No. 24.**

29. *Hymns for the Watchnight* (n.p., n.d.). (G.97. Although Green accepts this as an independent publication issued about 1746, it seems to have been issued after No. *28*; apart from the opening item, which comes from No. *7*, the pamphlet consists solely of items selected from the 19 'Hymns for the Watchnight' in Vol. II of No. *28*, nine in the order in which they there occur, together with a tenth selected from those originally passed over.) **Nos. 82–3*.**

30. *Hymns for New Year's Day, 1750* (Bristol, n.d.; 1749). (G.147; 7 items; reprinted with other dates on the title-page, and more frequently with no date.) **Nos. 88–9.**

31. *Hymns occasioned by the Earthquake, March 8, 1750* (London, 1750). (G.148, 148A; two separately published parts having 6 items in the first and 13 in the second; to a joint reprint in 1756, occasioned by the Lisbon earthquake of 1755, 3 further items were added.) **Nos. (90*), 242*–3.** Cf. pp. xix, xxii.

32. *Hymns and Spiritual Songs, intended for the use of real Christians of all denominations* (London, 1753). (G.165; 84 items selected from Nos. *1, 2,* and *7,* with some slight alterations; prepared by John Wesley as a general hymn-book for the Methodist Societies, and succeeded in 1761 by *Select Hymns* (No. *45*), and in 1780 by the famous *Collection* (No. *55*).) **Nos. 1, 14, 15, 17–19, 23, 25–6, 28.**

33. *Hymns for Social Worship, collected from various authors, and more particularly design'd for the use of the Tabernacle congregation, in London. By George Whitefield, A.B.* (London, 1753). (Whitefield compiled this hymn-book upon principles which led to the alteration of a number of the Wesley hymns. Being for 'social worship', singular pronouns usually became plural; eschewing long hymns Whitefield severely abridged a number of Wesley's, and in one case (**No. 10**) squeezed ten four-lined verses into five eight-lined, in order to make it *look* shorter. It has often been supposed that his other more general alterations—such as the transformation of 'Hark how all the welkin rings' to 'Hark! the herald angels sing' (**No. 8**)—were what John Wesley had principally in mind in his preface to the 1780 *Collection*, where he castigated re-writers of hymns. This is very unlikely, however, for Whitefield had then been dead almost ten years, and in any case Wesley did retain some of Whitefield's emendations. The 1st edn of Whitefield's *Hymns* contained 132 numbered 'Hymns for Public Worship', followed by 11 doxologies, etc, and 38 'Hymns for Society and Persons meeting in

Christian-Fellowship'. Of these, 30 hymns and 3 doxologies were by the Wesleys, while 83 hymns and 2 doxologies were by Watts.) **Nos. 8, 10, 12, 13, 18, 19, 32–3, 59, 62–3.**

34. *Catholick Spirit. A Sermon . . . by John Wesley, M.A.* (London, 1755). (G.170; appended is the poem 'Catholic Love'.) **No. 146.**

35. *An Epistle to the Reverend Mr John Wesley. By Charles Wesley, Presbyter of the Church of England* (London, 1755). (G.173.) **No. 257*.**

36. *An Epistle to the Reverend Mr George Whitefield. Written in the year MDCCLV. By Charles Wesley, A.M. Late Student of Christ-Church, Oxford* (London, 1771). (G. 277.) **No. 256*.**

37. *Hymns for the Year 1756. Particularly for the Fast-Day, February 6, 1756* (Bristol, 1756). (G.181; 17 items.) **Nos. 90*–1.**

38. *Hymns of Intercession for all mankind* (Bristol, 1758). (G.192; 40 items.) **Nos. 92, 261*–3.**

39. *Funeral Hymns* (London, 1759). (G.197; 43 items; a collection quite independent of source *22*. Cf. p. lv.) **Nos. 93, (250*), 252.**

40. *Hymns on the Expected Invasion* (n.p., 1759). (G.198; 8 items; re-issued in 1779, when another invasion threatened.) **No. 264*.**

41. *Hymns to be used on the Thanksgiving-Day, Nov. 29, 1759, and after it* (n.p., n.d.). (G.199; 15 items.) **No. 265.**

42. *Reasons against a Separation from the Church of England. By John Wesley, A.M. Printed in the year 1758. With hymns for the preachers among the Methodists (so called), by Charles Wesley, A.M.* (London, 1760). (G.201; 7 items.) **Nos. 266*–7.**

43. *A Collection of Psalms and Hymns, extracted from various authors, and published by the Reverend Mr Madan* (London, 1760). (170 numbered hymns, together with 8 unnumbered doxologies; of these, 89 hymns and 4 doxologies are by the Wesleys, and 4 other hymns are selected from their publications, though not written by them. This *Collection*, together with the Appendix of 23 hymns issued by Madan in 1763, furnished the chief source from which many hymn-books for a century derived their knowledge—and their altered texts—of the more familiar Wesley hymns.) **Nos. 8–10, 15, 19, 22–3, 32–3, 44, 53–4, 58–9, 61–4, 67, 69, 72, 80, 88, 92, 116.**

44. *Hymns for those to whom Christ is all in all* (London, 1761). (G.204; 134 items selected from Nos. *1, 2, 7, 9, 14, 26*, and *28*. The drop-title on p. 1 is simply 'Select Hymns'. Cf. No. *45*.) **Nos. 1–5, 11, 16, 29, 34, 68–9, 71, 75–80, 82, 121–2, 141.**

45. *Select Hymns: with Tunes annext: designed chiefly for the use of the people called Methodists* (London, 1761). (G.205; 133 items, with tunes, selected by John Wesley from previous publications—the hymns themselves are not exclusively by the Wesleys. This was the second important hymn-book for general use [cf. Nos. *32, 55*], and completely over-shadowed No. *44*, issued during the same year, probably by Charles Wesley. The 2nd edn, published in 1765, was 'corrected and enlarged', one item being omitted, and 17 added. From the 4th edn (1773) onwards, the hymns were sometimes published separately from the tunes, entitled *Select Hymns for the*

use of Christians of all denominations [G.208].) **Nos. 10, 11, 18, 30, 32–3, 43, 53–4, 56, 58–64, 69–70, 75–6, 81, 88, 116, 144.** (2nd edn 1765): **Nos. 15, 22–3, 28, 80, 92, 101, 158.**

46. *Short Hymns on Select Passages of the Holy Scriptures. By Charles Wesley, M.A. and Presbyter of the Church of England* (Bristol, 1762). (G.214; 2 vols, containing 1160 numbered hymns on the O.T. in Vol. I and a further 318 in Vol. II, together with 870 numbered hymns on the N.T.; in a posthumous 2nd edn [though not so called] the number of hymns was reduced both by omission and by fusion to 1328 and 817.) **Nos. 33, 94–102, 148, 149*–60, 162–4, 166–8, 171, 174–5, 177–8, 196–204, 248, 268.** Cf. pp. xxi, lvi.

47. *Hymns for Children* (Bristol, 1763). (G.223; 100 items; reprinted in 1766 and subsequently with the title *Hymns for Children and others of riper years.*) **Nos. 27, 103*–8, 270.**

48. *Hymns for the Use of Families, and on various occasions* (Bristol, 1767). (G.245; 166 items.) **Nos. 110–11, 205–9, 245, 254*–5.**

49. *Hymns on the Trinity* (Bristol, 1767). (G.246; 136 items based on the various sections of *The Catholic Doctrine of a Trinity proved by above an hundred short and clear arguments, expressed in the terms of Holy Scripture,* first published in 1756 by William Jones of Nayland, an enlarged 3rd edn appearing in 1767; appended are 52 'Hymns and Prayers to the Trinity'.) **Nos. 210–12.**

50. *An Elegy on the late Reverend George Whitefield, M.A., . . . By Charles Wesley, M.A., Presbyter of the Church of England* (Bristol, 1771). (G.278.) **No. 286.**

51. *Preparation for Death, in several hymns* (London, 1772). (G.285; 40 items.) **No. 213.**

52. *The Arminian Magazine. Consisting of extracts and original treatises on universal redemption,* Vol. I (London, 1778). (G.333; later annual volumes, G.338, 346, 356, 365, 372, 377, 383, 391, 395, 400, 405, 412, 417. This monthly magazine was launched by John Wesley with the set purpose of combating the extreme views of some Calvinist teachers; it continued (and still continues) with a much wider purpose. From the very first volume there were not only poems acknowledged as by Charles Wesley, but others left anonymous—an annoying habit of John Wesley. In the case of one given above, **No. 293,** the internal evidence of authorship was confirmed by the discovery of a mere fragment of the poem in Charles Wesley's handwriting; we are not so fortunate with similar items. In the *Magazine* for March 1779 John Wesley commenced reprinting selections from his brother's *Scripture Hymns* (No. 46), and 86 items appeared before the series ended in March 1783. In May 1789, just over a year after Charles Wesley's death, John Wesley commenced publication in the *Magazine* of items from his brother's manuscript Scripture hymns. These continued to appear after his own death; 35 from the first eight chapters of St Matthew (No. *94*) having appeared by August 1792, and one more from Acts (No. *93*) appearing in 1797— after which year the *Magazine* was renamed the *Methodist Magazine.* From 1797 to 1802 appeared Charles Wesley's versions of 32 Psalms, including the long series

on Psalm 119.) **Nos. 20, 22, 95–6, 98, 101, 162, 219, 230, 295*–6, 301, 306, 308, 334.**

53. *Hymns written in the time of the tumults, June 1780* (Bristol, 1780). (G.347; 13 items.) **No. 302*.**

54. *The Protestant Association. Written in the midst of the tumults, June 1780* (London, 1781). (G.357; 4 items.) **No. (302*).**

55. *A Collection of Hymns, for the use of the People called Methodists* (London, 1780). (G.348; 525 hymns selected, abridged, and revised by John Wesley. This volume, with Wesley's famous preface, dated 'Oct. 20. 1779', succeeded Nos. *32* and *45* as the general hymn-book for the Methodists. In these earlier volumes John Wesley had anticipated some of his revisions which became standardized through the 1780 *Collection*. A number of misprints were corrected, and further slight alterations made, in the 2nd edn of 1781 and the 3rd edn of 1782. This 3rd edn represents the book as it left John Wesley's hands, though it suffered many alterations in succeeding years, both in the numbers and the text of the hymns, alterations both authorized and (usually) unauthorized. This *Collection* formed the nucleus of all subsequent major Methodist hymn-books, particularly of those in the main stream of Wesleyan Methodism [Cf. Nos. *60–1, 63–6, 85, 100*].) **Nos. 1–3, 5, 6, 11–14, 17–19, 21–3, 25–6, 28–30, 34, 52, 58, 62–5, 68–70, 72, 74–80, 82, 85–8, 90–1, 94–7, 99–100, 103, 111, 113, 141, 143–4, 149, 245.**

56. *Hymns for the National Fast, Feb. 8, 1782* (London, 1782). (G.366; 15 items.) **No. 304*.**

57. *Hymns for the Nation in 1782* (n.p., n.d.). (G.367, 368; 2 parts, published separately; 9 + 8 items.) **Nos. (304*), 305, 314.**

58. *A Collection of Psalms and Hymns for the Lord's Day* (London, 1784). (G.378; by J. & C. Wesley; 118 items from No. *8*; originally issued as a companion to John Wesley's revision of the *Book of Common Prayer*, his *Sunday Service of the Methodists in the United States of America* (1784) [G.376]; enlarged by Dr Thomas Coke after Wesley's death it became the authorized 'Morning Hymn Book' for use where Methodists held a liturgical service.

N.B. There appears to be no copy of the 1st edn in the United Kingdom, and the collations are from my own copy of the 1788 edn, which is paged continuously with the *Sunday Service*.) **Nos. 31, 118.**

59. *Prayers for Condemned Malefactors* (London, 1785). (G.384; 10 items.) [Cf. Source *110*.]. **No. 229*.**

60. *A Pocket Hymn Book, for the use of Christians of all Denominations* (London, 1785). (G.385; 200 items; issued by John Wesley as a smaller version of No. *55*; 39 hymns from the larger *Collection* are reprinted, but the opportunity is taken to utilize some of the treasures omitted from the 1780 volume.) **Nos. 4, 15, 16, 28, 33, 43, 52, 59, 61–2, 81, 85, 89, 93, 96, 98, 111, 127–8, 142.**

61. *A Pocket Hymn Book, for the use of Christians of all Denominations* (London, 1787). (G.396; 250 items, arranged in a similar way to No. *55*; this volume was prepared to displace, not No. *61*, but a

pirated collection issued under the same title by Robert Spence of York.) **Nos. 8, 14, 17–19, 22–3, 29–30, 33–4, 52, 58, 62–5, 69–70, 72–3, 80–1, 85, 87–90, 92, 94–100, 111, 144–5, 149, 158, 245.**

62. *Hymns for Children* (London, 1787). (Given by Green as G.414, dated 1790, when a preface to the work was added by John Wesley; it is clearly dated 1787, however, and was advertised on the covers of the *Arminian Magazine* for November 1787 along with No. *61*, as 'A Small Pocket Hymn Book for the use of Children'; 44 items selected from No. *47*.) **Nos. 27, (103*), 108.**

63. *A Collection of Hymns for the use of the People called Methodists. By the Rev. John Wesley, A.M. . . . With a supplement* (London, 1831). (Scores of editions differing from the 1780 *Collection* had come into use by the first quarter of the nineteenth century, the desire for greater variety outstripping reverence for Wesley's original selection. Both enlargement and a greater degree of standardization were clearly desirable, and after several abortive attempts the official solution was provided in 1831. The original selection was reduced by 12 and enlarged by 21, while 6 of the hymns were divided into two parts, a net gain of 15. (The total appears to be 539, but is actually 540, two consecutive hymns being numbered '46'.] A further 21 'Additional Hymns' were appended, numbered 540–60. There was appended—and also published separately—a *Supplement* containing 209 hymns. The Preface to the *Supplement*, dated 9th November 1830, pointed out that its intention was to 'furnish a greater number of hymns suitable for public worship, for festivals, and for occasional services, than are found in that invaluable Collection'. These supplementary hymns were mainly by Charles Wesley, some being from his manuscripts; they also incorporate most of the 'Morning Hymn Book' (No. *58*). Henceforth this enlarged *Collection* and *Supplement*, containing 769 [actually 770] hymns numbered consecutively, was the standard Wesleyan hymn-book. Altogether it contained 623 hymns by Charles Wesley, and 30 by John Wesley.) **Nos. 1–3, 5, 6, 8–15, 17–23, 25–6, 28–30, 32, 34, 38–9, 45, 52–4, 57–8, 61–5, 68–72, 74–82, 85–101, 103, 109, 111, 113, 141, 143–4, 149, 245, 305.**

64. *A Collection of Hymns, for the use of the People called Methodists. By the Rev. John Wesley, M.A. With a New Supplement* (London, 1876). [From later edns 'New' and the date were omitted, and 'London, 1876' was appended to the Preface.] (The Wesleyan Conference of 1874 authorized the issue of a new *Supplement* to the 1780 *Collection*. This time the *Supplement* did not appear separately, but only as appended to still another revised edition of the original *Collection*, containing this time 539 hymns. The *Supplement* itself consisted of a further 487 hymns, making a total of 1026. Again there were some new accessions from Charles Wesley's manuscripts, but the main feature was a far wider use of hymns by over a hundred other composers, of both the eighteenth and the nineteenth centuries. Altogether 724 are noted as by Charles Wesley, and 26 as by John Wesley. There are omissions from both parts of the 1831 volume, as well as considerable additions.) **Nos.**

1–3, 5, 6, 8–15, 17–23, 25–6, 28–34, 38–9, 44–5, 52–4, 57–63, 65, 68–82, 85–103, 106, 109, 111, 113, 131, 141, 143–4, 149, 171, 245, 305, 334.

65. *The Methodist Hymn-Book* (London, 1904). (The new title given to the standard hymn-book of the Methodists of the early twentieth century signalized that a new era had begun in Methodist hymnology. John Wesley's name was dropped from the title-page, and of the total of 981 hymns Charles Wesley was credited with 446, John Wesley with 29. The whole 'shape' of the *Collection*, with contents-divisions based on the stages in the spiritual experience of the Christian, was discarded for an arrangement under main sections devoted to 'The Glory of God', 'The Gospel Call', 'The Christian Life', 'The Church', 'Time, Death, Eternity', 'Family Religion', and 'Special Occasions'. [There was an attempt, however, to retain something of the old flavour in the titles of the sub-divisions of 'The Christian Life'.] Even fuller use was made of the writings of recent authors. There was real justification for the employment of the generic term 'Methodist' in the title, for this volume was prepared not only by the Wesleyan Methodists, but by associated Methodist Churches—the Methodist New Connexion, the Wesleyan Reform Union, and the independent Wesleyan Methodist Conferences in Ireland and Australia.) **Nos. 1, 3, 5, 6, 8–15, 17–23, 25–30, 32–4, 38–9, 44–5, 52–3, 57–63, 65, 68–82, 85–9, 92–103, 109, 111, 141, 144, 149, 334.**

66. *The Methodist Hymn-Book* (London, 1933). (With the union of the main branches of British Methodism in 1932, a new hymn-book was obviously desirable. This was copyrighted in December 1933, though not actually published until the following year. The general form of the 1904 book was retained, and if in the interests of modernity the old phraseology describing 'The Christian Life' was discarded, in the interests of history John Wesley's preface was restored. The volume was greatly enriched from the collections of the other uniting bodies, and by other hymns both ancient and modern. Of the total of 984 hymns 243 are credited to Charles Wesley and 25 to John. Of the 50 'Verses' appended (sometimes comprising two verses) all but 8 are by the Wesleys.) **Nos. 1, 3, 5, 6, 8–15, 17–23, 25–7, 29–30, 32–4, 38–9, 44–5, 52–5, 57–63, 65, 68–80, 82, 85–9, 92–102, 106, 109, 111, 141, 143, 144, 149, 334.**

67. *Hymns Ancient and Modern* (London, 1861, &c.). (In spite of strong competition, the varying editions of *Hymns Ancient and Modern* may be regarded as constituting the basic Anglican hymn-book during the last hundred years. Of 273 hymns in the first edition of 1861 only 9 were by Charles Wesley, 3 more being added in the 'Appendix' (Hymns 274–386) of 1868. The 473 hymns in the revised and enlarged edition of 1875 contained the same 12 hymns by Charles Wesley, together with one by John Wesley. The edition of 1889, with its 'First Supplement' (Hymns 474–638) added a further 10 by Charles and 2 by John, and the 'Second Supplement' of 1916 (Hymns 639–779) also added 10 by Charles and 1 by John. The abortive edition of 1904 included in its new selection of

386

643 hymns 24 by Charles Wesley and 5 by John; of these 3 by
Charles and 2 by John there appeared for the first time, 2 by Charles
and 1 by John of these additions being carried over into the 1916
'Second Supplement'. The 1950 revision contains among its 636
hymns 28 by Charles and 4 by John, 7 of those by Charles being
here included for the first time. In the Schools Edn of 1958 Charles
Wesley is easily the best represented author, with 17 out of 266
hymns. Throughout these varying editions the text of the Wesley
hymns was treated freely, even in the 1950 edition, whose editors
set out to restore the original text of at least some of 'the great
Charles Wesley's hymns'.) **Nos. 8–10, 12, 13, 15, 17, 23, 25, 27, 30,
32–3, 44, 57–9, 63, 69, 77, 92–3, 96–7.** Cf. p. xviii.

68. *The Poetical Works of John and Charles Wesley; reprinted from the
originals, with the last corrections of the authors; together with the
poems of Charles Wesley not before published. Collected and arranged
by G. Osborn, D.D.* (London, 1868–72). (13 vols, containing some
4600 items published by the Wesleys and a further 3000 left in
manuscript by Charles Wesley. In spite of the wording of the title-
page, however, these volumes do not contain all the unpublished
verse of Charles Wesley, and there are actually a number of
omissions from his published verse. For this present volume a
further 1350 unpublished poems have been read. Dr Osborn's text
seems to be based on the first editions of the published works, but
he uses considerable freedom in modernizing. In order to avoid
duplication of poems which appeared in more than one publication
a few of the original works are not presented in their entirety, and
unfortunately it is sometimes the earlier work which thus suffers.
Volumes IX–XIII are the chief sinners, because of Dr Osborn's
method of massing together in strict biblical order both the published *Scripture Hymns* and other scriptural poems from various
manuscript sources, without any attempt at differentiation or
documentation; a score of poems published by Charles Wesley
himself are discarded without indication or with a brief note about
a 'superior version' being substituted from a manuscript source.
Nevertheless this work is a noble monument to the world's most
prolific hymn-writer, and the index to the first lines of all the verses
is immensely valuable—though here also care is needed, the
chief stumbling-block for the unwary being the omission of the *first*
lines of the poems contained in Vols. I–VIII.)

MANUSCRIPT SOURCES

N.B. Every manuscript is in the hand of Charles Wesley unless
the contrary is stated. Locations are appended, 'Bk. Room'
denoting the Methodist Book Room, City Road, London, E.C.1.
Of the manuscripts used in the text only the major ones are listed
below. For others see items **68, 91, 112, 143, 145, 230, 240, 244,
249, 254, 264, 275–6, 279, 288–90, 300–2, 306–7, 309, 319–20, 332,
334–5.**

69. *MS Miscellany Verses.* 12mo volume entitled by John Wesley

'Miscellany Verses' and in his hand throughout. It contains both
extracts from other authors and original verses, but apparently
nothing later than the date at the end, 'Feb. 6. 1729/30' (Bk. Room,
Colman Collection, Vol. I.) **No. 231*.**

70. *MS Clarke.* 12mo volume, with MS inscription by Dr Adam Clarke,
to whom it once belonged. It contains 99 items, together with
various notes in longhand and shorthand. This volume has a close
relationship with *MS Cheshunt*, though there are items in each
which are not in the other; both were apparently in use by Wesley
in 1743, and it appears that items were transcribed from this into
MS Cheshunt. (Bk. Room, MS 45.) **Nos. 11, 61–2, 72, 75, 79, 104,
118, 121–2, 129, 139.**

71. *MS Cheshunt.* 12mo volume, with contents and pagination in the
hand of Charles Wesley, together with pp. 165–217, but the remainder in the hand of three different scribes, sometimes with
revisions in Charles Wesley's hand. In the contents he lists 103
items, and there are a further 13 at the end. The MS seems to have
been compiled mainly in 1743: 2 items are included in No. *8,* 9 in
No. *9,* 2 in No. *10,* 6 in No. *16,* 4 in No. *26,* 83 in No. *28,* and
1 in No. *47.* Cf. *MS Clarke.* (Cheshunt College, Cambridge.) **Nos.
61–2, 72, 75, 79, 118, 121–2, 129–30, 135, 139.**

72. *MS Thirty.* 12mo volume, in the hands of Charles Wesley and a
scribe, the index being supplied by John Wesley. Most of the 108
items are endorsed in shorthand 'Tr[anscribed]' and 'snt ldi' [?
'sent to Lady Huntingdon']; most are published in volumes from
1743 onwards, the majority in *Hymns and Sacred Poems* (1749),
No. *28.* This volume also overlaps to some extent Nos. *70, 71.*
(Bk. Room, MS 30.) **Nos. 30, 32, 49, 59, 63, 69, 70, 79, 86–7,
120.**

73. *MS Shorthand.* 12mo volume, originally of about 100 leaves. All that
remain and many that have been torn out (from the evidence of
the stubs) were inscribed in shorthand. The only longhand words
by Charles Wesley are one on the back cover, and on the front
cover 'April 24 (the day!)'. On the remaining leaves are four long
poems, all unpublished, though one, 'An Epistle to a Friend, July
1743', appears in *MS Epistles* (No. *86*). (Bk. Room, MS 40.)

74. *MS Family.* 12mo volume with 20 pages numbered and written by
Charles Wesley. Many other pages, blank or with writing in a
later hand, have been torn out. No date, but probably in the 1740's.
The hymns comprise 2 for morning, 3 for evening, 1 'Looking unto
Jesus', 3 'Before Reading the Scriptures', and 17 Graces—26
items altogether. Some of these seem to have been adapted from
earlier poems, including two of John Wesley's translations from
the German. The basic type of revision was to change the first person singular pronouns to the plural, as if to compile a manual of
hymns for family use. (Bk. Room, MS 47.) **Nos. 13, 66–7.**

75. *MS Richmond Tracts.* 12mo volume comprising printed copies of
Nos. *10, 11, 22, 15, 16, 18, 17,* interleaved with many blank pages
between the various tracts. On the blank pages Charles Wesley
has written 24 hymns relating to the hymn-tracts immediately

preceding—2 'Hymns for the Year 1746' after Nos. *10* and *11*, 9 after No. *22*, 2 after No. *15*, 6 after No. *16*, 5 after No. *18*. Some of these had already been published, others remained unpublished. (Richmond College, Surrey.) **Nos. 8–10, 123.**

76A. *MS Fish.* 12mo volume bearing the bookplate of 'Selina Countess Dowager of Huntingdon', containing a copy of the *Collection of Psalms and Hymns* (2nd edn, 1743), No. *8*, bound up in the centre of many blank leaves. These have been numbered by Charles Wesley 1–142, 143–249. On them he has written 42 additional versions of Psalms, and the closing lines of another are on p. 7, the psalm itself having probably occupied the whole of the preceding pages, which are missing. This is the MS volume used by the Rev. Henry Fish for *A Poetical Version of nearly the whole of the Psalms of David. By the Rev. Charles Wesley, M.A.* (1854), and was used for the *Poetical Works* by his permission. Cf. *MS Psalms*, No. *77.* (Bk. Room, MS 38.)

76B. *MS Emory.* 12mo volume entitled 'C. Wesley's Version of the Psalms. 1750', containing an almost exact transcript of *76A*. The date is assumed from a note on the cover about items left by Wesley at Shoreham, the home of the Rev. Vincent Perronet, at Easter, 1750. Only the last three psalms and a few minor corrections are in Charles Wesley's hand. A note by the Rev. Thomas Jackson suggests that the amanuensis was Edward Perronet, but in fact the handwriting is almost certainly that of his lesser-known brother John. (Emory University, Atlanta, Georgia, U.S.A.)

77. *MS Psalms.* Vellum-bound 8vo volume, with spine inscribed 'Psalms / New Version'; foliated 1–239, with 36 unnumbered leaves. It is in the hand of an amanuensis, with occasional corrections by Charles Wesley himself, and contains 42 of his versions of the psalms. Gaps are left for other psalms, some of which have been filled by John Pawson from the works of Isaac Watts. There is some overlapping with *MS Fish*, No. *76*, but apparently not with other MSS nor with the published *Collection of Psalms and Hymns* (No. *8*). This volume was used as the basis for most of the psalm versions published posthumously in the *Arminian Magazine* (see No. *52*). From the inclusion of a 1747 letter transcribed by Charles Wesley, the volume was probably begun about that time, and in a letter of January 1749 he referred to 'My New Version of the Psalms'. (Bk. Room, MS 49.)

78. *MS Gwynne.* 12mo volume containing 25 pages in the hand of Miss Sarah Gwynne, who later married Charles Wesley. It contains 18 items from various authors (usually named) including 'Mr Charles Wesley'. Probably compiled *c.* 1747. (Bk. Room, Case VI, sermons vi.) **Nos. 59, 64.**

79. *MS Deliberative.* Thin 8vo volume, in wallpaper-covered boards, containing notes by Miss Sarah Wesley and Miss Eliza Tooth. Written during Charles Wesley's chequered courtship of Sarah Gwynne, and containing 17 items on 40 pages. (Bk. Room, Lamplough Collection.) **Nos. 238–9.**

80. *MS Friendship I.* 12mo volume of 112 pages, sewn, containing 27

items apparently selected for a publication on 'Christian Friends' and later incorporated in the appropriate section in *Hymns and Sacred Poems* (1749) (No. *28*), *via MS Friendship II*. (Bk. Room, MS X.) **Nos. 143-5, (238*).**

81. *MS Friendship II*. 12mo volume, entitled 'Hymns Sacred to Friendship', containing 31 items on 50 pages, in the exact order (with the exception of the last two) in which they were used in the appropriate section of *Hymns and Sacred Poems* (1749) (No. *28*). Based on No. *80*. (Bk. Room, Lamplough Collection.) **Nos. 143-5, (238*).**

82. *MS Courtship*. 8vo note-book, inscribed by Miss Sarah Wesley: 'These Hymns & Prayers were written by the Revd C. Wesley, when he had thoughts of marrying Miss Sarah Gwynne, who became his wife afterwards.' 10 items on 18 numbered pages, apparently transcribed from No. *79*, the first two also appearing in No. *83*. (Bk. Room, CW. MSS I [d].) **No. (238*).**

83. *MS Occasional*. 12mo volume entitled 'Hymns on Several Occasions'; 48 items on 88 pages, with a contents list. Most of the poems were used in *Hymns and Sacred Poems* (1749) (No. *28*), and some are included in Nos. *79, 82*, and *84*. (Bk. Room, MS 46.) **Nos. 73, 84A, 237, 238*-9.**

84. *MS Richmond*. 12mo volume with contents at front; 74 items on 131 numbered pages, and a further 20 not listed in the contents. In this volume Charles Wesley appears to have written up, probably soon after his marriage in 1749, poems composed at various times during the preceding decade. To these were added occasional verses as they were composed during the years 1749–51. A number of poems were left incomplete, with blank spaces for lines, parts of stanzas, or whole stanzas. In a few cases the poems show signs of later revision, and many are scored through and endorsed in shorthand 'Tr[anscribed]'. Most remained unpublished by Charles Wesley. (Richmond College, Surrey.) **Nos. 93, 104, 110, 130-4, 158, 206, 237, 244-8.**

85. *MS Colman 21*. 12mo volume in which John Wesley kept his sermon register, 1747–1761. From the other end he has transcribed some two hundred hymns, mainly from his brother's *Hymns and Sacred Poems* of 1749. In most cases only a few key words or key lines are given, in a highly abbreviated script. This seems to have been a preliminary selection for a standard hymn-book, such as the *Select Hymns* of 1761 and the *Collection* of 1780, which it anticipates in many of its readings. (Bk. Room, Colman Collection, Vol. XXI.) **Nos. 17-19, 21-2, 28, 30, 34, 52, 58, 61-3, 68-9, 71, 75, 77, 80, 82, 85-7, 144-5.**

86. *MS Epistles*. 8vo volume entitled 'Epistles to Moravians, Predestinarians and Methodists. By a Clergyman of the Church of England'. It comprises eight epistles in decasyllabic couplets, all but one of which (the 'Epistle to a Friend' which appears in *MS Shorthand*, No. *72*) seem to have been written in 1755 and prepared for publication in that year. That to John Wesley was actually published at the time (No. *35*), and that to George Whitefield after Whitefield's death (No. *36*). (Bk. Room, MS 9.) **Nos. 256*-7.**

87. *MS Travail.* A much-thumbed gathering of 12mo leaves, containing 8 items, the first six being in the hand of Mrs Charles Wesley. She also supplies the title, 'Hymns for a Woman draw[in]g near ye time of h[er travail]'. No. 8 is 'For a Sick Child'. (Bk. Room, CW. MSS I [f].) **No. 254.**

88. *MS Thanksgiving.* 12mo volume containing printed copies of Nos. *10* (1756 edn), *21, 31, 37, 38, 39, 22, 40.* To these are added by Charles Wesley in manuscript six hymns which were included in No. *41, Thanksgiving Hymns,* 1759. (Wesley's Chapel, London.)

89. *MS Six.* 12mo volume originally having some 200 pages, of which practically all have been cut out, leaving some stubs large enough to reveal fragments of writing in Charles Wesley's hand. Inside the cover is a contents list by him, noting poems as far as p. 44, the remainder of the list being torn out. Of the poems listed, 9 were published in *Funeral Hymns* (No. *39*); the remainder occur in *MSS Richmond* or *Misc. Hymns* (Nos. *84, 113*). Pages 21–6 remain in the volume, and on the back cover are inscribed a further two poems in shorthand, apparently jotted down during a journey in 1766. (Bk. Room, MS 6.) **No. 93.**

90. *MS Festivals.* A foolscap sheet, folded into four, containing 10 poems, mainly on Saints' Days, apparently addressed to the Mayor and Corporation of Bristol on the occasion of some annual festival. (Bk. Room, CW. Vol. IV, folio 71.) **Nos. 147, 258–60, 277.**

91. *MS Preachers.* A foolscap sheet folded into four, with 9 items under the title: 'Hymns for the M.P.' (Bk. Room, CW. MSS I [q], and CW. MSS IV, Fo. 80.) **No. 266.**

92. *MS John.* 4to volume, 'John' scratched on spine, containing on 467 pages over 800 items, of which 145 remain unpublished either in whole or in part. Wesley's shorthand notes show that he began this volume on 3rd December 1763, and finished it on 30th April 1764. (Bk. Room, MS 20.) **Nos. 178–82.**

93. *MS Acts.* 4to volume, with 555 pages, containing almost 1000 items, 302 of them unpublished either in whole or in part. This volume was commenced 'N[ov]. 13. 1764' and 'Finished, April 24, 1764'— which may mean 1763–4, but more probably 1764–5. At the end of the volume are Charles Wesley's records of the seven 'revisals' of the five volumes of Scripture poems. (Bk. Room, MS 21.) **Nos. 10, 183–95.**

94. *MS Matthew.* 4to volume, 'Matthew' scratched on spine. On 371 pages are some 800 poems, of which 65 remain unpublished in whole or in part. At the end Charles Wesley wrote in shorthand 'Finished March 8. 1766'. (Bk. Room, MS 23.) **Nos. 161–6.**

95. *MS Mark.* 4to volume, 'Mark' scratched on spine. On 195 pages are some 400 poems, of which 50 remain unpublished in whole or in part. Charles Wesley's shorthand notes show that the volume was begun 8th March 1766. (Bk. Room, MS 18.)

96. *MS Luke.* 4to volume, 'Luke' scratched on spine. On 367 pages are some 800 poems, of which 314 remain unpublished in whole or in part. Wesley's shorthand notes show that the volume was begun

on 8th April and 'finished April 29, 1766'. (Bk. Room, MS 19.) **Nos. 109, 169–73, 269.**

97. *MS Death*. 4to volume, comprising the following collections:

   (*a*) 'Hymns of Preparation for Death', pp. 1–44, containing 81 items, of which the first 40 were published in 1772 (No. *51*).

   (*b*) 'Hymns for Love', pp. 41–81, containing 34 items, which were first published (with some minor variations) in *Poetical Works*, Vol. VIII (No. *68*).

   (*c*) 'Funeral Hymns', pp. 1–115, containing 44 items, including epitaphs for Methodists dying between 1756 and 1787; most were published in *Poetical Works*, Vols. VI or VIII (No. *68*).

   (*d*) 'Mrs Horton', i.e. an elegy on her death in 1786; this covers 10 pages, with other pages removed. (See No. *117*.)

   (Bk. Room, MS 24.) **Nos. 64, 213–19, 288, 298.**

98. *MS Nursery*. Twelve 4to pages, on the first 6 of which are 7 items relating to young Samuel Wesley and his early days at Bristol. The MS was probably written in the early 1770's, and apparently with the assistance of young Samuel. (Bk. Room, CW. MSS III [b].) **Nos. 273–5, 289.**

99. *MS Intercession*. Four foolscap pages, containing 20 'Hymns of Intercession', later transcribed into *MS Misc. Hymns* (No. *113*). (Bk. Room, CW. Vol. IV, folios 68–70.) **Nos. 227–8, 317.**

100. *MS Collection*. 8vo volume in the hand of John Wesley, being the rough draft of the 1780 *Collection of Hymns*, No. *55*. The volume was finished on 16th April 1778. It is the successor to No. *85*, but much fuller in contents and less abbreviated in the script. (A facsimile page may be seen in *John Wesley's Journal*, Standard edn, VI. 259.) (Bk. Room, MS 14.)

101. *MS Howe*. 'The American War under the Conduct of Sr. W. H[owe']', in three parts, 615 lines of 'Hudibrastics'. This attack on Howe was probably written in 1779, while the House of Commons was making its fruitless inquiry into his dilatory tactics in the American War, and was probably based on information (and a viewpoint) supplied to Wesley by Joseph Galloway. (Bk. Room, CW. MSS I (a), a draft; and a fair copy at Richmond College, Surrey.)

102. *MS Preachers Extraordinary*. A gathering of 25 4to pages, containing 13 items, of which Nos. 5–11 had been incorporated in No. *42*; the last two are headed: 'For Some of the Preachers. Written in 1779.' Drafts or copies of most of these items are to be found in CW. MSS I (p), (q), or CW. Vol. IV, folios 72–3, all at the Bk. Room, and the poems were also incorporated in *MS Misc. Hymns* (No. *113*). Cf. Source *115*. (Bk. Room, CW. MSS I [i].) Nos. **249*, 266–7, 300.**

103. *MS Protestant Association*. The MS from which No. *54* was published. (Bk. Room, CW. MSS III [d].)

104. *MS American*. A bundle of 52 4to pages, on the back of one of which is inscribed 'Hymns & / Verses for 1782'. They contain 16 items, with which should be associated 3 other items under the heading 'Written in 1782' at another location. They were mostly connected with the American War, and were later transcribed into *MS*

Patriotism, No. *112*. Loose drafts of other associated poems are to be found in CW. MSS I and III at the Bk. Room. (Bk. Room, CW. MSS I [r, n].) **No. 313.**

105. *MS Scriptural Hymns.* 4to volume inscribed on the fly-leaf 'Scriptural Hymns / 1783 May 11'. 128 pages containing 126 items on the Old Testament, all but one of which (and a stanza of another) were incorporated in *Poetical Works*, Vols IX and X (No. *68*). There follow 139 pages on the New Testament, containing 128 items, of which all but 19 were fully incorporated in *Poetical Works*, Vols X–XIII. At the end is the note: 'Finished May 26. 1783.' The poems in this volume do not overlap in contents either the published *Scripture Hymns* (1762) (No. *46*) or the MS volumes on the Gospels and Acts (Nos. *92–6*). Many of them were directed against the folk who lightly claimed to have attained Christian Perfection. (Bk. Room, MS 25.) **Nos. 184, 220–6, 318.**

106. *MS Peace.* Four poems on four 4to pages entitled 'Occasioned by the Peace / 1783', bearing John Wesley's endorsement on the back, 'Verses on ye Peace / Keen enough!'. (Bk. Room, Lamplough Collection.) **No. 315.**

107. *MS Samuel Wesley, R.C.* A sewn gathering of 24 4to pages, containing 13 items headed by Miss Sarah Wesley's note: 'By the Revd C. Wesley: Verses on his Son Samuel on being made acquainted he had embraced the Roman Catholic Religion.' (pp. 1–2 are missing.) (Bk. Room, CW. MSS I [1].) **No. 324.**

108. *MS Ordinations.* 8vo volume, with various items in prose and verse relating to John Wesley's ordinations of Methodist preachers for America in 1784. The 10 poems on pp. 1–3, 136–30 (working backwards in the volume) were aimed particularly at Dr Thomas Coke. (Bk. Room, MS 48.) **Nos. 325*–9.**

109. *MS Revd X.* A gathering of eleven 4to pages entitled: 'To the Revd ——.' It is actually an attack on his brother John over the ordinations for America, in 248 lines of octosyllabic couplets. (Bk. Room, CW. MSS I [j].)

110. *MS Malefactors.* A foolscap folder of loose sheets inscribed outside: 'Malefactors.' Eight items, including one entitled: 'The Prayer of Condemned Malefactors—May 10. 1785.' Four of the items are included in No. *59*. (Bk. Room, CW. MSS I [h].)

111. *MS Brothers.* 8vo notebook, from which all but the last of nine poems are missing. (Bk. Room.) **No. 330*.**

112. *MS Patriotism,* and *MS Patriotism: Misc.* 4to volume inscribed inside front cover: 'Hymns & Verses on Modern Patriotism, & the American Rebellion and Independancy &c//Miscellaneous Poems.' Under the first heading are 145 pages containing 58 items, some of which were published in *Poetical Works*, Vol. VIII (No. *68*). Under the second heading are 44 pages, of which pp. 5–8 and 13–22 have been pulled out, and pp. 39–44 cut out. It has been possible to identify some of these fragments in other groups of MSS, so that at present a total of 26 items can be named as belonging to this section, a further 10 pages being still missing. A number of the items in both sections are known in draft or copy or

both (Bk. Room, MS 27.) **Nos. 84B, 271, 278, 280–5, 287, 291–4, 296, 301, 306–13, 315–16, 319, 321–3, 329, 331.**

113. *MS Misc. Hymns.* 4to volume, inscribed inside front cover, 'Miscellaneous Hymns', 316 pages containing 211 items. The subject matter covers dates ranging from 1747 to 1786; 131 items are unpublished, four of them occurring also in *MS Richmond* (No. *84*). (Bk. Room, MS 26.) **Nos. 112, 131, 227–9, 249–51, 253, 266–7, 272, 297, 299–300, 303, 317.**

114. *MS Misc., 1786.* Loose 8vo sheets, bluish paper, headed: 'Miscellaneous. Oct. 20, 1786.' There should be 40 pages, but pages 13, 14, 25–34, are missing. On the pages present there are 18 items. (Bk. Room, CW. MSS III [c, g].)

115. *MS Preachers, 1786.* 8vo bundle, 25 pages headed, 'Hymns for the Methodist Preachers in 1786', containing 17 unpublished items. Drafts are present in CW. MSS I (p, q). (Bk. Room, CW. MSS I [k].)

116. *MS Samuel Wesley.* A scrapbook mainly of items relating to Charles Wesley's son Samuel, including some of his father's verses in Samuel's hand. (Bk. Room.) **No. 325.**

117. *MS Henderson.* 4to bundle, headed: 'For John Henderson, April 8, 1787.' This contains 6 items, and is prefixed by an epitaph on Mrs Horton, and the number '11', showing that this MS was actually cut from the end of *MS Death* (No. *97*). (Bk. Room, CW. MSS III [f].)

AN ALPHABETICAL INDEX TO THE SOURCES LISTED ABOVE

CHARLES WESLEY'S METRES: NOTES AND INDEX

THE Introduction pointed out that one of the important claims of Charles Wesley to the attention of students lies in the great metrical variety of his verse, as well as in his sure command of the many stanzaic patterns which he employed. Ideally the metre of a poem should derive directly from the words used, and be inseparable from their pronunciation in normal speech, the poetic value consisting in their choice and arrangement. In this sense much (but by no means all) of Charles Wesley's verse is ideal. Even this 'ideal' verse, however, is liable to be read somewhat stumblingly and without full appreciation unless the reader has some idea of what the poet is about, is made quickly aware of the beat and pattern of the verse. This is particularly difficult for those whose taste has been limited to and by the jog-trot of unvarying iambic verse. Even if one is accustomed also to the more martial tramp of the trochaic line, and the rollicking abandon of the anapaest, there remains a frequent snare for the unwary reader of Charles Wesley in his mixing of the two main types of line, iambic and trochaic, in a single stanza. Unless one is on the look-out for this alternating beat, this syncopation in verse, much of Charles Wesley's best writing is likely to be denied its full impact, even though some of these 'mixed' metres may be read as if they were trochaic throughout. It is with such considerations in mind that the following notes and index have been prepared.

TERMINOLOGY

For many readers it may be desirable to define some of the terms used in prosody, the study of the technical aspects of verse. For others what is said here may seem both impertinent and inadequate. These must be encouraged to pass by on the other side, having first noted two points: (1) I use the term 'metre' not only in its restricted sense of 'the beat of the feet of the verse', but also in its wider sense as a convenient single word to summarize the complex combination of line-length, stanza-length, rhythmic pattern and rhyme-pattern, which differentiates one stanzaic pattern from another; (2) I use 'verse' or 'v.' in the text instead of 'stanza', and plead in justification not only Charles Wesley's own practice, but common usage.

No mechanical system of analysing verse is either adequate or foolproof, but it is convenient to describe modern English verse by the use of four main terms indicating the number of syllables and the position of the accent in the basic units (or feet) of each line. Admittedly this ignores much, the quantity and pitch of the sound, the duration of the syllable, and varying shades of emphasis. Nevertheless it provides a useful measuring-stick. This is particularly true of hymns, which to be sung satisfactorily must remain almost monotonously loyal to their basic metres. The four main types of feet may be exemplified thus:

Rising feet (i.e. from an unaccented to an accented syllable):

IAMBUS: '*be*fore'; 'Stup*end*/ous *height*/ of *heav'n*/ly *love*'

ANAPAEST: 'under*stand*'; 'What a *bless*/ing to *know*/ that my *Je*/sus is *mine*'

Falling feet (i.e. from an accented to an unaccented syllable):

TROCHEE: '*dy*ing'; '*Come* Thou / *long*-ex/*pec*ted / *Je*sus'

DACTYL: '*merrily*'; '*Pick* her up/ *tenderly* / . . .'
'*Fash*ioned so / *slenderly* / . . .'
(N.B. There is no example of a completely dactylic line in the whole of Charles Wesley's verse—and comparatively few in English verse as a whole. This foot is used much more frequently as a modulation in otherwise trochaic verse.)

Monosyllables are frequently used in place of a complete foot, as a regular feature of the verse-structure:
'*Christ* the / *Lord* is / *ris'n* to/*day*'

Modulations (i.e. variations within the basic verse-structure):
PYRRHIC (two relatively unstressed syllables):
'*Come*, and / [let us] / *sweetly* / *join*
Christ to / *praise* in / *hymns* di/*vine*;
Give we / *all*, with / *one* ac/*cord*,
Glory / [to our] / *common* / *Lord*'
SPONDEE (two almost equally stressed syllables):
'To *me* / with *thy*/ [*dear name*]/ are *giv'n*'
'In *weak*/ness *my* / [*almight*]/y *pow'r*'
CHORIAMBUS (in effect a trochee followed by an iambus, or a dactyl followed by a stressed monosyllable—a frequent modulation in iambic verse, especially at the beginning of a line):
'*O* for / a *thous*/and *tongues*/ to *sing*'
'*Jesus* / the *name*/ that *charms* / our *fears*'
'*Soldiers* / of *Christ*, / *arise*'
AMPHIBRACH (an iambus followed by an unstressed syllable, most common as a line-ending in couplets. Charles Wesley frequently wrote the tighter form of couplets without any example of the amphibrach, but in some of his lighter satirical verse he made considerable use of them, particularly in the form known as 'Hudibrastics'— Metre 97a):
'Ye *zeal*/ous *Cit*/izens / of *Lon*don,
Keep up/ your *Mob*, / or *ye*/ are *undone*'
(N.B. This also shows a pyrrhic in the first line and a spondee in the second. The misplacing of the accent in the last word in order to furnish a rhyme is quite deliberate, and is an integral part of the near-buffoonery of this type of verse.)

CLASSIFICATION

In classifying Charles Wesley's metres it seems impossible to devise a system which will show at a glance all the relationships between the various types, including the doubling and other variations of the basic stanza-forms. The grouping together even of those iambic forms which have the same number of syllables and lines is not fully satisfactory, for the varying rhyme-patterns lead to strong differences in 'feel', which is noticeable particularly in the six-8's forms—8.8.8.8.8 8 (Charles Wesley's favourite), 8 8.8.8 8.8, and 8 8.8 8.8 8. The following principles have been applied in the arrangement adopted, and applied in this order:

(1) List first the basic common metre and metres stemming directly from it.

(2) List first those with fewer syllables in their opening lines.

(3) List first the metres with fewer lines.

(4) List first metres with cross-rhyming, abab, etc., and then those with consecutive-rhyming, aabb, etc.

(5) Minor variants and a few major variants which were discovered after the book was set up in print have been listed in what seemed the most suitable position, and assigned a subsidiary letter as well as a number.

CONVENTIONS AND SYMBOLS

The number of syllables in each line of the stanza is shown in Arabic figures, and lines which do not rhyme with adjoining lines are separated from them by periods. The rhyme-pattern is shown separately by the letters corresponding to the lines. X and Y are used for lines which do not rhyme with any other, except accidentally. The basic metre of the line is shown by variations in the letters, thus:

A = iambic

A = a combination of iambic and anapaestic feet (rarely pure anapaestic)

a = trochaic

a = a combination of trochaic and dactylic

[D] added after syllables and rhyme-patterns indicates that the stanza is symmetrically double the size shown.

2* In the last column are given the numbers of the items in the volume which are examples of that metre. An asterisk added to the number indicates that in the introduction or notes to that item there is some mention of the metre.

INDEX

I. IAMBIC

Metre No.	Syllables per line	Rhyme-pattern	Examples
1.	8.6.8.6	ABAB	13, 17, 23, 74, 87, 111, 229, 246, 249, 297, 325–6
2.	4 4.6.8.6	AABAB	223
3.	4 4.6.4 4.6	AABCCB	156
4.	8 8.6.8 8.6	AABCCB	49, 63, 80, 91, 100, 122, 170, 206–7, 219, 224, 265, 267, 270, 272, 300, 303, 313, 315, 324
5.	8.6.8.6.8.6.8.6	ABABCDCD	71, 89, 93, 95, 98
6.	8.7.8.7	ABAB	289
7.	8.8.8.8	ABAB	6, 20, 35, 51, 77, 114, 118, 120, 192, 214, 218, 239, 244
8.	8 8.8 8	AABB	28, 62, 70, 72, 139, 278, 302, 318, 320
9.	8 8.8 8 8	AABBB	151

398

Metre No.	Syllables per line	Rhyme-pattern	Examples
10.	8.8.8.8.8 8	ABABCC	1, 5, 14, 25, 34, 47, 57, 76, 78, 94, 105, 109, 113, 132–3, 140, 146, 149, 161, 164B, 165, 171, 179, 188, 194, 196, 222, 227–8, 243, 252, 261–3, 266, 298, 310, 314, 317
11.	8.8.8.8.8 10	ABABCC	220
12.	8.8.8.8.10 12	ABABCC	184
13.	8 8.8.8 8.8	AABCCB	126–7, 198
14.	8 8.8.8 8.12	AABCCB	209
15.	8 8.8 8.8 8	AABBCC	106, 124, 143, 230, 236, 306, 323, 334
16.	8.8.8.8.8 8 8	ABABCCC	202
16a.	8 8.8 8.8 8 8	AABBCCC	273–4
17.	8.8.8.8.8.8.8.8	ABABCDCD	11, 84B, 96, 159, 172, 176, 191, 283
18.	8.8.8.8.8 8.8 8	ABABCCDD	164A
19.	8 8.8 8.8.8.8	AABBCDCD	148
20.	8 8.8 8.8 8.8 8	AABBCCDD	199, 268, 331
21.	8 8.10 12.8 8.10 12	AABBCCDD	208
22.	8 8.8.8 8.8 [D]	AABCCB [D]	128, 269
23.	6.6.6.6	ABAB	153
24.	6 6.6 6.6 6	AABBCC	102
25.	6.6.6.6.8 8	ABABCC	22*, 29, 39, 59, 144
26.	6 6.6 6.8 8	AABBCC	163, 193
27.	6.6.6.6.6.6.6.6	ABABCDCD	178
28.	6 6.6 6.6 6.6 6	AABBCCDD	213
29.	6 6.6 6.6 6.8 8	AABBCCDD	168
30.	6.6.8.6	ABAB	204, 235
31.	6.6.8.6.6.6.8.6	ABABCDCD	30, 43, 55, 85–6, 97, 99, 117, 134, 240, 299, 304
32.	6.6.6.6.8.6.8.6	ABABCDCD	141–2, 195, 211
33.	6.6.6.6.4 4.6.4 4.6	ABABCCDEED	136
34.	6.6.8.6.6.6.8.6 [D]	ABABCDCD [D]	186, 264
35.	7.6.7.6.7.6.7.6	ABABCDCD	169, 217
36.	7.7.4 4.7.7.7.4 4.7	XABBAYCDDC	33*, 40
37.	10 10 10	AAA	328
38.	10.10.10.10	ABAB	327
39.	10 10.10 10.10 12	AABBCC	332
40.	10.10.10.10.11 13	ABABCC	329
41.	10.10.10.10.10.10.10.10	ABABCDCD	271
42.	10 10.10 10.10 10.10 10	AABBCCDD	147, 258
43.	10 10.10 10.10 10.10 12	AABBCCDD	259–60
44.	8 8.8 10.10 8.8.6.10.10	AABBCCDEDE	277

399

II. TROCHAIC

Metre No.	Syllables per line	Rhyme-pattern	Examples
45.	7.7.7.7	abab	123
46.	7 7.7 7	aabb	8–10, 27, 46, 131, 201, 251
47.	7.7.7.7.7 7	ababcc	12, 58, 121, 255, 288
48.	7 7.7.7.7.7	aabcbc	167
49.	7 7.7 7.7 7	aabbcc	108, 216
50.	7.7.7.7.7.7.7.7	ababcdcd	15, 79, 177*, 221*
51.	7.7.7.7.7 7.7 7	ababccdd	155
52.	7 7.7 7.7 7.7 7	aabbccdd	18–19, 103, 215
53.	7 7.7 7.7 7.7 7.7 7	aabbccddeeff	7
54.	8.7.8.7.4.7	ababxb	92, 203
55.	8.7.8.7.7 7	ababcc	205
55a.	8 8.7.8 8.7	aabccb	335
56.	8.7.8.7.8.7.8.7	ababcdcd	44–5, 69, 81
57.	8.7.8.7.7 7.8 8	ababccdd	226
58.	8.3 3.6	abba	37*, 115–16, 238
59.	8.3 3.6.8.3 3.6	abbacddc	66–7, 110

III. TROCHAIC—DACTYLIC

As pointed out above, iambic verse, particularly in longer poems, is frequently written with reversed accents in the opening foot, thus giving what may be described as a trochee followed by an iambus, otherwise a choriambus. It would be possible, however, if the line stood by itself, to scan it as an opening dactyl followed by trochees, and the decision must be made on the basis of the context. In only one metre does Charles Wesley appear to have sustained an opening dactylic beat, in verse which otherwise seems to be trochaic—and even here the matter is open to a different interpretation. This is the famed 'Nancy Dawson' metre, which Wesley adopted from a popular but far from polite ballad. I have only discovered two other examples of this metre in addition to the one which began the experiment. It is noteworthy that eventually Charles Wesley re-wrote the original poem in a form which could more easily (but not faultlessly) be scanned as iambic. Cf. also No. 221 for a possible dactyl in the second foot.

| 60. | 8.7.8.7.8.7.8.7 | *ababcdcd* | 84A*, 130 |

IV. IAMBIC—ANAPAESTIC

Charles Wesley's anapaestic verse (as is common with other writers) is the least regular of all, though even here we should speak of more frequent modulations rather than definite irregularity. His basic five-syllabled and eleven-syllabled lines consist of an opening iambus and one or three anapaests. Occasionally one of the anapaests may become an iambus, thus reducing the syllables by one, but much more frequently the opening iambus becomes an anapaest, thus increasing the syllables by one. Indeed in his favourite iambic-anapaestic metre, 5.5.5.5.6.5.6.5, this is the basic pattern of the fifth and seventh lines. His eight-syllabled lines in Metre No. 68 remain constant to the pattern iambus-anapaest-anapaest.

The nine-syllabled lines, containing three anapaestic feet, occasionally modify the first foot to an iambus. Thus it will be seen that with hymns in the anapaestic metres the congregation must occasionally face the problem of tucking two syllables into one note of music—which seems to constitute more of a trial than putting the musical stress on an unstressed syllable— and less frequently of spreading two notes over one syllable. These variant forms should not be listed, however, as 'irregular' or as separate metres, nor even '5/6 5/6 11/12', as if the syllables were readily interchangeable. They are no more than modulations of the basic metre, which is therefore given quite simply as '5 5 11'.

Metre No.	Syllables per line	Rhyme-pattern	Examples
61.	5 5 11	*AAA*	50, 75
62.	5 5 11.5 5 11	*AAABBB*	61, 104, 212
63.	5 5.5 11	*AABB*	42, 48, 56
64.	5 5.5 11.5 5.5 11	*AABBCCDD*	60, 68, 83, 88, 112, 187
65.	5 5.9.5 5.9	*AABCCB*	73, 107, 245, 275
66.	5.5.5.5.6.5.6.5 (also set out as 10 10.11 11, with an internal rhyme)	*ABABCDCD*	16*, 21*, 26, 32, 36, 41, 190
67.	6 6.6 6.6 6.6 6	*AABBCCDD*	292
68.	8.8.8.8.8.8.8.8	*ABABCDCD*	52, 64*-5, 101
69.	11 11.11 11	*AABB*	129
70.	11 11.11 11.11 11	*AABBCC*	309
71.	11 11.11 11.11 11.11 11	*AABBCCDD*	312

V. MIXED IAMBIC AND IAMBIC-ANAPAESTIC

72.	7.7.5 5.8	XABBA	225

VI. MIXED IAMBIC AND TROCHAIC

The metrical forms which follow are among the most characteristic contributions of Charles Wesley to English verse. There seems to have been no major poet who used them with regularity before him, and few since. Their basic syllables per line are 8, 7, and 6. Various theories may be held about their individual origins. The 'Wesleyan 7 6 metres' (Nos. 85–6) can be scanned as if they were completely trochaic, with lines of 13 or 15 syllables split into two parts for the sake of the congregation's breath. On the other hand Wesley clearly desires a pause, however slight, at the end of almost every line, and we must take it therefore that he intended these also as 'mixed' metres, as are others without any peradventure.

It seems likely that the general idea of alternating the rising and falling rhythm in the lines of the same stanza came to Wesley from hearing (and later reading) the German hymns of the Moravians. German hymn-singing was at a much more advanced stage of development than English. In fact it could fairly be described as over-developed, with a bewildering profusion of metrical forms, some of them quite top-heavy and inflexible. Even though it is not possible to equate the German with the English metrical system, the parallels are there, and in the Herrnhut *Gesangbuch* of 1737 from which John Wesley translated there are over 250 different metres. Well over half of these are iambic, and the remainder fall into the categories of trochaic, anapaestic, and mixed iambic and trochaic. The latter include a number both in 7's and 6's and in 7's and 8's which, though not identical with Wesley's metres, may well have started his mind singing in broken rhythms.

Metre No.	Syllables per line	Rhyme-pattern	Examples
73.	4 4.6.7.5	AABab	137*
73a.	4 4.6.7.6	AABaB	138*
74.	4 4.7.7.7	AABaB	182 (Cf. 138*)
74a.	7.6.8 8.6	aBAAB	335
75.	6 6.7.7.7.7	AAbcbc	2*–4, 31, 173, 234
76.	7.7.7.7.8 8	ababCC	177
77.	7 7.7 7.8 8	aabbCC	152, 335
78.	7.8.8.8.8 12	aBABCC	279
78a.	7.7.7.8.10 12	abaBCC	335
78b.	7.6.7.8.10 12	aBaBCC	335
79.	8 7.6.8 8.6	AaBCCB	181, 183, 237*, 250
79a.	8 7.6.8.8.6	AaBCBC	125*
80.	8 8.8 8.7 7	AABBcc	158, 180
81.	8 8.7 8.8 8	AAbBCC	276
82.	7.7.7.7.7 8 8	ababcCC	154
83.	6.6.6.6.7 7.8 8	ABABccDD	200
84.	6 6.7 7.6.8 8.6	AAbbCDDC	175
85.	7.6.7.6.7.7.7.6	aBaBcdcD	38, 54, 82, 119, 145, 162, 241, 254
86.	7.6.7.6.7.8.7.6	aBaBcDcD	53, 90, 160, 185, 189, 210, 242
87.	7.7.7.7.7.6.7.6	aBaBcdcd	197
88.	7 7.7 7.7 7.7 8	aabbccdD	166
89.	7 7.7 7.7 7.8 8	aabbccDD	290
90.	7 7.7 8.7 7.8 8	aabBccDD	157
91.	7 8.7 7.7 7.8 7	aAbbccDd	150
92.	7 8.7 7.7 7.8 8	aAbbccDD	247–8
93.	7 8.7 8.7 8.8 8	aAbBcCDD	253
94.	7 7.7 7.7 7.8 8 8	aabbccDDD	174

VII. VARIED METRES

The first two categories which follow can hardly be classed as separate types of metre. The first arises (in two examples) from the introduction of some singing anapaestic stanzas as the closing portion of an iambic narrative. The second is really a demonstration of the fact that in Wesley's mind the 7's and 6's mixed metres to which the Nos. 85 and 86 have been assigned were almost variations one of the other, the only difference being the use in the sixth line of either a seven-syllabled trochee or an eight-syllabled iambus. Wesley felt it quite permissible to vary this sixth line as a form of modulation within either basic type. The third example stands in a different class. It is in fact an ode, wherein stanzas of varying patterns are combined to form a complex literary unit. Although these stanzas are by no means as elaborate as those of the normal Pindaric ode, and are far removed from the irregularities of the Cowleyan ode, nevertheless they do introduce four metrical patterns otherwise unknown in Wesley's writings.

94a.	Nos. 7 and 66 combined	**24***
94b.	Nos. 85 and 86 combined	**305**
94c.	Nos. 78a, 55a, 74a, and 78b combined (in first draft also 77 and 85? or 86?)	**335**

VIII. COUPLETS

Charles Wesley used the normal conventions of the classical school of eighteenth-century verse, as of Butler and others in the preceding century, by allowing himself frequent modulations, including amphibrachs, or by using a closing alexandrine in decasyllabic verse, or by varying his couplets with tercets.

Metre No.	Syllables per line	Rhyme-pattern	Examples
95.	Iambic 6's		**281**
96.	Trochaic 7's		**135**
97.	Iambic 8's (regular)		**295, 301, 311, 330**
97a.	Iambic 8's and 9's (Hudibrastics)		**282, 284, 294, 316**
98.	Iambic 10's (regular)		**231–2, 257, 287, 291, 296, 319, 321–2**
98a.	Iambic 10's (with closing alexandrines)		**233, 256, 280, 286, 293**
99.	Iambic-Anapaestic 11's and 12's		**307–8, 331**
100.	Iambic-Anapaestic 13's		**285**

INDEX OF FIRST LINES

N.B. Hymns or sub-sections beginning with a line other than the first line of the poem of which they form part are given in parentheses thus: '(O for a thousand tongues to sing) 17'.

404

407

GENERAL INDEX

This index includes the titles of the poems and their general subject matter. References to the various aspects of literary criticism discussed in the Introduction (such as Wesley's use of chiasmus) are given, but no attempt has been made to index the many examples of such features in the body of the work. Separate indexes are provided for sources (pp. 394–5), metres (pp. 398–403), and first lines (pp. 404–7). In those indexes the references are to the numbers assigned to the various items. Here the references are to pages.

411